Apocalypticism,
Prophecy, and
Magic in Early
Christianity

Apocalypticism, Prophecy, and Magic in Early Christianity

Collected Essays

DAVID E. AUNE

BakerAcademic
a division of Baker Publishing Group
Grand Rapids, Michigan

Paperback edition published in 2008 by Baker Academic
a division of Baker Publishing Group
P.O. Box 6287, Grand Rapids, MI 49516-6287
www.bakeracademic.com

Cloth edition first published in 2006 in Tübingen, Germany, by Mohr Siebeck GmbH & C. KG Tübingen

Printed in the United States of America

Library of Congress Cataloging-in-Publication Data is on file at the Library of Congress, Washington, DC

ISBN 978-0-8010-3594-4

To Charlie

Preface

The twenty essays collected here were published from 1981 through 2006 and center, as the title indicates, on the themes of apocalypticism, prophecy and magic in early Christianity. The three essays on aspects of Christian prophecy ("Charismatic Exegesis in Early Judaism and Early Christianity," "Christian Prophecy and the Messianic Status of Jesus," and "The *Odes of Solomon* and Early Christian Prophecy," are all studies that discuss in detail some of the special problems and issues that arose in connection with my monograph, *Prophecy in Early Christianity and the Ancient Mediterranean World* (Grand Rapids: Eerdmans, 1983), translated into Italian by Oscar Ianovitz as *La Profezia nel Primo Cristianesimo e il Mondo Mediterraneo Antico*, Biblioteca di storia e storiografia dei tempi biblici, 10 (Brescia: Paideia Editrice, 1996). My interest in early Christian prophecy was piqued while a member of the Seminar on Christian Prophecy of the Society of Biblical Literature Seminar, which met annually for a five-years during the mid-1970's, chaired first by Prof. M. Eugene Boring and later by myself. My initial interest in the Apocalypse of John was indeed sparked by an interest in the extent to which that Christian apocalyptic work was a witness to early Christian prophecy. The lion's share of the following essays, fifteen to be exact, center on aspects of my studies on the Apocalypse of John with some special forays into particular aspects of Jewish and Christian apocalypticism. Most of these essays were written in connection with a sixteen-year project that unexpectly grew into a three-volume commentary on the Greek text of the Apocalypse: *Revelation 1–5*, Word Biblical Commentary 52A (Waco: Word Books, 1997); *Revelation 6–19*, Word Biblical Commentary 52B, (Nashville: Thomas Nelson, Publishers, 1998), and *Revelation 17–22*, Word Biblical Commentary 52C (Nashville: Thomas Nelson, Publishers, 1998). This work was dedicated to two of my mentors and their wives, Peter and Inger Borgen and Martin and Marianne Hengel. Research on the commentary on the Apocalypse began in earnest during 1982–83 (at that point I was a Professor of New Testament at Saint Xavier College, Chicago), when I was named a visiting Fulbright professor at the University of Trondheim in Norway (the land of my forbears). My host at the University of Trondeim was Professor Peder Borgen, whose friendship, scholarship and enthusiasm made our stay there both profitable and memorable. Toward the conclusion of the commentary project (while on the Faculty of Theology at Loyola University of Chicago), I was the happy recipient of an Alexander von Humboldt Forschungspreis, making it possible to spend a year in Tübingen, Germany, in 1994–95, where my host was Professor Martin Hengel and his able wissenschaftliche Assistent, Jörg Frey (now a professor of New Testament on the Protestant faculty in Munich). The vast and detailed knowledge of Professor Hengel in the fields early Judaism and early Christianity, together with the impressive resources of the Theologicum at the University of Tübingen made this a very productive year indeed.

Oh yes, magic. Just two articles are devoted to the issue of magic and early Christianity ("The Apocalypse of John and Graeco-Roman Revelatory Magic" and "Magic in Early Christianity"). While I'm not quite sure how my interest in ancient magic began, I have continued to maintain an interest in this arcane subject and have written a number of dictionary articles on related issues and have given a number of lectures on various aspects of the subject. A major current project closely related to this interest in ancient magic is a commentary on the *Testament of Solomon*, a second or third century CE Christian composition with strong links to early Judaism and loaded with magical traditions. This project is under contract to Verlag Walter de Gruyer (Berlin and New York) and will be part of their series called "Commentaries on Early Jewish Literature." While I have written many other pieces on aspects of ancient magic, many of these were for reference works and are too technical for this collection of essays (e.g., articles on "Jeu," "Iao," "Jesus im Zauber," and "Kreis" for the *Reallexikon für Antike und Christentum*).

Each of the articles included in this volume have been published previously, with the exception of "Revelation 17: A Lesson in Remedial Reading," which I have given under various titles as a lecture. While the articles have all been reformatted to produce a homogeneous collection, and apart from the correction of a number of errors, they remain substantially unrevised. I have requested and received permission to republish the rest of the articles from the various publishing houses that own the copyrights to these articles. A list of the articles and their original sources follows.

"Understanding Jewish and Christian Apocalyptic" was first published by the Lutheran journal *Word & World* 25 (2005) 233–45 and the editor has granted me permission to republish the article.

"From the Ideal Past to the Imaginary Future: The Theme of Restoration in Jewish Apocalyptic Literature," written with the assistance of Eric Stewart, appeared in *Restoration: Old Testament, Jewish, and Christian Perspectives*, ed. James Scott (Leiden: Brill, 2001), pp. 147–177. Koninklijke Brill N.V. has granted permission to reprint this article.

"The Apocalypse of John and the Problem of Genre" originally appeared in *Semeia*, 36 (1986), 65–96., and the Society of Biblical Literature have given me permission to republish this article.

"Following the Lamb: Discipleship in the Apocalypse" was first published on pp. 269–84 in *Patterns of Discipleship in the New Testament*, ed. R.N.

Longenecker (Grand Rapids: Eerdmans, 1996), and the W. B. Eerdmans Publishing Company has granted permission to reprint this article.

"Qumran and the Book of Revelation" originally appeared in *The Dead Sea Scrolls after Fifty Years: A Comprehensive Assessment*, ed. P. W. Flint and J. C. Vanderkam (Leiden: Brill, 1999) 2.622–48, and Koninklijke Brill N. V. has granted permission to reprint this article.

"The Influence of Roman Imperial Court Ceremonial on the Apocalypse of John" was published in *Biblical Research*, 18 (1983), 5–26, and the editor of that journal has granted permission to reprint the article.

"Apocalypse Renewed: An Intertextual Reading of the Apocalypse of John" appeared on pp. 43–70 in *The Reality of Apocalypse: Rhetoric and Politics in the Book of Revelation,* edited by David L. Barr (Atlanta: Society of Biblical Literature, 2006), and the Society of Biblical Literature has granted me permission to reprint this article.

"The Apocalypse of John and Palestinian Jewish Apocalyptic" has just appeared in *Neotestamentica* 40 (2006) 1–33, and the editor, Jonathan Draper, has given his permission to reprint it.

"The Social Matrix of the Apocalypse of John" was initially published by *Biblical Research*, 26 (1981), 16–32, and the editor has granted permission to reprint it.

"Stories of Jesus in the Apocalypse of John" was published in *Contours of Christology in the New Testament*, ed. Richard N. Longenecker (Grand Rapids: Eerdmans, 2005), 292–319, and the W. B. Eerdmans Publishing Company has granted permission to reprint the article.

"The Form and Function of the Proclamations to the Seven Churches (Rev 2–3)" appeared in *New Testament Studies*, 36 (1990), 182–204, and the current editor, Judith Lieu, has given permission to reprint this article, on behalf of the copyright holder, Cambridge University Press.

"Revelation 5 as an Ancient Egyptian Enthronement Scene? The Origin and Development of a Scholarly Myth" was published on pp. 85–91 in *Kropp og Sjel: Festkrift til Olav Hognestad.* (ed. Theodor Jørgensen, Dagfinn Rian and Ole Gunnar Winsnes; Trondheim: Tapir Akademisk Forlag, 2000), and permission was obtained from Tapir Akademisk Forlag to reprint this article.

"The Prophetic Circle of John of Patmos and the Exegesis of Revelation 22:16" was originally published in *Journal for the Study of the New Testament*, 37 (1989), 103–116, and reprinted in S. E. Porter and C. A. Evans (eds.), *The Johannine Writings*, Biblical Seminar 32 (Sheffield: Sheffield Academic Press, 1995). Permission is granted by Sage Publications Ltd. to reprint this article for non-exclusive world rights in the English language only.

"God and Time in the Apocalypse of John" originally appeared in *The Forgotten God: The God of Jesus Christ in New Testament Theology: Essays in Honor of Paul J. Achtemeier on the Occasion of his Seventy-fifth Birthday*, ed. Frank J.

Matera and A. Andrew Das (Louisville: Westminster John Knox, 2002), © 2002 Westminster John Knox Press. Used by permission of Westminster John Knox Press.

"Charismatic Exegesis in Early Judaism and Early Christianity" first appeared on pp. 126–150 in *The Pseudepigrapha and Early Biblical Interpretation*, ed. J.H. Charlesworth and C.A. Evans (Sheffield: Sheffield University, 1993) and permission to reprint this article was granted by the copyright holder, Continuum International.

"Christian Prophecy and the Messianic Status of Jesus" was first printed in J.H. Charlesworth, ed., *The Messiah: Developments in Earliest Judaism and Christianity* (Minneapolis: Fortress, 1992), 404–422. Fortress Press, the copyright holder, granted permission to reprint this article.

"The Odes of Solomon and Early Christian Prophecy" first appeared in *New Testament Studies*, 28 (1982), 435–60, and permission to reprint the article was given by Dr. Judith Lieu, the current editor on behalf of the copyright holder, Cambridge University Press.

"The Apocalypse of John and Graeco-Roman Revelatory Magic" initially published in *New Testament Studies*, 33 (1987), 481–501, is reprinted by permission of the current editor, Dr. Judith Lieu, on behalf of Cambridge University Press, the copyright holder.

"Magic in Early Christianity" was published in *Aufstieg und Niedergang der römischen Welt*, edited by H. Temporini and W. Haase, Part II, 23/2 (Berlin and New York: Walter de Gruyter, 1980), pp. 1507–1557, and is reprinted by permission.

Finally, I would like to express my gratitude to a number of people who have made the present collection of essays possible. Two graduate assistants in the PhD program in Christianity and Judaism in Antiquity at the University of Notre Dame, Ardea Caviggiola Russo and Matthew Gordley scanned and corrected earlier articles for which I had no computer files. Prof. Dr. Jörg Frey, editor of Wissenschaftliche Untersuchungen zum Neuen Testament, has been encouraging me for several years to produce a collection of my essays on apocalypticism and the Apocalypse, and I thank him for his encouragement and friendship.

David E. Aune
University of Notre Dame

Table of Contents

Understanding Jewish and Christian Apocalyptic

1. Defining Apocalyptic

Francis Ford Coppola's disturbing film "Apocalypse Now" (1979), re-released in 2001 under the title "Apocalypse Now Redux" (with previously cut footage restored) is a frightening, surrealistic epic enabling viewers to experience the obscene violence that characterized the war in Vietnam. Coppola's juxtaposition of the term "apocalypse" with the adverb "now" is what Biblical scholars have called "realized eschatology," that is, events properly belonging to the *end* of the world are paradoxically experienced as *present*. "Apocalypse Now" implies that the appalling and obscene horrors experienced by those caught up in the conflict in Vietnam were at least a partially realization of the even more cataclysmic and violent eschatological events narrated (for example) in the Apocalypse (or Revelation) of John. Recently, journalists have repeatedly characterized the Tsunami disaster in the countries surrounding the Indian Ocean as "a catastrophe of *Biblical* proportions." Here the adjective "Biblical" (meaning "awesome"), is clearly a surrogate for "apocalyptic," alluding to the kind of massive destruction predicted by the Hebrew prophets and narrated in the eschatological visions of the Revelation of John.

The term "apocalyptic," an adjective functioning as a noun, is synonymous with the noun "apocalypticism," and both are transliterated forms of the Greek adjective ἀποκαλύπτικος, meaning "revelatory," while "apocalypse" is a transliteration of the Greek noun ἀποκάλυψις, "unveiling, revelation." The English words "reveal" and "revelation" are transliterations of the Latin verb *revelare* and noun *revelatio*. Apocalyptic or apocalypticism is a slippery term used in at least three different ways: (1) as a type of literature, (2) as a type of eschatology, and (3) as a type of collective behavior. Each of these categories needs some explanation.

Apocalyptic as Literature

The term "apocalypse" has become a common designation for a type of supernatural visionary literature depicting the imminent and catastrophic end of the world. "Apocalypse" was borrowed from the opening verse of the Revelation of John: "The revelation [the Greek term is ἀποκάλυψις or "apocalypse"] of Jesus Christ, which God gave him to show to his servants what must soon take place." This opening sentence, intended by the author to describe his work, was later shortened into the title found in modern Bibles: "The Revelation of John," or "The Apocalypse of John." Even though John the Apocalyptist used the term "apocalypse" to refer to the *content* of his book, i. e., what God had revealed to him, by the mid-19th century, German scholars such as Friedrich Lücke (1832) used the term "apocalypse" as a designation for an ancient type or genre of early Jewish and early Christian literature similar to Daniel and the Revelation of John. The book of Daniel (actually, only Dan 7–12) is the only apocalypse found in the Old Testament or Hebrew Bible, but many apocalypses were written in early Judaism, including *1 Enoch* (really a composite of five separate apocalyptic works), *2 Enoch*, *2 Baruch*, the *Sibylline Oracles* and the *Apocalypse of Abraham* (to name a few of the more important ones).[1] In addition to the Revelation of John, early Christians wrote several other apocalypses, including Hermas' *The Shepherd* (early 2nd cent. CE), the *Apocalypse of Peter* (before 150 CE), the *Ascension of Isaiah* (late 2nd cent. CE) and the *Apocalypse of Paul* (mid-3rd cent.CE).[2]

How can we describe the literary form of the typical apocalypse? New Testament scholars have debated this question endlessly during the last generation. With David Hellholm, it is helpful to think in terms of a literary form or genre under three aspects: form, content and function (e. g., form: a chair has four legs a seat and a back; content: it is typically made of wood or metal; function: it is used for sitting).[3] In *form*, an apocalypse is a first-person recital of revelatory visions or dreams, framed by a description of the circumstances of the revelatory experience, and structured to emphasize the central revelatory message. In *content*, an apocalypse involves the communication of a transcendent, often eschatological perspective on human experience. Finally, apocalypses typically have a threefold *function*: they legitimate the message through the appeal to transcendent authority by the author (i. e., it is from God), they create a literary surrogate of the author's revelatory experience for readers or hearers (i. e., God speaks to the modern reader just as he spoke to John), and they motivate the recipients to modify their views and behaviors in conformity with transcendent perspectives (i. e., they demand changed behavior).[4]

---

[1] Convenient English translations of nearly all the extant Jewish apocalypses can be found in the first volume of James H. Charlesworth (ed.), *The Old Testament Pseudepigrapha*, 2 vols. (Garden City, New York: Doubleday & Company, 1983–85).

[2] Convenient English translations of many early Christian apocalypses can be found in J.K. Elliott (ed.), *The Apocryphal New Testament: A Collection of Apocryphal Christian Literature in an English Translation based on M. R. James* (Oxford: Clarendon Press, 1993), and in the second volume of Wilhelm Schneemelcher (ed.), *New Testament Apocrypha*, translated by R. McL. Wilson (2 vols.; Cambridge: James Clark; Louisville: Westminster John Knox, 1991–92).

[3] David Hellholm, "The Problem of Apocalyptic Genre and the Apocalypse of John," *Semeia* 36 (1986) 13–64.

[4] David E. Aune, "The Apocalypse of John and the Problem of Genre," *Semeia* 36 (1986) 65–96. Reprinted below, pp. 39-65.

All extant Jewish apocalypses are pseudonymous, that is, they were written by unknown Jewish authors using the names of ancient Israelite or Jewish worthies as pen names, attributing them to such figures as Adam, Enoch, Abraham, Moses, Daniel, Ezra and Baruch. Only the two earliest Christian apocalypses, the Revelation of the John and *The Shepherd* by Hermas were written using the names of the actual authors. Later Christian apocalypses, such as the *Apocalypse of Peter* and the *Apocalypse of Paul* reverted to the earlier Jewish practice of pseudonymity. Why use pseudonyms? Some have suggested that the authors borrowed the credentials of ancient Israelite figures in order to insure that people would read their books at a time (2nd cent. BCE through the 1st cent. CE) when there was stiff competition from the books that wound up in the Hebrew canon of Scripture. Others have suggested that they identified themselves in an almost mystical way with the ancient Israelite whose identity they assumed.

Finally, apocalypses can be broadly characterized as *protest literature*. That is, they typically represent the perspective of an oppressed minority. It is difficult to reconstruct the social situations within which many apocalypses were produced because the use of pseudonyms and symbolism masked the specific social and political setting within which they wrote. With the Revelation of John and *The Shepherd* of Hermas, however, interpreters have an easier task, since both were written by specific named authors addressing specific situations. The language of persecution pervades the Revelation of John, suggesting to many that it was written either in the late 60's (during the Neronian persecution), or during the late 90's (during the Domitianic persecution). Research carried out during the last thirty years, however, has suggested a radically different understanding of the persecution issue. The persecution under Nero, terrible as it was, was restricted to Rome during the aftermath of the great fire of 64 CE, for which Christians were blamed (Tacitus *Annals* 15.44). The persecution under Domitian, under closer historical scrutiny, turned out to have been a myth fanned much later by retrospective Christian imagination.[5] Adela Yarbro Collins argued convincingly that the social situation in which the Revelation of John was written was that of a *perceived* (in contrast to a *real*) crisis.[6] Pressure exerted against Christians in Roman Asia toward the end of the 1st and the beginning of the 2nd cent. CE, is now recognized as having been random, local and sporadic (i. e., they were victims of terrorism), but not an official persecution of the type that occurred much later under the emperor Decius (249–51 CE). However, Christians in Roman Asia can be forgiven if they thought that the roof was about to fall in on them. The Revelation of John reflects that fear, linked to powerful symbols of the past used as types of the imminent eschatological persecution (e. g., the

---

[5] Leonard L. Thompson, *The Book of Revelation: Apocalypse and Empire* (New York and Oxford: Oxford University Press, 1990).

[6] Adela Yarbro Collins, *Crisis and Catharsis: The Power of the Apocalypse* (Philadelphia: The Westminster Press, 1984), 84–110.

figure of Antichrist was based in part on tyrants of the past such as Antiochus Epiphanes, the Seleucid ruler responsible for the religious persecution of Jews in the 160's BCE).

Apocalyptic Eschatology

"Apocalyptic eschatology" is the narrative theology characteristic of apocalypses, centering in the belief that (1) the present world order, regarded as both evil and oppressive, is under the temporary control of Satan and his human accomplices, and (2) that this present evil world order will shortly be destroyed by God and replaced by a new and perfect order corresponding to Eden before the fall. During the present evil age, the people of God are an oppressed minority who fervently expect God, or his specially chosen agent the Messiah, to rescue them. The transition between the old and the new ages will be introduced with a final series of battles fought by the people of God against the human allies of Satan. The outcome is never in question, however, for the enemies of God are predestined for defeat and destruction. The inauguration of the new age will begin with the arrival of God or his accredited agent to judge the wicked and reward the righteous, and will be concluded by the re-creation or transformation of the earth and the heavens. This theological narrative characterized segments of early Judaism from ca. 200 BCE to ca. 200 CE, a period when they were oppressed by foreign occupations, including the Greek kingdom of the Seleucids and then by the Romans. Knowledge of cosmic secrets and the imminent eschatological plans of God were thought to be revealed to apocalyptists through dreams and visions, some real, some fictional and some a combination of both. The apocalypses they wrote were primarily accounts of these visions, with the meaning made clear to the readers through use of the literary device of an "interpreting angel," who explained everything to the seer through a question-and-answer dialogue.

"Eschatology" has frequently been distinguished from "apocalyptic," and this distinction needs explanation. Eschatology is a term that began to be used in the 19th century as a label for that aspect of systematic theology which dealt with the future of the individual (death, resurrection, judgment, eternal life, heaven and hell), and topics relating to corporate or national eschatology, that is the future of the Jewish people (i.e., the coming of the Messiah, the great tribulation, the resurrection, the final judgment, the temporary Messianic kingdom, the re-creation of the universe) or the Christian church (all of these topics were adopted, yet at the same time subordinated to the hope of the Parousia or Second Coming of Christ).

A distinction has often been made between "prophetic eschatology" and "apocalyptic eschatology," underscoring continuities as well as changes in Israelite-Jewish eschatological expectation. "Prophetic eschatology" is regarded as an optimistic perspective anticipating God's eventual restoration of the original pristine conditions of human history by acting through historical processes. This view is well represented by Isa 2:4b (NRSV): "They shall beat their swords into plowshares, and their spears into pruning hooks; nation shall not life up sword against nation, neither shall they learn war any more." Prophecy sees the future as arising from the present, while apocalyptic eschatology regards the future as breaking into the present; the former is essentially optimistic, while the latter is pessimistic. "Apocalyptic eschatology" is pessimistic about the fate of the righteous in the present world order, and anticipates a cataclysmic divine intervention into the human world bringing history to an end, but thereafter a renewal of the world in which Edenic conditions will be restored.

Apocalypticism or Millenarian Movements

"Apocalypticism," or millennialism (a term derived from the thousand year reign of Christ described in Rev 20) is a form of collective religious behavior inspired by the belief that the world as we know it is about to end and drastic steps must be taken by an oppressed minority to prepare for an imminent catastrophe. Millennial or millenarian movements in third world societies have been studied extensively by anthropologists and sociologists, and the results of these studies have made it possible to understand the structure, function and motivations of ancient millennial movements.[7] Millenarian movements typically crystallize around a charismatic leader regarded as supernaturally endowed to lead his followers to accomplish group goals. The leaders of millenarian movements in ancient Palestine were typically labeled "prophets" and "messiahs" because they were thought by their followers (and themselves) to have been chosen by God and endowed with supernatural powers, like the prophets of old, to pave the way for the full realization of God's eschatological rule. Palestinian millenarian movements were "revitalistic movements," whose purpose was the revival of ancient Israelite religious and nationalistic ideals within an eschatological framework. Millennarian movements within first century Judaism were not uncommon, since the oppressive conditions of the Roman occupation provided a seedbed for religious revolt. Examples include the movement led by John the Baptist (who proclaimed the necessity of repentance in preparation for the imminent arrival of the kingdom of God) and the revolts of Theudas reported in Acts 5:36 and Josephus (*Antiquities* 20.5.1), and the unnamed Egyptian (mentioned in Acts 21:38 and Josephus *Antiquities* 20.169–72 and *Jewish War* 2.261–63). A showcase example of an early Jewish millenarian movement is the Qumran Community, who lived in expectation of the near end of the world, and whose library, the Dead Sea Scrolls, contains many texts produced by the community

[7] Bryan R. Wilson, *Magic and the Millennium: A Sociological Study of Movements of Protest among Tribal and Third-World Peoples* (New York: Harper & Row, 1973); Norman Cohn, *The Pursuit of the Millennium* (revised edition; Oxford: Oxford University Press, 1970).

that testify to their preoccupation with the end of days. Apocalypses themselves, however, which present themselves as esoteric wisdom, do not appear to have had any *direct* connection with the millenarian movements roughly contemporaneous with them (Dan 7–12 may be an exception). This view is strengthened by the fact that, although the Qumran Community has an obvious apocalyptic orientation, no member of the community appears to have written an apocalypse.

2. The Origins of Apocalyptic

The origins of apocalypticism in Judaism are disputed. Many have argued for a continuity between prophecy and apocalyptic, suggesting that apocalyptic was a logical historical development of Old Testament prophecy, perhaps as a result of national disillusionment associated with the post-exilic period (beginning ca. 538 BCE, with the return of some exiled Judahites from Babylon narrated in Ezra 1–2). In the post-exilic period, the returned Judeans were subject to foreign nations (Persia, followed by the Greek Ptolemaic and Seleucid empires, and eventually by the Romans), and tensions existed also within the Jewish community both in the eastern diaspora (where a sizable Jewish community remained until the rise of Islam in the 7th cent. CE) and in Judah.

Toward the end of the last century it became increasingly evident that prophecy and apocalyptic exhibit both continuity and discontinuity. The sharp contrast often thought to exist between them can be moderated by recognizing the fact that prophecy was not a stable phenomenon and exhibits development and change throughout the history of Israel and then in the postexilic period in Judah. Some sections of later prophetic books, such as Zech 1–6 (where an interpreting angel explains the meaning of visions to Zechariah), Isa 24–27, 56–66, Joel and Zach 9–14, have been aptly described as "proto-apocalyptic" works. A description of how proto-apocalyptic sections of the Old Testament served as a transition to Jewish apocalypses is convincingly presented by Old Testament scholar Paul D. Hanson.[8]

Others have argued that there was a fundamental break between prophecy and apocalyptic. The German scholar Gerhard von Rad (1901–1971), for example, rejected the view that the primary roots of apocalypticism were to be found in Israelite prophecy.[9] Describing apocalypticism as consisting in a belief in cosmic dualism, radical transcendence of God, esotericism and gnosticism, he proposed that apocalypticism arose out of the wisdom literature of the Old Testament. Considerably less popular is the minority view that apocalypticism was essen-

---

[8] Paul D. Hanson, *The Dawn of Apocalyptic: The Historical and Sociological Roots of Jewish Apocalyptic Eschatology* (revised edition; Philadelphia: Fortress Press, 1979).

[9] Gerhard von Rad, *Wisdom and Apocalyptic* (Nashville: Abingdon Press, 1972).

tially alien to Judaism and that it originated in Iran and had penetrated Jewish thought from the outside during the Hellenistic period (ca. 400–200 BCE).

3. Was Jesus an Apocalyptist?

Toward the end of the 19th century, liberal Protestant Biblical scholars in Europe and America tended to regard Jesus as a religious genius who taught such timeless truths as the universal fatherhood of God, the fact that all humankind were sisters and brothers, and the worth and potential of the individual. Wilhelm Hermann (1841–1905) and Adolf von Harnack (1851–1930) regarded Jesus' proclamation of the Kingdom of God as the rule of God in the hearts of humankind, while the great Albrecht Ritschl (1822–1889) and the social gospel movement he mentored saw it as the realization of an ideal society on earth. Albert Schweitzer (1875–1965), in a critical review of scores of 18th and 19th century lives of Jesus, exposed the extent to which well-meaning liberal scholars had projected their own theological views back into their reconstructions of the historical Jesus.[10] The liberal quest for the historical Jesus was carried out at a time when a negative attitude toward early Judaism as a legalistic and decadent religion was widely assumed, and Jewish apocalyptic literature was considered a particularly appalling development within Judaism. At the close of the 19th century, Johannes Weiss (1863–1914), a German Protestant New Testament scholar, took seriously the apocalyptic features of Jesus' proclamation of the imminent coming of the Kingdom of God, and wrote an influential monograph arguing that Jesus himself held an apocalyptic world view strikingly at odds with modern views.[11] In Schweitzer's critique of lives of Jesus, written a few years after the appearance of Weiss' book, he criticized the liberal quest for the historical Jesus as a bankrupt enterprise. However, he understood Jesus as a kind of wild-eyed apocalyptist who willingly died in a last-ditch attempt to force God to inaugurate his kingdom. "The historical Jesus," concluded Schweitzer, "will be to our time a stranger and an enigma."[12] Schweitzer's devastating critique coupled with the depiction of Jesus as an apocalyptic fanatic brought down the curtain on the writing of lives of Jesus on the Continent for nearly a generation.

Following the two world wars, interest in the historical Jesus picked up again in Germany, though interest had never really flagged in the United States and England. Scholars such as W. G. Kümmel argued convincingly that, unlike the typical apocalyptic emphasis on the future, Jesus taught that the Kingdom of

---

[10] Albert Schweitzer, *The Quest of the Historical Jesus* (New York: Macmillan, 1961; German original 1906).

[11] Johannes Weiss, *Jesus' Proclamation of the Kingdom of God*, translated by Richard Hiers and David L. Holland (Philadelphia: Fortress Press, 1971; German original 1892).

[12] Schweitzer, *The Quest of the Historical Jesus*, 399.

God was both present as well as future.[13] Though some English scholars (notably C.H. Dodd) tended to emphasize the presence of the Kingdom of God in the teaching of Jesus to the virtual exclusion of the future,[14] many if not most New Testament scholars in the 1960's and 1970's (some representative names include Joachim Jeremias, Norman Perrin and George Ladd) understood that Jesus saw a tension between present realization and future fulfillment of the Kingdom of God, making him far from a typical apocalyptist..

By the 1980's, the so-called Third Quest of the historical Jesus began to pick up steam.[15] This concern with the historical Jesus by a motley collection of scholars with widely different perspectives, has tended to focus on the critical importance of understanding Jesus in light of his Jewish context, regarded much more positively than it had been during the 19th century. Scholars who are associated with the Third Quest, such as John Meier, a professor of New Testament at the University of Notre Dame, tend to take the Jewish setting of eschatological message of Jesus very seriously, while at the same time recognizing that Jesus had his own very distinct message.[16] At the same time that the Third Quest began to crystallize into a trend, the Jesus Seminar, a group of critical scholars led by Robert Funk became active in a distinctive research program intended to recover the historical Jesus. Members of the Jesus Seminar (which includes such influential scholars as Marcus J. Borg and John Dominic Crossan) discounted the apocalyptic elements of the teachings of Jesus as a later development in early Christianity that obscured the earlier more historical character of Jesus as a non-eschatological teacher of wisdom. At the beginning of the 21st century then, two very different approaches to understanding the mission and message of Jesus are in play: Jesus the apocalyptic prophet vs. Jesus the Jewish sage. Those who regard Jesus as an apocalyptic prophet tend to view his teachings from the standpoint of the eschatological material found in the Gospels, while those who consider Jesus as a Jewish sage tend to make the ethical and proverbial teachings of Jesus the key to understanding his message.

4. Paul the Apocalyptist

One of the debated issues in modern the modern study of Paul is the extent to which it is appropriate to characterize Pauline thought as "apocalyptic." While there is widespread agreement that Paul was influenced by apocalyptic eschatol-

[13] W.G. Kümmel, *Promise and Fulfilment: The Eschatological Message of Jesus* (London: SCM Press, 1957).

[14] C.H. Dodd, *The Parables of the Kingdom* (New York: Charles Scribner's Sons, 1961).

[15] The Third Quest is chronicled by Ben Witherington, *The Jesus Quest: The Third Search for the Jew of Nazareth* (2nd edition; Downers Grove: InterVarsity Press, 1997).

[16] John Paul Meier, *A Marginal Jew: Rethinking the Historical Jesus* (3 volumes and counting; New York: Doubleday, 1991–2001).

ogy, the extent to which he modified apocalypticism in light of his faith in Christ is still debated. Rudolf Bultmann eliminated apocalyptic features from Paul's thought using what he called "critical theological interpretation" (*Sachkritik*). He argued, for example, that in 1 Cor 15:1–15, where Paul proposes a historical argument for the resurrection of Jesus, he has violated his own theological standards by embracing a motif of apocalyptic myth that he elsewhere demythologizes.[17] Following this same tack, Baumgarten suggested that Paul has demythologized apocalyptic traditions by consistently applying them to the present life of the community.[18]

The authors of Jewish apocalypses, though they typically concealed their identities behind pseudonyms, claimed to receive divine revelations through visions and they therefore structured the apocalypses they wrote as series of vision narratives. While there is no evidence that Paul himself wrote an apocalypse, he does claim to have received revelatory visions and had ecstatic experiences.[19] In Gal 1:12, in fact, he refers to his Damascus Road experience as an ἀποχάλυψις ("revelation") from Jesus Christ, and in 2 Cor 12:1 he speaks of "visions and revelations of the Lord," presumably describing his own experiences.

Again, though Paul probably did not write an apocalypse, he does include four relatively extensive apocalyptic scenarios (i. e., sequences of events that Paul expects to transpire in the eschaton) in his letters. Three of these scenarios center on the Parousia or Second Coming of Jesus (1 Thess 4:13–18; 2 Thess 1:5–12; 1 Cor 15:57–58). The fourth scenario, sometimes referred to as the "Pauline apocalypse," is found in 2 Thess 2:1–12, centering on the coming of the eschatological antagonist or Antichrist. Since 2 Thessalonians is widely considered to be pseudepigraphical, the two passages mentioned above found in that letter may reflect the apocalyptic eschatology of the Pauline school or circle rather than of Paul himself.

Like the Jewish apocalyptists, Paul holds a form of temporal dualism that contrasts the present evil age with the coming age of salvation (Gal 1:4; Rom 8:18; 1 Cor 1:26). Yet it is also apparent that Paul has considerably modified the sharp distinction usually made in apocalyptic thought between the present evil age and the age to come. Paul understood the death and resurrection of Jesus in the past as the cosmic eschatological event that separated "this age" (Rom 12:2; 1 Cor 1:20; 2:6) or "this present evil age" (Gal 1:4) from "the age to come." This means that though Paul regards himself as living in the present age, dominated by demonic powers, nevertheless because of the death and resurrection of Jesus

---

[17] Rudolf Bultmann, *Theology of the New Testament* (2 vols.; New York: Charles Scribner's Sons, 1951–55) I.295–96, 305.

[18] Jörg Baumgarten, *Paulus und die Apokalyptik* (Neukirchen-Vluyn: Neukirchener Verlag, 1975).

[19] Gal 1:11–17; 1 Cor 9:1; 15:8; see also Acts 9:1–9; 16:9; 18:9–10; 22:6–11, 17–21; 26:12–18; 27:23–24.

these evil powers have been defeated and are therefore doomed to pass away (1 Cor 2:6–7).

Paul's belief in the resurrection of Jesus the Messiah, convinced him that eschatological events had begun to take place within history, and that the resurrection of Jesus was part of the traditional Jewish expectation of the resurrection of the righteous (1 Cor 15:20–23). For Paul, the present time is just a temporary period between the death and resurrection of Christ on the one hand, and his return in glory on the other, in which those who believe in the gospel will share in the salvific benefits of the age to come (Gal 1:4; 2 Cor 5:17). This temporary period is characterized by the eschatological gift of the Spirit of God, experienced as present within the Christian community as well as individual believers (Rom 8:9–11; 1 Cor 6:19; 12:4–11; 1 Thess 4:8). While Paul did not explicitly use the phrase "the age to come," in 2 Cor 5:17 and Gal 6:15 he does use the phrase "new creation," which has apocalyptic associations (see Isa 65:17; 66:22; Rev 21:1). Though the final consummation is still future for Paul, the new age was present for Christians because the Messiah had come.

5. Apocalypse Now and Then

The strange, even bizarre, world of apocalypses and apocalypticism seems light years away from the world that most of us inhabit. The two Biblical apocalypses, Daniel and Revelation, have been influential throughout the history of the church particularly during periods of social unrest, dislocation and war. The lavishly illuminated commentary on Revelation compiled by Beatus of Liebana, Spain (8th cent. CE), saw the Arab invasion of Spain as anticipated in Biblical prophecy, and the enormously influential philosophy of history of Joachim of Fiore (ca. 1132–1202 CE), based in part on the Revelation of John, was a response to conflicts between the poor and the rich, the worldly and the spiritual, which tested the church of his day. More recently, the Revelation of John has had renewed influence when read by liberation theologians, with their fundamental concern for social justice. The works by Pablo Richard, Catherine and Justo González, and Jean-Pierre Ruiz, are just a few of many possible examples.[20] In the apposite words of Catherine and Justo González:[21]

> We are also part of a worldwide church that in many areas is living under circumstances similar to those of the first century. Injustice and idolatry are still rampant both in our

[20] Pablo Richard, *Apocalypse: A People's Commentary on the Book of Revelation* (Maryknoll: Orbis Books, 1995);Catherine Gunsalus González and Justo L. González, *Revelation* (Louisville: Westminster John Knox, 1997); Jean-Pierre Ruiz, "Biblical Interpretation from a US Hispanic American Perspective: A Reading of the Apocalpse," *El Cuerpo de Cristo: The Hispanic Presence in the US Catholic Church*, edited by Peter J. Cassarella and Raul Gomez (New York: Crossroad, 1998), 78–105.

[21] González and González, *Revelation*, 3.

society and throughout the world. For these reasons, it is good that the book of Revelation, with its dire warnings against those who would rather be comfortable or successful than faithful, is part of our New Testament.

The polyvalent symbolism of apocalypses has proven to be a two-edged sword, and the Revelation of John in particular (sometimes correlated with Daniel) has frequently been commandeered by sectarian movements which have perverted its message in support of destructive and pathological behavior. During the tragic Anabaptist rebellion in 1535, the rebels established a center at Münster, which they believed was chosen by God to be the site of the new Jerusalem, and tried to bring in the new age by force only to be defeated by a coalition of Roman Catholic and Lutheran troops. More recently, apocalyptic expectation fueled by David Koresh's bizarre interpretation of Revelation ended in the fiery destruction of the Branch Davidian compound at Waco, Texas on April 19, 1993, resulting in 86 deaths, including that of Koresh himself. A few years later, in 1997, thirty-nine members of the Heaven's Gate community at Rancho Santa Fe, California killed themselves, intending to board a hovering spaceship unencumbered by their human bodies, all this calculated to coordinate with the appearance of the Hale-Bopp comet. The two leaders of the cult, Marshall Applewhite (who had predicted the imminent end of the world in 1992) and Bonnie Lu Nettles, known as "Bo" and "Peep," identified themselves as the two lampstands of Rev 11.

Daniel and Revelation have exerted a perennial fascination among Protestant Fundamentalists, particularly premillennial dispensationalists (nurtured by the *Schofield Reference Bible*), who interpret these texts literally, regarding them as play-by-play coded descriptions of the historical events that were unfolding in the late 20th (now the 21st century). Examples of this kind of literalistic exegesis include Hal Lindsey's frequently revised bestseller, *The Late Great Planet Earth*, and the more recent dispensationalist commentary on Revelation by Tim LaHaye, both of whom have rejected conventional scholarly interpretations of Daniel and Revelation as liberal betrayals of the divinely inscribed message of those books.[22] LaHaye and Jim Jenkins, of course are co-authors of the enormously popular *Left Behind Series*, a series of (thus far) twelve books of "apocalyptic fiction," making lavish use of such symbols as the Rapture (understood as imminent), and the Antichrist and the Mark of the Beast (the latter has been understood by some as referring to the widespread use of universal product codes).

Despite the ways in which the Biblical apocalypses have been abused as various times throughout Christian history, Daniel and Revelation have important positive theological contributions to make to the modern church. Sermons on Revelation generally tend to focus on the sections of moral and spiritual exhorta-

[22] Tim LaHaye, *Revelation Unveiled* (Grand Rapids: Zondervan, 1999). A more scholarly dispensationalist approach to Revelation can be found in Robert L. Thomas *Revelation* (2 vols. Chicago: Moody Press, 1995).

tion found at the beginning and end of the book (Rev 1–3 and Rev 22), while the divine punishments narrated in the sequences of the opening of the seven seals, the blowing of the seven trumpets, and the pouring out of the seven vials are understandably given short shrift in pulpits (Rev 4–16). Yet these neglected chapters make an important contribution to the Christian knowledge of God. While elsewhere in the New Testament God is limited to a few lines in the Gospels as a heavenly voice at Jesus' baptism and transfiguration, in Revelation he is given two short but profound speeches. The shortest is found in Rev 1:8 and emphasizes God's comprehensive and transcendent sovereignty as the book begins (NRSV): "I am the Alpha and the Omega," says the Lord God, "who is and who was and who is to come, the Almighty." The longer divine speech is situated at the core of the book and summarizes the basic theological message of the entire work: God sovereignly rewards the righteous and judges the wicked (Rev 21:5–8; NRSV):

> And the one who was seated on the throne said, "See, I am making all things new." Also he said, "Write this, for these words are trustworthy and true." Then he said to me, "It is done! I am the Alpha and the Omega, the beginning and the end. To the thirsty I will give water as a gift from the spring of the water of life. Those who conquer will inherit these things, and I will be their God and they will be my children. But as for the cowardly, the faithless, the polluted, the murderers, the fornicators, the sorcerers, the idolaters, and all liars, their place will be in the lake that burns with fire and sulfur, which is the second death."

The divine self-predication "the Alpha and the Omega," found in both of these passages, is also a self-predication of Christ in Rev. 22:13. Similarly, the title "the Beginning and the End" used of God in Rev 21:5–8, is also applied to Christ in Rev. 22:13. These two observations, confirmed by many other passages in Revelation, argue that God and Christ share divine sovereignty.[23]

One of the more striking features of Revelation is the numerous throne scenes in the book, the most impressive of which is in Rev 4–5. There the author uses a kaleidoscope of imagery to convey the transcendent power and mystery of the God who rules over human history. For original readers whose faith had been shaken, in large part because they were innocent victims of terrorist attacks by their "neighbors," the author makes clear the fact that God remains in firm control of the events of history despite appearances to the contrary, and that the final victory will ultimately be theirs. Finally, the recurring waves of divine punishment inflicted on unbelieving humankind in Rev 4–16, present an aspect of the Biblical conception of God that many would just as soon forget. Yet the fact that God ultimately punishes wickedness (and there is plenty of it in the modern world), was understood by the original readers as a demonstration that the God of Abraham, Isaac, Jacob and Jesus is a God of justice as well as a God of love.

[23] David E. Aune, "God and Time in the Apocalypse of John," *The Forgotten God: Perspectives in Biblical Theology*, edited by A. Andrew Das and Frank J. Matera (Louisville: Westminster John Knox, 2002), 229–48. Reprinted below on pp. 261–79

From the Idealized Past to the Imaginary Future

Eschatological Restoration in Jewish Apocalyptic Literature

1. Introduction

The concept of "restoration" is rooted in the pre-modern perception of culture which explicitly and implicitly regarded the imagined past as the sole legitimate basis for appraising the legitimacy of the present and envisioning or shaping the future.[1] As religious literature, Jewish apocalypses were centrally concerned with the problem of evil and fallenness, with the ultimate solution projected into the eschatological or imaginary future where both the punishment and salvation of responsible moral agents would be meted out by God.[2] Salvation, the positive aspect of the solution, is a mythical conception which can be defined as the divinely determined restoration of individuals and the societies in which they are enmeshed to the ideal state which had once been possible for them to enjoy. The conception that the End should recapitulate the Beginning (the *Urzeit / Endzeit* or "protology" / "eschatology" pattern), which is understood as both perfect and paradigmatic, forms the basic horizon of the apocalyptic view of the world, for the imperfect present lies at the low point between the perfections of the distant past and the perfections of the imminent future. The eschatological and mythical focus of Jewish apocalyptic literature makes it appropriate to confine this inquiry to the ways in which apocalyptic conceptions of the paradigmatic past became the basis for imagining the future as a return to the past, for from the apocalyptic perspective all aspects of the existing world system are hopelessly debased and in need of divine reconstitution.

After first defining the specific corpus of Jewish apocalyptic literature which will be the focus of this investigation, I will sketch out the main clusters of restoration themes which will be investigated in that literature. The main sections of the paper will then consist of analyses of each of these clusters of themes.

---

[1] On the contrast between modernity and pre-modernity, see Göran Therborn, *European Modernity and Beyond: The Trajectory of European Society, 1945–2000* (London: Sage Publications, 1995) 3–5.

[2] An attempt to analyze the religious explanations for evil and death found in two late apocalypses is the study by T. W. Willett, *Eschatology in the Theodocies of 2 Baruch and 4 Ezra* (JSPSup 4; Sheffield: JSOT Press, 1989).

The major limitation in restricting this investigation to ten Jewish apocalypses is that the results cannot be generalized beyond this group of texts, while the major limitation of the thematic approach is the fact that the study of themes in Jewish apocalypses is beset with a host of critical problems that can only be briefly mentioned.

The term "apocalypticism" is a somewhat infelicitous modern designation for a worldview which characterized segments of early Judaism,[3] centering on the expectation of God's imminent intervention into human history to save his people and punish their enemies by destroying the existing cosmic order and by restoring or recreating the cosmos to its original pristine perfection. The apocalyptic worldview is characteristic of, though not limited to, a type of early Jewish and early Christian literature called "apocalypses." Arising from proto-apocalyptic segments of post-exilic OT prophetic literature,[4] the main corpus of Jewish apocalypses originated between 250 BCE and 150 CE, a period when Palestine was successively dominated by the Greeks and then the Romans. As an appropriate database for the present investigation, I will examine ten Jewish religious works widely regarded as apocalypses, and arrange them chronologically into earlier and later groups in order to see whether a rough diachrony reflects any differences. The early group consists of five apocalypses which originated from the late third century through the second century BCE:[5] (1) the Book of Heavenly Luminaries (*1 Enoch* 72–82), third cent. BCE, (2) the Book of Watchers (*1 Enoch* 1–36), late third cent. BCE, (3) Daniel (particularly the apocalyptic section in 7–12), 167–164 BCE, (4) the *Epistle of Enoch* (*1 Enoch* 92–104), between 175 and 167 BCE, including the *Apocalypse of Weeks* (93:1–10 + 91:11–18), between 175 and 167 BCE, (5) the *Book of Dreams* (*1 Enoch* 83–90), ca. 160 BCE, including the *Animal Apocalypse* (85–90), ca. 160 BCE.[6]

The later group of Jewish apocalypses, separated from the early group by 150 to 200 years, includes works which originated from (perhaps) the early first century through (perhaps) the middle of the second century CE: (1) the Similitudes of Enoch (*1 Enoch* 37–71), early first cent. CE,[7] (2) 2 *Enoch*,[8] first cent. CE or

[3] See the critique of the term "apocalyptic" by T. F. Glasson, "What is Apocalyptic?" *NTS* 27 (1980) 98–105.

[4] Paul D. Hanson, *The Dawn of Apocalyptic* (revised edition; Philadelphia: Fortress, 1979).

[5] The dates suggested are those cogently argued for by James C. VanderKam, *Enoch and the Growth of an Apocalyptic Tradition* (CBQMS 16; Washington, D.C. : The Catholic Biblical Association of America, 1984).

[6] Ferdinand Hahn regards the *Apocalypse of Weeks* and the *Animal Apocalypse* as the oldest sections of 1 Enoch, going back to the Maccabean period (*Frühjüdische und urchristliche Apokalyptik: Eine Einführung* (Neukirchen-Vluyn: Neukirchener Verlag, 1998) 47–51.

[7] Michael Knibb, "The Date of the Parables of Enoch: A Critical Review," *NTS* 25 (1979) 345–59, suggests a date late in the first cent. CE, but admits that the date is disputed and can be placed within the *terminus a quo* of 63 BCE and 135 CE as a *terminus ad quem*. Matthew Black, on the other hand dates the Similitudes early in the first cent. CE, based in part on the questionable assumption that the Synoptic Gospels exhibit literary dependence on the Similitudes ("The

later, (3) *4 Ezra*, late first cent CE (our concern here is only with the earlier Jewish work in 3–14, which is framed by later additions in 1–2, called *5 Ezra*, and 15–16, called *6 Ezra)*, (4) *2 Baruch*, late first cent. CE,[9] (5) *3 Baruch*, late first or early second cent. CE.[10] The last three are responses to the fall of Jerusalem to the Romans in 70 CE, but pseudepigraphically juxtapose this event with the earlier fall of Jerusalem to the Neo-Babylonians in 586 BCE.

Following the traumatic impact on Judean life and culture of the destruction of the temple of Solomon in 586 BCE, with the attendant political and economic subjugation to the Neo-Babylonian empire, and the forced exile of thousands from the upper classes to Babylonia, the hope for restoration became a frequent theme in early Jewish literature. One group of four themes has an obvious nationalistic orientation and includes such elements as the restoration of sovereignty over the land of Palestine, the restoration kingship, i. e., the reestablishment of theocratic monarchy in the ideal form of the Davidic messiahship, the regathering of the twelve tribes of Israel, and the final the restoration of the city of Jerusalem and the Temple. A second group of themes has a universalistic orientation, since they are not so much related to an idealistic conception of the specific experiences and institutions of historical Israel, as the first group, but to

Messianism of the Parables of Enoch: Their Date and Contribution to Christological Origins," *The Messiah: Developments in Earliest Judaism and Christianity*, ed. J. H. Charlesworth (Minneapolis: Fortress, 1992) 145–68.

[8] The dating of *2 Enoch* is problematic, for the work exists in a longer (A) and a shorter (J) recension, neither of which can be dated within reasonably narrow limits, nor is there agreement on which recension is earlier. Charlesworth's statement that specialists date the Greek original to the decades before 70 CE masks disagreements among concerned scholars, who often avoid the issue because of its complexity (J. H. Charlesworth, *The Pseudepigraphy and Modern Research with a Supplement* [SCS 7; Chico: Scholars Press, 1981] 104). Further, the translations of the shorter (A) and longer (J) recensions by F. I. Andersen are arranged synoptically so that both consist of 73 chapters, while the translation of the shorter recension alone by A. Pennington consists of 23 chapters, making comparison between these two translations of the shorter recension very difficult; F. I. Andersen, "2 (Slavonic Apocalypse of) Enoch," *The Old Testament Pseudepigrapha*, ed. J. H. Charlesworth (2 vols.; Garden City: Doubleday, 1983) 1.91–213; A. Pennington, "2 Enoch," *The Apocryphal Old Testament*, ed. H. F. D. Sparks (Oxford: Clarendon Press, 1984) 321–62. Pennington's translation is based on a critical text of the twenty-three chapter shorter recension in Slavonic with a French translation by A. Vaillant, *Le Livre des Secrets d'Hénoch: Texte Slave et Traduction Française* (Paris: Institute d'Études Slaves, 1952).

[9] While there is some kind of literary relationship between *4 Ezra* and *2 Baruch*, there is disagreement regarding which document is dependent on the other. While R. H. Charles and G. H. Box thought *2 Baruch* dependent on *4 Ezra*, more recently P. Bogaert argues that *4 Ezra* was dependent on *2 Baruch* (*Apocalypse de Baruch*, 1.26–7, 113–4, 284–8). In my view, Charles and Box were correct. A helpful synopsis of the two works was produced by Klaus Berger, *Synopse des vierten Buches Esra und der Syrischen Baruch-Apokalypse* (Tübingen: Francke, 1992).

[10] Daniel C. Harlow, *The Greek Apocalypse of Baruch (3 Baruch) in Hellenistic Judaism and Early Christianity* (SVTP 12; Leiden: Brill, 1996) 10, 12, 206.

themes of general significance, including the restoration of Edenic conditions and the restoration of creation.

These themes, though sometimes mentioned individually and treated independently, are obviously interrelated and are therefore frequently found in combination. For example, the themes of the regathering of the people and the restoration of the land are combined in Ezek 11:17: "I will gather you from the peoples ... and I will give you the land of Israel," while the themes of the restoration of the people and the city are combined in Ezek 48:30–35, where the twelve gates of the New Jerusalem are named after the twelve tribes of Israel. The restoration of the people of Israel would be inconceivable apart from their regathering in the land of Israel and the restoration of the cultic center in the Temple in Jerusalem. According to Zech 2:16, "The Lord will inherit Judas as his portion in the holy land and will again choose Jerusalem."

2. The Restoration of the Land

The Land theme is one of the more focal motifs in the Hebrew Bible,[11] and is a centrally important theological conception in prophetic literature. [12] It is a central political concept in the Hasmonean literature of the second century BCE,[13] but is somewhat diminished as a theological conception in several rewritten versions of the Bible, including *Jubilees*, the *Testament of Moses*, the *Biblical Antiquities* of Pseudo-Philo, and the *Antiquities* of Josephus.[14] By contrast, the themes of the land and the restoration of the land are relatively rare in Jewish apocalypses,[15] though they are often implicitly present, though bundled with other restoration themes such as the appearance of the Davidic Messiah and the eschatological regathering of the people of God. In *2 Bar* 40:2, for example, the themes of the restored ideal king, the regathering of the people and the land are juxtaposed: "He [the Messiah] will preserve the remnant of my people, gathered in the place that I have chosen."

In the apocalyptic section of Daniel (7–12), national restoration is reflected primarily in Dan 7:13–14, 22–27 in a way that lacks connection with such other

---

[11] Walter Brueggemann, *The Land: Place as Gift, Promise and Challenge in Biblical Faith* (OBT; Philadelphia: Fortress, 1977); W. Janzen, "Land," *ADB* 4.146.

[12] Walther Zimmerli, "Das 'Land' bei den vorexilischen und frühexilischen Schriftpropheten" and Robert Hanhart, "Das Land in der spätnachexilischen Prophetie," *Das Land Israel in biblischer Zeit: Jerusalem-Symposium 1981*, ed. Georg Strecker (Göttingen: Vandenhoeck & Ruprecht, 1983) 33–45, 126–40.

[13] Doron Mendels, *The Land of Israel as a Political Concept in Hasmonean Literature* (TSAJ 15; Tübingen: Mohr Siebeck, 1987).

[14] Betsy Halpern-Amaru, *Rewriting the Bible: Land and Covenant in Postbiblical Jewish Literature* (Valley Forge: Trinity Press International, 1994).

[15] W. D. Davies, *The Gospel and the Land: Early Christianity and Jewish Territorial Doctrine* (Berkeley and Los Angeles: University of California Press, 1974) 49–52.

restoration themes found in the same work, such as the hope of the restoration of Jerusalem (9:2, 25), the purification of the (second) Temple (9:17, 20, 24) and the hope of the restoration of the righteous through resurrection (12:1–2). Dan 7 contains Daniel's symbolic dream vision of four beasts representing four successive near eastern empires. The last empire will blaspheme God and persecute the righteous (7:25), but will eventually be judged and destroyed (7:26). Finally, according to Dan 7:27:

> And the kingdom and the dominion and the greatness of the kingdoms under the whole heaven shall be given to the people of the saints of the Most High; their kingdom shall be an everlasting kingdom, and all dominions shall serve and obey them.

While nothing is said explicitly about the theme of the regathering of dispersed exiles and their return to the land, the emphasis on the eschatological restoration of sovereignty by God's people clearly implies sovereignty in their Palestinian homeland. Daniel 7 is concerned primarily with the oppression experienced by Judeans living in Palestine under Ptolemaic and then Seleucid rule (particularly under Antiochus IV Epiphanes), an oppression that the group that produced Daniel thought could only be terminated by divine intervention. Judean national sovereignty will then be restored and, indeed, Judea will dominate all the kingdoms of the world.[16]

The four kingdoms of Daniel 7 were re-interpreted, apparently independently, in *4 Ezra* 11–12 (the vision of Daniel is explicitly mentioned in 12:11) and *2 Baruch* 39–40. In the interpretation of Ezra's fifth vision concerning the eagle, the lion who reproved the eagle in the vision (11:36–46) is identified as the Davidic Messiah (12:32), who will destroy the fourth kingdom and deliver the remnant of God's people, "those who have been saved throughout my borders, and he will make them joyful until the end comes" (12:34). Here it is clearly implied that the temporary messianic kingdom is located in Palestine. A parallel scenario is narrated in 9:1–12, though without mention of the Messiah, and it concludes similarly with the preservation of the survivors in Palestine as the concluding phrase indicates:

> And it shall be that every one who will be saved and will be able to escape on account of his works, or on account of the faith by which he has believed, will survive the dangers that have been predicted, and will see my salvation in my land and within my borders, which I have sanctified for myself from the beginning.

[16] It is interesting to note that John J. Collins has little to say in his extensive and detailed commentary on this relatively significant eschatological theme of the final sovereignty attained by the people of God by divine intervention (*Daniel: A Commentary on the Book of Daniel* [Hermeneia; Minneapolis: Fortress, 1993] 322–23).

These "survivors" are those who survived the Messianic woes, specifically the great eschatological battle fought by the Messiah (*4 Ezra* 12:34; 13:48–9).[17]

Similarly, according to *2 Bar* 39:1–40:3, the fourth in a series of world kingdoms (i. e., Rome) will be destroyed and their leader taken to Zion in chains to be judged by the Messiah who will judge him and execute him. The Messiah "will preserve the remnant of my people, gathered in the place that I have chosen" (40:2). His kingdom "shall stand for ever, until this world of corruption comes to an end and the times appointed are fulfilled" (40:3). Again, the location of this temporary messianic kingdom is clearly Palestine. A parallel scenario occurs in 29:1–30:5, which begins by predicting that the Messianic woes will affect everyone on earth, except for those who are in the holy land: "For at that time I will protect only those who are found in those days in this land" (29:2; cf. 71:1). This scenario continues by referring to the revelation of the Messiah (29:3), including an eschatological reading of the Behemoth-Leviathan myth (found in a non-eschatological form in *4 Ezra* 6:49–53) in which these monsters serve as food for the survivors, and describing how the survivors are also nourished by the miraculous fruitfulness of the earth and manna sent to earth from heaven (29:4–8). The Messiah then returns to glory, followed by the resurrection of the righteous (30:1–3).

The restoration of the land, while not occupying a central role in the eschatological scenarios of Jewish apocalypses, nevertheless provides the indispensable setting for the playing out of the eschatological drama.

3. The Restoration of Kingship: the Davidic Messiah

Following the capture of Jerusalem in 597 BCE, Jehoiakin king of Judah was deported to Babylonia and replaced by Zedekiah, another Davidide. After an abortive revolt, the city was recaptured in 586 BCE, the Temple destroyed and Zedekiah was deported to Babylon.[18] Following the termination of the monarchy, two different political tendencies developed in Judah and the diaspora, both with established roots in Israelite political tradition: restorative monarchism and theocracy.[19] Restorative monarchism was inspired in part by the promise of an unconditional and eternal covenant between Yahweh and David expressed in both prose (1 Sam 7) and poetry (Ps 89), and encouraged by the continued existence of the Davidic family in exile (Zech 12:7–8, 10, 12; 1 Chron 3:17–24). The

[17] Michael Stone, *Features of the Eschatology of IV Ezra* (HSS 35; Atlanta: Scholars Press, 1989) 103–4.

[18] John H. Hayes and J. Maxwell Miller, *Israelite and Judaean History* (Philadelphia: Westminster, 1977) 469–76.

[19] Joachim Becker, *Messianic Expectation in the Old Testament*, trans. David Green (Philadelphia: Fortress, 1980) 48–53.

royalists were even more concretely heartened by the appointment of Zerubbabel the grandson of Jehoiakin as governor of Judah (Hag 1:1; 2:1). Zerubabbel was identified by Haggai and Zechariah as the ideal Davidic king (Hag 2:20–23; Zech 4:6–10; cf. 3:8; 6:12), but despite the hopes they pinned on him, he must have ultimately disappointed them, for he disappears from the pages of history. David, the founder of the Davidic dynasty and the king with a legendary reputation, became the postexilic model for the ideal king in the eschatological restoration (Jer 30:8–9; 33:14–18; Ezek 34:23–24; 37:24–25; Zech 12:7–13:1).[20] Despite the hyperbole, the anticipation of a new David or a David *redivivus* was the expectation that the Davidic dynasty would be restored and continued, not that a final Davidic king would rule for ever.[21]

In the eschatological speculation which developed from the second century BCE on, the theocratic tendency (emphasizing the kingship of Yahweh) was dominant, but took two forms: theocracy *with* a restored monarchy (but subordinate to the priesthood) or theocracy *without* a monarchy, so that eschatological scenarios were generated both with and without a Davidic messiah. The picture is made more complex by the fact that messianism developed not only out of the idealization of the Davidic dynasty (the Messiah as a warrior), but also from the interpretation of the angelic "son of man" figure in Dan 7 (the Messiah as a cosmic judge) and input from the language of the Servant Songs of Isa 40–55, particularly in the Similitudes of Enoch and *4 Ezra*. Messianism, therefore, is not invariably present in all strands of early Jewish literature,[22] and is in fact entirely missing from the early group of apocalypses, including the Book of the Watchers (*1 Enoch* 1–36), the *Book of Heavenly Luminaries* (*1 Enoch* 72–82), the *Apocalypse of Weeks* (93:1–10 + 91:11–18), from Daniel[23] and from the *Book of Dreams* (*1 Enoch* 83–90), including the *Animal Apocalypse* (85–90).[24] Even among the later apocalypses, the figure of the Messiah is surprisingly absent from *2 Enoch* and *3 Baruch*.

---

20 A number of passages with similar sentiments are more controversial since they are often judged to be later interpolations: Amos 9:11; Micah 5:2–5; Isa 11:1–9; Jer 23:5–7; see John J. Collins, *The Scepter and the Star: The Messiahs of the Dead Sea Scrolls and Other Ancient Literature* (ABRL; New York: Doubleday, 1995) 24–6.

21 J.J.M. Roberts, "The Old Testament's Contribution to Messianic Expectations," *The Messiah: Developments in Earliest Judaism and Christianity*, ed. J.H. Charlesworth (Minneapolis: Fortress, 1992) 39–51.

22 James C. VanderKam, "Messianism and Apocalypticism," *The Encyclopedia of Apocalypticism*, Vol. 1: *The Origins of Apocalypticism in Judaism and Christianity*, ed. John J. Collins (New York: Continuum, 1998).

23 The son of man figure in Dan 7:13–14 is often regarded as a messianic figure on the basis of the later use of the imagery in this passage, particularly in *1 Enoch* 37–71, *4 Ezra* and the Gospels. The original meaning of this figure in Dan 7:13–14, however, is not messianic.

24 Past Messianic interpretations of various passages in the Animal Apocalypse (including the white bull of 90:37) are not convincing; see Patrick A. Tiller, *A Commentary on the Animal Apocalypse of I Enoch* (Atlanta: Scholars Press, 1993) 384, 387–9; against VanderKam, "Messianism and Apocalypticism,"199–200.

The figure of a Davidic Messiah, then, is found only in three of the later apocalypses, the Similitudes of Enoch (*1 Enoch* 37–71), *4 Ezra* and *2 Baruch*, all dating from the early first century to the early second century CE. Though the eschatology of these texts has been extensively studied, there still remain areas of vigorous disagreement among concerned scholars. In the present context I can only present the briefest overview of the role and function of the Messiah in these compositions.

The Similitudes of Enoch (*1 Enoch* 37–71), the earliest apocalypse to present developed messianic conceptions, announces the coming of the great judgment in which God, through his agent the Messiah, will vindicate his people and punish the wicked. Four different designations are used for the Messiah: the Righteous One (four times), the Anointed One (twice: 48:10; 52:4), the Chosen One (fifteen times), and the Son of Man (sixteen times).[25] The Son of Man designation has been drawn from Dan 7, while the titles Righteous One and Chosen one are based on the language of the servant songs in Isa 40–55. Throughout *1 Enoch* 37–71 there are a number of eschatological scenarios which center on the figure of the Messiah (38:1–6; 45:1–48:10; 51:1–5; 55:4; 61:8–13; 62:1–16; 69:27–29). The Messiah is frequently described as sitting on his throne in judgment (55:4; 61:8; 62:2; 69:27) or ruling in wisdom (45:1; 51:1–5), or as conquering the hostile nations in warfare (46:4–8). All these functions are analogous to those of the kings of Israel and Judah, who were regarded as the adopted sons of God and therefore divine plenipotentiaries on earth. It is probable that the author of the Similitudes thought of the Messiah as preexistent (39:6–7; 46:3; 48:2–3; 62:7; 70:1).[26]

The Messiah is a central figure in three eschatological scenarios found in the interpretations of the visions in *4 Ezra* (7:25–44; 12:31–34; 13:25–50).[27] In the first scenario (7:25–44), when "the city which now is not seen shall appear, and the land which now is hidden shall be disclosed" (7:26) and the Messiah and his company appear and prevail for 400 years, at the conclusion of which he and all those living on the earth will die (concluding the temporary messianic kingdom), after which the world will be renewed and the dead will be resurrected. God will then judge the wicked and reward the righteous (cf. 9:1–13). It is noteworthy that the Messiah plays no significant role in this scenario, as king, warrior or judge. In the second scenario (12:31–34), the Davidic Messiah is a warrior who defeats the fourth kingdom (Rome), denounces their ungodliness and destroys them, but

---

25 James C. VanderKam, "Righteous One, Messiah, Chosen One, and Son of Man in *1 Enoch* 37–71," *The Messiah: Developments in Earliest Judaism and Christianity*, ed. J.H. Charlesworth (Minneapolis: Fortress, 1992) 169–91.

26 Some argue that the language used in these passages may only imply divine foreknowledge, or that the "hiding" of the Son of Man is the suppression of his identity; see VanderKam, "Righteous One," 179–82.

27 See Stone, *Eschatology*, 97–141.

preserves the remnant of the people of God in the land (Palestine), "until the end comes, the day of judgment" (12:34). Again the temporary messianic kingdom is concluded by a judgment presided over by God himself. Here the Messiah plays the traditional roles of warrior and judge and his Davidic descent is mentioned (12:32), but this period of his ascendancy is neither characterized nor described, nor is there any mention of a resurrection before the final judgment. The third scenario (13:25–50), is doubtless the most complex, for this vision represents an elaborate re-interpretation of the Son of Man figure of Dan 7:13. While neither the designations Messiah nor Son of Man actually occur in *4 Ezra* 13, there is little doubt that the mysterious figures who is seven times called a "man" (13:3 [*bis*], 5, 12, 25, 32, 51) and twice called *filius meus*, "my servant,"[28] is modeled both after the Davidic Messiah, who appears elsewhere in *4 Ezra* and the figure of the son of man of Dan 7:13, who occurs nowhere else in the book.[29] The "man from the sea" in Ezra's vision (13:3–4) is interpreted as the revelation of God's servant (13:32). The hostile nations will gather to conquer him, but he will stand on the top of Mount Zion, where the heavenly Jerusalem will appear (13:34–35) and where he will reprove the assembled nations for their ungodliness and will destroy them by the law. He then gathers a peaceable multitude at Mount Zion (the nine-and-one-half tribes from exile), and "will defend the people who remain" showing them great wonders (13:39–50). The Messiah of *4 Ezra*, though his Davidic ancestry is mentioned (12:32), has no real royal features nor is his period of dominance characterized as a reign over a kingdom. The fact that there are two eschatological scenarios in which the Messiah is not mentioned (6:17–28; 9:1–13) suggests that the Messiah is not absolutely essential to the author's eschatological thought.[30]

"To describe the Messiah of *2 Baruch*," says Bogaert, with some exaggeration, "is not an easy task."[31] Compared to the complexities of the messianic figures of the Similitudes of Enoch and *4 Ezra*, however, the task seems at least feasible. The main problem is that of harmonizing the role of the Messiah presented in three eschatological scenarios in *2 Baruch*, i.e., one revelatory dialogue with the Lord (26:1–30:5) and two visionary narratives (36:1–40:4; 53:1–76:5). It is of some interest that the figure of the Messiah appears *only* in these three narratives. In the first scenario (*2 Bar* 26:1–30:5), after a series of twelve ordeals, the Messiah appears, followed by the reappearance of the two great monsters, Behemoth and Leviathan, to serve as food for the survivors. The earth will be miraculously fruitful and manna will return to earth from heaven. At the end

[28] Here *filius meus*, literally "my son," probably represents an original Hebrew עבד or παῖς meaning "servant," rather than Hebrew בן or Greek υἱός meaning "son." See Stone, *Fourth Ezra*, 207–13.

[29] Collins, *The Scepter and the Star*, 183–7.

[30] Stone, *Eschatology*, 140.

[31] Bogaert, *Baruch,* 1.415.

of this period the Messiah will return to heaven[32] (suggesting his preexistence and corresponding to the death of the Messiah in *4 Ezra* 7:29), followed by the resurrection of the righteous. In the second scenario (*2 Bar* 36:1–40:4), the fourth in a series of wicked kingdoms will be destroyed (i. e., Rome) and their leader taken to Zion in chains to be judged by the Messiah, whose kingdom is revealed, "and his kingdom shall stand for ever, until this world of corruption comes to an end and the times appointed are fulfilled" (40:3). The third scenario (*2 Bar* 53:1–76:5), consists of a lengthy historical survey of the ups and downs of the history of Israel leading to a final period of tribulation which concludes with the appearance of the Messiah (70:1–10). He will summon the nations together, sparing some and destroying others, depending on how they have treated Israel. He will then sit down in peace for ever on the throne of his kingdom in Edenic conditions. These three scenarios depict the Messiah as a military leader and judge who defeats and punishes the enemies of God's people and a king who reigns "for ever" until he returns to heaven, bringing the temporary messianic kingdom to an end.[33]

4. National Restoration: Regathering the People

One of the central themes of post-exilic Jewish eschatology was the nationalistic hope of the regathering of Israel.[34] This theme was often linked with the related themes of the recovery of the land and the reestablishment of the monarchy as in Ezek 37:21–23:[35]

> Thus says the Lord God: Behold I will take the people of Israel from the nations among which they have gone, and will gather them from all sides, and bring them to their own

---

[32] Bogaert, *Baruch,* 2.65.

[33] A. F. J. Klijn, "The Sources and Redaction of the Syriac Apocalypse of Baruch," *JSJ* 1 (1970) 75: "In all these cases [*2 Bar* 30:1; 40:1–3; 74:2–3] the author obviously tried to say that the times of the Anointed One belong to this world, the world of corruption. For this reason it has to come to an end to make place for the time of incorruption. This means that the author … presupposes a break between this world and the next one. The days of the Anointed One are a step in history in the direction of the incorruptible world. Then the final judgment takes place." Unfortunately, he later changed his views by taking the indefensible position that "the author … rejected the idea of a messianic kingdom on earth" ("2 (Syriac Apocalypse of) Baruch," *The Old Testament Pseudepigrapha*, ed. J. H. Charlesworth [2 vols.; Garden City: Doubleday, 1983] 1.619.

[34] Isa 11:11–13; 27:12–13; 43:5–6, 14–21; 49:6–7; 56:1–8; 60:3–7; 66:18–24; Jer 23:3–8; 29:10–14; 30:3; 31:10–11; 32:37–41; Ezek 11:17–20; 20:34; 34:11–16; 36:24; 37:1–28; Hos 11:10–11; Zeph 3:20; Zech 8:7–8; 10:6–12; Ps 106:47; 147:2; *Tob* 13:5, 13; 14:4–5; 2 Macc 1:27–29; 2:7, 18; *Jub.* 1:15–17; *T. Benj.* 9:2; 10:11; *T. Jos.* 19:4; *Shemoneh Esreh* 10; Philo *Praem.* 94–97, 162–72; *Bar.* 4:37; 5:5; Sir 36:11; 48:10; *Pss. Sol.* 11, 17:28–31, 50. See E. P. Sanders, *Jesus and Judaism* (Philadelphia: Fortress, 1985) 95–98.

[35] Other passages where these three overlapping themes are mentioned include: Jer 23:3–8; Ezek 34:20–31.

land; and I will make them one nation in the land, upon the mountains of Israel; and one king shall be king over them all; and they shall be no longer two nations, and no longer divided into two kingdoms.

Even though Ezekiel's immediate frame of reference is the destruction of Jerusalem and the exile which followed (586 BCE), his vision of the reunification of Israel includes the exiles from the Northern Kingdom which fell to the Assyrians nearly 150 years earlier (722–21 BCE). The realization of this hope would have necessitated the kind of radical divine intervention presupposed by his use of a resurrection metaphor in his vision of the valley of dry bones (Ezek 37:1–14). The regathering theme can also be linked to that of the reestablishment of the monarchy, as in Hos 3:5: "Afterward the children of Israel shall return and seek the Lord their God, and David their king; and they shall come in fear to the Lord and to his goodness in the latter days."

In the OT, those who will be regathered are sometimes designated by such general terms as [my/his/our] "people" (Zech 8:7–8; 2 Macc 1:27–29; 2:7), "sons and daughters [of Jerusalem]" (Isa 60:3–7), "the remnant of my flock" (Jer 23:3), or "my sheep" (Ezek 34:11–16). More frequently, however, an emphasis on the unity of Israel and Judah that existed in the days of David and Solomon is clearly implied in phrases like "the tribes of Jacob and the preserved of Israel" (Isa 49:6–7; Jer 31:10–11), by the use of the name "Israel" (Isa 43:5–7; cf. 43:1; Ezek 37:21; Zeph 3:20; cf. 3:14), "the descendants of the house of Israel" (Jer 23:8), "the tribes of Jacob" (Sir 48:10), or by simply juxtaposing the names "Ephraim" and "Judah" (Isa 11:11–13), or alternately "Judah" and "Joseph" (Ezek 37:15–19; Zech 10:6). The only OT text which specifically refers to the twelve tribes in contexts which presuppose their eschatological regathering is the naming of the twelve gates of the restored Jerusalem after the twelve tribes of Israel in Ezek 48:30–35 (cf. 11QTemple 18:14–16).

Among the earlier group of apocalypses, the theme of national restoration is conspicuous by its relative absence; it is touched on only in the *Animal Apocalypse* (*1 Enoch* 85–90) and Daniel. Perhaps the earliest reference to this theme is found toward the end of the elaborate allegory in the Animal Apocalypse (90:33):

And all who had been destroyed and scattered and all the wild beasts and all the birds of heaven assembled in that house. And the owner of the sheep rejoiced with great joy because they had all become good and they had returned to his house.

Here "all who had been destroyed" refer to the dead who have been resurrected for inclusion in the eschatological restoration, while the "scattered" refer to Jews of the diaspora.[36] The "house" is the New Jerusalem, not the temple.[37] In the Animal Apocalypse, "house" is first used of the wilderness tabernacle or camp

[36] Tiller, *Animal Apocalypse*, 380–1.
[37] Tiller, *Animal Apocalypse*, 45–7, 376.

(89:36) and later of Jerusalem (89:50); the author nowhere mentions the existence of a temple in the eschatological period.[38]

Among the later apocalypses, the theme of national restoration is strikingly absent from *2 Enoch* and *3 Baruch*, though it does occur in *4 Ezra* and *2 Baruch*. *4 Ezra* 13 contains an extensive eschatological vision of the coming of the Man from the Sea, i. e., the Messiah who defeats a host of hostile nations who have converged at Mount Zion. The vision concludes with the Man's assembly of a peaceable multitude (13:12–13), interpreted as a reference to the assembly of the nine-and-one-half[39] tribes who were exiled in Assyria (Manasseh is frequently referred to in the OT as a half tribe),[40] but who emigrated to a distant land called Azareth. On their way there they miraculously cross the Euphrates (13:44), alluding to Israel's miraculous crossing of the Red Sea (Exod 14:21–29). The interpretation concludes in 13:46–48:

> Then they dwelt there until the last times; and now, when they are about to come again, the Most High will stop the channels of the river again, so that they may be able to pass over. Therefore you saw the multitude gathered together in peace. But those who are left of your people, who are found within my holy borders, shall be saved.

The Exodus event is replicated yet a second time when the nine-and-one-half tribes return (cf. Isa 11:15–16; 43:16–17; or perhaps the allusion is to the miraculous crossing of the Jordan narrated in Josh 3:1–17). The reference to those who are left in the land refers to the survivors of the Messianic woes and the great eschatological battle between the Messiah and the hostile nations. The tradition of ten tribes surviving somewhere among eastern nations is preserved in a number of early Jewish sources (Josephus *Ant.* 11.133; *Sib. Or.* 2.171; *T. Moses* 3:4–9; 4:9). Apart from these texts in *4 Ezra* 13, however, there is no concern elsewhere in this apocalypse for eschatological nationalism.

2 Baruch contains four texts, in a variety of contexts, which touch on the theme of the regathering of the exiled tribes. The work opens with a reference to the two tribes of the Southern Kingdom whose sins have exceeded those of the ten tribes of the Northern Kingdom, which were carried off into captivity (1:2–3). The author refers elsewhere to the nine-and-one-half tribes (62:5; 77:17; 78:1) and the two-and-one-half tribes (63:3; 64:5). *2 Baruch*, like *4 Ezra*, exhibits a special concern for the nine-and-one-half tribes exiled from the Northern Kingdom in 722 BCE (62:5), who are addressed in the so-called Letter of Baruch

---

[38] Giovanni Bissoli, *Il Tempio nella Letteratura Giudaica e Neotestamentaria* (Studium Biblicum Franciscanum Analecta 37; Jerusalem: Franciscan Printing Press, 1994) 30–1.

[39] Michael Stone argues convincingly that the reading translated "nine and one half" (supported by Syriac, two Arabic and two Ethiopic MSS) is to be preferred to "ten" (supported by most Latin MSS and found in most English translations) or "nine" (supported by a few other MSS), *Fourth Ezra: A Commentary on the Book of Fourth Ezra* (Hermeneia; Minneapolis: Fortress, 1990) 404. See also Bogaert, *Baruch*, 1.343–44.

[40] That the Northern Kingdom consisted of ten tribes is found only in 1 Kgs 11:31, 35.

(*2 Bar* 78–87).[41] The letter is a summary of the contents of the book written to console those who have been carried away, assuring them that the situation will indeed be reversed in the future, and that God will act at the "consummation of the age" (83:7) to judge those who oppress them. Baruch encourages the exiles to "remember the law and Zion, the holy land and your brothers, and the covenant of your fathers" (84:8). In spite of their enormous losses, the author comforts his audience with the expectation that what they lost was corruptible, but what they will receive in its place is incorruptible (85:3–5):

> But now the righteous have been gathered to their fathers, and the prophets have fallen asleep, and we also have been exiled from our land: Zion has been taken from us, and nothing is left us now save the Mighty One and his law. But if we direct and dispose our hearts aright, *we shall retrieve everything that we have lost* [emphasis mine], and gain many more and much better things than we have lost. For what we have lost was subject to corruption, but what we shall receive is incorruptible.

The emphasis on God and his law as the sole possessions left to the people of Israel, was of critical importance for Judaism for the Torah became the primary substitute for the Temple and its cult in Judaism from 70 CE to the present day.

In Baruch's address to an assembly of his people, he tells them: "If, then, you direct your ways aright, you will not go as your brothers went [i. e., into exile]; but *they will come to you* [emphasis mine]" (77:6). Here he is referring to the future return of the nine-and-one-half tribes to whom he addresses the circular letter which concludes the book (78–87). Since, from the perspective of the author, the other two tribes or two-and-one half tribes are already present in the land, his eschatological concern actually embraces all twelve Israelite tribes. In the exordium of this letter he reiterates this theme of regathering (78:7):[42]

> For if you do this, he will remember you continually, he who always promised on our behalf to those who were far superior to ourselves, that he will never forget us or forsake us, but in the greatness of his mercy *will gather together again* those who have been dispersed [emphasis mine].

The possibility of regathering is based on the moral proviso that they obey the law of Moses. This connection is clearly made in 84:2:

> Remember how Moses at one time summoned heaven and earth to witness against you and said, "If you transgress the law you will be scattered, but if you keep it you will be firmly planted [*var. lect.*: you will be kept][43] in your land.

[41] Convincing arguments for considering the letter as part of the original composition of *2 Baruch* are found in P. Bogaert, *Apocalypse de Baruch: Introduction, Traduction du Syriaque et Commentaire* (SC 144–5; Paris: Le Cerf, 1969) 1.67–72, a view shared by F. J. Murphy, *The Structure and Meaning of Second Baruch* (SBLDS 78; Atlanta: Scholars Press, 1985) 28–29.

[42] Bogaert, *Baruch*, 2.143.

[43] Bogaert, *Baruch*, 2.155.

Earlier in the book, the themes of the regathering of the dispersed people and the land are brought together in 40:2: "He [the Messiah] will preserve the remnant of my people, gathered in the place that I have chosen."

Though the theme of the regathering of the exiles occurs just four times in *2 Baruch*, it is necessary to conclude that these references are not simply relics of apocalyptic tradition which the author has witlessly included in his work, but represent one thread of his eschatological expectation.

5. Jerusalem and the Temple

Jerusalem and the Temple were so closely associated that the mention of one often implicitly entails the other and the sanctity of the former was thought an extension of the latter. The OT conception of a restored, liberated and purified Jerusalem, liberally laced with hyperbole (Isa 52:1–2; 54:11–14; 60:10–14; Zech 2:6–12; *Tob.* 13:16–18),[44] became the basis for the imaginative descriptions of the eschatological or the heavenly Jerusalem. Ezekiel's vision of the restored Temple in Jerusalem (40:1–43:12) included a plan for the restoration of equal allotments of land to the twelve tribes (47:13–48:29), centrally symbolized in a powerful way by naming the twelve gates of the city after the twelve tribes of Israel (48:30–35).[45]

Ezek 40–48 had a significant impact on subsequent apocalyptic conceptions, though specific features of this eschatological vision were never reproduced without significant revision among later authors. The association of the names of the twelve tribes of Israel with the gates of the New Jerusalem (Ezek 48:30–35) is also found associated with the twelve gates of the Temple-City in the fragments of the Description of the New Jerusalem (4Q554 frag. 1,I.9–II.11),[46] the

---

[44] Leslie J. Hoppe, *The Holy City: Jerusalem in the Theology of the Old Testament* (Collegeville: Liturgical Press, 2000).

[45] In Ezekiel's vision of the square outer walls of the eschatological Jerusalem, there are three gates on each side (Ezek 48:16–17, 30–35), which the author claims are named after the tribes of Israel (Ezek 48:31), though in fact they are named after the sons of Jacob (i. e., Joseph and Levi are mentioned rather than Ephraim and Manasseh).

[46] There are six fragmentary Aramaic copies of the Description of the New Jerusalem: (1) 1Q32; (2) 2Q24 = 2QNew Jerusalem; (3) 4Q554 = 4QNew Jerusalem; (4) 4Q555 = 4QNew Jerusalem; (5) 5Q15 = 5QNew Jerusalem; (6) 11Q18 = 11QNew Jerusalem. In addition, 4Q232 is a Hebrew fragment which has some relationship to the Aramaic work; J. T. Milik, *The Books of Enoch: Aramaic Fragments of Qumrân Cave 4* (Oxford: Clarendon Press, 1976) 59. The fragments of the Description of the New Jerusalem have been subject to a detailed reconstruction and analysis by Michael Chyutin, who has integrated the fragments into a single composition (*The New Jerusalem Scroll from Qumran: A Comprehensive Reconstruction*. Journal for the Study of the Pseudepigrapha, Supplement Series 25; Sheffield: Sheffield Academic Press, 1997).

Temple Scroll (11QTemple 39.12–13; 40.11–14),[47] and the Apocalypse of John (Rev 21:9–22:9).[48] While in Ezek 40–48 and the Temple Scroll the emphasis in on the temple complex itself, in the Description of the New Jerusalem and Rev 21:9–22:9 the emphasis is on the city.[49] In all of these texts which focus on the eschatological Jerusalem, the striking emphasis on the twelve tribes of Israel reflects one of the central concerns of Jewish eschatology, the restoration of all Israel, which is repeatedly mentioned in post-exilic OT and early Jewish literature. The mention of the twelve tribes implies that the New Jerusalem is not simply a city but rather the focal point for the entire land.

Among the earlier group of apocalypses there are several references to the heavenly temple as well as to the restoration on earth of the city and the temple.[50] The Book of the Watchers contains a narrative of the heavenly ascent of Enoch to the throne of God (*1 Enoch* 14). On his way, Enoch passes through a series of heavenly structures, including a wall (14:9), an outer house (14:10–14) and an inner house (14:15–17). In the innermost structure, Enoch came upon the awesome spectacle of God seated on his throne, out from which rivers of fire flowed (14:18). It is generally recognized that this complex heavenly structure replicates the structure of the Solomonic Temple described in 1 Kgs 6.[51] Like the wilderness Tabernacle, the Temple of Solomon was thought to be constructed on the basis of a heavenly model. There is no suggestion in *1 Enoch* 14, however, that this heavenly temple would ever be revealed on earth.[52] In the elaborate al-

---

[47] Florentino García-Martínez, "The Temple Scroll and the New Jerusalem," *The Dead Sea Scrolls after Fifty Years: A Comprehensive Assessment*, ed. Peter Flint and James C. VanderKam (2 vols.; Leiden: Brill, 1998–99) 2.431–60.

[48] David E. Aune, "Qumran and the Book of Revelation," *The Dead Sea Scrolls after Fifty Years: A Comprehensive Assessment*, ed. P. W. Flint and J. C. VanderKam (2 vols.; Leiden: Brill, 1998–9) 2.629–41. Reprinted below, pp. 79–98.

[49] Though the relationship between the Description of the New Jerusalem and the Temple Scrolls is debated, neither document appears to have been a product of the Qumran sectarians. Arguments for excluding the Temple Scroll from the sectarian literature are proposed by Lawrence Schiffman, "The Temple Scroll in Literary and Philological Perspective," *Approaches to Ancient Judaism II*, ed. W. S. Green (Chico: Scholars Press, 1980) 143–58; H. Stegemann in "The Origin of the Temple Scroll," *Supplements to Vetus Testamentum* 40 (1988) 235–56; *idem*, "The Literary Composition of the Temple Scroll and Its Status at Qumran," *Temple Scroll Studies*, ed. G. J. Brooke (JSPS 7; Sheffield: JSOT Press, 1989) 123–89; Michael Wise, *A Critical Study of the Temple Scroll from Qumran Cave 11* (Studies in Ancient Oriental Civilization 49; Chicago: The Oriental Institute of the University of Chicago, 1990) 201–3.

[50] R. G. Hamerton-Kelly, "The Temple and the Origins of Jewish Apocalyptic," *VT* 20 (1970) 1–15.

[51] Martha Himmelfarb, "Apocalyptic Ascent and the Heavenly Temple," *Society of Biblical Literature Seminar Papers* (Atlanta: Scholars Press, 1987) 210–17. See also the depiction of the heavenly temple in the fragments of 4QShirShabb edited by Carol Newsom, *Songs of the Sabbath Sacrifice: A Critical Edition* (Atlanta: Scholars Press, 1985).

[52] In the last section of the Similitudes of Enoch, the seer is carried to the highest heaven where he sees the heavenly temple (*1 Enoch* 71:5–13), though as in *1 Enoch* 14 there is no indication that this temple will be revealed upon the earth.

legory of the *Animal Apocalypse* (which has a negative attitude toward the first temple, called a "high tower" in *1 Enoch* 89:73), the Lord of the sheep himself is presented as the builder of the new Jerusalem (*1 Enoch* 90:29), a notion which first occurs in this work.[53] In the *Apocalypse of Weeks,* weeks eight through ten describe eschatological events, including the fact that "a house will be built for the great king in glory for ever" in the eighth week (*1 Enoch* 91:22).

References to the eschatological Jerusalem and temple become more frequent in the later group of apocalypses, particularly in *4 Ezra* and *2 Baruch*, though both concepts are largely absent from the Similitudes of Enoch and *3 Baruch*.[54] In the fourth vision of *4 Ezra* (9:26–10:59), the preoccupation of the author, as throughout the entire book, is on the tragic fate of Jerusalem.[55] He encounters a woman weeping for her dead son, and rebukes her by explaining that the real reason for mourning is the desolation of the temple, Zion/Jerusalem and her people (10:5–24). The woman is then transformed before his eyes into a city (10:25–27). Elsewhere the author mentions a city or Zion which will be revealed at the end (7:26; 8:52; 13:36), suggesting that his vision of the established city in 10:25–27 is a visionary preview of the future revelation of the heavenly Jerusalem intended to comfort Ezra in his grief for the loss of the historical Jerusalem.[56] In the context of an eschatological scenario which includes the judgment of the hostile assembly of nations by the Messiah (13:37–38) and the regathering of the nine-and-one-half tribes in Zion (13:39–50), the heavenly Jerusalem seen by Ezra in the vision in 9:26–10:59 becomes a reality on earth: "And Zion will come and be made manifest to all people, prepared and built, as you saw the mountain carved without hands" (13:36). Since Zion or Jerusalem is inseparable from the land of Palestine, the restoration of the land is presupposed in these texts.

One of the ways in which *2 Baruch* deals with the catastrophe of the destruction of Jerusalem in 70 CE is by arguing that the earthly Jerusalem is not to be identified with the heavenly Jerusalem which is the true dwelling place of God (*2 Bar*. 4:3–6):

---

[53] Tiller, *Animal Apocalypse*, 45–47, 376. Hamerton-Kelly assumes incorrectly that the new house is the temple ("The Temple and the Origins of Jewish Apocalyptic," 2), whereas it must be the city alone, for the earlier temple is referred to as a tower, which is pointedly missing from the new house (see Tiller, *Animal Apocalypse*, 46–7, 376).

[54] On the problem of the absence of a heavenly temple in *3 Baruch* and its possible polemical implications, see Harlow, *The Greek Apocalypse of Baruch,* 71–75.

[55] Hermann Lichtenberger, "Zion and the Destruction of the Temple in 4 Ezra 9–10," *Gemeinde ohne Tempel, Community without Temple: Zur Substituierung und Transformation des Jerusalemer Tempels und seines Kults im Alten Testament, antiken Judentum und frühen Christentum*, ed. B. Ego, A. Lange and P. Pilhofer (Tübingen: Mohr Siebeck, 1999) 238–49.

[56] Stone, *Fourth Ezra*, 335–6; Bissoli's suggestion that the term "luogo" ("place") in 10:27 and 10:54 suggests the presence of a temple is overreaching (*Il Tempio*, 153–54).

Do you think that this is the city about which I said, On the palms of my hands have I engraved you [Isa 49:16]? This building which now stands in your midst, is not *the one that is to be revealed* [emphasis mine] that is with me now, that was prepared beforehand here at the time when I determined to make Paradise, and showed it to Adam before he sinned (though when he disobeyed my commandment it was taken away from him, as was also Paradise) ... And now it is preserved with me, as is also Paradise.

This is clearly a reference to a "pre-existent" temple that is to be found in the heavenly realm with God and which will eventually "be revealed" on earth.[57] However, this conception seems to contradict the tradition that the vessels of the earthly temple were hidden on earth until the last times, ostensibly to protect their purity (69:7–9; 80:2),[58] a tradition that presupposes the eventual restoration of the earthly temple. Murphy argues that the description of the heavenly temple is a condemnation of the earthly cult, and sees the heavenly sanctuary in opposition to the earthly temple.[59] He argues that "the real opposition is between earthly and heavenly, and not between present and future earthly Zion." Although the author does not elsewhere return directly to the subject of the heavenly Jerusalem ("the one that is to be revealed"), he does refer in 32:4 to the second temple which, after its destruction in 70 CE, "must be renewed in glory." Nevertheless 4:3–6, cited above, coheres with the author's characterization of the present world as transitory and the future world as permanent (44:8–9). The fall of Jerusalem is an example of the corruptibility of the present world (31:4–5), and in fact its destruction was brought about by God, not the Gentiles (7:1).

2 Bar 53:1–74:4 contains a lengthy eschatological vision of a series of six dark rain showers, or times of falsehood, and six bright rain showers, or times of truth (53:1–74:4), dominated by a historical review in which the eleventh dark shower represents the capture of Jerusalem and the destruction of the first temple in 586 BCE (67:1–9), while the twelfth bright shower represents the restoration of the city and the temple in 516 BCE, which functioned in basically the same way that the first temple did had prior to its destruction (68:5–6):[60]

And then after a short interval, Zion will be rebuilt, and its offerings will be restored again, and the priests will return to their ministry, and the Gentiles also will come and acclaim it. However, things will not be as they were in former times.

---

[57] Murphy, *Second Baruch*, 88, claims that nowhere in *2 Baruch* is it stated that the heavenly Jerusalem will descend to earth. Yet that seems to be exactly what is claimed here in *2 Bar* 4:3.

[58] This tradition is also found in 2 Macc 2:4–8; *Vitae prophetarum* 2:11–18; *4 Bar.* 3:8–11; see M. F. Collins, "The Hidden Vessels in Samaritan Traditions," JSJ 3 (1972) 97–116.

[59] Murphy, *Second Baruch*, 87.

[60] Bogaert, *Baruch*, 2.122; Klijn, "Baruch," 71; John J. Collins, *The Apocalyptic Imagination: An Introduction to the Jewish Matrix of Christianity* (New York: Crossroad, 1984) 172; Heinz-Martin Döpp, *Die Deutung der Zerstörung Jerusalems und des Zweiten Tempels im Jahre 70 in den ersten drei Jahrhunderten n. Chr.* (TANZ 24; Tübingen and Basel: A. Francke Verlag, 1998) 92–3, n. 53.

The dark showers which follow the twelfth bright showers represent the future, which consists of a period of warfare and chaos culminating in the assembly of hostile nations who will be judged by the Messiah and punished or rewarded depending on how they have treated Israel (71:1–72:6). The final bright showers represent the period following the Messiah's complete victory over all opposition in the world, when he sits down in peace for ever on the throne of his kingdom introducing an apparently permanent idyllic period (73:1–74:4). There is no mention of the fate of the restored temple mentioned in 68:5–6 (cited above), nor of the revelation of a heaven Jerusalem. The latter element, however, may be reflected in *2 Bar.* 32:2–4, where the author explicitly refers to two destructions of Jerusalem, the first in 586 BCE and the second in 70 CE, followed by a restoration:

> For after a little while the building of Zion will be shaken so that it may be built again. But that building [i. e., the rebuilt earthly temple] will not endure, but will after a time be razed to the ground, and it will remain desolate until the appointed time. And afterwards it must be renewed in glory and be made perfect for evermore.

The author has already referred to the heavenly Jerusalem as "the one that is to be revealed" (4:3), and here he apparently refers to the eschatological Jerusalem on earth (not the heavenly Jerusalem) as one that "must be renewed in glory and made perfect for evermore."[61] These are the only two references in *2 Baruch* to the eschatological Jerusalem and temple (references to it are strikingly absent from the messianic passages in *2 Bar*. 29–30, 39–40 and 70–74),[62] and some have tried to reconcile the apparent contradiction between author's references to a heavenly temple which will be revealed at the end and the restoration of the temple (implied in the inclusion of the legend of the miraculous preservation of the temple vessels in *2 Bar*. 80:2), by proposing that 32:2–4 is an interpolation.[63] While the author of *2 Baruch* was dependent on earlier material, particularly on eschatological traditions shared with *4 Ezra*, he failed to achieve consistency in his preservation of eschatological traditions concerning the restoration of Jerusalem. It is particularly striking that in the one revelatory dialogue (26:1–30:5) and two visionary narratives (36:1–40:4; 53:1–76:5), which have been inappropriately labeled "Messianic Apocalypses,"[64] and which center on the activity of the Messiah, that the restoration of Jerusalem and the Temple are not even

---

[61] Klijn, "Baruch," 70; Döpp, *Die Deutung der Zerstörung Jerusalems,* 92 (he understands *2 Bar* 32:2–4 to refer to the temple, though in fact it refers to Zion/Jerusalem which probably includes the temple).

[62] Murphy, "The Temple in Syriac Baruch," 682.

[63] Klijn, "Baruch," 70.

[64] L. Joseph Kreizer, *Jesus and God in Paul's Eschatology* (JSNTSupp 19; Sheffield: JSOT Press, 1987) 72.

mentioned, suggesting that such a restoration was not integral to the author's eschatological thought.[65]

6. Paradise Lost and Regained

Though story of Adam and Eve in the garden of Eden, narrated in Gen 2–3, is largely neglected in the rest of the Hebrew Bible, two poetic accounts in Ezekiel mention "Eden" and "the garden of God." In Ezek 28:11–19, an independent narrative of the fall of man is used as a poetic vehicle for a lament over the king of Tyre,[66] who is compared to a cherub whom God expelled from Eden, the garden of God, located on the holy mountain of God.[67] In Ezek 31:8–9, the trees in Eden, in the garden of God, are mentioned (though no special trees are singled out) only to emphasize the fact that they are nothing in comparison with the Lebanese cedar, i.e., the cosmic tree, a metaphor for the pharaoh of Egypt. Subsequent references to Paradise in Jewish literature are largely based on Gen 2–3, though allusions in Ezek 28 and 31 also play a lesser role. The location of Eden is an issue which later interpreters solve in various ways, though in Gen 2:10–14 itself, it is obvious that there is an attempt both to mystify the location of Paradise as well as to confirm its reality.[68] As a parenthetical note, the term "paradise" as a designation for the garden of Eden originated in the LXX, where the Hebrew term *gan* ("garden") was translated *paradeisos*, a Greek transliteration of a Median loanword which in Ptolemaic and Roman Egypt (where the LXX was translated), came to connote royal parks with many trees and suitable for walking.[69]

In the earlier group of apocalypses (all of which share a cosmology of a three-storey cosmos), Paradise tends to be located (as in Gen 2:10–14) in some far off, mysterious region of the earth. In the late third century BCE *Book of the Watchers* (*1 Enoch* 32:3–6), for example, toward the end of his journey to the east, Enoch comes to the Garden of Righteousness where he sees many wonderful trees, though one in particular stands out (32:5–6; trans. Knibb):

---

65 Murphy, *Second Baruch*, 104–5.

66 The hypothesis that the Israelites had an epic tradition of the story of the garden of Eden before Gen 2–3 (normally regarded as a Yahwistic account) was written is defended by Umberto Cassuto, *A Commentary on the Book of Genesis*, Part 1 (Jerusalem: Magnes Press, 1961) 71–96.

67 In this difficult passage, I am persuaded by the views of E. Noort, "Gan-Eden in the Hebrew Bible," *Paradise Interpreted: Representations of Biblical Paradise in Judaism and Christianity* (ed. G.P. Luttikhuizen; TBN 2; Leiden: Brill, 1999) 22–24, who argues that the LXX connects Ezek 28 with Gen 2–3.

68 Noort, "Gan-Eden," 33.

69 Jan M. Bremmer, "Paradise: From Persia, via Greece, into the Septuagint, *Paradise Interpreted: Representations of Biblical Paradise in Judaism and Christianity* (ed. G.P. Luttikhuizen; TBN 2; Leiden: Brill, 1999) 1–20.

And I said, This tree is beautiful! How beautiful and pleasing is its appearance! And the holy angel Raphael, who was with me, answered me and said to me, This is the tree of wisdom from which your old father and your aged mother, who were before you, ate and learnt wisdom; and their eyes were opened, and they knew that they were naked, and they were driven from the garden.

While this passage clearly alludes to Gen 3:6–7, 23, the Garden of the Righteous contains only the Tree of Knowledge. The Tree of Life is not mentioned, probably because it has already been located at the summit of the highest of seven mountains where the throne where God will sit in judgment is located (*1 Enoch* 24:1–6). The location of the Tree on a mountain is an allusion to Ezek 28:11–19. Access to this Tree of Life is prohibited and in the future will be restricted to the righteous (*1 Enoch 25:5–6*; trans. Knibb):

From its fruit life will be given to the chosen; towards the north it will be planted, in a holy place, by the house of the Lord, the Eternal King. Then they will rejoice with joy and be glad in the holy place; they will each drawn the fragrance of it into their bones, and they will live a long life on earth, as your fathers lived, and in their days sorrow and pain and toil and punishment will not touch them.

Thus while access to the Tree of Life was denied to Adam and Eve by driving them from the garden (Gen 3:22–24), in the future, access to the Tree of Life will reverse the sentence of death that Adam received by eating of the Tree of Knowledge. Further, it will be planted "by the house of the Lord, the Eternal King," i. e., on Mount Zion where the Temple of Solomon was located. The Book of Watchers, then, knows of a Garden of Righteousness which contains the Tree of Knowledge (located in one place), but not (as in the Biblical account) the Tree of Life (which is located in another place).[70]

Though the Similitudes of Enoch (first century CE) was the latest addition to the corpus comprising *1 Enoch*, it appears to share the archaic cosmology of the three-layer universe found in the other parts of this composite work, though Enoch says at one point that his spirit went up into the heavens (71:1), and it is later said that the spirit carried Enoch off to the highest heaven (71:5).[71] What is called "the place of the chosen and the righteous" is located somewhere on earth between the north and the west (*1 Enoch* 70:7–8). This place is variously designated a garden where the chosen and righteous (specifically Enoch) dwell

[70] E. J. C. Tigchelaar, "Eden and Paradise: the Garden Motif in some Early Jewish Texts (1 Enoch and Other Texts found at Qumran)," *Paradise Interpreted: Representations of Biblical Paradise in Judaism and Christianity* (ed. G. P. Luttikhuizen; TBN 2; Leiden: Brill, 1999) 47. P. Grelot argues that *1 Enoch* 1–36 reflects an attempt to harmonize the various traditions and allusions to the garden of God found in the Hebrew Bible ("La géographie mythique d'Hénoch et ses sources orientales," *RB* 65 [1958] 33–69).

[71] Adela Yarbro Collins, "The Seven Heavens in Jewish and Christian Apocalypses," *Cosmology and Eschatology in Jewish and Christian Apocalypticism* (JSJSupp 50; Leiden: Brill, 1996) 30.

(*1 Enoch* 60:8),[72] the Garden of Righteousness (*1 Enoch* 60:23) or the Garden of Life (*1 Enoch* 61:12) where the first fathers, who are chosen and righteous, dwell. There is a close similarity to Greek mythical conceptions of Elysion or the Islands of the Blessed, vaguely located in the far reaches of the world, where only exceptional heroes like Menelaus are admitted after death, while Hades was the postmortem destination of most mortals.[73]

Two of the later group of apocalypses reflect a newer cosmology of several heavens, five in *3 Baruch* (though there were probably seven originally),[74] seven in *2 Enoch* (A), and ten in *2 Enoch* (J), though only in *2 Enoch* is Paradise is located in a heavenly region. According to *2 Enoch* 8:1 (A & J); 43:2 (A), Paradise is located in the third heaven and among its many wonderful trees is the Tree of Life (8:3 [A & J), while the tree of knowledge is conspicuous by its absence. This heavenly paradise is the place prepared for the righteous (9:1 [A & J]), but the northern region of the third heaven is also a place for the torment of sinners (10:1–6 [A & J]. According to *2 Enoch 8–9* (A) [Andersen] = 5:1–10 (A) [Pennington], the paradise of the righteous is a heavenly realm, while in 8–9 (J) [Andersen] the paradise of Edem is specifically located in the third heaven, reflecting a cosmology of multiple heavens (ten according to *2 Enoch* 22:1 [J], but seven according to *2 Enoch* 20:1 [A & J]).[75] In *3 Baruch*, which also narrates an ascent through the various heavens, Baruch learns that the flood also ravaged Paradise, dislodging the vine planted by Sammael (the tree of the knowledge of good and evil of Gen 2–3), expelling it from Paradise (4:10). This very vine was planted by Noah and the wine produced from it became the source of many evils (4:11–17), so that the vine/tree continues to cause evil in the world. Only in the Christian interpolation in 4:15[76] is Paradise mentioned as the place where the righteous will dwell. Hades is located in the third heaven (4:3, 6; 5:3), but there is no indication where Paradise is located;[77] the location of the souls of the righteous is placed in the fourth heaven, around a pool (10:5).

In many respects the Tree of Life represents what was lost to humanity at the beginning of history, but is now available to the righteous at the end. *4 Ezra* also speaks of the tree of life in describing the future age and world. The tree of life is explicitly mentioned in 8:52. In the messianic age, "Paradise is opened, the tree of life is planted, plenty is provided, a city is built, rest is appointed, goodness is established and wisdom is perfected beforehand" for the sake of the

---

72 *Jub*. 4:23–4 also contains the tradition that Enoch was taken away to the garden of Eden and because of him the flood did not reach Eden.

73 Christine Sourvinou-Inwood, *'Reading' Greek Death to the End of the Classical Period* (Oxford: Clarendon Press, 1995) 32–56.

74 Harlow, *Baruch*, 41–50.

75 The location of Paradise in the third heaven is known to Paul (2 Cor 12:3–4) and is also found in *Apoc. Moses* 37:5.

76 Harlow, *Baruch*, 122–23.

77 Harlow, *Baruch*, 122, n. 36.

righteous. Fourth Ezra also mentions the "fruit of immortality" that is available to those who enter the "greater world" (7:13). These fruits are said to provide "abundance" and "healing" (7:152).

The tradition of the coming world in *2 Baruch*, however, contains an element not found in either of the other two apocalypses under consideration here, namely the reversal of the curse given by God to Adam and Eve in Genesis 3:14–19. There, God gave to Eve pain in childbirth and to Adam the toil of farming. In *2 Bar*. 73:7–74:1 this curse is lifted:

> And women will no longer have pain when they bear, nor will they be tormented when they yield the fruits of their womb. And it will happen that the reapers will not become tired, and the farmers will not wear themselves out, because the products of themselves will shoot out speedily, during the time that they work on them in full tranquility.

This passage reflects the ongoing concern for reproduction and the necessity for production of food in the Messianic age. More significant, though, is the fact that the author of *2 Baruch* sees a return to the Edenic state of Paradise as part of the restoration of the world in the end times.

7. The Restoration of Creation

Already in the early post-exilic period, Trito-Isaiah anticipated the miraculous eschatological renewal, of heaven and earth (Isa 65:17; cf. 66:22).[78] This particular restoration theme was picked up by two of the group of early apocalypses. The *Book of Heavenly Luminaries* is introduced by a reference to a new creation that will last forever (*1 Enoch* 72:1). This reference is ambiguous, however, for it is not clear whether renewal or replacement is involved (probably the former). The *Apocalypse of Weeks* strikes quite a different note by concluding with a clear allusion to the cosmic renewal tradition in Trito-Isaiah as well as an allusion to Isa 30:26 in *1 Enoch* 91:16 in which miraculous renewal is replaced with destruction and recreation: "And the first heaven will vanish and pass away, and a new heaven will appear, and all the powers of heaven will shine with sevenfold light." The "first earth" and the "new earth," however, are not mentioned, perhaps because the "new heaven" is the presumed abode of the righteous for

[78] Claus Westermann, *Isaiah 40–66: A Commentary* (Philadelphia: Westminster, 1969) 408, argues that Isa 65:17–18 refers to the miraculous renewal of heaven and earth (the world), not the destruction of heaven and earth followed by the creation of a new heaven and a new earth, which would be apocalyptic (as in Rev 21:1 and 2 Pet 3:13). Westermann's position is completely misrepresented by R. North, *TDOT* 4.241. The doubtful apocalyptic construal of Isa 65:17–18 is defended by J. D. Smart, *History and Theology in Second Isaiah: A Commentary on Is. 35, 40–66* (Philadelphia: Westminster, 1965) 280 (referring to the parallel in Isa 51:6, where the old heavens and old earth disappear like smoke.

ever.[79] In the context of the last judgment in the ninth and tenth weeks, The negative as well as the positive reformulation of Isa 65:17 here suggests that the creation of the new heavens and earth following the destruction of the old referred to in Rev 21:1 and 2 Pet 3:13 constituted allusions to *1 Enoch* 91:16 rather than Isa. 65–66.[80]

The same theme also occurs in the later apocalypses and apocalyptic traditions, normally with renewal rather than replacement in view.[81] According to the Similitudes of Enoch, both the heavens and the earth will be transformed in the eschaton (*1 Enoch* 45:4–5), and *2 Bar* 44:12 speaks of the coming hour "which abides for ever, and the new world which does not turn to corruption those who own its sway." *2 Bar* 57:2 refers to a "hope for a world to be renewed was then established and the promise of a life to come hereafter was implanted in men's hearts" (cf. *2 Bar*. 32:6; 49:3). The future transformation is called "the consolation of Zion" in *2 Bar*. 44:7, a phrase which evokes passages in Isaiah and Zechariah which anticipate the future restoration of Zion (Isa 40:1–11; Zech 1:14–17), a transformation which is dependent on the faithful observance of the law (77:6; 78:7; 84:2; 85:4).[82] Similarly *4 Ezra* 7:31 (which has no counterpart in *2 Baruch*), depicts a world which recapitulates the original creation: "And after seven days the world, which is not yet awake, shall be roused, and that which is corruptible shall perish." In *4 Ezra* 7:75, Ezra raises the issue of the postmortem fate of the soul: "Shall we be kept in rest until those times come when thou wilt renew the creation, or shall we be tormented at once?" The primary function of the eschaton can be encapsulated as the "retour" or "recommencement" (*2 Enoch* 13:14 [Vaillant]), "renewal" (*2 Enoch* 13:14 [Pennington]), "recommencement" (*2 Enoch* 40:1 = 13:14 (A) [Andersen]).[83] One eschatological theme of the Book of Watchers is the promise of God that the earth, which has been ruined by the corrupting teaching of the Watchers, will be restored (*1 Enoch* 10:7–9). Some authors exploit the parallel between the story of the flood as the end of one world and the beginning of another (Matt 24:37–39; 2 Pet 3:5–7; cf. *1 Clem*. 9:4 where παλιγγενεσία is used of the world after the flood).

One of the more significant ways in which the restoration of the original state of the world was conceptualized in Jewish apocalyptic was through the notion of two successive worlds or ages (the Hebrew word עוֹלָם can mean either "period

[79] M. Black, "The New Creation in 1 Enoch," *Creation, Christ and Culture: Studies in Honour of T. F. Torrance*, ed. R. McKinney (Edinburgh: T. & T. Clark, 1976) 17.

[80] J. T. Milik, *The Books of Enoch: Aramaic Fragments of Qumran Cave 4* (Oxford: Clarendon Press, 1976) 199; Black, "The New Creation in 1 Enoch," 17–18.

[81] *Jub*. 1:29; 4:26; Ps.-Philo *Bib. Ant*. 3:10; 16:3; *Tg. Onq*. Deut 32:12; 2 Cor 5:17; *Barn*. 15:8.

[82] John F. Hobbins, "The Summing up of History in 2 Baruch," *JQR* 89 (1998) 62–3.

[83] See the use of Greek terms which encapsulate the future transformation of the world, such as παλιγγενεσία, "restoration of all things"(Matt 19:28), or χρόνοι ἀποκαταστάσεως πάντων, "times of the restoration of all things" (Acts 3:21).

of time" or "age" and "world, though the latter meaning is only attested after 134 BCE),[84] the first corruptible and the second incorruptible. The conception of the Two Ages is a basic feature of the eschatological perspective of *4 Ezra*, and is mentioned in 6:7: "And I answered and said, 'What will be the dividing of the times? Or when will be the end of the first age and the beginning of the age that follows'?" (see also 6:34; 7:12–13, 50, 112–3; 8:1, 62).[85]

8. Concluding Observations

As the preceding discussion demonstrates, the eschatological conceptions found in Jewish apocalyptic literature are primarily expressed in narrative modes. The individual themes which we have examined, therefore, are characteristically embedded in eschatological scenarios from which they can only be separated artificially. Many if not most of the eschatological scenarios discussed in this article exhibit traditional and stereotypical features which were often retained by the authors of apocalypses despite exhibiting what appears to modern critics as contradictory, inconsistent, disordered, missing and even paradoxical elements when two or more of these scenarios are compared, even in the same author. This problem becomes particularly obvious in the case of several of the later apocalypses, particularly *4 Ezra* and *2 Baruch*. The very nature of eschatological thought seems resistant to consistency and coherence. Nevertheless at this point it is my intention to summarize the analysis of each of the seven restoration themes treated above.

1. The restoration of the land. Despite undoubted universalistic features, Jewish apocalypses exhibit strong and characteristic streaks of parochialism. One of the most basic of these is the dream of regaining sovereignty over the land of Palestine. The emphasis on the land as the indispensable arena for God's eschatological action pervades the eschatological scenarios of both the earlier and later groups of Jewish apocalypses examined above.

2. The restoration of kingship. Referring to *sovereignty* over the land implies some form of dominating leadership, whether theocratic or monarchic in conception. While both tendencies can be considered forms of eschatological restoration, the discussion above emphasized the restoration of an idealized Davidic kingship in the form of a "theocratic monarchianism," i. e., the Messiah as the agent of God's eschatological activity in domestic and international affairs (and therefore a dispensable figure). The Davidic Messiah appears only in the later group of Apocalypses, where he functions as God's agent in defeating, reproving, judging and executing the enemies of God and rewarding the

---

[84] E. Jenni, "Das Wort 'ôlam im Alten Testament," *ZAW* 65 (1953) 90–106.

[85] These passages are all discussed by Stone, *Eschatology*, 47–65.

righteous. He also presides enthroned over an idyllic period of peace, prosperity and abundance which is frequently a temporary period which concludes with the final great judgment of God. Messianic figures in early Judaism are various and complex, not least because they are amalgams of a variety of conceptions in addition to the idealized characteristics and functions of the Davidic kings.

3. Regathering the people. The imaginary and idealized original unity of the twelve tribes of Israel was a conception which fueled the eschatological imaginations of apocalyptic writers, though not to the degree that it dominated the thought of the postexilic writing prophets. The myth of the lost ten or nine-and-one-half tribes who would eventually be supernaturally reassembled in their Palestinian homeland found its fullest expression, for whatever reason, in the latest group of apocalypses, notably in *4 Ezra* and *2 Baruch*. The inclusion by Ezekiel of twelve gates in the eschatological Jerusalem named after the twelve tribes of Israel and pointedly symbolizing their eschatological regathering and unity was taken over in the subsequent apocalyptic visions of the Description of the New Jerusalem and the Temple Scroll (documents preserved at Qumran) as well as by the Christian author of the Apocalypse of John. Nevertheless there are apocalypses in which the theme of the regathering and restoration of the people of Israel is mysteriously ignored (*2 Enoch* and *3 Baruch*).

4. Jerusalem and the Temple. The sanctity and unity of Jerusalem and the Temple was a central theme of Jewish eschatological speculation, particularly following destruction of the first temple in 586 BCE, the profanation of the second temple during the period of the Maccabees, the perception of the profanation of the second temple by dissident Jewish groups following the Maccabean triumph, and the destruction of the second (or third) temple by the Romans in 70 CE. Although the spectrum of beliefs about the eschatological Jerusalem and the eschatological temple are represented only partially by the Jewish apocalypses analyzed above, the subject is treated at some length by two of the later apocalypses, *4 Ezra* and *2 Baruch*. In both, the necessity of obeying the law of God is essential is Judaism is to regain what she has lost. The revelation on earth of the eschatological Jerusalem is a central feature of the outlook of *4 Ezra*, while *2 Baruch* is more equivocal on the issue, apparently the existence of the incorruptible heavenly temple as consolation for the loss of the corruptible earthly temples.

5. Paradise lost and regained. The myth of Adam and Eve in the Garden of Eden, though largely ignored in the Hebrew Bible outside Genesis, provided the basis for a good deal of eschatological speculation. Eschatological salvation came to be conceptualized as idyllic existence in Paradise, access to which had been impossible after the expulsion of Adam and Eve. In the early group of apocalypses, which tend to presuppose an archaic cosmology characterized by a three-storey cosmos, Paradise is usually located in a remote corner of the earth and is often considered the refuge of the righteous dead. The attainment of

immortality became widely symbolized by access to the fruit of the Tree of Life, denied to Adam and Eve. In the later apocalypses, many of which presuppose the newer cosmology of seven heavens, Paradise is usually located in one of the seven heavens, often in the third heaven. The restoration of the righteous to Paradise is essentially a return to the beginnings of human history.

6. The restoration of the cosmos. Throughout apocalyptic literature there are indications that human sin has had an increasingly negative effect on the environment. Apocalyptic writers, often inspired by the prophetic anticipation of the renewal of heaven and earth expressed in Third Isaiah (65:17), frequently interpreted as a renewal of the cosmos, but occasionally as the replacement of the cosmos. While the emphasis on the renewal of the cosmos is found in some of the early apocalypses, the theme comes into its own in many of the later apocalypses, particularly *4 Ezra* and *2 Baruch*, in which the Two Age or Two World conception provides an explicit temporal framework for expressing the implicit contrast between the world as it is now and the world as it will be when God acts in a final and decisive manner to restore his creation to its original pristine state.

The Apocalypse of John and the Problem of Genre[1]

1. Approaching the Problem of Genre

Genre criticism is that aspect of comparative literature which attempts to understand literary works in relation to one another, both diachronically and synchronically. A literary genre consists of a group of texts which exhibit a coherent and recurring pattern of features constituted by the interrelated elements of form, content and function.[2] Satisfactory definitions and descriptions of particular genres are rare, not only because there has been so little agreement among literary critics regarding which specific literary qualities are generically significant, but also because of the diversity of perspectives brought to specific types of texts by scholars. The notion of "genre" has for the most part been based on intuitive or phenomenological judgments that particular groups of texts have closer affinities with each other than with texts which appear to belong to other groups. Consequently definitions of genres exhibit wide differences. In a useful article summarizing modern theoretical discussion of the problem of genre W. G. Doty concludes:[3]

> Generic definitions ought not be restricted to any one particular feature (such as form, content, etc.), but they ought to be widely enough constructed to allow one to conceive of a genre as a congeries of (a limited number of) factors. The cluster of traits charted may include: authorial intention, audience expectancy, formal units used, structure, use of sources, characterizations, sequential action, primary motifs, institutional setting, rhetorical patterns, and the like.

Although this synthesis of possible generic features represents the state of genre research a decade ago, its very lack of specificity and systemic integrity militates against its usefulness. At this point in research, it appears that real progress will be made only through the careful generic analysis of individual members of

---

[1] The original version of this paper was presented to the SBL Seminar on Early Christian Apocalypticism on December 19, 1983 in Dallas, Texas. A number of suggestions made by Hans Dieter Betz, the main respondent, and Adela Yarbro Collins (the chair of the Seminar) as well as other members of the Seminar have been incorporated into this version of the paper.

[2] The necessity of defining a particular genre in terms of form, content and function is argued persuasively by D.Hellholm, "The Problem of Apocalyptic Genre and the Apocalypse of John," Semeia 36 (1986) 13–64.

[3] W. G. Doty, "The Concept of Genre in Literary Analysis," *Society of Biblical Literature 1972 Proceedings*. 2 vols. Ed. L. C. McGaughy (Society of Biblical Literature, 1972) 439–40.

affiliated texts. The first part of the discussion below focuses on recent research on the apocalyptic genre, an area in which important strides have been made in the last decade. The second section argues that significant qualitative differences between ancient literature and modern (western) literature should make critics wary of forcing ancient texts to conform to modern expectations. The third part of the paper suggests that by their very nature ancient apocalypses exhibit a special literary character which necessitates a consideration of related revelatory genres as well as the phenomenology of ancient revelatory experience, and part four proposes a definition of the apocalyptic genre.

Before moving into the first part of the discussion, two important preliminary points need to be made. First, the conception of "mixed genres" is theoretically infelicitous and should be used only as a court of last resort, for if the notion of a *mixtum compositum* is too quickly applied to a problematic text, the possibility of achieving a generic understanding of the structure of the entire text is given up without a struggle. Second, the three-fold distinction between "apocalypses" (as literature), "apocalyptic eschatology" (as a world view), and "apocalypticism" (as a socio-religious movement) proposed recently by a number of scholars is an important step forward in the discussion of the genre of apocalypses and should be retained.[4] It can no longer be assumed that apocalypses were produced by apocalyptic groups who espoused a distinctive type of apocalyptic eschatology. The central concern of the writers of apocalypses was not apocalyptic eschatology so much as speculative knowledge generally, in which cosmology figured prominently.[5] It is therefore critically important to derive the content of the apocalypses, not from an external conception of apocalyptic eschatology, but rather from the study of the texts considered "apocalypses" themselves.

2. Recent Research on the Genre of Apocalypses

In a paper published in 1976, M. E. Stone observed:[6]

> Recent years have not seen any particularly great advances in the study of the apocalypses as a genre, although criticism of various individual works has been advanced at diverse points.

That assessment is no longer accurate. First, the work of the Society of Biblical Literature's Apocalypse Group, part of the SBL Genres Project, published the results of its collaborative research in Volume 14 of *Semeia* (1979), edited by

---

[4] M. E. Stone, "Lists of Revealed Things in Apocalyptic Literature." *Magnalia Dei: The Mighty Acts of God* ed. F. M. Cross, W. E. Lemke and P. D. Miller, Jr. (Garden City: Doubleday, 1976) 439–42; P. D. Hanson, "Apocalypticism." IDBSup. Nashville: Abingdon, 1976) 29–31.

[5] C. Rowland, *The Open Heaven: A Study of Apocalyptic in Judaism and Early* Christianity (New York: Crossroad, 1983) 49–72.

[6] Stone, "Lists of Revealed Things," 439.

the Group's chairman John J. Collins, with the title: "Apocalypse: The Morphology of a Genre." Second, the International Colloquium on apocalypticism, held in Uppsala in 1979, consisted of thirty-four papers (twelve on the problem of genre), published under the editorship of David Hellholm with the title *Apocalypticism in the Mediterranean World and the Near East.* Third, there is the significant work of David Hellholm himself, first in his published Uppsala dissertation (1980), and more recently his paper on "The Problem of Apocalyptic Genre and the Apocalypse of John" discussed in the SBL Seminar on Early Christian apocalypticism in 1982 in New York. Since all of these contributions to the discussion were made (or appeared) between 1979 and 1983, there has not been a sufficient interval for the contributors to interact critically with each other, or for their work to be assessed adequately by a broader spectrum of scholarship. In this section of the paper, I propose both to summarize and assess critically the contributions of J. J. Collins and D. Hellholm and then to point out some of the more significant contributions to the discussion made by participants in the 1979 International Colloquium on Apocalypticism.

The Proposal of J. J. Collins

Professor Collins has formulated a definition of the genre apocalypse which consists of what he considers the constant or invariable features of the genre:[7]

> "Apocalypse" is a genre of revelatory literature with a narrative framework, in which a revelation is mediated by an otherworldly being to a human recipient, disclosing a transcendent reality which is both temporal, insofar as it envisages eschatological salvation, and spatial insofar as it involves another, supernatural world.

Although the core elements of the genre are described in this definition, no specific apocalypse, Collins claims, can be understood properly without reference to a master paradigm which he has constructed, consisting of a lengthy list of the constituent features of apocalypses, divided into the following major categories, each of which describes an aspect of the form or content of apocalypses: (1) Manner of Revelation (i. e., form), (2) Content: Temporal Axis (i. e., content), (3) Content: Spatial Axis (i. e., content), (4) Paraenesis (i. e., content), and (5) Concluding Elements (i. e., form). Further, in addition to the core definition and the master paradigm of elements which are frequently, but not always, found in individual apocalypses, Collins proposes two main types of apocalypses, those with and those without an otherworldly journey (Types I and II respectively). Each type may be further specified by one of three features: (a) Those with a historical review, (b) Those with cosmic or political eschatology, and (c) Those with only personal eschatology.

---

[7] J. J. Collins, "Introduction: Towards the Morphology of a Genre," *Semeia* 14 (1979) 9.

This definition, master paradigm and typological grouping focus on the generic dimensions of *form* and *content.* On the relationship of the dimension of function to generic definition, Collins observes:[8]

> Further, while a complete study of a genre must consider function and social setting, neither of these factors can determine the definition. At least in the case of ancient literature our knowledge of function and setting is often extremely hypothetical and cannot provide a firm basis for generic classification. The only firm basis which can be found is the identification of recurring elements which are explicitly present in the texts.

While this description of the genre apocalypse is probably the most complete and systematic attempt to define the genre at the pragmatic level, it has not gone without criticism. David Hellholm, for example, who insists that the three dimensions of form, content and function must be integrated for a successful definition of a given genre, accepts Collins' definition (as a paradigmatically established definition), but proposes adding a statement dealing with *function:* "intended for a group in crisis with the purpose of exhortation and/or consolation by means of divine authority."[9] Further, Hellholm claims that while Collins himself has properly presented a hierarchization of recurring features of apocalypses (designated *semes/noemes* by Hellholm) in his master paradigm, he has failed to carry this insight out in practice. Although Hellholm's insistence on including the element of function is well-taken, I think he is wrong in claiming that Collins' master paradigm is hierarchically arranged, so that when he criticizes Collins for hierarchical inaccuracies in his paradigm he criticizes him for what he did not set out to do. Collins' master paradigm is only "hierarchically arranged" in the sense that it is in outline form, and the function of an outline, with its infinite capacity for subordination, is by definition "hierarchic."

Both Lars Hartman and E. P. Sanders have criticized Collins' proposal from different perspectives. Hartman lists four groups of genre constituents: (1) linguistic/stylistic constituents, (2) propositional constituents, (3) illocutionary features, and (4) socio-linguistic function, and claims that all the elements of Collins' master paradigm belong to the category of propositional constituents.[10] Hartman thinks that in dealing with propositional constituents one must not only consider such features as plot, themes and motifs (as Collins does), but also take into consideration the hierarchic structure and literary interrelations of those elements. Another critic of Collins' proposal is E. P. Sanders, who discusses the difficulties of regarding "genre" as a term appropriate for entire literary works

[8] Collins, "Introduction: Towards the Morphology of a Genre," 1–2.

[9] Hellholm, "The Problem of Apocalyptic Genre," 27.

[10] L. Hartman, "Survey of the Problem of Apocalyptic Genre,"*Apocalypticism in the Mediterranean World and the Near East,* ed. D. Hellholm (Tübingen: Mohr Siebeck, 1983) 329–43.

when applied to texts which are compiled.[11] Thus, he points out, Collins does not consider *1 Enoch* 91–104 an apocalypse, even though the other sections of *1 Enoch* are so categorized. Similarly, claims Sanders, Collins considers only *Jubilees* 23 an apocalypse, while other scholars (notably J. Carmignac) consider the entire document an apocalypse. He concludes that "a lot of the material is left out of the description. The questions of the whole and the parts and of composite works still leave problems for students of genre."[12] Sanders further criticizes Collins by noting the fact that the definition of what ought to constitute the basic elements in defining a genre proposed by W. G. Doty, part of which is quoted above,[13] has little relationship to the elements included by Collins.[14] However, this criticism erroneously assumes that Doty's synthesis of generically salient literary features is anything more than an eclectic summary of possibilities.

In sum, Collins' proposals represent an important step forward in research on the genre of ancient apocalypses, though two problematic features have surfaced: the problem of the *function* of the genre, and the problem of the hierarchical arrangement of various generically salient literary features of apocalypses. Further, despite the comprehensive character of Collins' definition, it remains inductive and descriptive. Thus it cannot deal with the virtualities or potentialities of the apocalyptic genre and shows little hermeneutical promise.

The Proposal of David Hellholm

The work of David Hellholm, mentioned above, constitutes another important step forward in genre research generally, and may provide a complement to the work of John J. Collins. Hellholm utilizes text-linguistic methodology, particularly as developed in Germany during the past two decades. His discussions and analyses are exceedingly complex, but the results are so important that New Testament scholars should become aware of his work and its implications. Hellholm is fully cognizant that language has paradigmatic as well as syntagmatic relations (i. e., form as well as content must be considered), and so he insists that the paradigmatic approach to defining the genre of apocalypses be supplemented by a syntagmatic approach.[15] Hellholm must make this concession since formal linguistic structures (syntagmatics) have no intrinsic meaning (pragmatics), and it is difficult to imagine a generic definition which ignored text-pragmatics.

---

[11] E. P. Sanders, "The Genre of Palestinian Jewish Apocalypses," *Apocalypticism in the Mediterranean World and the Near East,* ed. D. Hellholm. Tübingen: Mohr Siebeck, 1983) 447–59.

[12] Sanders, "The Genre of Palestinian Jewish Apocalypses," 454.

[13] W. G. Doty, "The Concept of Genre in Literary Analysis," 413–48.

[14] Sanders, "The Genre of Palestinian Jewish Apocalypses," 454–55.

[15] Hellholm, "The Problem of Apocalyptic Genre and the Apocalypse of John," 33.

In this macro-syntagmatic approach to the analysis of generic structures, Hellholm proposes two necessary and complementary steps in text analysis: (1) Division of the text into hierarchically arranged communication levels (the text-pragmatic aspect), and (2) Division of the text into hierarchical textsequences (the text-semantic aspect). The communication levels are of two types, those external to the text (between the sender and receiver, author and readers), and those internal to the text (between *dramatis personae*). Text sequences are signaled by several types of markers: (a) changes in "world" (this world; other world), (b) episode markers indicating time and change of time, localization and relocalization, (c) changes in grouping of actors, (d) renominalization (an actor referred to by a pronoun is reintroduced with a noun or name), (e) adverbs and conjunctions which relate clauses to each other. The identification of communication levels and textsequences together constitute the generic structures of the text. Hellholm has analyzed two apocalypses in this way, the *Shepherd of Hermas* (*Vis.* 1–4) in great detail,[16] and Revelation in considerably less detail. For Hermas *Vis.* 1–4, Hellholm proposes six levels of communication (from lowest to highest), excluding the title: (1) Between author and addressees, (2a) Between mediators of revelation and author, (2b) Between the bearers of revelation and addressees, (3) Between quotations from revealed books in the text and author, (3a) Between quotations from revealed books in the text and addressees, (4) Between the quoted saying of God and a quoted apocryphal prophetic book and addressees.[17] The texts which constitute the highest communication level are the most profoundly embedded texts in the apocalypse. Hellholm's next complementary step, the hierarchical ranking of textsequences, produces a scheme in five "grades," extending from the general to the particular:[18]

1. Introductory narrative
   Main visionary part
2. Four vision reports
3. Movement to place of this-worldly revelation
   Vision account
4. Preparation for vision
   Vision
5. Dialogue between revealer and human recipient
   Listening to or copying heavenly book/letter

[16] D. Hellholm, *Das Visionenbuch des Hermas als Apokalypse: Formgeschichtliche und texttheoretische Studien zu einer literarischen Gattung.* ConBNT 13/1. Lund: Gleerup, 1980) 11–13. Hellholm regards these four visions as constituting a unified apocalypse; the fifth vision is judged a redactional introduction to the *Mandates.*

[17] Hellholm, *Das Visionenbuch des Hermas als* Apokalypse, 190–91.

[18] Hellholm, *Das Visionenbuch des Hermas als* Apokalypse, 190–96.

Hellholm shows that the most embedded text on the communication level coincides with the location of the same embedded text at the fifth, or highest, grade of the textsequential structure. The most embedded texts in Herm. *Vis.* 1–4 which Hellholm has identified are Herm. *Vis.* 2.2.5 and 2.3.4:

(For the Master has sworn to his elect by his glory that) if there is still sin after this day has been fixed, they shall find no salvation; for repentance for the just has an end; the days of repentance have been fulfilled for all the saints, but for the heathen repentance is open until the last day.

The Lord is near those that turn to him, (as it is written in the book of Eldad and Modat, who prophesied to the people in the wilderness). (*LCL* translation)

Hellholm proposes that the function of this hierarchical embedment is the *authorization* of the message, and it is true that the first passage constitutes a clear expression of the central message of Hermas. He promises to discuss the genre of Hermas and the interpretation of specific texts in a forthcoming volume. Further, he intends to present an analysis of the levels of the macro-structure and functional communication levels of other apocalyptic texts.[19]

Yet some of Hellholm's conclusions are available, if only in a preliminary way in connection with his discussion of the genre of the Apocalypse of John in comparison with the earlier analysis of the *Shepherd* of Hermas. In presenting his analysis of the hierarchical communication levels in the Apocalypse of John, Hellholm proposes six such levels or grades:[20]

1. Prologue functioning as a title
2. Epistolary prescript
   Main revelatory part
   Epilogue in form of a visionary authentication by Christ
   Brief Epistolary postscript
3. Revelation without an other-worldly journey
   Revelation with an other-worldly journey
4. Pneumatic enrapture
   Visionary account itself
5. Introductory revelation reports
   Messages in written form
6. Separate message to the seven churches
   Summary revelation as *scriptura exterior* and the main revelation as *scriptura interior*

As in the case of Herm. *Vis.* 1–4, Hellholm finds that the text most profoundly embedded at the functional communication level coincides with the sixth, or

[19] Hellholm, *Das Visionenbuch des Hermas als* Apokalypse, 197.
[20] Hellholm, "The Problem of Apocalyptic Genre and the Apocalypse of John," 43–44.

highest, grade of the macro-structure of the Apocalypse of John. This text is Rev 21:5–8, a passage which expresses the book's central message:

> And he who sat upon the throne said, "Behold, I make all things new." Also he said, "Write this, for these words are trustworthy and true." And he said to me, "It is done! I am the Alpha and the Omega, the beginning and the end. To the thirsty I will give water without price from the fountain of the water of life. He who conquers shall have this heritage, and I will be his God and he shall be my son. But as for the cowardly, the faithless, the polluted, as for murderers, fornicators, sorcerers, idolaters, and all liars, their lot shall be in the lake that burns with fire and brimstone, which is the second death. (RSV translation)

In comparing his analyses of the Apocalypse of John and the *Shepherd* of Hermas, Hellholm claims that the phenomenon of embedment is a constitutive and invariant feature of the apocalyptic genre and that while equally deep embedments in other apocalypses cannot be expected, "… it does mean that some kind of hierarchic communication levels must be present."[21] In both apocalypses the most deeply embedded level of communication coincides with the highest grade of hierarchically ranked text sequences.[22]

Hellholm's syntagmatic approach to the description of generically salient features of ancient apocalypses is a methodologically sophisticated generic analysis of both the Apocalypse of John and the *Shepherd* of Hermas that has yielded some striking results. Hellholm's demonstration of the existence of parallel phenomena in the macro-structures of both texts suggests that he has made an important contribution to our knowledge of these texts as well as of the genre of ancient apocalypses generally. There are a number of issues which must be raised in connection with some of his proposals, however. The most obvious problem concerns the comparative nature of genre criticism. One or two syntagmatic analyses, striking though they may be in their convergences, cannot be generalized to include all the texts of that type until all (or at least many) have been syntagmatically analyzed. This is Hellholm's ultimate intention, but whether the results will support his claims regarding the two apocalypses he has already analyzed remains to be seen. Further, texts which are *not* commonly regarded as "apocalypses" must also be subject to syntagmatic analysis, for comparisons can be made confidently only when contrasts are clearly drawn as well.

A second problem lies in the relationship between paradigmatic and syntagmatic definitions of the apocalyptic genre. If the paradigmatic model must be supplemented by syntagmatic analysis (as Hellholm insists), what is the precise relationship between these two approaches to formulating a generic definition of apocalypses? This issue will be taken up again below, for one of the purposes of this paper is the integration of the results of Hellholm's syntagmatic analysis within the framework of a paradigmatic description of the apocalyptic genre.

---

[21] Hellholm, "The Problem of Apocalyptic Genre and the Apocalypse of John," 45.
[22] Hellholm, "The Problem of Apocalyptic Genre and the Apocalypse of John," 52–3.

Yet a third problematic area is the matter of determining just what degree of embedment and what degree of hierarchically arranged partial texts should be regarded as constitutive for the apocalyptic genre. Any ancient text which recounts a visionary experience within which statements by a revealer or a dialogue occur will exhibit several grades of embedment. In the NT this phenomenon is found not only in Revelation but also in the gospels, Acts and letters as well (e. g., 2 Cor 12). By way of illustration, let me propose a preliminary analysis of one of the acts of the martyrs not normally considered an apocalyptic text, the *Martyrdom of Perpetua and Felicitas*.[23] Excluding the title, this text exhibits three levels of communication: (1) Between the author and the addressees, (2) Between the martyrs and the addressees, and (3) Between the principal figures in the visions and the martyrs. In attempting to rank partial texts in a hierarchical series of grades, I propose the following levels (with references in parentheses):

1. Prologue (1)
   Narrative introduction (2)
   Visionary part (3–13)
   Narrative conclusion (14:1–21:10)
   Epilogue (21:11)
2. Revelation without an otherworldly journey
   Revelation with an otherworldly journey
3. Five vision reports (4:1–10; 7:1–10; 7:11–8:4; 10:1–12; 11:1–13:8)
   Narrative interludes (3:1–9; 5:1–6:8; 9:1–3)
4. Autobiographical written vision reports
5. Prayer preceding vision
   Vision report
   Explication of vision

In this analysis the fifth grade of hierarchically arranged text sequences coincides with the third level of communication, yet this phenomenon occurs frequently within the text at no apparently significant junctures. Despite the tentative nature of this analysis, two mutually exclusive observations can be made: either this analysis suggests that the syntagmatic analysis which Hellholm regards as constitutive for apocalypses is also exhibited in other types of ancient texts, or,

[23] This text is not considered in the survey of early Christian apocalypses by A. Yarbro Collins. The omission of this text from consideration is based on Professor Yarbro Collins' view (expressed at the Seminar mentioned in note 1), that a supernatural revealer, a necessary feature of apocalypses, is missing. This phenomenon, however, is present in the fifth vision report (11:1–13:8), though not in the first four vision reports. Yarbro Collins also regards apocalypses as first-person reports of revelatory experiences; since the author of the *Martyrdom* is relating the visionary experiences of *others* the work is not an apocalypse. H. Musurillo (*The Acts of the Christian Martyrs: Introduction, Texts and Translations* [Oxford: Clarendon Press, 1972] xxv) regards the composition as an apocalypse.

the *Martyrdom of Perpetua and Felicitas* should be regarded as belonging to the apocalyptic genre.

Relevant Contributions from the Uppsala Colloquium.

Four of the twelve essays in the section entitled "The Literary Genre of Apocalypses" in the volume of the Uppsala Colloquium proceedings are particularly relevant to the present discussion. The essays by Hartman and Sanders have already been discussed briefly above. The essay by John J. Collins also makes an important contribution to the discussion.[24]

Reiterating the definition discussed above, Collins focuses on *2* (Slavonic) *Enoch, 3* (Greek) *Baruch* and the *Testament of Abraham* (Rec. A, 10–15; Rec. B, 8–12). He concludes that the function of *2 Enoch* is hortatory, *3 Baruch* gives a perspective on the fall of Jerusalem minimizing its importance in the light of an individualized eschatology, and the *Testament of Abraham* gives a perspective on death in light of God's mercy. All, however, have a significant paraenetic aspect. Collins makes the following generalization:

> The coherence of these works does not lie in their precise function, but in their underlying conceptual structure: the belief in another, heavenly, world, already existing and in a definite judgment of every individual after death. This structure constitutes the premises for more specific argument.[25]

While only *3 Baruch* can be related to a political crisis, all the texts appeal to transcendent reality as the most profound reality and as the final goal of humanity. The universalism of these apocalypses suggests that they cannot be identified with the sectarian views of particular conventicles.

In another significant essay, Hans Dieter Betz examines the literary sources on the ancient oracle of Trophonius and shows how afterlife mythology exerted an increasingly strong influence on accounts of consultations.[26] Betz proposes that the oracular dialogue, or *erotapokrisis,* found in literary accounts of consultations, developed from simpler oracular inquiries. In Plutarch's *De genio Socratis* 589F–592E, the story (*mythos*) of Timarchus' inquiry at the oracular grotto of Trophonius (his descent-and-return reflects the death-and-rebirth experience of mystery initiations) is preceded by a *logos* and concluded by a paraenetic interpretation of the *mythos.* Betz shows that an elaborate underworld mythology, influenced by Orphic-Pythagorean mythology, had become attached to many

---

[24] J.J. Collins, "The Genre Apocalypse in Hellenistic Judaism," *Apocalypticism in the Mediterranean World and the Near East*, ed. D. Hellholm (Tübingen: Mohr Siebeck, 1983) 531–48.

[25] Collins, "The Genre Apocalypse in Hellenistic Judaism," 544.

[26] H.D. Betz, "The Problem of Apocalyptic Genre in Greek and Hellenistic Literature: The Case of the Oracle of Trophonius," *Apocalypticism in the Mediterranean World and the Near East*, ed. D. Hellholm (Tübingen: Mohr Siebeck, 1983) 577–97.

Greek oracles. Betz observes that *mythos* refers to a specific literary genre attested in Plato and thereafter only fragmentarily until it reappears in Plutarch.[27] In Plato, *mythos* has a particular nature and function: (1) *Mythos* can do what *logos* cannot do, namely, speak of matters beyond the human world in human language. (2) The notion of the immortality of the soul, impossible to deal with in rational speech, "requires a confrontation with the destiny of one's own soul, and to bring this about is the purpose of *mythos.*"[28] (3) The experience of fear, generated by the *mythos* (including, e.g., the punishment of the wicked in the underworld), motivates people to live good lives. (4) "Like a magical charm the *mythos* must be told again and again."[29] Plutarch's eschatological myths, argues Betz, are representative of the genre *mythos* at the end of the first century CE, and the changes since Plato lie primarily in the areas of: (1) the increasing influence of Orphic-Pythagorean netherworld mythology, (2) the growing importance of cosmic visions, and (3) recent developments in ideas about the soul, divination and supernatural beings. *Mythos* is oracular narrative which stimulates man to explore its meaning. For Plutarch eschatological myths, which must be allegorically interpreted, function in several ways: (1) They explain the cause of conversion (here the case is Aridaeus-Thespesius in *De sera num. vind.* 563B ff.), and confront the hearer with the ancient notion that "responsibility belongs to the chooser; God is not responsible" (Plato *Rep.* 10. 617E). (2) The shock-like experience of fear motivates man to live a good life. (3) *Mythos* produces the correct view of the gods, i.e., faith, while *logos* has functioned to awaken rational thought in the soul.

3. Special Features of Ancient Mediterranean Literature

Modern analyses of ancient texts usually proceed under the assumption that literature, particularly "good" literature, possesses certain essential qualities which transcend the specific culture and circumstances of its origin and reflect matters universal to human experience. On that basis, literary critical methods and perspectives which "work" with modern literature are automatically assumed to apply to ancient texts as well. But when an entire period in the history of Greco-Roman literary culture (the second century CE), can be labeled "mediocre" and "decadent," it is readily apparent that modern tastes and perspectives have precluded a sympathetic understanding and evaluation of ancient literature.[30] The scholarship of Peter Brown has done much to rescue late antiquity from such

27 H. D. Betz, "The Problem of Apocalyptic Genre," 585–95.
28 H. D. Betz, "The Problem of Apocalyptic Genre," 588.
29 H. D. Betz, "The Problem of Apocalyptic Genre," 588.
30 B. A. van Groningen, "General Literary Tendencies in the Second Century CE" *Mnemosyne* 18 (1965) 41–56.

pejorative labels and shown it instead to be an era of remarkable cultural change and creativity. Further, dramatic differences between archaic and modern society and thought have been amply demonstrated in the work of Moses I. Finley on ancient economy and democracy.[31] Models based on modern assumptions, when applied to ancient society and culture, may serve to mask the distinctive features of ancient life and thought. The purpose of this section is to suggest that the problem of the genre of ancient texts must be approached in a manner sensitive to the ancient cultural systems which such literature reflects. Four major areas of concern involve the problem of orality and textuality (involving the relationships between literature and rhetoric and texts and performance), the relationship between the whole and the part in literary texts, and the possible connections between literature and religious cults.

Orality and Textuality

Literature and rhetoric were so closely connected in the ancient world that many modern assumptions about the nature of ancient texts are misleading. It can be said, without exaggeration, that "all classical Greek authors composed for the ear."[32] The numerous (and entertaining) excurses in the first six books of Herodotus' *History of the Persian Wars*, for example, appear to be included precisely because the author wrote with the intention of public recitation, and indeed polished his material by delivering the same lectures many times.[33] Further, Thucydides' reliance upon speeches as a primary means for understanding the motivations of great men and their role in influencing historical events is scarcely conceivable in isolation from the great development in rhetoric and oratory in the Athens of his day. The dramatic effect created by the oral performance of these works, using first-person narratio, capitalized on the illusion of the author's actual presence (Plutarch *De gloria Ath.* 347A–B).[34] Ancient authors normally composed aloud,[35] and the advice of Dio Chrysostom (end of first, beginning of second centuries CE) illustrates the continuing affinity between oratory and writing:

> Writing, however, I do not advise you to engage in with your own hand, or only very rarely, but rather to dictate to a secretary. For, in the first place, the one who utters his

[31] M.I Finley, *Economy and Society in Ancient Greece*. New York: Viking, 1982) ix–xxvi.

[32] W. B. Stanford, *The Sound of Greek: Studies in the Greek Theory and Practice of Euphony* (Berkeley and Los Angeles: University of California Press, 1967) 4.

[33] For an impressive analysis of Herodotus' style and compositional techniques, see H. R. Immerwahr, *Form and Thought in Herodotus*, American Philological Association Monographs, 23 (Cleveland: American Philological Association, 1966).

[34] C. W. Fornara, *The Nature of History in Ancient Greece and Rome* (Berkeley and Los Angeles: University of California Press, 1983) 31, 130.

[35] J. Balogh, "'Voces Paginarum:' Beiträge zur Geschichte des lauten Lesens und Schreibens," *Philologus* 82 (1927) 84–109, 213.

thoughts aloud is more nearly in the mood of a man addressing an audience than one who writes, and, in the second place, less labor is involved. (Dio Chrysostom *Or.* 18.18; LCL translation)

One of the features of ancient reading which closely links literature to rhetoric is the fact that texts were almost always read aloud, and authors knew that their works would be "performed" in such a manner and could design them accordingly. Ancients who read "silently" (i. e., making no audible sound, but with their lips moving) were an elite minority including Aristotle, Julius Caesar, Ambrose and Augustine.[36] Thus in many ancient texts, the terms "hear" and "read" are often used as synonyms, a phenomenon which occurs in Rev 1:3.[37] The intimate relationship, not only between writing and rhetoric but also between literature and oral performance suggests the importance of the rhetorical handbooks of antiquity for students of ancient literature. It is likely that all of the compositions in the NT were written expressly for public, oral performance. Even the *Shepherd* of Hermas, a cumbersome text by any account, was intended for public presentation (Herm. *Vis.* 2.4.3; cf. 1.3.3–4). Orality played an explicit role in the composition of the Apocalypse of John, for the entire document was written expressly for public performance (Rev 1:3; 22:18), and each of the seven proclamations of Rev 2–3 are presented as dictated to the author, as are many other segments of the book (cf. Rev 21:5). The fact that both the Apocalypse of John and the *Shepherd* of Hermas were intended for oral performance before Christian congregations *constitutes a unique feature of these two apocalypses.* There is some evidence from late Jewish apocalypses to suggest that an audience is envisaged, e. g. the use of plural forms of address,[38] but parallels to the specific prescriptions for performance found in the Apocalypse of John and the *Shepherd* of Hermas are notably absent. The feature of dramatic public performance, then, appears to be an innovative factor in the function of early Christian apocalypses. Types of ancient literature (such as apocalypses) which utilize "first-person" narratives are a particularly appropriate vehicle for reenacting the original speech experience within the framework of a public performance.

---

[36] On Julius Caesar, cf. Plutarch *Brutus* 5.3; on Ambrose, cf. Augustine *Conf.* 6.3; on Augustine, cf. Augustine *Conf.* 8.12, where it states that he read Romans "i silentio." On the subject of ancient reading, see (in addition to Balogh) G. L. Hendrikson, "Ancient Reading." *Classical Journal* 25 (1929/30), 182–90, E. S. McCartney, "On Reading and Praying Audibly," *Classical Philology* 43 (1948) 184–87, and B. M. W. Knox, "Silent Reading in Antiquity," *Greek, Roman & Byzantine Studies* 9 (1968) 421–35. Knox corrects some exaggerations found in Balogh.

[37] Herodotus 1.48; Augustine *Ep.* 147; *Conf.* 10.3; Cassiodorus *Inst. div. lec.* 1.29; J. Balogh, "'Voces Paginarum," 206–210; Hendrikson, "Ancient Reading," 182–90.

[38] Public recitation is implied in *Apocalypse of Zephaniah* 8:5: "Now, moreover, my sons, this is the trial because it is necessary that the good and evil be weighed in the balance" (Charlesworth: 1.514). Public recitation however, is not enjoined by the author, a *prima facie* impossibility if the fiction of pseudonymity was to be retained. Lebram (173) has observed that the post-Biblical apocalypses are "a *literary* revelation … a revelation intended to be read and not heard."

The Whole and the Part

The composite character of some apocalypses necessitates a consideration of the problem of the whole and the part in ancient literature. J. J. Collins, for example, does not regard *1 Enoch* 91–104 as an apocalypse (though the rest of *1 Enoch* is), and he considers *Jub* 23, *T. Levi* 2–5 and *T. Abr.* 10–15 as apocalypses, though not the rest of those documents.[39] David Hellholm regards only Herm. *Vis.* 1–4 as an apocalypse, and not Herm. *Vis.* 5 or the rest of the *Shepherd of Hermas*.[40] Generally, apocalyptic vision reports are constituent elements of larger texts in Greco-Roman literature,[41] while in Jewish and Christian tradition they tend to exist in discrete form. Since modern genre theory (representing many literary and linguistic perspectives) tends to emphasize the "gestaltist" unity of literary texts (i. e., the whole is greater than the sum of its parts),[42] there is no satisfactory framework with which to deal with "compilations" other than resorting to the view of "mixed genres."

In ancient Greek and Israelite literature, tension existed between literary compositions which exhibited a striking degree of unity of both plot and structure (e. g., epic, tragedy, comedy, and biblical books such as Ruth, Esther and Jonah), and those which exhibited a looser, more episodic structure or were used as vehicles to frame other, shorter, literary forms (examples from Greco-Roman literature include history, biography, and "antiquities," and in the Bible the "historical" section, running continuously from Genesis through 2 Kings). These two styles of literary macrostructures may be designated *periodic* and *paratactic* respectively, following a useful distinction made by Aristotle.[43] The periodic

[39] J. J. Collins, "The Jewish Apocalypses." *Semeia* 14 (1979) 21–49.

[40] Hellholm, *Das Visionenbuch des Hermas als Apokalypse*, 11–13.

[41] H. W. Attridge, "Greek and Latin Apocalypses." *Semeia* 14 (1979) 159.

[42] The "gestaltist" character of texts is treated in great detail by E. Güttgemanns, *Candid Questions Concerning Gospel Form Criticism* (Pittsburgh: Pickwick Press, 1979) 259–97. E. D. Hirsch's notion of "intrinsic genre," is "that sense of the whole by means of which an interpreter can correctly understand any part in its determinacy" (*Validity in Interpretation* [New Haven: Yale University Press, 1967] 86). The same credo is articulated by a very different literary critic, J. M. Ellis: "An interpretation, then, is a hypothesis about the more general organization and coherence of all the elements that form a literary text. The most satisfying interpretation will be that which is the most inclusive," J. M. Ellis, *The Theory of Literary Criticism: A Logical Analysis*. Berkeley and Los Angeles: University of California Press, 1974) 202. Text-linguists too ascribe to this conception as this quotation from W. Raible suggests; Raible claims that neither sentences nor text sequences of various degrees "have *per se* any function but only obtain their function from a superior totality, e. g. (with regard to tones) within a melody or, as far as texts are concerned, within a superior unit of meaning" (quoted in Hellholm, The Problem of Apocalyptic Genre, 175).

[43] Aristotle uses the phrases εἰρομένη λέξις, i. e., "continuous" or "running style," and the περίοδος λέξις, i. e., "periodic style" (*Rhet.* 1409A–B). E. Norden, *Agnostos Theos*: Untersuchungen zur Formengeschichte religiöser Rede (Darmstadt: Wissenschaftliche Buchgesellschaft, 1956), 367–79, derived the style of early literature from two types of grammatical relationships, καί-sentences (i. e., paratactic), and δέ-sentences (i. e., periodic). For a discussion of

(or, hypotactic) style has a beginning and an end and is the style reflecting the influence of oratory on writing.[44] The paratactic style, on the other hand, has no natural stopping places and ends when there is no more to say on the subject. The effect of parataxis is discontinuity, since the integrity of various members of the chain are preserved at the expense of the unity of the whole. Herodotus and the early Greek logographers, like the historical books of the OT, exhibit paratactic macrostructure.

During the Hellenistic and Roman periods the tension between the two styles of composition continued. While rhetorical theory exerted a powerful influence on literature, a number of types of prose narratives continued to be composed paratactically, including dialogues, various types of history and biography and the novel. Unfortunately, modern scholars have virtually ignored macrostructural composition techniques in these and other ancient narrative genres. Some of the more characteristic features of paratactic composition, such as ring composition, or chiasmus (i. e. close correspondence between statements which frame a literary unit in a composition), and related devices such as *inclusio,* are *never discussed in the rhetorical handbooks,* though they were important structuring devices. Paratactic macrostructure was more characteristic of popular literature (such as the Greek novel and the NT gospels and Acts), though even among educated writers it was used (such as the historians Polybius, Dionysius of Halicarnassus and Josephus, and some of the dialogues of Plutarch and Lucian).[45]

There was a greater exploitation during this period of the elastic and framing qualities inherent in the paratactic character of particular genres, and the inclusion of a wide variety of constituent literary forms within larger, more encompassing "host" or "inclusive" genres became commonplace.[46] Under such

paratactic composition in Herodotus, see Immerwahr, 1–16, 46–78. For a comparison between the paratactic styles of the Greek historians and OT literature, see J. van Seters, *In Search of History: Historiography in the Ancient World and the Origins of Biblical History* (New Haven: Yale University Press, 1983) 35–38.

[44] *Narratio,* when used in contexts other than forensic oratory, e. g., historiography, can be structured in terms of a drama according to Cicero *De inventione* 1.27; cf. *Ad. Herennium* 1.12–13. Historians could give dramatic unity to their narratives if they wrote monographs on very restricted sequences of related events. Polybius is an opponent of such "tragic history" (2.56.1–16), and looks down on those who write historical monographs instead of universal history, as he does; see K. Sacks, *Polybius On the Writing of History*, Classical Studies, 24 (Berkeley and Los Angeles: University of California Press, 1981) 96–121. For the influence of drama on narrative fiction, the novel, see B. Perry, *The Ancient Romances* (Berkeley and Los Angeles: University of California Press, 1967) 105–164.

[45] Lucian's emphasis on a smoothly progressing historical narrative in which each unit is like a link in a chain (*Hist. conscr.* 55; cf. G. Avenarius, *Lukians Schrift zur Geschichtsschreibung* (Meisenheim am Glan: Anton Hain, 1956) 105–164, suggests that the historians he implicitly criticizes were clumsily paratactic.

[46] H. Dubrow, *Genre* (New York and London: Methuen, 1982) 116, coins the phrase "host genre" for a genre, "one of whose roles is to provide a hospitable environment for the other form or forms that are regularly incorporated within them."

circumstances, notions of an overall gestaltic unity are anachronistic, for in texts exhibiting a paratactic macrostructure, the constituent literary forms (or *logoi*) of which the whole is constructed have their own disconcerting dominance. An apocalypse, then, can exist as an independent text or as a constituent part of a host genre, and must be recognized on its own terms in either setting.[47]

Literature and Cult

In describing the function of a given text and the genre to which is belongs, it is often helpful (though often difficult) to reconstruct the socio-religious setting of author and readers. The quest for the original *Sitze im Leben* of ancient religious texts in particular has proven a vexing problem for scholars, and "solutions" have often been excessively speculative. Of special concern here are texts which may "encode" cultic practices, i. e., transform them into a system of symbolic equivalents fully comprehensible only to members. One such theory, proposed by Karl Kerenyi (1962, originally published in 1927), broadened by Reinhold Merkelbach, and all but universally rejected by scholars, discerns an intimate relationship between the ancient novel and Hellenistic mystery religions. Merkelbach proposed that the novel was in fact a mystery text, completely comprehensible only to initiants. The themes of separation, wandering, trials, apparent death and ultimate reunion (characteristic of all Greek novels), reproduce the myth of Isis and Osiris. Yet the theory founders on the fact that human experience exhibits basic patterns which are reflected in ritual and myth as well as in the novel.[48] A similar theory has been proposed for the Jewish novel *Joseph and Aseneth,* that it reflects a Jewish mystery initiation, but this too has not been well received.[49] Evidence for the existence of a Jewish mystery cult has also been proposed for the dream of Moses in the *Exogoge* of the Jewish tragedian Ezekiel (lines 68–89), but this too has met with resistance.[50]

[47] The argument of Sanders, that partial texts should not be regarded as apocalypses is therefore without substance (454).

[48] For two short but telling critiques of Merkelbach's hypothesis, see B. P. Reardon, *Courants littéraires grecs des IIe et IIIe siedes apries J.-C.* (Paris: Les Belles Lettres, 1971) 393–99, and T. Hägg, *The Novel in Antiquity* (Berkeley and Los Angeles: University of California Press, 1983) 101–104.

[49] This view is favored by M. Philonenko, *Joseph et Aseneth: introduction, texte critique, traduction et notes*, SPB, 13 (Leiden: E. J. Brill, 1968) 89–98. For a comprehensive critique, see D. Sänger, *Antikes Judentum und die Mysterien: Religionsgeschichtliche Untersuchungen zu Joseph und Aseneth*, WUNT, 2/5 (Tübingen: Mohr Siebeck, 1980).

[50] This was proposed by L. Cerfaux, "Influence des Mystères sur le Judaisme Alexandrin avant Philo," L. Cerfaux, *Recueil Lucien Cerfaux*, BETL, 6 (Gembloux: J. Duculot, 1954), 85–88 and accepted by E. R. Goodenough, *By Light, Light: The Mystic Gospel of Hellenistic Judaism* (New Haven: Yale University Press, 1935) 289–91. For a critique see J. J. Collins, *Between Athens and Jerusalem: Jewish Identity in the Hellenistic Diaspora* (New York: Crossroad, 1983) 207–211.

Less well-known, perhaps, is Richard Reitzenstein's proposal that *Corpus Hermeticum* 13 constitutes a *Lese-Mysterium,* i.e., a "literary mystery" (as a surrogate for an actual mystery cult), in which the author acts as a mystagogue and the reader can experience initiation (i.e., regeneration) through the use of imagination.[51] While nothing in the tractate suggests that it is intended to effect regeneration in the reader (the injunctions to secrecy in 13.13, 22 militate against it), it does appear to serve both as a reminder of a past experience of regeneration and perhaps of the cultic setting in which it occurred.[52]

These examples suggest that while the relationship between literary texts and cults may be complex and speculative, it is a factor which cannot be ignored. The Apocalypse of John and the *Shepherd* of Hermas, both explicitly intended for public presentation, possibly within the setting of Christian worship (revelation is part of worship, 1 Cor 14:26), potentially can be described generically in terms of their cultic function.

4. The Generic Virtualities of Apocalypses and the Apocalypsae of John

The Special Character of Apocalypses

One of the reasons that it has proven so difficult to move from theoretical discussions of genre constituents to the description of discrete genres is that each genre must be analyzed in its own terms and not in terms of an eclectic list of literary qualities derived from the description of many individual genres (such as that proposed by W.G. Doty). In the preceding section the apocalyptic genre was placed in its ancient literary setting. At this point I will describe some of the special features of apocalypses which must be considered in any generic description of apocalypses.

Vision Reports and Revelatory Magic

A crucial issue in understanding the generic character of ancient apocalypses is the problem of determining the literary parameters within which a comparative analysis may be carried out fruitfully. There are two types of literature relevant for an investigation of the generic affinities of the Apocalypse of John: (1) ancient vision reports, commonly designated "apocalypses," including Christian, Greco-Roman, Greco-Egyptian, Iranian and Greco-Persian apocalypses in ad-

[51] R. Reitzenstein, *Die hellenistischen Mysterienreligionen*, 3. Aufl. (Stuttgart: Teubner, 1927) 51–52, 64–65, 242–45.

[52] W.C. Grese, *Corpus Hermeticum XIII and Early Christian Literature*, SCHNT 5 (Leiden: Brill, 1979) 201–2.

dition to Jewish apocalypses, and (2) ancient ritual prescriptions describing the techniques, possibilities and benefits of visionary revelatory experience, including (on the Jewish side), the texts dealing with Merkavah mysticism and (on the Greco-Roman side), the magical papyri whose chief concern is revelatory magie.[53] Both types of ancient revelatory literature are relevant for understanding the genre of the Apocalypse of John.

First, regardless of the problem of the authenticity of revelatory experiences narrated in apocalypses (in my view an insoluble problem), they were composed in conformity with ancient cultural patterns and expectations. This suggests that regardless of the stereotypical literary formulations, structures and imagery, the context in which such texts must be understood is that of the *phenomenology of revelatory experience*. Texts describing the ritual techniques for achieving revelatory visions and those which narrate revelatory visions describe two complementary phases of revelatory experience. To be sure, the apocalyptist is never overeager to publish his revelatory techniques along with the account of his visions, but we cannot on that account assume (using the argument from silence) that the author of an apocalypse did not employ such techniques. Nor should scholars succumb to the temptation to formulate theological judgments which value spontaneity and disapprove of "apocalyptogenic" technique.[54] The Merkavah literature and the Greek magical papyri provide the ritual procedures for achieving revelatory visions without including a narrative of the visions themselves. Apocalypses, on the other hand, narrate the vision while generally omitting all but brief references to the preparatory ritual procedures. Some apocalypses do provide hints of the ritual techniques preparatory to the reception of visionary revelations, but these hints merely suggest that the authors knew more than they chose to reveal.[55]

Second, there are important phenomenological similarities between the literature containing preparatory ritual procedures for receiving revelations and

---

[53] Magical divination was a major concern of ancient Greco-Roman magic to judge by the many magical procedures which deal with this type of magic. The most comprehensive discussion of the subject remains that of Hopfner. For an overview of the role of the magical diviner, see David E. Aune, *Prophecy in Early Christianity and the Ancient Mediterranean World.* (Grand Rapids: Eerdmans, 1983), 44–47.

[54] J. Maier (*Vom Kultus zur Gnosis* [Salzburg: Otto Mueller, 1964], 17), for example, claims that the revelatory experiences typical of those narrated in apocalypses occurred spontaneously, while the visions anticipated in the Merkavah literature and the magical papyri were obviously based on the initiative of man and induced through complex theurgic techniques; cf. M. Smith, "Observations on Hekhalot Rabbati," *Biblical and Other Studies,* ed. A. Altmann (Cambridge: Harvard University Press, 1963), 155–56.

[55] 4 Ezra 3:1–36 narrates a long preparatory prayer for revelation (cf. Dan 9:3; 10:2–3), and the preparatory procedure of fasting and mourning for seven days, concluded by a preparatory prayer are found in 4 Ezra 5:20–30; 6:31–59; 9:23–37; 13:50–51. In *Herm. Vis.* 2.1.1, Hermas is seized by the Spirit after prayer, and fasting and prayer precede revelatory experiences in *Herm. Vis.* 2.2.1; 3.1.1–2. In Greek apocalypses, preparatory rituals are also only briefly mentioned; cf. Betz, "The Problem of Apocalyptic Genre," 581.

apocalyptic literature. A number of scholars have emphasized the relationship between Jewish apocalypses and Merkavah mysticism in particular.[56] In spite of differences in emphasis (apocalypses tend to focus more on eschatological and cosmological themes, while Merkavah literature focuses on the mysteries of heaven and the throne of God), there is tentative agreement that Merkavah mysticism emerged from Jewish apocalypticism.[57] Further, in addition to the apparently close relationship between the Merkavah texts, particularly the Hekalot literature[58], and Jewish apocalypses, it is important to recognize the close phenomenological relationship between the Merkavah texts and the Greek magical papyri,[59] and now made even more apparent by the Jewish magical text *Sepher ha-Razim.*[60]

Third, the texts prescribing ritual procedures for procuring revelatory visions and those narrating such visions (i. e. apocalypses) in addition to sharing a similar conceptual world, also share similar constituent literary forms. One example is the oracular dialogue, commonly found in both Greco-Roman and Jewish apocalypses, a form suggested in prescriptions for magical revelation found in the magical papyri. Here are two examples of this phenomenon from a Demotic magical papyrus:[61]

> You cause him (i. e., the boy medium) to say to Anubis "The god who will inquire for me to-day, let him tell me his name." When he stands up and tells you his name, you ask him concerning everything you wish.

---

[56] I. Gruenwald, "The Jewish Esoteric Literature in the Time of the Mishnah and the Talmud," *Immanuel* 4 (1974), 37–46; idem, *Apocalyptic and Merkavah Mysticism* (Leiden: E. J. Brill, 1979), 29–72; Rowland, *The Open Heaven,* 271–348 (where he treats esoteric Judaism within the framework of apocalyptic); P. Alexander, "3 (Hebrew Apocalypse of) Enoch," *Old Testament Pseudepigrapha,* ed. J. H. Charlesworth (2 volumes; Garden City, New York: Doubleday & Company, 1983–86), 1.235. Elsewhere Alexander suggests that Gnosticism and Merkavah mysticism have a common ancestor in Jewish apocalyptic and a mediator in synchretistic magic ("Comparing Merkavah Mysticism and Gnosticism," *Journal of Jewish Studies* 35 (1984), 17. The *Apoclypse of Abraham,* according to G. Scholem, "more closely resembles a Merkabah text than any other in Jewish apocalyptic literature" (*Jewish gnosticism, Merkavah Mysticism, and Talmudic Tradition* [New York: Jewish Theological Seminary, 1965], 23, and Rowland, *Open Heaven,* 15, 344–45).

[57] P. Alexander, "3 (Hebrew Apocalypse of) Enoch." Pp. 223–315.

[58] The Hekalot literature is surveyed in Scholem: *Jewish Gnosticism,* 1–8. The contents of many of these documents is summarized by Gruenwald, 1979: 127–234.

[59] Scholem, *Jewish Gnosticism,* 75–83; M. Smith, "Observations on Hekhalot Rabbati," 142–60.

[60] Gruenwald, *Apocalyptic and Merkavah Mysticism,* 225–34, summarizes the content of *Sepher ha-Razim,* even though he claims that "magic as such does not directly belong to our subject matter" (225). This Jewish magical text is now available in English translation by Morgan, *Sepher Ha-Razim: the Book of Mysteris* (Chico: Scholars Press, 1983).

[61] H. Griffith and L. Thompson, *The Demotic Magical Papyrus of London and Leiden.* London: H. Grevel. Republished under the title *The Leiden Papyrus: An Egyptian Magical Book* (New York: Dover, 1974), 33, 123.

"The god who will ask for me, let him put forth his hand to me and let him tell me his name." When he tells you his name, you ask him as to that which you desire. When you have ceased asking him as to that which you desire, you send him away. (Griffith and Thompson: 33, 123)

The revelatory dialogue anticipated in these introductory preparations was to have begun with a question regarding the identity of the inspiring divinity (clearly a more pressing question in a pagan than in a Jewish or Christian setting, given the crowd of possibilities), and an answer introduced with the phrase "I am," a self-disclosure formula occurring frequently in the magical papyri. When we turn to apocalyptic literature, the same phenomenon occurs occasionally at the beginning of the composition. In Jewish apocalypses it occurs in *Apoc. Abr.* 9:1–4 and *3 Enoch* 3:1–3; in Greek apocalypses it occurs in *Corpus Hermeticum* 1.2 and Lucian *Icar.* 13; in Gnostic apocalypses in *Apoc. Paul* 18:21 and *Apocry. John* 2:11–15. The three narrative vision accounts of Paul's conversion in Acts all begin with a similar question-and-answer dialogue (*erotapokrisis*), in which the revealer identifies himself with an "I am" formulation. Finally, in Revelation, the "I am" self-disclosure formula plays a significant role in the opening chapter (Rev 1:8, 17–20), where it is oracular and functions both to identify and to legitimate the revealer and the revelations which follow.

The Reveal/Conceal Dialectic

Although revelatory texts from antiquity must be interpreted within the structural framework of the particular religious traditions of which they are expressions, it is nevertheless possible to speak of a "reveal"/"conceal" dialectic which pervades ancient Mediterranean revelatory literature. It consists of the paradox that the hidden, now revealed, nevertheless remains concealed, a phenomenon described by Paul Tillich:[62]

Only what essentially is concealed, and accessible by no mode of knowledge whatsoever, is imparted by revelation. But in thus being revealed it does not cease to remain concealed, since its secrecy pertains to its very essence; and when therefore it is revealed it is so precisely as that which is hidden.

This dialectic finds frequent expression in ancient apocalypses. Despite the fact that the "hidden" now appears "revealed," the literary presentation of revelation is expressed in obscure modes so that the substance of the revelation is not clarified once-and-for-all. Rather, it becomes a vehicle capable of providing new revelations for the audience (when the apocalypse is orally performed), or for the individual reader (when studied). This is a generic feature characteristic of apocalypses including the Apocalypse of John and the *Shepherd* of Hermas. One

[62] P. Tillich, "Die Idee der Offenbarung." *ZTK* 35 (1927) 406.

of the generic virtualities of apocalyptic genre is the possibility of maximizing audience/reader participation in the revelatory experience.

Though parables, as such, are not utilized in the Apocalypse of John, they do play a prominent role in the *Shepherd* of Hermas, where the term itself in its various forms occurs thirty-two times. The view of parables reflected in Hermas, where they are particularly emphasized in the section called "Similitudes" (*parabolai*), is very similar to that found in Mark 4:11–12 in terms of their function: both to reveal and conceal divine truth (cf. Herm. *Mand.* 10.1.3–6). While it is commonly held that *Hermas'* use of parables is dependent upon synoptic tradition, it is more likely that there was an apocalyptic convention in Judaism which preferred parables for their paradoxical ability both to reveal and conceal divine truth. This suggests that one of the literary forms constituting the apocalyptic repertoire, the parable, was used in apocalypses precisely because of their essential affinity and mutual compatibility.

In the Apocalypse of John, the reveal/conceal dialectic comes to expression in the phenomenon that only rarely are visions accompanied by explanations (Rev 1:20; 7:13–17; 17:6b–18), an uncommon characteristic in apocalypses in which revelatory dialogues (*erotapokriseis*) between the revealer and the visionary, which are explicitly explanatory, are the rule. Further, in the Apocalypse of John the three passages which contain explanations do not reveal much. Rev 1:20 discloses just two basic equivalencies (seven stars = seven angels of the churches; seven lampstands = seven churches). Rev 7:13–17 simply explains that the great host in white are those who have come out of the great tribulation, i. e., martyrs, and Rev 17:6b–18 interprets the great harlot seated upon many waters in such enigmatical terms that the interpretation is made obviously pertinent only to political matters. This minimal use of explanation in the rehearsal of visionary sequences suggests that the ingenuity and imagination of the audience is allowed greater challenge and fuller scope than in the case of most apocalypses. This in turn suggests that the author wanted to achieve the fullest possible degree of audience participation. Though extensive visionary scenes are narrated, the author's only real literary control over the direction of the audience's response (aside from the negligible impact of the three passages just discussed), is exerted through his creative utilization of hymns and hymn-like choral passages to develop a commentary on the direction and significance of the narrated eschatological visions.

Yet another expression of the reveal/conceal motif in revelatory literature is through explicit references to the *limitations* of revelatory knowledge. There is a tendency in oracular dialogues, and hence in apocalypses which incorporate this form, to emphasize the fact that an oracular question is either improper, should not be answered at all, should be delayed, or that the answer given to the seer should not be relayed to his audience. In Rev 10:4, we read: "And when the seven thunders had sounded, I was about to write, but I heard a voice from heaven saying, 'Seal up what the seven thunders have said, and do not write it down.'" Here John is put into a position of claiming to know more than he can reveal, much as Paul "heard things that cannot be told, which man may not utter" (2 Cor 12:4). The statement in Rev 10:4 is significant, because a refusal to reveal all lends credibility to what is disclosed, placing as it does a limit on what can be revealed, i. e., revelation never involves full disclosure. Similar passages occur in a wide range of Christian, Jewish and Greco-Roman apocalypses and revelatory literature (Herm. *Vis*. 1.3.3; 3.3.4; T. Sol. 6:6; Lucian *Alex*. 43; Plutarch *De genio Socratis* 22; *4 Ezra* 4:10 f., 21, 52). These occurrences of apocalyptic secrecy are phenomenologically related to the necessity of maintaining secrecy in connection with initiation into mystery religions (an initiation which could often include various stages of revelatory experience). One is not the *source* of the other, but both are expressions of the phenomenology of revelatory experience. In cultic experience as well as in revelatory literature, the revealed/concealed dialectic is a pervasive phenomenon in ancient perceptions of revelatory experience.

The Genre of the Apocalypse of John

In any specification of a genre, the definition, if possible, should be formulated in terms of form, content and function. Although the description of the form or function or content of the apocalyptic genre may, if taken separately, apply to other types of literature, when taken together they should describe only apocalypses. The proposed definition of the apocalyptic genre, with special reference to the Apocalypse of John, is as follows: (1) *Form*: an apocalypse is a prose narrative, in autobiographical form, of revelatory visions experienced by the author, so structured that the central revelatory message constitutes a literary climax, and framed by a narrative of the circumstances surrounding the revelatory experience(s). (2) *Content:* the communication of a transcendent, often eschatological, perspective on human experience. (3) *Function:* (a) to legitimate the transcendent authorization of the message, (b) by mediating a new actualization of the original revelatory experience through literary devices, structures and imagery, which function to "conceal" the message which the text "reveals," so that (c) the recipients of the message will be encouraged to modify their cognitive and behavioral stance in conformity with transcendent perspectives. Each of these aspects will now be discussed in greater detail.

The Form of Apocalypses

Three aspects of the definition of the form of apocalypses proposed above require special comment: autobiographical style, the structuration or segmentation of vision reports, and the central revelatory message as a literary climax. First, the autobiographical style of apocalypses requires emphasis since this feature is an important aspect of the *legitimation* of the revelatory experience (see under function), and the first-person style in oral performance enables the audience to experience the vividness and vitality of the original revelatory experience. Unlike pseudonymous apocalypses in the eastern Mediterranean tradition, two Christian apocalypses, the Apocalypse of John and the *Shepherd* of Hermas, were written by persons personally known to their addressees so that the intended public recitation of these revelatory writings would take on a different significance than the recitation of a pseudonymous work. The historical reviews, presented as predictions, which form a central structural feature of many Jewish apocalypses (together with pseudepigraphy), enables the reader to see the predictions as applicable to his own day and situation. John and Hermas accomplish this in an alternate way without recourse to either pseudepigraphy or historical reviews.[63] Second, the notion that the literary climax of an apocalypse coincides with the central message is one of the virtualities of the apocalyptic genre, the successful execution of which lies in the abilities and skill of the individual author. Segmentation can refer to a variety of literary strategies. Such apocalypses as the *Shepherd* of Hermas, sections of *1 Enoch, 2 Baruch* and 4 Ezra, utilize a sequence of vision reports which are kept distinct from each other through literary markers, whereas a single, extensive vision report dominates the body of the Apocalypse of John, 4:1–22:5.[64] If the segmented or episodic presentation of vision narrative is a generically salient feature of apocalypses generally, the literary segmentation used by the author of the Apocalypse of John appears generically imposed. Another common form of segmentation in apocalypses is achieved by successive movement through the heavens to the highest heaven of all (usually the seventh). This obtains for the dreams which constitute *2 Enoch* 1–38, *3 Enoch,* the conceptual world of Merkavah mysticism, *Sepher ha-Razim,* and others.

The assertion that the central message of an apocalypse coincides with a literary climax expresses in paradigmatic terms the proposal of Hellholm that the texts of the Apocalypse of John and the *Shepherd* of Hermas in which the most embedded text at the highest communication level coincides with the highest grade of hierarchically arranged text sequences constitute the central messages of these apocalypses. Ring composition and chiasmic structures are also used in apocalypses to direct the attention of the audience to the texts within such frames. Apocalypses use these surface markers to enable the audience to progress from the periphery of the revelatory experience to the "innermost" or highest mystery which the author wishes to communicate. One of the more

[63] J. J. Collins, J. J."Pseudonymity, Historical Reviews and the Genre of the Revelation of John," *CBQ* 39 (1977) 329–43.

[64] J. S. Hanson, "Dreams and Visions in the Graeco-Roman World and Early Christianity." Section II, Vol. 23, Part 2, pp. 1395–1427 in *Aufstieg and Niedergang der römischen Welt.* Ed. H. Temporini and W. Haase (Berlin: W. de Gruyter, 1980), Section II, vol. 23.2, 1422–23.

common devices used for this purpose in ancient apocalypses is the otherworldly journey whereby the seer ascends through the various spheres or heavens to the uppermost heaven where the crowning revelation is found, usually the vision of God himself.[65] In the Apocalypse of John, of course, this culminating revelatory experience is delayed, for in John's vision of the throne room in Rev 4–5, the one sitting upon the throne is described only with vague imagery (4:3), and 5:1 mentions only that a scroll was in his hand. Thus the vision of God is skillfully delayed until the penultimate chapter, when the one seated upon the throne finally speaks (21:5–8). These formal structures for highlighting the central message of the author closely relate to an aspect of the *function* of apocalypses discussed below.

The Content of Apocalypses

The content of apocalypses, considered at an appropriately abstract level, overlaps with the content of other forms of ancient revelatory literature. Thus ancient revelatory literature communicates a transcendent perspective on human experience. The revelatory message is necessitated by the perception of discrepancy between ideology and reality perceived by the author and communicated to his audience. Apocalypses belong to a narrower grouping of revelatory literature which includes an *eschatological* in addition to a transcendental perspective on human affairs. Cosmic or individual eschatology is characteristic of Jewish, Christian, and Greco-Roman apocalypses, and some revelatory discourses (e. g. the *Sibylline Oracles*). J. Carmignac omits any reference to eschatological salvation in his definition of the apocalyptic genre, which he describes as "a literary genre which presents, through characteristic symbols, revelations either concerning God, or concerning angels or demons, or concerning their supporters, or concerning the instruments of their activity."[66] Carmignac expresses general agreement with the definition proposed by J. J. Collins except that he does not regard eschatological salvation as essential to apocalypses. It is apparent that he errs by defining eschatology too narrowly so that individual eschatology is left out of consideration.

The Function of Apocalypses

In most discussions of the function of apocalyptic literature, the notion of "function" is frequently understood, explicitly or implicitly, as "*social* function," i. e., as a quest for the original *Sitz im Leben,* or life setting of apocalypses. Apoca-

---

[65] C. Rowland, *The Open Heaven: A Study of Apocalyptic in Judaism and Early* Christianity (New York: Crossroad, 1983) 84.

[66] J. Carmignac, "Qu'est-ce que l'apocalyptique? Son emploi à Qumran." *RevQ* 10 (1979) 20.

lypses are often, and not incorrectly, understood as a form of protest literature in which the oppressed rights of a minority are legitimated by divine revelation. Yet it is precisely this aspect of apocalyptic literature most often hidden from the view of modern scholars and in many cases irrecoverable. The concept "function," however, has many meanings, necessitating a distinction between *literary* function and *social* function.[67] The literary function of an apocalypse is concerned only with the implicit and explicit indications within the text itself of the purpose or use of the composition. The social function of an apocalypse, from this perspective, would include not only its original (implicit and explicit) purpose (if recoverable), but also the entire history of varied utilization which it (as any other literary text) has experienced.

The description of the function of apocalypses in the definition above proposes three complementary literary functions of apocalypses, of which the first is the legitimation of the transcendent authorization of the message. This is a very important aspect of the function of apocalypses (as perhaps of all revelatory literature), for in many cases it suggests that an appeal to transcendent authority is necessitated by either the impossibility or ineffectiveness of an appeal to more rational or mundane structures of thought or authority. It is certainly true sociologically that persons or groups on the margins of society have sought to appeal to the transcendent through various forms of vision-trance and possession-trance to receive enhanced status, justification for innovative social programs and ideologies[68]

The second aspect of our functional definition proposes that apocalypses mediate a new actualization of the original revelatory experience through literary devices, structures and imagery which function to "conceal" the message which the text purportedly "reveals." That is, the skillful apocalyptic writer may portray the revelatory experience which he purportedly had with such literary skill (particularly enhanced through public performance) that the intended audience may indeed participate in the original experience to such an extent that the experience is "re-presented" or re-actualized for them. Further, the peculiar idiom of apocalypses (perhaps more characteristic of those in the east than the west) is to thinly conceal what it purports to reveal so that the audience may themselves have the experience of decoding or deciphering the message. Apocalypses stand in a unique relationship to revelatory experience, for it is they which provide continuing access to a past, ordinarily irretrievable, type of religious experience. Just as cults can protect and isolate the sacred from the profane by placing it at the center of both ritual and spatial barriers, so the central message of an apocalypse can lie at the center of or at the climax of a

[67] J. J. Collins, "The Apocalyptic Technique: Setting and Function in the Book of Watchers." *CBQ* 44 (1982) 92–4,110–11.

[68] I. M. Lewis, *Ecstatic Religion: An Anthropological Study of Spirit Possession and Shamanism* (Boston: Penguin Books, 1971).

series of literary devices intended to protect the sacred character of the revelatory message from the profane hearers and readers. Just as an initiant makes his way through various cultic barriers into the *adyton* where the focal religious experience will be staged, so the audience of such revelatory literature as the Apocalypse of John is brought through various literary structures and devices into the innermost recesses of the secrets which an apocalypse is designed to convey. The phenomenon of profound embedment of the focal message of the Apocalypse functions to conceal, as it were, that message within the innermost recesses of the composition. The movement from one level of communication to another, then, is a device utilized by the author to replicate the original revelatory experience in a literary, rather than a ritual or spatial, idiom, thereby maximizing the participation of the audience in the performance of the Apocalypse within the framework of public performance, possibly within framework of worship. That is, the author does not merely *narrate* the substance of the divine revelation he has received to his audience, he provides the audience with a literary vehicle so that they can, in effect, relive the experience of the seer and thereby appropriate for themselves the revelatory message.

The third aspect of our functional definition of the apocalyptic genre focuses on the purpose of apocalypses in terms of their role in encouraging cognitive and behavioral modifications based on the message communicated from the transcendent world. In this sense apocalypses are basically ideological, and are basically paraenetic even though the specifically paraenetic features appear at first sight to be in short supply.[69] Viewed from this perspective, paraenesis, though existing in its own distinctive literary forms, exhibits an affinity for apocalypses which are particularly concerned with behavioral aspects of human experience. Hans Dieter Betz has shown that one of the theoretically explicit functions of Greco-Roman apocalypses is to motivate changes in life-style through the shock-like experience of fear based on a journey to the afterlife or the nether world, an experience which can be shared by those who hear the story.[70] Apocalyptic vision reports in Judaism and early Christianity function analogously. The message of the Apocalypse of John centers on the promise of final salvation for believers and terrible punishment which will be meted out to unbelievers (Rev 21:5–8). The author who wrote Rev 22:18–19 (though there are compositional problems at this point), wanted to threaten those who might add to or delete from the book. A central purpose of the author was to motivate the audience to pursue a life of faithfulness and purity in order to avoid the punishments awaiting those who follow the wrong path.

---

[69] J.C.H. Lebram, "The Piety of the Jewish Apocalypses," *Apocalypticism in the Mediterranean World and the Near East,* ed. D. Hellholm (Tübingen: Mohr Siebeck, 1983) 173.

[70] H.D. Betz, "The Problem of Apocalyptic Genre in Greek and Hellenistic Literature: The Case of the Oracle of Trophonius," *Apocalypticism in the Mediterranean World and the Near East,* ed. D. Hellholm (Tübingen: Mohr Siebeck, 1983) 595.

5. Conclusions

Recent research on the problem of the genre of ancient apocalypses has made important strides. In particular, the paradigmatic description of the genre by John J. Collins and the syntagmatic analysis of the macrostructure of two Christian apocalypses by David Hellholm have provided two very different yet complementary approaches to the problem. In this article I have implicitly rejected Hellholm's proposal that the addition of "exhortation and/or consolation" to J. J. Collins' definition provides an adequate statement on function, and proposed instead a more comprehensive description of the function of the Apocalypse of John, based on what I consider the implications of Hellholm's own proposals. The profound embedment of the speech of God summarizing the central message of the Apocalypse (Rev 21:5–8) is the core of a literary structure which is a surrogate for the cultic barriers which separate the profane from the sacred, the hidden from the revealed. The Apocalypse of John is a literary replication of the original and unique revelatory experience of John the Seer which, when performed in a public, probably even a cultic setting, communicates the author's paraenetic message with divine authority.

Following the Lamb

Discipleship in the Apocalypse

Throughout the history of Christianity there have been, and continue to be, countless situations in which the followers of Christ have experienced various forms of opposition and hostility resulting not only in physical and emotional suffering, but even death. The Apocalypse of John was written at the end of the first century or the very beginning of the second century AD in response to one such situation of hostility against Christians, whether real or anticipated. The author portrays Rome and its emperors as the willing accomplices of Satan who try in vain to destroy the people of God. The three series of eschatological plagues depicted in the book – the seven seals in 6:1–8:1; the seven bowls in 8:2–11:19; the seven trumpets in 15:1–16:21 – are presented as divine punishments directed at those responsible for the persecution of God's people (cf. 6:12–17; 16:5–6; 18:4–8). The persecutors become the persecuted, and when the enemies of God and his people are finally conquered in decisive eschatological battles (19:11–21; 20:7–10), the last judgment takes place (20:11–14), followed by the triumphal appearance of the New Jerusalem on a transformed earth.

Until recently it has generally been accepted that the Johannine Apocalypse arose in the context of the persecution of the Christian church by the Roman emperor Domitian (AD 81–96). That was the explicit view of Eusebius of Caesarea, and early third-century Christian historian (*Ecclesiastical History* 3.17; 4.26.5–11), which was repeated and embellished by later Christian authors. Of late, however, studies have shown that much of Domitian's negative reputation is undeserved and that no persecution was sponsored by that emperor against Christians, whether officially or unofficially. Two possible ways of relating this new information to the interpretation of the Apocalypse of John, therefore, are open: the author of this writing perceived a degree of anti-Christian hostility that did not conform to actual experience, or, more probably, the persecution reflected in the Apocalypse was the result of sporadic local opposition to Christianity, which sometimes ended tragically – as in the case of Antipas of Pergamum (cf. 2:13), who is the only martyr specifically mentioned in the entire book.

John of Patmos, the author-editor of the Apocalypse, was centrally concerned with Christian discipleship, which he explored in a variety of ways against the dark background of anti-Christian sentiment in the Roman province of Asia at the end of the first century AD It was his view, given the existing or imminent social and political situation of the Christians of Anatolia, that death was the almost inevitable consequence for those who remained faithful to the demands of the word of God and were faithful to Jesus.

The theme of discipleship in the Apocalypse of John has two focal points: the present and the future. Present and future are related in the Apocalypse not only in the general sense that the present will soon become the future, but in the more specific sense that the future will be qualitatively *different* from the present. It is for this kind of future that theologians in the early nineteenth century coined the term *eschatology*.

The emphasis on discipleship in the present is concentrated in 1:1–3:22 and 22:10–21, sections which frame the book and deal primarily with the historical situation of the seven Christian congregations to whom John addressed his prophetic book. The future or eschatological dimensions of discipleship, however, are the focus of 4:1–22:9, the main part of the book, which deals with the unfolding eschatological plan of God for the world. The present and future dimensions of discipleship are closely related in the Apocalypse, with discipleship in the future being based on discipleship in the present.

An exhaustive study of discipleship in the Apocalypse of John is not possible in this short chapter. One passage and two groups of passages are, however, crucial, and need to be treated here. The central passage is 14:1–5, which speaks of the 144,000 and is centrally important for an understanding of how the author views the nature of Christian discipleship. One group of passages speaks of "victory," with that victory being presented as possible only through apparent defeat and death. The other group of passages has to do with obedience to the commands of God and witnessing to the salvific significance of Jesus.

1. Characteristics of Discipleship in 14:1–5

Rev 14: 1–5 narrates an eschatological scene in which John sees a vision of the Lamb standing on Mount Zion with 144,000 people who have the name of the Lamb and of God written on their foreheads. Down through the centuries, readers of the Apocalypse have puzzled over the identification of the 144,000. The number is obviously symbolic, not literal. But does this group represent Jewish Christians (cf. 7:4–8), or an elite group of Christians, such as the martyrs, or the entire people of God? While it seems logical to identify them with the 144,000 mentioned in 7:4, there is a strong grammatical argument that stands in the way of such an equation. For in 7:4 the Greek phrase behind the number 144,000 lacks a definite article, indicating that the author there was introducing an unknown entity to his audience. But when the number 144,000 is next mentioned in 14:1, it also lacks the definite article – thereby suggesting that the author did not regard this group as identical with the group mentioned in 7:4. The 144,000 are mentioned again in 14:3, this time with the "anaphoric" definite article, so called because it "refers back" to the previous mention of the 144,000 in 14:1.

Another interpretive problem is whether the scene takes place on earth or in heaven – that is, is "Zion" to be understood literally of the earthly Jerusalem or metaphorically of heaven (cf. Gal 4:26; Heb 12:22; 5 *Ezra* 2:42–48; *Targum of Isaiah* 24:23; 31:4)? Early Jewish apocalyptic traditions depict the Messiah on Mount Zion, where he will annihilate the enemies of Israel, which have gathered there for battle (e. g., *4 Ezra* 13:33–36; 2 *Baruch* 40:1–3; cf. Isa 40:9–11). The original readers, who were familiar with Jewish apocalyptic expectations, would probably have connected the 144,000 celibate males who stood with the lamb on Mount Zion with the eschatological army gathered to repulse the onslaught of the heathen nations. What the author of the Apocalypse appears to have done with this traditional eschatological scenario is to use it in a metaphorical way, as did the author of Hebrews (12:22), so that the earthly struggle of the people of God is juxtaposed with a scene of their heavenly triumph. On such a reading of 14:1–5, the 144,000 are depicted as prepared to do battle and win, but the notion of "victory" means that they (like their Lord) must be killed. So while the Lamb is not literally in their midst, he will be in their midst in the heavenly Mount Zion when they have conquered the Beast by laying down their lives (as in 7:9–17 and 15:2–4). This way of reading the passage will be reinforced in the following discussion.

John of Patmos provides his readers with a threefold characterization of the 144,000 in 14:4–5, each introduced with the stereotypical phrase "these [are]" – with each of these characterizations being important for an understanding of the author's view of Christian discipleship. First "*these are those* who have not polluted themselves with women, for they are chaste." Second, "*these are those* who follow the Lamb where he would go." Third, "*these are those* who have been redeemed from humanity, the firstfruits for God and the Lamb, and in their mouth no lie was found; they are blameless." Each of these characterizations requires elaboration in what follows.

Discipleship and Celibacy

The first characterization of the 144,000 focuses on their sexual asceticism: "These are those who have not polluted themselves with women, for they are chaste [*parthenoi*]" (14:4a). The contrast between the 144,000 and the "polluting" influence of women indicates that they are all males. The notion that men can be polluted by women is offensive in modern Western societies, since it not only implies a superior status for males, but also suggests that women are sources of impurity and so constitute a constant danger for males. This viewpoint, which is frequently found in Third World countries, was not, however, uncommon in antiquity. For example, in the Mishnah, which was codified about 200 CE by Rabbi Judah the Prince, women are considered a necessary evil because procreation is impossible without them. Yet they are also viewed as a major source of ritual impurity for their rabbinic spouses, whose lives revolved about the central concern of ritual purity. The term "pollution" as it is used in the Mishnah, of course, has to do primarily with ritual purity rather than moral purity, though the two were not always distinguished.

The context for this emphasis in Rev 14:4 on sexual purity or virginity (the term *parthenoi,* which we have translated "chaste," literally means "[male] virgins," a term rarely applied to males) is one of discipleship. As such, it points the reader to the discipleship sayings of the Synoptic Gospels, some of which emphasize sexual asceticism – particularly those in Luke's Gospel. In Mark 10:29, seven types of renunciation are mentioned for disciples of Jesus: home, brothers, sisters, mother, father, children, and fields. All seven are repeated in Matt 19:29, but they are reduced to five in Luke 18:29, with the interesting addition of *wives*: house, wife, brothers, parents, and children – though Geza Vermes argues that "house" in Mark 10:29 and Matt 19:29 is synonymous with "wife," since in vernacular Aramaic "one belonging to his house" is the wife of the owner.[1]

More expressly, in the Q passage in Luke 14:26–27, *wives* are also included in a list of things that the followers of Jesus must "hate" though wives are not mentioned in the parallels in Matt 10:37–38 or *Gospel of Thomas* 53. In the Q parable of the Great Supper (Luke 14:15–24; Matt 22:1–14), only Luke includes recent marriage as an excuse not to attend the banquet, thereby giving marriage a negative connotation (marriage is not mentioned as an excuse in the parallel in *Gospel of Thomas* 64). According to Matt 19:12, there are three types of eunuchs, eunuchs by birth (i. e., males born without normal sexual organs), those made eunuchs (i. e., emasculated males), and "those who have made themselves eunuchs for the sake of the Kingdom of Heaven" (through either self-emasculation or, more probably, voluntary celibacy). The Lukan version of the question about the resurrection (Mark 12:18–27; Matt 22:23–33; Luke 20:27–40) emphasizes celibacy, the "angelic life" for those who will be accounted worthy to attain to the age to come and the resurrection (Luke 20:34–36). And a definite correlation between discipleship and sexual abstinence characterizes the various apocryphal *Acts of the Apostles* that originated in Asia Minor in ca. AD 175–225.

We must ask whether the virginity of the 144,000 should be understood literally or metaphorically, though it is a thorny issue. The metaphorical interpreta-

[1] Geza Vermes, *Jesus the Jew (*New York: Macmillan, 1973) 246, note 79.

tion of virginity in this passage has been motivated, in part, by the Protestant rejection of celibacy as a legitimate expression of moral or religious virtue. It is also facilitated by the fact that in the Old Testament unchastity is a frequent metaphor for the act of turning away from the true worship of God and embracing the worship of idols (cf. Jer 3:2; 13:27; Ezek 16:15–58; 23:1–49; 43:7; Hos 5:4; 6:10). Perhaps here, too, virginity is a metaphor for faithfulness to God.

Another possible interpretation is linked with the apocalyptic expectation of an attack on Zion or Jerusalem in the eschaton by heathen armies. The 144,000, who are gathered around the Lamb on Mount Zion, may represent the eschatological army of the Messiah (cf. 20:9). From this perspective their celibacy could be understood within the context of the requirement for temporary sexual abstinence demanded of participants in a holy war as prescribed in the Old Testament (cf. 1 Sam 21:4–5; 2 Sam 11:11–12; Deut 23:9–14). In the Qumran community, which flourished from the mid-second century BCE until it was destroyed by the Romans in 68 CE, there was a close link between the celibacy apparently practiced by the community and holy war theology (1QM 7:3–6; cf. Philo, *Apology* 11.14–17; Pliny, *Natural History* 5.15; Josephus, *War* 2.120–21).

Following the Lamb

The 144,000 are further characterized in 14:4b as "those who follow [*hoi akolouthentes*] the Lamb wherever he would go." The unusual metaphor of the Lamb who is also Shepherd, presupposed here, is expressed explicitly in 7:17: "The Lamb in the midst of the throne will shepherd [*poimanei*] them and guide them to springs of living water." The title "Lamb," in this context, is used in place of the more conventional early Jewish metaphor of the Messiah as the Shepherd of the eschatological people of God (cf. *Psalms of Solomon* 17; *Fragmentary Targum* on Exod 12:42; see also Isa 40:11; Ezek 34:23). The connection between "Messiah" and "Shepherd" lies in the fact that the term *Messiah,* "anointed one," originated as a designation for the king of Israel or Judah, while the term "Shepherd" was a stock metaphor for "king" (cf. 2 Sam 7:7; Isa 44:28; Jer 3:15; 10:21; 25:34–36; Micah 5:4; Nahum 3:18). The figure of a shepherd is used of Jesus several times in the New Testament (cf. Matt 15:24; 25:32; Mark 14:27–28 = Matt 26:31–32; Luke 19:10; John 10:2, 11, 12, 14; Heb 13:20; 1 Pet 2:25).

Of central interest here is the use of the verb "follow" (*akolouthein*). In the New Testament this verb occurs primarily in the Gospels (seventy of seventy-nine occurrences). It has two literal meanings: "follow" in the sense of "go behind" and "follow" in the sense of "accompany." By figurative extension, it also means "be a disciple of," in the sense of adhering to the teachings or instructions of a leader and promoting the cause of that leader. It is striking that this figurative meaning of "follow" is found in the New Testament only in the four Gospels and in Rev 14:4.

Furthermore, the phrase ("where he would go" in 14:4 suggests that the 144,000 follow the Lamb regardless of the cost – with the Lamb depicted in the Apocalypse as the one who was slaughtered and who thereby ransomed people for God (5:9, 12; 13:8). And one implication of true discipleship in the canonical Gospels is the possibility of dying for one's adherence to Jesus (cf. Matt 10:38 = Luke 14:27; Mark 8:34–35 = Matt 16:24–25 = Luke 9:23–24; Luke 17:33; John 12:25–26; 1 Pet 2:21; Rev 12:11). Furthermore, following the Lamb wherever he goes includes the necessity of forsaking everything, including normal marital relationships (see above).

The phrase "those who follow the Lamb wherever he would go [*hoi akolouthentes tō arniō hopou an hypagē*]" appears, therefore, to be modeled on Gospel traditions that speak of discipleship, particularly the introduction to the Q saying in Luke 9:57–58 (= Matt 8:19–20): "As they were going along the road a man said to him [Jesus], 'I will follow you wherever you go.'" This phrase probably indicates the early existence of a very simple, yet potentially profound, generic conception of discipleship – that is, that those who are Jesus' disciples "follow Jesus wherever he goes."

Such a conception of discipleship reappears in the second century in *Acts of Paul* 25, where Thecla, a female follower of Paul, says to him: "I will shave my head and follow you wherever you go." The same phrase, probably alluding to Rev 14:4, occurs in a letter of the churches of Lyons and Vienne (from the mid-second century CE), where it is said of the Christian martyr Vettius Epagathus that "he was and is a true disciple of Christ, following the Lamb wherever he goes" (preserved in Eusebius, *Ecclesiastical History* 5.1.10).

Similarly worded sayings occur in the Fourth Gospel. In John 13:36 Jesus is reported to have said: "Where I go you are unable to follow [*akolouthēsai*] me now, but you will follow me later." Here discipleship clearly means following Jesus to death (cf. 21:18–19). John 13:36 is thematically linked to 12:26: "If any one serves me, he must follow [*akoloutheitē*] me; and where I am there shall my servant be also." Finally, in John 14:3 Jesus speaks of the eventual reward for disciples who follow him to death: "Where I am you may be also. And you know the way I am going." These Johannine passages, it appears, provide versions of the tradition found in Rev 14:4, though without the latter's apocalyptic features. According to this tradition true discipleship means following Jesus to the death, with the promise of then sharing Jesus' relationship with the Father.

Firstfruits for God and the Lamb

The third clause that describes the 144,000 is found in 14:5 and consists of three characteristics, the first and the last of which are closely related: "These are those who have been redeemed from humanity, the firstfruits [*aparchē*] for God and the Lamb. In their mouth no lie was found. They are blameless." The term "firstfruits" (*aparchē*) is usually explained as a metaphor drawn from the sacrificial language of the Old Testament, where it refers to the first and best portion of agricultural produce, which represents the entire crop and is ritually presented to God (cf. Exod 23:19; 34:22; Lev 23:9–14; Num 28:26–27; Deut 16:9–12). Though the Hebrew terms for "firstfruits" are never applied to individual people or animals in the Old Testament (the term "firstborn" being used instead), in the New Testament "firstfruits" (*aparchē*) is always used metaphorically, often of people. In Rom 16:5, for example, Paul speaks of Epaenetus as "the firstfruits of Asia" – that is, just as the firstfruits of the wheat, barley, or grape harvest represented the entire harvest, so Epaenetus represented the first of many converts to Christianity from Asia Minor (cf. 1 Cor 16:15; 2 Thess 2:13; Jas 1:18). This may suggest that the 144,000, numerous as they were, are but the first of a much larger number of faithful Christians.

But the number 144,000 is obviously symbolic. It probably represents the complete number of the people of God: the twelve tribes of Israel times the twelve apostles (12 × 12 = 144) times 1,000 (representing completeness, totality, and perfection) = 144,000. So if the number 144,000 represents the complete number of the people of God on earth, construing the metaphorical significance of the "firstfruits" as the first and best of an even larger number hardly seems to be on the right track.

It is generally overlooked that sacrificial or cultic terms meaning "firstfruits" are even more common in the cultures of the Greco-Roman world than in the Old Testament and early Judaism. The Greek term *aparchai* and the Latin term *primitiae*, both meaning "firstfruits," refer to animal as well as vegetable sacrifices and offerings (cf. Herodotus 4.71; Sophocles, *Trachiniae* 183, 761; Thucydides 3.85; Isocrates, *Archidamus* 96). More directly relevant, however, is the fact that the phrase "firstfruits consisting of people" (*aparchē anthrōpōn*) was used of human beings (sometimes captives) who were actual offerings presented to the gods, who then either became temple servants or were freed (cf. Plutarch, *Theseus* 16.2; *Quaestiones Graecae* 298 f.; *De Pythiae oraculis* 402a; Diodorus Siculus 4.66).

Against this Greco-Roman background, the 144,000 of Rev 14:1–5 can be regarded not as the first and best representatives of a larger number, but rather as actual sacrificial offerings to God and the Lamb. That they are designated in verse 5 as "blameless" (*amōmos*), a term often used of flawless sacrificial victims (cf. Exod 29:1; Lev 1:3; 4:3; 5:15; 22:21; Ezek 43:22–23; Philo, *Legum allegoriae* 1.50; Heb 9:14; 1 Pet 1:19), suggests that they are themselves destined to be sacrificial victims – that is, through martyrdom. And that "no lie was found in their mouth" (14:4b; cf. Zeph 3:13, where the phrase is applied to the remnant of Israel) does not mean simply that they were honest, but rather that they refused to acknowledge the claims of the Beast on their lives and chose to remain faithful to God and to the Lamb (cf. 14:9, 11; 15:2).

In the Old Testament and early Judaism an extremely large vocabulary was devoted to the notions of deceit and treachery, suggesting that lying (along with idolatry, murder, and sexual immorality) was considered one of the major vices. Paradoxically, there is not a single law in the Old Testament that forbids lying generally, though there are injunctions against bearing false witness and perjury (Exod 20:16; Lev 19:12; Prov 21:28). In the Old Testament, God is associated with truth and idolatry is associated with lying, and by the late Second Temple period this was transposed into the association of God with truth and Satan with lying (cf. 1QS [Manual of Discipline] 4:9; 10:22; John 8:41–47; Rom 3:4; Titus 1:22).

2. The Paradoxical Meaning of Victory

In Revelation 5, one of the most dramatic scenes of the Apocalypse, the universal quest for someone worthy to open the scroll sealed with seven seals ends with the introduction of "the Lion of the tribe of Judah" by one of the twenty-four elders. In that introduction, "the Lion of the tribe of Judah" is also called "the Branch of David, who has conquered [*enikēsen*] and can open the scroll" (v 5), using descriptive titles that were clearly drawn from traditional designations of the Davidic Messiah. Paradoxically, however, when John looks more closely at this figure, what he actually sees is "a Lamb standing as though slaughtered" (v 6). Then in the hymnic section that follows, the reader learns that the reason the Lamb alone is worthy to open the sealed scroll is that he was slaughtered and by that sacrificial act has ransomed people for God from all parts of the world (v 9). Thus it is the *death* of Jesus (under the metaphor of the Lamb) that is understood as his victory – which is a theological conception very close to the statement attributed to Jesus in John 16:33: "I have conquered [*enikēka*] the world." This dual presentation of the salvific function of Jesus as the crucified Messiah, which has been aptly called the irony of kingship through crucifixion, is not unique to the Apocalypse but of central theological significance in other major sections of the New Testament as well (e.g., 1 Cor 1:23–24). Martin Luther designated these two complementary aspects of the work of Christ as the *theologia crucis* ("theology of the cross") and the *theologia gloriae* ("theology of glory"). The atoning death of Christ, conceptualized as conflict resulting in victory, reflects the classic idea of the atonement, according to which Christ fought against and triumphed over all the evil powers in the world, under whom human beings were in bondage and suffering – and so decisively triumphing over those powers, he reconciled the world to God. The victory achieved by Jesus through suffering and death becomes a central paradigm for discipleship in the Apocalypse. This correlation between the experience of Jesus and the demands of discipleship is made explicit in the final words to the church of Laodicea in 3:21 : "As for the one who conquers [*ho nikōn*], I will authorize that one to sit with me on my throne, just as I conquered [*enikēsa*] and sat with my Father on his throne." And like this conclusion of the proclamation to Laodicea (3:14–22), each of the other six proclamations to the churches of Roman Asia concludes with a promise to "the one who conquers" (2:7, 11, 17, 26; 3:5, 12).

A more oblique way of correlating the death of Jesus with the victory of Christians is articulated in the context of the hymn of rejoicing in 12:11: "They conquered [*enikēsan*] him [Satan] through the blood of the Lamb and by the word of their testimony, and they did not love their lives to the point of death." The verb "conquer, be victorious" (*nikan*) occurs seventeen times in the Apocalypse. When the exalted Jesus is the subject of this verb (as in 3:21 and 5:5), it means that he conquered *through death*. And it means precisely the same thing where it is used (eleven times) elsewhere in the Apocalypse of Christians, explicitly in 12:11 and implicitly in eight other places (2:7, 11, 17, 26, 3:5, 12, 21 [twice]). Likewise, the theme of martyrs "conquering" (*nikan*) their besiegers and torturers by nobly facing suffering and death appears in 4 Macc 6:10: "And like a noble athlete the old man, while being beaten, was victorious [*enika*] over his torturers" (see also 7:4b; 9:6, 30; 11:20; 16:14; 17:15). In 4 Macc 1:11, in a summary passage, it is said that "by their endurance [*hypomonē*] they [the Jewish martyrs] conquered [*nikēsantes*] the tyrant."

3. The Commands of God and the Witness to Jesus

At the conclusion of the narrative about the Woman, the Child, and the Dragon in Revelation 12, the Dragon (= Satan) in enraged because his attempts to destroy the Woman (here representing the people of God) have been unsuccessful. He then turns his anger toward the offspring or seed of the Woman (representing Christians), who are described as "those who keep the commands of God" [*tōn tēroutōn tas entolas tou theou*] and maintain the witness of Jesus [*echontōn tēn martyrian Iēsou*]" (v 17). A close parallel occurs in an abrupt parenetic exhortation in 14:12: "This indicates that the perseverance of God's people involves keeping the commands of God [*hoi tērountes tas entolas tou theou*] and the faith of Jesus [*tēn pistin Iēsou*]." These statements constitute a remarkable definition of Christian faith in which the validity of the traditional commands of God (i. e., the Torah), understood from a Christian perspective, is seen as *complementary* rather than antithetical to the requirements of "the witness of Jesus" or "the faith of Jesus." Furthermore, both of these sayings, as well as their parallels elsewhere in the Apocalypse, occur in contexts of persecution.

It is not completely clear, however, what each of these statements really means (we have translated them literally to reveal their ambiguity). Should the "commandments of God" be understood to refer in a restricted way to the Decalogue, or more generally to the Torah? Furthermore, does the phrase focus on either the ceremonial or the ethical requirements of the Decalogue, or does it have in mind the entire Torah? And what is the "witness" or "testimony" of Jesus? Does it refer to the witness borne *by* Jesus (taking "of Jesus" as a subjective genitive), or is it the witness or testimony of Christians *about* Jesus that is in view (taking "of Jesus" as an objective genitive)?

There is a striking parallel to these two statements in 12:17 and 14:12 in 1QpHab (the Qumran commentary on Habakkuk) 8:1–3: "Its interpretation pertains to *all the doers of the Law* in the House of Judah, whom God will rescue from the House of Judgment for their tribulation and *their fidelity to the Teacher of Righteousness*." Here the phrase "the doers of the Law" corresponds to "those who keep the commands of God" in Rev 12:17 and 14:12, while "their fidelity to the Teacher of Righteousness" corresponds to "the witness of Jesus" in 12:17 and "the faith of Jesus" in 14: 12. This parallel suggests that the latter phrase should be construed as an objective genitive, that is, as "faith in Jesus" or (more probably) "faithfulness to Jesus."

In Jewish martyrological literature, adherence to the commands of God is one of the major reasons that martyrs give for their willingness to suffer and die rather than compromise their faith (cf. 1 Macc 1:60–63; 2 Macc 7:1–3; 3 Macc 1:23; 4 Macc 5:16–17,29; 6:18; 7:8; 9:1–2; Pseudo-Philo, *Biblical Antiquities* 38:2). In such contexts, "obeying the commands of God" refers primarily to sociological markers of Jewish identity, including circumcision, dietary laws, Sabbath observance, and avoidance of any participation in pagan sacrificial rituals (cf. Dan 3:3–18; 1 Macc 1:60–63). In early Christianity, on the other hand, "keep the commandments of God" (e. g., *Barnabas* 4:11) came to have a very particular meaning – that is, the *ethical* as opposed to ceremonial commands of the Torah. Thus while for early Judaism the Law included the entire Torah, for early Christian authors the central part of the law was the second table of the Decalogue, its ethical commandments, and the love command.

In the New Testament and other early Christian literature, the phrase "keep the commandments" occurs quite frequently (e. g., Matt 19:17; John 14:15, 21; 15:10; 1 John 2:3; 3:22, 24; 5:3; Hermas, *Mandates* 7.7.5; 12.3.4; 12.6.3; *Similitudes* 5.1.5; 5.3.3), almost always in a positive sense. Paul also speaks quite positively of "obeying the commandments of God" (1 Cor 7:19) – though he excludes circumcision, which is certainly part of the Torah, unless his focus was on the ethical rather than on the ceremonial laws (cf. Rom 7:8; 13:8–9). And even though the ethical requirements of the Torah may be thought to play a negative theological role (e. g., Rom 7:7–11), in general they are regarded in an overwhelmingly positive light in early Christianity as the revealed will of God (cf. Rom 7:12). Paul's negative perception of "the works of the law" was, in fact, sometimes – though not entirely (cf. Rom 3:20; 7:7–25) – restricted to the distinctive socio-religious markers of Judaism: circumcision, food regulations, and Sabbath observance.

There was a tendency in early Christian thought, beginning with Jesus himself, to see the whole Law as encapsulated in either the two commands to love God and to love one's neighbor (Mark 12:28–31 = Matt 22:36–40; *Didache* 1:2; Justin, *Dialogue* 93.2; Theophilus, *Ad Autolycum* 2.34), or in the single command to love one's neighbor (Rom 13:9–10; Gal 5:14; Jas 2:8). This tendency to summarize the Law under a single rubric or two was also prevalent in Judaism. The command to love one's neighbor was, of course, not part of the Decalogue, but derived from Lev 19:18 (cf. Lev 19:33–34; Deut 10:19). This love command took on a significant theological role in the New Testament (1 Thess 4:9; Rom 13:8–10). So in the context of these considerations, it is probable that "keeping the commandments of God" in Rev 12:18 and 14:12 should be regarded as referring exclusively to the *ethical* requirements of the Torah.

The phrases "the witness of Jesus" (12:17) and "the faith of Jesus" (14:12) can be construed in a number of ways. In 20:4 the martyrs are clearly referred to in a similar way: "those who had been beheaded because of their witness to Jesus and because of the word of God." Here, as in 12:17 and 14:12, the relationship of these Christians to both Jesus and God is described in a very particular way. The phrase "the word of God" is doubtless a more general designation for "the commandments of God," and refers to the will of God revealed in the Torah. A closely related text is in 6:9, where John sees the souls of those slain "because of the word of God and because of the witness [*martyrian*] which they bore." Here the absence of the qualifying genitive "of Jesus" which is present in the other parallels in the Apocalypse, indicates that "witness" (*matryria*) refers to the witness expressed in word and deed borne by those faithful Christians who experienced martyrdom.

There are several expressions in the Apocalypse, which are set out in similar couplets, that contain variations of this phrase:

1:2 Who bore witness to the message from God,
that is, the witness borne by Jesus [*tēn martyrian Iēsou Christou*]
1:9 Because of the word of God
and my witness to Jesus [*tēn martyrian Iēsou*].
6:9 Because of the word of God
and because of the witness which they bore.
20:4 Because of their witness to Jesus [*tēn martyrian Iēsou*] and because of the word of God.

Two additional parallel couplets contain just one of the lines of the parallels listed above:

12:17 Who keep the commandments of God
and maintain their witness to Jesus [*tēn martyrian Iēsou*].

19:10 Who maintain the witness to Jesus *[tēn martyrian Iēsou]*.
For the witness to Jesus is the spirit of prophecy.

So while the Greek phrase *tēn martyrian Iēsou,* literally, "the witness of Jesus" can be an objective genitive, and therefore translated "the witness about Jesus" or "the witness to Jesus," it can also be translated as a subjective genitive – that is, "the witness borne by Jesus."

There are several instances in the Apocalypse where a genitive dependent on "witness" (*martyria)* should be construed as a subjective genitive (e.g., 1:2; 11:17; 12:11; cf. 6:9), but there are other instances where it seems contextually appropriate to construe the genitive as an objective genitive (e.g., 12:17; 14:12; 17:6; 19:10 [twice]; 20:4). More specifically, the phrase "the witness of Jesus" (*martyria Iēsou*) occurs five times in the Apocalypse (1:2, 9; 12:17; 19:10; 20:4), and only in 1:2 does it appear appropriate to translate the phrase as a subjective genitive – and there "the witness borne by Jesus" appears to be identical with the contents of the prophetic book that John has written.

In the other occurrences of the phrase "the testimony/witness of Jesus" (*martyria Iēsou),* it is the testimony or witness of Jesus that is in view – presumably referring to the testimony that Jesus maintained during his trial (cf. Matt 27:11–14; Mark 15:1–5; Luke 23:1–12; John 18:19–24, 33–38), which can be characterized as either evasive answers (except for Mark 14:62), silence, or profound response (cf. John 18:33–38). Furthermore, construing "witness" (*martyria*) as a subjective genitive would mean that it would be one of the very few references to the historical Jesus in the Apocalypse (along with 1:5; 2:8; 5:6; 11:8). Finally, since the statements found in 6:9; 11:7; 12:11; and 17:6 all unambiguously emphasize the fact that the testimony is borne by Christians, the focus of that testimony must be the salvific significance of Jesus.

4. Concluding Observations

Without treating the subject of discipleship in the Apocalypse of John in any exhaustive fashion, we have attempted to focus on three important groups of texts that deal with this theme. Rev 14:1–5 is a centrally important text for understanding the author's views on the nature of Christian discipleship. Christians who have given their allegiance to God and are consequently symbolically and indelibly marked with the name of God and of the Lamb on their foreheads "follow the Lamb wherever he goes." In the context this does not refer to green pastures and springs of water (as in 7:17) but rather to a willingness to suffer and die as a consequence of faithfulness to God and the Lamb. Just as this language of discipleship has been turned into a metaphor for death, so the designations "firstfruits for God and the Lamb" and "blameless" (14:5) underscore the sacrificial calling of these faithful followers of the Lamb.

Paradoxically, the term "victory" in the Apocalypse refers to a victory achieved through apparent defeat and death. The exalted Jesus is paradigmatic for Christian disciples. But the victory he has achieved is based on the sacrificial death that he experienced (5:9), and so those who conquer as he conquered will be rewarded by sitting with him on his throne (3:21).

Finally, John's view of a Christian disciple is of one who is obedient to the commands of God (by which the ethical commands of the second table of the Decalogue are likely in view) and witnesses to the salvific significance of Jesus. There is no dichotomy between law and grace – a Pauline theological problem that is remarkably absent from the Johannine apocalypse. Rather, obedience to the will of God as mediated by the Torah is considered complementary to the demands of faith in Christ.

Qumran and the Book of Revelation

1. Introduction

In most discussions of the influence of the Qumran scrolls on the New Testament, the focus is on particular figures (John the Baptist and Jesus of Nazareth), on themes (eschatology, messianism, biblical interpretation), and on texts or groups of texts (the Fourth Gospel, the Pauline Letters, the Synoptic Gospels).[1] The fact that little if any emphasis is given to the Revelation of John is somewhat surprising, particularly in view of the apparent relevance of the War Scroll (1QM), one of the earliest Qumran documents to be published. There are, of course, many references to the Dead Sea Scrolls in scholarly literature which illuminate or provide additional background for one or another point of interpretation in Revelation.[2] Helpful as these may be, the possibility of discovering more substantive structural or thematic parallels which illuminate major features of the text is even more desirable.

One way of assessing the impact which the Dead Sea Scrolls have had on the study of the Revelation of John is the use to which the Dead Sea Scrolls are put in commentaries. In the 1975 commentary on Revelation by J. Massyngberde Ford, there are some 200 references to various texts in the Dead Sea Scrolls.[3] In view of the fact that virtually all of the Scroll texts have been available for a number of years now, a survey of more recent commentaries proves disappointing. One of the more recent full-scale German commentaries on Revelation is that of Heinz Giesen (1997),[4] who cites forty-seven Qumran texts, although the

---

[1] One of the earlier assessments of the light shed on the New Testament by the Qumran scrolls was Krister Stendahl (ed.), *The Scrolls and the New Testament* (New York: Harper, 1957). The topics covered are very similar to the more recent synthetic discussions of the subject. See, for example, J. Trebolle Barrera, "The Qumran Texts and the New Testament," in F. García Martínez and J. Trebolle Barrera, *The People of the Dead Sea Scrolls. Their Writings, Beliefs and Practices* (Leiden: Brill, 1995) 203–32; James C. VanderKam, *The Dead Sea Scrolls Today* (Grand Rapids: Eerdmans, 1994) 159–85.

[2] A useful synthesis of illuminating parallels found between the Dead Sea Scrolls and Revelation during the first wave of Qumran studies is found in Herbert Braun, *Qumran und das Neue Testament* (2 vols., Tübingen: Mohr Siebeck, 1966) 1.307–26.

[3] J. Massyngberde Ford, *Revelation* (AB 38; Garden City: Doubleday, 1975).

[4] Heinz Giesen, *Die Offenbarung des Johannes* (RNT; Regensburg: Friedrich Pustet, 1997).

obviously relevant "Description of the New Jerusalem" texts are conspicuous by their absence.

2. Apocalyptic and Apocalypses

The Book of Revelation is widely assumed to belong to the literary genre "apocalypse," reflecting an "apocalyptic" ideology. It is well-known that the modern generic term "apocalypse" derives from the opening titular sentence of this book: Ἀποκάλυψις Ἰησοῦ Χριστοῦ, "the revelation of Jesus Christ" (Rev 1:1).[5] In this context, however, ἀποκάλυψις (which occurs only here and in the inscription) is not a generic designation, but rather a description of work's contents. The inscription, ἀποκάλυψις Ἰωάννου or "Apocalypse of John" (a second century formulation originally located at the end of the book but then moved to the beginning with the transition from roll to codex), is simply a shortened form of the title or first sentence of the book with no generic intentions. Yet whether through the influence of the Apocalypse of John or other documents which have not survived, the designation ἀποκάλυψις came to be used in a quasi-generic sense of works with a revelatory character, though they rarely conform to the modern generic conception of "apocalypse."[6] Although the modern designations "apocalypse" and "apocalyptic" represent modern conceptions applied to ancient texts and ideologies,[7] their usefulness in enabling modern scholars to understand ancient genres and ideologies is not automatically invalidated. "Apocalypticism" is a term used of the types of eschatological belief systems reflected in the canonical apocalypses Daniel 7–12 (Aramaic: 7:1–28; Hebrew: 8:1–12:13) and Revelation, and in such other early Jewish apocalypses as *1 Enoch* (a composite text containing five originally separate apocalypses), 2 *Enoch,* 2 *Baruch, 4 Ezra* and the *Apocalypse of Abraham.*

Since the modern use of the term has been so varied, it would be helpful to define "apocalyptic" in terms of four differing but related aspects: (1) "Apocalyptic eschatology," a *world of beliefs and symbols* based on a cosmic dualism

---

[5] Friedrich Lücke (1852) was the first scholar to use the term "apocalypse" (Rev 1:1) as a generic designation for works similar to Revelation such as Daniel, *1 Enoch; 4 Ezra* and 2 *Baruch.* See Helge S. Kvanvig, *Roots of Apocalyptic: The Mesopotamian Background of the Enoch Figure and of the Son of Man* (WMANT 61; Neukirchen-Vluyn: Neukirchen Verlag, 1988) 40, 56.

[6] In an otherwise excellent article by Morton Smith, "On the History of ΑΠΟΚΑΛΥΠΤΩ and ΑΠΟΚΑΛΥΨΙΣ," in D. Hellholm (ed.), *Apocalypticism in the Mediterranean World and the Near East* (Tübingen: Mohr Siebeck, 1983) 9–20, the author does not discuss the particular problems of the term ἀποκάλυψις in the superscription and title of Revelation.

[7] Bruce J. Malina (*On the Genre and Message of Revelation: Star Visions and Sky Journeys* [Peabody, MA: Hendrickson, 1995] 12) argues that the terms "apocalypse" and "eschatological apocalyptic" are "theological jargon of the past century that fossilize perception and misdirect interpretation."

of good and evil centering on the expectation of the imminent end of the world. (2) "Apocalyptic movement," a *form of collective behavior* based on those beliefs and symbols. (3) "Apocalypse," a *type of literature* which consists of a pseudonymous autobiographical report of a supernatural revelation mediated by an angel or other heavenly being concerning the end of the world (in some apocalypses the visionary ascends to heaven, while in others the heavenly revealer comes to earth). (4) "Apocalyptic imagery," the *language of apocalyptic eschatology,* i. e. themes and motifs found in a variety of literary settings but no longer used in the context of a coherent apocalyptic world view.[8]

The history of the Qumran community stretches from murky beginnings in the second century BCE, and continues on until the destruction of Khirbet Qumran by the Romans in 68 CE. Until recently there was a widespread consensus that throughout this entire period the community was an apocalyptic movement based on an apocalyptic eschatology,[9] understood to consist in a strong conviction of the imminence of the end correlated with a belief in cosmic dualism. While this consensus has been challenged recently on a number of fronts,[10] the debate necessarily centers on those documents which can be claimed to have originated with the Qumran sectarians (e. g. 1QS, 1QM, 1QH and the pesharim) – i. e. works containing clusters of terms and ideas linked to the Qumran community.[11] This is in contrast to clearly non-sectarian documents (e. g. *1 Enoch, Jubilees, Tobit*) – i. e. documents which do not contain terminology reflecting the distinctive perspective of the Qumran community,[12] as well as the Biblical manuscripts. However, the value of Qumran sectarian literature for understanding the Book of Revelation is not dependent on the viability of a diachronic socio-historical reconstruction of the Qumran community and its literary activity (desirable as that is), so much as on an assessment of the relevance of each sectarian or non-sectarian document for illuminating aspects of Revelation.

---

[8] This categorization is based on the threefold distinction of "apocalypse," "apocalyptic eschatology," and "apocalypticism" introduced by Paul Hanson ("Apocalypticism," *IDBSupp,* 28–34), but then revised and expanded by D. E. Aune (*The New Testament in Its Literary Environment* [LEC 8; Philadelphia: Westminster, 1987] 227).

[9] Other possible apocalyptic movements include the *maskilim* of the Maccabean era whose perspective is reflected in the book of Daniel, and the hypothetical movements behind the apocalypses of *1 Enoch* and *Jubilees;* however, none of these can be described as organized communities in a way analogous to the Essene group at Qumran (see John J. Collins, "Was the Dead Sea Sect an Apocalyptic Movement?," in L. H. Schiffman [ed.], *Archaeology and History in the Dead Sea Scrolls: The New York University Conference in Memory of Yigael Yadin* [JSPSup 8; JSOT/ASOR Monographs 2; Sheffield: JSOT Press, 1990] 28–35).

[10] The main features of the debate are summarized by Collins, "Was the Dead Sea Sect an Apocalyptic Movement?" 25–27.

[11] See D. Dimant, "The Qumran Manuscripts: Contents and Significance," in D. Dimant and L. H. Schiffman (ed.), *Time to Prepare the Way in the Wilderness: Papers on the Qumran Scrolls by Fellows of the Institute for Advance Studies of the Hebrew University, Jerusalem, 1989–1990* (STDJ 16; Leiden: Brill, 1995) 27–29 (the distinctive terms are listed in notes 10–13).

[12] Dimant, "Qumran Manuscripts," 29–30.

There is general agreement among scholars that the Qumran community, throughout its entire history, was an apocalyptic or eschatological movement,[13] a view which has been disputed only occasionally.[14] It is striking, therefore, that very few apocalypses are actually to be found among the more than two hundred individual documents that make up the corpus of literature that was produced at Qumran.[15] Further, *not a single document which has been identified as an apocalypse appears to have originated within the Qumran community*,[16] even though many typically apocalyptic themes and motifs pervade much of the literature produced by the sectarians.[17] Among previously-known apocalypses found at Qumran are fragments of four of the five apocalypses making up *1 Enoch* (only the Parables or Similitudes of Enoch are missing),[18] as well as fragments of Daniel, *Jubilees*,[19] and the Aramaic *Levi Document* (in two scrolls: 4Q213 = 4QTLevi[a] ar; and 4Q214 = 4QTLevi[b] ar).[20] None of these documents was produced by the Qumran community. However, the fact that they possessed and used them suggests that they found them compatible with their eschatological perspective.

---

[13] See L.H. Schiffman, *The Eschatological Community of the Dead Sea Scrolls: A Study of the Rule of the Congregation* (SBLMS 38; Atlanta: Scholars Press, 1989), whose study focuses on 1QSa; Collins, "Was the Dead Sea Sect an Apocalyptic Movement?," 25–51; more recently, see John J. Collins, *Apocalypticism in the Dead Sea Scrolls* (London and New York: Routledge, 1997).

[14] H. Stegemann, "Die Bedeutung der Qumranfunde für die Erforschung der Apokalyptik," in Hellholm (ed.), *Apocalypticism in the Mediterranean World and the Near East*, 513–14, 525.

[15] See D. Dimant, "Apocalyptic Texts at Qumran," in E. Ulrich and J. VanderKam (ed.), *The Community of the Renewed Covenant* (CJA 10; Notre Dame: University of Notre Dame Press, 1994) 175–91.

[16] This judgment is based on the survey of Qumran manuscripts by Dimant, "Qumran Manuscripts," 23–58.

[17] See, for example, Sapiential Work A (represented by seven fragmentary copies: 1Q26, 4Q415, 416, 417, 418a, 418b, 423), as analyzed by Torleif Elgvin, "Early Essene Eschatology: Judgment and Salvation according to Sapiential Work A," in D. W, Parry and S.D. Ricks (ed.), *Current Research and Technological Developments on the Dead Sea Scrolls: Conference on the Texts .from the Judean Desert, Jerusalem, 30 April 1995* (STDJ 20; Leiden: Brill, 1996) 126–65. The author sees Sapiential Work A as a bridge between the apocalyptic Enochic literature and the clearly defined sectarian community.

[18] J.T. Milik, *The Books of Enoch: Aramaic Fragments of Qumran Cave* 4 (Oxford: Clarendon Press, 1976).

[19] *Jubilees* is presented as an extensive revelation to Moses by the angel of the presence which is a rewritten form of Genesis and parts of Exodus, There is little eschatological material, with the exception of *Jubilees* 23 which is an *ex eventu* prophecy of events from Abraham to the Maccabean rebellion culminating in an eschatological crisis that results in a cosmic transformation. Though it differs in content and eschatological emphases from other apocalypses, *Jubilees* is a pseudepigraphic revelatory writing which should nevertheless be categorized as an apocalypse; see J.J. Collins, "The Jewish Apocalypses," *Semeia* 14 (1979) 32; M.E. Stone and J.C. Greenfield, "Aramaic Levi Document," in G. Brooke et al. (ed.), *Qumran Cave 4: XVII. Parabiblical Texts,* Part 3 (DJD 22; Oxford: Clarendon Press, 1996) 1–72.

[20] For further details, see H.W. Hollander and M. de Jonge, *The Testaments of the Twelve Patriarchs: A Commentary* (SVTP 8; Leiden: Brill, 1985) 17–20, 458–60.

Several other Dead Sea Scroll texts, previously unknown, have been labeled apocalypses by various scholars. Many of these are fragmentary, making an assessment of their genre difficult. Further, with one exception, none shares the distinctive terminology found in the major sectarian compositions,[21] which makes it doubtful that they were produced by the sectarians themselves. (1) The exception is 1 QM (the *War Scroll*), the sectarian document which is dominated by apocalyptic eschatology. However, despite the fact that it anticipates the final series of eschatological conflicts between the Sons of Light and the Sons of Darkness, 1 QM is not written in the style of a revelatory narrative (i. e. as an apocalypse), but rather as a rule book.[22] (2) 4Q246 (4Q Aramaic Apocalypse) is a text that was first edited by Émile Puech who labeled it an apocalypse.[23] In this much-discussed eschatological document, in which the titles "son of God" and "son of the Most High" both occur, perhaps as messianic epithets, a succession of kingdoms is predicted, culminating in a final kingdom over which a son of God will reign. While the document apparently contains the interpretation of a dream or vision, with similarities to the interpreted dreams of the court tales found in Daniel 1–6, no mention is made of a heavenly revealer, and since both the beginning and end of the text are missing, no clear judgments about genre can be made.[24]

(3) In 4Q552, 4Q553 (4QFour Kingdoms[a,b]) the seer sees four trees, apparently representing four kingdoms. Devorah Dimant categorizes this text as an apocalypse even though, like 4Q246, it lacks the generic features of the apocalyptic genre with the exception of the interpreted dream or vision.[25] (4) The "Description of the New Jerusalem," a work extant in seven fragments (1Q32; 2Q24 [2QNew Jerusalem]; 4Q554 [4QNew Jerusalem[a]]; 4Q555 [4QNew Jerusalem[b]]; 5Q15 [5QNew Jerusalem]; 11Q18 [11QNew Jerusalem]; and 4Q232), has been widely and correctly, in my view, categorized as an apocalypse (this work is discussed in more detail below).[26] (5) 4Q521 (4QMessianic Apocalypse),[27] another work edited by Puech and labeled by him as an apocalypse, refers to the idyllic

[21] This evaluation is based on the survey of Dimant, "Qumran Manuscripts," 23–58.

[22] Collins, *Apocalypticism in the Dead Sea Scrolls,* 10.

[23] É. Puech, «Fragment d'une apocalypse en araméen (4Q246 = pseudo-Dan[d]) et le 'Royaume de Dieu,»' *RB* 99 (1992) 98–131 + pl. I; idem, «4QApocryphe de Daniel,» in Brooke *et al., Qumran Cave 4:XVII* (DJD 22), 165–84 + pl. XI. This text is also discussed by F. M. Cross, who assumes that it is an apocalypse: "Notes on the Doctrine of the Two Messiahs at Qumran and the Extracanonical Daniel Apocalypse (4Q246)," in Parry and Ricks (ed.), *Current Research and Technological Developments on the Dead Sea Scrolls,* 1–13.

[24] Collins, *Apocalypticism in the Dead Sea Scrolls,* 9.

[25] Dimant, "Apocalyptic Texts," 185.

[26] M. E. Stone, "Apocalyptic Literature," in *idem* (ed.), *Jewish Writings of the Second Temple Period* (CRINT 2.2; Assen: Van Gorcum; Philadelphia: Fortress, 1984) 425; Dimant, "Apocalyptic Texts," 182–84.

[27] É. Puech, "Une apocalypse messianique (4Q521)," *RevQ* 15/4 (1992) 475–522 + pls. I–III; «4QApocalypse Messianique,» in idem, *Qumrân Grotte* 4: *XVIII. Textes Hébreux (4Q521–4Q528, 4Q576–4Q579)* (DJD 25; Oxford: Clarendon Press, 1998) 1–38 + plates I–III.

eschatological future and the resurrection from the dead, but does not appear to be an apocalypse in its present fragmentary form.

(6) 4Q385, 386, 387, 388, 391 (4QPseudo-Ezekiel), which Dimant (who is editing these fragments) considers to be three separate compositions.[28] Pseudo-Ezekiel is a rewriting of the prophecies of the book of Ezekiel, including dialogues between the prophet and God set in Ezekiel's time. The revelatory dialogue and the eschatological character of some of these fragments bring this composition very close to the apocalyptic genre. However, since the characteristic terminology and emphases of the core group of sectarian texts are missing, there is little doubt that these fragments had a non-sectarian origin. (7) 4Q543, 544, 545, 546, 547, 548 (4QVisions of Amram), a work in six fragmentary copies, narrates a vision of Amram in which two angelic beings, the angel of darkness and angel of light, are contending and he has a dialogue with them. The work appears to be an apocalypse,[29] but like most of the other texts we have surveyed, does not share the distinctive terminology of the core group of sectarian texts. Devorah Dimant has identified ten of the twenty-five Aramaic works found in Cave 4 as apocalypses or visionary narratives. However, *sensu stricto,* while these texts are certainly eschatological (with the exception of "Description of the New Jerusalem"), they lack the motif of a heavenly revealer mediating supernatural revelations about heavenly secrets and final events to a mortal recipient of revelation.

How can it be that an apocalyptic or eschatological community which existed for nearly two centuries and which possessed apocalypses originating outside the community, did not themselves produce apocalypses? This problem is compounded by the fact that most, if not all, of the constituent features of apocalypses and apocalyptic eschatology occur in the various literary genres produced by the Qumran sectarians themselves, though the apocalyptic genre was apparently never used by members of the community. The answer to that question may be relatively simple. Since all Jewish apocalypses are pseudepigraphal, their acceptance and circulation depended on the assumption of authenticity on the part of the audience for whom they are intended. This presupposes a degree of social separation between author and audience, for such pseudepigraphal compositions can hardly arise within a particular community unless the author's actual identity remains concealed behind the *nom de plume* of an ancient Israelite worthy. The Revelation of John, the earliest Christian apocalypse, is one rare instance in which the author has foregone the normally generic feature of pseudepigraphy in the interest of directing exhortation to an audience with whom he is well-acquainted. Much may be said for Jonathan

---

[28] D. Dimant, "The Apocalyptic Interpretation of Ezekiel at Qumran," in I. Grunewald *et al.* (ed.), *Messiah and Christos: Studies in the Jewish Origins of Christianity Presented to David Flusser* (TSAJ 32; Tübingen: Mohr Siebeck, 1992) 31–51.

[29] Collins, "Jewish Apocalypses," 48.

Z. Smith's proposal that the typical Jewish apocalypse was the product of individual scribal activity rather than the product of community interests and concerns.[30]

3. The New Jerusalem

Some of the more illuminating literary parallels between the Qumran scrolls and the Revelation of John are found in the six fragmentary groups of a work written in Aramaic entitled "Description of the New Jerusalem"[31] (henceforth "DNJ"), which together with the *Temple Scroll*,[32] are part of a tradition linking the description of the eschatological temple and city in Ezekiel 40–48 with that of the New Jerusalem in Rev 21:9–22:9. The fragments of the DNJ have recently been subjected to a detailed reconstruction and analysis by Michael Chyutin, who has integrated them into a single composition.[33] Given the number and diversity of these pieces, this is obviously a very speculative procedure – yet the results carry conviction.

---

30 J.Z. Smith, "Wisdom and Apocalyptic," in B.A. Pearson (ed.), *Religious Syncretism in Antiquity: Essays in Conversation with Geo Widengren* (AAR and the Institute of Religious Studies, University of California, Santa Barbara, Formative Contemporary Thinkers 1; Missoula, MT: Scholars Press, 1975) 131–56.

31 There are six fragmentary Aramaic copies of the Description of the New Jerusalem: (1) 1Q32. Text: J.T. Milik, "Description de la Jérusalem Nouvelle (?)," in D. Barthélemy and J.T. Milik, *Qumran Cave 1 (DJD* I; Oxford: Clarendon Press, 1955) 134–35 + pl. XXXI. (2) 2Q24 (2QNew Jerusalem). Text: M. Baillet, "Fragments araméens de Qumrân 2. Description de la Jérusalem Nouvelle," *RB* 62 (1955) 225–45 + pls. II–III; *idem*, "Description de la Jérusalem Nouvelle," in M. Baillet, J.T. Milik and R. de Vaux, *Les 'Petites Grottes' de Qumran: Exploration de la falaise les grottes 2Q, 3Q, 5Q, 6Q, 7Q, a 10Q, Le rouleau de cuivre* (DJD 3; Oxford: Clarendon Press, 1962) 84–89 + pl. XVI. English translation: F. García Martínez, *The Dead Sea Scrolls Translated: The Qumran Texts in English* (Leiden: Brill, 1994) 129. (3) 4Q554 (4QNew Jerusalem[a]). Text: J. Starky, "Jérusalem et les manuscrits de la mer Morte," *Le Mond de la Bible* 1 (1977) 38–40; K. Beyer, *Die aramäischen Texte vom Toten Meer: Ergänzungsband* (Göttingen: Vandenhoeck & Ruprecht, 1994) 95–104. English translation: García Martínez, *Dead Sea Scrolls,* 129–31. (4) 4Q555 (4QNew Jerusalem[b]). English translation: García Martínez, *Dead Sea Scrolls Translated,* 131. (5) 5Q15 (5QNew Jerusalem). English translations: García Martínez, *Dead Sea Scrolls Translated,* 131–33; G. Vermes, *The Dead Sea Scrolls in English* (3rd ed., London: Penguin, 1987) 271–73. (6) 11QI8 (11QNew Jerusalem). English translation: García Martínez, *Dead Sea Scrolls Translated,* 133–35. In addition, 4Q232 is a Hebrew fragment which has some relationship to the Aramaic work; see Milik, *The Books of Enoch,* 59.

32 On 11QT[a], see F. García Martínez, "The Temple Scroll: A Systematic Bibliography 1985–1991," in J. Trebolle Barrera and L. Vegas Montaner (ed.), *The Madrid Qumran Congress: Proceedings of the International Congress on the Dead Sea Scrolls, Madrid 18–21 March 1991* (2 vols., Leiden: Brill; Madrid: Editorial Complutense, 1992) 2.393–403.

33 Michael Chyutin, *The New Jerusalem Scroll from Qumran:* A *Comprehensive Reconstruction* (JSPSup 25; Sheffield: Sheffield Academic Press, 1997).

Thus far scholars have utilized the DNJ in only limited and suggestive ways in their analyses of Rev 21:9–22:9.[34] While neither the terms "Jerusalem" nor "new Jerusalem" actually occur in the fragments of DNJ, there is little doubt that the work focuses on the eschatological city of Jerusalem and the temple. It is, of course, true that the name "Jerusalem" occurs neither in Ezekiel 40–48 (which substitutes the name שמה יהוה ["Yahweh is There"] in Ezek 48:35), nor in the Temple Scroll. The connection between the DNJ and the Temple Scroll is debated, though neither document appears to have been a product of the Qumran sectarians.[35] B. Z. Wachholder argues that the DNJ is dependent on 11QT[a] (i.e. 11QTemple),[36] while M. Wise – followed by M. Broshi – argues that 11QTa is dependent on the DNJ.[37] J. Licht and F. García Martínez, on the other hand, maintain that there is neither a literary nor programmatic relationship between the two works.[38] Three observations can be made about this debate. First, contrary to Wachholder, it appears that DNJ was compiled earlier than 11QT[a].[39] Second, while literary dependence of 11QTa on DNJ is doubtful, both works are clearly dependent on Ezekiel 40–48. Third, both compositions reflect an opposition to the existing temple cultus and share common traditions relating to an ideal or eschatological city and temple. The DNJ was an extremely popular text at Qumran given the fact that six Aramaic copies of parts of this work have been found in Caves 1, 2, 4, 5 and 11. This apparently pre-Qumranic text is the

[34] See H. Reichelt, *Angelus interpres-Texte in der Johannes-Apokalypse* (Frankfurt am Main: Peter Lang, 1994) 203–206; U. Sim, *Das himmlische Jerusalem in Apk 21,1–22,5 im Kontext biblisch-jüdischer Tradition und antiken Städtebaus* (BAC 25; Trier: Wissenschaftlicher Verlag, 1996) 64–67. In the most recent full-scale commentary on Revelation to appear in Germany (H. Giesen, *Die Offenbarung des Johannes*), no mention is made of the DNJ texts.

[35] Though most scholars, following Yigael Yadin ("The Temple Scroll – The Longest and Most Recently Discovered Dead Sea Scroll," *BAR* 10 [1984] 32–49), maintain that the Temple Scroll was produced by the Qumran sectarians, arguments for excluding this composition from the sectarian literature are proposed by Lawrence Schiffman, "The Temple Scroll in Literary and Philological Perspective," in W. S. Green (ed.), *Approaches to Ancient Judaism* II (Chico, CA: Scholars Press, 1980) 143–58; H. Stegemann, "The Origin of the Temple Scroll," in J.A. Emerton (ed.), *Congress Volume, Jerusalem 1986* (VTSup 40; Leiden: Brill, 1988) 235–56; *idem*, "The Literary Composition of the Temple Scroll and Its Status at Qumran," in G. J. Brooke (ed.), *Temple Scroll Studies* (JSPSup 7; Sheffield: JSOT Press, 1989) 123–89; Michael Wise, *A Critical Study of the Temple Scroll from Qumran Cave 11* (SAOC 49; Chicago: Oriental Institute of the University of Chicago, 1990) 201–3.

[36] *The Dawn of Qumran: The Sectarian Torah and the Teacher of Righteousness* (HUCM 8; Cincinnati: Hebrew Union College Press, 1983) 96.

[37] Wise, *Temple Scroll,* 61–86; M. Broshi, "Visionary Architecture and Town Planning in the Dead Sea Scrolls," in Dimant and Schiffman (edd.), *Time to Prepare the Way in the Wilderness,* 10–11.

[38] J. Licht, "An Ideal Town Plan from Qumran: The Description of the New Jerusalem," *IEJ* 29 (1979) 45–59; F. García Martínez, "The 'New Jerusalem' and the Future Temple of the Manuscripts from Qumran," in idem, *Qumran and Apocalyptic: Studies on the Aramaic Texts from Qumran* (STDJ 9; Leiden: Brill, 1992) 180–85.

[39] The dating of DNJ is partially dependent on its perceived relationship to the Temple scroll. Wise dates its composition to the third or early second century BCE *(Temple Scroll,* 86).

closest thing to an apocalypse among the Dead Sea Scrolls, apart from such previously known texts as *1 Enoch.*[40]

In the largest fragmentary copy, 5Q15,[41] an unnamed visionary (perhaps Ezekiel) is escorted around the city which will stand upon Zion by an unidentified guide (perhaps an angel), who carries a measuring rod that is seven cubits long (i. e. 3.2 m or 10.5 feet). The narrative is written in the first-person singular of the visionary and the guided tour begins outside the city. The guide measures the rectangular wall enclosing the city which is 140 *res* (sing. רס or ריסא, pl. ר[א]סין)[42] along the eastern and western sides, and 100 *res* long on the northern and southern sides. Since the exact length of the *res* is uncertain, scholars have had to resort to informed speculation. M. Broshi uses a rounded figure of 1 cubit = 50 cm, close to the average of the long and short cubits, and estimates that the city wall of 140 × 100 *res* is *ca.* 30 km × 21 km = 630 square km,[43] while F. García Martínez calculates that 1 *res* = 63 reeds = 441 cubits = 229 meters, so that the length and width of the rectangular wall surrounding the New Jerusalem would be 32 km × 23 km = 736 square km.[44] The wall has twelve gates (each is 21 cubits wide), with three on each side (cf. Ezek 48:33–34; 11QT[a] 39:12–13; 40:11–14; 4Q554), and 480 posterns (each 14 cubits wide), with one postern for each stadion. Each gate is flanked by two towers, each of which is 35 cubits square.

The inside of the city is constructed like a chessboard, with 192 insulae or blocks, each 357 cubits square, and consisting of a square row of houses enclosing an inner court, each with a second floor. Each housing-block has a tower with a spiral staircase and each has four gates, one in the middle of each side. The city is orthogonal (i. e. the streets intersect at right angles), a design with origins in ancient Egypt and with more immediate antecedents in the Hellenistic town planning introduced by Hippodamus.[45] A system of orthogonal narrow streets 42 cubits in width separates the insulae. The broader main street runs east-west and is 126 cubits wide, while the somewhat narrower main street running north-south is 92 cubits wide. In addition, there are two more east-west streets which are 70 cubits wide and two north-south streets which

---

40 García Martínez ("The 'New Jerusalem'," xi, xiii) refers to both 4Q246 and the Description of the New Jerusalem fragments as apocalypses.

41 G. Vermes, *The Dead Sea Scrolls,* 271–73; J. Fitzmyer and H. Harrington, A *Manual of Palestinian Aramaic Texts* (BibOr 34; Rome: Biblical Institute Press, 1978) 54–61.

42 A *res* in DNJ is divided into 352 royal or long cubits (Chyutin, *New Jerusalem Scroll,* 75), though the exact length of these cubits is not known.

43 M. Broshi, "Visionary Architecture and Town Planning," in D. Dimant and L. H. Schiffman (ed.), *Time to Prepare the Way in the Wilderness: Papers on the Qumran Scrolls by Fellows of the Institute for Advanced Studies of the Hebrew University, Jerusalem,* 1989–90 (STDJ 16; Leiden: Brill, 1996) 9–22, esp. 12.

44 García Martínez, "The 'New Jerusalem'," 192–93.

45 M. Chyutin, "The New Jerusalem: Ideal City," *DSD* 1 (1994) 71–97, and *idem, The New Jerusalem Scroll,* 113–30.

are 67 cubits wide. This network of streets divides the city into 16 large blocks, each measuring 35 × 25 *res* or stadia, and each consisting of 12 insulae for a total of 192 insulae.

In Rev 21:9–22:9, the figure of an *angelus interpres* appears for the second time in the narrative. However, in this context, unlike his first appearance in 17:1–18, the *angelus interpres* has very little to explain to the seer, and none of what he says can actually be considered interpretive. In fact, the only statement attributed to this angel (if one excludes the narrative possibility that he is the speaker in 22:6, 10–11) is an invitation to the seer in 21:9: "Come and I will show you the bride, the wife of the lamb." Thus the angel's principal task is to "show" the seers certain things, and this is emphasized by the phrase ἔδειξέν μοι ("then he showed me") which occurs twice (21:10a; 22:1a). The *angelus interpres* in Rev 21:9–22:9 functions in three ways: (1) he measures the architecture, (2) he makes occasional comments, and (3) he leads the seer from place to place. These same three functions characterize the mysterious "man" of Ezekiel 40–48 and the unidentified guide in DNJ. The various Qumran fragments of the "Description of the New Jerusalem" thus have many parallels to Rev 21:15–21, not least the frequent occurrences of variations on the phrase ואחזיני, "then he showed me."[46]

In Rev 21:12 the New Jerusalem is described as having a wide and high wall with twelve gates, each inscribed with the names of "the twelve tribes of the sons of Israel." The mention of the twelve tribes implies that the New Jerusalem is not simply a city, but rather the focal point for the entire land. This arrangement corresponds to Ezekiel's vision of the square outer walls of the eschatological Jerusalem (4,500 cubits on each side) with three gates on each side (Ezek 48:16–17, 30–35); these are purportedly named after the tribes of Israel (Ezek 48:31), but in fact are named after the sons of Jacob (i. e. Joseph and Levi are specified, not Ephraim and Manasseh).

The DNJ, like the Temple Scroll, is inspired by Ezekiel 40–48, although the sequence of names for the gates in Ezek 48:30–35 is very different from that in 4Q554. In this DNJ text, the city has twelve gates, each named after one of the sons of Jacob in the following order:[47] South: Simeon, [Levi], and Judah; West: Joseph, [Benjamin], and Reuben; North: [Issachar, Zebulon, and Gad]; East: Dan, Naphtali, and Asher (4Q554 1 i 12-ii 9). This order conforms generally to that found in 11QT^{a} 39: 12–13; 40:11–14.

The ideal eschatological city and/or temple complexes detailed in Ezekiel 40–48, the DNJ, the Temple Scroll and Revelation 21 are all gigantic, though in the case of DNJ and the Temple Scroll it is not possible to determine the exact

---

46 2Q24 1 3; 4Q554 1 ii 15; iii 20; 4Q555 1 3; 5Q15 1 i 2, 15; ii 6; and 11Q18 16 6; 18 1.

47 The names of seven of the twelve gates survive in the text.

metric equivalent of the cubit.[48] (1) *Ezekiel 40–48*. In Ezekiel, the outer court of the temple was surrounded by a square wall, measuring 500 cubits on each side (40:5; 42:15–20; 45:2). The walls of the city itself form a gigantic square 4,500 cubits on each side, with three gates on each side named after the twelve tribes of Israel (48:30–35). (2) *Description of the New Jerusalem*. The city in DNJ is a rectangle, measuring 140 *ris* or stadia on the east and west and 100 *ris* or stadia on the north and south, thus forming a rectangle with a perimeter of from 100,000 cubits to somewhat over 200,000 cubits,[49] depending on the number of cubits per *res*.[50] (3) The *Temple Scroll*. In the Temple Scroll, the sanctuary complex consists of three concentric squares: (a) The inner court, or court of priests, measures 300 cubits on a side; (b) The middle court, or court of men, measures 500 cubits on a side; (c) The outer court, or court of Israel, measures 1700 cubits on a side, with a total perimeter of 6,800 cubits.[51] Such a structure would equal the size of the Hasmonean city of Jerusalem![52]

In all of these texts that focus on the ideal or eschatological temple, there is a striking emphasis on the twelve tribes of Israel. The association of the names of the twelve tribes with the gates of the New Jerusalem in each text (Ezek 48:30–35; 4Q554 I i 9–ii 11; 11QT[a] 39:12–13; 40:11–14) anticipates the final realization of one of the central concerns of Jewish eschatology: the restoration of all Israel, which is repeatedly mentioned in post-exilic OT and early Jewish literature.[53]

The New Jerusalem of Revelation 21 and the city of the DNJ texts also share an emphasis on the precious stones and metals which are part of the building material used in the construction of these eschatological structures. The earliest references to precious stones used in the rebuilding of Jerusalem are found in Isa 54:11–12 and Tob 13:16. Gold overlay was used on parts of the Herodian temple (Josephus, *War* 5.201, 205, 207–208; *m. Mid.* 2.3), a feature taken up in 11QT[a] (36:11; 39:3; 41:15). The city in DNJ is described as having buildings

[48] Five different metrical equivalents to the cubit in the Temple scroll, which vary from 0.42 meters to 0.56 meters, are considered by J. Maier, "The Architectural History of the Temple in Jerusalem in the Light of the Temple Scroll," in Brooke (ed.), *Temple Scroll Studies*, 24–25.

[49] Wise, *Temple Scroll*, 82.

[50] See the comments on the *res* on p. 87 above.

[51] J. Maier, *The Temple Scroll: An Introduction, Translation & Commentary* (JSOTSup 34; Sheffield: JSOT Press, 1985) 63–64, 144 (diagram); *idem*, "Architectural History," 50.

[52] M. Broshi, "The Gigantic Dimensions of the Visionary Temple in the Temple Scroll," *BAR* 13 (1987) 36–37; Wise, *Temple Scroll*, 82.

[53] Deut 30:3–4; Neh 1:9; Isa 11:12; 27:12–13; 49:5–6; 56:1–8; 60:3–7; 66:18–24; Jer 31:8, 10 [LXX 38:8, 10]; 32:37 [LXX 39:37]; Ezek 11:17; 20:34, 41–42; 34:11–16; 36:24; 37:11–14, 21–28; Hos 11:10–11; Ps 106:47; 147:2; Tob 13:5, 13; 14:6–7; 2 Macc 1:27–29; 2:7, 18; *Jub.* 1:15–17; *T. Benj.* 9:2; 10:11; *1 Enoch* 57; 90:33; Philo, *Praem.* 94–97, 162–72; Bar 4:37; 5:5; Sir 36:11; 48:10; *Pss. Sol.* 11; 17:28–31, 50; *4 Ezra* 13:12–13, 39–47; 2 *Baruch* 78:5–7; *T. Jos.* 19:4; *Shemoneh Esreh* 10; *m. Sanh.* 10:3; 1QM 1:2–3, 7–8; 11QT[a] 18:14–16; 4Q504 [4QWords of the Luminaries[a]] frgs. 1–2 vi 10–13; Matt 23:37; cf. Mark 13:27 (a Christian adaptation of this motif). See E. P. Sanders, *Jesus and Judaism* (Philadelphia: Fortress, 1985) 95–98.

of sapphire, ruby and gold (4Q554 2 ii 15), and the streets are paved with white stone, alabaster and onyx (5Q15 I 2 6–7). In Revelation, the New Jerusalem is described as a whole as having the appearance of jasper, clear as crystal (21:11), or of gold, clear as glass (21:18). Similarly, the city's twelve foundations are each made of a variety of precious and semi-precious stones (21:19–20). This may be an embellishment of OT texts which refer to the use of huge costly stones for the foundation of Solomon's temple (1 Kgs 5:17; 7:10). Utopian cities constructed of precious stones and metals are not found only in Israelite-Jewish tradition, however; Lucian speaks of a city of gold surrounded with an emerald wall with seven gates, each constructed of a single plank of cinnamon, with a river of myrrh running through it (*Verae historiae* 2.11).

4. The Temple and Ritual Purity

The particular group of Essenes who formed the Qumran community had separated themselves from the temple in Jerusalem because of what they considered a laxity in ritual purity and the use of an unlawful ritual calendar (CD 20:22–23; 4QMMT),[54] although they accepted the basic validity of the temple cult and anticipated its eschatological renewal. In the interim there was a tendency to describe the community as a temple.[55] Just as the temple was the center of purity for Second Temple Judaism in general, so the assembly of sectarians itself formed a substitute center of ritual purity for the group. In lQS in particular, the notion of the community as an eschatological temple comes to expression a number of times (5:4–7; 8:4–10; 9:3–6), with Israel (= laymen) as the holy place and Aaron (= priests) as the holy of holies.

The anti-temple attitude expresses itself in different ways in these texts. In Ezekiel 40–48, the fact that the temple has been destroyed provides the context for the prophet's vision of an ideal or eschatological temple. Both the DNJ and the Temple Scroll are formulated in opposition to the existing temple cult, which they correct by visualizing an ideal or eschatological temple. The implicit opposition to the existing city and temple as reflected in both the DNJ and the Temple Scroll suggests why these texts found a sympathetic reading among the Qumran community. In Rev 21:9–22:9, the emphasis is exclusively on the city, and the author calls attention to the absence of a temple from city's midst (Rev

---

54 García Martínez and Trebolla Barrera, *The People of the Dead Sea Scrolls,* 32–35.

55 Bertil Gärtner, *The Temple and the Community in Qumran and the New Testament: A Comparative Study in the Temple Symbolism of the Qumran Texts and the New Testament* (SNTSMS 1; Cambridge: Cambridge University Press, 1965); R.I. McKelvey, *The New Temple: The Church in the New Testament* (London: Oxford University Press, 1969) 46–53; Georg Klinzing, *Die Umdeutung des Kultus in der Qumrangemeinde und im Neuen Testament* (SUNT 7; Göttingen: Vandenhoeck & Ruprecht, 1971) 50–93.

21:22).[56] In both Ezekiel and the Temple Scroll, the major emphasis is on the temple complex itself, while in DNJ the emphasis is on the city.

In the Temple Scroll, the ritual status of temple and holy city is such that they form a temple-city unit so that the purity requirements normally applying to the temple are extended to the entire city.[57] Thus, according to the *halakhah* in 11QT^a 45:7–18, the following conditions cause impurity and exclude people from the temple-city: (1) nocturnal emissions, (2) sexual intercourse,[58] (3) blindness,[59] (4) bodily discharges, (5) contact with the dead and (6) leprosy.[60] A regimen of ablutions is prescribed for those who incur any of these forms of impurity and are in consequence consigned to a special area reserved for them east of the temple-city (11QT^a 46:16–18). In Lev 15:16–18 the period of impurity for those who have nocturnal emissions or engage in sexual intercourse is one day, but the temple-city requires a purification ritual lasting three days (11QT^a 45:7–12).[61]

In Revelation, the New Jerusalem, though explicitly lacking a temple (21:22),[62] nevertheless clearly functions as a temple-city with "the glory of God as its light

---

[56] A very different view of Rev 21:22 is proposed by David Flusser, "No Temple in the City," in *idem, Judaism and the Origins of Christianity* (Jerusalem: Magnes, 1988) 454–65. Flusser argues that Rev 21:22–23 is not based on opposition to the temple, but rather on the combination of two midrashic units, the second of which is based on Ps 132:17 where the phrase "I have prepared a lamp for my Messiah" occurs, and the first on Isa 60:19 which refers to the Lord as the everlasting light of Jerusalem. He proposes that these two midrashic units are fused in a midrash on Ex 27:20 (as also in Rev 21:22–23): The Holy One said to Israel: 'In this world you needed the light of the Temple, but in the world to come because of the merit of the above-mentioned lamp (Ex. 27:20) I will bring you the King Messiah, who is compared to a lamp, as it is written: There I will make a horn to sprout for David, I have prepared a lamp for my Messiah' (Ps 132: 17).

[57] F. García Martínez, "The Problem of Purity: The Qumran Solution," in García Martínez and Trebolle Barrera, *People of the Dead Sea Scrolls,* 138–57.

[58] There is a close parallel in CD 12:1–2: "Let no man lie with a woman in the city of the sanctuary [בעיר המקדש] to defile the city of the sanctuary with their pollution," translated by J. Baumgarten and D. Schwartz, "Damascus Document (CD)," in J. H. Charlesworth (ed.), *The Dead Sea Scrolls. Hebrew, Aramaic, and Greek Texts with English Translations,* Vol. 2: *Damascus Document, War Scroll and Related Documents* (PTSDSS 2; Tübingen: Mohr Siebeck; Louisville: Westminster John Knox, 1995) 4–57, esp. 51.

[59] In the Bible this regulation is limited to priests (Lev 21:17–20; cf. 1QM 7:4–5; 1QSa 2:3–11), suggesting the tendency to extend the regulations for priestly purity to the people generally. See García Martínez, "The Problem of Purity," 146–47.

[60] Two forms of ritual uncleanness not mentioned are menstruation and parturition in the case of a woman (see *TDOT* 5.336–37).

[61] Jacob Milgrom ("Studies in the Temple Scroll," *JBL* 97 [1978] 512–13), who cites Yadin to the effect that the three-day purification is modeled after the purification commands relating to the encampment of Israel at Sinai (Exod 19:10–15).

[62] In Judaism, the eschatological expectation of a New Jerusalem generally implied a New Temple. The explicit denial of a temple in the New Jerusalem in Rev 21:22 is therefore surprising and has been frequently understood to reflect an anti-temple stance in strands of early Christianity. The traditions of Jesus' "cleansing" of the Temple and predictions of its destruction are frequently thought to reflect such a stance. Yet Jesus' act of "cleansing" the temple makes more sense if it is understood as a symbolic action anticipating its destruction (though not impugning

and its lamp is the Lamb" (21:23).[63] Impurity is also barred from this city, according to 21:27: "But nothing unclean [πᾶν κοινόν] shall enter it; nor anyone who practices abomination or falsehood." At the conclusion of Revelation there is a short list of those who are excluded from the city (22:15): "Outside are the dogs and sorcerers and fornicators and murderers and idolaters, and everyone who loves and practices falsehood." Despite the brevity of these two lists,[64] they exhibit a strikingly common pattern. Both begin with what appears to be an exclusively *ritual* category, which is then followed by a list of *moral* transgressors. Given the unlikelihood that a Christian author would regard ritual and moral impurity as equally defiling, we are left with two possibilities: (1) The author understands the ritual prescriptions metaphorically in moral terms,[65] or (2) The author incorporates a source in which ritual impurity and moral transgression are regarded as equally defiling.[66] It is not easy to choose between these two possibilities, for both may be valid.

While the generic category of κοινός might be expected to subsume various other categories of ritual impurity, the author appears to shift gears and provides, rather, a list of those people who are excluded from the city because of their immoral behavior. Closely parallel to Rev 21:27, with its exclusion of anything impure from the eschatological Jerusalem, is the pronouncement in 11QT[a] 47:3–6:

> The city which I will sanctify, installing my name and my temple [within it] shall be holy and shall be clean from all types of impurity [לכול טמאה] which defile it. Everything that there is in it shall be pure and everything that goes into it shall be pure.[67]

The phrase כול טמאה is virtually identical with πᾶν κοινόν in Rev 21:27 and even the contexts are similar since both imply the perfect purity of the eschatological Jerusalem. Jan Fekkes has argued convincingly, on the basis of diction and context, that Rev 21:27 alludes to Isa 52:1b:[68] כי לא יוסיף יבא בך עוד ערל וטמא

its purity and legitimacy), as well as implying its eschatological restoration (Mark 11:15–19 = Matt 21:12–13 = Luke 19:45–48; see James D. G. Dunn, *Unity and Diversity in the New Testament: An Inquiry into the Character of Earliest Christianity* [Philadelphia: Westminster, 1977] 324). It is striking that sayings of Jesus predicting the destruction of the existing temple and its replacement by an eschatological temple are widespread in the tradition (Mark 13:2 = Matt 24:2 = Luke 21:6; Mark 14:58 = Matt 26:61; Mark 15:29 = Matt 27:40; John 2:18–22; Acts 6: 14). Following E. P. Sanders *(Jesus and Judaism* [Philadelphia: Fortress, 1985] 61–76), it is likely that the action and the saying formed an original unity, i. e. the saying interpreted the action.

[63] W. J. Harrington, *Revelation* (Sacra Pagina; Collegeville: The Liturgical Press, 1993) 218; H. Giesen, *Die Offenbarung des Johannes,* 135.

[64] The only common feature of these two short lists is the phrase "the one who practices falsehood" ὁ ποιῶν ψεῦδος).

[65] In the Hebrew Bible, טמא is used metaphorically of idolatry and sin *(TDOT* 5.337–41).

[66] This suggests that the source was incorporated without any thoroughgoing redaction.

[67] García Martínez, *Dead Sea Scrolls Translated,* 168.

[68] Jan Fekkes, *Isaiah and Prophetic Traditions in the Book of Revelation; Visionary Antecedents and their Development* (JSNTSup 93; Sheffield: Sheffield Academic Press, 1994) 273–74.

("For there shall no more come into you [Jerusalem] the uncircumcised and the unclean," thus *RSV*). The Septuagint translates Isa 52:1 somewhat woodenly: οὐκέτι προστεθήσεται διελεῖν διὰ σοῦ ἀπερίτητος καὶ ἀκάθαρτος, which exhibits little verbal similarity to Rev 21:27. However, like Rev 21:27, Isa 52:1b is formulated negatively; it includes a verb meaning "to come," whose goal is the holy city, and specifically prohibits the entrance of the unclean person or thing.[69]

The prediction that unclean persons or things will not enter the eschatological Jerusalem occurs only in Isa 52:1 and Isa 35:8 in the entire OT. Both Isa 52:1 and 35:8 represent an extension of the kind of postexilic prohibition found in Ezek 44:9, where participation in temple ritual is forbidden the foreigner (i. e. the non-proselyte who is "uncircumcised in heart and flesh," cf. Isa 56:3–8).[70] Isa 52:1 is also quoted in 4Q176 (4QTanhumin) 8:3, an anthology of texts largely from Deutero-Isaiah on the topic of comfort. While Rev 21:27 probably alludes to Isa 52:1, no such allusion is present in the close parallel found in 11QT^a 47:3–6,[71] which suggests that the exclusion of the unclean from the eschatological Jerusalem was a conception not restricted to the exegesis of Isa 52:1 and 35:8. Moreover, *Ps. Sol.* 8:8–13 condemns priests whose immorality and impurity profaned the temple and the sacrifices, a charge that is closely paralleled by CD 5:6–8.

Finally, since the "temple" was used both at Qumran and in early Christianity as a metaphor for the community of salvation in the end time, is there any indication that temple-city in 11QT^a, the city in the DNJ, or the New Jerusalem in Rev 21:9–22:9 symbolize their respective communities? In the first two cases the answer must be negative. There is no indication in either the Temple Scroll or the DNJ that the eschatological city or temple symbolized a community. On the other hand, a number of scholars have argued that the New Jerusalem in Revelation symbolizes the Christian community.[72] The strongest evidence for this view is the identification of the new Jerusalem as "the bride the wife of the Lamb" (21:9–10a; cf. 21:2–3), when compared with the earlier identification of

---

69 The adjective טמא, when used as a noun, can mean "impure one" or "impure thing" (Isa 52:1), just as the phrase πᾶν κοινόν in Rev 21:27 is neuter and therefore means "every impure thing."

70 Parallel to Ezek 44:9 is 4QFlorilegium (4Q174) 1:3–4, "This (refers to) the house in which shall never enter [...] either the Ammonite, or the Moabite, or the Bastard, or the foreigner, or the proselyte, never, because there [he will reveal] to the holy ones" (García Martínez, *Dead Sea Scrolls Translated,* 136).

71 The identification of the sources of 11QT^a, particularly the Hebrew Bible, has been investigated in detail by Michael Wise (*Temple Scroll,* 205–42), who categorizes 11QT^a 47:3–18 as free composition.

72 For further details and discussion, see R. J. McKelvey, *The New Temple,* 167–76; W. Thüsing, "Die Vision des 'Neuen Jerusalem' (Apk 21,1–22,5) als Verheissung und Gottesverkündigung," *TTZ* 77 (1968) 17–34; R. H. Gundry, "The New Jerusalem: People as Place, Not Place for People," *NovT* 29 (1987) 254–64.

the wife of the Lamb as the saints (19:7–8). This is supported by the numerical symbolism of the enormous dimensions of the city, which is 12,000 stadia long, wide and high (21:16). At Qumran, there is ample evidence that "the men of the community" regarded themselves as a temple of God, an intermediate situation in which they rejected the existing temple cult and lived in expectation of the rebuilding of the true and unpolluted eschatological temple.[73]

5. The Eschatological War

A final eschatological holy war is a frequent motif in prophetic and apocalyptic scenarios of the series of events which bring the present age to a decisive end (Ezek 38:7–16; 39:2; Joel 3:2; Zech 12:1–9; 14:2; 1 *Enoch* 56:5–7; 90:13–19; 99:4; *Jub.* 23:23; *4 Ezra* 13:33–34; *Sib. Or.* 3.663–68).[74] The most detailed description of this eschatological conflict in early Jewish literature is found in the War Scroll, the most extensive form of which is in 1QM.[75] This text narrates the eschatological war in which the Sons of Light, who belong to the lot of God, are opposed by the Sons of Darkness, whose leader is Belial. The War Scroll deals with the final series of seven future battles between the forces of God and Satan which will last forty years. In three preliminary battles the Sons of Light will have the advantage; in three the Sons of Darkness will have the advantage; then in the seventh and final battle, the hand of God will prevail and the Sons of Darkness will be utterly destroyed (1QM 1:13–16). Despite the presence of many apocalyptic features, the War Scroll is not in the form of an apocalypse, but is rather a rule book bearing a close resemblance to the Greco-Roman "tactical treatise," which provides instructions on how a war should be conducted.[76] There are many similarities between the military organization and practices of the *War Scroll* and of 1–2 Maccabees.[77]

The theme of combat pervades the Revelation of John,[78] taking a variety of forms. One of these consists of a number of fragmentary narratives which describe the gathering of eschatological armies in order to annihilate God's people

---

[73] B. Gärtner, *The Temple and the Community in Qumran.*

[74] See especially R. Leivestad, *Christ the Conqueror: Ideas of Conflict and Victory in the New Testament* (London: SPCK, 1954) 3–18; and A. Yarbro Collins, *The Combat Myth in the Book of Revelation* (HDR 9; Missoula, MT: Scholars Press, 1976).

[75] In addition to 1QM (1Q33), there are six additional fragmentary copies of the War Scroll (4Q491–496), as well as the War-Scroll like fragment 4Q497; see J. Duhaime, "War Scroll," in Charlesworth (ed.), *Damascus Document, War Scroll, and Related Documents,* 80–83.

[76] Duhaime, "War Scroll," 84; *idem*, "The War Scroll from Qumran and the Greco-Roman Tactical Treatises," *RevQ* 13/49–52 (Carmignac Memorial, 1988) 133–51; M. Avi-Yonah, "The War of the Sons of Light and the Sons of Darkness and Maccabean Warfare," *IEJ2* (1952) 1–5.

[77] Duhaime, "War Scroll," 88–89.

[78] A. Yarbro Collins, *The Combat Myth in the Book of Revelation.*

and detail the decisive eschatological battle that eventually ensues (16:12–16; 17:14; 19:11–21; 20:8–9). These brief narrative fragments are not part of a consistent scenario, but contain various contradictory features, such as the location of the battle and the identity of the combatants. This suggests that the narrative fragments were drawn from a variety of written and oral sources and traditions by the author.[79] According to Rev 16:16, the location of this battle is Armageddon; then in 20:9 the enemy (described as the hosts of Gog and Magog in 20:10) surrounds "the beloved city" (i. e. Jerusalem) where the "camp of the saints" is located (based on Ezek 38:12, where Gog and his allies converge on the "center of the world," i. e. Jerusalem).[80] The enemy is variously described as "the kings of the east" (16:12),[81] often thought historically to denote the Parthian threat, or "the kings of the whole world" (16:14), or "the ten kings" (17:12–14). In the brief narrative in Rev 20:7–10, the enemy is alternately described as "the nations in the four quarters of the earth" (v. 8), and "the hosts of Gog and Magog" (v. 9), led by the unholy trinity consisting of the Devil, the Beast, and the False Prophet (v. 10).

In 1QM it is clear that the adversaries of the "Sons of Light" in the eschatological battle are "all nations" (15:1; 16:1), also called "all the nations of wickedness" (15:2), presumably a coalition led by the "king of the Kittim" (15:2). The enemies of the Sons of Light are identified with the traditional biblical enemies of Israel, though the name Kittim (perhaps a generic term for Israel's ancestral foes) occurs with particular frequency. In 1QM 1:1–7, Edom, Moab, the sons of Ammon, the Kittim of Asshur, the Kittim in Egypt, and the sons of Japhet are mentioned, while in 1QM 2:10–14, the list of enemies includes: Aram-Naharaim, the sons of Lud, the sons of Aram, Uz, Hul, Togal, Mesha, the sons of Arphaxad, the sons of Asshur and Persia, the Kadmonites, Elam, the sons of Ishmael, and Ketura, Ham, Japhet. These may be ciphers for the enemies of Israel during the Greco-Roman period, though their latter-day equivalents are far from obvious. Unlike Revelation, these enemies do not assemble a vast

---

[79] On the source-criticism of Revelation, which is too complex a topic for inclusion in this discussion, see D. E. Aune, *Revelation* (WBC 52A; Dallas: Word Books, 1997) cv–cxxxiv.

[80] In Rev 20:9, the phrase "the camp of the saints" is interpreted as "the beloved city," i. e. Jerusalem. According to 4Q394–98 (4QMMT B) 34–35, Jerusalem is called the "camp" (מחנה), and in line 68 "the holy camp"; מחנה is used fourteen times in 1QM to refer to a fortified military camp. The phrase "peace of God in the camps of his holy ones" (1QM 3:5), which is to be inscribed on the camp trumpets just before the eschatological war, is the plural Hebrew equivalent of the singular "the camp of the holy ones" (Rev 20:9). This suggests that the latter phrase originated in early Judaism within the context of speculation about the eschatological war; see C. F. Fensham, "'Camp' in the New Testament and *Milhamah*," *RevQ* 4/16 (1964) 562. However, it is not clear whether "holy ones" in 1QM 3:5 refers to God's people or angels; perhaps it includes both (S. Lambergits, "Le sens de QDWSYM dans les textes de Qumran," *ETL* 46 [1970] 24–39).

[81] In OT prophetic texts the enemies of Israel are described as coming from the north (Jer 1:15; 4:6; 6:22) or from the east (Isa 41:2; 46:11; Dan 11:44).

coalition and march to the place of battle, but rather are confronted seriatim by the armies of Israel. A further difference is that in the War Scroll, the holy angels are said to be with the army of the sons of light (1QM 1:10; 7:6; 19:1), while in Revelation there is never a hint that human beings and angels fight together in any eschatological battle.

There are two other textual units in Revelation, each exhibiting particular dependence on holy war traditions of the OT;[82] however, both do not explicitly reflect the combat theme, but instead appear to presuppose it. Here I am referring to the two passages that mention the 144,000 (7:1–9; 14:1–5). Rev 7:1–9 reads like a military census of the tribes of ancient Israel (cf. Numbers 1–3),[83] referring to 12,000 sealed from each of the twelve tribes of the sons of Israel, for a total of 144,000.[84] The reference to all twelve tribes presupposes an eschatological setting subsequent to the regathering of the twelve tribes;[85] this presupposition is shared with the author-editors of 1QM, where all twelve tribes participate in the final series of eschatological battles (1QM 5:1–2), in language also dependent on Numbers 1–3.[86] If the group in Rev 7:1–9 is identified with the innumerable multitude described in 7:10–17 (as most contemporary scholars do), then we have a vast army of martyrs depicted both before and after their "victory" over the enemy through martyrdom,[87] although the conflict itself is not mentioned. In my view, however, the 144,000 of 7:1–9 are *not* identical with the innumerable multitude in heaven of 7:10–17, but rather constitute the remnant of Christians living at the end of days who are chosen to participate in the final eschatological conflict.[88] The eschatological army of Rev 7:1–9 does not consist of martyrs, but of followers of Jesus who will actively participate in the final conflict in a way generally similar to the role of Israel in the War Scroll.

The other passage referring to the 144,000 is Rev 14:1–5, which contains a scene depicting the Lamb on Mount Zion with the 144,000, and appears to be a fragment of the beginning of an eschatological battle narrative emphasizing Jerusalem as the focal point (thus also 20:9).[89] The members of this group are

---

[82] This is emphasized in the recent commentary by C.H. Giblin, *The Book of Revelation: The Open Book of Prophecy* (GNS 34; Collegeville: Liturgical Press, 1991).

[83] Bauckham, "The Apocalypse as a Christian War Scroll," 217–18.

[84] The list of the twelve "tribes of the sons of Israel" in Rev 7:1–9 is unlike any other similar list in the OT or early Jewish literature.

[85] See n. 53 above for references to the eschatological regathering of the tribes of Israel in early Jewish and early Christian literature.

[86] See P.R. Davies, *1QM, the War Scroll from Qumran: Its Structure and History* (BibOr 32; Rome: Biblical Institute Press, 1977) 28, 30–31.

[87] This is also the view of Bauckham, "Apocalypse as a Christian War Scroll," 215–29.

[88] For several arguments supporting this position, see D.E. Aune, *Revelation, ad loc.*

[89] The close parallels between Rev 14:1–5 and *4 Ezra* 13:25–50 (which narrates the eschatological assault of the nations on Mount Zion and describes the Son of the Most High, the Man from the Sea, who will destroy them with fire) suggests the original content of the fragment in Rev 14:1–5.

identified as celibate males (14:4), which reflects the ancient requirement for sexual abstinence by holy warriors (Deut 23:9–14; 1 Sam 21:5; 2 Sam 11:9–13), and is comparable to the lifelong celibacy practiced by many Essenes.[90] While the location of the series of future battles narrated in 1QM is not clear, the overview of the war in 1QM 1:1–7 indicates that the Sons of Light will return from the wilderness to encamp in the wilderness of Jerusalem (1QM 1:3), after which the point of departure for the armies of the Sons of Light will be Jerusalem (1QM 3:11; 7:4).

Richard Bauckham has argued at length that the Revelation of John is a "Christian War Scroll" (based on the model provided by 1QM), in which the author has revised Jewish traditions about a final eschatological battle against evil which has already been decisively won by the witness and death of Christ. The author of Revelation, he argues, uses the metaphor of warfare which he derives from apocalyptic traditions about the final messianic war and reinterprets them as a metaphor of Christian witness and martyrdom. John presents the Messiah as a military victor (Rev 5:5–6), but reinterprets that tradition in terms of his sacrificial death for the redemption of people from all nations (5:9–10). Bauckham suggests that eschatological holy war traditions took two forms. In the first form, the victory is won by God alone or with his heavenly armies (the tradition which predominates in apocalyptic), which I will call the *passive* model. In the second, the people of God play an active role in physical warfare against their enemies (a striking example being found in 1QM), which I will call the *active* model.[91] Bauckham focuses on several texts: (1) The conquering Messiah (Rev 5:5–6); (2) The messianic army (7:2–14); (3) The Lamb and his army (14:1–5). He argues that each of these texts makes use of holy war language, while transferring the meaning of that language to non-military means of triumphing over evil. In other words, victory is achieved, just as it was by Jesus, through faithful witness and martyrdom.

While Bauckham's central thesis that in Revelation the notion of "victory" is often reinterpreted to refer to the suffering and martyrdom of faithful witnesses to Jesus (a view found earlier in Jewish martyrological traditions) is surely correct, all eschatological conflict in Revelation cannot be reinterpreted or demythologized in such a manner. Bauckham fails to draw into his discussion those passages in which the motif of the eschatological battle is mentioned *explicitly* through the brief and often truncated narratives mentioned above (16:12–16; 17:14; 19:11–21; 20:8–9). A few comments on each of these texts would be in order.

---

[90] A. Marx, "Les racines du célibat essénien," *RevQ* 7/27 (1971) 323–42.

[91] Bauckham, "Apocalypse as a Christian War Scroll," 210–11. Apocalyptic texts in which the righteous act as agents of divine retribution include *1 Enoch* 90:19; 91:12; 95:3, 7; 96:1; 98:12; *Jub.* 23:30; and *Apoc. Abr.* 29.17–20. See also 1 Cor 6:2–3.

In Rev 16:12–16, the kings from the east or the kings of world assemble at Armageddon "for the battle on the great day of the Lord Almighty" (16:14). Nothing is said concerning the opponents of this coalition of kings, and the text ends abruptly with no mention of the actual battle itself. *In Rev 17:14* (which reads like a continuation of 16:12–16), a coalition of ten kings wages war on the Lamb, but he conquers them. Those who are with the Lamb are "called and chosen and faithful." While it is not explicitly said that "those with him" participate in the battle, this seems to be implied, thus making this brief narrative an example of the *active* model of the eschatological holy war. *In Rev 19:11–21*, the Messiah appears as a rider on a white horse followed by the armies of heaven, who battle the kings of the earth with their armies" (v. 19), which is an example of the *passive* model. While the battle itself is not narrated, the result is that the beast and the false prophet are captured and the rest are slaughtered by the sword which came out of the rider's mouth (vv. 15, 21).[92] The role of the rider on the white horse is emphasized, but no specific role is given to the heavenly armies. *In Rev 20:8–9*, which in many respects is a doublet of 19:17–21, the hosts of Gog and Magog besiege the camp of the holy ones and the beloved city, but are destroyed by fire from heaven (reminiscent of *4 Ezra* 13:10–11). The Devil, their leader, is then thrown into the lake of fire and sulphur.

With the possible exception of 17:14 which reflects the *active* model,[93] these texts conform to the tendency in apocalyptic literature to emphasize the *passive* model (i.e. the role of God and his angels in the eschatological battle), and to ignore the role, if any, of God's people of God in the conflict. Furthermore, none of these passages demythologizes the eschatological battle in terms of the "victory" that is experienced by the individual follower of Jesus in suffering and dying for his or her faithfulness to him.

1QM remains as a striking example of the *active* model of the eschatological war, while Revelation reflects a much more complex combination of sometimes contradictory eschatological perspectives. The *active* model is reflected (or presupposed) in Rev 7:1–9; 14:1–5; 17:14, while the *passive* model is evidenced in Rev 16:12–16; 19:11–21; 20:8–9.

---

[92] The "sword of his mouth" of Rev 19:15 appears to be a metaphor which is interpreted literally as a weapon used to slay the enemy army in Rev 19:21. In a closely related text (4 Ezra 13:10–11), an analogous weapon, "the breath of flame" from the mouth of the Man from the Sea, is first described as a weapon which is used to slay the enemies of the people of God. But later this weapon is interpreted as the word of judgment and rebuke that is given to the assembled peoples of the world.

[93] For an argument that the saints are enjoined to seek vengeance on their enemies in Rev 18:6–7, see S.M. Elliott, "Who is Addressed in Revelation 18:6–7?" *BR* 40 (1995) 98–113.

The Influence of Roman Imperial Court Ceremonial on the Apocalypse of John

I.

The author of the Apocalypse was thoroughly convinced that the claims of Caesar were antithetical to those of Christ. So convinced that he regarded any compromise as impossible and any accommodation as blasphemy. So convinced that he produced an elaborately designed and ingeniously crafted literary work in which he both heightened and schematized that antithesis to persuade his wavering readers that his perceptions were not only right, they coincided with the perspective of God himself.[1] Basic to the structure of John's thought is his conception of the Dragon and the Beast (theriomorphic symbols of Satan and Caesar) as a diabolic duo who function as counterfeit counterparts to God and the Lamb. Students of the Apocalypse, both ancient and modern, have interpreted the book in the setting of a real or imminent persecution of the Christians in Asia Minor based on their refusal to participate in the required rituals of the imperial cult. Domitian (81–96 CE), the emperor who insisted on the designation *dominus et deus* (Lord and God), is usually (and probably correctly) regarded as the emperor whose rule provoked John to respond with the composition of the Apocalypse. Two aspects of this common view require revision, though it is not possible in this paper to provide the appropriate demonstrations. First, there does not appear to have been an officially sponsored general or even local persecution of Christians during the reign of Domitian. Second, Christians appear to have experienced sporadic persecution, not because they refused to participate in emperor worship, but simply because they were Christians. [2]

Even though there is general recognition that the Apocalypse is pervaded by a scheme of cosmic and eschatological events based on the antithesis of Satan and Caesar to God and the Lamb, the subtlety and deftness of John's literary design has not always been sufficiently appreciated. Accordingly, the thesis of this paper is that John's description of the heavenly ceremonial practiced in the

---

[1] D.E. Aune, "The Social Matrix of the Apocalypse of John," *BR* 26 (1981) 16–32. Reprinted below, pp. 175–89.

[2] G.E.M. de Ste Croix, "Why were the Early Christians Persecuted?" *Studies in Ancient Society*, ed. M.I. Finley (London: Routledge and Kegan Paul, 1974) 210–249; *idem*, *The Class Struggle in the Ancient Greek World* (Ithaca: Cornell University Press, 1981) 396.

throne room of God bears such a striking resemblance to the ceremonial of the imperial court and cult that the latter can only be a parody of the former. While this thesis may not appear particularly controversial, I have found it extraordinarily difficult to demonstrate. However, I take no little comfort in the fact that the major competing view, namely that the heavenly liturgy of the Apocalypse is a projection of the liturgy of the Christian church on earth, is even more difficult to sustain. One difficulty I have encountered is the fragmentary nature of our knowledge of imperial court ceremonial of the first and early second centuries CE. Fortunately, this subject has been brilliantly discussed by the Hungarian classical historian, Andreas Alföldi in a lengthy 1934 article entitled "Die Ausgestaltung des monarchischen Zeremoniells am romischen Kaiserhofe."[3] A second difficulty is based on the fact that John was not, it appears, unduly constrained by reality; the heavenly world, of course, is an ideal world in which perfect correspondence to earthly realities can neither be expected nor desired. The throne room ceremonial of the Apocalypse, it appears, is a pastiche of images and conceptions drawn from Israelite-Jewish kingship traditions and ideologies, from Hellenistic kingship traditions and from Roman Imperial court and ruler ceremonial. Roman imperial court ceremonial itself, it must be observed, was heavily influenced by Hellenistic divine ruler traditions. Yet a third difficulty is the problem of how a provincial resident of the eastern Mediterranean world could possibly know enough about the ceremonial of the imperial court to use it as a model for the ceremonial of the heavenly throne room. First, the Roman emperors were not anchored to the city of Rome, but often visited cities in the Italian peninsula and various provincial cities, though our knowledge of their travels is limited for the earlier period. Where they went their court went with them, so that citizens of various areas, particularly those of the upper classes, were exposed to imperial ceremonial, particularly that of the *adventus,* i. e., the "arrival" of the emperor at a particular city. Second, the main task of the Roman emperor was to dispense justice through reading written petitions, hearing cases orally, and receiving embassies from various cities.[4] Firsthand exposure to the imperial court was therefore, over the years, experienced by hundreds and thousands of provincial residents. Third, popular images of the imperial court and the protocol required there circulated in such literature as the Acts of the Pagan Martyrs (*Acta Alexandrinorum*). Fourth, the ideology of the Roman divine monarchy was expressed in both Greek and Latin panegyric and in the rhetorical works of the Second Sophistic;[5] these compositions, often performed publicly for purposes

---

[3] Republished in Andreas Alföldi, *Die monarchische Repräsentation im römischen Kaiserreiche* (Darmstadt: Wissenschaftliche Buchgesellschaft, 1970) 1–118.

[4] On the role of the emperor generally, see Fergus Millar, *The Emperor in the Roman World (31 BC–AD 337)* (Ithaca: Cornell University Press, 1977). For a description of such an embassy, see Philo *De legatione ad Gaium*.

[5] The earliest panegyric, written to the emperor Trajan, is that of Pliny the Younger, written

of mass entertainment, were effective means of communicating basic notions of what the imperial court and the emperor who presided over it were like. Fifth, Roman art and coinage were vehicles for imperial propaganda, and can be used to understand when and where particular images and conceptions were popular.[6] In all these ways, residents of Asia Minor (the most important center for rhetoric and one of the areas in which the imperial cult was strongly entrenched) could have absorbed a combination of real and ideal images and conceptions of the character and function of the ceremonial of the imperial court.

In interpreting the throne room ceremonial of the Apocalypse as an idealized projection of imperial court ceremonial, I must reject the widely-held notion that the heavenly liturgy of the Apocalypse is a projection of the liturgy of the earthly church.[7] While few scholars propose that the entire Apocalypse constitutes such a liturgy (as M. H. Shepherd), many regard the throne room ceremonial (including the hymns and acclamations located throughout the Apocalypse) as having an origin in Christian liturgy or as representing fragments of such a liturgy. While it cannot be disputed that certain liturgical expressions and formulas, such as the Amen, the Halleluia and the Sanctus were a definite part of early Christian liturgy, one cannot simply assume that major segments of the heavenly liturgy of the Apocalypse accurately reflect Christian worship. Historians of late antiquity are cognizant of the important influence which the imperial cult exerted upon Christian liturgy,[8] yet what is true of the fourth century is not necessarily true of the first. In the following pages I will not attempt to refute the liturgical reflection theory directly, but will rather attempt to replace it with a hypothesis which I think is more probable.

---

and presented in the Roman senate in 100 CE. A manual of how to write panegyric is preserved in the *Peri Epideiktikon* in the late second/early third century rhetorician Menander. See also Ilona Opelt, "Zum Kaiserkult in der griechischen Dichlung," *Rheinisches Museum fur Philologie* 103 (1960) 43–56. Particularly for the later Empire, see Sabine G. MacCormack, *Art and Ceremony in Late Antiquity* (Berkeley and Los Angeles: University of California Press, 1981), where the focus is on art and Latin panegyric, and their depiction of the major imperial ceremonies of *adventus, consecratio* and *accessio.*

[6] On the view that imperial coin types were deliberately intended to convey a message, however simple, see C. H. V. Sutherland, "The Intelligibility of Roman Imperial Coin Types," *JRS* 49 (1959) 46–55.

[7] This view is held by M. H. Shepherd, *The Paschal Liturgy and the Apocalypse* (London: Lutterworth, 1960); Oscar Cullmann, *Early Christian Worship* (London: SCM Press, 1953) 7 f.; Ralph P. Martin, *Worship in the Early Church* (Grand Rapids, Eerdmans, 1975) 45 f.; T. Harnack, *Der christliche Gemeindegottesdienst im apostolischen und altkatholischen Zeitalter* (Erlangen: Theodor Bläsing, 1854) 161. Eric Peterson, *The Angels and the Liturgy* (New York: Herder and Herder, 1964) 1–13.

[8] Ramsey MacMullen, *Paganism in the Roman Empire* (New Haven: Yale University Press, 1981) 82. On pp. 73–94 he has an excellent section on "How the Divine World was Envisioned."

II.

The main vision report of the Apocalypse (4:1 through 22:5) begins with a relatively detailed description of the heavenly throne room where John experiences a magnificent concatenation of sights, sounds and odors (Rev 4–5). The entire vision report of the Apocalypse is apparently perceived from the vantage point of the throne room, for the narrative again and again refers to features found in the throne room (e. g., the altar, 6:9; the innumerable host before the throne, 7:9–17; the offering of incense on the altar before the throne, 8:3–5; and so on). There are a number of constituent elements of the heavenly throne room ceremonial in Rev 4–5 which require explanation. Encircling the throne of God are twenty-four elders (πρεσβύτεροι) sitting upon twenty-four thrones with golden crowns on their heads and clothed with white garments. Voices and thunder emanate from the throne itself, where God sits in splendor, but is not described. Before the throne are seven burning torches (interpreted as the seven spirits of God), and a sea of glass, like crystal. Around each side of the throne are four living creatures with many eyes (a lion, an ox, one with a human face and an eagle). All of these beings are constantly engaged in a heavenly liturgy involving ceaseless repetition of the Sanctus (4:8), and a doxology uttered by the twenty-four elders who prostrate themselves before the one seated on the throne and cast their crowns before the throne. Later, John sees the Lamb standing as though slain, between the throne and the living creatures and among the elders (5:6). Later we learn that a golden altar stands before the throne (8:3), upon which incense rather than victims are offered. The throne room is, in effect, a temple (14:15, 17). The overall impression gained from the throne room scene in Rev 4–5 is that it is a beehive of activity. Several features of John's description require further comment and explanation; these include: (1) the role of God, (2) the arrangement, behavior and appearance of those present in the throne room, (3) the function of the hymns and acclamations in the throne room ceremonial, and (4) the use of honorific titles and symbols applied to both God and the Lamb.

In the ancient near east, the conception of the gods in the heavenly world was based largely on projections of native kingship ideology and conventions into the heavenly world. The same was true for the classical world. The *Odyssey* begins with a scene in the council chamber of Zeus on Olympus (1.22–95), the protocol of which parallels that of the assembly of Ithacans called by the young Telemachos shortly thereafter (2.1–256). In the Roman world, God (Jupiter Optimus Maximus) is conceptualized as surrounded by armies, commanders, prefects, governors and messengers; all agents used by the supreme god to maintain control and communication over the universe in general and the world of man in particular. In Rome, which had a centralized monarchy unknown in the Greek world until the Hellenistic and Roman periods, Jupiter and his Council were conceptualized in terms of the emperor and his court; heaven was even called the "palatial" (Ovid *Met.* 1.175–76; *Ars Amat.* 3.119).

The primary role of the Roman emperor, from the time of Julius Caesar on, was that of rendering justice; this corresponds to the ancient conception that Zeus and Jupiter were guarantors of justice and that they provided sanctions supporting the maintenance of the laws and customs of humanity. The judicial task of the Roman emperor, as of provincial governors, involved responding to a constant flow of letters and petitions from everywhere in the empire to the emperor, wherever he happened to be. The emperors' responses came to be regarded as legal precedent; the publication of the extensive correspondence between Pliny and Trajan is a case at point. The emperor also heard cases orally, received embassies with both oral and written petitions from all over the empire. In discharging this enormous task, the emperor (and his lesser counterparts, the provincial governors) were surrounded by friends (*amici*) and advisors (*consilium*) whose task it was to aid him in his role of dispensing justice.[9] Further, emperors were, like consuls, accompanied by lictors bearing fasces, and by other *apparitores* (public servants), and sat between the consuls on their bench.[10] According to Fergus Millar,[11] "in the eyes of the subject the essential role of the *amici* was to be visibly present with the emperor in receiving delegations or petitions or, above all, in giving judgment." This popular image is reflected in the *Acta Isidori* (one of the acts of the pagan martyrs):

> The sixth day of Pachon: the second day. Claudius Caesar hears the case of Isidorus, the gymnasiarch of Alexandria v. King Agrippa in the … gardens. With him sat twenty senators (and in addition to these) sixteen men of consular rank, the women of the court also attending … Isidorus' trial.[12]

In sum, the role of the emperor was passive; most of the contacts which he had with his subjects was of the "petition-and-response" variety.[13]

Similarly, the role of God in the Apocalypse is essentially passive. Though he is seated upon his throne in the heavenly temple, he is not described, and is not presented as speaking until the climax of the vision report, in Rev 21:5–8; this brief speech, which is directed to John, focuses on the reward of the righteous and the punishment of the wicked. The primary role of God in the Apocalypse, in fact, appears to be that of dispensing justice in the sense of punishing past breaches of divine law and rewarding the righteous (11:18; 14:7; 16:7; 18:8; 19:2, 11; 20:12, 13). The souls of the martyrs under the altar in the throne room

---

[9] Millar, *Emperor*, 3–12.

[10] Millar, *Emperor*, 208.

[11] Millar, *Emperor*, 119.

[12] H. Musurillo, *Acts of the Pagan Martyrs* (Oxford: Clarendon Press, 1954) 18–26. Further descriptions of the emperor and his court are found in Philostratus *VS* 2. 30; P. Oxy. 3019, 3020. Additional references are cited by Fergus Millar, *Emperor,* 120.

[13] Millar, *Emperor*, 6.

are depicted as crying out for justice to God (6:10): "O Sovereign Lord, holy and true, how long before thou wilt judge and avenge our blood on those who dwell on the earth?" Further, just as the princeps as depicted in Roman art surrounded by his council and holding a *libellus,* i.e., a petition or letter in the form of an open scroll, so God is seen to be holding a βιβλίον in his right hand (5:1). None of these general similarities, of course is decisive, but the parallels do provide a general context in which John's vision of the throne room ceremonial can be understood.

III.

A great deal of speculation regarding Rev 4–5 revolves about the problematic identity of the twenty-four elders. They have been variously identified as the righteous of the old covenant viewed as elders of the heavenly church, redeemed and transformed men, representations of the twenty-four star gods of the Babylonian pantheon, or as a special class of angelic or heavenly beings.[14] The interpretive difficulties are clearly indicated by Wilhelm Bousset who, after surveying the many possibilities, concluded that the Apocalyptist was dependent on an ancient traditional image which we no longer understand.[15] John's distinctive vision of twenty-four elders, clad in white and wearing gold crowns, suggests that they are depicted for a special effect. I am convinced that attempts to "identify" the twenty-four elders, while understandable, are misguided. The elders, I think, have no separate "identity" or "meaning," but are part of a constellation of images which includes their garments and crowns, their singing of hymns and shouts of acclamation, their προσκύνησις before the throne and their utilization of harps and bowls of incense.

The number twenty four can be regarded, I think, as a symbol of cosmic kingship without suggesting any more specific intention than the doubling of the number twelve, a number in which the Apocalyptist has great interest. The elders encircle (κυκλόθεν) the throne of God, themselves seated on twenty-four thrones. In a circle in closer proximity to the throne of God are the four living creatures (κύκλῳ τοῦ θρόνου), who have eyes facing within and without, toward God upon his throne, and toward the elders (ἔμπροσθεν καὶ ὄπισθεν, v. 6, and κυκλόθεν καὶ ἔσωθεν, v. 8). Even closer to the throne of God is the encircling rainbow (κυκλόθεν, v. 3). On occasion, even the outer ring of twenty-four elders is itself encircled by great hosts of angels (5:11 κύκλῳ τοῦ θρόνου καὶ τῶν ζῴων

[14] See the survey of views in G. Bornkamm, *TDNT* VI, 668 f. The views summarized above are far from exhaustive; the number twenty four is also thought by some to combine the twelve apostles with the twelve patriarchs (or their angelic representatives).

[15] Wilhelm Bousset, *Die Offenbarung Johannis* (Göttingen: Vandenhoeck & Ruprecht, 1906) 247.

καὶ τῶν πρεσβυτέρων, and again in 7:11: κύκλῳ τοῦ θρόνου καὶ τῶν πρεσβυτέρων καὶ τῶν τεσσάρων ζῴων). The cosmic symbolism inherent in circular constructions is well-known;[16] here John heightens the symbolism of cosmic kingship by envisioning God on his throne in the center of three and four concentric circles. God is depicted, not unnaturally, as the *axis mundi.* In addition to using the symbolism of concentric circles and the doubling of the number twelve, John envisions seven flaming torches before the throne in Rev 4:5. This number is also an important structuring element in the Apocalypse bearing both the notion of completeness and cosmic symbolism (i. e., the number of planetary spheres). This conscious accumulation of cosmic symbolism is crafted by the author in order, I believe, to emphasize the cosmic kingship in magnificent transcendence of God.

While I am playing with numbers, let me indulge myself a bit more in a brief discussion of the cosmic significance of the New Jerusalem depicted in Rev 21:9–27, with its twelve gates, twelve foundations and its cubical shape (12,000 stadia in length, width and height). Centuries earlier, Plato had proposed an ideal city to be founded in the center of the country (*Leges* 5. 745bff.). The surrounding land was to be divided into 5,040 tracts, a number which is the product of 1 × 2 × 3 × 4 × 5 × 6 × 7. The people are then divided into twelve tribes, with twelve clans in each tribe. Cosmic laws and proportions thus penetrate the city; according to Plato:

> Our whole number has twelve subdivisions, and the tribal number also has twelve; and each such portion must be regarded as a sacred gift of God, conformed to the months and to the revolution of the universe. (*Leges* 771b, LCL trans.).

While I am not suggesting that the Apocalyptist was influenced by Plato, I am convinced that the ancients, in literature, art and architecture, consciously adapted cosmic symbolism into their structures. In contrast to John's New Jerusalem, which is an enormous cube constructed according to cosmic proportions, Herodotus reports that Ecbatana, the royal city of the Median empire, had seven concentric circuit-walls painted (from outermost to innermost), white, black, purple, blue, scarlet, silver and gold (Herodotus 1.98; cf. W. W. How and J. Wells, A *Commentary* on *Herodotus* [Oxford: The Clarendon Press, 1928] I, 104).

After Alexander had taken his seat on the Persian throne under the "golden heavenly canopy" (τὸν χρυσοῦν οὐρανίσκον, Plutarch *Alex.* 37. 7; Diodorus Siculus 17. 66), the Hellenistic kings incorporated cosmic and astral imagery as visible symbols of their divine rule. Demetrius Poliorcetes, the son of Antigonus, is described as having worn a garment with golden stars and the twelve signs of

[16] See H. P. L'Orange, *Studies on the Iconography of Cosmic Kingship* in *the Ancient World* (Oslo: H. Aschehoug & Co., 1953).

the Zodiac.[17] Herod Agrippa I, who died of an acute case of divinization according to Acts 12:20–23, was clothed in royal robes which Josephus describes as a silver garment which reflected the sun in a dazzling manner (*Ant.* 19. 343–46). The fact that the cosmic symbolism of such apparel and furnishing was transparent to many ancients is suggested by Josephus' extensive explanation of the cosmic symbolism of the Israelite priestly vestments and ritual objects within the Tabernacle/Temple (*Ant.* 3. 179–87).

The Roman imperial ruler cult was, as we have suggested above, profoundly influenced by the traditions associated with Hellenistic kingship, though the more extravagant forms of the Roman ruler cult were found in the eastern provinces rather than within Rome itself. Nero, after the great fire of 64 CE, embarked on an enormous and extravagant building project in which he constructed for himself the famous Golden House. A central feature of this house, according to Suetonius, was a revolving rotunda: "The main banquet hall was circular and constantly revolved day and night, like the heavens" (*Nero* 31. 2; LCL trans.). Further, Nero was represented by statues, some of which were gold, as Apollo-Helios, and on occasion he even acted the part of this divinity in person. Nero also reportedly wore a Greek cloak adorned with golden stars, perhaps similar to that worn by Demetrius Poliorcetes.[18] An earlier emperor, Claudius, is reported to have worn a golden robe as well (Tacitus *Annals* 12.51). In the Apocalypse, God is never described, nor is it ever intimated that his garments were embroidered with cosmic symbols. Yet John does see "one like a son of man," with a golden girdle and with seven stars in his right hand (1:12–16); it is further reported that "his face was like the sun shining in full strength" (1:16). At the end of John's vision, he makes this observation in describing the New Jerusalem:

> And the city has no need of sun or moon to shine upon it, for the glory of God is its light, and its lamp is the Lamb (Rev 21:23).

And again he observes:

> And night shall be no more; they need no light of lamp or sun, for the Lord God will be their light, and they shall reign for ever and ever (Rev 22:5).

These comparisons suggest that both the heavenly throne room envisioned by John, as well as God and the Lamb are described in images replete with cosmic imagery suggesting exaltation and majesty. The fact that Nero himself depicted himself as Apollo-Helios and was enthroned in a cosmic hall suggests an obvious antithesis between the two. The latter must be regarded as a counterfeit of the former.

---

[17] Plutarch *Dem.* 41. 4–5; cf. L. Cerfaux and J. Tondriau, *Le culte des souverains dans la civilisation Gréco-Romaine* (Tournai: Desclée, 1957) 184.

[18] Suetonius *Nero* 25; Stephan Lösch, *Deitas Jesu und Antike Apotheose* (Rottenburg: Adolf Bader, 1933) 13–16. Lösch sees a special connection between the Mithras-Helios-Apollo imagery and the spectacular garments of Herod Agrippa I.

IV.

The imagery of twenty-four elders clothed in white with crowns on their heads would suggest, above all, the appropriate ritual apparel for worship to a Greek audience. White was the sacred color among the ancients which was regarded as pleasing to the gods (Plato *Leges* 12. 956a; Cicero *De leg.* 2. 18). The presentation of gold crowns to a sovereign was a ceremony inherited by the Romans from the traditions of Hellenistic kingship.[19] Arrian reports a relevant anecdote from the life of Alexander:

> Embassies (πρεσβεῖαι) also in the meantime came from Greece, and their envoys (πρέσβεις), themselves crowned, came forward and crowned Alexander with golden crowns. as if they had come on a sacred embassy to honour some god (*Anab. Alex.* 7. 23; LCL trans.).

This suggests the Greek practice of honoring gods with crowns, though they were usually made of laurel or myrtle (Aelius Aristides *Orat.* 47. 44). In Palestine itself, Josephus reports that an embassy (πρεσβεῖαν) from Hyrcanus and the Jewish people met Antony at Ephesus and presented him with a golden crown (*Ant.* 14. 304–323). The Roman emperor was customarily presented with gold crowns by the senate (and provincial cities) on the occasions of accessions, consulships, victories and anniversaries.[20] A scene similar to that described above by Arrian is found at the time of the emperor Maximinus in the early third century CE:

> The Italian cities sent delegations (πρεσβεΐας) of their prominent citizens dressed in white, wearing laurel wreaths and all bringing with them the statues of their local gods and any golden crowns that were among their dedications (*Herodian* 8. 7. 2; LCL trans.).

In the Apocalypse, it is only the twenty-four elders who present crowns to the one seated on the throne, and it is perhaps not insignificant that in Roman custom the *populus Romanus* itself did not offer gold crowns to the emperor.[21] Taken separately, white garments can symbolize purity (3:4 f.; 6:11; 7:9, 13), just as crowns can symbolize victory (2:10; 3:11), yet John's symbols are frequently polyvalent. The heavenly scene of the twenty-four elders throwing down their crowns before the throne has no parallel in Israelite-Jewish literature, and become comprehensible only in light of the ceremonial traditions of Hellenistic and Roman ruler worship.

---

[19] See the detailed study by Theodor Klauser, "Aurum Coronarium," *Gesammelte Arbeiten zur Liturgiegeschichte, Kirchengeschichte und Christlichen Archäologie,* Hrsg. Ernst Dassmann, Jahrbuch für Antike und Christentum. Ergänzungsband 3 (Münster Westfalen: Aschendorffsche Verlagsbuchhandlung, 1974) 292–309.

[20] MacCormack, *Art and Ceremony,* 58; Millar, *Emperor*, 140–43.

[21] Millar, *Emperor*, 142. On the presentation of crowns, see Livy 37. 46. 4; 38. 37. 4; 39. 7. 1; Plutarch *Aem.* 34. 5; Pliny *Hist nat.* 33. 16. 54.

As a footnote, let me suggest an interesting parallel to the number twenty four which, as far as I know, has not been proposed. Roman magistrates were permitted to be accompanied by the number of lictors bearing fasces which corresponded to the degree of imperium which they had been granted. The purpose of these lictors, in addition to acting as bodyguards, was to announce the approach of the magistrates they accompanied.[22] Consuls were permitted twelve lictors. Augustus apparently had twelve lictors from Actium (31 BCE to 23 BCE), though it is possible that he had twenty-four lictors until 27 BCE.[23] At any rate the standard number of twelve lictors, indicative of the degree of imperium, was doubled by Domitian to twenty four.[24] These lictors, of course, were not crowned, nor did they wear white robes. They did, however, constitute part of the official crowd of public servants which constantly surrounded the emperor.

The twenty-four elders are frequently depicted as prostrating themselves before the throne of God (4:10; 5:8; 7:11; 11:16; 19:4), an act of worship which was accompanied by casting down crowns before God, hymning, shouting acclamations, etc. While the practice of προσκύνησις, or prostration, originated in eastern oriental monarchies, it became a widely practiced part of royal ceremonial in the courts of Hellenistic kings. King Prusias of Bithynia, employing the ritual forms of his own court in the Roman senate, is described as having bowed himself to the ground before the senators with the words "Hail savior gods!" (Livy 45.44; Polybius 30.16). The practice of the ritual of προσκύνησις before early Roman emperors is incontrovertible. In Dio's account of the self-presentation of Tiridates I before the emperor Nero in 66 CE we read:

> And I have come to thee, my god, to worship (προσκυνήσων) thee as I do Mithras. The destiny thou spinnest for me shall be mine; for thou art my Fortune and my Fate (Dio Cassius 63. 5. 2; LCL trans.).

There is also evidence that the Roman senators performed ritual προσκύνησις (accompanied by hymns and acclamations) before the empty throne of the living emperor Gaius:[25]

> The senators, nevertheless, went up to the Capitol, in a body, offered the regular sacrifices, and did obeisance (προσεκύνησαν) to the chair of Gaius that was in the temple (Dio Cassius 59. 24. 3–4; LCL trans.).

This practice may have been performed before the empty throne which represented Julius Caesar's monarchy toward the end of the Republic.[26] However,

---

[22] Theodor Mommsen, *Römisches Staatsrecht* (3. Aufl.; Leipzig: Verlag S. Hirzel, 1887) I, 355 f.

[23] Mommsen, *Römisches Staatsrecht*, I, 387, n. 5.

[24] Mommsen, *Römisches Staatsrecht*, I, 388; Alföldi, "Die Ausgestaltung des monarchischen Zeremoniells," 102; Dio Cassius 67. 4. 3; Suetonius *Dom*. 4.

[25] Alföldi, "Die Ausgestaltung des monarchischen Zeremoniells," 60.

[26] Dio Cassius 45. 6. 5; 53. 30. 61; Lily Ross Taylor, *The Divinity of the Roman Emperor*, 87, n. 15; Stephan Weinstock, *Divus Julius*, 283.

the quotation from Dio Cassius just cited, goes on to include another important feature of the Roman imperial Court ceremonial:

The same course was followed the next year also; but at the time of the events just narrated they assembled in the senate-house after these ceremonies, though no one had convened them, and yet transacted no business, but merely wasted the whole day in laudations to Gaius and prayers in his behalf. (Dio Cassius 59. 24. 5; LCL trans.).

This mention of hymns of praise in the court ceremonial brings us to the subject of the hymns in the Apocalypse.

V.

One very important feature of the ceremonial of the heavenly throne room in the Apocalypse is the inclusion of about fifteen hymns or hymn-like compositions at various junctures in the author's vision report. These hymns or hymn-like compositions include 4:8c; 4:11; 5:9b–10; 5:12b; 5:13b; 7:10b; 7:12; 11:15b; 11:17–18; 12:10b–12; 15:3b–4; 16:5b–7b; 19:1b–2; 19:5b; 19:6b–9.[27] They are often arranged so that two or three hymn-like segments are placed together in an antiphonal arrangement (e.g., 4:8–11; 5:8–14; 7:9–12; 11:16–19; 16:5–7; 19:1–4, 5–8), so that there are in total eight choral interludes in which the hymns play a significant role. From the perspective of genre criticism, these "hymns" present a number of difficulties. Some of them can be more accurately described as doxologies (cf. 5:13; 7:10, 12; 19:1), or acclamations or a combination of the two.[28] For present purposes, however, these form-critical issues are not relevant.

In harmony with the view that the heavenly liturgy in the Apocalypse is a reflection of the earthly liturgy of the church, the hymns of the Apocalypse have been regarded as fragments of Christian liturgical hymns which the author has inserted at appropriate points in his vision report.[29] Recent research, however, suggests that the hymns of the Apocalypse are literary compositions by the author.[30] Like the speeches in Acts, however, the hymns appear to be one device

---

[27] Klaus-Peter Jörns, *Das hymnische Evangelium* (Güttersloh: Gerd Mohn, 1971) 19.

[28] An excellent form-critical discussion of the hymns is found in Reinhard Deichgräber, *Gotteshymnus und Christushymnus in der frühen Christenheit* (Göttingen: Vandenhoeck & Ruprecht, 1967) 44–59. The doxologies of the Apocalypse are sometimes used as acclamations, e.g. Rev 7:10, 12; 19:1 (Deichgräber, 35). E. Peterson, *The Angels and the Liturgy*, 5 f., describes Rev 5:9 f. as an *epinikion*, i.e., a victory ode.

[29] E. Peterson, *The Angels and the Liturgy*, 11 f.; J. Kroll, *Die christliche Hymnodik bis zu Klemens von Alexandreia* (2. Aufl.; Darmstadt: Wissenschaftliche Buchgesellschaft, 1968) 16 f.

[30] G. Delling, "Zum gottesdienstlichen Stil der Johannesapokalypse," *NovT* 3(1959) 134 f.; R. Deichgräber, *Gotteshymnus und Christushymnus*, 58 f.; Jörns, *Das hymnisch Evangelium*, 178 f.

whereby the plot of the narrative is moved along.[31] There are, to be sure, traditional elements and phrases and motifs which have been incorporated into the hymns by the author, not only from Christian traditions, it appears, but also from pagan traditions as well.[32] The setting for all of the hymns appears to be the throne room in heaven, though that is not always completely clear (cf. 5:8–14). Those who participate in the singing of hymns or the chanting of acclamations include the four living creatures (4:8; 5:8; 7:11), the twenty-four elders (4: 10; 5:8; 7:11; 11:16; 16:5), the martyrs (6:10), every creature in the universe (5:13), one or more angels (5:11; 7:11; 16:5), and the great multitude of victorious Christians (7:9 f.; 15:2 f.; 19:1, 6), and finally a mysterious heavenly voice (11:15).

Hymns were integral features of the cults of all ancient Mediterranean religions.[33] Hymns were customarily reserved for the gods. When they were addressed to men (i.e., those who were alive or who had once been alive), the implication was that they were equal with the gods (ὥσπερ θεός; ἰσόθεοι τιμαί). Appian (*Bella civ.* 146) records that Antony made a eulogy to Caesar, whom he "hymned as a god in heaven" (ὡς θεὸν οὐράνιον ὕμνει). Lysander is remembered as the first Greek whom the cities honored as a god; they erected altars and made sacrifices to him "as to a god" (ὡς θεῷ), the first also to whom songs of triumph (παιᾶνες) were sung (Plutarch *Lys.* 18. 3). Songs of praise were addressed to Antony, along with the offering of incense, a ritual which suggests, according to Lily Ross Taylor, that "like every conqueror of the East, Antony was hailed as divine."[34] For the historian of early Christianity, this calls to mind the famous description by Pliny the Younger of the liturgical practices of Christians in Bithynia, who "chant verses alternately among themselves in honour of Christ as if to a god (*quasi deo*)."[35] Here the phrases *carmen dicere* ("to sing a song") and *Christo quasi deo* ("to Christ as god") suggest that a hymn of praise is meant, and that antiphonal singing of such hymns is the specific form of presentation. The NT hymns which have been isolated on form-critical grounds by scholars (e.g. Phil 2:5–11; Heb 1:3; Col 1:15–20; 1 Tim 3:16, etc.),[36] differ considerably in both form and content from the hymns of the Apocalypse. They are not addressed to Christ, but adhere to the third-person singular style, and they do not

---

[31] This is demonstrated in Jörns, *Das hymnische Evangelium*.

[32] For an emphasis on the traditional elements in the hymns, see J. O'Rourke, "The Hymns of the Apocalypse," *CBQ* 30 (1968) 399–409. H.D. Betz, "On the Problem of the Religion-Historical Understanding of Apocalypticism," *Journal for Theology and the Church* 6 (1969) 134–56, regards the "judgment doxology" of Rev 16:5–7 as including traditional elements from Hellenistic syncretism.

[33] MacMullen, *Paganism in the Roman Empire*, 15–24.

[34] Lily Ross Taylor, *The Divinity of the Roman Emperor* (Middletown, Connecticut: American Philological Association, 1931) 108. She refers to Plutarch *Ant.* 24; Strabo 14. 648, 674; Appian *Bella Civilia* 5. 7.

[35] A.N. Sherwin-White, *The Letters of Pliny: A Historical and Social Commentary* (Oxford: The Clarendon Press, 1966) 705.

[36] Deichgräber, *Gotteshymnus und Christushymnus*, 106–196.

exhibit any features of realized eschatology, a pervasive characteristic of the hymns of the Apocalypse.[37]

One of the oldest preserved hymns composed in honor of a living person regarded as divine, is the hymn to Demetrius Poliorcetes, preserved by the historian Duris of Samos and quoted in Athenaeus (*Deipnosophistae* 6. 253d–f), a paean sung by the Athenians upon the arrival (parousia/adventus) of Demetrius in their city in 291 BCE. I quote here only the first twelve lines of the surviving fragment:

The greatest and the dearest of the gods are present in our city.
The same lucky moment has brought them here, Demeter and Demetrius.
She has come to celebrate the holy mysteries of Kore;
he is present, joyous as befits the god, beautiful and with laughter.
An august picture is revealed – his friends all around him,
he himself in the middle: they like stars, but like the sun he.
Hail to thee, O son of the mighty god Poseidon and of Aphrodite![38]

Hellenistic kingship ideology and tradition was decisive for shaping both the Roman principate as well as the Roman image of the seven kings of Rome's early monarchy. Victorious Roman generals in the eastern Mediterranean were accorded divine honors as were the Hellenistic princes before them. In a papyrus preserving two edicts of Germanicus, dated 19 CE, the adopted son of Augustus declares to the Egyptians:

Your goodwill, which you display on all occasions when you see me, I welcome, but your acclamations (ἐκφωνήσεις) which for me are invidious and such as are addressed to the gods (ἰσοθέους), I altogether deprecate.[39]

The early emperors, particularly when visiting or represented in the eastern provinces, were accustomed to receiving divine honors in terms of sacrifices, offerings of incense, processions, priesthoods, hymns and acclamations. Even in Rome, however, claims to divinity and the encouragement of divine honors were consistently part of the imperial program beginning with Julius Caesar himself.[40] In the *Res Gestae Divi Augustae* 10, we read (LCL trans.): "By decree of the senate my name was included in the Salian hymn," a step which was interpreted by Dio Cassius (51. 20. 1) as a way of regarding Augustus as equal to the gods.

Little is known in detail about the hymns and acclamations accorded the Roman emperors during the first century. According to Andreas Alföldi:

---

37 Leonard L. Thompson, "Cult and Eschatology in the Apocalypse of John," *JR* 49 (1969) 348 f. This feature is also found in the Odes of Solomon; see D. E. Aune, "The Odes of Solomon and Early Christian Prophecy," *NTS* 28 (1982) 235–60. Reprinted below, pp. 320–46.

38 Translation of Victor Ehrenberg, "Athenian Hymn to Demetrius Poliorcetes," in *Aspects of the Ancient World: Essays and Reviews* (Oxford: Blackwell, 1946) 179.

39 A. S. Hunt and C. C. Edgar, *Select Papyri* II (LCL; Cambridge: Harvard University Press, 1934) 77.

40 Weinstock, *Divus Julius*, 282–84.

The customary acclamations of the senate which served as hymnic praise of the ruler, reached a peak in designating him as a deity. Unfortunately we have only reports regarding such acclamations of Nero and Caracalla, and so we are not quite able to follow the rise of this already cultic mode of honor.[41]

We have already mentioned the report found in Dio Cassius about the behavior of the senate during the reign of Gaius Caligula, in which they prostrated themselves before the emperor's empty throne and sang praises and uttered prayers on his behalf for an entire day (Dio 59. 24. 5). Nero, in fact, had a group of five thousand equestrians, called Augustiani, who followed him everywhere and provided hymns and acclamations which emphasized his divinity.

Then it was that Roman knights were first enrolled under the title of Augustani, men in their prime and remarkable for their strength, some, from a natural frivolity, others from the hope of promotion. Day and night they kept up a thunder of applause, and applied to the emperor's person the voice and epithets of deities (Tacitus *Annals* 14.15).[42]

Some emperors, such as Tiberius and Claudius, urged restraint in the offering and acceptance of such divine honors, while others, such as Nero and Caligula, were notorious in their encouragement of them.

The penetration of the Hellenistic-Roman ruler cult ideology and traditions into first century CE Palestine is exemplified by the acclamation accorded Herod Agrippa I by the people of Tyre and Sidon after an oration: And the people shouted, 'The voice of a god, and not of men!'" (Acts 12:22; cf. the parallel account in Josephus *Ant.* 19. 343–46).[43] Though few acclamations addressed to the early emperors have survived, there is a late document, the *Gesta Senatus Urbis Romae* (discovered in 1820 and subsequently prefixed to the Theodosian Code), in which a series of acclamations (together with a notation of the number of times each acclamation is to be repeated) has been preserved:

The assembly shouted;
"Augustuses of Augustuses, the greatest of Augustuses!"
  Repeated eight times.
"God gave You to us! God save You for us!"
  Repeated twenty-seven times.
"As Roman Emperors, pious and felicitous, may You rule for many years!"
  Repeated twenty-two times.

---

[41] Weinstock, *Divus Julius,* 282–84.

[42] See also Dio 61. 20. 2–4; 63. 8. 3; 63. 15. 2; 63. 18. 3; Suetonius *Nero* 20. 3; cf. Alföldi, "Die Ausgestaltung des monarchischen Zeremoniells," 82, and Dominique Cuss, *Imperial Cult and Honorary Terms in the New Testament* (Fribourg: The University Press, 1974) 77–81.

[43] Stephan Lösch, *Deitas Jesu und Antike Apotheose: Ein Beitrag zur Exegese und Religionsgeschichte* (Rottenburg: Adolf Bader, 1933) 6–38, in which the history-of-religions background of this text is thoroughly discussed.

"For the good of the human race, for the good of the Senate, for the good of the State,
for the good of all!"
Repeated twenty-four times.
"Our hope is in You, You are our salvation!"
Repeated twenty-six times.
"May it please our Augustuses to live forever!"[44]

Such acclamations, however, were not reserved for emperors alone, but were also a constant feature of the public life and activities of provincial governors. Like the emperors, governors were acclaimed whenever they entered and left a city, when they appeared at the theaters and when they drove through the streets.[45]

In considering briefly the individuals and groups which are presented as singing the hymns included in the Apocalypse, we noted that the hymnic doxology of Rev 5:12 is uttered by a vast throng:

Then I looked, and I heard around the throne and the living creatures and the elders the voice of many angels, numbering myriads of myriads and thousands of thousands, saying with a loud voice, "Worthy is the Lamb who was slain, to receive power and wealth and wisdom and might and honor and glory and blessing."

In Rev 5:13, which culminates in a doxology, the chorus is even greater:

And I heard every creature in heaven and on earth and under the earth and in the sea, and all therein, saying,
"To him who sits upon the throne and to the Lamb be blessing and honor and glory and might for ever and ever."

Similarly, the hymn in Rev 7:9–12 is sung by a vast host:

And after this I looked, and behold, a great multitude which no man could number, from every nation, from all tribes and peoples and tongues, standing before the throne and before the Lamb, clothed in white robes with palm branches in their hands, and crying out with a loud voice, "Salvation belongs to our God who sits upon the throne and to the Lamb!"

Again, the hymn in Rev 19:6b–8 is introduced in v. 6a in this way:

Then I heard what seemed to be the voice of a great multitude, like the sound of many waters and like the sound of mighty thunderpeals, crying, "Hallelujah! For the Lord our God the Almighty reigns…"

---

[44] Clyde Pharr, *The Theodosian Code and the Novels and the Sirmondian Constitutions* (New York: Greenwood Press, 1952) 3–7. Though the acclamations date from the year 429 CE, both the practice and the sentiments can be placed with confidence toward the second half of the fourth century, if not earlier; cf. O. Hirschfeld, "Die römische Staatszeitung und die Akklamationen im Senat," *Kleine Schriften* (Berlin: Weidmannsche Buchhandlung, 1913) 689–97.

[45] J. H. W. G. Liebeschuetz, *Antioch: City and Imperial Administration in the Later Roman Empire* (Oxford: The Clarendon Press, 1972) 208–210.

Each of these hymnic pieces is concerned with particular aspects of the reign of God or of the Lamb (or of God and the Lamb together). The studied way in which the author attributes these hymns and acclamations to vast throngs of beings suggests that they should be understood in relation to the ancient *argumentum e consensus omnium*, i. e., the argument from universal agreement (or, the "forty-million Frenchmen cannot be wrong" argument). The consent of the governed in the making of emperors was taken very seriously in antiquity, both in reality and in imperial propaganda designed to justify or legitimate the assumption of power on the part of particular emperors. This emphasis on universal consent is expressed by Augustus in the *Res Gestae Divi Augusti* 34, where a formula occurs which will be repeated many times during the principate of Augustus and his successors: "*per consensum universorum potitus rerum omnium,*" "by universal consent taking control of all things." According to Klaus Oehler:[46]

> In the Roman principate the consensus motif won worldwide significance for the first time. It was of fundamental importance for the establishment of the authority of the principate.

The agreement of three powerful groups, the senate, the equestrians and the people, was the basis upon which the principate of Augustus was founded.[47] The importance of the principle of *consensus omnium* is evident in the propagandistic use of a series of "consensus coins" minted by Augustus and his successors. On a denarius of 16 BCE, the legend reads "*Imperatori Caesari Augusto communi consensus*."[48] An example of the *consensus humani generis* is reported by Suetonius of the accession of Gaius Caligula: "When he (Gaius) entered the city, full and absolute power was at once put into his hands by the consent of the senate and of the mob" (*Caligula* 14; LCL trans.). Galba, one of three short-term emperors of the chaotic year 69 CE, claimed in an address to Piso that he had been called to the imperium by the consent of gods and men: "*deorum hominumque consensu ad imperium vocatum*" (Tacitus *Hist*. I. 15; cf. Pliny *Pan.* 68. I). The inevitable addition of the *consensus deorum* to the *consensus humani generis* was a step which had been taken much earlier in the first century. The Roman historian Valerius Maximus, in his *Factorum ac dictorum memorabilium libri IX* (written between 28 and 32 CE), is dedicated to Tiberius: "*penes quem hominum dorumque consensus maris ac terrae regimen esse voluit, certissima salus patriae, Caesar*."

For our understanding of this motif in the Apocalypse of John, it is particularly significant that the importance of the *consensus omnium* as a constitutional basis for imperial legitimacy was strongly emphasized during the period following

46 Klaus Oehler, "Der Consensus Omnium als Kriterium der Wahrheit in der antiken Philosophie und der Patristic," *Antike und Abenland* 10 (1961) 111.

47 Oehler, "Der Consensus," 113.

48 H. Mattingly, *The Roman Imperial Coinage* (London: Spink, 1923), I, plate 3.

the fall of Nero.[49] This heightened emphasis on the *consensus omnium* is related to the numismatic evidence for the sudden appearance of emphasis on "imperial security" evinced by a series of coins which first appear in Nero's last year (65 CE), bearing the legend "*Securitas Augusti*," and later "*Securitas Populi Romani*."[50] The tradition of the *consensus omnium* was fundamental, not only for legitimating imperial accession, but also for the ceremonial connected with the *adventus*, i. e., the arrival of the emperor, or on a lesser scale and with lesser pomp, that of a provincial governor or visiting dignitary:

> Whenever a governor entered the city he would expect the leading citizens to meet him outside the gates. If the council did not turn up in strength this might have serious consequences for its members. The councillors in turn would be entitled to expect that the governor should descend from his carriage to greet them. The crowd that welcomed the governor mirrored the social order of the town. In turn, he would pass senators and ex-governors, *officiales*, councillors, advocates, and teachers, and after passing the gates he would hear the acclamations (εὐφημίαι) *of the people*.[51]

This expression of the *consensus omnium* emphasizes its representative character, as does the suggestions of the third century rhetorician Menander for the appropriate elements to include in the epilogue to an imperial panegyric:

> (You say), for instance, "We have all gone out to meet you for your welcome, with our whole families, children, old men and men in their prime, the priestly families, the city council and the people at large. We were all glad in our hearts (and expressed it) with acclamations (ταῖς εὐφημίαις) calling you our savior and wall, a most radiant star, and children called you their nourisher and the savior of their parents.[52]

At least part of the rationale for this carefully orchestrated emphasis on *consensus omnium* in ceremonies of *accessio* and *adventus* is due to the widespread assumption among the Romans that imperial honors, to be both acceptable and legitimate, had to be conferred by others, not claimed by the emperor himself.[53] According to H. U. Instinsky, speaking of the period extending from the first through the third centuries CE, "There is an essential distinction between the emperor designating himself and others so speaking and addressing him."[54] From this perspective, Domitian's purported self-designation *dominus et deus* is less a new direction in imperial ideology as it is a tasteless violation of propriety.

---

[49] Oehler, "Der Consensus," 114.

[50] Hans Ulrich Instinsky, *Sicherheit als politisches Problem des römischen Kaisertums* (Baden-Baden: Verlag für Kunst und Wissenschaft, 1952).

[51] Liebeschuetz, *Antioch*, 208 f.

[52] Menander *Peri epideiktikōn* (L. Spengel, ed., *Rhetores Graeci*, III, 381); trans. S. MacCormack, *Art and Ceremony*, 20.

[53] Werner Hartke, *Römische Kinderkaiser. Eine Strukturanalyse römischen Denkens und Daseins* (Berlin: Akademie-Verlag, 1951) 105 f.

[54] Hans Ulrich Instinsky, "Kaiser und Ewigkeit," *Hermes* 77 (1942) 348; cf. M. P. Charlesworth, "Some Observations on Ruler Cult, Especially in Rome," *HTR* 28 (1935 15.

In the introductory narrative segments which precede the hymns and acclamations of the Apocalypse cited above (Rev 5:12 f.; 7:9–12; 19:6b–8; cf. 19: 1a, 4), it is apparent that the sovereignty and power of God and the Lamb are affirmed by vast multitudes of beings. In Rev 19:5: a voice from the throne intones "Praise our God, all you his servants, you who fear him, small and great." Here the phrase "small and great" is an idiom found frequently in the Apocalypse and in the Old Testament.[55] It refers to those who come from various social stations, a significance clarified by Rev 13:16. "Also it causes all, both small and great, both rich and poor, both free and slave, to be marked on the right hand or the forehead" (cf. 19:18). During the late first century, when the *argumentum e consensu omnium* had become particularly important in imperial propaganda, it is striking that the Apocalyptist should emphasize both the social breadth as well as the numerical strength of those who celebrate the sovereignty and power of both God and the Lamb. Indeed, those who proclaim the eternal kingship of God and the Lamb are more numerous and more representative than those who are depicted as participating in the rituals of imperial *accessio* and *adventus*.

VI.

The conflict between Caesar and Christ is nowhere more evident than in the honorific titles which were applied to both; titles which have the greatest religious and theological significance tend to be those which express or imply divinity. Terms used frequently of both include the following: (1) god, (2) son of god (i. e., *divi filius*, υἱὸς θεοῦ), (3) god made manifest, (4) lord, (5) lord of the whole world, (6) lord's day (*Sebaste* is pagan, while Κυριακή is Christian), (7) savior of the world, (8) epiphany, (9) imperator.[56] According to Adolf Deissmann,

> The cult of Christ goes forth into the world of the Mediterranean and soon displays the endeavour to reserve for Christ the words already in use for worship in that world, words that had just been transferred to the deified emperors or had perhaps even been invented in emperor worship. Thus there arises a polemical parallelism between the cult of the emperor and the cult of Christ, which makes itself felt where ancient words derived by Christianity from the treasury of the Septuagint and the Gospels happen to coincide with solemn concepts of the Imperial cult which sounded the same or similar.[57]

---

[55] Rev 11:18; 13:16; 19:5; 18; 20:12; cf. Gen 19:11; Deut 1:17; 25:13 f.; 1 Sam 5:9; 20:2; 30:2, 19; 1 Kgs 22:31, etc.

[56] Keith Hopkins, "Divine Emperors or the Symbolic Unity of the Roman Empire," in *Conquerors and Slaves* (Cambridge: The University Press, 1978) 199, n. 3; Adolf Deissmann, *Light from the Ancient East* (New York and London: Hodder & Stoughton, 1910) 346–69; Dominique Cuss, *Imperial Cult*, 63–71. The titles King of kings and Lord of lords (Rev 17:14; 19:16) are discussed in Deissmann, *Light*, 367–68.

[57] Deissmann, *Light*, 346.

Only two emperors are known to have applied to term "god" to themselves, Gaius (Philo *Leg. ad Gaium* 353), and Domitian (Suetonius *Dom.* 13.2; Martial 5. 8. I; 7. 34. 8; Pliny *Pan.* 33. 4; 78. 2; Dio Chrysostom 45. 1; Dio Cassius 67. 13. 4). The phrase in the doxology of Rev 4:11, "You are worthy, Lord and God (ὁ κύριος καὶ ὁ θεὸς)," is often seen, probably correctly, as a Christian reaction to imperial propaganda. The official title of the Roman emperor, "Imperator," was alternately rendered in Greek with the terms βασιλεύς, κύριος and δεσπότης while in Latin *rex* and *dominus* were preferred.[58] Yet, as J. H. W. G. Liebeschuetz has observed, "No ceremony ever took place to deify a living ruler since as far as the state religion of the Roman people was concerned, the emperor was not part of the pantheon."[59] Further, there is no evidence to suggest that the average Roman thought that the emperor possessed supernatural powers, could hear and answer prayers, influence the weather or the harvest or act at a distance.[60] The imperial cult was, as Keith Hopkins has maintained, a symbol of the unity of the Roman Empire.[61] The same point is emphasized by Liebeschuetz:

> The whole Roman system turned on loyalty and under the principate the object of loyalty had become personalized in the emperor. How to evolve and communicate loyal attitudes among people spread over a vast area and to keep them focused on a remote ruler who was scarcely ever seen was a problem which a great territorial empire had to solve ... The loyalty of the inhabitants of the Roman Empire was recreated by the ceremonies taken from religion: festivals, processions, temples, statues, altars, sacrifices, even very occasionally mysteries, focused men's attention on their remote sovereign as in their original context they had focused it on the remote gods.[62]

Julius Caesar's self-conscious designs on transforming his role into that of a divine king were based on the Hellenistic conceptions of divine kingship which increasingly pervaded Rome during the later Republic and even influenced the late Republican conception of the earlier Roman kingship.[63] The posthumous deification of Julius Caesar in 42 BCE in a bill sponsored by the Triumvirs and passed by the Senate began a long tradition of post-mortem deification, or apotheosis, ritualized in the rite of *consecratio*.[64] The antithesis of *consecratio* (i. e., *damnatio memoriae*) was always possible, since *consecration* must always be ratified or enacted by a *senatus consultum* (n. b. that the *consecratio* of Julius

---

[58] Albert Wifstrand, "Autokrator, Kaisar, Basileus," *DRAGMA* (Lund: C. Gleerup, 1939) 529–39.

[59] J. H. W. G. Liebeschuetz, *Continuity and Change in Roman Religion* (Oxford: The Clarendon Press, 1979) 74.

[60] Liebeschuetz, *Continuity and Change*, 75.

[61] Hopkins, "Divine Emperors," 197–242.

[62] Liebeschuetz, *Continuity and Change*, 77.

[63] Taylor, *The Divinity of the Roman Emperor*, 58–77; on p. 76, Ms. Taylor observes: "There can be no doubt of Caesar's own interest in the recognition of his divinity." This view has not been universally accepted, though recently it has been persuasively argued in a massive discussion of the evidence by Weinstock, *Divus Julius*.

[64] MacCormack, *Art and Ceremony*, 93–158.

Caesar occurred two years after his death). The effect of the new status of *divus Iulius* was the legitimation of Octavian as *divi filius,* i.e., son of the divine Julius. It must be remembered that prior to the *consecratio* of Julius Caesar, the terms *deus* and *divus* were virtually synonymous.[65] After 42 BCE, *divus* came to be used exclusively of a god who has once been a mortal. The divinity of his adopted father was so important to Octavian that the weapons he used in fighting the Perusian war were inscribed with the name *Divum Iulium,* a datum which calls to mind the inscription "King of kings and Lord of lords" on the thigh (where the sword hangs) of the rider in Rev 19:16. Though Liebeschuetz claims that Roman emperors were "not thought to be divine in the same sense as Jupiter,"[66] they certainly appear to have come very close. The traditional epithets of Capitoline Jupiter, i.e., Optimus Maximus (Best and Greatest), are attributed by Pliny the Younger to Trajan.[67] From 103 CE on, Trajan was designated *Optimus* on coins. Caligula too was called Jupiter, or pretended to be Jupiter.[68] Suetonius related that Gaius assumed the designation *optimus maximus Caesar* (*Cal.* 22. 1), and it appears that he was greeted as *Jupiter Latiaris* (Suetonius *Cal.* 22. 2; Dio Cassius 59. 28. 5). These pieces of evidence suggest that the antithetical claims of Caesar and Christ did not first appear during the late first century during the reign of Domitian, but characterized the imperial cult from its inception under Augustus.

VII.

In this paper I have adduced a number of arguments and demonstrations which strongly suggest that John's depiction of the ceremonial in the heavenly throne room has been significantly influenced in its conceptualization by popular images of Roman imperial court ceremonial. For the most part, the individual constituents of that ceremonial used by John in his depiction of the heavenly ceremonial have been heightened, expanded and given even greater cosmic significance. The result is that the sovereignty of God and the lamb have been elevated so far above all pretensions and claims of earthly rulers that the latter, upon comparison, become only pale, even diabolical imitations of the transcendent majesty of the King of kings and Lord of lords. The limitations of this paper prevent me from expanding upon the thesis presented in but a preliminary way here.[69] I have had no intention of denying or in any way minimizing the

[65] Weinstock, *Divus Julius*, 391.

[66] Liebeschuetz, *Continuity and Change*, 75.

[67] Pliny *Pan.* 88. 8–9; cf. 2. 7; 88. 4, 7; *Ep.* 2. 13. 8; 3. 13. 1.

[68] Dio Cassius 59.26.5, 8; 28.8; 30.1.

[69] I will present a detailed and enlarged defense of the thesis presented in this paper in a commentary on the Apocalypse currently in preparation.

influences which the Israelite-Jewish Biblical and post-Biblical traditions have exerted upon the Apocalyptist. I have sought to suggest indirectly, however, that John's thought world is sufficiently syncretistic that its complexities cannot be understood apart from a consideration of the traditions of the Graeco-Roman world of which he and his communities were part. If the proposals presented in this paper prove persuasive, the widespread view that the heavenly liturgy depicted in the Apocalypse is a reflection, or projection, of the earthly liturgy of the Christian churches of western Asia Minor will have to be radically revised, or, even better, abandoned.

An Intertextual Reading of the Apocalypse of John

1. Intertextuality as a Critical Method

Intertextuality plays a central role in both the production and reception of texts, so that critics can focus on either the author who constructed the text or the reader who reconstructs the text, or both. Intertextuality is a way of reading a text that sees it as a network of references to other texts, a phenomenon which may be approached at the levels of the word, the phrase and the sentence, but which becomes particularly evident in terms of larger textual units within a composition which have parallels or analogues in the constituent literary units of other texts. In the initial sequential reading of a text, connections with other textual units known to the reader are forged, which may upon the completion of the reading task lead the reader to an association with analogous self-contained literary texts, i. e., to a conception of the genre to which a given text belongs.

From the standpoint of intertextuality, a particular text only exists as part of a larger literary tradition, or "canon" (culture itself can be considered an intertext). A given text is part of a web of relationships with earlier texts which must be known in order to fully understand the focal text, at least from the perspective of the author who constructed it and the readers who reconstruct it. Texts are necessarily written and read in light of the familiarity which both authors and readers have of earlier texts. The writers of texts use a variety of strategies as they write in the light of a circle of texts which they consider significant. Intertextuality is not as concerned with identifying the sources of a document as it is with understanding the impact and function of both earlier and contemporary texts in a given text. In fact, texts take on distinctive features when they intentionally deviate from their precursors, and this may suggest the particular function of a textual unit.

Normally intertextuality centers on the modern reader (i. e., the literary critic as reader), and the intertext out of which the text is read and understood is the one known to that reader. An intertextual reading is not usually limited to the intertext of the author or to that of the original readers. In this paper, however, I will focus on the intertextual reconstruction of the Apocalypse of John by a hypothetical original circle of readers. While the intertext of the modern critical reader is (at least theoretically) completely accessible to that reader, any attempt to reconstruct the intertext of the original readers can only be partially and imperfectly realized. While no two early Christian readers would have understood the Apocalypse in precisely the same way (since their knowledge of precursor texts would necessarily have been different), it seems likely that particular congregations of readers would have a relatively homologous understanding of the Apocalypse because of their shared knowledge of antecedent texts. The modern critic, on the other hand, can never become fully aware of the range of ancient responses to the Apocalypse for the simple reason that many (perhaps even most) of the precursor texts which the ancient reader would have assumed have been lost and are consequently unknown to us. Though some might regard our focus on the reader of the late first and early second century CE as inappropriate, in my view it is a completely legitimate enterprise which does not, however, invalidate other approaches to the response of readers to this particular text. Indeed, there can be no privileged approach to the reading and understanding of written texts. In the present context it is not possible to provide a detailed analysis of all of the intertexts which might have shaped the responses of an ancient reader to the Apocalypse of John. In what follows, however, I will provide a sequential survey of the various textual units which comprise the Apocalypse, and make suggestions regarding the particular precursor texts which might very well have guided readers during the late first and early second centuries CE.

2. Aspects of the Literary Character of the Apocalypse

The Participant Transmitter

The textual history of most early Jewish and early Christian apocalypses suggests that the popular conception of the task of the ancient "copyist" as a faithful transcriber and transmitter of a stable sacred text is largely an imaginary construction. For many early Jewish and early Christian scribes, the task of recopying a text provided the opportunity (perhaps even the obligation) to rewrite that text.[1] In many instances it is even likely that the primary motivation for recopying a text was based on the desire to *rewrite* that text, since scribes often appear to have had agendas of their own.[2] In such instances the reader's response was transmuted (or transmogrified) into the literal recreation of the text, suggesting that the modern distinction between author and reader may

[1] For a discussion of the same phenomenon in the history of Gospel manuscripts, see David C. Parker, *The Living Text of the Gospels* (Cambridge: Cambridge University Press, 1997). For a more recent discussion of the creative role of scribes, see Kim Haines-Eitzen, *Guardians of Letters: Literacy, Power, and the Transmitters of Early Christian Literature* (Oxford and New York: Oxford University Press, 2000).

[2] For examples of theological motivations exhibited by scribes, see Bart D. Ehrman, *The Orthodox Corruption of Scripture: The Effect of Early Christological Controversies on the Text of the New Testament* (New York and Oxford: Oxford University Press, 1993).

not apply in a straightforward way to certain types of ancient compositions including apocalypses. Unlike many other early Christian apocalypses, all the manuscripts of the Apocalypse of John appear to derive from one exemplar. The eventual canonical status of the Apocalypse may be the major reason why earlier versions have not survived. Source criticism (see below) can provide a way of reconstructing how the author and his predecessors responded to the texts and partial-texts which he (and they) revised.

Source Critical Issues

During the last two centuries, many source critical theories of the origin of the Apocalypse have been generated by scholars struck by the many aporias, doublets, pleonastic phrases, glosses and grammatical peculiarities which permeate the text. While a holistic literary approach to the Apocalypse may choose to bracket out these problematic features (or even attempt to explain such textual phenomena in a way that makes an appeal to the hypothetical sources and redactional techniques of the author unnecessary), sooner or later these features of the Apocalypse must be dealt with. The Apocalypse is far from a finished, unified composition, and it is my view that only a careful source critical analysis can explain the many peculiarities of the text.[3]

Types of Intertexts, Real or Imagined

The following three types of intertexts certainly do not exhaust the literary precursors within which the Apocalypse of John could be read, but they are among the more significant.

1. Old Testament Allusions. From the perspective of the ancient reader, the Apocalypse signaled its relationship to various precursor texts in a variety of ways. One way was certainly the allusions to the OT which permeate the composition. The most recent edition of the Nestle-Aland Greek text uses its margins to suggest that there are 734 quotations or allusions to the OT in the Apocalypse, though this number is somewhat excessive. Another, more complex way in which the OT functions as the intertext of the Apocalypse is in the replication of structures found in various OT compositions.

2. The Anaphoric Definite Article. One very particular way in which the author reflects an intertext within which he wrote (whether written or oral) is betrayed by his use of the anaphoric definite article. Part of the style of apocalyptic literature is the use of already familiar persons and things drawn from stock apocalyptic imagery which are introduced the first time with the definite

---

[3] I have proposed such an analysis in David E. Aune, *Revelation 1–5* (WBC 52; Dallas: Word Books, 1997) cv–cxxxiv.

article.[4] Each of the following seventeen nouns occurs with the definite article upon its first occurrence, apparently because the author assumes that the readers are already familiar with the reality which the substantive represents: (1) οἱ ἑπτὰ ἄγγελοι οἳ ἐνώπιον τοῦ θεοῦ ἑστήκασιν, "the seven angels who stand before God" (8:2, 6, 8, 10, 12, 13; 9:1, 13, 14). (2) οἱ τέσσαρες ἄγγελοι οἱ δεδεμένοι ἐπὶ τῷ ποταμῷ τῷ μεγάλῳ Εὐφράτῃ, "the four angels who are bound at the great river Euphrates" (9:14). (3) ὁ αἐτός, "the eagle" (12:14). (4) αἱ ἑπτὰ βρονταί, "the seven thunders" (10:3). (5) ἡ γυνή, "the wife [of the Lamb]" (19:7; 21:9). (6) ἡ εἰρήνη τῆς γῆς, "the peace of the earth" (6:4). (7) τὸ θηρίον, "the Animal" (11:7). (8) ἡ ἶρις, "the rainbow" (10:1). (9) ἡ κιβωτὸς τῆς διαθήκης, "the ark of the covenant" (11:19). (10) οἱ δύο μάρτυρές μου, "my two witnesses" (11:3). (11) ἡ πλατεῖα τῆς πόλεως τῆς μεγάλης, "the street of the great city" (11:8). (12) τὰ ἑπτὰ πνεύματα, "the seven spirits" (1:4; 3:1; 4:5; 5:6). (13) ὁ πόλεμος, "the war" (16:14). (14) ἡ πορνή, "the whore" (17:1, 15, 16; 19:2). (15) τὸ τέκνον, "the child" (12:4). (16) ὁ υἱὸς τοῦ θεοῦ, "the son of God" (2:18). (17) τὸ φρέαρ τῆς ἀβύσσου, "the shaft of the abyss" (9:1).

3. Constituent Literary Forms. A third type of intertext consists of the constituent literary units within a composition which the reader has encountered in other texts. This analysis focuses on the sequential identification of what initially appear to be coherent units of text containing codes which trigger in the reader a particular set of intertextual associations. When a different set of associations are triggered, it is apparent that a new unit of text with a different set of codes is before the reader. Discrete units of text are usually introduced with recognizable formulas which prepare the reader to look for new associations. The intertext within which each unit of text is read suggests both similarities and differences to the reader. However, while these units might initially appear to be relatively independent, the process of reading and association quickly makes connections between contiguous textual units (by virtue of their sequential proximity, the repetition of formulaic phrases encountered earlier, and by virtue of verbal and thematic associations which the reader discovers during process of reading and rereading, or hearing and rehearing). It is precisely the retrospective association of what initially appeared to be discrete textual units which brings readers to associate this text, more or less in its entirety, with other discrete texts in their experience. Further, it is important to consider a dimension of reading often neglected, i. e., interactive reading or reading aloud as a social experience in which the verbal and behavioral responses of the audience constitute signals productive

[4] Josef Schmid, *Studien zur Geschichte des griechischen Apokalypse-Textes* (Munchen: Karl Zink Verlag, 1955) II, 194–5; G. Mussies, *The Morphology of Koine Greek as Used in the Apocalypse of St. John: A Study in Bilingualism* (NovTSup 27; Leiden: E.J. Brill, 1971) 187–8.

of a more homogeneous experience than one might otherwise expect in readers who belong to a social network, but who read the text in isolation from others.[5]

3. Intertextual Analysis of the Apocalypse

In this section of the paper it is my intention to discuss twenty-one major textual units within Rev 1–22 for the purpose of suggesting the various associations which the original circle of readers might have had with each discrete literary form.[6] This level of generic intertext is particularly important for analyzing a composition such as the Apocalypse of John precisely because of the conventional, episodic, highly stylized and formulaic character of Jewish and Christian apocalypses generally.

1. Rev 1:1–3. Ancient expectations regarding the function of the opening sentence of Rev are revealed in Epiphanius *Pan.* 1.1.1:[7]

> The authors of old used to give hints of the subject they were to treat in the prefaces or remarks which they composed as a sort of title. Hence we too shall use this style in writing our preface for you, beloved brothers, and we shall briefly summarize the essential matter of [our work composed?] against the sects.

This suggests the obvious, namely, that Rev 1:1–3 functions as a title, and conforms to the ancient tendency to describe the essential contents of a literary work. In content, however, this text clearly suggests that the composition it introduces is a particular type of literary text, namely one which mediates divine revelation. Revelatory literature is a broad category of texts clearly identifiable by both form and content.[8] Similar titles or introductory sentences occur in both prophetic and apocalyptic works (Jer 1:1–2; Ezek 1:1–3; Amos 1:1; *1 Enoch* 1:1; 93:1–3; *3 Apoc. Bar. praef* 1–2). When the author claims that the revelation of Jesus Christ was made known to him by an *angel* that would have suggested immediately the stock apocalyptic figure of the *angelus interpres*, though no such figure actually appears until 17:1–18 and 21:9–22:11 (the conclusion of this section is difficult to specify). The content of the revelation, "what must soon take place" (v. 1), underlines the imminence of the revealed events, and the fact that "the time is near" (v. 3) indicates that eschatological events are in view. By

[5] Cf. Linda Dégh and Andrew Vázsony, "Legend and Belief," *Folklore Genres,* ed. Dan Ben-Amos (Austin and London: University of Texas Press, 1976) 100–103 in which the interaction of those who narrate legends and their audience is considered an essential feature of the legend genre.

[6] The seven proclamations of Rev 2–3 are considered subunits within a single major unit of text.

[7] Philip R. Amidon (trans. and ed.), *The Panarion of St. Epiphanius, Bishop of Salamis: Selected Passages* (New York: Oxford University Press, 1990) 5.

[8] David E. Aune, *The New Testament in its Literary Environment* (Philadelphia: Westminster, 1987) 231–38.

describing his composition as "prophetic words" (cf. 22:7, 10, 18, where the parallel phrase "prophetic book" occurs), the author was undoubtedly encouraging the reader to associate this work with earlier prophetic books in the Israelite and early Jewish tradition. The concluding emphasis on obeying the message of the book (v. 3) emphasizes the paraenetic function of the work that is certainly more characteristic of prophecy than of apocalyptic. Since the present version of the Apocalypse is characterized as "prophetic words" or "prophetic oracles" which must be obeyed (1:3), and yet that were revealed by an *angelus interpres* (1:1), the original readers would readily have associated the title as a combination of prophetic and apocalyptic features.

2. Rev 1:4–5a is an epistolary prescript which is abruptly introduced, since such prescripts *never* follow titles. The fact that this one does would very probably have triggered *literary* associations, i. e., this particular letter is meant to be "published" in the sense of copied many times for distribution and circulation. Since this composition contains an epistolary prescript near the beginning, the ancient reader would have expected an epistolary closing formula at the end and would not have been disappointed (22:21). While it is certain that these epistolary formulas reflect a distinctive early Christian adaptation of liturgical formulas, it is not clear that this adaptation was (as many maintain) a Pauline innovation. Regardless of their origin, these epistolary formulas would connect the Apocalypse with the role and function of other early Christian letters, particularly the Pauline letters. In the salutation in v. 4, the author does not simply identify the source of grace and peace as God, but rather as "the one who is and who was and who is coming," a formula that modifies the widespread "Dreizeitenformel" used of God in the Hellenistic world by changing the timeless "who will be" to the eschatological "who is coming," i. e., "who will come." The jarring solecism ἀπὸ ὁ ὤν, "from the one who is," provides a foretaste of coming grammatical incongruities. Despite the fact that the Apocalypse is framed with epistolary conventions, the entire text does not appear to have been affected by epistolary features.[9]

Excursus: Ugo Vanni connects the units of text in Rev 1:4–8 in a very different way. He has suggested that Rev 1:4–8 reflects a "liturgical dialogue," and that recognition of this fact solves the problem of the apparent lack of unity in this section.[10] He points to several

[9] Contrary to the view of Martin Karrer, *Die Johannesoffenbarunq als Brief* (Göttingen: Vandenhoeck & Ruprecht, 1986).

[10] Ugo Vanni, "Un esempio di dialogo liturgico in Ap 1:4–8." *Bib* 57 (1976) 453–467; *idem*, *L'Apocalisse: Ermeneutica, exegesi, teologia* (Bologna: Edizione Dihoniana, 1988) 101–113. The schema which Vanni finds is the following ("Dialogo Liturgico," 460 f.; *L'Apocalisse*, 107 f.):

Lector (ὁ ἀναγινώσκων):
4b Grace to you and peace
from him who is and who was and who is to come,
and from the seven spirits who are before his throne,

features which suggest the presence of such a dialogue: (1) Rev 1:3 has revealed the existence of a reader or lector and a group of listeners, the assembly. (2) The two amens (vv. 6, 7) lend a liturgical flavor to the passage. (3) An abrupt change of person occurs in the passage between 1:4–5a (χάρις ὑμῖν, "grace to you," a second-person plural pronoun), and 1:5b–6 (τῷ ἀγαπῶντι ἡμᾶς καὶ λύσαντι ἡμᾶς ... καὶ ἐποίησεν ἡμᾶς, "to the one who loved *us*, and washed *us* ... and made *us*," three first-person plural pronouns). Attractive though this proposal is, it is highly speculative since there are no analogous liturgical dialogues in existence in early Christianity which might prove the actual existence of such a liturgical genre.]

3. Rev 1:5b–6 is a doxology which is liturgically sonorous yet appropriate following an epistolary prescript, since Gal 1:1–5 exhibits a close parallel. Doxologies are frequently used to conclude early Jewish and early Christian religious compositions (3 Macc 7:23; 4 Macc 18:24; Tob 14:15; *1 Clem* 64:2; *2 Clem* 20:5) or to conclude a constituent unit of text, particularly in letters (Rom 11:36; 1 Tim 1:17; 1 Pet 4:11; *1 Clem* 20:12; 32:4; 38:4). The inclusion of this doxology would probably have increased the liturgical expectations of the reader, a fact which gives some weight to Vanni's suggestions.

4. Rev 1:7–8 contains what appear to be two prophetic oracles (the first ends with a climactic ναί, ἀμήν). The first (v. 7) is a third-person prediction of the coming of Jesus Christ using the words of Dan 7:13 and Zech 12:10b. The second (v. 8) is a brief first-person speech of the Lord God in which he uses the "I am" formula to claim that he is the Alpha and the Omega, and to reiterate the revised "Dreizeitenformel" (v. 4), perhaps to authenticate the ultimate source of the revelation that John is transmitting. Both of these oracles reinforce the propriety of the phrase "words of prophecy" which the author used to characterize his work, though the first appears to be predominantly apocalyptic (focusing as it does on

---

5 and from Jesus Christ the faithful witness, the firstborn from the dead, and the ruler of kings on earth.

Assembly (οἱ ἀκούοντες):
To him who loves us
and has freed us by his blood
6 and made us a kingdom, priests to his God and Father,
to him be glory and dominion for ever and ever. Amen.

Lector:
7 Behold, he is coming with the clouds
and every eye will see him,
every one who pierced him;
and all tribes of the earth will wail on account of him.

Assembly:
Even so. Amen.

Lector:
8 I am the Alpha and the Omega
– says the Lord God –
who is and who was and who is to come,
the Almighty.

the parousia), while the second has predominantly prophetic associations (i. e., in divine self-predications in Isaiah).

5. Rev 1:9–20 is a relatively short first-person singular narrative of a vision of the exalted Christ in which John receives a command to write what he sees in a book and send it to the seven Christian congregations. This narrative style is maintained throughout the rest of the work, and is generally characteristic of apocalyptic or prophetic vision or dream reports, an important factor contributing to their authenticity. Yet it has often been noted that while Jewish and Christian apocalypses are pseudonymous, the Apocalypse of John is apparently not. While there is no reason to suspect that John was aware of the pseudonymous character of all earlier apocalypses, he would have been cognizant of the fact that among the putative authors of apocalypses, none wrote later than Ezra. John's self-consciously autobiographical style, therefore, may be linked to prophetic books. The command to "write what you see" is given twice (and expressed in two different ways: v. 11: ὃ βλέπεις γράψον; v. 19: γράψον οὖν ἃ εἶδες), and then reiterated through the repetition of the aorist imperative γράψον in the introduction to each of the seven proclamations. Similar commands to write also occur in 14:13; 19:9 and 21:5. Two major aspects of this epiphany may well have impressed the readers: (1) it identifies the exalted Jesus with the Ancient of Days through allusions to Dan 7:9–14 and 10:5–9,[11] and (2) it provides divine legitimation for the composition of the Apocalypse through the reiterated command to write down the visions which John is about to see. Commands issued by God or angels to write down a revelatory message occasionally occur in the OT and early Jewish texts (Isa 30:8; Exod 34:27–28; Deut 31:19, 21; *Jub.* 1:5–7; cf. Tob 12:20; *4 Ezra* 14), though they are much more frequent in Greco-Roman texts (Plato *Phaedo* 4.60e–61b; Callimachus *Aetia* 1.1.21–22; Propertius 3.3; Cicero *Academica priora* 2.16.51; Pausanias 1.21.2; Pliny *Ep.* 3.5.4; Aelius Aristides *Or.* 48.2; Dio Cassius 73.23.2). The author's autobiographical style (1:9) is characteristic of prophetic self-consciousness, while the command to write is a more general phenomenon characteristic of ancient revelatory literature. Rev 1:9–20 is not an inaugural call (comparable to the call narratives in Isa 6, Jer 1 or Ezek 1–3), for John is not called to a new vocation but rather commissioned for a particular task.

6. Rev 2:1–3:22. By the time the reader has finished the vision of commission narrated in 1:9–20, there is no reason to expect that the exalted Christ will dictate seven individual messages to each of the seven congregations. This section

[11] This identification of the human figure with the Ancient of Days in Dan 7:13 was already assumed in Mss. 88 and 687, the only two extant LXX manuscripts of Daniel. Cf. the reading of Dan 7:13 in Ms. 967 (A. Giessen, *Der Septuaginta-Text des Buches Daniel,* 108): ηρχετο ως υιος ανθρωπου και ως παλαιος ημερω(ν) παρην και οι παρεστηκοτες προσηγαγον αυτω ("he came like a son of man and like the Ancient of Days was present, and those who were near approached him").

consists of seven units of text, often incorrectly styled "letters" which share an extraordinarily large number of stereotypical formulas. This literary device has no parallels in other apocalypses, and must therefore be regarded as one of the author's more innovative moves. In all probability, early Christian readers would have associated these seven closely related textual units with royal or imperial decrees which were preserved on stone in important urban centers throughout the Roman province of Asia, and which the author has freely adapted for use in the present context.[12] Since each of the seven "proclamations" (a more appropriate designation than "letters") is dictated by the exalted Jesus, who knows the intimate details of each of the seven Christian communities, these texts clearly fit the general rubric of revelatory literature, though there are no close parallels in other Jewish or Christian apocalypses. Since the language used by the exalted Jesus in these proclamations is in a subtly higher register than that of the rest of the Apocalypse, Jesus is presented as more eloquent than the author.[13] The reading and rereading of the entire text suggests that using the form of royal or imperial proclamations is in fact part of the author's strategy of contrasting God and Christ with the Roman emperor, who is but a diabolical imitation of the former. Further, these proclamations are permeated with paraenesis (2:4–6, 14–16, 20–22; 3:14, 15–19) and in that respect they have a strikingly prophetic character, for paraenesis is almost entirely lacking in apocalypses.[14]

7. Rev 4:1–6:17 (and 8:1) constitutes an extended throne vision narrative which begins with the heavenly ascent "in spirit" of the author, followed by a vision of the throne of God and the liturgy of angelic beings in the heavenly court. It is introduced somewhat abruptly, though the abruptness is mitigated by the continuity in trumpet-like voices (1:10; 4:1). Though the reader has been given no hint that such a visionary ascent is in the works, such ascents, coupled with visions of the heavenly throne room, are stock features of many apocalypses. According to a cosmology widespread in the Hellenistic world, the earth was

[12] David E. Aune, "The Form and Function of the Proclamations to the Seven Churches (Revelation 2–3)," *NTS* 36 (1990) 182–204. Reprinted below, pp. 212–32.

[13] The adversative particle ἀλλά occurs frequently in Hellenistic Greek literature, but just thirteen times in Rev, of which eight of those instances occur in Rev 2–3 (2:4, 6, 9 [2x], 14, 20; 3:4, 9). The common connective particle δέ also occurs three times Rev 2–3 (2:5. 16, 24), and just four times in the rest of Rev. These two stylistic features suggest that the author is providing the words of the exalted Christ with what he regarded as a dignified style; cf. J. A. L. Lee, "Some Features of the Speech of Jesus in Mark's Gospel," *NovT* 27 (1985)1–26. Also relevant is the fact that while 73.8% of the 337 sentences in Rev begin with καί, Rev 2–3 contains 44 sentences, just nine of which begin with καί, i. e., 20.5%. Not a single sentence begins with καί in the Proclamation to the Ephesians, and the other occurrences of καί occur only at the beginning of each proclamation (2:8, 12, 18; 3:1, 7, 14), with the exception of the Proclamation to Thyatira, where καί is used at the beginning of three of the eight sentences in the Proclamation (2:21, 23, 26).

[14] For a qualification of this generalization, see J. C. H. Lebram, "The Piety of Jewish Apocalyptists," *Apocalypticism in the Mediterranean World and the Near East,* ed. David Hellholm (Tübingen: Mohr Siebeck, 1983), 171–210.

the lowest part of the cosmos surrounded by seven planetary spheres; in the early Jewish version of this cosmology, God's throne was located in the seventh heaven. Surprisingly, this cosmology is absent from John's conception, which is apparently that of the older cosmology of a three-tiered universe consisting of heaven above, earth beneath, and the underworld below the earth (Rev 5:3, 13). Throne visions function in one of at least six different ways, i.e., (1) as *enthronement* scenes (Dan 7:13–14; *4 Ezra* 2:42–48; Ezekiel the Tragedian *Exagoge* 68–82; *Odes of Sol.* 36; cf. Rev 3:21, (2) as *judgment* scenes (Dan 7:9–12; *1 Enoch* 25:3; 45:3; 47:3–4; 62:1–6; *Apoc. Moses* 22:1–29:6; Matt 19:28–30 [and par. Luke 22:28–30]; 25:31–46; Rev 20:4–6; 20:11–15), (3) as *commission* scenes (1 Kgs 22:19–22; Job 1:6–12; 2:1–6; Isa 6:1–13; Ezek 1:4–3:11; *1 Enoch* 14:8–16:4; *Asc. Isa.* 10:1–16; cf. Rev 3:21), (4) as *eschatological heavenly festal gathering* scenes (Rev 7:9–12; Heb 12:22–24; *Odes of Sol.* 36), (5) as *the goal of Merkavah mysticism* (*3 Enoch* 1:6–12; 7:1; cf. *Sepher ha-Razim* 7 [ed. M. Morgan, 81–86]), and (6) as a *literary device* used for commenting on earthly events in the narrative, much like the chorus in Greek tragedy (1 Kgs 22:19–20; Job 1:6–12; 2:1–6; Rev 4:1–6:17; 11:15–18; 14:1–5; 19:1–8).

Since throne visions typically functioned in one of the six ways mentioned above, the readers might well wonder about the purpose of this particular throne vision. Rev 4:1–6:17 is a textual unit which presents the readers with three distinct subunits. (1) In 4:1–11 the author relates his vision of God enthroned and the angelic liturgy in the heavenly court room. One group of heavenly beings, the twenty-four elders, is found only in the Apocalypse; the quest for their identity has been the cause for much fruitless speculation. The four cherubim, or "living creatures," however, are familiar from many parts of the OT, where they often function as the divine throne, though John's description of the cherubim differs significantly from how they are depicted in the OT. In Ezekiel's initial vision (Ezek 1:4–28), the four cherubim figure significantly, and the competent reader would have been aware of this text. While in Ezekiel each of the four cherubim has four faces, the cherubim of the Apocalypse are each unique: one looks like a lion, one like an ox, one with a human face, and one like a flying eagle (4:7). While the cherubim of Ezekiel and the Apocalypse are "covered with eyes" (symbolizing divine omniscience), the cherubim in Ezekiel are each associated with a wheel, together constituting the four-wheeled divine throne-chariot (Ezek 1:15–21). The narrative pace is leisurely and serves to slow down and even delay the narrative. There is a degree of suspense in this narrative, for the function of the throne vision has not yet become clear. (2) In 5:1–14 a short drama is enacted in which the slain Lamb, first paradoxically identified as the lion of the tribe of Judah (v. 5), is found worthy to open the scroll. The figure of the Lamb is not found in any other Jewish or Christian apocalypse, and constitutes an innovation on the part of the author. The first of twenty-nine occurrences of ἀρνίον in 5:6 is anarthrous, suggesting that the author assumed that this figure was unfamiliar to the readers. In 5:6–14, the author gradually focuses on the Lamb, and carefully builds up the suspense to the point where the scroll actually begins to be unsealed. The reader remains in suspense, for the function of the throne scene has not yet become clear. (3) In 6:1–17, when the seals are opened, it becomes obvious that this throne vision constitutes an unusual form of judgment scene. The four horsemen bring waves of slaughter upon the people of the earth, though no basis for these punishments has yet been given (motivations for behavior are often missing from apocalypses; here the apocalyptic framework permits the reader to assume that those who dwell on the earth are irredeemably wicked). Finally in vv. 9–11, an implied motive for the preceding judgments appears to have been divine revenge for the slaughter of Christians. After the opening of the sixth seal (6:12–17), the reader is left hanging, since only six of the seven seals have been opened, while an entirely different scene begins in 7:1 (the readers' expectation that the seventh seal will be opened is of course eventually fulfilled in a rather strange, anticlimactic way in 8:1).

8. Rev 7:1–17 is introduced abruptly because the reader expects the opening of the seventh seal, which is postponed until 8:1. Rev 7:1–17 consists of two distinct, but related,[15] textual units, 7:1–8 and 7:9–17. The first unit, Rev 7:1–8, consists of three subunits of text. (1) The first is an *angelic epiphany*, a form which occurs three more times in Rev (8:2; 15:1; 20:1–3), and each time exhibits a similar structure: (a) Introductory phrase: καὶ εἶδον. (b) Object of vision: ἄγγελον or ἀγγέλους. (c) Brief description of the action of the angel(s). (d) Followed by an abrupt change of subject. The author presents these brief angelic epiphanies as an outside observer; the angel(s) he sees and whose action he describes neither interact with him nor he with them. This is a peculiar form with few if any parallels in Jewish or Christian apocalyptic literature, though they seem appropriate in the context of a vision report. (2) Rev 7:2–3 contains an *angelic speech*. This form occurs eight more times in Rev (10:1–7; 14:6–7; 14:8; 14:9–11; 14:14–16; 14:18–20; 18:1–3; 19:17–18), and again has few parallels in Jewish and Christian apocalyptic literature. The *angelic speech* in Rev exhibits the following structural features: (a) Introductory phrase: καὶ εἶδον. (b) Object of vision: ἄλλον ἄγγελον. (c) The angel moves (ascends, descends, flies, emerges) to the center of the action. (d) The angel "cries with a loud voice." (e) The angel utters a brief statement on divine authority which must be understood as divine commentary on events in the eschatological drama. (3) Finally, the roster of the 144,000 who are sealed is given in 7:4–8 (though the sealing scene itself is omitted between vv. 3 and 4), which somewhat surprisingly consists of a list of twelve Israelite tribes, from each of which 12,000 are selected for this magical ritual of divine protection. Whether the readers understand the 144,000 to be

[15] A similar two-part structure occurs in *1 Enoch* 39:6–40:10.

Christians of pagan and/or Jewish origin, the list of tribes serve to underscore the continuity between Judaism and Christianity.

Rev 7:9–17 is yet another throne vision, in this instance one which functions as an eschatological heavenly festal gathering scene (Rev 14:1–5; Heb 12:22–24;[16] *4 Ezra* 2:42–45; 13:5–50; *Odes of Sol.* 36). This type of throne vision dramatizes the final gathering before the heavenly throne of God of all the righteous in the company of the angelic beings engaged in the celebration of the victory and majesty of God. The constituent motifs in Heb 12:22–24 indicate the typical elements found in this scene: (1) Mount Zion, the heavenly Jerusalem (the setting), (2) an innumerable angelic host in festal gathering, (3) the assembly of the first-born, (4) God the judge of all, (5) the assembly of righteous people, apparently distinct from "the assembly of first-born," (6) Jesus, and (7) the sprinkled blood (implying the figurative presence of the ark).

9. Rev 8:2–9:21 centers on a series of seven plagues which are inflicted on the earth and its inhabitants, unleashed by the blowing of seven trumpets. The strikingly anticlimactic opening of the seventh seal in 8:1 is followed by two short angelic epiphanies, the first consisting of the brief introduction of the seven trumpet angels (v. 2), and the second consisting of a brief scene involving an angel at the heavenly altar who casts fire down upon the earth (vv. 3–5). This serves to emphasize the point (like the throne vision in 4:1–6:17) that divine retribution originates in heaven, i. e., with God. As in the case of the seven seals, there is an interruption (10:1–11:14) before the blowing of the seventh trumpet (11:15–18). There is a widespread tendency, which is essentially correct, to understand the seven trumpet plagues (and the seven bowl plagues in 16:1–21), as an eschatological counterpart to the ten plagues inflicted by Moses upon the Egyptians. Though the particular schema found in Rev 8:2–9:21 (with 11:15–18) has no counterpart in other Jewish or Christian apocalypses (and so must be considered an innovation by the author), the constituent features are all thoroughly at home in Jewish apocalypticism. First, there is the tendency to conceive of the end of the world as a time when God will punish the unrighteous inhabitants of the world with plagues (ten are enumerated in *Apoc. Abr.* 30:3–8; *T. Dan* 5.8).[17] Second, there is (the admittedly rare) use of trumpet blasts as a structuring device for eschatological events (*Apoc. Zeph.* 9–12), though the trumpet did become a minor though staple feature of early Jewish and early Christian apocalyptic imagery (Isa 27:3; Zech 9:14; 1 Thess 4:16; 1 Cor 15:52; *Did* 16:6), often associated with eschatological judgment (Isa 58:1; Joel 2:2–3; Zeph 1:15–16; *4 Ezra* 6:23; *Sib. Or.* 4.174 f.; *Apoc. Mos.* 22:3; *Par. Jer.* 3:2; 4:1;

[16] In Heb 12:22–24 this type-scene is used metaphorically (cf. Heb 12:18: "you have not come to what may be touched"), a fact which suggests that it was widely familiar in early Jewish and early Christian circles.

[17] Though the Egyptian plagues were a recurring theme in early Jewish literature, they are rarely interpreted eschatologically.

Apoc. Zeph. 12:1; *Grk. Apoc. Ezra* 4:36). Third, there is the observable tendency to reduce the ten plagues of Exodus to seven (Ps 78:43–51; Ps 105:27–36; Amos 4:6–11; Artapanus [Eusebius *Praep. evang.* 9.27.1–37]; Wis 11:1–19:9; cf. *T. Benj.* 7:1–4; *m. Abot* 5.8). Nevertheless, though some of the trumpet plagues resemble some of the plagues of Exodus, the correlation is far from striking. This thoroughly apocalyptic section concludes on a prophetic note in 9:20–21, which seems to imply that the people punished could have repented, but chose not to do so.

10. Rev 10:1–11:2 is a unit of text consisting of three separate sections; the first two are linked only by virtue of the fact that a single angel and a voice from heaven figure prominently in both episodes. Since the author had already interrupted the opening of the seventh seal, it comes as no great surprise that he interrupts the blowing of the seventh trumpet with two major units of text, 10:1–11 and 11:1–14. It does come as a surprise, however, that in a passage which functions to delay the blowing of the seventh trumpet, the angelic revealer expressly swears that there will be no more delay (10:6). The first episode (10:1–7) looks like a cross between an *angelic epiphany* and an *angelic speech* (see above under Rev 7:1–8), though with one major difference: in both episodes John interacts with the heavenly voice, and in the second episode he interacts with the angelic revealer as well. The peculiarity of the content of this episode[18] suggests that it was composed entirely by the author for its present context and that he followed no obvious exemplars. At the end of the first episode the readers would very likely anticipate the blowing of the seventh trumpet, particularly since "there will be no more delay" (10:6b). The second episode (10:8–11) appears to have been consciously modeled after that part of the prophetic call of Ezekiel found in Ezek 2:8–3:3, and would be naturally understood as a prophetic commission by those familiar with that text. The fact that it functions as a prophetic commission is made clear in 10:11: "you must again prophecy about many peoples and nations and tongues and kings." This section therefore contributes to the perception of the author as a prophet in the tradition of the OT prophets.[19] The third episode occurs in 11:1–2 (though it is difficult to decide whether v. 2 or v. 3 concludes the section).[20] Rev 11:1–2 should be construed as a continuation of 10:8–11 (no typical Johannine formulas suggest a new unit of text), for John is given a measuring

---

[18] This section has all the features of an *angelic speech,* were it not for the fact that what the angel says is not recorded, and when John begins to write down the response of the seven thunders, he is explicitly commanded not to write down what they said.

[19] The author s prophetic role is also emphasized in Rev 22:16; cf. David E. Aune, "The Prophetic Circle of John of Patmos and the Exegesis of Revelation 22:16," *JSNT* 37 (1989) 103–116. Reprinted below, pp. 250–60.

[20] The problem is that there is a brief speech, apparently by God or Christ (cf. "*my* two witnesses" in v. 3a) in vv. 1b–3. What the voice says in v. 3, however, has no logical connection with what was said in vv. 1b–2, but seems to belong to vv. 4–13. It may well be that the author has intentionally created this dovetail joint to link vv. 1–2 to vv. 4–13.

rod and told what to measure and what not to measure; this is the language of commission, and is therefore appropriately placed after 10:8–11.

11. The abrupt appearance of Rev 11:3–13 is mitigated by the fact that in vv. 1b–3, the brief speech of God or Christ slides from one subject to another, from a command to measure the temple to a prediction that the two witnesses will prophecy for 1,260 days (from a source-critical perspective this is an obvious seam). The reader expects the delayed blowing of the seventh trumpet to occur momentarily, but this event continues to be delayed. Rev 11:3–13 exhibits a literary character quite different from anything which the reader has yet confronted in the Apocalypse. It is not presented as a vision (the author's characteristic "I saw" is conspicuous by its absence), but rather as a prophetic narrative, which appears to begin as a commentary on Zech 4:1–14, though that passage soon disappears from view. The quasi-visionary form of 11:3–13 is suggested by the clusters of verb tenses. There are thirty-six verbs in Rev 11:3–13. The author begins with three future tenses in v. 3, then shifts largely to the present tense in vv. 4–6 (eight verbs). He shifts back to the future in v. 7 (three verbs), then back largely to the present in vv. 8–10 (five verbs). The future tense (usually characteristic of predictions in apocalyptic literature) appears just once in v. 10, then twelve aorists are used in vv. 11–13. This phenomenon of a shifting from one group of tenses to another is characteristic of Johannine vision reports,[21] and while it may provide criteria for source critical analysis, an intertextual approach to this peculiar style suggests that the original readers would probably understand 11:3–13 as at least the functional equivalent of a vision. It appears to be the first of several scenarios borrowed from Jewish apocalyptic folklore (similar material occurs in close proximity in Rev 12 and 13). While several parallel texts suggest that John's readers were familiar with the story of the martyrdom of the two witnesses (note the occurrence of the anaphoric article used with the first occurrence of the phrase "my two witnesses" in 11:3),[22] a particularly close parallel is found in a text preserved in Lactantius *Div. Inst.* 7.17. The parallels

---

[21] G. Mussies, *The Morphology of Koine Greek as Used in the Apocalypse of John* (NovT-Sup 27; Leiden: E.J. Brill, 1971) 330–36, 340.

[22] Two such texts are found in *Apoc. Elijah* 4:7–17 and 14:9–15:7. The *Apoc. Elijah* is probably late (150 to 275 CE), and 4:7–19 may be dependent, at least in part, on Rev 11:3–13. However, *Apoc. Elijah* 14:9–15:7 is a doublet featuring the woman Tabitha and that appears to be independent of Rev 11:3–13 (P. Chester Beatty 2018; trans. Pietersma): "The young woman whose name is Tabitha will hear that the shameless one has made his appearance in the holy places. She will dress in her linen clothes and hurry to Judea and reprove him as far as Jerusalem, and say to him, 'O you shameless one, O you lawless one, O you enemy of all the saints!' Then the shameless one will become angry with the young woman. He will pursue her to the region of the setting of the sun. He will suck her blood in the evening and toss her onto the temple, and she will become salvation for the people. At dawn she will rise up alive and rebuke him saying, 'You shameless one, You have no power over my soul, nor over my body, because I live in the Lord always, and even my blood which you spilled on the temple became salvation for the people.'"

can be seen more clearly in a synoptic presentation in which the only change in order is the placement of Rev 11:6 before 11:5:[23]

Rev 11:3–12	*Lactantius 7.17.1-8*
v. 3 I will permit my two witnesses to prophecy	1 Now, when the end of these times is imminent, a great prophet will be sent by God to convert men to a recognition of God,
	and he will have the power of working miracles.
v. 6a They have power to shut up heaven that rain might not fall during the period when they prophesy.	2 Wherever men will not hear him, he will close heaven and will hold back the rains.
v. 6b They also have power over the waters, that is, to turn to blood.	he will change water into blood and will torture them with thirst and hunger.
v. 5 If anyone wants to harm them, fire proceeds from their mouths and utterly destroys their enemies.	2 and fire will proceed from his mouth and burn whoever will attempt to hurt him.
v. 7 When they finish their witness, the Beast who ascends from the abyss will wage war on them that he might conquer them and kill them.	3 This one will fight against the prophet of God; he will conquer and kill him
v. 9 but people would not permit their bodies to be buried	and suffer him to lie unburied.
v. 11 Now after three-and-a-half days a spirit of life from God entered into them so that they stood on their feet with the result that great fear fell on those who saw them.	But after the third day, he will rise again.
v. 12 They heard a loud voice from heaven saying to them: 'Come up here.' They ascended to heaven on a cloud while their enemies looked on.	and will be taken into heaven while all look on and marvel.

[23] Here is the entire passage in Lactantius *Div. Inst.* 7.17 (trans. M. F. McDonald, *Lactantius*, 517 f.): "Now, when the end of these times is imminent, a great prophet [*magnus propheta*] will be sent from God to convert men to recognition of God, and he will have the power of working miracles. Whenever men will not hear him, he will close heaven and will hold back the rains; he will change water into blood, and will torture them with thirst and hunger; and fire will proceed from his mouth and burn whoever will attempt to hurt him. By these prodigies and powers, he will convert many to the worship of God. When these works of his have been carried out, another king will rise from Syria, born of the evil spirit, the overthrower and destroyer of the human race, who will destroy the remains of that previous evil one together with itself. This one will fight against the prophet of God; he will conquer and kill him and suffer him to lie unburied. But after the third day, he will rise again and will be taken into heaven while all look on and marvel."

There are several reasons for supposing that Lactantius is dependent here on the Oracles of Hystaspes[24] or some otherwise unknown Jewish source and *not* on Rev 11:3–13, based on a comparison of these two texts. (1) A single prophet is found in Lactantius, compared with two prophets in Revelation (2) The result of closing the heavens and turning the waters into blood in Lactantius is to torment people with hunger and thirst, while this effect is absent from Revelation (3) The narrative in Rev is consistently told with verbs in past tenses, while that in Lactantius is told using future tenses. (4) The text in Revelation contains a number of explanatory glosses none of which appear in the account of Lactantius. (5) The narrative in Lactantius continues on to describe events similar to those in Rev 13:1–10 but lacks allusions to Rev 11:14–12:17. (6) Since Lactantius lived from ca. 250–325 it is not impossible that he may have been influenced by the text of Revelation, yet he does not elsewhere reflect a very profound knowledge of that work.[25]

Assuming, then, that Rev 11:3–13 was a particular eschatological scenario with which the readers were familiar, what might they have made of it? First, the prophetic role of the two witnesses is clear, and that prophetic role appropriately follows the prophetic commissions in 10:8–11 and 11:1–2. Second, like other eschatological scenarios from Jewish apocalyptic folklore, the participants in the melodramatic conflict are not named, so that the readers can only speculate on their identity. Indeed, the author appears to encourage such speculation.

12. In Rev 11:15–18 the seventh trumpet is finally blown. Presumably, it was in order to avoid the problem of relating Rev 11:19–12:17 to 11:3–13 (i.e., the chronological order in the eschatological scheme is thereby obscured) that the author has inserted the blowing of the seventh trumpet with its consequences. However, rather than introduce an expected seventh set of plagues, it rather signals the introduction of a brief (and relatively awkward) throne vision which

---

[24] The view of David Flusser, "Hystaspes and John of Patmos," *Irano-Judaica: Studies Relating to Jewish Contacts with Persian Culture Throughout the Ages* (ed. S. Shaked; Jerusalem, Ben Zvi Institute for the Study of Jewish Communities in the East, 1982) 12–75.

[25] Outside of *Div. Inst.* 7.17, Lactantius appears to reflect an awareness of Revelation when he speaks of the second resurrection after a thousand years (*Div. Inst.* 7.26.5–7; cf. Rev 20:11–13, though the term "second resurrection" does not occur in Revelation). A comparison between Lactantius *Epitome* 66.9 (a later work in which the *Divine Institutes* are presented in abbreviated form) reflects an alteration of what he had originally written in *Div. Inst.* 7.17.7 apparently made in light of Rev 13:16. Lactantius was thoroughly familiar with classical sources, and also with the Sibylline Oracles and Hermetic writings (R.M. Ogilvie, *The Library of Lactantius* [Oxford: Clarendon Press, 1978] 28–36), and even with early Christian extra-canonical literature (Ogilvie, 105–8), but less familiar with the Bible (Ogilvie, 96–110, where he concludes that the 73 Biblical quotations in *Div. Inst.* 4 are closely related to Cyprian's *Ad Quirinum,* though Lactantius cannot have drawn these quotations from the *Ad Quir.* in its present state). Outside of *Div. Inst.* 7 (with its 73 quotations of the Bible), the rest of *Div. Inst.* contains just 7 quotations (Ogilvie, 107 f.), and the other works of Lactantius contain no Biblical quotations at all (with the exception of the later *Epitome*).

begins as something John *hears* in heaven (vv. 15b–16), but soon turns into a throne vision which John apparently *sees,* complete with a thanksgiving hymn sung by the twenty-four elders (the other denizens of the heavenly court are, for the nonce, absent).

13. In Rev 11:19–12:17 the author inserts another eschatological scenario which centers on the conflict between the Woman and the Dragon. Because this section is immediately preceded by the episode involving the blowing of the seventh trumpet (11:14–18), the reader is somewhat insulated from the problem of the relationship between the story of the two witnesses (11:3–13) and the story of the Woman and the Dragon (11:19–12:17), both with regard to chronology and characters. There is no continuity in *dramatis personae*, who are for the most part not named (challenging the ingenuity of the readers). In 12:7–9, however, the combatants are specifically named Michael and the Devil or Satan. In the rest of the story, the identities of the Messiah, i. e., Christ (v. 3) and faithful Christians (v. 17b) are obvious. The author has apparently sandwiched two stories together by placing the narrative of Satan's defeat and expulsion from heaven, complete with commentary by the heavenly "chorus" (vv. 7–12) into the frame of the narrative of the Woman and the Dragon (vv. 1–6, 13–17). Adela Yarbro Collins and others before her have demonstrated the pre-Christian existence of the component elements of these combats in Greco-Roman and Jewish folklore. Important as this recognition is for the source criticism of the Apocalypse, it is also important for reconstructing the intertext within which the Apocalypse was read. Variants of two stories familiar to the readers, the Leto-Apollo-Python myth and the protological combat myth in which angels who remained faithful to God expelled rebel angels from heaven, have been linked in such a way as to demonstrate that pre-Christian myth contains basic truths about the Christian dispensation. Again, this complex scenario is not introduced or punctuated by the phrases typically used to introduce vision reports, such as "I saw," or "I saw, and behold" (the unusual introduction in v. 1, "A great sign appeared [ὤφθη] in heaven," is not simply a parallel expression, since in 15:1 the author begins a new segment with the phrase "And I saw another great and marvelous sign in heaven"). Further, the narrative style departs considerably from that of other vision reports in the Apocalypse. There are forty-five verbs in Rev 12, thirty-four are aorists (the basic narrative tense), two are perfects (N. B. the fusion of aorist and perfect indicatives in Hellenistic Greek), nine are presents; the future tense does not occur. Rev 12:1–17, therefore, would certainly not be understood as a vision report by the original readers.

14. Rev 13:1–18, in contrast to 11:3–13 and 11:19–12:17, is explicitly cast in the form of a vision report divided up into two major segments, one concerning the Beast from the Sea (vv. 1–10), and the other concerning the Beast from the Land (vv. 11–18). Since the Beast from the Sea has seven heads and ten horns (v. 1), the readers would immediately identify it with the great red Dragon of

12:3. But this first impression is not correct, since the Dragon is very quickly distinguished as both different from and superior to the Beast from the Sea (v. 2b). The seven heads and ten horns of the latter must rather be attributed to family resemblance. Despite the awkwardness of vv. 1–2 read as a continuation of 11:19–12:17, it is obvious that the original readers would have understood 13:1–18 precisely as a continuation of that story. Among the known protological and eschatological myths of Jewish apocalyptic there is no close parallel to Rev 13. The reader would probably be aware, however, that the author has selected some elements from the early Jewish Leviathan and Behemoth myths (*1 Enoch* 60:7–11, 24; *4 Ezra* 6:49–52; *2 Apoc. Bar.* 29:4; b.B. Bat. 74b–75a), and combined them with motifs from the eschatological antagonist myth. The eschatological Antagonist myth appears to have had two primary variants, one of which was based on the tradition of the godless tyrannical ruler (largely dependent on the depiction of Antiochus IV in Daniel), and the other of which was based on the figure of the false and seductive prophet. These traditions are presented separately in Rev 13:1–10 and 13:11–18 respectively, but blended (for example) in 2 Thess 2:3–12. In Christian apocalyptic, a presentation of the antics of the eschatological Antagonist was perhaps *de rigueur* (this figure is noteworthy by his absence in Rev 11:3–13, though he is present in parallel eschatological scenarios such as Lactantius *Div. Inst.* 7.17). The author's retention of *two* eschatological Antagonists very probably corresponds to his desire to encourage the reader to speculate about the particular identities of the *dramatis personae* in these traditional myths (this reaches a high point with the gematria puzzle in v. 18).

15. Rev 14:1–20. The composition and structure of Rev 14 is extraordinarily complex and consists of six self-contained units of text framed by one of the author's favorite introductory formulas which is frequently used to introduce a new subject in 14:1: "I saw and behold," and at the end by the phrase in 15:1: "Then I saw another sign" (referring back to 12:1, 3), which also indicates a new subject. The Six units of text include: (1) 14:1–5, (2) 14:6–11, (3) 14:12, (4) 14:13, (5) 14:14–20, each of which presents a unique set of problems (14:12 and 14:13 will not be discussed here). Rev 14:1–5 provides an effective contrast to the terrifying developments narrated in Rev 13. The reader would naturally link the 144,000 with the earlier mention of the same number of those sealed in Rev 7:4–8. The entire pericope is introduced with the formula "I saw, and behold" (v. 1), and is followed by three structural segments: (1) the earthly vision of the 144,000 in v. 1, (2) the audition of the New Song sung in heaven in vv. 2–3, which constitutes a brief throne vision, and (3) the interpretive explanation in vv. 4–5 which elaborates on the identity of the 144,000 using three οὗτοι clauses.

Rev 14:6–11 is a group of three angelic visions (vv. 6–7, 8, 9–11), all introduced with the phrase "then I saw" (v. 6), and concluded when the author inserts an explanatory statement in v. 12. Each of the angelic visions is introduced by the mention of a new angelic revealer, the second and third of which are specifically enumerated: "another angel" (v. 6), "another angel, a second one" (v. 8), and "another angel, a third one" (v. 9).

Rev 14:14–20 is introduced with one of the author's customary formulas for beginning a new subject, "I saw and behold" (v. 14), and concludes in v. 20, which is followed by an introductory phrase indicating the beginning of a major new section of the composition "I saw another sign" (15:1). Rev 14:14–20 consists of two units, the first in vv. 14–17, and the second in vv. 17–20, which are essentially doublets:

Rev 14:14–17		*Rev 14:17–20*	
v. 14	figure with sickle seated on cloud	v. 17	figure with sickle comes out of temple
v. 15a	another angel comes out of the temple	v. 18a	another angel comes out from the altar
v. 15b	calls with loud voice to first figure	v. 18b	calls with loud voice to first figure
v. 15c	"Put in your sickle" [πέμψον τὸ δρέπανόν σου]	v. 18c	"Put in your sickle" [πέμψον σου τὸ δρέπανον]
v. 15d	to harvest	v. 18d	to gather clusters
v. 15e	for harvest is ripe	v. 18e	for grapes are ripe
v. 16a	first figure used his sickle on the earth	v. 19a	first angel used his sickle on the earth
v. 16b	the earth was reaped	v.19b	vintage of earth gathered

The parallelism ceases with vv. 19c–20, where the imagery of the grape harvest is continued by mentioning the "great wine press of the wrath of God," into which the grapes are placed. The juxtaposition of the imagery of the grain harvest and the grape harvest as metaphors for divine judgment in vv. 14–20 is also found in Joel 3:13: "Put in the sickle, for the harvest is ripe. Go in, tread, for the wine press is full. The vats overflow, for their wickedness is great."[26]

16. Rev 15:1–16:21 is a unit of text in the form of a vision report which narrates the plagues unleashed by the seven bowl angels. It is important to observe that the first readers would hardly have anticipated another round of plagues, particularly after the result of the seventh trumpet (11:14–18), which signals heavenly rejoicing over the commencement of God s reign. This section begins with a title (15:1), and thereafter there are two subunits of text: (1) 15:2–8, a scene in the heavenly temple which narrates the commission of the seven bowl angels, and (2) 16:1–20, the plagues in the bowls are poured out upon the earth. These seven bowl plagues have rough parallels with the seven trumpet plagues,

26 Elsewhere the cutting of the grape clusters and/or the treading of the vintage is used alone as a metaphor for divine judgment (Isa 63:1–6; Jer 25:30–31), as is the metaphor of the grain harvest and/or the image of the threshing floor (Isa 17:4–5; Jer 51:33; Micah 4:13; Matt 3:12 [= Luke 3:17]; Matt 9:37–38 [= Luke 10:2; *Gosp. Thom.* 73]; Mark 4:29; cf. Gal 6:7–9).

to the extent that the earliest readers would very probably have understood them together.

17. Rev 17:1–18 is a very distinctive textual unit in the Apocalypse, though it is part of a larger section consisting of 17:1–19:10 (this become evident only when the careful reader has read 19:9–10 and has become aware that the mention of the angel in 17:1–18 is part of an *inclusio* framing 17:1–19:10 (see below). This realization will be reinforced in an even more forceful way when the competent reader comes to recognize the parallel structure which exists between 21:9–22:9 and 17:1–19:10. However, since the first reader would not be aware of this when reading 17:1–18, it is appropriate to discuss 17:1–19:10 in terms of its three constituent parts (17:1–18 and 18:1–19:10). As we begin reading 17:1–18 it is clear that it is an angelic revelation consisting of a vision (17:1–6) paired with an interpretation by the angelic guide (17:7–18). Even though the role of the *angelus interpres* has been accentuated in the title in 1:1 (and reappears at the end in 22:8, one of several clues linking the larger units of text), only in Rev 17 does this stock figure of apocalyptic literature appear in his stereotypical role (note that in 21:9–22:5, though John has an angelic guide, the guide offers no interpretation of what the author sees and hears). This particular vision report involves the transport of the visionary "in the spirit" to a remote location, a motif apparently based on the Elijah cycle which in turn influenced Ezekiel (cf. 1 Kgs 18:12; 2 Kgs 2:16; Ezek 3:14; 40:2; Rev 21:10; Hermas *Vis.* 1.1.3; 2.1.1). Another distinctive feature of this vision lies in the fact that it is a *tableau,* i. e., there is no movement in what John sees. It is very likely that the vision itself in vv. 3–6 is an *ekphrasis,* i. e., a description of a work of art. The work of art in question, probably a marble bas relief or series of bas reliefs, survives only on a series of bronze sestertii of Vespasian minted in 71 CE.[27] The reverse depicts the goddess Roma in military dress seated on the Seven Hills of Rome, with a parazonium in her left hand and her right foot touches the anthropomorphic figure of the river god Tiber. The readers, familiar with this marble bas relief and its numismatic counterpart as instruments of imperial propaganda, would have shared this inside allegorical joke with the author. While *ekphraseis* in the restricted sense of "descriptions [of a work of art]" are not typical of apocalypses, a description of a painting does occur in *Apoc. Abr.* 21:7–29:21, while Hermas *Vis.* 3 and *Sim.* 6 and 9 appear to reflect *ekphraseis* in dependence on the *Tabula* of Cebes. By the Second Sophistic (second cent. CE), there were two major ways in which *ekphraseis* were used in literature. One approach centers on the necessity of understanding and interpreting the work of art itself, while the other (with examples in Cebes and Lucian) stresses the hidden meanings conveyed by the work of art

[27] F. Castagnoli, "Note Numistiche," *Archeologia Classica* 5 (1953) 104–111; R. Beauvery, "L'Apocalypse au risque de la numismatique. Babylone, la grande Prostituée et le sixième roi Vespasien et la déese Rome," *RB* 90 (1983) 243–60.

which can usually be made clear through allegorical interpretation.[28] While the allegorical meaning of some *ekphraseis* is obvious, in others the meaning must be carefully explained. In Lucian's *Hercules* and Cebes' *Tabula,* the narrator is puzzled over the meaning of the work of art, not unlike the surprise and wonder expressed by John in v. 6b over what he has just seen in vv. 1–6a. Though Rev 17 is probably the result of a complex redactional process, in its present form it a represents a particular type of apocalyptic vision report, while in content it uses a contemporary piece of propagandistic Roman art as an allegorical vehicle for a forceful condemnation of Rome; the conventionality of the vision report is combined with the unconventionality of the *ekphrasis* at its core.

18. In the poetic parallelism of Rev 18:1–19:10, the prose style in the Apocalypse reaches its highest and most lyrical level. This textual unit consists of two parts, 18:1–24, centering on a proleptic vision of the fall of Babylon, followed by a scene-shift to a heavenly court scene in which the inhabitants rejoice over the destruction. The mention of the fall of Babylon evokes memories of the destruction of Jerusalem by the Babylonians on the Ninth of Ab in 586 BCE, a memory which survives in modern Jewish synagogue liturgy linked, as it is in the Apocalypse of John, with the fall of Jerusalem in 70 CE. For the author, however, "Babylon" is a symbol for the present world power, Rome, responsible for the fall of Jerusalem in 70 CE. In 18:1–24, the strophes are arranged to produce a particular effect on the readers. After announcing the fall of Babylon (vv. 1–3), events *preceding* that fall are narrated (vv. 4–7), after which events *subsequent* to the fall are described (vv. 8–21), first in future tenses in vv. 8–11 (seven future verbs), and then, following v. 18, exclusively in past tenses. Finally, the prophecy that Babylon will be destroyed is reiterated in v. 21. Three different types of poetic composition are connected in celebration of the fall of Babylon: (1) a ritual lament (vv. 1–3, 9–20; strikingly reminiscent of ritual laments over Tyre in Ezek 26:15–18 and 27:1–8, 26–36), interrupted by (2) a command to flee (vv. 4–8; cf. Jer 4:4–5; 6:1; 48:6–8; 50:8–10; 51:6–10; 51:45–48), and (3) a symbolic action and its interpretation: an angel casts a millstone into the sea, comparing it with the violence attending the overthrow of Babylon (vv. 21–24; cf. prophetic symbolic actions in 1 Kgs 22:11; 2 Kgs 13:14–19; Isa 7:10–12). The literary forms in this chapter are strikingly dependent on the writing prophets of the OT (the pervasive influence of Jeremiah is particularly prominent) rather than on early Jewish apocalyptic traditions. The author uses these biblical allusions to create a shared destiny of Israel and the followers of Jesus.

Rev 19:1–10 consists of three subunits (19:1–4, 5–8, 9–11), all of which are introduced with the auditory formula "After this, I heard." The first unit consists of an initial hymn or praise (introduces another scene from the heavenly throne

[28] Shadia Bartsch, *Decoding the Ancient Novel: The Reader and the Role of Description in Heliodorus and Achilles Tatius* (Princeton: Princeton University Press, 1989) 22–31.

room consisting of an initial hymn rejoicing over the destruction of Babylon-Rome (19:1b–3), followed by an affirmative response from the twenty-four elders and the four cherubim (19:4). The readers' emotional response to the exquisitely detailed description of the destruction of Babylon-Rome would naturally have been one of joy over the deserved misfortune of others, and this response is validated by the similar reaction of the denizens of the heavenly court. The second subunit of this section (19:5–8) is a call to praise (19:5), paired with a hymnic response (vv. 6–8), a hymnic continuation of the auditory throne scene which began in 19:1b–4. In this hymnic response, a puzzling bit of information is provided for the reader: "Let us rejoice and exult and give him the glory, for the marriage of the Lamb has come, and his bride has made herself ready" (19:7). This reference to "the marriage of the Lamb" has the anaphoric definite article before a phrase that has not occurred earlier in the book, an indication that the author is assuming that the expression is already known to the readers (whether it actually is or not). This phrase occurs just twice in the Apocalypse, here and in v. 9, and is not mentioned later. The phrase is amplified somewhat by the mention of the "bride" in v. 7, which is later picked up when the New Jerusalem is referred to under the metaphor of the bride in 21:2, 9 which is striking because it clearly suggests to the reader the metaphorical nature of the New Jerusalem itself.[29] The metaphors of Christ as the bridegroom and the people of God as the bride were relatively widespread in early Christianity. For example, the metaphor of the (Corinthian) church as a chaste virgin to Christ as husband occurs in 2 Cor 11:2. This metaphor is picked up again in Eph 5:25–32, where the archetype for the appropriate relationship between husbands and wives is the self-sacrificial love of Christ for the church. He cleanses her by his death and is thereby able to present her to himself at his return as a pure bride. The Synoptic tradition also seems to equate the figure of the bridegroom with Christ in a parabolic context (Mark 2:20; Matt 9:15b; Luke 5:35; cf. *Gos. Thom.* 104).

The third subunit consists of vv. 9–11 in which the author is commanded by an angel to write down a beatitude: "Blessed are those who are invited to the wedding banquet of the Lamb" (v. 9), thereby emphasizing the reference in the immediately preceding hymn to the marriage of the Lamb and the preparation of the bride for that event in v. 7. The new element here is the specific mention of the "banquet" (δεῖπνον) of the wedding of the Lamb, an emphasis found only here in the Apocalypse. This metaphor was readily comprehensible, however, as a variant of the widespread tradition of the Messianic banquet,[30] that is, the metaphor of an eschatological meal (a time of gladness and rejoicing) to which

---

[29] Robert H. Gundry, "The New Jerusalem: People as Place, not Place for People," *Novum Testamentum* 29 (1987) 254–64.

[30] J. Priest, "A Note on the Messianic Banquet," *The Messiah: Developments in Earliest Judaism and Christianity*, edited by James H. Charlesworth (Minneapolis: Fortress Press, 1992) 222–238.

those blessed with final salvation are invited by God or his accredited agent. The beatitude in v. 9 is reminiscent of Luke 14:15: "Blessed is he who shall eat bread in the kingdom of God," and the later parallel in the *Acts of Philip* 135: "Behold, the dinner is prepared, and blessed is the one who has been invited." While the wedding banquet of the Lamb is mentioned only in the Apocalypse, the imagery would have been immediately evident to the competent reader.

This command is followed by John's awestruck prostration before the angelic revealer, who immediately forbids him to do so, but rather enjoins him to worship God alone (v. 10b), a reference to the Shema. The whole subunit is introduced with the phrase "And the angel said to me" (v. 9a). But which angel? Upon reflection, this can only refer to one of the seven bowl angels who provided John with a revelatory visit to the wilderness in 17:1–3a). For the first time it becomes clear that 17:1–19:10 are not just an unconnected series of textual units. The author has formed an *inclusio* by mentioning the *angelus interpres* at the beginning and end of the larger unit. Yet this unit is not simply a way of linking a group of subunits together, but also introduces new and proleptic information, namely the reference to the invitation to the marriage supper of the Lamb (19:7, 9).

19. The next literary unit is Rev 19:11–21:8, consisting of three constituent subunits: (1) a description of the divine warrior and his conquests (19:11–21), (2) the defeat of Satan (20:1–10), and (3) the vision of the judgment of the dead (20:11–15). The first subunit has two parts and opens with a clear marker of a new episode: "Then I saw heaven opened" (19:11); the second part of the passage is introduced with the phrase "then I saw an angel standing in the sun" (19:17). The reader is scarcely prepared for the introduction of the main character in this section, the rider on the white horse who rides out from heaven clad in blood-stained garments at the head of a heavenly army (19:11–14). Despite the mysterious character of this new figure, the author links him with familiar titles, such as "Faithful and True" (v. 11; cf. 1:5; 3:14), "the Word of God" (v. 13; reminiscent of the Johannine Logos in John 1:1–2, 14; 1 John 1:1), and "King of kings and Lord of lords" (v. 16; 17:14 where it is a title of the Lamb). In v. 15, the warrior is further described as having a sharp sword proceeding from his mouth with which to strike down the nations, a metaphor for judgment found earlier in the Apocalypse (1:16; 2:12, 16) and clearly associated with the exalted Christ. The allusion to Ps 2:9 in v. 15, "he will rule them with a rod of iron" is a messianic passage already mentioned twice earlier (2:26; 12:5). These titles and descriptions leave little doubt in the reader that the heavenly warrior is none other than the exalted Jesus Christ who leads an eschatological assault against the enemies of God.

The second part of 19:11–21 is found in vv. 17–21, which begins with the angel's proleptic announcement of victory over the kings and mighty men of the earth, using the negative image of "the great supper of God" at which the birds of heaven are invited to feast on the corpses of the defeated enemies of

God (vv. 17–18). The "great supper of God" is therefore the antithesis of "the marriage banquet of the Lamb," since the latter is a metaphor of salvation while the former is a metaphor of divine judgment. It is typical of the Apocalypse that scenes of conflict are described in the briefest possible way, if they are mentioned at all, and that is true of this passage as well. In v. 19, we learn that the enemies of God are gathered to make war against the divine warrior and his army, and abruptly in v. 20, the feast and the false prophet are captured and cast into the lake of fire. The episode concludes with the grisly scene of the birds feasting on the flesh of the defeated army.

The second subsection is the capture and ultimate defeat of Satan (20:1–3, 7–10), which frames an enigmatic "judgment scene" (no one is actually judged and the judges are never identified) in which the martyrs come to life and reign with Christ for a thousand years (vv. 4–6), labeled "the first resurrection" (v. 6). The motifs of this section consist of (1) an imprisonment of the malefactors followed by (2) a long interval, and concluding with (3) the end of the period of imprisonment with a final punishment. This same sequence is described protologically as the imprisonment and final punishment of Azazel and his associates in *1 Enoch* 10:4–14. In the opening scene the enemy is described with many of his aliases as "the dragon, that ancient serpent, who is the Devil and Satan" (these same aliases are used as a fulsome way of identifying the dragon in 12:9, leaving no doubt in the mind of the reader the identity of this great enemy of God. The millennial reign of the resurrected martyrs with Christ underscores the high value that God puts on those who die for their faith, supported by the beatitude in v. 6: "Blessed and holy are those who share in the first resurrection; over these the second death has no power, but they will be priests of God and of Christ, and they will reign with him a thousand years."

The third and final scene in Rev 20:1–10 narrates the release of Satan from prison, his role in deceiving the nations and raising up armies to march on "the camp of the saints and the beloved city" (v. 9). The author has deftly combined a reference to Jerusalem besieged by her enemies, now understood metaphorically as followers of Jesus who are persecuted for their faith. The motif of a repulsed attack upon Jerusalem is a part of a Zion theology that frequently surfaces in the OT (Pss 46, 48, 76; Isa 17, 29; Joel 2, 4; Zech 12, 14). Similarly, the attempt of kings and their armies to surround and conquer Jerusalem and the temple is a motif found frequently in Jewish and early Christian literature (*Sibylline Oracles* 3.657–58; *1 Enoch* 56:5–8; *4 Ezra* 13:5–11, 33–38; Luke 19:43–44; 21:20).[31] The allusion to these nations under the names "Gog and Magog" would remind the competent reader of the prophetic narrative in Ezek-

[31] Lars Hartman, *Prophecy Interpreted: The Formation of Some Jewish Apocalptic Texts and of the Eschatological Discourse Mark 13 par.* (Lund: Gleerup, 1966) 77–101 ("The Tumult and Assault of the Heathen").

iel 38–39,[32] where a hostile nation from the north will attack the peaceful and unsuspecting inhabitants of Palestine "in the latter days" (Ezek 38:8–16), but this nation will be completely defeated. The reader would naturally regard the event narrated in 20:7–10 as the fulfillment of an ancient prophecy of the defeat of God's enemies at the end of days. Oddly, the destruction of the hostile nations mentioned in 19:17–21 has been forgotten. The destruction of this hostile force by fire from heaven, a metaphor with OT antecedents, including the defeat of Gog and Magog (Ezek 38:22; 39:6; cf. Zeph 1:18; 3:8), underscores God's direct involvement from heaven in destroying his enemies.

The third subsection is Rev 20:11–15, which centers on the final judgment, is introduced with a magnificent theophanic scene: "Then I saw a great white throne and the one who sat on it; the earth and the heaven fled from his presence, and no place was found for them." This single verse is an excellent example of the theophany form,[33] which consists of just two parts, the coming of the deity and the reaction of nature. The frequency with which this form is found in the OT and early Jewish literature would mean that the competent reader would be very familiar with it (Judg 5:4–5; Pss 18:7–15; 68:7–8; Amos 1:2; Micah 1:3–4; Sirach 16:18–19; 43:16–17; 1QH 3.32–36). The focus of this judgment scene, introduced with an "And I saw" (v. 12), is on the opening of the heavenly books, including the book of life, which are then used as a basis for judging the dead. The author has used the traditional Jewish apocalyptic image of the opening of the books (Dan 7:10; cf. Ps 56:8; Isa 65:6; Jer 22:30; Mal 3:16; *Jub* 30:22; 36:10; *Ascension of Isaiah* 9:22), presumably one book for recording the deeds of the righteous and the other for recording the deeds of the wicked, and juxtaposed these books with the book of life (v. 12). The book of life has already been mentioned in the Apocalypse (3:5; 13:8; 17:8). In some way, the book of life is the decisive record, for the passage concludes with the statement that "anyone whose name was not found written in the book of life was thrown into the lake of fire."

20. The primary focus of the Apocalypse is introduced in Rev 21:1–22:9 which consists of an elaborate descriptive vision of the results of the transformation of the world centering on the New Jerusalem which descends from heaven to earth. This passages consists of an introductory subsection (21:1–8) followed by a relatively long subsection focusing on the New Jerusalem (21:9–27), and concluding with a subsection focusing on the river water of life flowing from the throne of God, and the Edenic trees on each side of the river . Rev 21:1–8 is an introductory subsection that first describes the transition to the new world order complete with the replacement of the first heaven and the first earth by a new

---

[32] Sverre Bøe, *Gog and Magog: Ezekiel 38–39 as Pre-text for Revelation 19,17–21 and 20,7–10* (WUNT 2. Reihe, 135; Tübingen: Mohr Siebeck, 2001).

[33] Jörg Jeremias, *Theophanie: Die Geschichte einer alttestamentlichen Gattung* (Neukirchen: Neukirchener Verlag, 1965).

heaven and a new earth and the descent of the New Jerusalem to earth (vv. 1–4), followed by a section containing a speech of God which effectively summarizes the message of the entire book: how God sovereignly rewards the righteous and judges the wicked (vv. 5–8):

And the one who was seated on the throne said, "See I am making all things new." Also he said, "Write this for these words are trustworthy and true." Then he said to me, "It is done! I am the Alpha and the Omega, the beginning and the end. To the thirsty I will give water as a gift from the spring of the water of life. Those who conquer will inherit these things, and I will be their God and they will be my children. But as for the cowardly, the faithless, the polluted, the murderers, the fornicators, the sorcerers, the idolaters, and all liars, their place will be in the lake that burns with fire and sulfur, which is the second death.

Since elsewhere in the book God speaks only in 1:8, this relatively lengthy divine pronouncement is extremely important. The competent reader will recognize the fact that this speech is a summative pastiche of phrases and motifs found earlier in the book. The fact that God makes all things new is a clear allusion to Isa 43:19, anchoring the transformation of the world in Old Testament prophecy. The divine title "the Alpha and the Omega," suggesting God's sovereign control over all creation, was mentioned in 1:8a, and will be referred to in 22:13 where is a title belonging to Christ, not God. The title "the Beginning and the End," essentially synonymous with "the Alpha and the Omega" will occur again in 22:13, where it too will be used to refer to Christ. The motif of providing the thirsty with the water of life was referred to in 7:17 as the eschatological role of the Lamb. The motif of conquering is of course a central emphasis in each of the seven proclamations to the church in Rev 2–3. The concluding list of sinful practices has numerous parallels with the ten commands which the competent reader would not miss.

Rev 21:9–22:9 is dominated by the guided tour that the interpreting angel gives the author. The passage begins in 21:9–10 when one of the seven bowl angels offers to show John "the bride, the wife of the Lamb," clearly a metaphor for the New Jerusalem which is in turn is a metaphor for the people of God.[34] This passage is clearly reminiscent of Rev 17:1, where another (or the same?) bowl angel offers to provided a guided tour of the harlot seated on the beast with seven heads and ten horns. This literary clue signals the structural parallelism between17:1–19:10 and 21:9–22:9, cleverly designed by the author to frame the passages of battle, destruction and judgment in 19:11–21:8.[35] Among the finds from Qumran are a number of fragments of several copies of a document which has been called "Description of the New Jerusalem." The parallels between these texts and Rev 21:9–22:9 are so striking that it seems quite likely that the

---

34 Gundry; "The New Jerusalem."

35 C.H. Giblin, "Structural and Thematic Correlations in the Theology of Revelation 16–22," *Biblica* 55 (1974) 487–504.

author of the Apocalypse was familiar with something very similar to these apocalyptic texts.[36] The heavenly or eschatological Jerusalem and the temple were, of course, very important motifs in early Judaism. These two motifs were closely related. In the wake of the destruction of Jerusalem in 586 BCE, Ezekiel envisioned the reconstruction of an eschatological temple in Ezek 40–48. In yet another strand of expectation, according to the scenario imagined in *1 Enoch* 90:28–29, the existing temple is razed and replaced with a new one built by God himself (cf. *2 Apoc. Bar.* 31:5–32:4). The New Testament contains a critique of the "temple made with hands" (Acts 7:48–50; 17:24), which is juxtaposed to the temple "made without hands," i. e., built by God (Mark 14:58; Heb 9:11, 24; Philo *Spec. Leg.* 1.66–67). The New Jerusalem is mentioned once earlier in the Apocalypse, in 3:12 where it is a metaphor for the full attainment of salvation: "I will write on you [the one who conquers] the name of my God, and the name of the city of my God, the new Jerusalem that comes down from my God out of heaven." While the expectation of an eschatological temple (the core, after all, of Ezekiel's vision in Ezek 40–48) would be traditional in early Judaism, a new and unexpected element in John's vision is his insistence that there is no temple in the eschatological Jerusalem (21:22–27). Regardless of the various reasons scholars have given for the absence of the temple in John's vision of the eschatological Jerusalem, it is clear that the author envisages a totally new reality, namely that the Lord God Almighty and the Lamb constitute the true temple of the New Jerusalem (21:22). Temples symbolize both the distance and the proximity of the worshiper and his or her god or gods. This dichotomy is shattered by the continuous presence of God and Christ with their people making temple imagery unnecessary and outmoded.

The third subsection within Rev 21:9–22:9 centers on the river of the water of life flowing from the throne of God and watering the miraculous trees along its banks. The reason that heaven is referred to as Paradise is based on the widespread belief in early Judaism that the Garden of Eden, from which Adam fell, was not in fact a mysterious place on earth, but rather a heavenly realm (Paul, for example, reflects the belief that Paradise was in the third heaven; see 2 Cor 12:1–4). Since human beings were expelled from Paradise at the beginning of human history, the expectation that admission would again be granted to Paradise by a restored human race became a widespread element of Jewish apocalyptic thought.

21. The concluding section of the Apocalypse is the very complex composition found in Rev 22:10–21, often colorlessly identified as the epilogue. Unlike the references in Dan 8:26 and 12:4, 9, where the seer is told to seal up the book,

[36] David E. Aune, "Qumran and the Book of Revelation," *The Dead Sea Scrolls after Fifty Years: A Comprehensive Assessment*, ed. Peter W. Flint and James C. VanderKam (2 vols.; Leiden: Brill, 1998–99), 2.622–48, esp. 629–36. Reprinted above, pp. 79–98

John is commanded to do precisely the opposite: "Do not seal up the words of the prophecy of this book, for the time is near" (v. 10). Contradicting this ancient apocalyptic motif, the author emphasizes the immediate and timely relevance of the revelatory visions he has just described, and in so doing emphasizes the nearness of the end. The words which follow seem to be a clumsy concatenation of statements with no clear indication of who is speaking and why. One suggestive solution proposed by Ugo Vanni and reiterated by his student M.A. Kavanaugh is that this concluding section of the Apocalypse represents a liturgical sequence with an antiphonal character, i.e., a liturgical dialogue.[37] Ancient readers would have picked up the literary clues immediately and understood that this concluding section of the Apocalypse was carefully designed to fit into a worship setting. That is, the author designed the book to cohere with current liturgical practices in order to secure a hearing for his revelatory vision. Part of an introit liturgy has been detected in 22:10–21, with parallels in similar introit liturgies in *Didache* 10:6 and 1 Cor 16:22.

Toward the end of this section, a complex text occurs which should apparently be considered the words of the exalted Christ (22:18–20):

> I warn everyone who hears the words of the prophecy of this book:
> if anyone adds to them,
> God will add to that person the plagues described in this book;
> If anyone takes away from the words of the book of this prophecy,
> God will take away that person's share in the tree of life and in the holy city,
> which are described in this book.

This final substantive paragraph in the Apocalypse consists of three literary forms crafted into a unity: (1) the integrity formula (don't add, don't take away, don't change), which is phrases as (2) two conditional curse formulas combined with the *lex talionis*, the principle of retributive justice (if anyone does x, God will repay him or her with y), and (3) a liturgical invocation ("Amen! Come Lord Jesus!"). Each of these literary forms, taken separately, was widely known throughout the ancient Mediterranean world. The integrity formula was typical of treaties between nations and cities, used in the covenant (or treaty) language of Deut 4:2: "You must neither add anything to what I command you nor take away anything from it, but keep the commandments of the Lord you God with which I am charging you." John was trying to copyright his Apocalypse, fearing that someone would be tempted to fiddle with the written account of his revelatory visions. The importance which he placed on the revelation which he had received from God through Jesus Christ was underscored by the curse formulas juxtaposed with the integrity formula. Finally, the liturgical invocation, "Amen!

[37] Ugo Vanni, *La struttura letteraria dell'Apocalisse* (Brescia: Morcelliana, 1980) 109–15, 298–302; M.A. Kavanaugh, *Apocalypse 22:6–21 as Concluding Liturgical Dialogue* (Rome: Pontifical Gregorian University, 1984).

Come Lord Jesus!" (v. 19), sounds a note which the author has underscored throughout his book: Jesus is coming soon! (1:7; 2:16; 3:11; 16:15). The concluding verse reminds us that the lengthy composition we have just read is a letter: "The grace of the Lord Jesus be with all the saints. Amen" (22:21), the salutation of which occurs in 1:4–6.

4. Conclusions

After this guided tour through the literary forms of the Apocalypse with suggestions regarding the intertextual associations which formed the context within which it might have been read and understood by the original readers, it is time to ask whether anything of significance has been learned, or whether you, dear reader, have not been led down the garden path (where angels fear to tread) by a *magister interpres.*

From the perspective of the original reader, it has become obvious that the sequence of literary forms in the Apocalypse conforms to no known ancient literary conventions.[38] Since the author rarely provides signals anticipating what he will do next, the readers either had no way to anticipate what would occur next or were in fact as surprised as we are by new turns in the narrative. Since the Apocalypse, whatever else it may be, is certainly an example of ancient revelatory literature, it is worth wondering whether the original readers would have thought that such abrupt literary moves were consonant with their understanding of the appropriate ways of narrating divine revelation.

Perhaps the most interesting result of our survey is the phenomenon that in the Apocalypse, literary forms which had come to be associated either with apocalyptic or prophetic literary traditions (but not general enough to be associated with both), have been synthesized through juxtaposition. It is critical at this juncture to define what I understand by "prophecy" and "apocalyptic." Perhaps the most significant way in which prophecy can be differentiated from apocalyptic is *sociologically.* In contrast to apocalypticism, prophecy does not rigidly distinguish between the righteous and the wicked, but rather assumes that the wicked may repent and change their ways, and that the righteous require admonition, censure and exhortation to encourage them to remain faithful or to repent and return to the fold. Apocalypticism, on the other hand (i. e., the religious ideology within the context of which apocalypses were written), is a perspective generally thought to have been espoused by an oppressed minority which clearly distinguished the righteous from the wicked and anticipated an

[38] This statement must be qualified by the admission that the problem of the literary patterns evident in the sequence of constituent literary forms in apocalypses is a subject which has not been investigated.

eschatological denouement, in which they would be rewarded and the wicked punished.

By placing apocalyptic traditions within a prophetic framework (Rev 1–3 and 22:6–20), and by juxtaposing apocalyptic with prophetic elements throughout the entire composition, the author appears to have attempted to give a new lease on life to apocalyptic traditions which could not and did not long retain their vitality in early Christianity because of their indissoluble association with nationalistic myths connected with the royal ideology of ancient Israel. Apocalypses, the primary repository of apocalyptic traditions, were largely a scribal phenomenon perforce divorced from real settings because of their pseudepigraphical character. This suprahistorical perspective of apocalyptic literature generally appears to have been mitigated in the Apocalypse of John through the incorporation of prophetic concerns which have a historical orientation. The Apocalypse of John is one of the only apocalypses for which the author, audience and setting is generally known because it is not concealed in the work itself, though that setting is not reflected in the hardcore, genre-bound apocalyptic sections of the work.

The Apocalypse of John
and Palestinian Jewish Apocalyptic

1. Introduction

In several respects, the Apocalypse of John is an anomaly. First of all, the Apocalypse of John is clearly a *Christian* apocalypse which bears more generic similarities to early *Jewish* apocalypses than to other (admittedly later) Christian apocalypses such as the *Shepherd* of Hermas and the Apocalypses of Peter and Paul. There are, in fact, instances in which Christian traditions are conspicuous by their absence (Rev 12:1–6; 19:11–21). Second, unlike all other Jewish and Christian apocalypses – with the single exception of the *Shepherd* of Hermas – the Apocalypse of John is not pseudepigraphical, but rather was written in the name of its actual author. Third, the Apocalypse of John was composed in the Roman province of Asia, though the Jewish apocalypses with which it has the closest generic affinities were all almost certainly written in Palestine. No Jewish apocalypse appears to have originated in the Jewish Diaspora.

These three strikingly anomalous features of the Apocalypse of John require explanation. It is the purpose of this paper to explore these problematic issues within the context of an examination some of the many motifs which the Apocalypse of John shares with Palestinian Jewish apocalyptic and apocalypses.

2. The Apocalypse of John and Jewish Apocalypses

It is well known that the generic term "apocalypse" was derived from the first sentence of the Apocalypse of John Ἀποκάλυψις Ἰησοῦ Χριστοῦ, "the revelation of Jesus Christ" (Rev 1:1).[1] In this context, however, ἀποκάλυψις (which occurs only twice in the entire book; here and in the inscription) is not a *generic* designation, but rather a description of the *contents* of the work. The inscription, Ἀποκάλυψις Ἰωάννου, "the Apocalypse of John" (presumably a second

[1] Friedrich Lücke (1852) was the first scholar to use the term "apocalypse" in Rev 1:1 as a generic designation for works similar to Revelation such as Daniel, *1 Enoch*; *4 Ezra* and *2 Baruch*; see Helge S. Kvanvig, *Roots of Apocalyptic: The Mesopotamian Background of the Enoch Figure and of the Son of Man* (WMANT 61; Neukirchen-Vluyn: Neukirchen Verlag, 1988) 40, 56.

century formulation originally placed at the end of the book but then moved to the beginning with the transition from roll to codex), is simply a shortened form of the title or first sentence of the book with descriptive rather than generic intentions. However, whether through the influence of the Apocalypse of John or other documents which have not survived, the designation ἀποκάλυψις came to be used relatively quickly in a quasi-generic sense of works with a revelatory character, though such works rarely conform to the modern generic conception of "apocalypse."[2] While the modern designations "apocalypse" and "apocalyptic", then, really represent modern conceptions applied to ancient texts and ideologies, i.e., they are etic rather than emic designations,[3] that does not mean that these designations are unhelpful.

There is some consensus among modern scholars that the literary category "apocalypse" at least includes Dan 7–12, *1 Enoch* (a composite text containing five originally separate apocalypses), *4 Ezra*, *2 Baruch* and the Apocalypse of John.[4] Though there are many other works which should be included in this category (e.g., *2 Enoch*, *3 Enoch*, the *Apocalypse of Abraham*, *Testament of Levi* 2–5, *3 Baruch*, *Apocalypse of Zephaniah*) we will restrict the first major part of our discussion (III. Shared Apocalyptic Motifs) to the first group of texts.

It is striking that three of the early Jewish works generally considered to be apocalypses by modern scholars – the Similitudes of Enoch (*1 Enoch* 37–71), *4 Ezra* and *2 Baruch* – were composed in the first century, the last two almost certainly after the fall of Jerusalem in 70 CE and are roughly contemporary with the final composition of the Apocalypse of John, written ca. 90 CE. Two authors of recent commentaries on *4 Ezra*, Jacob M. Myers and Michael Stone, in company with most other scholars, place the composition of *4 Ezra* after the fall of Jerusalem in 70 CE, during latter part of the reign of Domitian (81–96 CE).[5] Pierre Bogaert, the author of a detailed commentary on *2 Baruch*, reflects scholarly consensus in arguing that *2 Baruch* was written in response to the destruction of the Second Temple in 70 CE.[6] The dating of the Similitudes of Enoch is more problematic. M.A. Knibb (whom I follow) tentatively dates the

---

[2] In an otherwise excellent article by Morton Smith, "On the History of ΑΠΟΚΑΛΥΠΤΩ and ΑΠΟΚΑΛΥΨΙΣ," *Apocalypticism in the Mediterranean World and the Near East*, ed. D. Hellholm (Tübingen: Mohr Siebeck, 1983) 9–20, the author not discuss the particular problems of the term ἀποκάλυψις in the inscription and title of Revelation.

[3] Bruce J. Malina, *On the Genre and Message of Revelation: Star Visions and Sky Journeys* (Peabody: Hendrickson, 1995) 12, argues that both "apocalypse" and "eschatological apocalyptic" are "theological jargon of the past century that fossilize perception and misdirect interpretation."

[4] John J. Collins, "Introduction: Toward the Morphology of a Genre," *Semeia* 14 (1979) 3.

[5] Jacob M. Myers, *I and II Esdras: Introduction, Translation and Commentary* (Anchor Bible; Garden City, New York: Doubleday, 1974) 129–131; Michael Stone, *Fourth Ezra: A Commentary on the Book of Fourth Ezra* (Hermeneia; Minneapolis: Fortress, 1990) 10.

[6] *Apocalypse de Baruch: Introduction, Traduction du Syriaque et Commentaire* (SC 144 and 145; Paris: Le Cerf, 1969) 1.270–95.

Similitudes of Enoch toward the end of the first century CE, though he readily admits that the date is disputed and can be placed within the wider boundaries of 63 BCE and 135 CE.[7] The late first century CE date is supported by the fact that fragments of four of the five apocalypses comprising *1 Enoch* have been found at Qumran with the exception of the Similitudes of Enoch.[8] While this is not a decisive argument for dating the Similitudes late in the first century CE, it is part of a cumulative argument supporting such a dating. While most scholars date the composition of the Apocalypse of John to the latter part of the reign of the Roman emperor Domitian, i. e., ca. 95 CE,[9] some propose a date a bit later during the reign of Trajan (98–117 CE), while others argue that it was written earlier, soon after the death of Nero in 68 CE. Since all these datings fall into a relatively close range in the late first or early second century, the issue need not be argued in detail.

The distinction between the traditions reflected in the Apocalypse of John and those found in Palestinian Jewish apocalypses is somewhat more blurred than many suppose. First, the distinction between "Jewish" and "Christian" is largely anachronistic for the first century CE, before hard and fast boundaries were drawn between Judaism and Christianity.[10] The so-called "parting of the ways" between Judaism and Christianity which supposedly occurred ca. 85 CE, was not a single event but rather the result of a series of unconnected conflicts which occurred over a relatively wide geographical area which unfolded from ca. 90–130 CE.[11] There is no evidence in the Apocalypse of John, at any rate, that the author made a rigid distinction between Jews and Christians, despite his diatribe against "those who call themselves Jews but are not" and "those of the synagogue of Satan" (Rev 2:9; 3:9). Second, all of the Palestinian Jewish apocalypses which have come down to us were in fact preserved by Christians who must have considered them essentially compatible with Christianity since they introduced remarkably few revisions or interpolations into the texts they

---

[7] "The Date of the Parables of Enoch: A Critical Review," *New Testament Studies* 25 (1979) 345–59. Matthew Black argues for a date earlier than the composition of the Synoptic Gospels (i. e., presumably well before 70 CE), since in his view the New Testament conception of the session of the Son of Man at the right hand of God (Mark 14:62; Matt 19:38; 25:31) is based on the Elect Son of Man messianism of the Similitudes of Enoch ("The Messianism of the Parables of Enoch: Their Date and Contribution to Christological Origins," *The Messiah: Developments in Earliest Judaism and Christianity*, ed. J. H. Charlesworth [Minneapolis: Fortress, 1992] 145–68). Black's date is based on the questionable assumption that the Synoptic Gospels exhibit literary dependence on the Similitudes of Enoch.

[8] James C. VanderKam, *The Dead Sea Scrolls Today* (Grand Rapids: Eerdmans, 1994) 37–39.

[9] See the extensive discussion in David E. Aune, *Revelation* (World Biblical Commentary, 52A, 52B, 52C; Nashville: Thomas Nelson, 1997–98) 1.lvi–lxx.

[10] John J. Pilch, "No Jews or Christians in the Bible," *Explorations* 12 (1998) 3.

[11] See Graham Stanton, "Aspects of Early Christian-Jewish Polemic and Apologetic," *New Testament Studies* 31 (1985) 377–92.

transmitted.[12] A major exception is *4 Ezra*, with a core Jewish apocalypse in *4 Ezra* 3–14 transmitted in a Latin version framed by two Christian compositions, *4 Ezra* 1–2 = *5 Ezra* and *4 Ezra* 15–16 = *6 Ezra*. Third, source criticism has frequently been used to account for the striking Jewish character of the Apocalypse of John. Some scholars, particularly in the late nineteenth and early twentieth centuries, proposed that the Apocalypse of John was made up of one or more Jewish apocalypses which were Christianized and supplemented to various extents. Others have proposed more plausibly that the author made use of sources which originated in Judaism but which were shorter and more fragmentary.[13] Even though it is theoretically possible to identify and analyze the sources used in a document such as the Apocalypse of John (and I plead guilty to have tried to do so), the task of reconstruction is extraordinarily difficult and inevitably subjective.

3. Shared Apocalyptic Motifs

There are a number of apocalyptic motifs which the Apocalypse of John shares with Palestinian Jewish apocalypses, which for the purposes of this section of the paper are limited to the Similitudes of Enoch (*1 Enoch* 37–71), *4 Ezra* and *2 Baruch*. Some of the motifs shared by the Apocalypse of John and Jewish apocalypses have been examined by Richard Bauckham, who is one of the few who have explored this important but neglected area of study.[14] While it is evident that some kind of "intimate relationship" (the phrase of Stone) exists between *4 Ezra* and *2 Baruch*, there is no agreement on the precise nature of this relationship.[15] R.H. Charles[16] and Bruno Violet[17] argued that *2 Baruch* used *4 Ezra* as a source, while Bogaert argued the opposite,[18] even suggesting that *4 Ezra* in turn "appears to know" the Apocalypse of John, which was itself dependent on *2 Baruch*.[19] Bogaert's theory of the relationship between these three compositions can be diagrammed as follows:

---

[12] Marinus de Jonge, "The so-called Pseudepigrapha of the Old Testament and Early Christianity," *The New Testament and Hellenistic Judaism*, ed. Peder Borgen and Søren Giversen (Peabody: Hendrickson, 1997) 59–71.

[13] Source critical theories applied to the Apocalypse of John are reviewed in Aune, *Revelation*, 1.cx–cxvii.

[14] Richard Bauckham, "The Use of Apocalyptic Traditions," in *The Climax of Prophecy: Studies on the Book of Revelation* (Edinburgh: T. & T. Clark, 1993) 38–91.

[15] Stone, *Fourth Ezra*, 39.

[16] R.H. Charles, *The Apocalypse of Baruch* (London: A. and C. Black, 1896).

[17] Bruno Violet, *Die Esra-Apokalypse (IV. Esra)* (Die griechischen christlichen Schriftsteller; Leipzig: J.C. Hinrichs, 1910) l.

[18] Bogaert, *L'Apocalypse syriaque de Baruch*, 1.26–27, 113–14, 284–88.

[19] P.-M. Bogaert, "Les Apocalypses contemporaines de Baruch, d'Esdras et de Jean,"

2 Baruch → Apocalypse of John

↓ ↓

4 Ezra

R. H. Charles argued that the author of the Apocalypse was literarily dependent on several Jewish apocalyptic texts, including the Testament of Levi, *1 Enoch* and the *Assumption* (or *Testament*) *of Moses*.[20] His relatively early dating of the Similitudes of Enoch (either 94–79 BCE or 70–64 BCE), made it easy for him to suppose that the author of the Apocalypse of John could have been literarily dependent on the Similitudes. Most scholars, however, have not thought it likely that the Apocalypse was dependent on the texts of the Similitudes, *4 Ezra* or *2 Baruch*. Swete's critique of Charles' claims is still valid: "Here it is enough to say that they [i. e., the parallels] shew the writer of the Christian Apocalypse to have been familiar with the apocalyptic ideas of his age, they afford little or no clear evidence of his dependence on Jewish sources other than the books of the Old Testament."[21]

These shared motifs can logically be explained in one of three ways: (1) the Apocalypse of John is literarily dependent on a particular Jewish apocalypse, (2) a particular Jewish apocalypse is dependent on the Apocalypse of John, or (3) similar motifs shared by the Apocalypse of John and other Jewish apocalypses are based on a common written or oral apocalyptic tradition. In the past, scholars have been quick to propose various theories of literary dependence. More recently, as a result of more stringent standards for judging quotations and allusions, relationships other than direct literary dependence have been more seriously entertained.

The passages in the Apocalypse of John which Charles and others have thought dependent on Jewish apocalypses provide the opportunity for evaluating the source of such parallel passages. Our concern will be limited to those three apocalypses which are nearly contemporary with the Apocalypse of John, namely *1 Enoch* 37–71, *4 Ezra* and *2 Baruch*.

L'Apocalypse johannique et l'Apocalyptique dans le Nouveau Testaxment, ed. J. Lambrecht (BETL, 53; Gembloux: J. Duculot, S. A.; Leuven: University Press, 1980) 54–56, 67.

20 *A Critical and Exegetical Commentary on the Revelation of St. John* (2 vols.; Edinburgh: T. & T. Clark, 1920) 1.lxv, lxxxii–lxxxiii. The ten passages in 1 Enoch on which he claims that the Apocalypse of John is dependent are the following: 1 Enoch 9:4; 14:15; 18:13; 46:1; 47:3–4; 48:9; 51:1; 62:3, 5; 86:1; 99:7.

21 Henry Barclay Swete, *The Apocalypse of St John: The Greek Text with Introduction, Notes and Indices* (Grand Rapids: Eerdmans, 1908) clviii.

(1) *The Terror of Humanity before the Throne of Judgment* (Rev 6:15–16; *1 Enoch* 62:3–5).

Rev 6:15–16: The kings of the earth and the important people and the generals and the wealthy and the powerful and every slave and free person hid themselves in the caves and in the mountain rocks. They said to the mountains and the cliffs, "Fall on us and hide us from the One who sits on the throne and from the wrath of the Lamb, because the great day of his wrath has come, and who is able to withstand it?"

1 Enoch 62:3–5 (trans. Knibb): And on that day all the kings and the mighty and the exalted, and those who possess the earth, will stand up; and they will see and recognize how he sits on the throne of his glory ... and pain will come upon them as (upon) a woman in labour for whom giving birth is difficult ... And one half of them will look at the other, and they will be terrified, and will cast down their faces, and pain will take hold of them when they see that Son of a Woman sitting on the throne of his glory.

These two passages have clear similarities and differences.[22] Similarities: (1) They share the common apocalyptic motif of the terror of all humankind before the throne of judgment. (2) In *1 Enoch* 37–71, the phrase "the kings and the mighty and the exalted and those two dwell on the earth" (*1 Enoch* 62:3) is a stereotypical phrase referring to everyone (62:1, 3, 6, 9; 63:1, 12; 67:8). A very similar phrase occurs in Rev 6:15: "The kings of the earth and the important people and the generals and the wealthy and the powerful and every slave and free person" (similar lists occur twice elsewhere in the Apocalypse of John with essentially the same meaning: 13:16; 19:18). These phrases may allude to the LXX text of Isa 34:12 where the phrase "the kings and rulers and great ones" (with nothing corresponding to it in the Massoretic text) is found in a context of judgment. (3) In Rev 6:15–16, God occupies the throne of judgment, though the Lamb is somehow also involved in judgment (see the next section below). In *1 Enoch* 62:3–5, God is initially seated on the throne of judgment (62:2–3), while the Son of Man is suddenly referred to as "sitting on the throne of his glory." There is one major differences between these passages: Different OT passages are alluded to: Rev 6:15–16 is based on allusions to Isa 2:19–21 and Hos 10:6, while *1 Enoch* 62:3–5 alludes to the image of the woman in labor in Isa 13:8.

The allusions to different OT passages in these two texts discourages the hypothesis of a direct literary relationship between them. However, the three impressive similarities suggest that both texts are dependent on a relatively fixed oral or written source. Since the existence of an *oral* apocalyptic tradition cannot easily be substantiated, it appears more likely that both the Apocalypse of John and the Similitudes of Enoch are dependent on a common *written* source, which each author partially reformulated in a distinctive way.

---

[22] These passages are discussed by Knibb, "Parables of Enoch," 356.

(2) *The Messiah Seated on the Throne of God Judging the Wicked* (Rev 3:21; 6:16; 22:1, 3; *1 Enoch* 45:3; 51:1; 55:4; 61:8).

Rev 3:21: As for the one who conquers, I will allow him to sit with me on my throne, just as I also conquered and sat with my Father on his throne.

Rev 6:16: They said to the mountains and the cliffs, "Fall on us and hide us from the One who sits on the throne and from the wrath of the lamb, 17 because the great day of their wrath has come, and who is able to withstand it?"

Rev 22:1: He showed me a river of living water, sparkling like crystal, flowing from the throne of God and of the Lamb.

Rev 22:3: The throne of God and of the Lamb will be in the city, and his servants will worship him.

[*Matt 19:28* (NRSV): Jesus said to them, "Truly I tell you, at the renewal of all things, when the Son of Man is seated on the throne of his glory, you who have followed me will also sit on twelve thrones, judging the twelve tribes of Israel."]

[*Matt 25:31–32* (NRSV): When the Son of Man comes in his glory, and all the angels with him, then he will sit on the throne of his glory. 32 All the nations will be gathered before him, and he will separate people one from another as a shepherd separates the sheep from the goats.]

1 Enoch 45:3 (trans. Knibb): On that day the Chosen One will sit on the throne of glory, and will choose their works, and their resting-placed will be without number; and their spirits within them will grow strong when they see my Chosen One and those who appeal to my holy and glorious name.

1 Enoch 51:1 (trans. Knibb): And in those days the Chosen One will sit on his throne, and all the secrets of wisdom will flow out from the counsel of his mouth, for the Lord of Spirits has appointed him and glorified him.

1 Enoch 55:4 (trans. Knibb): "You powerful kings, who dwell upon the dry ground, will be obliged to watch my Chosen One sit down on the throne of my glory, and judge, in the name of the Lord of Spirits, Azazel and all his associates and all his hosts."

1 Enoch 61:8 (trans. Knibb): And the Lord of Spirits set the Chosen One on the throne of his glory, and he will judge all the works of the holy ones in heaven above, and in the balance he will weigh their deeds.

1 Enoch 62:2, 5 (trans. Knibb): 2 And the Lord of Spirits sat on the throne of his glory, and the spirit of righteousness was poured out on him, and the word of his mouth kills all the sinners and all the lawless, and they are destroyed before him … 5 And one half of them will look at the other, and they will be terrified, and will cast down their faces, and pain will take hold of them, when they see that Son of Man sitting on the throne of glory.

1 Enoch 69:26–29 (trans. Knibb): And they had great joy, and they blessed and praised and exalted because the name of that Son of Man had been revealed to them. 27 And he sat on the throne of his glory, and the whole judgment was given to the Son of Man, and he will cause the sinners to pass away and be destroyed from the face of the earth. 28 And those who led astray the world will be bound in chains, and will be shut up in the assembly-place of their destruction, and all their works will pass away from the face of the earth. 29 And from then on there will be nothing corruptible, for that Son of man has appeared and has sat on the throne of his glory, and everything evil will pass away and go from before him; and the word of that Son of Man will be strong before the Lord of Spirits.

The traditional eschatological motif of God (the Lord of Spirits) as the enthroned judge is mentioned three times in the Similitudes (*1 Enoch* 47:3; 60:2; 62:2). However, the motif of the Chosen One or the Son of Man, seated on the "throne of glory," i.e., the throne of God, occurs seven times in the Similitudes (45:3; 51:1; 55:4; 61:8; 62:5; 69:27, 29). In four of these passages the enthronement of Chosen One or the Son of Man is combined with the theme of judgment (55:4; 61:8; 62:5; 69:27–29). In the OT, reference is occasionally made to the king sitting on the throne of Yahweh, and in early Judaism the Messiah is frequently depicted as an eschatological judge (e.g., *T. Judah* 24:4–6; *4 Ezra* 12:32; *2 Bar* 40:1–3). A particularly significant reference is found in *1 Enoch* 61:8, where it is said that the Lord of Spirits set the Elect One on his [i.e., God's] throne of glory. This unique theologoumenon can be traced with some likelihood to the Messianic interpretation of Ps 110:1, which combines the themes of enthronement and judgment: "The Lord says to my Lord: 'Sit on my right hand, till I make your enemies your footstool.'"[23] The same theologoumenon occurs also in the New Testament in Matt 19:28 and 24:31–32, where it is explicitly predicted that the Son of Man will sit on the throne of his glory. While the possessive pronoun "his" could refer to the Son of Man, i.e., it is his throne, it is also possible that "his" refers to God and means that the Son of Man will sit on God's throne of glory. While the possessive pronoun is ambiguous, it appears that in the Similitudes of Enoch the Chosen One or Son of Man is also understood as sitting on God's throne of glory.[24] Matthew Black has used this evidence to argue that the Similitudes of Enoch are earlier than the Synoptic Gospels and that the distinctiveness of this theologoumenon suggests that the Synoptics were literarily dependent on the Similitudes. Of the four passages in the Apocalypse of John cited above, one refers to the enthronement of Christ with God on his throne (3:21), while the other three refer either directly (22:1, 3) or indirectly (6:16) to the Lamb seated on the throne with God. Only in Rev 6:16, however, is the motif of judgment present. We have already proposed that Rev 6:15–16 is dependent on a written source used also *1 Enoch* 62:3–5. The other passages referring to co-enthronement in the Apocalypse do not use the motif of judgment, nor is the figure enthroned with God identified as the Son of Man.

[23] Johannes Theisohn, *Der auserwählte Richter: Untersuchungen zum traditionsgeschichtlichen Ort der Menschensohngestalt der Bilderreden des Äthiopischen Henoch* (SUNT, 12; Göttingen: Vandenhoeck & Ruprecht, 1975) 93–98

[24] Black, "The Messianism of the Parables of Enoch," 154–55.

(3) *The Cry for Vengeance and the Numerus Iustorum* (Rev 6:9–11; *1 Enoch* 47:1–4; *4 Ezra* 4:33,35–37; *2 Bar* 23:4–5a).[25]

Rev 6:9–11: When he broke the fifth seal, I saw underneath the altar the souls of those slain because of the word of God and because of the witness which they bore. They cried out loudly saying, "O Master, holy and true, how long will it be until you judge and avenge our deaths caused by those who dwell on the earth?" Then each of them was given a white robe, and they were told that they should rest a while longer until the number of their fellow servants, that is, their brothers who were to be killed as they were, would be complete.

1 Enoch 47:1–4 (trans. Knibb): And in those days the prayer of the righteous and the blood of the righteous will have ascended from earth before the Lord of Spirits. 2 In these days the holy ones who dwell in the heavens above will unite with one voice, and supplicate, and pray, and praise, and give thanks, and bless in the name of the Lord of Spirits, because of the blood of the righteous which has been poured out, and (because of) the prayer of the righteous, that it may not cease before the Lord of Spirits, that justice may be done to them, and (that) their patience may not have to last for ever… . 4 And the hearts of the holy ones were full of joy that the number of righteousness had been reached, and the prayer of the righteous had been heard, and the blood of the righteous had been required before the Lord of Spirits.

4 Ezra 4:33, 35–37 (NRSV): 33 Then I answered and said, "How long? When will these things be?" Why are our years few and evil?" … 35 Did not the souls of the righteous in their chambers ask about these matters, saying, "How long are we to remain here? And when will the harvest of our reward come?" 36 And the archangel Jeremiel answered and said, "When the number of those like yourselves is completed."

2 Baruch 23:4–5 (Charlesworth, *OTP* 1.629): For when Adam sinned and death was decreed against those who were to be born, the multitude of those who would be born was numbered. And for that number a place was prepared where the living ones might live and where the dead might be preserved. No creature will live again unless the number that has been appointed is completed. For my spirit creates the living, and the realm of death receives the dead. And further, it is given to you too hear that which will come after these times. For truly, my salvation which comes has drawn near and is not as far away as before.

A quick survey of these four passages indicates that they are linked by the motifs of the reward of the righteous dead and the death of the predestined number of the righteous as an event which must occur before Good will act. In Rev 6:9–11, *1 Enoch* 47:1–4 and *4 Ezra* 4:33–37, the righteous dead ask about their vindication or reward and are given an answer involving the future completion of the complete number of the righteous dead.[26]

In Rev 6:9–11 and *1 Enoch* 47:1–4 the dead are the righteous who have been killed by their enemies and pray for vindication and are answered with the *numerus iustorum* formula. In *4 Ezra* 4:33–37 they are the righteous dead, while

[25] Bauckham, "Apocalyptic Traditions," 48–56; Aune, *Revelation*, 2.406–413.
[26] Bauckham, "Apocalyptic Traditions," 52.

in *2 Bar* 23:4–5 they are simply all the dead. Rev 6:9–11 has a special formal link with *4 Ezra* 4:33–37 by an entreaty attributed to the righteous dead in direct discourse introduced by the phrase "How long?", commonly used in impatient prayer in the OT (Pss 6:3–4; 13:1–2; 35:17; 74:9–10; 79:5; 80:4; 89:6; 1 Macc 6:22), and also used in apocalyptic contexts about when the end will arrive (Dan 8:13; 12:6; *2 Bar* 21:19; 81:3 [MS c only]; *4 Ezra* 6:59). Stone considers *4 Ezra* 4:35–36a to reflect the author's use of a source, and the author may have therefore have structured 4:33 on the "how long?" pattern of 4:35,[27] a proposal which is unnecessary. Bauckham suggests the possibility of the following possible literary relationship between these texts: *1 Enoch* 37–71 → Revelation → *4 Ezra* → *2 Baruch*, he thinks that the relationship between these four texts is not the result of direct literary dependence but rather as a result of dependence on a common tradition which had already taken particular forms in the sources used by each apocalypse.[28]

(4) *The kings from the east are supernaturally instigated to march on the holy city* (Rev 16:12–16; 19:19–21; 20:7–10; *1 Enoch* 56:5–7).

Rev 16:12–16: The sixth angel poured his bowl on the great river Euphrates, and its water was dried up in order to prepare the way for the kings from the east. 13 And I saw three foul spirits like frogs coming from the mouth of *the dragon, from the mouth of the beast, and from the mouth of the false prophet.* 14 These are demonic spirits, performing signs, which go abroad to the kings of the whole world, to assemble them for the battle on the great day of God the Almighty.... 16 And they assembled them at the place that in Hebrew is called Harmagedon.

Rev 19:19–21: "Then I saw the beast and the kings of the earth and their armies assembled to wage war with the one mounted on the steed and with his army. *The beast was captured and with him the false prophet who performed signs on his authority, which he deceived those who received the brand of the beast and who worshiped his cultic image; they were both hurled alive into the lake of fire burning with sulfur.* The rest were slain with the sword projecting from the mouth of the one mounted on the steed, and all the birds feasted on their carrion.

Rev 20:7–10: When the thousand years are completed, Satan will be released from his prison 8 and will go out to deceive the nations that are at the four corners of the earth, God and Magog, to assemble them for battle. Their number is like the sand of the sea. 9 They marched up across the breadth of the earth and surrounded the encampment of the people of God, the beloved city. Then fire came down from heaven and devoured them. 10 *And the devil who deceived them was cast down into the lake of fire and brimstone where the beast and the false prophet were, so that they were tormented day and night for ever.*

1 Enoch 56:5–7 (trans. Knibb): And in those days the angels will gather together, and will throw themselves towards the east upon the Parthians and Medes; they will stir

---

27 Stone, *Fourth Ezra*, 96–97.

28 Bauckham, "Apocalyptic Traditions," 54.

up the kings, so that a disturbing spirit will come upon them, and they will drive them from their thrones; and they will come out like lions from their lairs, and like hungry wolves in the middle of their flocks. 6 And they will go up and trample upon the land of my chosen ones, and the land of my chosen ones will become before them a tramping-ground and a beaten track. 7 But the city of my righteous ones will be a hindrance to their horses, and they will stir up slaughter among themselves, and their (own) right hand will be strong against them; and a man will not admit to knowing his neighbour or his brother, nor a son his father or his mother, until through their death there are corpses enough, and their punishment – it will not be in vain. 8 And in those days Sheol will open its mouth and they will sink into it; and their destruction – Sheol will swallow up the sinners before the face of the chosen.

Of the three passages in the Apocalypse cited above, the first two constitute a single source which has been interrupted in order to accommodate an extensive section on Babylon in Rev 17–18. The first fragment in Rev 16:12–16 ends without narrating the actual assembly of the kings and the ensuing eschatological battle, while the second fragment in Rev 19:19–21 provides both. Together these passages constitute a doublet of Rev 20:7–10; the italized phrases are probably the additions to the source used by the author of the Apocalypse. The same eschatological scenario characterizes the two passages: a malevolent supernatural being or beings instigates the kings of the east to assemble and march to the holy city where they are supernaturally defeated by God and/or his Messiah. This same scenario characterizes *1 Enoch* 56:5–7, which designates the enemy specifically as the Parthians and the Medes. This identification has been the basis of attempts to date the Similitudes. Sjöberg argued that this text was written shortly after the capture of Jerusalem by the Parthians in 40–37 BCE,[29] while J. C. Hindley, argued that it reflected Trajan's campaign against the Parthians in 113–17 CE.[30] These are just two of many proposals, none of which has proven decisive. *1 Enoch* 56:5–7 also reflects the defeat of the enemy before the holy city, and therefore appears to be based on Sennacherib's abortive campaign against Jerusalem in 701 BCE (Isa 36:1–37:38 = 2 Kings 18:13–19:37). The motif of "trampling" on the holy land, is applied to the holy city in Zech 12:3 ("and Jerusalem will be trampled on by the Gentiles until the times of the Gentiles are fulfilled"), a passage which is alluded to in both Luke 21:24 and Rev 11:2. In *1 Enoch* 56:5–7, the holy city is inviolate. The fate of the enemy host is depicted through a combination of two traditions, one emphasizing the self-destruction of the enemy forces, while in the other tradition Sheol opens up and swallows them.

---

[29] E. Sjöberg, *Der Menschensohn im Äthiopischen Henochbuch* (Lund: Gleerup, 1946) 39.

[30] J.C. Hindley, "Towards a Date for the Similitudes of Enoch. An Historical Approach," *New Testament Studies* 14 (1968–69) 551–65.

A comparison of the use of this motif in the Similitudes and the Apocalypse of John suggests that no mutual literary dependence is probable, but rather both texts have used this motif in distinctive ways.

(5) *The Leviathan-Behemoth Myth* (Rev 13:1–18; *1 Enoch* 60:7–11, 24; *4 Ezra* 6:49–52; *2 Bar* 29:4).

Rev 13:1–18: I saw a beast rising up out of the sea, with ten horns and seven heads, and on its horns were ten diadems and on its heads were blasphemous names… . 11 Then I saw another beast ascending from the earth, and it had two horns like a ram, but it sounded like a dragon.

1 Enoch 60:7–11, 24 (trans. Knibb): And on that day two monsters will be separated from one another: a female monster, whose name (is) Leviathan, to dwell in the depths of the sea above the springs of the waters; 8 and the name of the male (is) Behemoth, who occupies with his breast an immense desert, named Dendayn, on the east of the garden where the chosen and righteous dwell, where my great-grandfather was received, who was the seventh from Adam, the first man whom the Lord of Spirits made. 9 And I asked that other angel to show me the power of those monsters, how they were separated on one day and thrown, one into the depths of the sea, and the other on to the dry ground of the desert… . 24 And the angel of peace who was with me said to me: "These two monsters, prepared in accordance with the greatness of the Lord, will be fed that the punishment of the Lord … will not be in vain."

4 Ezra 6:49–52 (NRSV): Then you kept in existence two living creatures; the one you called Behemoth and the name of the other Leviathan. 50 And you separated one from the other, for the seventh part where the water had been gathered together could not hold them both. 51 And you gave Behemoth one of the parts that had been dried up on the third day, to live in it, where there are a thousand mountains; 52 but to Leviathan you gave the seventh part, the water part; and you have kept them to be eaten by whom you wish, and when you wish.

2 Baruch 29:2–4 (trans. Charlesworth, *OTP*, 1.630): For at that time I shall only protect those found in this land at that time. 3 And it will happen that when all that which should come to pass in these parts has been accomplished, the Anointed One will begin to be revealed. 4 And Behemoth will reveal itself from its place, and Leviathan will come from the sea, the two great monsters which I created on the fifth day of creation and which I shall have kept until that time. And they will be nourishment for all who are left.

The beast from the sea and the beast from the land of Rev 13 clearly reflect the Jewish myth of Leviathan, the female monster from the sea, and Behemoth, the male monster from the desert, even though the beasts are not given their traditional names in the text. Further, the myth of the beast from the sea and the beast from the land are combined with other motifs associated with the eschatological antagonist, so that the beast from the sea is depicted as a godless, tyrannical ruler, while the beast from the land is presented as a lying prophet. It is striking that the Leviathan-Behemoth myth is referred to in only three

Palestinian Jewish apocalypses, *1 Enoch* 37–71, *4 Ezra* and *2 Baruch*, where they are explicitly named and rudiments of the myth are mentioned. The Leviathan-Behemoth myth has both protological features (i. e., they were created on the fifth day of creation) and eschatological features (they will serve as food for the righteous in the eschaton). More complete forms of this myth, inspired by Gen 1:21, are found in the Talmud and Midrashim and have been synthesized by Ginsberg. According to Gen 1:21, the great sea monsters were created on the fifth day, when God separated the pair, appointing Leviathan to inhabit the sea (Job 41:1–34; Ps 104:25–26; *Apoc. Abr.* 21:4; *Ladder of Jacob* 6:13), and Behemoth the land (Job 40:15–24; *4 Ezra* 6:51). Missing from Revelation, but present in our three focal Jewish apocalypses as well as in rabbinic versions of the story, is the expectation that Leviathan and Behemoth will ultimately serve as food for the righteous in the eschaton (*1 Enoch* 60:24; *4 Ezra* 6:52; *2 Baruch* 29:4; cf. *b. B. Bat.* 75a).

While literary dependence could be proposed for the passages focusing on the Leviathan-Behemoth myth in the *Similitudes of Enoch, 4 Ezra* and *2 Baruch*, the vague and general reference to the myth in Rev 13 indicates only that the author or his sources were aware of the traditional features of the myth.

4. The New Jerusalem

In this section I will depart from a tight focus on the Similitudes of Enoch, *4 Ezra* and *2 Baruch* and extend the inquiry to include the traditions of the eschatological Jerusalem found in the Qumran documents called "Description of the New Jerusalem" and the Temple Scroll. Though both *4 Ezra* and *2 Baruch* (not the Similitudes of Enoch) mention the eschatological Jerusalem, the similarities between the New Jerusalem in the Apocalypse of John, the Description of the New Jerusalem and the Temple scroll are more detailed and striking and raise the problem of the relationship between these three texts.

First let me provide an overview of the relevant sections of *4 Ezra* and *2 Baruch*:

4 Ezra 7:26 (NRSV): For indeed the time will come, when the signs that I have foretold to you will come to pass, that the city that now is not seen shall appear [Latin, Syriac: that the bride shall appear], and the land that now is hidden shall be disclosed.

4 Ezra 8:52 (NRSV): Because it is for you that paradise is opened, the tree of life is planted, the age to come is prepared, plenty is provided, a city is built, rest is appointed, goodness is established and wisdom perfected beforehand.

4 Ezra 10:25–27a (NRSV): While I was talking to her, her face suddenly began to shine exceedingly; her countenance flashed like lightning, so that I was too frightened to approach her, and my heart was terrified. While I was wondering what this meant, 26 she suddenly uttered a loud and fearful cry, so that the earth shook at the sound. 27 When I looked up, the woman was no longer visible to me, but a city was being built, and a place of high foundations showed itself.

4 Ezra 10:44 (NRSV): The woman whom you saw is Zion, which you now behold as a city being built [Latin: as an established city].

4 Ezra 13:36 (NRSV): And Zion shall come and be made manifest to all people, prepared and built, as you saw the mountain carved out without hands

2 Baruch 4:1–7 (Charlesworth, *OTP*, 1.622): And the Lord said to me: "This city will be delivered up for a time, And the people will be chastened for a time, And the world will not be forgotten. 2 Or do you think that this is the city of which I said: On the palms of my hands I have carved you? 3 It is not this building that is in your midst now; it is that which will be revealed, with me, that was already prepared from the moment that I decided to create Paradise. And I showed it to Adam before he sinned. But when he transgressed the commandment, it was taken away from him – as also Paradise. 4 After these things I showed it to my servant Abraham in the night between the portions of the victims. 5 And again I showed it also to Moses on Mount Sinai when I showed him the likeness of the tabernacle and all its vessels. 6 Behold, now it is preserved with me – as also Paradise. 7 Now go away and do as I command you.

The heavenly Jerusalem is mentioned briefly six times in *4 Ezra* (7:26; 8:52; 10:25–27, 42, 44; 13:36); it is pre-existent, has a special holiness, is linked with the Messianic kingdom and will appear at the end.[31] The single reference to the heavenly Jerusalem in *2 Bar* 4:1–7 makes a careful distinction between the earthly Jerusalem and the pre-existent city which God prepared when he created Paradise. Together, the passages in *4 Ezra* and *2 Baruch* reveal the prevalence of the conception of the heavenly Jerusalem which is used to relativize the fate of the earthly Jerusalem. In *4 Ezra* and the Apocalypse of John, the New Jerusalem appears on earth, presumably a motif that presupposes the destruction of the earthly Jerusalem.

Some of the more illuminating literary parallels between the Apocalypse of John and the Qumran scrolls are found in the six groups of fragments of a work written in Aramaic entitled "Description of the New Jerusalem"[32] (henceforth

[31] Michael Stone, *Features of the Eschatology of IV Ezra* (Harvard Semitic Studies, 35; Atlanta: Scholars Press, 1989) 101–2.

[32] There are six fragmentary Aramaic copies of the Description of the New Jerusalem: (1) 1Q32; text: J.T. Milik, *DJD* 1:134–35. (2) 2Q24 = 2QNew Jerusalem; text: M. Baillet, "Fragments araméens de Qumrân 2. Description de la Jérusalem Nouvelle," *RevB* 62 (1955) 225–45, plates I II; M. Baillet, *DJD* III, 84–89, plate XV; English translation: F. García Martínez, *The Dead Sea Scrolls Translated: The Qumran Texts in English* (Leiden: Brill, 1994) 129. (3) 4Q554 = 4QNew Jerusalem[a]; text: J. Starky, "Jerusalem et les manuscrits de la mer Morte," *Le Mond de la Bible* 1 (1977) 38–40; K. Beyer, *Ergänzungsband*, 95–104; English translations: García Martínez, *Dead Sea Scrolls*, 129–31. (4) 4Q555 = 4QNew Jerusalem[b]; English translation: García Martínez, *Dead Sea Scrolls*, 131. (5) 5Q15 = 5QNew Jerusalem; English translation: García Martínez, *Dead Sea Scrolls*, 131–33; G. Vermes, *The Dead Sea Scrolls in English* (3rd ed.; London: Penguin, 1987) 271–73. (6) 11Q18 = 11QNew Jerusalem; English translation: García Martínez, *Dead Sea Scrolls*, 133–35. In addition, 4Q232 is a Hebrew

DNJ), which together with the Temple Scroll[33] (henceforth TS), are part of a tradition linking the description of the eschatological temple and city in Ezekiel 40–48 with the description of the New Jerusalem in Rev 21:9–22:9. Here are a few selections from some of the relevant portions of each document, though each document is so extensive that these selections can only convey something of the flavor of the complete texts:

Rev 21:9–16 (NRSV): Then one of the seven angels who had the seven bowls full of the seven last plagues came and said to me, "Come, I will show you the bride, the wife of the Lamb." 10 And in the spirit he carried me away to a great, high mountain and showed me the holy city Jerusalem coming down out of heaven from God. 11 It has the glory of God and a radiance like a very rare jewel, like jasper, clear as crystal. 12 It has a great, high wall with twelve gates, and at the gates twelve angels, and on the gates are inscribed the names of the twelve tribes of the Israelites; 13 on the east three gates, on the north three gates, on the south three gates, and on the west three gates. 14 And the wall of the city has twelve foundations, and on them are the twelve names of the twelve apostles of the Lamb. 15 The angel who talked to me had a measuring rod of gold to measure the city and its gates and walls. 16 The city lies foursquare, its length the same as its width; and he measured the city with his rod, twelve thousand stadia; it length and width and height are equal.

Ezek 40:30–35 (NRSV): These shall be the exits of the city: On the north side, which is to be four thousand five hundred cubits by measure, 31 three gates, the gate of Reuben, the gate of Judah, and the gate of Levi, the gates of the city being named after the tribes of Israel. 32 On the east side, which is to be four thousand five hundred cubits, three gates, the gate of Joseph, the gate of Benjamin, and the gate of Dan. 33 On the west side, which is to be four thousand five hundred cubits, three gates, the gate of Gad, the gate of Asher, and the gate of Naphtali. 35 The circumference of the city shall be eighteen thousand cubits. And the name of the city from that time on shall be, The Lord is There.

11Q19 = 11QTemple 39.11–16; 40:11–13 (trans. García Martínez and Tigchelaar, *DSS*, 2.1259): And the names of the gates of this [cou]rtyard are according to the name[s] 12 of the children of Is[ra]el: Simeon, Levi and Judah to the East; [Reu]ben, Joseph and Benjamin to 13 the South; Issachar, Zebulun and Gad to the West; Dan, Naphtali and Asher to the North. And between one gate and another 14 the measurement is: from the North-east corner up to the gate of Simeon ninety-nine cubits; and the gate, 15 twenty-eight cubits; and from this gate up to the gate of {...} Levi, ninety-nine 16 cubits; and the gate, twenty-eight cubits; and from the gate of Levi up to the gate of Judah ... 40.11 In [it] there will be three gates to the East, and three to the South, and three 12 to the West, and three to the North. And the width of the gates will be fifty cubits and their height seventy 13 cubits.

5Q15 = 5QNew Jerusalem, frag. 1, col. 1, lines 2–5 (trans. García Martínez and Tigchelaar, *DSS*, 2.1137–41): Also [he showed me the mea]surements of [all the] blo[cks. Be-

fragment which has some relationship to the Aramaic work; J. T. Milik, *The Books of Enoch: Aramaic Fragments of Qumrân Cave 4* (Oxford: Clarendon Press, 1976) 59.

[33] On 11QTemple, see F. García Martínez, "The Temple Scroll: A Systematic Bibliography 1985–1991," *The Madrid Qumran Congress: Proceedings of the International Congress on the Dead Sea Scrolls, Madrid 18–21 March 1991*, ed. J. Trebolle Barrera and L. Vegas Montaner (2 vols.; Leiden: Brill; Madrid: Editorial Complutense, 1992) 2.393–403.

tween one block and another there is the street,] six rods wide, forty-two cubits. 3 [And] the main [street]s [which] from East [to West; the] wid[th of the street, of two] of them is ten rods, sev[enty cubits;] and the third, 4 [the one which passes to the lef]t of [the] tem[ple he mea]sured; eighte[en] rods wide, one hund[red and twent]ty-six cubits.

4Q554 (4QNJ^a ar – 4QNew Jerusalem, frag. 1, col. 1, lines 9–22 (trans. García Martínez and Tigchelaar, *DSS*, 2.1107): In the S[ou]th 10 [...] ... and they are all different from 11 [another ... from the] East [corner] which is too the North 12 [...] thirty-five stadia. And 13 [this door is called the door of] Simeon; and from this door up [to] the central door 14 [he measured thirty-five stadia; and] this door is which is called the door of 15 [Levi. And he measured from this door up to the S]outh [door:] thirty-five stadia; 16 [and this door is called the door of Judah. And from] this door he measured up to the [southweastern] corner: 17 [thirty-five stadia. And] from *Blank* this corner to the West 18 [he measured to the door 25 stadia; and this door] is called the door of Joseph. 19[...And from this door he measured to the central door:] 25 [stadi]a; and 20 [this door is called the door of Benjamin. And from] this [do]or he measured up to the door 21 [25 stadia; and this door is called] the door of Reuben and [from] this [do]or 22 [he measured up to the West corner: 25 stadia. And] from this corner he measured up to

The fragments of the DNJ have recently been subject to a detailed reconstruction and analysis by Michael Chyutin, who has integrated the fragments into a single composition.[34] Given the number and diversity of the fragments, this is obviously a highly speculative procedure, yet the results are persuasive. Thusfar scholars have utilized the DNJ in only limited and suggestive ways in their analyses of Rev 21:9–22:9.[35] While neither the terms "Jerusalem" nor "new Jerusalem" actually occur in the fragments of DNJ, there is little doubt that the work focuses on the eschatological city of Jerusalem and its temple. It is of course also true that the name "Jerusalem" occurs neither in Ezek 40–48 (which substitutes the name יהוה שמה, "Yahweh is There" in Ezek 48:35), nor in the TS. The connection between the DNJ and the TS is debated, though neither document appears to have a product of the Qumran sectarians.[36] Wachholder ar-

34 Michael Chyutin, *The New Jerusalem Scroll from Qumran: A Comprehensive Reconstruction* (JSNTSup, Supplement Series 25; Sheffield: Sheffield Academic Press, 1997).

35 See H. Reichelt, *Angelus interpres-Texte in der Johannes-Apokalypse* (Frankfurt am Main: Peter Lang, 1994) 203–6; U. Sim, *Das himmlische Jerusalem in Apk 21,1–225:5 im Kontext biblisch-jüdischer Tradition und antiken Städtebaus* (Bochumer Altertumswissenschaftliches Colloquium 25; Trier: Wissenschaftlicher Verlag, 1996) 64–67. In the most recent full-scale commentary on Revelation to appear in Germany, no mention is made of the DNJ texts: Heinz Giesen, *Die Offenbarung des Johannes* (Regensburger Neues Testament; Regensburg: Friedrich Pustet, 1997).

36 Though most scholars, following Yigael Yadin, maintain that the Temple Scroll was produced by the Qumran sectarians, arguments for excluding the Temple Scroll from the sectarian literature are proposed by Lawrence Schiffman, "The Temple Scroll in Literary and Philological Perspective," *Approaches to Ancient Judaism II*, ed. W. S. Green (Chico: Scholars Press, 1980) 143–58; H. Stegemann in "The Origin of the Temple Scroll," *Supplements to Vetus Testamentum* 40 (1988) 235–56; *idem*, "The Literary Composition of the Temple Scroll and Its Status at Qumran," *Temple Scroll Studies*, ed. G. J. Brooke (JSPS 7; Sheffield: JSOT Press, 1989) 123–89; Michael Wise, *A Critical Study of the Temple Scroll from Qumran Cave 11*

gues that the DNJ is dependent on 11QTemple,[37] while Wise followed by Broshi argue that 11QTemple is dependent on the DNJ.[38] Licht and García Martínez, on the other hand, maintain that there is neither a literary nor programmatic relationship between the two works.[39] Three observations can be made about this debate. First, contrary to Wachholder, it appears that DNJ was compiled earlier than 11Q Temple.[40] Second, while literary dependence of 11QTemple on DNJ is doubtful, both works are clearly dependent on Ezek 40–48. Third, both works reflect an opposition to the existing temple cultus and share common traditions relating to an ideal or eschatological city and temple. The DNJ was an extremely popular text at Qumran given the fact that six Aramaic copies of parts of this work have been found in caves 1, 2, 4, 5 and 11. This apparently pre-Qumran text is the closest thing to an apocalypse among the Dead Sea Scrolls, apart from such previously known texts as *1 Enoch*.[41]

In the largest fragmentary text, 5Q15 (Vermes, DSS, 271–73; Fitzmyer and Harrington, *Aramaic Texts*, 54–61) an unnamed visionary (perhaps Ezekiel) is escorted around the city which will stand on Zion by an unidentified guide (perhaps an angel), who carries a measuring rod which is seven cubits long, i.e., 10.5 feet. The narrative is written in the first-person singular of the visionary and the guided tour begins outside the city. The guide measures the rectangular wall enclosing the city which is 140 res (singular רס or ריסא, plural ר[א]סין)[42] along the eastern and western sides, and 100 res long on the northern and southern sides. Since the exact length of the *res* is uncertain, scholars have had to resort to informed speculation. M. Broshi uses a rounded figure of 1 cubit = 50 centimeters, close to the average of the long and short cubits, and estimates that the city wall of 140 × 100 *res* is ca. 30 km × 21 km = 630 square km,[43] while

(Studies in Ancient Oriental Civilization 49; Chicago: The Oriental Institute of the University of Chicago, 1990) 201–3. Yigael Yadin argued that 11QTemple was a sectarian document in "The Temple Scroll – The Longest and Most Recently Discovered Dead Sea Scroll," *Biblical Archaeology Review* 10 (1984) 32–49.

[37] B.Z. Wachholder, *The Dawn of Qumran: The Sectarian Torah and the Teacher of Righteousness* (Cincinnati: Hebrew Union College, 1983) 96.

[38] Wise, *Temple Scroll*, 61–86; M. Broshi, "Visionary Architecture and Town Planning in the Dead Sea Scrolls," *Time to Prepare the Way in the Wilderness: Papers on the Qumran Scrolls Presented by Fellows of the Institute for Advanced Studies of the Hebrew University, Jerusalem, 1989–1990*, ed. D. Dimant and L.H. Schiffman (STDJ 16; Leiden: Brill, 1995) 10–11.

[39] J. Licht, "An Idea Town Plan from Qumran: The Description of the New Jerusalem," *IEJ* 29 (1979) 45–59; F. García Martínez, "The 'New Jerusalem' and the Future Temple of the Manuscripts from Qumran," *Qumran and Apocalyptic: Studies on the Aramaic Texts from Qumran* (Leiden: Brill, 1992) 180–85.

[40] The dating of DNJ is partially dependent on its perceived relationship to the Temple scroll. Wise dates its composition to the third or early second century BCE (*Temple Scroll*, 86).

[41] García Martínez (1992:xi, xiii) refers to both 4Q246 and the Description of the New Jerusalem fragments as apocalypses.

[42] The *res* in DNJ is divided into 352 royal or long cubits (Chyutin, *New Jerusalem Scroll*, 75), though the exact length of these cubits is not known.

[43] "Visionary Architecture and Town Planning," 12.

F. García Martínez calculates that 1 *res* = 63 reeds = 441 cubits = 229 meters, so that the length and width of the rectangular wall surrounding the New Jerusalem would be 32 km × 23 km = 736 square km.[44] The wall has twelve gates (each is 21 cubits wide), three on each side (cf. Ezek 48:33–34; 11QTemple 39.12–13; 40.11–14; 4Q554), and 480 posterns (each is 14 cubits wide), one postern for each stadion. Each gate is flanked by two towers, each of which is 35 cubits square.

The inside of the city is constructed like a chessboard, with 192 insulae or blocks, each 357 cubits square, and consisting of a square row of houses enclosing an inner court, and each with a second floor. Each housing block has a tower with a spiral staircase and each has four gates, one in the middle of each side. The city is orthogonal, i. e., the streets intersect at right angles, a design virtually impossible in Palestine, but with origins in ancient Egypt and with more immediate antecedents in the Hellenistic town planning introduced by Hippodamus.[45] A system of orthogonal narrow streets 42 cubits in width separate the insulae. The main street runs east-west and is 126 cubits wide, while the somewhat narrower main street which runs north-south is 92 cubits wide. In addition there are two more east-west streets which are 70 cubits wide and two north-south streets which are 67 cubits wide. This network of streets divides the city into 16 large blocks, each 35× 25 *ris* or stadia, each consisting of 12 insulae, with a total of 192 insulae.

In Rev 21:9–22:9, the figure of an *angelus interpres* appears for the second time in the narrative. However, in this context, unlike his first appearance in 17:1–18, the *angelus interpres* has very little to explain to the seer, none of which can actually be considered interpretive. In fact, the only statement attributed to this angel is an invitation to the seer in 21:9: "Come and I will show you the bride, the wife of the lamb." Thus the angel's principal task is to "show" the visionary certain things and this is emphasized by the phrase καὶ ἔδειξέν μοι ("then he showed me") which occurs twice (21:10a; 22:1a). The *angelus interpres* in Rev 21:9–22:9 functions in three ways: (1) he measures the architecture, (2) he makes occasional comments, and (3) he leads the seer from place to place. These same three functions characterize the mysterious "man" of Ezek 40–48 and the unidentified guide in DNJ. The various Qumran fragments of the "Description of the New Jerusalem" have many parallels to Rev 21:15–21, not least of which are the frequent occurrences of variations on the phrase ואחזיני, "then he showed me."[46]

44 "The 'New Jerusalem'," 192–93.

45 M. Chyutin, "The New Jerusalem: Ideal City," *Dead Sea Discoveries* 1 (1994) 71–97, and *idem*, *The New Jerusalem Scroll*, 113–30.

46 2Q24 frag. 1, line 3; 4Q554 frag. 1, col. 2, line 15; col. 3 line 20; 4Q555 frag. 1, line 3; 5Q15 frag. 1, col. 1, lines 2, 15; col. 2, line 6; 11Q18 frag. 16, line 6; frag. 18, line 1.

In Rev 21:12, the New Jerusalem is described as having a wide and high wall with twelve gates, each inscribed with the names of "the twelve tribes of the sons of Israel." The mention of the twelve tribes implies that the New Jerusalem is not simply a city but rather the symbolic focal point for the entire land. This arrangement corresponds to Ezekiel's vision of the square outer walls of the eschatological Jerusalem (4,500 cubits on each side) with three gates on each side (Ezek 48:16–17, 30–35), purportedly named after the tribes of Israel (Ezek 48:31), though in fact named after the sons of Jacob (i. e., Joseph and Levi are mentioned rather than Ephraim and Manasseh).

The DNJ, like the TS is inspired by Ezek 40–48, though the sequence of the names of the gates in Ezek 48:30–35 is very different from DNJ 4Q554. In the latter text, the city has twelve gates, each named after one of the sons of Jacob named in the following order (the names of seven of the twelve gates survive in the text): South: Simeon, [Levi], Judah; West: Joseph, [Benjamin], Reuben; North: [Issachar, Zebulon, Gad]; East: Dan, Naphtali, Asher (4Q554). This order conforms generally to that of 11Q Temple 39.12–13; 40.11–14.

The ideal or eschatological city and/or temple complex detailed in Ezek 40–48, the DNJ, the TS and Rev 21 are all gigantic, though in the case of DNJ and the TS it is not possible to determine the exact metric equivalent of the cubit.[47] (1) *Ezekiel 40–48*. In Ezekiel, the outer court of the temple was surrounded by a square wall, 500 cubits on each side (40:5; 42:15–20; 45:2). The walls of the city itself forms a gigantic square 4,500 cubits on each side, with three gates on each side named after the twelve tribes of Israel (48:30–35). (2) *Description of the New Jerusalem*. The city in DNJ is a rectangle, measuring 140 *ris* or stadia on the east and west and 100 *ris* or stadia on the north and south, making a rectangle with a perimeter of almost 100,000 cubits, 18.67 miles by 13.33 miles.[48] (3) *Temple Scroll*. In the TS, the sanctuary complex consists of three concentric squares: (1) the inner court, or court of priests measures 300 cubits on a side, (2) the middle court, or the court of men, measures 500 cubits on a side, and (3) the outer court, or the court of Israel, measures 1700 cubits on a side, with a total perimeter of 6,800 cubits,[49] a structure which would equal the size of the Hasmonean city of Jerusalem.[50]

In all of these texts which focus on the ideal or eschatological temple, there is a striking emphasis on the twelve tribes of Israel. The association of the names

---

[47] Five different metrical equivalents to the cubit in the Temple scroll, which vary from .42 meters to .56 meters, are considered by J. Maier, "The Architectural History of the Temple in Jerusalem in the Light of the Temple Scroll," *Temple Scroll Studies*, ed. G. J. Brooke (JSPSupp 7; Sheffield: JSOT Press, 1989) 24–25.

[48] Wise, *Temple Scroll*, 82.

[49] J. Maier, *The Temple Scroll: An Introduction, Translation & Commentary* (JSOTSuppl 34; Sheffield: JSOT Press, 1985) 63–64, 144 (diagram); *idem*, "Architectural History," 50.

[50] M. Broshi, "The Gigantic Dimensions of the Visionary Temple in the Temple Scroll," *BAR* 13 (1987) 36–37; Wise, *Temple Scroll*, 82.

of the twelve tribes of Israel with the gates of the New Jerusalem in each of these texts (Ezek 48:30–35; 4Q554 frag. 1, I.9–II.11; 11QTemple 39.12–13; 40.11–14), anticipates the final realization of one of the central concerns of Jewish eschatology, the restoration of all Israel, which is repeatedly mentioned in post-exilic OT and early Jewish literature.[51]

The New Jerusalem of Revelation 21 and the city of the DNJ texts also share an emphasis on the precious stones and metals which are part of the building material used in the construction of these eschatological structures. The earliest references to precious stones used in the rebuilding of Jerusalem are found in Isa 54:11–12 and Tob 13:16. Gold overlay was used on parts of the Herodian temple (Josephus *War* 5.201, 205, 207–8; *m. Mid.* 2.3), a feature picked up in 11QTemple (36.11; 39.3; 41.15). The city in DNJ is described as having buildings of sapphire, ruby and gold (4Q554 frag. 2, II.15), and the streets are paved with white stone, alabaster and onyx (5Q15 frag. 1, II.6–7). In Revelation, the New Jerusalem is described as a whole as having the appearance of jasper, clear as crystal (21:11), or as gold, clear as glass (21:18). Similarly, the twelve foundations of the city were each constructed of a variety of precious and semi-precious stones (21:19–20). This may be an embellishment of OT texts which refer to the use of huge costly stones for the foundation of the temple of Solomon (1 Kgs 5:17; 7:10). Utopian cities constructed of precious stones and metals are not found only in Israelite-Jewish tradition, however, for Lucian speaks of a city of gold surrounded with an emerald wall with seven gates each constructed of a single plank of cinnamon with a river of myrhh running through it (*Verae historiae* 2.11).

The particular group of Essenes who formed the Qumran community had separated themselves from the temple in Jerusalem because of what they considered a laxity in ritual purity and the use of an unlawful ritual calendar (CD 20.22–23; 4QMMT),[52] though they accepted the basic validity of the temple cult and anticipated its eschatological renewal. In the interim there was a tendency to describe the community as a temple.[53] Just as the temple was the center of

---

51 Deut 30:3–4; Neh 1:9; Isa 11:12; 27:12–13; 49:5–6; 56:1–8; 60:3–7; 66:18–24; Jer 31:8, 10 [LXX 38:8, 10]; 32:37 [LXX 39:37]; Ezek 11:17; 20:34, 41–42; 34:11–16; 36:24; 37:11–14, 21–28; Hos 11:10–11; Ps 106:47; 147:2; Tob 13:5, 13; 14:6–7; 2 Macc 1:27–29; 2:7, 18; *Jub.* 1:15–17; *T. Benj.* 9:2; 10:11; *1 Enoch* 57; 90:33; Philo *De praem. et poen.* 94–97, 162–72; Bar 4:37; 5:5; Sir 36:11; 48:10; *Pss. Sol.* 11; 17:28–31, 50; *4 Ezra* 13:12–13, 39–47; *2 Baruch* 78:5–7; *T. Jos.* 19:4; *Shemoneh Esreh* 10; *m. Sanh.* 10:3; 1QM 1.2–3, 7–8; 11QTemple 18.14–16; 4Q504 [= 4QWords of the Luminaries[a]] frags. 1–2, VI.10–13; Matt 23:37; cf. Mark 13:27 (a Christian adaptation of this motif); see E. P. Sanders, *Jesus and Judaism* (Philadelphia: Fortress, 1985) 95–98.

52 Florentino García Martínez and Julio Trebolla Barrera, *The People of the Dead Sea Scrolls: Their Writings, Beliefs and Practices* (Leiden: Brill, 1995) 32–35.

53 Bertil Gärtner, *The Temple and the Community in Qumran and the New Testament: A Comparative Study in the Temple Symbolism of the Qumran Texts and the New Testament* (SNTSMS 1; Cambridge: Cambridge University, 1965); R.J. McKelvey, *The New Temple:*

purity for second temple Judaism generally, so the assembly of sectarians itself formed a substitute center of ritual purity for the sectarians. In 1QS in particular, the notion of the community as an eschatological temple comes to expression a number of times (5.4–7; 8.4–10; 9.3–6), with Israel (= laymen) as the holy place and Aaron (= priests) as the holy of holies. The anti-temple attitude expresses itself in different ways in these texts. In Ezek 40–48, the fact that the temple has been destroyed provides the context for the prophet's vision of an ideal or eschatological temple. Both the DNJ and the TS are formulated in opposition to the existing temple cult, which they correct by visualizing an ideal or eschatological temple. The implicit opposition to the existing city and temple reflected in both the DNT and the TS suggests why these texts found a sympathetic reading in the Qumran community. In Rev 21:9–22:9, the emphasis is exclusively on the city and the author calls attention to the absence of a temple from the midst of the city (Rev 21:22).[54] In both Ezekiel and the TS, the major emphasis is on the temple complex itself, while in DNJ the emphasis is on the city.

In the Temple Scroll, the ritual status of temple and the holy city is such that they form a temple-city unit so that the purity requirements which normally apply to the temple are extended to apply to the entire city.[55] Thus according to the *halakhah* in 11QTemple 45.7–18 the following conditions cause impurity and exclude people from the temple-city: (1) nocturnal emissions, (2) sexual intercourse,[56] (3) blindness,[57] (4) bodily discharges, (5) contact with the dead, and (6) leprosy.[58] A regimen of ablutions is prescribed for those who incur any of

The Church in the New Testament (London: Oxford University Press, 1969) 46–53; Georg Klinzing, *Die Umdeutung des Kultus in der Qumrangemeinde und im NT* (SUNT 7; Göttingen: Vandenhoeck & Ruprecht, 1971) 50–93.

54 A very different view of Rev 21:22 is proposed by David Flusser, "No Temple in the City," *Judaism and the Origins of Christianity* (Jerusalem: Magnes Press, 1988), 454–65, who argues that Rev 21:22–23 is not based on opposition to the temple, but is rather based on the combination of two midrashic units, the second based on Ps 132:17 in which the phrase "I have prepared a lamp for my Messiah" occurs, and the first on Isa 60:19 which refers to the Lord as the everlasting light of Jerusalem. Flusser argues that these two midrashic units are fused in a midrash on Ex 27:20 (as they also are in Rev 21:22–23): "The Holy One said to Israel: 'In this world you needed the light of the Temple, but in the world to become because of the merit of the above mentioned lamp (Ex. 27:20) I will bring you the King Messiah, who is compared to a lamp, as it is written: "There I will make a horn to sprout for David, I have prepared a lamp for my Messiah" (Ps. 132:17).'"

55 Florentino García Martínez, "The Problem of Purity: The Qumran Solution," in García Martínez and Trebolle Barrera, *People of the Dead Sea Scrolls*, 138–57.

56 There is a close parallel in CD 12.1–2 (trans. Baumgarten and Schwartz): "Let no man lie with a woman in the city of the sanctuary [בעיר המקדש] to defile the city of the sanctuary with their pollution."

57 In the Bible this regulation is limited to priests (Lev 21:17–20; cf. 1QM 7.4–5; 1QSa 2.3–11), suggesting the tendency to extent the regulations for priestly purity to the people generally; see García Martínez, "The Problem of Purity: The Qumran Solution," 146–47.

58 Two forms of ritual uncleanness not mentioned are menstruation and parturition in the case of a woman (see *TDOT* 5.336–37).

these forms of impurity and who are in consequence consigned to a special area reserved for them east of the temple-city (11QTemple 46.16–18). While in Lev 15:16–18 the period of impurity for those who have nocturnal emissions or have sexual intercourse is one day, the temple-city requires a three-day purification ritual (11QTemple 45.7–12).[59]

In Revelation, the New Jerusalem, though explicitly lacking a temple (21:22),[60] nevertheless clearly functions as a temple-city with "the glory of God as its light and its lamp is the Lamb" (21:23).[61] Impurity is also barred from this city, according to 21:27: "But nothing unclean [πᾶν κοινόν] shall enter it, nor any one who practices abomination or falsehood." At the conclusion of Revelation there is a short list of those who are excluded from the city (22:15): "Outside are the dogs and sorcerers and fornicators and murderers and idolaters, and every one who loves and practices falsehood." Despite the brevity of these two lists,[62] they exhibit a strikingly common pattern. Both lists begin with what appears to be an exclusively *ritual* category ("nothing unclean," and "dogs"), which is then followed by a list of *moral* transgressors. Given the unlikelihood that a Christian author would regard ritual and moral impurity as equally defiling, we are left with two possibilities: (1) the author understands the ritual prescriptions metaphorically in moral terms,[63] or (2) the author incorporates a source in which ritual impurity and moral transgression are regarded as equally defiling.[64] It is not easy to choose between these two possibilities, for both might be true.

---

[59] Jacob Milgrom, "Studies in the Temple Scroll," *JBL* 97 (1978) 512–13. Milgrom cites Yadin to the effect that the three-day purification is modelled after the purification commands relating to the encampment of Israel at Sinai (Exod 19:10–15).

[60] In Judaism, the eschatological expectation of a New Jerusalem generally implied a New Temple. The explicit denial of a temple in the New Jerusalem in Rev 21:22 is therefore surprising and has been frequently understood to reflect an anti-temple stance of strands of early Christianity. The traditions of Jesus' "cleansing" of the Temple and predictions of the destruction of the Temple are frequently thought to reflect an anti-temple stance. Yet Jesus' act of "cleansing" the temple makes more sense if it is understood as a symbolic action anticipating its destruction (though not impugning its purity and legitimacy), as well as implying its eschatological restoration (Mark 11:15–19 = Matt 21:12–13 = Luke 19:45–48; see J. D. G. Dunn, *Unity and Diversity in the New Testament: An Inquiry into the Character of Earliest Christianity* [Philadelphia: Westminster, 1977] 324). It is striking that saying of Jesus predicting the destruction of the existing temple and its replacement by an eschatological temple are widespread in the tradition (Mark 13:2 = Matt 24:2 = Luke 21:6; Mark 14:58 = Matt 26:61; Mark 15:29 = Matt 27:40; John 2:18–22; Acts 6:14). Following Sanders, it is likely that the action and the saying formed an original unity, that is, the saying interpreted the action (see E. P. Sanders, *Jesus and Judaism* [Philadelphia: Fortress, 1985] 61–76).

[61] W. J. Harrington, *Revelation* (Collegeville: The Liturgical Press, 1993) 218; Giesen, *Die Offenbarung des Johannes*, 135.

[62] The only common feature of these two short lists is the phrase "the one who practices falsehood (ὁ ποιῶν ψεῦδος).

[63] In the Hebrew Bible, טמא is used metaphorically of idolatry and sin (*TDOT* V, 337–41).

[64] This suggests that the source was incorporated without thoroughgoing redaction.

While the generic category of κοινός might be expected to subsume various other categories of ritual impurity, the author appears to shift gears and provides rather a list of those people who are excluded from the city because of their immoral behavior. Closely parallel to Rev 21:27, with its exclusion of anything impure from the eschatological Jerusalem, is the pronouncement in 11QTemple 47.3–6 (trans. García Martínez, *Dead Sea Scrolls*, 168):

> The city which I will sanctify, installing my name and my temple [within it] shall be holy and shall be clean from all types of impurity [כול טמאה] which defile it. Everything that there is in it shall be pure and everything that goes into it shall be pure.

The phrase כול טמאה is virtually identical with πᾶν κοινόν in Rev 21:27, and even the contexts are similar since both imply the perfect purity of the eschatological Jerusalem. Jan Fekkes has argued convincingly on the basis of diction and context, that Rev 21:27 alludes to Isa 52:1b:[65] כי לא יוסיף יבא בך עוד ערל וטמא (RSV: "For there shall no more come into you [Jerusalem] the uncircumcised and the unclean"). However, like Rev 21:27, Isa 52:1b is formulated negatively, it includes a verb meaning "to come," the goal of which is the holy city, and specifically prohibits the entrance of the unclean person or thing.[66] The prediction that unclean persons or things will not enter the eschatological Jerusalem occurs only in Isa 52:1 (and Isa 35:8) in the entire OT. Both Isa 52:1 and 35:8 represent an extension of the kind of postexilic prohibition found in Ezek 44:9, where participation in temple ritual is forbidden the foreigner (i. e., the non-proselyte who is "uncircumcised in heart and flesh," cf. Isa 56:3–8).[67] Isa 52:1 is also quoted in 4Q176 = 4QTanhumin 8.3, an anthology of texts largely from Deutero-Isaiah on the topic of comfort. While Rev 21:27 probably alludes to Isa 52:1, no such allusion is present in the close parallel in 11QTemple 47:3–6,[68] suggesting that the exclusion of the unclean from the eschatological Jerusalem was a conception not restricted to the exegesis of Isa 52:1 and 35:8. *Psalms of Solomon* 8:8–13 condemns priests whose immorality and impurity profaned the temple and the sacrifices, a charge closely paralleled by CD 5.6–8.

---

[65] Jan Fekkes, *Isaiah and Prophetic Traditions in the Book of Revelation; Visionary Antecedents and their Development* (JSNTSuppl 93; Sheffield: Sheffield Academic Press, 1994) 273–74.

[66] The adjective טמא, used as a noun, can mean "impure one" or "impure thing" in Isa 52:1, just as the phrase πᾶν κοινόν in Rev 21:27 is neuter and therefore means "every impure thing."

[67] Parallel to Ezek 44:9 is 4QFlorilegium = 4Q174 1.3–4 (trans. García Martínez, *Dead Sea Scrolls*, 136): "This (refers to) the house in which shall never enter [...] either the Ammonite, or the Moabite, or the Bastard, or the foreigner, or the proselyte, never, because there [he will reveal] to the holy ones."

[68] The identification of the sources of 11QTemple, particularly the Hebrew Bible, has been investigated in detail by Wise, *Temple Scroll*, 205–242, who categorizes 11QTemple 47.3–18 as free composition.

Without question the Description of the New Jerusalem, the Temple Scroll and the Apocalypse of John exhibit some striking similarities, many of which are explicable by common dependence on Ezek 40–48. All three texts contain descriptions of the future Jerusalem in which the city is presented as an enormous square temple-city complex with twelve gates named after the twelve tribes of Israel or the twelve sons of Jacob. While the Apocalypse of John simply states that the three gates on each of the four sides of the city are named after "the twelve tribes of the sons of Israel" (Rev 21:12), an unusual phrase which is also found in Rev 7:4, where it is followed by a unique list of eleven sons of Israel and one tribe (Manasseh). The names of the twelve city gates of the Description of the New Jerusalem are identical with those of the Temple Scroll, but both differ from the names in Ezekiel. This suggests a literary relationship between the DNJ and the TS. Only the DNJ and the Apocalypse of John feature an angelic guide with a measuring rod, probably based on the model of Ezek 40–48. In the TS it is God who narrates the measurements of various parts of the Temple-City complex. While these texts share many common features, there is no clear indication of a direct literary relationship, except perhaps between the DNJ and the TS. The heavenly existence of the holy city is emphasized in *2 Baruch* as in the Apocalypse of John, while its appearance on earth is a motif shared by *4 Ezra* and the Apocalypse of John. Thus the Apocalypse has combined emphases in *2 Baruch* and *4 Ezra* with those of Ezek 40–48, the Description of the New Jerusalem and the Temple Scroll.

5. Conclusion

The apocalyptic motifs which the Apocalypse of John shares with the three first century CE Palestinian Jewish apocalypses on the one hand, and with the Description of the New Jerusalem and Temple Scroll on the other (the latter two documents almost certainly date from the first and more probably the second century BCE), are generally to be accounted for, not through literary dependence, but as independently drawn from a written or oral stream of Palestinian Jewish apocalyptic traditions. An analogy to this somewhat vague proposal is the Fourth Gospel, which obviously shares particular traditions with the Synoptic Gospels, though direct literary dependence appears highly unlikely. Though the Apocalypse is written in the province of Roman Asia, it is permeated with the motifs and literary conventions of Palestinian Jewish apocalyptic. This investigation supports the suggestion that the author was not only an immigrant from Palestine, perhaps in the wake of the second Jewish revolt, but that he was a card-carrying Jewish apocalyptist. Since a close analysis of the Apocalypse of John betrays an intimate knowledge of many apocalyptic sources and traditions, it appears likely that the author read, and perhaps even owned a modest library of Palestinian apocalyptic literature. Whether he began his career as a Christian apocalyptist or whether he began as a Jewish apocalyptist who only later became a follower of Jesus of Nazareth, can never be known with certainty, though in my view the latter seems more inherently probable. At any rate, no other Christian author (so far as we know) ever attempted to produce an apocalypse so generically similar to the generally recognized corpus of Palestinian Jewish apocalypses as the Apocalypse of John.

The Social Matrix of the Apocalypse of John

The Apocalypse of John, more than any other NT document, has provoked an enormous number of diverse, often bizarre, schemes of interpretation. The chief reasons doubtless include the inherent polyvalence of its mythopoetic language and the recurring psychosocial relevance of its apocalyptic vision. The recent emergence of a more empathetic approach to the general phenomenon of apocalypticism (as literature, ideology and social movement), in both its Jewish and Graeco-Roman forms, has apparently encouraged new interest in the Johannine Apocalypse. This resurgence of interest in ancient apocalyptic has often been combined with another emerging focus in Biblical studies, the sociological approach to Israelite-Jewish and early Christian history and literature.[1]

1. The Social Dimensions of Early Christian Literature

Many NT scholars have attempted to approach early Christian history and literature from a sociological perspective in recent years,[2] yet the results of these studies are often disappointing. Certainly no great strides will be made by those combining shallow NT scholarship with sociological naiveté ("let the reader understand"). For present purposes, an important distinction must be made between the *sociological* approach to early Christianity and the *social-historical* approach. Sociology is the systematic attempt to formulate general rules governing human behavior through the study of social institutions, social interaction and social relationships. Given the empirical character of sociological research (particularly in the American sociological tradition), early Christianity cannot be the object of primary analytical research. It can only be the object of sociological research in the sense that theoretical models, formulated on the basis of modern empirical studies, may be applied secondarily to relevant data of early Christian history and literature. The secondary application of sociological theory

---

1 Observe the emphasis on the social function of apocalypticism in P. D. Hanson, *The Dawn of Apocalyptic* (Philadelphia: Fortress Press, 1975), and J. J. Collins, *The Apocalyptic Vision of the Book of Daniel* (Missoula: Scholars Press, 1977).

2 R. Scroggs, "The Sociological Interpretation of the New Testament: The Present State of Research," *NTS*, 26 (1980), 164–79; D. J. Harrington, "Sociological Concepts and the Early Church: A Decade of Research," *TS*, 41 (1980), 181–90.

is primarily of heuristic value in that it enables the scholar to see correlations, functions and explanations which would not otherwise be apparent.[3] It also provides unlimited scope to the imagination.

The *social-historical* approach to ancient literature and history, on the other hand, can either use a particular text as a window through which to view the social realities of which it was part, or the social dimensions of the text can be explored with a view to providing a more adequate understanding of the text itself.[4] Without denigrating the utility of sociological models, our discussion of the social matrix of the Apocalypse of John constitutes a modest attempt to unravel the social history of that text. I propose to explore the social dimensions of three interrelated elements presented to us by the Apocalypse: (1) the literary self-presentation of the author, (2) the author's conception of the nature and character of the Christian communities he addresses, and (3) the character of the interactions and relationships between the author and his readers.

2. The Self-Presentation of the Author

The fact that John addressed a lengthy apocalyptic letter, not to an individual but to seven Christian communities in western Asia Minor, implies that the author assumes a higher status than his addressees. Yet the author does not capitalize on this implication; he simply reveals that his name is "John" at the beginning and end (1:1, 4, 9; 22:8). He does not label himself in the prescript in any way other than "his (i. e., God's) servant" (1:1). The notion of "servant," often used to characterize the authors of early Christian letters, is not necessarily a title suggestive of lowliness and humility, but may be understood from OT usage as an honorific title.[5] Through stereotypical usage in the prescripts of Christian letters (nearly always implicitly addressed to those of lower social status than the authors), the designation "servant" had doubtless come to connote one of superior status (Phil. 1:1; Jas. 1:1; Jude 1), particularly when combined with the term "apostle" (Rom. 1:1; Tit. 1:1; 2 Peter. 1:1). At the beginning of the exordium, John further identifies himself as "your brother and companion in the

---

[3] For the Apocalypse, see J. Gager's attempt to view the mythic structure of the book in terms of psychoanalytic function in *Kingdom and Community: The Social World of Early Christianity* (Englewood Cliffs, New Jersey: Prentice-Hall, Inc., 1975) 49–57.

[4] See W. J. Cahnman and A. Boskoff (eds.), *Sociology and History: Theory and Research* (New York: The Free Press, 1964). This approach is emphasized by A. J. Malherbe, *Social Aspects of Early Christianity* (Baton Rouge: Louisiana State University Press, 1977) 11–20, and an excellent example of the fruitfulness of this approach is found in Malherbe's student, R. F. Hock, *The Social Context of Paul's Ministry: Tentmaking and Apostleship* (Philadelphia: Fortress Press, 1980).

[5] *TDNT,* 2.268, 276 f.; E. Käsemann, *Commentary on Romans* (Grand Rapids: Eerdmans, 1980) 5.

tribulation, kingdom and endurance in Jesus" (1:9). While this "John", whoever he may be, does not provide himself with compelling credentials, he does make a sustained attempt to identify himself with his readers. An important rhetorical feature of the Apocalypse, therefore, is the author's attempt to establish a sympathetic rapport with his readers.[6]

The Apocalypse is written, as are Jewish and Graeco-Roman apocalypses generally, in the first person as a subsequent narrative in which the author uses past tenses to tell his story, separated from the narrated events by an indeterminate period of time. The urgency of John's message suggests a short interval between vision experience and vision report, a view reinforced by the occasional switch to the present indicative (12:2, 4; 16:14; 19:9, 11), a device intended either to make the report more vivid or (more likely) to emphasize the relative contemporaneity of story time.[7] The strict concurrence between story sequence and narrative sequence, characteristic of the Apocalypse, contributes to the overall impression of verisimilitude. The Apocalypse presents the reader with both a real narrator and a real audience. Remarkably, John did not resort to the traditional apocalyptic device of pseudonymity, characteristic of all other Jewish and Christian apocalypses (with the exception of the *Shepherd of Hermas*), in order to attract attention and claim authority for his composition.[8] Again unlike the typical Jewish apocalypse, the destination of the Apocalypse is clearly indicated and the historical situation of the recipients hinted at. Though we cannot expect that the author was conscious of the pseudonymous nature of Jewish apocalyptic literature within which tradition he stood, his use of the device of subsequent narration in the first person (common in apocalyptic literature), takes on a markedly different character than the narrative of an author consciously adopting the fictional perspective of an ancient worthy. John frequently uses the first person singular of aorist verbs for seeing and hearing throughout the vision report found in 4:1 through 22:5.[9] Six times he uses the phrase "after this I saw (and behold)" (4:1; 7:1, 9; 15:5; 18:1; 19:1) as a formal device to introduce substructure; "I saw" is found thirty-two times, "I heard" twenty-six times, "I saw and behold" eight times and "I saw and heard" twice. Though John very occasionally takes upon himself the role of analyst or commentator (cf. 6:9; 7:13–17; 9:6; 13:9–10;

[6] The establishment of rapport between speaker and audience was one of the more important of ancient rhetorical conventions in judicial oratory; cf. Quintilian *Inst.* 3.8.7; 3.8.48; 11.1.1–93; Cicero *De or.* 3.10.37. Cf. G. Kennedy, *The Art of Persuasion in Greece* (Princeton: Princeton University Press, 1963) 136, 150.

[7] G. Genette, *Narrative Discourse: An Essay in Method* (Ithaca: Cornell University Press, 1980) 220.

[8] J. J. Collins, "Pseudonymity, Historical Reviews and the Genre of the Revelation of John," *CBQ,* 39 (1977), 329–43.

[9] The view that the body of the Apocalypse constitutes one extended vision report is also held by J. S. Hanson, "Dreams and Visions in the Graeco-Roman World and Early Christianity," *Aufstieg und Niedergang der römischen Welt,* (ed. H. Temporini and W. Haase; Berlin: W. de Gruyter, 1980) 2.23.2, pp. 1422 f.

14:4–5, 12; 20:6), he generally limits himself to a straight sequential narrative report. This autobiographical character of the Apocalypse has the function of encouraging the acceptance of the vision report at face value. Further, John does not exhort or admonish his readers using his own authority, but attributes paraenesis to the Risen Lord. At the same time, John does not feign ignorance of the meaning of any of the features of his vision, a typical dialogical device often occurring in revelatory literature.[10] John never asks the meaning of any features of his vision experience; occasionally however, interpretations are volunteered by the revealer (1:20; 7:13–17; 17:6b–18), giving the impression that they are included for the sake of the reader, not the author.

John does not designate himself a "prophet" (προφήτης) in the Apocalypse, though he certainly implies that he plays that role in describing the Apocalypse as a "prophecy" (προφητεία) in 1:3; 22:7, 10, 18, 19. He comes close to designating himself a prophet when he attributes these words to the revelatory angel in 22:9: "I am your fellow servant, and of your brethren the prophets." Here it appears that John is one of a number of prophets who may constitute a prophetic circle or guild. This is confirmed in 22:16, where John is clearly part of a group whose task is the communication of revelation to the churches: "I Jesus sent my angel to testify these things to you (ὑμῖν) for the churches."[11] Though John is certainly making an indirect claim to the role of prophet, his failure to make the claim explicit should not be regarded as fortuitous. John's chief opponent in the churches is "Jezebel," who calls herself a prophetess (2:20). This direct claim to prophetic authority by "Jezebel" is countered by John's greater claim to mediate divine revelation from Jesus Christ to the seven churches.

By emphasizing the common features which he and his readers share, John ensures the acceptance of his prophetic revelation. In effect, he "democratizes" the churches by emphasizing that all believers are kings and priests (1:6; 5:10), and that all (whether prophets, martyrs or Christians in general) are obliged to remain faithful to the testimony of Jesus and the word of God (1:2, 9; 6:9; 12:17; 19:10; 20:4). This egalitarian notion of the fundamental role of all Christians comes to expression whenever John lists some of the constituent elements of the church. The first of these "lists," all of which occur in hymnic contexts, is found in 11:18:

> The nations raged, but your wrath came,
> and the time for the dead to be judged,
> for rewarding your servants, the prophets and saints,
> and those who fear your name, both small and great.

[10] See H. Dörrie and H. Dörries, "Erotapokriseis," *RAC*, 6 (1966) 342–70.

[11] E. Schüssler Fiorenza, "Apokalypsis and Propheteia: The Book of Revelation in the Context of Early Christian Prophecy," *L'Apocalypse johannique et l'Apocalyptique dans le Nouveau Testament,* (ed. J. Lambrecht; Leuven: The University Press, 1980) 120 f.

The last two lines refer to Christians in general as "thy servants," and "those who fear thy name." "Prophets and saints" appear to constitute two separate but overlapping groups within the church as do the "small and great."[12] Since the phrase "small and great" is an idiom occurring frequently in the Apocalypse and the OT and means a group comprised of those from various social stations,[13] a difference in social status is suggested for the parallel phrase "prophets and saints." John twice refers to the martyrdom of prophets and saints (16:6; 18:24), and again the designations refer to two groups, both of which together with the "small and great" constitute the church as a whole. In 18:20 the phrase "saints and apostles and prophets" is placed in a context suggesting that all three groups share the same basic obligations and responsibilities. The apostles referred to should probably be understood as itinerant Christian missionaries (cf. 2:2; *Did.* 11:3–6).[14] Yet while John views all Christians as sharing the same basic privileges and obligations, that does not mean that prophets and apostles merely exemplify the potential inherent in all Christians.[15] John's calculated attempt to emphasize the common features he shares with his readers has misled some scholars by encouraging them to conclude that all Christians are potential prophets or that the church has a basically prophetic character.

Biblical scholars often define the prophetic role so that an inaugural call or commission is an essential feature.[16] The Hebrew word נבי, thought by many to have originally meant "one called," has encouraged the view that a divine call is integral to the prophetic role.[17] While OT prophetic literature does contain a number of call narratives (cf. Isa. 6:1–13; Jer. 1:4–10; Ezek. 1:1–3:11), the hypothesis that *all* Israelite prophets, whether court prophets, temple prophets or free prophets, began their careers with an inaugural vision cannot be demonstrated. The stereotypical features of many of the OT call narratives has led scholars to suspect that such accounts have a primarily social function by providing validation and legitimation for the prophet as a true spokesman of Yahweh.[18] The Apocalypse contains two call narratives, one in 1:9–20 and the second in 10:8–11:2. The first call narrative, however, is not an *inaugural* vision,

[12] A. Satake, *Die Gemeindeordnung in der Johannesapokalypse* (Neukirchen-Vluyn: Neukirchener Verlag, 1966) 39, 52 f.

[13] In the Apocalypse see 11:18; 13:16; 19:5, 18; 20:12; in the OT see Gen 19:11; Deut 1:17; 25:13 f.; 1 Sam 5:9; 20:2; 30:2, 19; 1 Kgs 22:31, etc.

[14] Satake, *Gemeindeordnung,* 56, 135.

[15] Against the conclusions of D. Hill, "Prophecy and Prophets in the Revelation of St. John," *NTS,* 18 (1971–72), 411–14.

[16] G. Ahlström, "Prophecy," *Encyclopedia Brittanica,* 15th ed., Macropaedia, XV, 62; D. Hill, *New Testament Prophecy* (Atlanta: John Knox Press, 1979) 8 f.

[17] W. F. Albright, *From Stone Age to Christianity,* 2nd ed. (Garden City, New York: Doubleday, 1957) 305.

[18] N. Habel, "The Form and Significance of the Call Narrative," *ZAW,* 77 (1965), 317; J. Blenkinsopp, *Prophecy and Canon: A Contribution to the Study of Jewish Origins* (Notre Dame: University of Notre Dame Press, 1977) 144 f.

but rather constitutes a commission to perform a specific prophetic task not only that of writing proclamations to the seven churches, but also relaying the vision report in 4:1–22:5, "the things that shall be hereafter" (1:19). The second call narrative in 10:8–11:2 functions as a resumption of the earlier call.[19] Now John may have introduced his lengthy vision report with a call narrative for formal reasons; however, the call narrative appears to legitimate John as a receiver and transmitter of revelatory visions. The call narratives in the Apocalypse, then, correlate with other rhetorical features which indicate that one of John's primary objectives was to secure the complete acceptance of his apocalyptic letter as a revelation of Jesus Christ.

Some NT scholars have regarded John as a unique type of early Christian prophet standing closer to Israelite-Jewish prophetic traditions than to those which developed in early Christianity.[20] If this view is correct, it means that the Apocalypse is not a very good source for our knowledge of early Christian prophets and prophecy. Some of the main arguments for regarding John as a unique Christian prophet are these: (1) He plays a special role in mediating divine revelation to other prophets; this function sets him above or at least apart from his prophetic colleagues. (2) John claims an authority comparable only with that claimed by apostles. (3) While NT prophets stand under the authority of the community (1 Cor. 12:10; 14:29), John's prophetic message, like that of the OT prophets, stands over and above the community. The truth of his message cannot therefore be questioned, for it is declared reliable and true by God himself (21:5; 22:6). (4) In the Apocalypse, predictions of the eschatological future are central and exhortations are marginal, while in the prophecy reflected in the Pauline letters, exhortation and admonition are central while predictive prophecy is only incidental. (5) John is the only one of his prophetic colleagues who wrote a prophetic book.

Yet these arguments are not persuasive. In defense of the representative character of John as an early Christian prophet, the following points can be made:[21] (1) Specialized social roles, such as those of the early Christian apostle, prophet, teacher, bishop, elder and deacon, are not created by those so designated, but are traditional and conventional categories meaningful within particular social settings. This suggests that John's presentation of himself as a prophet and as the author of a prophetic proclamation would have been accepted as such by the Christian communities he addressed only if his mode of speech and behavior

---

[19] A. Yarbro Collins, *The Combat Myth in the Book of Revelation* (Missoula: Scholars Press, 1976) 20.

[20] G. Friedrich, *TDNT,* VI, 849f.; D. Hill, "Prophecy and Prophets," 406–411; *idem,* "Christian Prophets as Teachers or Instructors in the Church," *Prophetic Vocation in the New Testament and Today,* ed. J. Panagopoulos (Leiden: Brill, 1977) 119–20.

[21] The article by E. Schüssler Fiorenza mentioned in note 11 above treats this entire subject in a thorough and convincing manner.

and particularly his literary self-presentation were recognizably and characteristically categorizable as "prophetic." (2) John apparently did receive a divine revelation which he relayed to prophetic colleagues who in turn transmitted it to the churches of western Asia Minor (1:1; 22:16; cf. 2:1, 8, 12, etc.). Yet prophetic groups are not uncommon in early Christianity; some appear to have functioned largely within settings of corporate worship (cf. Acts 13:1–3; 1 Cor. 14:29–32), while others functioned outside that context. In Hermas *Vis.* 2. 4. 3, for example, the Ancient Lady gives the following instructions to Hermas:

> You shall therefore write two little books and send one to Clement and one to Grapte. Clement shall then send it to the cities abroad for that is his duty; and Grapte shall exhort the widows and orphans; but in this city you shall read it yourself with the elders who are in charge of the church.

Though there is no indication that Clement and Grapte function as prophets (Hermas does not even make that claim for himself),[22] they do serve as emissaries whose task was the transmission of Hermas' revelation to various Christian groups. Perhaps more pertinent is the practice of the pagan "prophet" Alexander of Abonuteichos as reported by Lucian (*Alex.* 36):

> No sooner did Alexander get Italy in hand than he began to devise projects that were ever greater and greater, and send oracle-mongers (χρησμολόγοι) everywhere in the Roman Empire, warning the cities to be on their guard against plagues and conflagrations and earthquakes; he promised that he would himself afford them infallible aid so that none of these calamities should befall them.

During the Roman period χρησμολόγοι were not only regarded as collectors and interpreters of oracles,[23] but also as prophets or spokesmen for divinities (Philo *De spec. leg.* 4.52). The apparent pattern of John's relationship with his prophetic colleagues, then, is not unique when compared with similar practices in the Graeco-Roman world. (3) The argument that John stands over the churches he addresses like an OT prophet, while NT prophets were subject to community authority has several weaknesses. The image of the OT prophet used for the comparison is based exclusively on the role of the free prophet, and even then ignores the existence of various criteria found throughout the OT for distinguishing the true from the false prophet.[24] Even though John claims divine authority for his message, and appends conditional curses for those who might tinker with his prophetic proclamation (22:18–19), we simply do not know how his message was received. The late acceptance of the Apocalypse into the canon of the Syrian

---

[22] There are many examples of prophets and diviners in the ancient world who claimed that they were not prophets and diviners; see Amos 7:14 (cf. Y. Hoffmann, "Did Amos Regard Himself as a *Nabi'*?" *VT,* 27 (1977), 209–212); Zech 13:5; *Odyssey* 1.200 ff.; Philostratos *Vita Apoll.* 4.44.

[23] See M. P. Nilsson's review of J. H. Oliver, *The Athenian Expounders of the Sacred and Ancestral Law,* in *AJP,* 71 (1950) 422.

[24] See J. L. Crenshaw, *Prophetic Conflict* (Berlin: W. de Gruyter, 1971).

church proves that it did not receive universal approval by all Christians. Early Christian prophets characteristically claimed divine authority for their messages, yet there is no reason to regard the claims of Agabus (Acts 21:11) or Ignatius of Antioch (*Philad.* 7:1) as in any way inferior to those of John the Prophet. John had not been unopposed in the past (cf. 2:14 f., 20–23), and it is presumably for the purpose of overcoming a reluctance to accept and act on his message that he so carefully focuses on the divine authority of that message. (4) The differences between the types of Christian prophecy reflected in the Pauline letters (particularly 1 Cor. 11–14) and the Apocalypse of John have been overstated.[25] For Paul, exhortation and edification are the general objectives of intramural Christian communication, not just the task of prophets or other specially-endowed persons. Similarly, prediction for Paul (cf. 1 Thess. 4:13–18), no less than for John the prophet, serves to meet the present information and emotive needs of Christians. (5) While John is the author of an impressive piece of revelatory literature which combines Jewish and Graeco-Roman apocalyptic traditions with early Christian prophetic traditions, it is an argument from silence to claim that his colleagues did not produce revelatory books.

In summary, John's self-presentation in the Apocalypse is very carefully and calculatingly constructed to obliquely legitimate his prophetic role by making indirect claims and by emphasizing those values, norms and behaviors which he and the Christians of western Asia Minor shared and by securing the absolute and unconditional acceptance of the divine authority of his apocalyptic message.

3. The Congregations Addressed by John

The church polity reflected in the Apocalypse constitutes an erratic boulder on the terrain of the social history of early Christianity in western Asia Minor. Though the author addresses a lengthy apocalyptic letter to seven congregations, not once does he refer, overtly or covertly, to such traditional local officials as bishops, presbyters or deacons. The author refers only to God's "servants the prophets and saints" (11:18), "the blood of the saints and prophets" (16:6), "saints, apostles and prophets" (18:20), and "the blood of prophets and saints" (18:24). Here "saints" is a generic term for Christians, and "prophets" and "apostles" (always found in the plural) apparently constitute identifiable groups within the general framework of "saints." The "elders" (πρεσβύτεροι) seem to refer to heavenly, angelic beings with no relationship to the presbyterial structure of the earthly church (4:4, 10; 5:5, 6, 8, 11, 14; 7:11, 13; 11:16; 14:3;

[25] G. Dautzenberg, *Urchristliche Prophetie: Ihre Erforschung, ihre Voraussetzungen im Judentum und ihre Struktur im ersten Korintherbrief* (Stuttgart: Kohlhammer Verlag, 1975) 40–42; E. Schüssler Fiorenza, "Apokalypsis and Propheteia," 111–13.

19:4).[26] Further, the "angels" to whom each of the seven proclamations are addressed have been regarded as the bishops or leaders of the churches.[27] While most interpreters regard these "angels" as heavenly beings who function as counterparts to the earthly communities, a few hold that they are the prophetic messengers sent to each community. The more probable view, it seems to me, is that recently proposed by E. Schüssler Fiorenza, that the seven angels to whom the proclamations are addressed are the visionary counterparts of the prophets of each community.[28]

If John has revealed the polity of the seven churches, it would appear that they are directed by prophets, and perhaps apostles, without any other form of local official. When we compare this congregational polity with that of other early Christian communities in Asia Minor (using the evidence of Acts, Colossians, Ephesians, 1 Peter, the Pastorals, the Johannine Letters, the Ignatian letters and the letter of Polycarp to the Philippians), we can draw certain conclusions:[29] (1) The congregational polity reflected in these documents naturally exhibits diversity since they were written over the span of a half century. (2) With the exception of the Johannine letters the polity in these documents diverges dramatically from the Apocalypse. (3) If a continuum of simple to complex polity were constructed, the Apocalypse and the Johannine letters should be placed at the lower end of the scale, the Pastorals and the Ignatian corpus at the upper end and the remaining documents scattered at various points in between.

Given the possibility that several varieties of Christianity flourished in Asia Minor and that various changes occurred from 60 to 120 CE to affect Christian communities both internally and externally, several possible solutions to the problem of the relationship between the ecclesiastical polity of the Apocalypse and other Christian literature of Asia Minor have been proposed. (1) The prophets of the Apocalypse (including John), constitute the only office bearers in the churches addressed; if so, these groups are likely constituted of Jewish-Christian immigrants from Palestine. (2) The church polity of the Apocalypse in which prophets play a central role, is an ideal portrait or literary fiction rooted in conceptions from an earlier period in Christian history. (3) The monarchical episcopate reflected in the Ignatian letters, which reflects the ecclesiastical polity of Syria-Palestine, has been imaginatively projected on the churches of Asia Minor by Ignatius. (4) John intentionally ignored local church officials since his role as a mediator of divine revelation transcended local community concerns and because his message was directed to the entire community not just its leaders. Let us briefly take up each of these possibilities.

---

[26] Satake, *Gemeindeordnung,* 137–50.

[27] The various perspectives on this issue are reviewed in Satake, *Die Gemeindeordnung,* 150–55.

[28] E. Schüssler Fiorenza, "Apokalypsis and Propheteia," 120 f.

[29] See the succinct review in Satake, *Gemeindeordnung,* 1–18.

The first view, that prophets were the only officials of the seven churches, has been proposed by Günther Bornkamm and defended in a monograph by his student, Akira Satake.[30] The origin of this church polity is traced by these scholars to an ancient apocalyptic tradition from Palestine, to a period antedating the control of the Jerusalem church by James.[31] This proposal fails, however, since it is difficult to imagine such an immigrant community uninfluenced by Pauline tradition and evenly scattered throughout western Asia Minor. Further, the notion that these prophets were regarded as "office bearers" (*Amtsträger*) is faulty, and the theory assumes that John reveals the basic polity of the seven churches.

Against the second theory, that the polity of the Apocalypse is a literary fiction, it must be argued that John's use of his real name instead of a pseudonym militates against this view, and the description of the situations of each of the seven churches gives the appearance of verisimilitude.[32]

The third view, recently proposed by William Schoedel and taken up by Elizabeth Schüssler Fiorenza, that Ignatius' monarchical episcopate was at home only in Syria-Palestine and was ideally projected onto the five Asia Minor churches addressed by Ignatius, appears to contain an element of truth. Nevertheless we must remember that Ignatius mentions many specific individuals by name, often associating them with a particular ecclesiastical office. He mentions the bishop Damas, the presbyters Bassus and Apollonius and the deacon Zotion, all from Magnesia (*Magn.* 2:1); he refers to Onesimus, bishop of Ephesus (*Eph.* 1:3), and the deacon Byrrhus (*Eph.* 2:1; cf. *Philad.* 11:2; *Smyrn.* 12:1), Polybius bishop of Tralles (*Trall.* 1:1), Philo a deacon from Cilicia and Rheus Agathopous a deacon who accompanied Ignatius (*Philad.* 11:1; *Smyrn.* 10:1; cf. *Smyrn.* 13:1; *Philad.* 11:1). In a letter of Polycarp to the Philippians, the epistolary prescript reads "Polycarp and the presbyters with him to… "; Valens is mentioned as a former presbyter in Polycarp *Phil.* 11:1. This evidence suggests that while Ignatius might have tended to idealize and tighten the conception of the monarchical episcopate, he did not project its basic elements onto the churches of Asia Minor at the beginning of the second century CE.

The fourth proposal appears to me to be the most probable solution to the problem. First, the Apocalypse is a letter addressed to a cluster of seven churches; like many other early Christian letters this one is addressed to a group by an individual. Early Christian epistolary conventions did not necessitate the acknowledgement of the status, role, authority or even the existence of local

---

30 G. Bornkamm, *TDNT,* VI, 669 f.; A. Satake, *Gemeindeordnung.* The view that the communities of the Apocalypse represent a Jewish Christianity of Palestinian origin was earlier expressed by W. Bauer, *Rechtgläubigkeit and Ketzerei im ältesten Christentum,* 2. Aufl. (Tübingen: Mohr Siebeck 1964) 88.

31 Satake, *Gemeindeordnung,* 194.

32 J. M. Court, *Myth and History in the Book of Revelation* (Richmond: John Knox Press, 1979) 20–42.

officials. References to local officials, such as Paul's mention of bishops and deacons in Phil. 1:1, often appear fortuitous. Second, it is a fundamental error to regard John the prophet as an "office bearer"; he claims only to mediate divine revelation, and his only authority lies in the faithful communication of the message with which he was entrusted. Evidence from early Christian literature suggests that prophets were never fully integrated into the organizational structure of the local churches, even though they occasionally played an important role in communal worship. In the lists of spiritually gifted persons or offices in Pauline or Deutero-Pauline literature, emphasis is placed either on the *supralocal* nature of such leadership roles as apostle, prophet and teacher (1 Cor. 12:28 f.; Eph. 4:11), or on their *foundational* function as past leaders (Eph. 2:20; 3:5; cf. Ign. *Philad.* 9:1). In the Apocalypse, the foundational function of apostles is emphasized in 21:14, while that of OT prophets is hinted at in 10:7; the other references to prophets and apostles all focus on the supralocal character of those roles. The emphasis on apostles, prophets and teachers as supralocal leaders does not mean, as Harnack contended, that early Christianity had a rational and coherent international organizational structure. Rather, it suggests that the ideological unity of the many scattered congregations of Christians found concrete expression in the view that God himself (through Jesus and/or the Spirit) was the central authority of the church and whose will and purposes were expedited by specially endowed persons. The emphasis placed on this supernatural unity and coherence of the church appears to have diminished in varying ways (compare Ignatius with Hermas), probably in relation to the increase in the complexity and visibility of the local and regional institutionalization of early Christianity. Third, the close relationship between the saints (or Christians in general) and the prophets in the Apocalypse appears to be a rhetorical ploy John used to gain a hearing for himself and his revelatory message. By placing himself on the same plane with those he addressed, he abandoned any appeal to personal or official authority by focusing on his role as a faithful and inspired intermediary of divine revelation. Since he does not articulate with local organizational structure (whatever that may have been), he cannot use it to facilitate or justify his external intervention into the life of local congregations. Indeed, the very fact that he communicates through the genre of an apocalypse indicates that he either does not have or cannot use personal authority as the basis for his appeal. Fourth and finally, if John was an itinerant prophet (a notion that shall be discussed below), he would have been dependent on local officials and owners of houses in which congregations met for a proper reception (cf. 2 and 3 John). The absence of any criticism of local officials may be partially understood as a desire not to alienate those upon whom he might someday be dependent.

In summary, John reveals very little about the congregational polity of the local congregations he addresses. While this may be partially inadvertent, it appears primarily the result of John's concerted emphasis on the supralocal character of the saints, apostles and prophets. As a prophet, his intervention into the local affairs of each of the seven churches must be viewed, not as an attempt on his part to meddle or swing his weight about, but rather to faithfully mediate divine revelation with truthfulness and accuracy.

4. John's Relationship to the Seven Churches

If we have correctly understood the *Tendenz* of the Apocalypse, it appears that John's major objective was the presentation of himself and his message in such a way that the focus would be on the message that would be recognized as legitimate and authoritative by the churches. John could not presume but had to ensure such recognition and acceptance. As an heir of Jewish and Graeco-Roman apocalyptic traditions, John was an advocate of passive resistance to prevailing religious and cultural values, norms and behaviors of Roman Hellenism. This resistance was encouraged by the seductive vision of God's cosmic triumph over the Roman empire and her satanic allies in the spiritual world.

Since John addressed the seven proclamations in Rev 2–3 to seven particular communities and gives evidence of familiarity with the situation of each, the fact that he was personally known to the communities is inescapable. John was probably an itinerant prophet in the sense that he traveled a restricted circuit to a limited number of Christian congregations. Modern views of early Christian prophets generally cast them into the role of either *itinerant* prophets (reflecting an early Christian Palestinian prophetic tradition), or *community* prophets (reflecting Hellenistic tradition). This typology, however, is an oversimplification.[33] The appropriate framework for understanding the itinerant character of early Christians and their leaders is the recognition of the astonishing degree of mobility which characterized Graeco-Roman society during the first centuries CE.[34] First century Judaism, with an enormous Diaspora population (various estimates range from four to seven million), had an effective international network of communication through the active maintenance of contacts between the many Jewish communities that dotted the Graeco-Roman world. Christianity emerged within Judaism and became heir to many practices regarding travel and communication. The evidence from early Christian literature suggests that there were at least three types of itinerant prophets in early Christianity: (1) the prophet who traveled to a particular place to execute a divine commission (Acts,

[33] This view is represented by U.B. Müller, *Prophetie and Predigt im Neuen Testament* (Gutersloh: Verlagshaus Gerd Mohn, 1975) 19–23.

[34] L. Casson, *Travel in the Ancient World* (Toronto: Hackert, 1974) 122, 127, 147f.; W.M. Ramsey, "Roads and Travel (in the New Testament)," *Hastings Dictionary of the Bible,* V, 375–402; *idem, Letters to the Seven Churches* (New York: Hodder & Stoughton, 1904) 15–20; A.J. Malherbe, *Social Aspects of Early Christianity,* 62–70.

Shepherd of Hermas), (2) the prophet who traveled a circuit with some regularity (John the Prophet), and (3) prophets whose wandering was an enactment of the ascetic values of homelessness, lack of family ties and the rejection of wealth and possessions (Peregrinus, prophets of the *Didache*, and prophets of the Q-Community).

Apart from John's familiarity with the situation of each of the seven churches, the only specific indication of any previous relationship is found in the proclamation to the church at Thyatira. Referring to the prophetess "Jezebel," Jesus through his prophet John declares: "I gave her time to repent" (2:21). This may be regarded as a reference to an earlier oracle directed to Jezebel herself by John, or perhaps by one of the members of his prophetic circle.[35] Though there is no convincing evidence to suggest that John had resided in one of the seven communities, a number of considerations point in the direction of Ephesus as his home base. John had his visionary experience on Patmos, off the coast of Miletus, closest to Ephesus of any of the seven churches. An ancient tradition associates both John the Apostle and John the Presbyter with Ephesus (Eusebius *Hist. eccl.* 3.39.5–7; 7.25. 16; Jerome *De uir. inl.* 9). Further, it is the Ephesian church that had rejected the Nicolaitan heresy and which had tested and rejected the false apostles (2:2), who may have represented the Nicolaitan views. Since scholars are agreed that the Nicolaitans mentioned in the proclamations to Ephesus and Pergamum are identical with the movement represented by "Jezebel" in Thyatira, it appears that John's opposition to this movement had been more successful in Ephesus than anywhere else. It is not improbable that John himself led the opposition to the Nicolaitans in Ephesus prior to his departure for Patmos.

John's relationship to the congregations of western Asia Minor may be suggested by the model of "Jezebel" and her entourage in Thyatira. On the other hand, it can be argued that "Jezebel" is simply portrayed as exercising a considerable influence in Thyatira, but that she did not in fact chair a prophetic circle. Yet in view of the fact that the Nicolaitans mentioned in the letters to Ephesus and Pergamum are probably part of the movement sponsored by "Jezebel" of Thyatira, it is not improbable that "Jezebel's" prophetic circle consisted of colleagues who are influential in Pergamum and who have been less than successful in Ephesus. Since "Jezebel" and the Nicolaitans are associated by John with such practices as sexual immorality and eating meat sacrificed to idols – and these are regarded as innovative forms of behavior by John – it is likely that "Jezebel" and her colleagues legitimated these innovative practices through prophetic pronouncements. The mention of Balaam who taught Balak to place a stumbling

[35] W. Bousset, *Die Offenbarung Johannis* (6. Aufl.; Göttingen: Vandenhoeck & Ruprecht, 1906) 219; R.H. Charles, *A Critical and Exegetical Commentary on the Revelation of St. John* (Edinburgh: T & T. Clark, 1920) 1.71; E. Lohmeyer, *Die Offenbarung des Johannes,* (2. Aufl.; Tübingen: Mohr Siebeck 1953) 28; G.R. Beasley-Murray, *The Book of Revelation* (London: Oliphants, 1974) 21; U.B. Müller, *Prophetie and Predigt,* 69.

block before the sons of Israel that they might eat food sacrificed to idols and practice immorality, confirms this view, for Balaam was a paradigmatic false prophet in both early Jewish and early Christian literature.

John's intense opposition to "Jezebel" and the Nicolaitans appears to have been grounded, not only in the pagan practices they encouraged, but also in the prophetic role they played in legitimating their behavior. John's battle with the Nicolaitans and "Jezebel" was, in a word, a conflict between prophets. If we review the proclamations to the seven churches with this conflict in view, many of the congregations appear to be constituted (from John's perspective) of two to three tendencies or parties. The conflict is not really over immorality and the eating of sacrificial meat alone, but over the stance toward cultural and religious accommodations which these practices represent. John, with his apocalyptic tradition of nonconformity and opposition to the influence of the dominant alien culture, represents a conservative approach to the question of accommodation to paganism. He has allies in the churches of Ephesus, Smyrna and Philadelphia; some in Thyatira (2:24 f.), and few in Pergamum, Sardis (3:4) and Laodicea.

"Jezebel" and the Nicolaitans represent liberal tendencies in these churches, and they appear to have had their strongest influence in the churches of Pergamum and Thyatira and to have been generally unsuccessful in Ephesus. The majority of Christians, however, seem to belong to a centrist tendency or party, which has not yet moved into the camp of the Nicolaitans, but that (from John's perspective) has departed from the works done at first (2:5), or whose works are imperfect in God's sight (3:2), or who are neither cold nor hot (3:15 f.). If this centrist party dominated most of the churches of Asia Minor, these congregations would clearly have provided a battleground for the divinely-legitimated movements led by John on the one hand and "Jezebel" and the Nicolaitans on the other. Scholars have erred, I think, in their tendency to anachronistically conceptualize many deviant movements within early Christianity as Gnostic;[36] that label has little intrinsic justification when applied to the Nicolaitan movement in the churches of western Asia Minor. Since John's anti-Roman apocalyptic tradition is by definition opposed to all cultural accommodation, it is likely that "Jezebel" and the Nicolaitans do not share that tradition. Yet their use of prophecy to legitimate accommodationism suggests that they also stood within some kind of definite prophetic or oracular tradition. One important feature of the Apocalypse which has not yet been treated with the detail it deserves is the marked anti-magical polemic which pervades it.[37] Revelatory magic is the subject of a great quantity of magical papyri preserved from the first through the fourth centuries CE. Using this material, Eric Peterson demonstrated how the

[36] E. Schüssler Fiorenza, "Apocalyptic and Gnosis in the Book of Revelation," *JBL,* 92 (1973) 565–81.

[37] See D. E. Aune, "Magic in Early Christianity," *Aufstieg und Niedergang der römischen Welt*, (ed. H. Temporini and W. Haase, Part II, 23.2 Berlin: W. de Gruyter, 1980) 1555 f.

Shepherd of Hermas, even though the author polemicized against such practices (cf. *Mand.* xi), has been profoundly affected by notions associated with Hellenistic revelatory magic.[38] It is not unlikely that the opponents of John stood in the tradition of Hellenistic revelatory magic themselves.

In summary, John the prophet, like "Jezebel" his Nicolaitan opponent, belongs to an association of prophets found in many if not most of the communities addressed by the Apocalypse. Many of these communities are dominated by a centrist party which neither espouses the kind of cultural and religious accommodation advocated by the Nicolaitan prophets, nor the kind of strict nonconformist behavior advocated by John the prophet. The Apocalypse constitutes a final, culminating statement of the values, norms and behaviors advocated by John in which the author seeks acceptance by his readers of the divine revelation he mediates. In that revelation the position of John's opponents is attacked and a definitive statement of his apocalyptic vision of God's final defeat of Rome, her satanic allies, and the cultural accommodationists is promulgated under the name of the Risen Lord of the church.

38 E. Peterson, "Beiträge zur Interpretation der Visionen im Pastor Hermae," *Frühkirche, Judentum und Gnosis* (Rom, Freiburg u. Wien: Herder, 1959) 254–70.

Stories of Jesus in the Apocalypse of John

1. Introduction

In looking to the Apocalypse of John for an answer to the question "Who is Jesus Christ?" the problem is how to begin. Since this is an essay and not a book, it is necessary to find a manageable way to deal with a potentially expansive subject. Inasmuch as the Apocalypse, like the Gospels and Acts, consists primarily of narrative discourse (with a heavy blend of description), I will discuss the Christology of the Apocalypse from the methodological standpoint of narrative theology. While theological claims are intentionally embedded in the narratives and descriptions of the Apocalypse, as they are in the Gospels and Acts, stories and descriptions cannot easily be translated into ideas, nor is that translation necessarily desirable. The meaning of a concrete event (in history or in story) is the series of events with which it is causally related, not a supposedly "deeper" allegorical or symbolic reading of the events, characters, and actions that constitute a realistic narrative. The Christological debates of the fourth and fifth centuries centered on metaphysical issues, including such ontological categories as the nature, substance, and being of Christ. There was, however, little focus on the work of Christ during this period, and it was precisely the work of Christ that was the primary concern of the New Testament authors. While the Christological doctrines which emerged from this period have largely determined the perspective from which the Church reads the Bible,[1] these categories are more at home in exposition and dialogue (the question-and-answer was an early format for theological discussion) than in either narration or description. Unless we wish to turn the Gospels and the Apocalypse into something they are not, it is simply not acceptable to sever meaning from the mutual implications of events in the order of their narration.

Before proceeding further, it is appropriate at this point to present a brief overview of the literary character of the Apocalypse. The author has imposed an artificial literary unity on his work by presenting the whole as a single, extensive vision report which is introduced in 1:9 and concludes somewhat uncertainly at 22:20. The external narrative unity provided by this overarching vision report

[1] George Lindbeck, *The Nature of Doctrine: Religion and Theology in a Postliberal Age* (Philadelphia: Westminster, 1984) 74.

does not guarantee the unity of the episodes which constitute it. Further, this lengthy vision report is framed as a letter with an epistolary prescript (1:4–5a), and concludes with a grace benediction (22:21). Despite recent arguments to the contrary, this does not mean that the material framed by these formal epistolary elements is epistolary in character. This letter-framework is further subordinated to a meta-textual introduction (1:1–3) which is "meta" because it self-consciously refers to the text which follows, much as a title prefixed or suffixed to a literary work. This introductory paragraph in Rev 1:1–3, which has no analogies in ancient letters, is an auctorial innovation that overrides the formal epistolary features signaling that what follows is a vision narrative rather than a letter.

2. The Uses of Discourse in the Apocalypse

Progression and cohesion are the most basic rhetorical features of both written texts and oral traditions. The focus in this essay is on the first two of the four basic types of progression or discourse used in written texts: narrative, description, exposition and dialogue. Though the Apocalypse of John is dominated by narrative discourse (the main feature of which is temporal progression), it is quite different from the type of narrative discourse which characterizes the Gospels and Acts. Most scholars now recognize that, despite certain distinctive features, the Gospels are basically similar in literary form to Hellenistic biographical literature, while Acts (or Luke-Acts) has close affinities to Hellenistic historiography. The Apocalypse of John, on the other hand, is associated with the apocalypse genre of early Jewish and early Christian revelatory literature. Since types of discourse, with some limits, typically cross generic boundaries, it is not surprising that the narrative discourse in the Apocalypse, functions in a markedly different way than it does in the Gospels and Acts.

Narrative Discourse

There are four major characteristics of narrative discourse in apocalypses in general and the Apocalypse of John in particular, which distinguish it from narrative discourse in the Gospels and Acts. First and most importantly, the Apocalypse of John narrates a Master Story or Grand Narrative into which believers can read their own stories in a way analogous to how many in the last hundred and fifty years have inscribed their own stories into such seductive alternate Master Stories as Marxism, Darwinism and Freudianism. The Master Story reflected in the Apocalypse is actually a mythically formulated account of two different and conflicting sets of stories, the story of the People of God (i. e., the story of the followers of Jesus Christ) paired with the story of the Evil Kingdom (i. e., the story of the Roman empire and those under its domination). Both are set in the natural world. The Master Story of the Apocalypse is generated by the conflict between these two rival stories, which are significant primarily because they mask a paired opposing set of supernatural stories of cosmic significance: the conflict between the story of God and Jesus set over against the story of Satan. This Master Story, like all other stories, has a plot which focuses on the resolution of conflict, and it is the intersection of these two stories which generates the conflict. In this case the conflict is resolved with the ultimate triumph of God with Jesus and the followers of Jesus over Satan and the people of the Roman Empire who blindly and obstinately follow him. This Master Story is a Christian rewriting of an early Jewish Master Story typically found in early Jewish apocalypses, which is unapologetically utopian, and is intended by the author to be received as the true story of the world. This Christian Master Story is larger, longer and stronger than the individual stories of those followers of Jesus who first heard it read aloud in worship, for it not only includes everything, but also tells the hearers who they are while assuring them that things cannot fail to turn out better. The dramatic (or melodramatic) character of the Apocalypse invites the hearers to identify themselves in the story and in so doing to subordinate their own stories to that of the Master Story. The appropriate term for moving from a failed Master Story (the story of the Roman Empire and those under its domination) to a new Master Story (the story of the victory of God through Jesus Christ) or for subordinating one's own story to the Master Story is "conversion."

The second major characteristic of narrative discourse in the Apocalypse is that, unlike most other narrative genres, the narrative sequences or episodes in the Apocalypse, while exhibiting internal temporal progression, are sometimes linked by expressions indicative of temporal succession, but often are not. For example, the *dramatis personae* in the story of the Woman, the Child and the Dragon in Rev 12:1–17, the Dragon excepted, are found nowhere else in the book, and the story itself is connected only tenuously with the story of the Beast from the Sea and the Beast from the Land which follows in Rev 13. Further, the rather nightmarish tale of the enslavement of a willing world by the two Beasts in Rev 13, is suspended by an enigmatic conclusion in which the riddle of the mysterious number of the Beast is posed but not answered (13:18). The threads of this interrupted narrative are eventually picked up again and finally brought to a conclusion when the Rider on the White Horse captures the two Beasts (the second is a.k.a. the False Prophet), consigns them into the lake of fire and slaughters the armies of the kings of the earth (19:11–21). Thus while some of the narrative episodes in the Apocalypse appear to be *disjecta membra*, they are all explicitly or implicitly segments woven into the Master Story. They are all there for a reason.

Third, like all stories, the Gospels, Acts and the Apocalypse each have a beginning, middle and end. While the story world of the Gospels and Acts is set in the *past*, the story world of the Apocalypse of John is set primarily in the *future*. However, paradoxically, the canonical and ecclesial setting of the Gospels means that even though the story of Jesus has a literary "end" in each of them (the empty tomb in Mark, the resurrection appearance of Jesus to the eleven in Matthew, the ascension of Jesus in Luke, and the resurrection appearances in John), each Gospel nevertheless remains open and is perpetuated in the story of the people of God or the Church, a story which continues to be shaped by the story of Jesus.[2] This means that the Gospels too function as a Master Story, since whatever narrative gaps they have are filled in by the people of God who read them in public worship in the context of the overarching Master Story which they already know and own.

While the future is normally considered open since the possibilities it holds out have yet to be realized (though here "openness" is admittedly a modern conception), the future in the Apocalypse of John is essentially closed, for it concludes with a vision of the final triumph of God with Jesus, forever united with the people of God in the New Jerusalem in a renovated heaven and earth. We are told how the Master Story ends, even though its ending lies in the future. There is an important sense in which the Apocalypse is the appropriate work to conclude the Christian biblical canon, for it is the only biblical book (including the Gospels) which draws everything to a final and decisive conclusion.

Fourth, the Gospels and Acts consist of what Hans Frei has designated "realistic narrative," i. e., they are history-like and set in a recognizable, real world. The narrative episodes of the Apocalypse, however, are "mythical narratives," i. e., they are highly symbolic and imaginative stories placed in settings in heaven or in the future (or both) which the living have not yet experienced. "Realistic narrative" or "history-like narrative" for Frei is "mimetic" (following Erich Auerbach), a quality which has nothing to do with the common distinction between fiction and nonfiction (i. e., story and history), for "realistic narrative" is found in both categories. It is tempting to mistake the "realistic narrative" of the Gospels for history, a move which Frei thinks led to the "eclipse" of Biblical narrative.[3] Since the visions of the Apocalypse are not set in the real world it is of course less tempting to read them (as many have) as history written in advance. Finally, for Frei, "realistic narrative" carries no hidden meaning, but simply means what it says. Events in "realistic narrative" are not interchangeable symbols. One of the central characteristics of "mythical narrative," however, is precisely the fact that events are interchangeable symbols, and the narrative embodies a subtext encoded in story form. This subtext is the Master Story.

Since realistic narrative, though found throughout the Bible, is not the only type of discourse in Scripture, Frei might be faulted for ignoring the other main forms of discourse, i. e., for being reductionistic by limiting all forms of

---

[2] Gerard Laughlin, *Telling God's Story: Bible, Church, and Narrative Theology* (Cambridge: Cambridge University Press, 1996) 85.

[3] Hans W. Frei, *The Eclipse of Biblical Narrative: A Study in Eighteenth and Nineteenth Century Hermeneutics* (New Haven: Yale University Press, 1974) 11–12

discourse to narrative, and even for ignoring other types of Biblical narrative such as apocalyptic. However, like the realistic narrative of the Gospels, the Apocalypse cannot be reduced to ideas or timeless truths, but rather must be read in terms of a more basic narrative – the Master Story – which it implies. Since even descriptive discourse in the Apocalypse presupposes the basic realistic narrative of the Master Story (as we shall see below), I think that Frei has correctly identified realistic narrative as the hermeneutically significant key to understanding the Bible.

Descriptive Discourse

Like most narrative genres, the Apocalypse uses other types of discourse in subordinate ways. One of the more important of these is description, a type of discourse which in apocalypses is organized spatially, usually from the point of view of the revealer or the visionary. Description is a central feature of most apocalypses, for visual aspects of revelatory experience can only be imagined by the hearer through verbally communicated word-pictures. Relatively long descriptive passages occur, therefore, with some frequency (1:12–16; 4:2–11; 7:9–12; 9:7–11; 10:1–3; 15:5–8; 17:3–6; 19:11–16; 21:10–22:5), along with other shorter passages too numerous to mention. The symbolic character of descriptive discourse more frequently than not presupposes a story or can only be appropriately understood within the context of a story already known to the hearers. When John looks toward the throne of God, for example, and sees "a Lamb standing as though slain, with seven horns and seven eyes" (5:6), these symbols obviously represent the story of the death, resurrection and cosmic sovereignty of Jesus Christ.

Two of the more extended descriptive passages center on Jesus Christ, but both could hardly differ from each other more than they do. The first is the description of the One like a Son of Man (1:12–16), while the second is that of the Rider on the White Horse (19:11–16). Despite their differences, both descriptive passages make sense within the context of the Master Story known to the hearers, but not with each other.

Expository Discourse

The Apocalypse also contains some lengthy passages of expository discourse, primarily at the beginning of the book (1:1–3, 4–5a, 5b–8; 2:1–3:22), but here also the exposition makes sense only in light of a story known to the hearers. Progression in expository discourse is based primarily on various types of logical progressions which link a series of statements, questions or commands together. In the New Testament, expository discourse is concentrated in the epistolary literature, but these often have a dialogical character as well, for example, when

Paul or the author of James make use of diatribe style. There are, to be sure, a few quasi-dialogical passages in the Apocalypse as well (7:13–17; 17:6b–18; 22:8–17), though this type of discourse is more common in Jewish apocalypses which feature an *angelus interpres* in dialogue with the visionary, a literary device all but absent from the Apocalypse. Dialogical progression is primarily marked by questions and answers as well as affirmations and negations.

3. Opening Gambits

The Title (Rev 1:1–3)

The first thing that the first hearers of the Apocalypse of John heard on the occasion of its inaugural reading was the title and a beatitude bundled together in a short meta-textual unit of expository discourse (Rev 1:1–3). While this is a rich and complex text, my present concern is only the christological signals which this passage might have sent to the original hearers and how it might have prepared them for what follows.

The name "Jesus Christ" occurs twice in this title, and elsewhere in the book only in the epistolary prescript which immediately follows in 1:5. "Jesus Christ" in all three references is a proper name for that Jesus who is the object of Christian faith, with no hint that the designation "Christ" may have gained currency earlier as a Messianic title predicated of Jesus in confessional contexts, i.e., "Jesus is the Christ," meaning "Jesus is the Messiah" (John 11:27; 20:31; Acts 17:3; 1 John 2:22; 5:1). "Jesus Christ" as a proper name is a characteristic usage of Paul (the earliest extant Christian author), who never uses the term "Christ" (i.e., "Messiah") as a predicate of "Jesus." All three references to "Jesus Christ" in the Apocalypse link him closely with God as the following discussion will indicate.

The title "the Christ" or "the Messiah" occurs four times in the body of the Apocalypse (11:15; 12:10; 20:4, 6), always referring to the exalted Jesus, always with the definite article (and so should be translated "the Messiah"), always closely linked with the cognate Greek terms for "kingdom" and "to reign," three times in tandem with names for God (11:15; 12:10; 20:6), twice in hymnic contexts (11:15; 12:10), and once in a beatitude (20:6). This leaves a single instance where "the Christ" occurs in a narrative context (20:4: "they came to life and reigned with the Messiah a thousand years"). Three of the four contexts in which the term "the Messiah" is used (11:15; 12:10; 20:6) suggest that the final victory of God is conceived only by and with Jesus Christ.

The first three words in Rev 1:1 can be translated "This is a revelation from Jesus Christ," a phrase which characterizes the entire Apocalypse of John as divine in origin. This revelation is further described as having been given to

Jesus Christ by God for the purpose of disclosing to the servants of God those end-time events which will shortly occur. The Lamb's reception of the sealed scroll from the One seated on the throne in Rev 5:7 (discussed below) is certainly an appropriate dramatization of this opening clause in the Apocalypse.

The fact that God imparted this revelation exclusively to Jesus Christ has several implications. First, Jesus Christ is not a figure of the past alone, but also – and more importantly – of the present. This point is reinforced by the vision of one like a son of man in 1:9–20, which will be discussed in more detail below. Second, Jesus Christ functions as the sole mediator of divine revelation. He functions, as it were, as the Director of Communications for the heavenly court. He is also, after God himself, the central divine actor in the Master Story which follows, though he appears in a number of guises and with a number of aliases, all of which transparently refer to Jesus Christ for the believing hearers who have subscribed to the Master Story.

According to Rev 1:2, John testifies to "the word of God and the testimony borne by Jesus Christ," a phrase which can also be translated "the word of God, that is, the testimony borne by Jesus," thus referring to a single message. If I have correctly construed the linking "and" as epexegetical or explanatory, then "the word of God," a widely-used OT term for divine revelation, is equated with "the testimony borne by Jesus." Understood in this way, this clause is another way of saying that God has given the revelation to Jesus Christ, and "the testimony borne by Jesus Christ" is precisely that of the revelation transmitted to John, i.e., the contents of the Apocalypse, as the qualifying phrase "whatever he saw" indicates.

Epistolary Salutation (Rev 1:4–5a)

In the expository salutation of the epistolary prescript in Rev 1:4–5a, John greets the churches in Asia with "grace and peace" from God (using the very special designation "the One who is and was and who will come"), from the seven spirits before the throne, and "from Jesus Christ, the faithful witness, the firstborn from the dead, and the ruler of the kings of the earth." Again, God and Jesus Christ are closely linked, separated by the reference to the seven spirits before the throne (apparently the seven archangels). This epistolary salutation has close links with those used by Paul, though the sources of grace and peace for him are typically limited to "God the Father and the Lord Jesus Christ" (Rom 1:7; 1 Cor 1:3; 2 Cor 1:2; Gal 1:3; Phil 1:2; Phile 3), with no intervening reference to any other supernatural being or beings.

Each element of an epistolary prescript was typically susceptible to expansion (a close parallel to Rev 1:4–5a is found in Gal 1:4), and here the name "Jesus Christ" in the salutation is expanded by three appositional phrases, "the faithful witness, the firstborn from the dead, and the ruler of the kings of the earth."

Though the author is still using expository discourse, these three phrases are a succinct way of summarizing the distinctive events in the story of Jesus. "The faithful witness" refers to his death (preceded by his testimony before hostile leaders), "the firstborn from the dead" refers to his resurrection, and "the ruler of the kings of the earth" refers to the certainty of his future cosmic triumph over all opposition when he truly becomes "King of kings and Lord of lords" (Rev 17:14; 19:16). These three events are simply placed in sequential order with no indication of a causal relationship, though a narrative is clearly implied. The content of this part of the epistolary prescript can be summarized in this way: death of Christ + resurrection of Christ + sovereignty of Christ (the plus sign indicates that the events are placed in sequential order with no indication of causal relationships).

The Doxology (Rev 1:5b–6)

The epistolary prescript in 1:4–5a is closely followed by a doxology, a pattern also found in Gal 1:5. While early Christian doxologies were almost exclusively addressed to God, this one is exceptional in that it is directed to Christ (the doxology in 5:13 is directed to both God and Christ). It is therefore a liturgical or quasi-liturgical witness to the phenomenon of the worship of Jesus which Richard Bauckham has rightly emphasized. Though Jesus is not explicitly named, the content makes it certain that it is directed to Jesus Christ:

> To the one who loved us
> And freed us from our sins by his blood,
> And made us a kingdom,
> Priests to his God and Father.
> To him is the glory and power for ever. Amen.

Here the author abruptly switches from expository to narrative discourse, for this doxology is essentially a narrative centering on two significant episodes in the story of Jesus, his liberating death and the formation of those who experienced that liberation into a group, i. e., the Church. The content of this doxology can be summarized in this fashion: Christ's liberating death → formation of a liberated people (the arrow indicates that the event to the left of the arrow is understood as causing the event to the right of the arrow). Yet a closer examination of the doxology suggests that this schema can be expanded with the addition of two actions: Christ's anticipatory love for his people → Christ's liberating death → formation of a liberated people → the worship of God. The phrase "the one who loved us" is striking, for it refers to the motivation of the historical Jesus to sacrifice his life on behalf of others. It is thus one of the few references to the historical Jesus found in the Apocalypse. This doxology is one of a number of formulaic passages in the New Testament which coordinate the love of Jesus (reflecting the motivation for his voluntary death) with the death of Jesus (Gal 2:20: "who loved me and gave himself for me"; cf. Eph 5:2, 25). Here Christ's self-giving love is personalized by Paul who regards himself (and no doubt others like him) as the object of the voluntary death of Jesus Christ. Emphasis on the voluntary, sacrificial nature of the death of Christ and the salvific benefits of that death were central features of early Christian catechesis (Mark 10:45 = Matt 20:28; John 10:11; Gal 1:4; 1 Tim 2:6; 1 John 3:16). The doxology in Rev 1:5b–6 is similar to the hymn-like statement in Titus 2:13–14, though "love" is substituted for "gave": "Jesus Christ, who gave himself for us to redeem us from all iniquity and to purify for himself a people of his own who are zealous for good deeds."

4. The Lamb in Rev 4:1–8:1

Rev 4:1–8:1 is a narrative unit which consists of a lengthy heavenly throne room scene in two parts (4:1–11 and 5:1–14), followed by a narrative of the breaking of the seven seals by the Lamb and the resultant plagues which afflict the people of the world (6:1–17, 8:1). The Lamb dominates the entire narrative unit even when he does not appear to be present. This narrative is "interrupted" in a puzzling way between the breaking of the sixth and seventh seals by a two-part vision: the sealing of the 144,000 on earth (7:1–8), followed by the heavenly throne room and the innumerable host worshiping God (7:9–17).

The Heavenly Throne Room (Rev 4:1–11)

The vision of the heavenly throne room in Rev 4, apart from a brief narrative setting in v. 1, consists almost entirely of descriptive discourse (vv. 2–11). The One seated on the throne is described as appearing like jasper and carnelian, while a rainbow which looked like an emerald surrounds the throne, from which comes thunder, lightning, and strange noises. All these symbols are attempts to capture the majesty and power of God, who is further described as surrounded by seven torches of fire (i. e., the seven spirits of God), the four living creatures and the twenty-four elders, all engaged in unending worship. While a first reading of Rev 4 turns up no reference to Jesus, this reading will have to be revised in light of Rev 5.

The Investiture of the Lamb (Rev 5:1–14)

The essentially static scene of Rev 4 becomes the prelude to the brief dramatic episode in Rev 5, the quest for one who is worthy to unseal the mysterious scroll (5:1–7), and the subsequent investiture of the Lamb (5:8–13). The chapter begins with a close-up shot of a single object in the right hand of God, a mysterious scroll sealed with seven seals. An angelic herald of the heavenly court asks if there is anyone who is worthy to open this scroll, but no one can be found throughout the entire cosmos. This fruitless cosmic job-search is obviously staged to emphasize the unique qualifications of the Lamb. John himself weeps that no one worthy can be found, but is comforted by one of the twenty-four elders who declares that the lion of the tribe of Judah, the root of David, has conquered and is therefore qualified to break the seals and open the scroll (5:5). Looking more closely, John sees, between the throne of God and the four living creatures and the twenty-four elders, "a Lamb, standing as though slain, with seven horns and seven eyes, which are the seven spirits of God sent out to all the earth" (5:6). As soon as the seven spirits of God are mentioned, we realize that the Lamb was present in the heavenly throne room all along, though initially unrecognized. In 4:5, "the seven torches of fire" are interpreted as "the seven spirits of God," just as the seven eyes of the Lamb are interpreted as "the seven spirits of God sent out to all the earth" (5:6). The seven torches of fire are the seven eyes of the Lamb.

John has juxtaposed two symbolic descriptions in vv. 5–6, each representing a widely-known story. The initial description of the Lamb identified him with traditional language as the Messiah, who must be of Davidic ancestry, and whose main function is to liberate Israel from Gentile oppressors, i.e., "who has conquered" (5:5). Yet this "Messianic" figure is reinterpreted through his depiction as a slain, yet living Lamb, with seven horns and seven eyes. This somewhat grotesque imagery succinctly summarizes a competing story, the story of Jesus who, though he has all the qualifications of the Messiah of Jewish expectation, has conquered through death, but yet lives. The narrative implied in this second symbolic description can be summarized in this way: Death of the Lamb (= conquest) + Resurrection of the Lamb. This reflects the simplest theological abbreviation of the significance of the mission of Jesus Christ, the temporal juxtaposition of the motifs mentioning the fact of death of Jesus and fact that God raised him from the dead (Acts 3:15; 4:10; 5:30; 10:39–40; 13:28–30; Rom 4:24; 1 Cor 15:3–4).

The scene of the investiture of the Lamb (5:7–14), begins with his reception of the sealed scroll from the hand of God, but is thereafter dominated by a profound and complex scene of worship in which the Lamb is extolled with a hymn of praise. This antiphonal hymn consists of the basic two actions in the story celebrated in the doxology of 1:5b–6, namely the liberating death of Jesus and the formation of a new people constituted by those who were liberated (5:9–10, 12) – the italicised words are repeated in the passage quoted after this one:

> You are worthy to receive the book and open its seals,
> because you were slain and you redeemed for God by your death,
> People from every tribe and tongue and people and nation,
> and made them for our God a kingdom and priests.

> Worthy is the Lamb who was slain to receive
> *power* and wealth and wisdom
> and might and *honor* and *glory* and *praise*.

The underlying narrative events expressed in this hymn are the following: redemptive death of the Lamb → formation of a redeemed people for God → worship of the sovereign Lamb. The absence of a reference to the resurrection of Jesus is striking, and requires further explanation.

God is depicted in this entire throne room scene as a remarkably passive figure despite the awesome power and majesty attributed to him. The Lamb's reception of the sealed scroll from the right hand of God surely places him in an obviously subordinate position to God and yet at the same time God is apparently unable to act, or perhaps better, chooses not to act, apart from the mediation of the Lamb. Thus, just as Rev 1:1–2 makes in clear that Jesus Christ is the exclusive transmitter of divine revelation to the servants of God in the world, so Rev 4–5 makes it clear that he is also, under the metaphor of the Lamb, the exclusive agent of God who alone is in a position to see God's intentions realized in the world.

Those who heard the hymn of praise in Rev 5:9–10, 12, would instantly recall the earlier hymn sung in praise of God which concluded Chapter 4 (v. 11)–the common terms of adoration shared by these hymns are italicised:

> Worthy are you, our Lord and God,
> To receive *glory* and *honor* and *power*,
> Because you created all things
> And by your will they existed, yes were created.

God is honored primarily for his creative work, while Jesus Christ, as the Lamb, is celebrated for his redemptive death and his establishment of the Church. This juxtaposition of the creative activity of God, the redemptive death of Christ and the establishment of the new people of God is precisely the pattern of the hymn to Christ in Col 1:15–20. While the first stanza (vv. 15–17) describes Christ's role as the image of the invisible God, the firstborn of all creation and the agent through which God created the cosmos, the second stanza (vv. 18–20) centers on Christ as the founder of the Church whose death became the basis for reconciling human kind with God:

> He is the head of the body, the Church;
> He is the beginning, the first-born from the dead,
> that in everything he might be preeminent.
> For in him all the fullness of God was pleased to dwell,
> and through him to reconcile to himself all things,
> whether on earth or in heaven,
> making peace by the blood of his cross.

If the hearers failed to catch the significance of the parallel hymns to God and to Christ, the author gives them a final chance with the doxology jointly addressed to God and the Lamb which concludes Chapter 5, again italicizing the terms of adoration shared with the previous passages quoted above (v. 13):

> To the One who sits on the throne and to the Lamb
> be *praise* and *honor* and *glory* and *power* for ever.

This joint doxology is a powerful statement of the unique relationship between the One seated on the throne and Jesus Christ.

What does the scroll sealed with seven seals symbolize? There have been a variety of answers to this question, none of which have commanded general agreement. At a basic level, the scroll must represent the will or intention of God for the world, and that intention – at least in its initial phase – is dramatized in the story of the breaking of the seven seals. The author provides a clue at the conclusion of the catastrophes inflicted on the world with the breaking of the seventh seal, when he has the people of the earth implore the mountains and rocks to hide them "from the One who sits on the throne and from the wrath of the Lamb, because the great day of his wrath has come" (6:16–17). Those who are being punished know the program, that it is none other than God himself who is inflicting divine punishment upon them with the Lamb acting as his exclusive agent.

The Lamb Breaks the Seven Seals (Rev 6:1–17; 8:1)

We must now turn to the narrative of the breaking of the seven seals by the Lamb described in Rev 6:1–17, 8:1. This entire section consists of seven brief narratives, each initiated by the Lamb's serial breaking of the seven seals. This is obviously part of a literary pattern which serves as means for introducing the particular effects associated with each seal. The breaking of the first seal is introduced with the phrase "Then I saw when the Lamb broke the first of the seven seals" (6:1), but the Lamb is represented thereafter simply by the third-person singular verb "he broke" (6:3, 5, 7, 9, 12; 8:1), without the renominalization that one might expect (i. e., the explicit mention of the Lamb as subject of the verb "break"). Particularly striking is the failure of the author to remind the readers of the subject of the verb "break" in 8:1, which follows the extended "interruption" of 7:1–17. However, much more than a formal literary pattern is involved here, for central to the narrative theology of the Apocalypse is the sovereign will of God mediated to the world by Jesus Christ who, through his role in breaking each of the seven seals, functions as the agent of God in punishing a disobedient world.

The first four seals constitute a group in which each of the four living creatures calls forth a cavalier who visits a particular type of destruction and devastation upon the earth (6:1–8). This series of four divine judgments upon the earth is relieved by the breaking of the fifth seal which shifts the focus from plagues inflicted on the wicked to the righteous, slain for their fidelity to the word of God and who now cry out to God for vengeance (6:9–11). If the earliest hearers of the Apocalypse identified themselves with anyone in this melodramatic narrative of the seven seals, it would have been with these martyrs rather than with those afflicted by the waves of plagues send by God to punish their wickedness. In fact, the author gives the reader little choice in the matter. None of them would want to experience the terrible plagues by which God punishes the ungodly. Yet the only option the readers have is to identify with the *martyrs*, not with ordinary Christians who survive. He is, in effect, using a literary strategy to push their commitment to God and to Jesus to the point that they identify themselves with those willing to lay down their lives for their faith.

The opening of the sixth seal (6:12–17) initiates a series of earthquakes and cosmic catastrophes which terrifies the people of the earth, who try to flee from the calamities which have overtaken them. Together they cry to the mountains and the rocks (6:16–17):

> Fall on us and hide us from the One who sits on the throne and from the wrath of the Lamb, because the great day of his wrath has come, and who is able to withstand it?

Here the author uses the collective voice of the people of the world in a short expository passage to reiterate succinctly to the hearers what they already know, namely, that God has initiated payback time and that the Lamb is his exclusive agent in mediating that plan in the world.

Focus on the People of God (Rev 7:1–17)

The position and meaning of the interjected vision in Rev 7 has been a perennial problem for interpreters. For many, it provides an answer to the plaintive cry of those doomed to experience divine punishment in Rev 6:17: Who can stand before the wrath of God and the Lamb? The first part of Rev 7 is set on earth and focuses on the sealing of the 144,000 (7:1–8), which surely represents salvation in one form or other, despite arguments over the identity of the 144,000. The second part of Rev 7 is set in heaven and centers on the innumerable host who have come out of the great tribulation (7:9–17), a group that surely represents the saved. The hearers of the Apocalypse could easily have identified themselves with either group; with the 144,000 because they are still in the world, as are the readers, and with the innumerable host, because though they are dead – many if not all as victims of violence – they have experienced the ultimate salvation which is the object of hope for all of God's people.

In this interruptive section, it is significant that the Lamb, who figures prominently as the agent of God in the narrative from 5:1–8:1, is mentioned three times in the second half of the passage (7:9–17). (1) The first mention occurs in the context of the cry of victory addressed to God and the Lamb: "Victory belongs to our God who sits upon the throne, and to the Lamb" (7:10). This *Siegesruf* constitutes a proleptic celebration of the cosmic victory of both

God and the Lamb; both are mentioned because such a victory is not possible apart from the role played by the Lamb. (2) The second is found in the speech of the *senior interpres* in which he tells the seer that the innumerable multitude consists of those "who came from the great tribulation. They washed their robes and made them white in the blood of the Lamb" (7:14). The Great Tribulation is one of the plotted eschatological events which, together with other historical and eschatological events, forms part of the Master Story which is never fully articulated but expressed tantalizingly in bits and pieces throughout the Apocalypse. This reference to the liberating effects of the death of Christ has already been mentioned in the doxology in Rev 1:5b–6 as well as in the hymn of praise to the Lamb in Rev 5:9–10, 12. (3) The last reference is found in the conclusion of the heavenly elder's speech where he tells John that "the Lamb in the midst of the throne will be their shepherd, and he will lead them to springs of living water" (7:17). The dual focus on the foundation of the new people of God based on the liberating death of Jesus has already been referred to in the two passages just mentioned (Rev 1:5b–6 and 5:9–10, 12). The presence of the Lamb with his redeemed people is further dramatized in Rev 14:1–5, where the seer describes a vision of the 144,000, each with the names of the Lamb and his Father inscribed on their foreheads. The language of discipleship familiar from the Gospels is evoked in v. 4: "It is these who follow the Lamb wherever he goes; these have been redeemed from humanity, servants devoted to God and the Lamb."

Thus each of these three references to the Lamb evokes a different phase of the Master Story: (1) The Lamb sharing the cosmic victory with God (7:10), (2) The death of the Lamb which provides the basis for victory (7:14), and (3) The Lamb as the center of a redeemed people (7:17).

To this point in Rev 4:1–8:1, the emphasis has been upon judgment rather than salvation, though the hymn of praise sung by the heavenly chorus in Rev 5:9–10, 12, emphasizes the liberation of people by the death of the Lamb and the complementary foundation of a new people of God. The presentation of white robes to the souls under the altar also represents salvation for the faithful martyrs. Just as the Lamb, by his liberating death has created a new people constituted by those who are his obedient followers, so his death has also qualified him to function as God's agent in the destruction of those who are disobedient to him. Salvation, of course, is more pleasant to contemplate than judgment, and while a preoccupation with the latter is certainly theologically unfashionable, both are part of the biblical depiction of the role of Jesus Christ.

5. Stories Implied in Descriptions

Despite the dominance of narrative discourse in the Apocalypse of John, there are (as we have seen) some relatively long descriptive passages. Two of these are descriptions of Jesus Christ in the context of symbolic visions. Though he is not explicitly named in either visionary description, his identity is not in doubt. The descriptive sections in both passages introduce a larger textual unit which concludes with a relatively extensive section of narrative discourse. The heavily symbolic and mythic character of these descriptive passages suggests that they imply existing narratives known to the hearers.

One like a Son of Man (1:9–20)

The first is the vision of "the one like a son of man" in 1:9–20, beginning with a lengthy descriptive passage in (1:12–16). This descriptive passage is in part repeated and augmented in the introductory sections to each of the seven proclamations where parts of the description are repeated by the exalted Christ (2:1, 8, 12, 18; 3:1, 7, 14). For the sake of convenience, I will put a translation of the descriptive section below in the left-hand column, with the parallels in the introductions to the seven proclamations in the right-hand column. The *italicized* words and phrases are not found in the other column, while the *underlined* words and phrases are common to both columns.

Figure 1: Rev 1:12–19 and Parallels in Rev 2–3

Rev 1:12–19	*Rev 2–3*
12 Then I turned to see the voice speaking to me. Upon turning around I saw seven golden menorahs, 13 and in the midst of the menorahs,	2:1 Thus says the one … who walks in the midst of the seven golden menorahs
one like a son of man [Dan 7:13; 10:16] *wearing a long robe and with a golden sash encircling his chest* [Dan 10:5]. 14 *His head, that is, his white hair, was like white wool, like snow* [Dan 7:9],	
and his eyes were like a flame of fire [cf. Dan 10:6c],	2:18 Thus says *the Son of God* whose eyes are like a flame of fire
15 and his feet were like bronze [Dan 10:6d] *when smelted in a furnace, and his voice was like the sound of cascading water* [Dan 10:6e].	and his feet as burnished bronze
16 In his right hand he had seven stars,	2:1 Thus says the one who holds the seven stars in his right hand 3:1 Thus says the one who has *the seven spirits of God, namely the seven stars.*
and a sharp double-edged sword projecting from his mouth,	2:12 Thus says the one with the sharp double-edged sword. [Cf. 2:16 I will come to you soon and war

and *his face was like the sun shining in full strength* [cf. Dan 10:6b].	against them with the sword of my mouth.]
17 And when I saw him, I fell at his feet as though dead, and he placed his right hand upon me, saying: “Stop being afraid.	
I am the First and the Last, 18 even the Living One,	2:8 Thus says the First and the Last,
and I was dead, but behold I now live *for ever and ever*,	the one who died, but came to life.
and I have the keys *to Death and Hades*.	3:7 Thus says *the Holy One the True One*, the One who has the key *of David, who opens so that no one can shut, and shuts so that no one can open*
	3:14 Thus says *the Master Workman, the faithful and true Witness, the Origin of the creation of God*.

In the preceding synopsis, it can be readily seen that there are many features in the description and exposition in Rev 1:9–20 which have no counterpart in the Christological predications found in the introductions to the seven proclamations. Similarly, there are Christological predications in the seven proclamations (underlined) which have no counterpart in Rev 1:9–20. Further, the Christological predicates in Rev 2–3 are dependent on both the descriptive and expository sections.

Rev 1:9–20 itself is comprised of two units of text, the description of “one like a son of man” (1:12–16), and an expository speech which includes several striking “I”-predications. There is a surprising disjunction between the two sections, for none of the “I” self-predications in the expository section have a counterpart in the descriptive section.

The figure described as “one like a son of man” (1:13) is not further identified in 1:9–20, but is called the Son of God in the Christological predicate in 2:18 (the only occurrence of that title in the Apocalypse). It is striking that the designation “son of man” is not repeated in the historical predicates in Rev 2–3, a fact which suggests that the author does not connect the anarthrous phrase “a son of man” with the Son of Man traditions in the Gospels. It is clear that the phrase “one like a son of man” is a direct allusion to either Dan 7:13 (where “one like a son of man” comes to the Ancient of Days) or Dan 10:16, 18 (where the phrase refers to the angelic figure described in Dan 10:5–6). Perhaps the most unusual feature of the allusion to Dan 7:10, 13 is the fact that the description is apparently dependent on an exegetical tradition of Dan 7 in which the two figures of the Ancient of Days and the one like a son of man are merged into a single figure. This exegetical tradition is represented in Dan 7:13 in the only two extant LXX manuscripts of Daniel (MS 967 and MS 88) which I translate literally:

He came like a son of man
and like the Ancient of Days was present,
and those who were near approached him.

Here the two figures are identified in a synonymous couplet. This is one of several instances in the Apocalypse where Jesus Christ (under various guises) is described using language normally or appropriately used only of God.

The story implied in the description of the figure in Rev 1:9–16 is limited to four features: (1) the designation "one like a son of man," (2) the sharp two-edged sword which proceeds from his mouth, (3) the seven golden menorahs, and (4) the seven stars he holds in his right hand. If the son of man designation is intended to remind the hearers of the judgment scene in Dan 7:9–14, this coheres well with the symbol of the two-edged sword proceeding from his mouth, a symbol occurring nowhere in Daniel, but which is twice mentioned in connection with the Rider on the White Horse in Rev 19:15, 21. Here the sword is a metaphor for the tongue, i. e., the word of Christ used in reproof and admonition (cf. *4 Ezra* 13:10, 37–38; 2 Thess 2:8). These two features combine to imply the story of Christ's role in the final judgment, a theme occurring frequently in early Christian literature (Acts 10:42; 17:31; Rom. 2:16; 1 Cor. 4:4–5; 2 Cor 5:10; 2 Thess. 1:7–10; 2 Tim. 4:1; 1 Pet. 4:5; *2 Clem.* 1:1; *Barn.* 5:7 7:2; 15:5; Polycarp *Phil.* 2:1; *Ep. Diogn.* 7:6; Justin *Dial.* 118.1; 132.1). One such version of the role of Christ in the eschatological judgment is 2 Cor 5:10:

For we all must appear before the tribunal of Christ, so that each might receive what [he or she did] while living, in proportion to what he or she did, whether good or bad.

In the context of Rev 1:9–3:22, however, the judgment of Christ is not directed to human beings in general at the last judgment, but rather toward the Christian communities of Roman Asia in the present.

The seven golden menorahs and the seven stars which the exalted Christ holds in his right hand both represent the seven churches (1:20), and dramatize the close link between Christ and his people. In fact, this is a dramatization of the second part of the two-part story which we found earlier in the implied story in the doxology of Rev 1:5b–6, in which the liberating death of Jesus becomes the basis for the creation of a new people of God. The same two-part story was celebrated in the hymn of praise to the Lamb in 5:9–10, 12.

Rev 1:9–20 concludes in vv. 17–20 with a brief but complex expository speech of the exalted Christ which contains two statements, each with three motifs. The first is an "I am" (ἐγώ εἰμι) predication: "I am the First and the Last, even the *Living* One" (1:17b–18a). The second statement shares but a single motif with the first one (underlined): "I was dead, but behold I now *live* for ever and ever, and I have the keys to Death and Hades" (vv. 18b). Both statements are based, at least in part, on a temporal continuum and that means that they imply a story.

"I am the First and the Last" is a title which occurs three times in the Apocalypse and always as a self-predication of the exalted Christ (1:17; 2:8; 22:13). It is a clear allusion to the Hebrew text of Isa 44:6b, where it is part of a lengthy speech attributed to God (Isa 42:14–44:23) in which, toward the end, God emphasizes his absolute sovereignty. The fact that such a predication is fully appropriate only to the God of Israel, complements the blended description in Rev 1:13–14 of "one like a son of man" with the Ancient of Days in Dan 7:10–13, which also implies some kind of equal status for God and Jesus Christ.

The "and" introducing the third element, "the Living One," should be almost certainly be regarded as epexegetical or explanatory (as we have translated it above) suggesting that "the First and the Last" is also "the Living One." This phrase is probably a double entendre, for it calls to mind numerous OT passages referring to the God of Israel as "the living God" (Deut 5:26; 1 Sam 17:26; Jer 10:10; Dan 6:27), yet is followed in v. 18 with a reference to the death and resurrection of Jesus, who by virtue of the latter event is truly "the living one." [While I am aware that the title "the First and the Last" as a self-predication of the exalted Christ is juxtaposed in Rev 22:13 with two other titles used primarily of God "the Alpha and the Omega" (1:8; 21:6), and "the Beginning and the End" (21:6), I have recently treated this subject in a lengthy essay elsewhere and have neither the space nor time to recapitulate those reflections here.]

Turning to the second Christological statement in Rev 1:17–20, the exalted Jesus says, "I was dead, but behold I now live for ever and ever, and I have the keys to Death and Hades" (v. 18b). The death and resurrection of Jesus Christ constitutes a theological abbreviation of the central story of early Christian faith, the Master Story to which each believer subordinates his or her own individual story. The phrase "I have the keys to Death and Hades" refers to the cosmic sovereignty to which Jesus has attained following the act of God raising him from the dead. All three elements are featured in the brief description of the Lamb in Rev 5:6, which was "standing as though slain, with seven horns and seven eyes, which are the seven spirits of God sent out into all the earth" (5:6). Here "standing" refers to the fact that he is now living, despite the fact that he was slain, and the seven eyes understood as "the seven spirits of God sent out into all the earth" is another symbolic way of emphasizing the sovereignty of Jesus Christ.

The Divine Warrior (19:11–21)

The second extensive description of the exalted Christ in the Apocalypse is found in the vision of the Rider on the White Horse (19:11–21), widely thought to represent the Parousia of Christ. Like Rev 1:9–20, this vision narrative begins with a lengthy descriptive passage (19:11–16), and then concludes with a truncated narrative of the defeat and destruction of the Beast, the False Prophet and the armies of their allied kings (19:17–21). Again for the sake of convenience,

I will put a translation of the descriptive section below in the left-hand column, with parallels from other passages in the Apocalypse in the right-hand column (Figure 2). Close parallels are underlined.

Figure 2: Rev 19:11–16 with Parallels

Rev 19:11–16	*Parallels in Revelation*
11 I then saw heaven open, and behold a white steed, and the person mounted on it is faithful and true.	3:14 Thus says the Master Workman, the faithful and true Witness 1:5 faithful witness 3:7 Thus says the Holy One, the True One,
With justice he judges and wages war.	
12 Now his eyes were like a flame of fire [Dan 10:6c], and on his head were many diadems with a name inscribed that no one knows but he himself. 13 He was dressed in a garment stained with blood [Isa 63:1, 3b], and his name was called the Word of God. 14 The heavenly armies followed him on white steeds, wearing white, pure linen.	1:14b His eyes were like a flame of fire
15 From his mouth projected a sharp sword that he might smite the nations with it [Isa 11:4],	1:16b from his mouth issued a sharp two-edged sword
and he himself will rule them with an iron crook [Ps 2:9],	12:5 one who is to rule all the nations with an iron crook [Ps 2:9] 2:27 he [the conquering believer] shall rule them with a crook of iron
and he himself will tread the winepress, of the furious wrath of God the Almighty [Isa 63:3]	14:19b the great winepress of the wrath of God
16 And he has upon his robe, that is, upon his thigh, a name inscribed, "King of kings and Lord of lords."	17:14 the Lamb … is Lord of lords and King of kings

This text begins with a detailed description of a divine warrior (heavily dependent on the depiction of God as a warrior in Isa 63:13 owing much to the and expansive messianic periphrasis in the Targum, wearing garments bloodied from battle and complete with the wine-press as a metaphor for destruction), who is identified by three positive designations and one negative one (19:11–16): (1) He is "Faithful and True" (19:11), (2) he has "a name inscribed which no one knows but himself" (v. 12), (3) his name is the "Word of God" (v. 13), and (4) he is called "King of kings and Lord of lords" (v. 16).

Let us look briefly at each of these: (1) The adjectives "faithful" and "true" are used of Jesus elsewhere in the Apocalypse (1:5; 3:7, 14). (2) The fact that he has a name known to no one but himself (like the conquering believer in 2:17) is enigmatic, but may allude to the true name of God, unknown to all but himself. (3) The designation "Word of God" conveys the idea that the Rider on the White Horse, alias Jesus Christ, represents the will or intention of God in the world. The three motifs of the Word of God, the sharp sword symbolizing that word, and the death which he dealt out, are all juxtaposed in Wis 18:15–16 which provides evidence that this combination of motifs is traditional:

> Thy all-powerful word leaped from heaven,
> from the royal throne
> Into the midst of the land that was doomed,
> A stern warrior carrying the sharp sword
> of thy authentic command,
> And stood and filled all things with death,
> And touched heaven while standing on the earth.

The narrative of the eschatological battle (19:17–21) is strangely truncated, for the preparations for the battle are related (vv. 17–19), followed by a narrative of the aftermath of the battle (vv. 20–21), but with no explicit mention of the battle itself. Rev 17:14 is another text in the Apocalypse which briefly narrates the final eschatological battle exhibits a similar "before and after" pattern:

> They [the ten kings who cooperate with the Beast] will fight against the Lamb, and the Lamb will conquer them, because he is Lord of lords and King of kings, and those with him are called and elect and faithful.

Perhaps the first feature of this text which strikes us when comparing it with Rev 19:11–21, is that there the Rider on the White Horse is named "King of kings and Lord of lords" (19:16), while here the Lamb is called "Lord of lords and King of kings (17:14). The order is reversed but the title is essential the same. These two texts look like versions of the same eschatological event: the Beast and his allies are conquered by a protagonist accompanied by a host. There are also some differences: The protagonist in Rev 17:14 is the Lamb; the protagonist in Rev 19:11–21 is the Divine Warrior. Both are transparent guises for Jesus Christ.

If this episode represents the Parousia, as most commentators suppose, it is distinctive, for the only motif it shares with other Parousia passages in the NT and early Christian literature is the fact that the protagonist is accompanied by a heavenly host. Absent are references to the Son of Man figure, his coming with clouds, the sounding of the trumpet, and the gathering of the elect (1 Thess 4:13–17; 2 Thess 2:1–12; Mark 13:26–27 = Matt 24:30–31; Mark 14:62 = Matt 26:64; Rev 1:7; *Did.* 16:7–8; cf. Matt 25:31–46). Descriptions of the Parousia in early Christian literature, however, suggest that it is understood as a polyvalent event which can be recounted in a variety of ways depending on the rhetorical situation. The emphasis can focus exclusively on the *salvific* aspects of the Parousia (1 Thess 4:13–17; Mark 13:26–27), accent the *judgmental* aspect while including a *salvific* aspect (1 Thess 1:7–10; Matt 24:30–31), balance *salvation* with *judgment* (2 Thess 2:1–12), or emphasize an exclusively *judgmental* aspect (Mark 14:62 = Matt 26:64; Rev 1:7; 19:11–21). The emphasis on the judgment and destruction of the enemies of God in Rev 19:11–21 is captured by the motto in v. 11: "with justice he judges and wages war." Though no mention is made of the people of God, their situation in the world or their eschatological salvation, it is still possible to regard this as a Parousia narrative, given the variety of performancial variants.

The description and narrative in Rev 19:11–21 center on one significant eschatological which concludes the Master Story of the triumph of Jesus Christ, namely acting as God's agent in his role as the future judge of the world in rebellion against God.

5. Concluding Summary

"Who is Jesus Christ?" is obviously a loaded question, since it already implies an answer. The verb "is" means that Jesus Christ is not a figure of the past, but that he is also – and more importantly – a figure of the present. The name "Jesus Christ," itself, with its submerged reference to Messianic status, is not primarily the name of an historical figure, but of the Lord and Savior of the Church, investing him with ultimate religious significance. It is entirely appropriate, however, for a person of faith to direct this question to the Apocalypse of John. But as central as Jesus Christ is to faith, faith is a Master Story, and such stories do not consist of a single character. While the Master Story is never narrated in a complete form in the Apocalypse of John, it is the presupposition which underlies the entire narrative. While I have not presented a complete account of the ways in which the Master Story makes its appearances in the Apocalypse, I have attempted to approach several important textual units from a narrative theological perspective.

Even though Hans Frei's exploration of the identity of Jesus focuses on a theological reading of the Gospels, his conclusions appear equally applicable to our reading of the Apocalypse of John:[4]

> Jesus' very identity involves the will and purpose of the Father who sent him. He becomes who he is in the story by consenting to God's intention and by enacting that intention in the midst of the circumstances that devolve around him as the fulfillment of God's purpose.

[4] Frei, Hans. *The Identity of Jesus Christ: The Hermeneutical Bases of Dogmatic Theology*. (Philadelphia: Fortress, 1975).

Though the Apocalypse, unlike the Gospels, does not consist of "realistic narrative," but rather "mythical narrative," the author's dramatization of the role of Jesus Christ in the guise of the Lamb appears to reiterate the story of Jesus as found in the Gospels.

As one might expect, the death and resurrection of Jesus constitute focal events in the Master Story of the Apocalypse (as they do in the Gospels), but are rarely mentioned in isolation from other events. The epistolary salutation refers to Jesus Christ as the faithful witness, the firstborn from the dead, and the ruler of the kings of the earth, referring to his death + resurrection + cosmic sovereignty, juxtaposed but not plotted. A similar series of motifs is found among the self-predications of the one like a son of man. In claiming that "I was dead, but behold now I live for ever and ever, and I have the keys to Death and Hades" (1:17–18), the death + resurrection + cosmic sovereignty pattern is repeated, still with no causal links between the events. Another pattern of events is referred to in the doxology in 1:5b–6: "To the one who loved us and freed us from our sins by his blood, and made us a kingdom, priests to his God and Father." This is a causal pattern: atoning death → creation of a people. The same pattern is evident in the hymn of praise in Rev 5:9–10, 12 as well. Lurking at the edges in the reference to "his God and Father," is a central feature of the Master Story of Jesus in the Apocalypse: his role as an agent of God in carrying out God's intentions in the world which is developed more fully in Rev 4:1–8:1.

The lengthy narrative unit in Rev 4:1–8:1 centers on the figure of the Lamb. The narrative in Rev 5:1–6:17; 8:1 reveals that only the Lamb is qualified to act as an agent for God, whose intentions for the world apparently cannot be realized without the mediation of the Lamb. The Lamb "completes" or "complements" God, as it were, in his relation to the cosmos. This suggests a pattern of events different from those summarized above: conquering death → agent of God's will for the cosmos → conquest of the enemies of God.

There are two very different descriptions of Jesus Christ under the guise of the "one like a son of man" (Rev 1:9–20), and the Divine Warrior (Rev 19:11–21). Both descriptions, however, describe the protagonists in language normally thought appropriate only for God. The one like a son of man is the present Lord of the Church whose will (which must be understood as the intention of God) is made known through revelation to his servant John for the reproof, admonition and exhortation of his people in the world. The Divine Warrior is the agent of God, the "Word of God" who inflicts punishment on the enemies of God and thereby achieves cosmic sovereignty as "King of kings and Lord of lords." This pattern consists of two elements conquest of God's enemies → cosmic sovereignty.

The Form and Function of the Proclamations to the Seven Churches (Revelation 2–3)[1]

A satisfactory solution to the twin problems of the *internal* literary structure of the proclamations to the seven churches in Rev 2–3, and the *external* literary form to which they have the closest generic relationship continues to challenge New Testament scholarship. It is of course theoretically possible to limit a literary analysis to the texts in Rev 2–3 based on intrinsic criteria alone. In practice, however, most analyses have been dialectical attempts to understand the intrinsic literary features of the seven proclamations in the light of the clues provided by one or another comparable literary form. This kind of contextual investigation is unavoidable for Rev 2–3 in view of the many repetitive and formulaic words and phrases which, in addition to denotative or designative meanings, have a variety of connotative or associative meanings requiring exploration and assessment. Some recent categories for explaining aspects of Rev 2–3 include the revelatory letter,[2] prophetic speech forms,[3] the covenant formulary[4] or one of the types of Greek oratory.[5]

---

[1] Presented to the Apocalypse Seminar at the annual meeting of the Studiorum Novi Testamenti Societas at Cambridge, England on August 8–12, 1988.

[2] Klaus Berger, "Apostelbrief und apostolische Rede: Zum Formular frühchristlicher Briefe," *ZNW* 65 (1974) 212–19; Ulrich B. Müller, "Literarische und formgeschichtliche Bestimmung der Apokalypse des Johannes als einem Zeugnis frühchristlicher Apokalyptik," *Apocalypticism in the Mediterranean World and the Near East,* ed. David Hellholm (Tübingen: J. C. B. Mohr [Paul Siebeck] 1983) 601, n. 6a.

[3] The most detailed form critical analysis of the Rev 2–3 in terms of constituent types of prophetic speech is by Ulrich B. Müller, *Prophetie und Predigt im Neuen Testament: Formgeschichtliche Untersuchungen zur urchristlichen Prophetie* (Gütersloh: Gerd Mohn, 1975).

[4] W. H. Shea, "The Covenantal Form of the Letters to the Seven Churches," *AUSS* 21 (1983) 71–84, suggests that the seven proclamations were modeled after the covenant formulary found in the OT and the ancient Near East. Analyzing the seven proclamations from this perspective, he proposes that they exhibit five structural elements: (1) Preamble, (2) Historical Prologue, (3) Stipulations, (4) Witness, (5) Blessing and Curse. Shea has forced the structure of the seven proclamations into a framework which is essentially alien to them (the seven proclamations deal primarily with a temporary situation rather than the legal establishment of a long-term relationship), and his verse-by-verse analysis reveals far too many exceptions to the overall schema. Nevertheless he does divide the οἶδα-clause into at least two components, the historical prologue and the stipulations (even though the latter category is, in my view, inappropriate). Shea's covenant schema has been extended to the whole of Rev by Kenneth A. Strand, "A Further Note on the Covenant Form in the Book of Revelation," *AUSS* 21 (1983) 251–64.

[5] John T. Kirby, "The Rhetorical Situations of Revelation 1–3," *NTS* 34 (1988) 197–207.

The purpose of this article is not primarily to review or critique previous analyses of Rev 2–3, but rather to build on existing research in order to provide a more satisfactory intrinsic literary analysis of the seven proclamations themselves as well as to link them with regard to both form and function to the specific literary genre which served the author as a literary model. The thesis of this paper is that the seven proclamations constitute a mixed genre created by the author.[6] The literary *genre* or *kind* to which the seven proclamations belong is that of the *royal* or *imperial edict,* while the *mode* is that of the prophetic form of speech called the *parenetic salvation-judgment oracle.*[7]

1. Structural Features of the Seven Proclamations

There is now widespread agreement that the seven proclamations never existed independently of Revelation, but were designed specifically for their present literary setting by the author-editor at a final stage in the composition of the entire work. Despite their ostensible destinations, they were clearly intended to complement one another and to be read and heeded by the other congregations.[8]

In this article Kirby proposes to analyze Rev 2–3 in accordance with the method of rhetorical criticism popularized by George A. Kennedy, *New Testament Interpretation through Rhetorical Criticism* (Chapel Hill: University of North Carolina, 1984). He suggests that the seven proclamations, while they have some judicial elements, are essentially deliberative, like the entire book (p. 200). He finds the fourfold structure of proem, narration, proposition and epilogue in each of the proclamations. While this analysis is somewhat problematic (e. g., his analysis of the function of the proem is problematic; he insists on the inclusion of a *narratio* section which is rare in the *genos sumbouleutikon;* he fails to understand the function of the *propositio* section; he does not explain the absence of the *probatio* section; he fails to see that the "epilogue" section has no typical rhetorical function at all), he does offer a more satisfactory way of understanding the οἶδα-clause. Since the seven proclamations contain praise and blame (*genos epideiktikon*) as well as exhortation to good behavior and dissuasion from bad behavior (*genos sumbouleutikon*), it is difficult to understand how Kirby avoids dealing with the problem of a *mixtum compositum.*

[6] Cf. Alastair Fowler, *Kinds of Literature: An Introduction to the Theory of Genres and Modes* (Cambridge: Harvard University Press, 1982). Fowler's distinction between *kinds* (*genres*), *modes* and *subgenres* makes it possible to understand how the generic features of various literary kinds can be combined into a *mixtum compositum. Modes* differ from *kinds* in that the external structure of the latter is absent from the former (pp. 106–111). Thus a "comic novel" is a novel in kind but a comedy in mode. "In short," writes Fowler on p. 107, "when a modal term is linked with the name of a kind, it refers to a combined genre, in which the overall form is determined by the kind alone". The seven proclamations could therefore be designated as "prophetic edicts".

[7] David E. Aune, *Prophecy in Early Christianity and the Ancient Mediterranean World* (Grand Rapids: Eerdmans, 1983) 326.

[8] This is clear from the proclamation formulas with which each proclamation concludes: "Let the one who has ears hear what the Spirit declares to the churches [ταῖς ἐκκλησίαις]" (2. 7, 11, 17, 29; 3.6, 13, 22), and by the statement in 2.23: "And all the churches [αἱ ἐκκλησίαι] shall know that I am the one who searches both mind and heart."

The seven proclamations contrast sharply with the literary matrix in which they are set in several ways. Two striking features which accentuate this contrast include (1) the heavy concentration of stereotypical phrases and formulas which provide the basic structure of the proclamations, and (2) the concentration of unusual grammatical and stylistic features.

From an intrinsic standpoint it is clear that the seven proclamations share seven stereotypical features: (1) the *adscriptio,* (2) the command to write (these first two features are often taken together), (3) the τάδε λέγει formula, (4) the Christological predications, (5) the οἶδα-clause (which introduces the *narratio* of each proclamation and is extremely varied in content), (6) the proclamation formula, and (7) the promise of victory. In addition there is an eighth feature, the *dispositio* ("arrangement") which must be distinguished from the οἶδα-clause, even though the transition is not assigned a stereotyped linguistic marker.

1. *The Adscriptio.* The *adscriptio* and the command to write appear to be part of the literary setting of each of the proclamations, since the actual messages to each of the churches begin only after the τάδε λέγει formula. Further, the second element of the "write and send" formula (a variation of the OT "go and tell" formula, both of which are types of prophetic commission formulas)[9] is omitted since the seven proclamations are part of a larger composition in an epistolary framework (1.4–6; 22.6–21) in which the complete formula has already been expressed in 1.11: γράψον … καὶ πέμψον.[10]

There are several significant features of the *adscriptiones. First,* there are some problematic textual variants which perhaps suggest that the *adscriptiones* were not originally as stereotypical in form as they now appear,[11] a feature that coheres with the author's tendency to vary rather than slavishly replicate formulaic phrases. Modern editors of the Greek text, like some ancient copyists (though not the scribes who wrote A and C), have tended to assume that all the *adscriptiones* must be identical. Thus while Nestle-Aland[26] (along with most modern critical editions) prefers τῷ ἀγγέλῳ τῆς ἐν τῷ δεῖνι ἐκκλησίας,[12] Westcott

[9] The *commission formula,* a longer form of the messenger formula, is found in several basic patterns in the OT: (1) "Say to X, thus says Y," (2) "Go and say to X, thus says Y" (Jer 2. 1–2), and (3) "[Go and] say to X [messenger formula absent]" (Isa 6:9; Jer 8:4); cf. Aune, *Prophecy in Early Christianity,* 90, 330.

[10] Cf. Hermas *Vis.* 2.4.3: γράψεις οὖν δύο βιβλαρίδια καὶ πέμψεις.

[11] A relatively full survey of the textual evidence is found in R.H. Charles, *A Critical and Exegetical Commentary on the Revelation of St. John* (Edinburgh: T. & T. Clark, 1920) 2.244; in J. Delobel, "Le texte de l'Apocalypse: Problèmes de méthode," *L'Apocalypse johannique et l'Apocalyptique dans le Nouveau Testament*, ed. J. Lambrecht (Leuven: The University Press, 1980) 159 n. 34, and in R. Berger, "NT[26] und die neutestamentliche Textkritik," *TR* 52 (1987) 42–5.

[12] Also preferred by UBSGNT[3], Tischendorf and Bernhard Weiss, *Die Johannes-Apokalypse. Textkritische Untersuchungen und Textherstellung* (Leipzig: J.C. Hinrichs, 1891) *ad loc.* While τῆς is supported by the majority of MSS in the *adscriptiones* to all the proclamations, in 2:12; 3:7, 14, it is attested by all the important witnesses. Charles, noting that the textual

and Hort and Charles suspected that all the proclamations originally read τῷ ἀγγέλῳ τῷ ἐν τῷ δεῖνι ἐκκλησίας.[13] The phrase τῆς ἐν τῷ δεῖνι ἐκκλησίας, however, apparently violates a stylistic "rule" of the author that a prepositional phrase can precede an anarthrous noun but cannot stand between the article and its noun.[14] That very "violation" may suggest the traditional character of the *adscriptiones*. *Second*, it is inconceivable that the *adscriptio* in the dative placed before the *superscriptio* should be conceived as an epistolary feature, since that form is limited almost exclusively to epistolary petitions, complaints and applications sent from an inferior to a superior.[15] *Third*, the author's unique literary device of addressing each proclamation to an ἄγγελος who functions as the *alter ego* of the Christian community, despite the fact that this literary fiction is not consistently maintained,[16] nevertheless suggests his literary creativity. Fourth, apart from the Ephesian *adscriptio*, all the rest begin with καί, which at least superficially coheres well with the paratactic Hebraistic style which the author uses in constructing Greek sentences. Yet of the 44 sentences found in the Nestle-Aland[26] text of Rev 2–3, only 10 begin with καί (22.7%). The entire text of Rev, however, has 337 sentences, of which 245 (73.79%) begin with καί. While the type of

evidence for an original τῷ becomes weaker and virtually nonexistent for 3:1, 7, 14, suggested that the self-confidence of the copyists increased as they wrote (*Revelation*, 2.244).

[13] The grammatically appropriate definite article τῇ," which goes with ἐκκλησίᾳ," has the strongest supporting textual attestation and is therefore preferred by Nestle-Aland[26] and UBSGNT[3]. Yet in 2:1 τῷ replaces τῆς in A and C (their agreement usually indicates a superior reading) and 1854, and therefore was preferred by Westcott & Hort and Charles, *Revelation*, I, cxx. In Rev 2:8, 18, τῷ rather than τῆς is attested in A, and in 3:1 by 046.

[14] Charles, *Revelation*, I, clvii; the same view is held by H. B. Swete, *The Apocalypse of St. John*, 3rd ed. (New York: Macmillan, 1908) 23, and Ernst Lohmeyer, *Die Offenbarung des Johannes*, 3. Aufl. (Tübingen: Mohr Siebeck, 1970) 21. Wilhelm Bousset, *Die Offenbarung Johannis*, 6. Aufl. (Göttingen: Vandenhoeck & Ruprecht, 1906) 176, however, cites Rev 2:1 (representing the other *adscriptiones*) as an exception to this rule. He is followed by Josef Schmid, *Studien zur Geschichte des griechischen Apocalypse-Textes* (München: Karl Zink, 1955–6) 2.197 f. Schmid noted that the article before ἐκκλησίας is more difficult to dispense with than the repetition of the article modifying τῷ ἀγγέλῳ, since the author *could* have written τῷ ἀγγέλῳ τῷ τῆς ἐν Ἐφέσῳ ἐκκλησίᾳ," but probably found it easier to eliminate the τῷ than the τῆς (*Studien*, 2.198).

[15] F. J. Exler, *The Form of the Ancient Greek Letter of the Epistolary Papyri* (Washington, D. C.: Catholic University of America, 1923) 65–7. More recently, John L. White, *The Form and Structure of the Official Petition* (Missoula: Scholars Press, 1972).

[16] Even though each of the seven proclamations addresses each angel-church directly as an individual entity using second-person singular pronouns and verb forms, the address occasionally shifts to second-person and third-person plural forms. This occurs when a particular group within a church is addressed (e. g., those ἐξ ὑμῶν about to be jailed in Smyrna, 2:10; those in Pergamon who hold (κρατοῦντας) the teaching of Balaam, 2:14, and those who hold (κρατοῦντες) the teaching of the Nicolaitans, 2:15; those in Thyatira who have not accepted the teaching of Jezebel (many second- and third-person plural forms, 2. 20–22; those who do not hold the teaching of Jezebel are directly addressed in 2:24 with an explicit shift of address: ὑμῖν δὲ λέγω. In several instances the author seems to forget his angelic addressee and refers to the entire community using second-person plural forms, i. e., in 2:10 (ἵνα πειρασθῆτε καὶ ἕξετε); 2:13 (παρ' ὑμῖν); cf. 2:20 (τοὺς ἐμοὺς δούλους).

discourse in Rev 2–3 consists of dialogue rather than narrative, this still does not explain the author's avoidance of καί at the beginning of clauses in these chapters. Similarly δέ, probably the most frequent conjunction in classical Greek, occurs just seven times in Rev, but three times in Rev 2–3 (2:5, 16, 24). Again, the stronger adversative particle ἀλλά, found just thirteen times in Rev, occurs eight times in Rev 2–3 (2:4, 6, 9 [2x], 14, 20; 3:4, 9). Despite the fact that the significance of these statistics is somewhat mitigated by the repetitive character of the seven proclamations, these minor syntactical features combine to suggest that the author is either intentionally varying his style or (less probably) that the author of these chapters is not the author of the body of Revelation.

2. *The Command to Write.* Expressed by the aorist imperative verb γράψον, the command to write is found in each of the seven proclamations between the adscriptio and the τάδε λέγει formula. Since τάδε is the object of the verb λέγει of which the subject is a Christological predication in the nominative, the entire discourse introduced by τάδε also functions as the object of the verb γράψον, indicating the secondary character of the literary connections to the narrative framework. γράψον has already occurred twice before in 1:11, 19 where it frames the vision report of 1:9–20, and three more times in insertions (14:13; 19:9; 21:5). While literary accounts of supernatural revealers commanding human recipients to write the substance of their revelations are found in Judaism,[17] such introductory divine commands are more frequent in Greco-Roman texts in which the gods command various individuals, usually through the medium of a dream, to write books.[18] The many occurrences of this phenomenon suggest that the claim of receiving a divine commission in a dream to write a literary composition had become a stock literary device providing divine legitimation for such compositions.[19] In Menander Rhetor 2. 17, the author recommends that a hymn to Apollo begin with a claim to divine inspiration, clearly suggesting the stereotypical literary character of this motif.[20]

---

[17] Exod 17:14 [LXX καταγράψον]; 34:27; Isa 8:1; 30:8 [verbally similar to Rev 1:11; cf. also Josh 24:26]; Jer 30:2 [LXX 37. 2]; 36:2, 28 [LXX 43:2, 28]; Hab 2:2; Tob 12:20; *4 Ezra* 14: 5 f., 22–48.

[18] Plato, *Phaedo* 4. 60e–61b; Callimachus, *Aetia* 1.1.21–22; Propertius 3.3; Cicero, *Academica priora* 2.16.51 (quoting Ennius, *Annales* 5); Pausanias 1.21.2 (Dionysius appeared in a dream to Aeschylus while he was gathering grapes and urged him to write tragedy); Pliny, *Ep.*, 3.5.4 (Nero Claudius Drusus, who had died in 9 BC, appeared to Pliny the Elder in a dream urging him to write the history of Germany); Aelius Aristides, *Or.* 48.2; Dio Cassius 73.23.2 (where the author claims that καί μοι καθεύδοντι προσέταξε τὸ δαιμόνιον ἱστορίαν γράφειν, "and while I was sleeping the god commanded me to write history"); in 79.10.1–2, Dio claims that the deceased Severus appeared to him and ordered him to write about the life of Caracalla; POxy. 1381, col. 8, lines 160–70.

[19] J.B. Stearns; *Studies of the Dream as a Technical Device in Latin Epic and Drama* (Lancaster: Lancaster Press, 1927) 1–7.

[20] D.A. Russell and N.G. Wilson (eds.), *Menander Rhetor: Edited with Translation and Commentary* (Oxford: Clarendon, 1981) 207–9.

3. *The τάδε λέγει Formula.* τάδε, a neuter plural accusative form of the demonstrative pronoun ὅδε, was obsolete in Koine Greek, and therefore had connotations or associations of *archaism* very similar to the now obsolete English phrase "thus saith." Apart from its widespread use as a quotation formula used for commenting on earlier authorities,[21] this intentional archaism had at least two other associations for ancient readers: as a (prophetic) messenger formula (i. e., a Septuagintism occurring more than 250 times in the LXX rendering the Hebrew phrase כה אמר יהוה), and as a proclamation formula characteristic of Persian royal diplomatic communications, primarily letters and edicts (some embedded in the OT; others preserved in inscriptions in western Anatolia) and the later edicts issued by Roman magistrates and emperors. In an illuminating discussion of the literary function of the introductory formula ὁ δεῖνα τάδε λέγει (and variations), Detlev Fehling has demonstrated how this third-person formula is used to justify the use of the first person in the text which follows it.[22]

As a prophetic speech form in early Christianity, τάδε λέγει occurs only in Acts 21:11 and (in a slightly modified form) in Ignatius, *Philad.* 7.3 (τὸ δὲ πνεῦμα ἐκήρυσσεν λέγον τάδε). The formula was also occasionally used to introduce Greek oracles: τάδε λέγει Ζεύς is attributed to the priestess of Zeus at Dodona as an introduction to oracular speech;[23] the προφήτης of Zeus-Ammon introduced an oracle with the formula τάδε λέγει Ἄμμων;[24] a saying of Bacchus (the male counterpart to Sibyl) is introduced by the formula Βάκχος ἔλεξε τάδε.[25] While such uses of the formula are comparatively rare in Greek sources (and the first two examples follow the normal Semitic and Hebraising LXX word order: object, verb, subject), the fact that they occur at all suggests that the formula was recognizable throughout the ancient Mediterranean world as a prophetic or oracular locution. The formula is also used to introduce promulgations of sacral law, as in Lucian *Saturnalia* 10: "Thus says [τάδε λέγει] Cronosolon, priest and prophet of Cronus, and giver of laws for his festival."

The τάδε λέγει formula is also used to introduce Persian decrees and letters (Herodotus 1.69; 3.40, 122; 5.24; 7.150; 8.140; 9.21; Thucydides 1.129.3: ὧδε λέγει βασιλεὺς Ξέρξης Παυσανίᾳ) which can be communicated either in oral or written form.[26] The form ὁ δεῖνα τῷ δεῖνι τάδε λέγει or ὧδε λέγει found in these

---

[21] Dionysius of Halicarnassus, *Ant. Rom.* 7.72.9; Heraclitus frag. 112 (ed. Kahn): διὸ καὶ Ἡράκλειτος οὕτως εἴρηκεν; in Rom 10:6 Paul introduces a quotation from Deut 9:4 with οὕτως λέγει.

[22] Detlev Fehling, "Zur Funktion und Formgeschichte des Proömiums in der älteren griechischen Prosa," ΔΩΡΗΜΑ: *Dauer und Überleben des antiken Geistes* (Athens: Griechische Humanistische Gesellschaft, 1975) 61–75.

[23] A. Adler, ed., *Suidae Lexicon* (Leipzig: Teubner, 1928–38) II, s. v. Δωδώνη.

[24] Plato, *Alcibiades* 2.149b.

[25] *Palatine Anthology,* Garland of Philip 36.2.

[26] Gunnar Rudberg, "Zu den Sendschreiben der Johannes-Apokalypse," *Eranos: Acta Philologica Suecana* 11 (1911) 175–6.

decrees is not, as G.A. Gerhard maintained,[27] an adaptation of the style of Persian kings, but was rather an indigenous fifth century Greek formula.[28] This style characterizes both royal decrees and letters issued by the Achaemenid chancery. In the five columns of the Behistan inscription of Darius, each of its seventy-three sections begins with the stereotyped introductory phrase *θatiy Darayavauš xšayaθiya*, literally "Declares Darius the king."[29] The style was occasionally imitated in fictional letters, doubtless because of the oriental flavor of the locution, e.g., "The king of kings, great Artaxerxes says to the Coans thus [τάδε λέγει],"[30] or "Thus says [ὧδε λέγει] Amasis to Polycrates,"[31] or "Amasis king of the Egyptians says [λέγει] to Bias wisest of the Greeks" (Plutarch, *Sept. sap. conv.* 151b), or βασιλεὺς θεὸς μέγας Δαρεῖος καὶ ἐνθῶν ρκ" κύριος 'Αλεξάνδρῳ τάδε λέγει, "Thus says Darius the great king and god and lord of 120 satrapies to Alexander" (*Historia Alexandri Magni,* ed. Kroll, 1.40.2). Several Persian edicts are quoted in the OT with τάδε λέγει as the introductory formula in the LXX (2 Chron 36. 23; 1 Esdr 2:3; Jud 2:5; Esth 3:13); a variant formula is οὕτως εἶπεν in Ezra 1:2. In *Ant.* 11.26, Josephus (apparently rewriting Ezra 4:7 and 1 Esdr 2:25 [LXX 2:21]) inserts the τάδε λέγει formula in a communication attributed to Cambyses, though it is not found in his sources. Since these decrees are of universal application (i.e., they are valid throughout the Achaemenid empire), they have no specific address. The verb of declaration in Roman edicts is usually λέγει/λέγουσι (*dicit/dicunt*). In one instance this occurs in the form οὕτως λέγουσιν (Appian, *Bella civilia* 4.2.8, the edict of the triumvirs on proscription, 43 BCE), but this edict was explicitly translated (perhaps freely) from Latin into Greek by Appian (*Bellum civile* 4. 2.11).

4. *The Christological Predications.* The speaker is identified by a series of varied titles and characterizations which provide literary links with the vision narrated in 1:9–20.[32] In four instances functional attributes of Christ are introduced with the substantival participle ὁ ἔχων, twice belonging to the semantic

---

[27] "Untersuchung zur Geschichte des griechischen Briefes I, *Philologus* 64 (1905) 53.

[28] M. van den Hout, "Studies in Early Greek Letter-Writing," *Mnemosyne* 4 (1949) 25 ff.; H. Koskenniemi, *Studien zur Idee und Phraseologie des griechischen Briefes bis 400 n. Chr.* (Helsinnki: Akateeminen Kirjakauppa, 1956) 156. Van den Hout's view is rejected by Detlev Fehling, "Zur Funktion und Formgeschichte des Proomium" 63, n. 5 though he admits that he had no access to the article.

[29] Roland G. Kent, *Old Persian: Grammar, Texts, Lexicon,* 2nd ed. (New Haven: American Oriental Society, 1953) 116–34. *θah-* is a verb meaning "declare, say," while the suffix *-ti* indicates the third-person singular in the present tense system.

[30] Ps.-Hippocrates, *Ep.* 8; Rudolph Hercher, *Epistolographi Graeci* (Paris: Editore Ambrosio Firmin Didot, 1873) 290.

[31] Hercher, *Epistolographi Graeci,* 100.

[32] For Rev 2:1, cf. 1:16; 2:8, cf. 1:17 f.; 2:12, cf. 1:16; 2:18, cf. 1:14; 3:1, cf. 1:4, 16; 3:7, cf. 1:18; 3:14, cf. 1:5.

subdomain of Have, Possess, etc. (2:18; 3:1b),[33] and twice belonging to the subdomain of Grasp, Hold (2:12b and 3:7b; cf. the synonym ὁ κρατῶν in 2:1, which belongs to the same semantic subdomain).[34] This has the effect of introducing a certain symmetry with the concluding proclamation formulas, each of which also begins with ὁ ἔχων. However, unlike the order typical of royal letters and edicts, the *name* of the exalted Christ is never given (though in 2:18 he is identified as the Son of God); name-play, of course, is characteristic of Rev. The cumulative effect of these titles and characterizations is to unify the seven proclamations as pronouncements of the exalted Christ who appeared to John in 1:9–20.

5. *The Narratio.* The so-called οἶδα-clause introduces the *narratio* section, i.e., a description of the situation of each community in the past and/or the present which serves as the basis for the *dispositio* or response which immediately follows. It consists of the following segments of each proclamation: (1) 2. 1–4, 6, (2) 2:9, (3) 2:13–15, (4) 2:19–20, (5) 3:1b, 4, (6) 3:8, (7) 3:15. In each case the content of the *narratio* is governed by the semantic significance of οἶδα, so that the finite verbs in this section are limited to past and present tenses in the indicative. It is important to emphasize the fact that the οἶδα-clause is not identical with the central message of each proclamation.[35] Like the *dispositio* section which immediately follows, it is extremely varied, making use of a number of optional forms.

In Greek literary letters, verbs of perception such as οἶδα, ἀκούω and πυνθάνομαι are not infrequently used to introduce the opening section of the letter body;[36] these verbs of perception belong to the semantic domains of

---

[33] Johannes P. Louw and Eugene A. Nida, *Greek-English Lexicon of the New Testament Based on Semantic Domains* (New York: United Bible Societies, 1988) I, § 57.1.

[34] Louw and Nida, *Greek-English Lexicon,* I, § 18.6.

[35] Ferdinand Hahn, "Die Sendschreiben der Johannesapokalypse: Ein Beitrag zur Bestimmung prophetischer Redeformer," *Tradition und Glaube: Das frühe Christentum in seiner Umwelt,* ed. G. Jeremias, H.-W. Kuhn and H. Stegemann (Göttingen: Vandenhoeck & Ruprecht, 1971) 370–7, proposes that the "οἶδα-Abschnitt" consists of six major elements collectively rooted in early Christian prophecy: (1) Recognition and/or censure of the present situation of each community. (2) Criticism often but not always begins with the expression ἀλλὰ ἔχω κατὰ σου. (3) Demand for repentance, characteristically expressed μνημόνευε οὖν. (4) The revelatory word, often introduced with ἰδού, functioning as a proclamation of judgment or a promise of salvation. (5) A motif with three variations, characteristically expressed with the phrase ἔρχομαι ταχῦ, also functioning as a promise of salvation or an announcement of judgment. (6) An admonition mentioning what each community "has" and should guard against.

[36] οἶδα: Dionysius Antiochenus, *Ep.* 39 (Hercher, *Epistolographi Graeci,* 266); Isocrates, *Ep.* 1. 2, 2. 1 (Hercher, 319 f.), 9. 1 (Hercher, 333); Ps.-Phalaris *Ep.* 8 (Hercher, 410); Ps.-Socrates, *Ep.* 17.1 (Hercher, 622); ἀκούω: Diogenes, *Ep.* 15, 17, 20 (Hercher, 239 f.); Dionysius Antiochenus, *Ep.* 65 (Hercher, 271); Isocrates, *Ep.* 5.2 (Hercher, 327); Ps.-Phalaris, *Ep.* 45 (Hercher, 419), 92 (Hercher, 435); Ps.-Pythagoras, *Ep.* 4.1, 5.1 (Hercher, 603 f.); Ps.- Socrates, *Ep.* 12 (Hercher, 618); πυνθάνομαι: Ps.-Heraclitus, *Ep.* 7 (Hercher, 283; Abraham J. Malherbe, ed., *The Cynic Epistles* [Missoula: Scholars Press, 1977] 200); Ps.-Phalaris, *Ep.* 56 (Hercher, 422), 109 (Hercher, 440); Ps.-Thales, *Ep.* 1 (Hercher, 740); οὐκ ἠγνόουν: Ps.-Phalaris, *Ep.* 84 (Hercher, 432).

Learn and Know which considerably overlap.[37] Ignatius of Antioch twice uses aorist forms of γινώσκω to begin letters (*Magn.* 1:1: γνούω; *Trall.* 1:1: ἔγνων). A functional parallel is found in the Pauline thanksgiving periods in which Paul's knowledge of the behavior of the community became an occasion for praise directed to God on their behalf. Yet the term οἶδα also suggests the kind of divine omniscience mediated by prophets; this association is made more plausible in view of the motto found in 2:23: "I am he who searches mind and heart."

There are two stereotypical phrases which occur in the *narratio* in some but not all of the proclamations. First, the phrase σου τὰ ἔργα which occurs four times immediately following οἶδα in Rev 2:19; 3:1, 8, 15 (cf. 2:2 where οἶδα τὰ ἔργα σου occurs in the same position), and once independently in 3:2.[38] The οἶδα-clause makes it clear that the exalted Christ is aware of the conduct of all members and factions of each of the seven congregations. The second phrase, ἀλλὰ ἔχω κατὰ σοῦ [ὀλίγα] ὅτι is found three times in 2:4, 20, 24). The general approval (praise is too strong a term) implied in statements immediately following the οἶδα in five of the proclamations (2:2–3; 2:9; 2:13; 2:19; 3:8) is contrasted with the criticism introduced by the contrastive adversative particle ἀλλά (an alternate device is the use of paradox in 3:1 b: "I know your works; you have the name of being alive, and you are dead"). Two positive formulations of this phrase (ἀλλὰ τοῦτο ἔχεις ὅτι in 2:6, and ἀλλὰ ἔχεις ὀλίγα ὀνόματα in 3. 4) break the pattern in that they *follow* the *dispositio* in 2:5 and 3:4 respectively, but refer to past or present situations in those communities with verbs in the present tense. Yet there can be little doubt that the author has intentionally used these positive and negative versions of this saying as an *inclusio* to frame the *dispositio.*

6. *The Dispositio.* This is the central section of the proclamations, the reason for which they were written.[39] It is closely connected to the *narratio,* which serves as the basis for assertions made in the *dispositio.* Unlike the other

[37] Louw and Nida, *Greek-English Lexicon* I, § 27.1–26; 28.1–16.

[38] Rev has 302 instances of a possessive pronoun in the genitive *following* an articular noun, as opposed to just 11 occurrences of a personal pronoun in the genitive *preceding* an articular noun. Seven of the eleven instances of the latter pattern occur in Rev 2–3: (σου τὰ ἔργα (2. 19; 3. 1, 2, 8, 15); σου τὴν θλῖψιν (2. 9); μου τὸν λόγον (3. 8). Outside of Rev 2–3 the pattern occurs four times (10:9; 14:18; 18:5, 14). In the LXX, the possessive pronoun in the genitive following an articular noun occurs 149 times in the case of τὸ ἔργον, but just once with the possessive pronoun in the genitive preceding an articular noun (Wis 6:3: ὑμῶν τὰ ἔργα). The possessive pronoun in the genitive occurs just once between the article and the noun it governs (Exod 36. 4: κατὰ τὸ αὐτοῦ ἔργον). On this problem see A. Wifstrand, "A Problem Concerning the Word Order in the New Testament," *ST* 3 (1949) 172–84.

[39] The term *dispositio,* was used by Quintilian for the effective and unified arrangement of the various elements of a speech (*Institutio oratoria* 3.3.1). Here the term is derived from the terminology for parts of documents in medieval diplomatics; cf. Åke Fridh, *Terminologie et formules dans les Variae de Cassiodore* (Stockholm: Almqvist & Wiksel 1956) 9 f., since the terms fit the peculiar characteristics of edicts; see below. The terms *propositio* and *probatio* typically following the *exordium* of juridical speeches and the *exordium* and *narratio* of

stereotypical features of the seven proclamations, the *dispositio* is not formally marked with a stereotypical phrase used consistently in all seven proclamations. Yet this section is marked with the use of imperatives and future indicatives (though futuristic presents such as ἔρχομαι, βάλλω and μέλλω do occur). The following sections of the seven proclamations function as *dispositiones:* (1) 2:5–6, (2) 2:10, (3) 2:16, (4) 2:22–25, (5) 3:2–4, (6) 3:9–11, (7) 3:16–20. Four of them are introduced with imperatives (μνημόνευε, 2:5; μηδὲν φοβοῦ, 2:10; μετανόησον, 2:16 γίνου γρηγορῶν καὶ στήρισον, 3:2), while three are introduced with future indicatives (or present indicatives which function as future indicatives): ἰδοὺ βάλλω, 2:22;[40] ἰδοὺ διδῶ ... [digression] ... ἰδοὺ ποιήσω, 3:9; μέλλω σε ἐμέσαι [following a causal clause],[41] 3:16.

The term μνημόνευε occurs six times (2.5, 16, 21 [2x], 22; 3:19) and is twice linked to μετανόησον (2:5; 3:3). This emphasis on remembering the past constitutes the idealization of the past implying that all perceived forms of slippage including the appearance of dissident views and behaviors are based on a nostalgic conception of the purity of the pristine era (compatible with the composition of Revelation later rather than earlier in the first cent. CE). The demand for repentance is also frequently mentioned in the *dispositiones.* Repentance is often found in a conditional "but if not" contrast (2:5a: μετανόησον ... εἰ δὲ μή; 2:5b: ἐὰν μὴ μετανοήσῃς; 2:16: μετανόησον οὖν· εἰ δὲ μή; 2:22: ἐὰν μὴ μετανοήσωσιν; 3.3: καὶ μετανόησον. ἐὰν οὖν μὴ γρηγορήσῃς), which introduces the threat of imminent eschatological judgment. This threat of judgment is identified with negative aspects of the Parousia in the phrase ἔρχομαι σοι (2:5, 16; 3:3), or ἥξω ὡς κλέπτης (3:3).[42] In 2:16, the negative effects of the Parousia are directed toward a dissident faction in the community, the Nicolaitans: "If not, I will come to *you* soon [ἔρχομαί σοι ταχύ] and war against *them* [καὶ πολεμήσω μετ" αὐτῶν] with the sword of my mouth" (alluding to 1:16b). Christ will come to the *community,* and punish the Nicolaitans.

7. *The Proclamation Formula.* This formula, cast in the third person, occurs at the end of each of seven proclamations (2:7, 11, 17, 29; 3:6, 13, 22), and in a variant form in 13:9 (Εἴ τις ἔχει οὖς ἀκουσάτω), where the formula introduces rather than concludes an oracle, and a functionally related form occurs in 13:18 (ὁ ἔχων νοῦν ψηφισάτω). The present imperative ἀκουσάτω is used transitively, with the entire clause beginning with the interrogative pronoun τί functioning as the object: "what the Spirit says to the churches" (in the Synoptic tradition,

deliberative speeches are inappropriate categories to describe the central sections of the seven proclamations.

40 βάλλω obviously functions as a future since it is parallel to ἀποκτενῶ in 2:23.

41 This pattern is repeated in the same proclamation in 2:17–18: ὅτι λέγεις ὅτι ... συμβουλεύω.

42 See the discussion in Traugott Holtz, *Die Christologie der Apokalypse des Johannes* (Berlin: Akademie-Verlag, 1962) 206–8:

however, ἀκούειν is always used *intransitively* in such formulas). The referent of this phrase is ambiguous. Formulated in the third person, it appears to introduce a new speaker, the Spirit, for the first Promise of Victory formula which follows it in 2:7b is formulated in the first person (all of these formulas except the one in 2:11b are formulated in the first person). Yet that cannot be the author's intention, for when the order of the Promise of Victory formula and the Proclamation formula in the last four proclamations is reversed, it is clear that a new speaker has not been introduced. The Spirit is therefore closely associated with the exalted Christ in the proclamations to the seven churches, perhaps as the prophetic Spirit who mediates the words of the exalted Christ.[43] The fact that the verb of declaration is again λέγει lends symmetry to each proclamation.

Placed at the conclusion of the seven proclamations this expression functions as a *proclamation* formula, i. e., as an injunction to an audience to pay attention to the message which has been (or will be) delivered. The formula has no close verbal parallel in ancient literature with the exception of the parable tradition found in the Synoptic Gospels. When the proclamation formula concludes an oracle it functions as a *prophetic signature.*[44] Proclamation formulas (variously phrased) often introduce OT prophetic oracles with expressions such as "Hear the word of Yahweh" (1 Kgs 22:19; Amos 7:16; Jer 29:20). Proclamation formulas, originally derived from use in public assemblies and courts of law (cf. Mic 6:2; Jer 2:4) were used to introduce legal teaching (Prov 4:1; Job 13:6; 33:1, 31; 34:2, 16; Isa 49:1; 51:4), and instruction in wisdom (Deut 32:1; Prov 7:24; Psa 49:1; Isa 28:23). The formula "He who has ears, let him hear" (and variants) is an aphorism rooted in the Jesus tradition, where it occurs in six variant versions.[45] These (probably intentional) allusions to sayings of Jesus presuppose that they had a firm place in the liturgy of the early Christian communities in Anatolia so that their use could authenticate the author's revelatory encounter with the exalted Jesus.

8. *The Promise of Victory*. This formula, like the Christological predications, exhibits variety in form and structure. The most obvious variation is its location

---

[43] The exalted Christ and the Spirit are not identical however (cf. 14:13; 22:17), for the Spirit is active in the earthly community as the representative of the exalted Jesus who will come in the near future; cf. Holtz, *Die Christologie der Apokalypse des Johannes,* 208–11:

[44] In early Christian literature other examples of the prophetic signature are found only in 1 Cor 14:37–38 and Odes Sol 3. 10–11; cf. D.E. Aune, "The Odes of Solomon and Early Christian Prophecy," *NTS* 28 (1982) 438 f. The appeal to "Open your ears" functions as an introductory proclamation formula in Odes Sol 9. 1.

[45] Variations of the formula occur seven times in the Synoptic Gospels (Mark 4:9, 23; Matt 11:15; 13:9, 43; Luke 8:8; 14:35), and five additional times as variant readings (Mark 7:16; Matt 25:29; Luke 8:15; 12:21; 13:9; 21:4). In non-canonical literature the formula occurs six times in *Gos Thom.* 8, 21, 24, 63, 65, 96, once as an introductory formula (*Gos Thom.* 24), the other instances as conclusions to parables. The formula also occurs once in *Acts of Thomas* 82, twice in the *Gospel of Mary* (BG 8502, 7.9–10; 8.10–11), and four times in *Soph. Jes. Chr.* (CG III, 97.21–23; 98.22–23; 105.10–12 107.18–108.1.

after the proclamation formula at the end of the first three proclamations (2:7b, 11b, 17b), but before the proclamation formula in the last four (2:26–27; 3:5, 12, 21), suggesting their close relationship. The author is concerned to place a present substantival participle from νικάω at the very beginning of the sentence, even though he used three different syntactical constructions to do so: (1) In the phrase τῷ νικῶντι δώσω αὐτῷ in 2:7 and 17, the substantival participle τῷ νικῶντι is a dative of respect, while αὐτῷ is the indirect object of δώσω. (2) In 2:11 and 3:5 ὁ νικῶν is the subject of a verb. (3) In 2:26; 3:12, 21, ὁ νικῶν functions as a nominative absolute or pendant nominative, a construction functionally parallel to (1). The element of reward is evident in the phrase δώσω αὐτῷ is found four times in the promise of victory (2:7b, 17b, 26; 3:21).

2. The Seven Proclamations as "Prophetic" Letters

There is at least one judgment which should be clear from the outset: whatever genre or genres the seven proclamations represent, they exhibit few features derived from the Hellenistic epistolary tradition.[46] Further, the seven proclamations do not rigidly replicate the generic features of any known ancient literary form, either individually or in terms of a grouping of seven.[47] While the author was certainly not without literary models, he has not chosen to follow them slavishly.

There are many examples from the ancient world of letters used to communicate divine revelation, i. e., oracles or prophecies.[48] With some justification, then, one can speak of "prophetic letters" or "oracular letters". Yet unlike the evident epistolary framework of Rev itself (1:4–5; 22:21), the seven proclamations in

---

[46] Adolf Deissmann regarded the seven messages in Rev 2–3 as *epistles* rather than letters; *Bible Studies* (Edinburgh: T. & T. Clark, 1901) 54; he was followed by William M. Ramsay, *The Letters to the Seven Churches* (London: Hodder & Stoughton, 1904) 38 f. In fact, they are neither. Kirby, "Rhetorical Situations," 200, claims that the letters "owe some of their formal features to the Hellenistic epistolary tradition". Yet he does not specify just what these formal features are nor do any of the many secondary sources referred to in an extensive footnote support his contention. The prescripts of Hellenistic letters (even when preserved in inscriptions, where abbreviation sometimes occurs) regularly consist of the sender's name in the nominative, the recipient's name in the dative (indirect object), and the salutation χαίρειν; they regularly conclude with a stereotypical expression of greeting.

[47] A fact recently emphasized by several scholars including Lars Hartman, "Form and Message: A Preliminary Discussion of 'Partial Texts' in Rev 1–3 and 22,6 ff.," *L'Apocalypse johannique et l'Apocalyptique dans le Nouveau Testament,* ed. J. Lambrecht (Leuven: The University Press, 1980) 142, and Martin Karrer, *Die Johannesoffenbarung als Brief: Studien zu ihrem literarischen, historischen und theologischen Ort* (Göttingen: Vandenhoeck & Ruprecht, 1986) 159 f.

[48] Aune, *Prophecy in Early Christianity,* 72–3; references to prophetic letters in the ancient Near East, other than those discussed below, are found in M. Dijkstra, "Prophecy by Letter (Jeremiah XXIX 24–32)," *VT* 33 (1983) 319–22.

Rev 2–3 betray no single feature of the Pauline or early Christian epistolary tradition. They do, however, use what could be construed as a Near Eastern epistolary prescript, i.e., the archaic τάδε λέγει formula.

The royal archives of the ancient kingdom of Mari contained cuneiform documents in Akkadian covering the period ca. 1800–1760 BCE. Some of these included cuneiform letters containing advice to king Zimri-Lin from the gods of Mari sent to him by "prophets".[49]

A collection of five texts written on ostraca with a similar function has survived from Hellenistic Egypt, ca. 168 BCE.[50] The five texts include rough and final drafts of a letter to the king. One of the rough drafts (text B) reads:

> Regarding the matters disclosed to me by the thrice-great god Hermes concerning oracles for the sovereign, I wish to announce that (the insurgent) Egyptians will quickly be defeated and that the king is to advance immediately to the Thebaid.

The final draft is formulated in epistolary form:

> To King Ptolemy and to King Ptolemy the Brother and to Queen Cleopatra the Sister, greetings. Horus the priest of Isis at the sanctuary of Sebenutos in the city of Isis wishes to make an announcement about certain oracles to the sovereigns, that (the insurgent) Egyptians will be defeated quickly and that the king is to advance immediately to the Thebaid.

Yet these ancient texts from Mari and Hellenistic Egypt provide evidence only that prophetic or oracular advice could be communicated in epistolary as well as oral form without the epistolary format influencing the form and content of the message.

Prophetic letters are occasionally found in the OT and early Jewish literature.[51] 2 Chron 21:12–15 (cf. Josephus, *Ant.* 9.99–101) contains a letter attributed to Elijah the prophet containing an announcement of judgment introduced with the traditional prophetic messenger formula "thus says the Lord". Most of these "prophetic" letters are associated with Jeremiah and his scribe Baruch.[52] The letters in Jer 29, like the letter of Elijah in 2 Chron 21:12–15, are all prophetic

---

[49] H.B. Huffmon, "Prophecy in the Mari Letters," *BA* 31 (1968) 101–24; F. Ellermeier, *Prophets in Mari und Israel* (Herzberg: Erwin Jungfer, 1968); E. Noort, *Untersuchungen zum Gottesbescheid in Mari* (Neukirchen-Vluyn, 1977). For a bibliography and a selection of translations, see W. Beyerlin, *Near Eastern Religious Texts Relating to the Old Testament* (Philadelphia: Westminster, 1978) 122–8.

[50] T.C. Skeat and E.G. Turner, "An Oracle of Hermes Trismegistos at Saqqara," *Journal of Egyptian Archaeology* 54 (1968) 199–208. The five texts were published the next year in *Sammelbuch griechischer Urkunden aus Ägypten* 10 (1969) 159–60, no.10574; texts B and E only are translated in this essay.

[51] Klaus Berger, "Apostelbrief und apostolische Rede: Zum Formular frühchristlicher Briefe," *ZNW* 65 (1974) 212–19.

[52] Jer 29:4–23 [LXX 36:4–23], 24–28 [LXX 36:24–28], 30–32 [LXX 36:30–32] (Dijkstra argues that Jer 29:24–32 is a single letter); 2 *Apoc. Bar.* 77:17–19; 78–87; *Ep Jer*; *Par Jer* 6:15–7:4; 7:24–35.

oracles in epistolary form introduced with prophetic rather than epistolary formulas.[53] A. S. van der Woude has argued that the prophecy of Nahum was originally in epistolary form (the term ספר in the superscription means "letter").[54] Elsewhere in early Jewish literature the association of divine revelation with epistolary form is found in *1 Enoch* 91–108, the so-called *Epistle of Enoch*. The Greek text of 1 Enoch 100.6 refers to the entire composition as Ἐπιστολὴ Ἑνώχ, "The Epistle of Enoch."[55]

Klaus Berger, after discussing the phenomenon of the prophetic letter as a constituent form included in larger literary forms in the OT and early Jewish literature, observes that "The letters of Revelation are therefore primarily to be regarded as exemplars of the gattung of the prophetic letter which never died out completely."[56] Berger does not, however, suggest that this prophetic-letter tradition served as a literary model for the whole of Revelation. However, the great diversity in form and content exhibited in the "prophetic letters" ascribed to Elijah, Jeremiah, Baruch and the more problematic Epistle of Enoch, argue against the supposition of a unified prophetic-letter tradition or genre in early Judaism. Berger's proposal, then, sheds no real light either on the "letters" in Rev 2–3 or the total epistolary form of Revelation.[57] Further, after examining the Hellenistic, Christian and Gnostic texts which are in any way comparable to Revelation, Karrer concludes that while Revelation moves within the context of the epistolary form of communication and within the possibilities inherent in ancient apocalyptic and revelatory literature, it was directly influenced by *none* of these roughly contemporary "parallel" literary phenomena.[58]

3. The Seven Proclamations as Prophetic Speech

Both Ferdinand Hahn and Ulrich B. Müller have argued that the seven proclamations of Rev 2–3 are rooted in early Christian prophetic speech. Both consider the τάδε λέγει formula as identical with the prophetic messenger formula of OT

[53] Dennis Pardee, *Handbook of Ancient Hebrew Letters* (Chico: Scholars Press, 1982) 175–8, 181.

[54] A. S. van der Woude, "The Book of Nahum: A Letter Written in Exile," *OTS* 20 (1977) 108–26.

[55] J. T. Milik, *The Books of Enoch: Aramaic Fragments of Qumran Cave* 4 (Oxford: Clarendon, 1976) 47–57, though see Matthew Black, *The Book of Enoch or I Enoch* (Leiden: Brill, 1985) 283 for appropriate qualifications.

[56] Berger, "Apostelbrief," 214. More recently, Berger has little to say about the literary form of the seven proclamations; cf. *Formgeschichte des Neuen Testaments* (Heidelberg: Quelle & Meyer, 1984) 302 f.; "Hellenistische Gattungen im Neuen Testament," *Aufstieg und Niedergang der römischen Welt,* Part II, Vol. 25/2 (New York and Berlin: Walter de Gruyter, 1984) 1361 f.

[57] Karrer, *Die Johannesoffenbarung als Brief,* 49–59.

[58] Karrer, *Die Johannesoffenbarung als Brief,* 66.

prophecy. Hahn has proposed that Rev 2–3 reflects a single form of prophetic speech which has a relatively fixed sequence of elements, but which also exhibits limited variation. Müller, on the other hand, has identified each of the proclamations as a type of prophetic sermon, which contains two basic forms of prophetic speech, the paraenetic sermon of repentance (*Busssparaklese*), and the sermon of salvation (*Heilspredigt*).[59] The first type is more common in Rev 2–3, and 2:1–7 reveals its basic form: accusation (2:4), admonition (2:5a), and conditional threat of judgment (2:5b). With many variations Müller finds this form in 2:12–17, 18–29; 3:1–6, 14–22. The sermon of salvation, on the other hand, is found in relatively pure form in 2:8–11, and combined with the paraenetic sermon of repentance in 3:1–6. Müller traces the basic form of the paraenetic sermon of repentance back to early Judaism through John the Baptist (Matt 3:7–10; Luke 3:7–9), to the speech of admonition in apocalyptic literature (e.g. *1 Enoch* 91:3–10; *Jub* 7:20–29; 36:3–11).

In my own earlier work on the forms of early Christian prophetic speech, I identified a complex form with a correspondingly complex label: *paraenetic salvation-judgment oracles*.[60] While this type of prophetic speech had its roots in early Judaism, it developed distinctive Christian features. In continuity with the introverted character of early Jewish apocalypticism, these oracles were directed primarily to members of the Christian community, and for that reason they exhibit a strong emphasis on moral exhortation. Proper behavior is negatively sanctioned with threats of judgment and exclusion, and positively sanctioned by promises of salvation and reward. This type of early prophetic speech exhibits great variety due to the diversity in the concrete situations experienced by the groups addressed. Most of the constituent features of this form must be regarded as *optional elements* rather than as fixed formal characteristics. The seven proclamations of Rev 2–3 fit this flexible prophetic form,[61] though the stereotypical formulas are doubtless the product of the literary artifice of the author rather than the result of the rigid reproduction of the oral style of early Christian prophetic speech. If the author has in fact cast these proclamations in the form of imperial edicts, their artificial literary character is made more probable.

4. The Seven Proclamations as Imperial Edicts

A number of scholars have suggested that the τάδε λέγει formula corresponds to the style of royal decrees promulgated by the great Persian kings and the imperial edicts issued by Roman magistrates and emperors as well as to the OT

[59] Müller, Prophetie und Predigt, 47–104.
[60] Aune, *Prophecy in Early Christianity,* 326.
[61] Aune, *Prophecy in Early Christianity,* 274–88.

prophetic messenger formula.[62] The only sustained attempt to argue that the seven proclamations conform both in form and content to royal or imperial edicts was published in 1911 by Gunnar Rudberg.[63] Rudberg observed that the same juxtaposition of praise and censure found in the seven proclamations (except those to Smyrna, 2:8–11 and Philadelphia, 3:7–13), occurs in an inscribed decree or letter of Darius I from Magnesia (see below).[64] He also noted that while the formula τάδε λέγει κύριος (like οὕτως λέγει κύριος and εἶπε κύριος) was used in the LXX for divine pronouncements, τάδε λέγει also introduced the rescripts and letters of Persian kings, and corresponded to the simple λέγει formula in the edicts of Roman magistrates and emperors.[65] Rudberg concluded that John used this form, consciously or unconsciously, to present the exalted Christ as a king addressing his subjects.[66]

The formal difference between edicts and letters is simply that the prescript of the former consists of the form ὁ δεῖνα λέγει or ὁ δεῖνα κελεύει (i.e., *imperator dicit*), while the prescript of letters consists of the formula ὁ δεῖνα τῷ δεῖνι χαίρειν.[67] *Edicta* (the Greek equivalent of *edictum* was διάταγμα, cf. Plutarch *Marcellus* 14.7), were public announcements by an emperor or higher magistrates setting forth orders or policies.[68] They were one of four types of judicial decisions by the emperor which were given the general designation *constitutiones;* the others were *mandata* (internal directives to officials in the imperial service), *decreta* (actual judicial decisions pronounced at the emperor's court), and *rescripta* (the imperial correspondence).[69] *Edicta,* the usual form for all communications directed toward the general public, were very heterogeneous.[70]

---

62 Ethelberl Stauffer, *Christus und die Caesaren: Historische Skizzen,* 5. Aufl. (Hamburg: Friedrich Wittig, 1960) 198; J. Lähnemann, "Die sieben Sendschreiben der Johannes-Apokalypse," *Studien zur Religion und Kultur Kleinasiens*, ed. S. Sahin, E. Schwertheim u. Wagner (2 vols.; Leiden: Brill, 1978), 526; Hanns Lilje, *Das letzte Buch der Bibel: Eine Einführung in die Offenbarung Johannes,* 7. Aufl. (Hamburg: Furche-Verlag, 1961) 82; Kirby, "Rhetorical Situations," 200; E.A. Judge in G.H.R. Horsley, *New Documents Illustrating Early Christianity* (North Ryde: Macquarie University, 1981) 40. Johannes Lindblom proposed that the *Orakelformel* "thus says the Lord" could be traced back to both the *Proklamationsformel* of ancient Near Eastern edicts and to the introduction to the message brought by a messenger (*Die Literarische Gattung der prophetischen Literatur* [Uppsala: Lundequist, 1924] 103 f.).

63 Gunnar Rudberg, "Zu den Sendschreiben der Johannes-Apokalypse," *Eranos* 11 (1911) 170–9.

64 Rudberg, "Sendschreiben," 172 f.

65 Rudberg, "Sendschreiben," 173–76.

66 Rudberg, "Sendschreiben," 179.

67 Wilhelm Larfield, *Griechische Epigraphik,* 3. Aufl., Handbuch der klassischen Altertumswissenschaft 1.5 (München: C.H. Beck, 1914) 427–32.

68 T. Kipp, "Edictum," *RE* 5, cols. 1940–8.

69 Adolph Berger, *An Encyclopedic Dictionary of Roman Law* (Philadelphia: American Philosophical Society, 1953), *s. v. Constitutiones principum.*

70 Wolfgang Kunkel, *An Introduction to Roman Legal and Constitutional History,* 2nd ed. (Oxford: Clarendon, 1973) 127 f. For examples of published decrees see Victor Ehrenberg and A.H.M. Jones, *Documents Illustrating the Reigns of Augustus and Tiberius,* 2nd ed.

Rescripta consisted of two types, the imperial letter or *epistula*,[71] and the marginal decision of the emperor, or *subscriptio* (written at the bottom of the actual petition or *libellus*). Edicts are formal and public, whereas letters are informal and private. Further, imperial edicts did not have universal application, but were valid only for the region and people for whom they were promulgated.[72]

Building on the research of Åke Fridh on the rhetoric of sixth century decretal forms attested in the letters found in the *Variae* of Cassiodorus,[73] Margretta Benner focused on a rhetorical analysis of 37 edicts and about 100 allusions to edicts primarily of the first century CE.[74] The propriety of such a rhetorical analysis of early imperial edicts is suggested by the advice of the Stoic philosopher M. Cornelius Fronto to Marcus Aurelius, where the matter of formulating edicts is specifically mentioned:[75]

> Which of them [earlier emperors between Tiberius and Vespasian] could address people or Senate in a speech of his own? Which draw up an edict [*edictum*] or a rescript [*epistulam*] in his own words ... Now *imperium* is a term that not only connotes power but also speech, since the exercise of *imperium* consists essentially of ordering and prohibiting. If he did not praise good actions, if he did not blame evil actions, if he did not exhort to virtue, if he did not warn off from vice, a ruler would belie his name and be called imperator for no purpose.

(Oxford: Clarendon, 1976) nos. 302, 311 (a series of five edicts of Augustus), 314 (Josephus, *Ant.* 16.162–65), 320; E. Mary Smallwood, *Documents Illustrating the Principates of Gaius, Claudius and Nero* (Cambridge: The University Press, 1967) no.368, 375 (edicts of Claudius), 377 (with the distinctive *superscriptio* Διάταγμα Καίσαρος), 380 (edict of the proconsul of Asia with ἐκήρυξεν as the verb of declaration), 381, 382, 383, 391 (edicts of the prefect of Egypt), 392 (edict of the proconsul of Sardinia); E. Mary Smallwood, *Documents Illustrating the Principates of Nerva, Trajan and Hadrian* (Cambridge: The University Press, 1966) 459, 461 (edicts of the prefect of Egypt), 462 (edict of Hadrian). All of these documents are translated in A. C. Johnson, P. R. Coleman-Norton and F. C. Bourne, *Ancient Roman Statutes: A Translation with Introduction, Commentary, Glossary and Index* (Austin: University of Texas, 1961).

[71] For a collection and discussion of *epistulae,* see Robert K Sherk, *Roman Documents from the Greek East: Senatus Consulta and Epistulae to the Age of Augustus* (Baltimore: Johns Hopkins, 1969) 186–364; a discussion of the form *of epistulae* is found on 189–97.

[72] A. N. Sherwin-White, *The Letters of Pliny: A Social and Historical Commentary* (Oxford: Clarendon, 1966) 651.

[73] *Terminologie et formules dans les Variae de Cassiodore* (Göteborg: Acta Universitatis Gothoburgensis, 1956).

[74] *The Emperor Says: Studies in the Rhetorical Style of Edicts of the Early Empire* (Göteborg: Acta Universitatis Gothoburgensis, 1975); for a critique see Michael Winterbottom, *Gnomon* 49 (1977) 419–20.

[75] *Ep. ad Verum Imp.* 2.1; C.P. Haines, *Marcus Cornelius Fronto,* LCL (Cambridge: Harvard University, 1929) 11, 138 f. For a summary of the rhetorical tasks of the emperor see Fronto, *Ep. ad M. Antionium, De eloquentia* 1.5 (Haines, 11, 59): "For it falls to Caesar to carry by persuasion necessary measures in the Senate, to address the people in a harangue on many important matters, to correct the inequities of the law, to dispatch rescripts [*litteras*] throughout the world, to take foreign kings to task, to repress by edicts [*edictis*] disorders among the allies, to praise their services, to crush the rebellious and to cow the proud." Both passages are mentioned in Benner, *The Emperor Speaks,* 10.

While the principle rhetorical *genus* of edicts may be that of the *genus deliberativum*,[76] the authority of the ruler or magistrate means that the inclusion of the persuasive element is almost entirely voluntary rather than necessary. Further, the presence of praise and blame (*genus demonstrativum*) as well as exhortations to pursue the good and avoid the bad (*genus deliberativum*) found in the quotation from Fronto above suggests that edicts are inevitably a *mixtum compositum*. The first formal element of the edict is the *praescriptio* ("introduction"), which gives the title(s) and name(s) of the issuing magistrate, followed by a verb of declaration, in Latin *dicit/dicunt* ("he says," "they say") and in Greek λέγει or λέγουσι ("he says, declares," "they say, declare").[77] The main function of the *praescriptio* is to state the authority by which an edict is issued. The text of the edict then follows with the magistrate speaking in the first person with the addressees addressed in the second person plural, as if the edict were being read to them (which originally, of course, it was). Unlike the recipients of a letter, they are not formally addressed by proper names either in the *praescriptio* or in the remaining sections of the decree. The body of the edict can consist of the following elements, not all of which are invariably present:[78] (1) the *prooemium*, "preface" (intended to produce benevolence and interest in the addressees), (2) the *promulgatio*, "proclamation" (a "publishing" phrase such as "I make known that," etc.), (3) the *narratio* (a clear, short account of the state of the matter, the facts which caused the enactment, etc.), (4) the *dispositio*, "arrangement" (the central part of the document expressing the decision), and finally, (5) the *sanctio*, "sanction," or *corroboratio*, "corroboration" (end clauses whose purpose is to bring about the observance of the enactment). The *praescriptio*, with the verb of declaration, is the only formal characteristic which always occurs in imperial edicts.[79] Each of the seven proclamations begins with a *praescriptio* similar to that found in imperial edicts with the exception that the verb of declaration normally *follows* the name and titles of the issuing emperor or magistrate(s) in imperial edicts, but *precedes* the titles and predicates of Christ in the seven proclamations. Yet there are exceptions, such as Xerxes' letter to Pausanias in Thucydides 1.129.3: ὧδε λέγει βασιλεὺς Ξέρξης Παυσανίᾳ and the parody of a proclamation of sacral law by Cronus in the guise of a priest in Lucian *Saturnalia* 10: Τάδε λέγει Κρονοσόλων. In addition to names and titles, Roman edicts can contain participial phrases in the *praescriptio* which further characterize the authority of the author(s), e. g. Appian *Bellum civile* 4.2.8: "Marcus Lepidus, Mar-

[76] Benner, *The Emperor Speaks*, 22 (though she recognizes the problems inherent in attempting to categorize the edicts).

[77] Cf. Hugh J. Mason, *Greek Terms for Roman Institutions: A Lexicon and Analysis* (Toronto: Hakkert, 1974) 127; Fergus Millar, *The Emperor in the Roman World* (Ithaca: Cornell University, 1977) 221 f.

[78] For an analysis of thirty-seven decrees using this schema, cf. Benner, *The Emperor Speaks*, 33–175.

[79] Benner, *The Emperor Speaks*, 26.

cus Antonius, and Octavius Caesar, chosen by the people [οἱ χειροτονηθέντες] to set in order and regulate the republic." Again, imperial edicts lack an *adscriptio,* but the *adscriptiones* in Rev 2–3 are not part of the proclamations proper.

No counterpart to the *prooemium* is found in any of the seven proclamations, though its absence is appropriate in eastern provinces where the traditions of absolute sovereignty of the Persian monarchs and then the Hellenistic kings were predominant.

The *narratio,* which occurs with great frequency in Roman edicts, often has the character of reported information (*renuntiatum est nobis*). The *narratio* has a clear functional counterpart in the οἶδα-clauses in each of the seven proclamations. Like the epistolary parallels to οἶδα discussed above (pp. 14 f.), in which terms from closely related semantic domains such as ἀκούειν, γινώσκειν, ἐπιγινώσκειν, and πυνθάνεσθαι are used to introduce the *narrationes* of royal and imperial edicts. One particularly relevant example is the edict of Claudius quoted in Josephus *Ant.* 19. 280–284:

Tiberius Claudius Caesar Augustus Germanicus, of tribunician power, declares [λέγει]: "Since I have known [ἐπιγνούώ] from the beginning that the Jews in Alexandria called 'Alexandrians' were joint-colonizers with the Alexandrians."

Another relevant document is a letter of Darius 1:[80] Βασιλεῦ [βα]σιλέων Δαρεῖος ὁ Ὑστάσπεω Γαδάται δούλῳ τάδε λέγε[ι], πυνθάνομαί σε τῶν ἐμῶν ἐπιταγμάτων οὐ κατὰ πάντα πειθαρχεῖν ("The king of kings Darius Hystaspes to his servant Gadatas says the following: "I have learned that you did not obey my commands in every respect'"). In this inscription, πυνθάνομαι ('I have learned', a historic present), with the infinitive introducing indirect discourse, functions much like the οἶδα of the seven proclamations. Though the original must have been inscribed during the lifetime of Darius (521–486 BCE), this particular inscription dates to the first half of the second century CE, perhaps as a replacement for a badly weathered one, a fact which reveals how important such inscriptions continued to be during a much later period. Similarly, in an inscription of Hadrian,[81] the *narratio* is introduced with a participial construction using πυθόμενος.[82]

80 O. Kern, *Die Inschriften von Magnesia am Maeander* (Berlin: W. Spemann, 1900) no.115; reprinted with brief but informative notes in W. Dittenberger, *Sylloge Inscriptionum Graecarum,* 3. Aufl. (Hildesheim: Georg Olms, 1960 [*1915–24]) I, no. 22, and conveniently reprinted with bibliography and notes in Russell Meiggs and David Lewis, *A Selection of Greek Historical Inscriptions to the End of the Fifth Century B. C.* (Oxford: Clarendon, 1969) no.12.

81 Smallwood, *Documents of Nerva*, no. 462; analyzed in Benner, *The Emperor Speaks*, 161 f.

82 In a fictional letter from Amasis to Polycrates preserved in Herodotus 3.40, we find a *narratio* introduced with the infinitive πυνθάνεσθαι and containing a positive and negative element very similar to the *narrationes* of the seven proclamations: "Amasis to Polycrates says the following: [ὧδε λέγει]: It is pleasant to learn [πυνθάνεσθαι] of the well-being of a friend and ally, but [δέ] I do not like these great successes of yours." Similarly in Herodotus 3.122,

The *dispositio* is uniformly found in each proclamation, except that it is not introduced with the customary ordaining verb meaning "I command," etc., but is influenced by the conditional style of prophetic speech consisting of ethical exhortations, usually matched by conditional threats. In the inscribed letter of Darius to Gadatas briefly discussed above, Darius goes on to praise Gadatas for cultivating Syrian fruit trees in Ionia (ἐπαίνω σὴν πρόθεσιν), lines 8–17, but threatens to punish him for attempting to tax Apollo's sacred gardeners (ὅτι δὲ τὴν ὑπὲρ θεῶν μου διάθεσιν ἀφανίζεις, etc.), lines 17–29. Thus the *narratio* has both a positive and negative element as in the seven proclamations.

Finally, statements with a function similar to the *sanction* or *corroboratio* of Roman edicts are regularly found at the close of each proclamation in the conditional promise of victory.

5. Conclusions

The seven proclamations addressed to each of the seven churches located in the Roman province of Asia were "public" proclamations; each was read by all the other congregations. They are not at all typical of the kinds of literary forms usually included in apocalypses. Since most apocalypses are written under the names of ancient Israelite worthies, they usually conceal the actually circumstances of their origin. The implicit function of *these* proclamations, however, is to demonstrate that the risen Christ, speaking through the prophet John in the Spirit, knows precisely the situation of each and every one of the seven communities. These proclamations have often been inaccurately characterized as letters, though it is true that there was a closer resemblance between letters and edicts issued by the Achaemenid chancery than those issued by Roman magistrates and emperors. Both letters and edicts issued by rulers with absolute powers have the force of law. The seven proclamations of Rev 2–3 are similar in form to ancient royal or imperial *edicts*, in that they exhibit formally and structurally similar *praescriptiones*, *narrationes*, *dispositiones* and *sanctiones*. In content, however, the *narrationes* and *dispositiones* exhibit the complex characteristics of the *paraenetic salvation-judgment* oracles widely used by early Christian prophets.

One oracular deity, Zeus at Heliopolis, replied in the form of *rescripta* ("written replies") to sealed *diplomata*, i.e., folded tablets with written instructions, or *codicilii*, i.e., written responses (Macrobius *Sat.* 1.23.14–16; referring to a consultation of Trajan). This is a parallel example of how the ancients could

---

the verb πυνθάνεσθαι again introduces the *narratio*: "Oroetes to Polycrates says thus: 'I have learned [πυνθάνομαι] that you are planning ambitious enterprises.'" Again, at the beginning of the *narratio* of a late edict of Statian (367–70 CE) reads "I speak not from hearsay alone … for I have learned …" (Johnson, Coleman Norton and Bourne, *Ancient Roman Statutes*, no. 316).

depict the governing activity of Zeus mediated by divine revelation using the imagery of the Roman emperor and his varied forms of communication with his subjects. John has used this form to create prophetic proclamations issued by the King of kings and Lord of lords to his subjects. John has consciously employed the form of the royal or imperial edict as part of his strategy to emphasize the fact that Christ is the true king in contrast to the Roman emperor who is both a clone and a tool of Satan.

Revelation 5 as an Ancient Egyptian Enthronement Scene?

The Origin and Development of a Scholarly Myth[1]

During the lengthy period that I worked on an extensive commentary on the Revelation of John,[2] beginning in 1982–83 when as a Fulbright professor I was a colleague of Olav Hognestad in the Department of Religion at the University of Trondheim, I discovered a number of fascinating "commentary traditions," that is, information of various kinds which is found in many commentaries on Revelation, which appears to have been derived and adapted from earlier commentaries, but which have little or no basis in fact. One clear example of a "commentary tradition" is the widespread opinion among commentators (commenting on Rev 1:9) that Patmos was a Roman penal colony or place of banishment, based on the evidence of Pliny *Historia naturales* 4.12.69.[3] R.H. Charles claims that the passage in Pliny "states that it was used as a penal settlement by the Romans."[4] Ernst Lohmeyer, probably following Wilhelm Bousset,[5] states that "Wie andere Sporaden (Gyara, Seriphus) ist es von den Römern als Verbannungsort benutzt worden (Plin. n. h. 4. 12. 23),"[6] and Heinrich Kraft follows him when he claims that Pliny "die Insel als Verbannungsort kennt."[7] None of these scholars appear to have actually read Pliny *Historia naturales* 4.12.69, for the passage says only "Patmus circuitu XXX," "Patmos, 30 miles in circumference." While I have not traced the pedigree of this "commentary tradition" back further than Swete and Bousset, I suspect that it did not begin with them. This is one of many instances of commentators reading earlier commentators and accepting

[1] *Amico et socio Olav Hognestad: ad multos annos, amice*!

[2] David E. Aune, *Revelation*, Word Biblical Commentary 52A–C (3 vols.; Nashville: Thomas Nelson, 1997–98).

[3] Henry Barclay Swete, *The Apocalypse of St John: The Greek Text with Introduction and Notes* (3rd ed.; London: Macmillan, 1908) 12.

[4] R.H. Charles, *A Critical and Exegetical Commentary on the Revelation of St. John* (2 vols.; Edinburgh: T. & T. Clark, 1920) 1.21.

[5] Wilhelm Bousset, Die Offenbarung Johannis, KEK 16 (6th ed.; Göttingen: Vandenhoeck & Ruprecht, 1906) 192;

[6] Ernst Lohmeyer, *Die Offenbarung des Johannes*, HNT 16 (3. Aufl.; Tübingen: Mohr-Siebeck, 1970) 15.

[7] Heinrich Kraft, *Die Offenbarung des Johannes*, HNT 16a (Tübingen: Mohr-Siebeck, 1974) 40. He cites the Pliny reference in a garbled way as *Naturgeschichte* 4,12,13, instead of 4,12,23.

their reading of ancient texts, apparently making no attempt to verify earlier interpretations of those texts. The focus of this paper will be on a more complex instance of "commentary tradition," the origin and development of an ancient Egyptian enthronement ritual as a model for understanding the significance of the throne scene in Revelation 5.

At the beginning of the Twentieth Century, a number of scholars influenced by the presuppositions of the history-of-religions school expressed the view that the depiction of the Lamb in Revelation 5 was based on ancient mythical models. Alfred Jeremias suggested a background in the ancient Near Eastern myth of the battle and victory of the "year god," perhaps in the specific form of the myth of Marduk who gained control of the tablets of destiny.[8] Gunkel saw the more general pattern of "the enthronement of a new god," one who could gain control of both heaven and earth through his great magical powers; the sealed scroll therefore represented a magical book.[9] Gunkel was followed by Bousset, who, like Alfred Jeremias, refers to the Marduk myth.[10] Following the suggestion of Hermann Gunkel, a number of scholars have argued that Revelation 5 depicts the enthronement of Christ based on the pattern of the coronation of a a new ruler.[11] Eduard Lohse combines two views of Revelation 5, maintaining that Rev 5:1–5 constitutes a commission scene in the heavenly court, while Rev 5:6–14 is an enthronement scene.[12] Heinrich Giesen, on the other hand,[13] following H.-P. Müller,[14] argues that Rev 5 conforms to the schema of the commission stories in the OT, like those found in 1 Kings 22:19–22 and Isa 6:1–10. He finds it unnecessary to appeal to a enthronement schema to understand Rev 5 and does not mention that such a view is widely held. Among more recent commentators, G.K. Beale devotes a few sentences to supporting the view that Rev 5 is an enthronement scene primarily because it is based on the enthronement scene in Dan 7, and claiming that W.C. van Unnik's arguments against this view are unsuccessful.[15]

---

[8] Alfred Jeremias, *Babylonisches im Neuen Testament* (Leipzig: Hinrichs, 1905) 13–14, 17–18.

[9] Hermann Gunkel, *Zum religionsgeschichtlichen Verständnis des Neuen Testaments* (Göttingen: Vandenhoeck & Ruprecht, 1903) 62–63.

[10] Bousset, *Die Offenbarung Johannis*, 259.

[11] D.W. Hadorn, *Die Offenbarung des Johannes*, THKNT 18 (Leipzig: Deichtert, 1928) 78; Ernst Lohmeyer, *Die Offenbarung des Johannes*, HNT 16 (3rd ed.; Tübingen: Mohr-Siebeck, 1970) 51–52; Traugott Holtz, *Die Christologie der Apokalypse des Johannes* (2nd ed.; Berlin: Akademie Verlag, 1971) 27–54; J.M.P. Sweet, Revelation (Philadelphia: Westminster, 1979) 121–27.

[12] Eduard Lohse, *Die Offenbarung des Johannes* (Göttingen: Vandenhoeck & Ruprecht, 1976) 44.

[13] Heinrich Giesen, *Die Offenbarung des Johannes*, RNT (Regensburg: Verlag Friedrich Pustet, 1997) 159–60.

[14] H.-P. Müller, "Die himmlische Ratsversammlung. Motivgteschichliches zu Apc 5,1–5," *ZNW* 54 (1963) 254–67.

[15] G.K. Beale, *The Book of Revelation*, NIGTC (Grand Rapids: Eerdmans, 1999) 356–57.

For many scholars, the notion that the enthronement of the Lamb provides the basic structure for the action of Rev 5 is apparently unproductive. While Johannes Behm observed that "one is reminded of the solemn act of ascending the throne of a divine ruler in oriental myths, an act which inaugurates the new age" (referring to the view of Lohmeyer), he does not further explore the hermeneutical possibilities of an enthronement schema.[16] While Robert H. Mounce laconically observes in his comments on 5:7 that the act of the Lamb receiving the scroll from the one seated on the throne is "not to be taken as the coronation of the risen Christ,"[17] though he does not mention who does construe the passage in that way. Other commentators either do not mention the enthronement motif at all,[18] or else may refer to Christ as enthroned but do not discuss the issue of whether or not Rev 5 is structured in conformity to an enthronement ceremony of some sort.[19] Heinrich Kraft, who entitles Rev 5 as "Die Inthronisation des Lammes," observes that the transfer of the sealed scroll designates the Lamb as king of the end time, but he does not mention the notion of an enthronement ceremony in his comments on the text.[20] Similarly, J. P. M. Sweet entitles the pericope consisting of Rev 5:1–14 "The enthronement of the Lamb,"[21] and later suggests that 5:11 (evoking Daniel 7:9–14) describes the enthronement of the Lamb, though he does not expand on this in his verse-by-verse treatment of the text and does not mention the issue of an enthronement ceremony which might provide a structure for Rev 5.[22]

G. R. Beasley-Murray claims that Rev 5 reflects the three stages of an ancient enthronement ceremony: exaltation, presentation, enthronement. The exaltation is the conquest of the Lamb referred to in 5:5, the presentation in 5:6 and the enthronement or bestowal or authority in 5:7.[23] For the three-stage enthronement ceremony, Beasley-Murray cites no authority, but rather directs the reader to his notes on Rev 5 where he makes the following claim in his comments on 5:8: "We are evidently expected to understand that on receiving the scroll the Lamb took his seat on the throne with God (cf. 3:21). The enthronement-ceremony,

16 Johannes Behm, *Die Offenbarung des Johannes*, NTD 11 (Göttingen: Vandenhoeck & Ruprecht, 1935) 36.

17 Robert H. Mounce, *The Book of Revelation*, NICNT (rev. ed.; Grand Rapids: Eerdmans, 1998) 134.

18 G. B. Caird, *The Revelation of St. John the Divine*, HNTC (New York: Harper & Row, 1966); George Wesley Buchanan, *The Book of Revelation: Its Introduction and Prophecy*, New Testament Series (Lewiston, Queenston and Lampeter: Mellen Biblical Press, 1993).

19 M. Eugene Boring, *Revelation*, IBC (Louisville: John Knox, 1989) 106; Wilfrid J. Harrington, O. P., *Revelation*, Sacra Pagina 16 (Collegeville: The Liturgical Press, 1993).

20 Heinrich Kraft, *Die Offenbarung des Johannes*, HNT 16a (Tübingen: Mohr-Siebeck, 1974) 111.

21 Sweet, *Revelation*, 121.

22 Sweet, *Revelation*, 126.

23 G. R. Beasley-Murray, *The Book of Revelation*, NCB (rev. ed.; Grand Rapids: Eerdmans; London: Marshall, Morgan and Scott, 1978) 110.

therefore, now reaches its climax."[24] Although Beasley-Murray does not mention the source of this three-fold enthronement schema, an earlier work that he cites in other connections does exhibit just such a schema. Traugott Holtz begins his discussion of the enthronement scene in Rev 5 by referring to an ancient Egyptian three-stage enthronement ritual, which he claims forms the basic structure of Rev 5.[25] This three-part schema consists of the following elements, according to Holtz: (1) *Erhöhung* ("elevation" or "exaltation"), the stage at which the new king receives divine status thorough a solemn symbolic action. This symbolic action is not actually narrated, but is referred to as an event which has previously taken place in the speech of the elder in v. 5, who declares that the Lion of the tribe of Judah has conquered (= been exalted) and consequently now has the authority to break the seals. (2) *Präsentation* ("presentation"): the deified king is now presented to the assembly of the gods, corresponding to v. 6 in which the slaughtered Lamb stands in the midst of the four cherubim and the twenty-four elders. (3) *Inthronisation*, ("enthronement"): royal power and authority are then transferred to the new king; this corresponds to the Lamb taking the sealed scroll from the hand of one seated on the throne in the presence of the heavenly assembly in v. 7. There are at least two questions which arise in response to this use of a three-fold enthronement schema by Holtz in his analysis of Rev 5. First, could it be that an "Egyptian" enthronement ritual has influenced the way that John composed Rev 5? Second, why use the term "enthronement" when the Lamb in fact does not ascend the throne? In Beasley-Murray's reading of Rev 5, of course, the fact that the Lamb sat down with God upon his throne is presupposed. It is often argued that in Rev 3:21, the victory and enthronement of the Lamb are mentioned explicitly, and that therefore enthronement in Rev 5 should be presupposed.

The source which Holtz cites for the enthronement ritual schema is Joachim Jeremias, who understands the Christological hymn in 1 Tim 3:16 from the perspective of the ancient oriental ceremony of the enthronement of a king, specifically as it is attested for Egypt.[26] The ancient Egyptian enthronement ritual, according to Jeremias, consists of three actions: (1) The new king receives divine status by means of a solemn symbolic action: *Erhöhung*. (2) The now divinised king is presented to the assembly of the gods (*Präsentation*). (3) Thereafter sovereignty is transferred to him (*Inthronisation*). According to Jeremias, this ancient ritual was gradually fixed into a schema which continued to exist in the first century AD, even though such enthronement ceremonies were no longer in actual use. For Jeremias, this enthronement schema provides the key for understanding the peculiar order of the statements in this pre-Pauline

---

[24] Beasley-Murray, *Revelation*, 126.

[25] Holtz, *Christologie*, 28.

[26] Joachim Jeremias, *Die Briefe an Timotheus und Titus*, NTD 9 (Göttingen: Vandenhoeck & Ruprecht, 1963) 23–25.

Christological hymn. There has been a favorable response to the use of the three-stage enthronement ritual to illuminate 1 Tim 3:16 on the part of some scholars,[27] while others express more caution.[28] Jeremias' labored explanation of how an ancient three-stage Egyptian enthronement ritual, though no longer in use, still had currency as a literary pattern in the first century AD does not inspire confidence, particularly when one asks where the evidence for such an assumption is to be found.

For the source of this three-stage enthronement ritual, Jeremias cites Eduard Norden, though by parenthetical mention of the surname only.[29] After some searching I discovered that Jeremias was probably referring to Norden's book *Die Geburt des Kindes* (Leipzig: Teubner, 1924). In that book, Norden was primarily concerned with using the ancient Egyptian three-stage enthronement ritual for interpreting Vergil's *Fourth Ecloque*,[30] though he refers in passing to the Christological hymn in 1 Tim 3:16, and it was perhaps this brief reference that caught the eye of Jeremias.[31] Norden's source for the three-stage enthronement ritual was derived from the work of the French Egyptologist Alexandre Moret.[32] In her book *Du charactère religieux de la royauté pharaonique* (Paris: E. Leroux, 1902), Moret provides a synthetic discussion of ancient Egyptian enthronement ritual consisting of the three stages of *Élevation*, *Proclamation* and *Intronisation*. However, Moret's reconstruction of ancient Egyptian enthronement ritual is based on a variety of sources spanning nearly two millennia, since *no connected account of Egyptian coronation ritual has survived.*[33] Moret's synthesis was based on Pyramid Texts, temple reliefs from the New Kingdom, the Ramesseum Dramatic Papyrus and other scattered sources.[34]

---

[27] Ceslas Spicq, *Les Épitres Pastorales* (Paris: J. Gabalda, 1947) 108–9; Reinhard Deichgräber, *Gotteshymnus und Christushymnus in der frühen Christenheit: Untersuchungen zu Form, Sprache und Stil der frühchristlichen Hymnen* (Göttingen: Vandenhoeck & Ruprecht, 1967) 134–36; Martin Dibelius and Hans Conzelmann, *The Pastoral Epistles*, Hermeneia (Philadelphia: Fortress, 1972) 63.

[28] J.N.D. Kelly, *The Pastoral Epistles*, BNTC (New York: Harper & Row, 1963) 92; P. Dornier, *Les Épitres Pastorales* (Paris: J. Gabalda, 1969) 71.

[29] Jeremias, *Briefe*, 24.

[30] Norden, *Geburt*, 116–28.

[31] It is interesting that Norden does not mention the three-stage ancient Egyptian enthronement ritual in his analysis of 1 Tim 16 in *Agnostos Theos: Untersuchungen zur Formengeschichte religiöser Rede* (Darmstadt: Wissenschaftliche Buchgesellschaft, 1956 [originally published in 1912, then reprinted in 1923]) 254–63.

[32] Norden, *Geburt*, 119.

[33] Inscriptions from the 18th dynasty in the palace of Deir-el-Bahari do present a relatively detailed account of the enthronement of Hatshopsitou, and there are also bas-reliefs which depict particular moments in enthronement ceremonies; see Alexandre Moret, *Rois et dieux d'Égypt* (Paris: Armand Colin, 1925) 19–31.

[34] On these sources, see Henri Frankfort, *Kingship and the Gods: A Study of Ancient Near Eastern Religion as the Integration of Society and Nature* (Chicago: University of Chicago, 1948) 123–39; H.W. Fairman, "The Kingship Rituals of Egypt," *Myth, Ritual, and Kingship:*

While tomb reliefs do depict select moments in coronation ceremonial, the order of these events remains a matter of scholarly speculation. Hans Bonnet has reconstructed an ancient Egyptian enthronement ceremonial consisting of five acts, though he does not claim that they occurred in a particular order:[35] (1) *Erwählung* ("election"), (2) *Einführung* ("inauguration"), (3) *Krönung* ("coronation"), (4) *Herrschaftsantritt* ("assumption of rule") or *Thronbesteigung* ("ascent to the throne"), and (5) *Festzügen* ("processions"). This reconstruction bears surprisingly few similarities to that by Alexandre Moret which had, through Norden and Jeremias, such a significant impact on the modern understanding of the composition of Rev 5. Bonnet's three separate actions of *Krönung*, *Herrschaftsantritt* and *Thronbesteigung* all appear to be subsumed under Moret's single category of *Intronisation*, while *Festzügen* is the closest approximation to Moret's *Proclamation*. More recent discussions of enthronement ritual in ancient Egypt focus on two central ritual actions, "Königskrönung"[36] and "Thronbesteigung,"[37] though these were probably significant moments in a relatively complex series of ritual actions. It is important to realize that both the three-stage ritual proposed by Moret and adopted by Norden and the five-element ritual suggested by Bonnet are modern reconstructions that would not and could not have been known in the first century AD. The idea that the author of Revelation 5 could have had access to such a fixed ancient enthronement ritual is neither possible nor plausible.

In the title of this article, I used the phrase "origin and development." Thus far I have focused on the origins of the three-stage Egyptian or oriental enthronement ceremony referred to frequently by commentators on Revelation 5. I want to conclude this brief study of the perpetuation of a "commentary tradition" with little basis in fact, by considering the development of this imaginary ancient enthronement ritual in the comments of Jürgen Roloff on Revelation 5.[38] Roloff agrees that in Rev 5 the action of God with respect to Jesus is developed "nach einem festen dreistufigen Schema, das dem Thronbesteigungsritual orientalischer Könige nachgebildet war: *Erhöhung* – *Herrschaftsübertragung* (bzw. Übergabe des Herrschernamens) – *Präsentation* des neuen Herrschers vor den ihm huldigenden Untertanen."[39] Like other commentators who use this schema, Roloff does not indicate the source of this fixed three-stage enthronement ritual. It is, in fact, not likely that Roloff could cite such a source, for the order of his version

Essays on the Theory and Practice of Kingship in the Ancient Near East and in Israel, ed. S. H. Hooke (Oxford: Clarendon Press, 1958) 74–104.

[35] Hans Bonnet, *Reallexikon der ägyptischen Religionsgeschichte* (2nd unveränderte Aufl.; Berlin and New York: Walter de Gruyter, 1971) 396–98.

[36] W. Helck and E. Otto (eds.), "Königskrönung," *Lexikon der Ägyptologie* 3:531–33.

[37] Helck and Otto, "Thronbesteigung," *LexÄgypt* 6:529–32

[38] Jürgen Roloff, *Die Offenbarung des Johannes*, Zürcher Bibelkommentare 18 (Zürich: Theologischer Verlag, 1984).

[39] Roloff, *Offenbarung*, 72.

of the enthronement ritual – *Erhöhung, Herrschaftsübertragung, Präsentation* – represents a departure in order from the normal version of the schema reviewed above: *Erhöhung, Präsentation, Inthronisation* (for Roloff, *Herrschaftsübertragung* appears to be the equivalent of *Inthronisation*). According to Roloff, Rev 5:5 functions as a description of the *Erhöhungsgeschehens* ("exaltation event"), vv. 6–7 described the *Herrschaftsübertragung* ("assumption of rule"), while vv. 8–14 constitute the *Präsentation des Herrschers* ("presentation of the ruler") in the homage paid by the heavenly court.[40] Roloff has reordered the stages of enthronement by reversing stages two and three found, for example, in the summary of Traugott Holtz' analysis found above. The reason for this rearrangement seems clear enough. Roloff has rearranged the schema to better fit the text. While Holtz regards v. 6 as the *Präsentation* (the Lamb is seen standing before the throne and the four cherubim and the twenty-four elders), while Roloff correctly thinks that the *Präsentation* stage is more appropriately represented by vv. 8–14, in which the four cherubim and the twenty-four elders sing praises to the one seated on the throne and to the Lamb. However, just because this fits the category more suitably is hardly a sufficient reason for rearranging an ancient oriental enthronement ceremony which the author describes as a "*festes* dreistufiges Schema," a "*fixed* three-stage schema" (emphasis mine).

The purpose of this paper has not been to determine whether or not the dramatic events narrated in Rev 5 should be understood as focusing on the enthronement of the Lamb, a view represented by many of the scholars whose work has been reviewed briefly in this article. There are a number of other scholars who have argued against this view at some length.[41] Rather, I have attempted to demonstrate that the widely-used schema of a fixed three-fold ancient Egyptian or oriental enthronement ceremonial did not exist in the first century AD and could not therefore have the model which the author of Revelation used to structure the dramatic narrative of Revelation 5.

---

40 Roloff, *Offenbarung*, 72.

41 W.C. van Unnik, "'Worthy is the Lamb': The Background of Apoc. 5," *Mélanges Bibliques en hommage au R.P. Béda Rigaux*, ed. A. Descamps et al. (Gembloux: Duculot, 1970) 445–61; Aune, *Revelation*, 1.332–38.

Revelation 17

A Lesson in Remedial Reading

1. Introduction

The Revelation of John is arguably the quintessential apocalypse, not least because the first word in the book, Ἀποκάλυψις, was made the anachronistic eponym for the entire genre early in the Nineteenth Century. Revelation 17, which narrates the vision of a prostitute seated on a scarlet beast with seven heads and ten horns, followed by a step-by-step unpacking of the complex symbolic meaning of the vision by the author's angelic guide, has in turn, the most typically apocalyptic features within of this complex work. In this paper, I will focus on Revelation 17 as an "intertext." That is, I will propose a reading of this text which does not regard it as an isolated or self-contained text (after the fashion of the nearly defunct New Criticism which still lives on in the narrative criticism of many New Testament scholars), but rather as part of a complex web of earlier texts with which the author is in dialogue. The focal "text" is the numismatic image of Dea Roma seated on the Seven Hills of Rome (which preserves the major features of a lost frieze or sculpture-group), the "reading" of which the author transformed into an anti-Roman parody, refracted through his understanding of several anti-Babylon passages in the Hebrew Bible.

Intertextuality is essentially a theory of reading which accounts for the basic intelligibility of a text in terms of the prior existence of other texts as well as general literary codes and conventions, and authors may also play with those conventions through pastiche, plagiarism, imitation, allusion, citation, parody, satire, and irony. Since Julia Kristeva coined the term "intertextuality" in 1969, it has been used and developed in a number of directions. One theoretical development of particular interest to me is Gerard Genette's program of "transtextuality" or the "textual transcendence of the text," which he defines as "all that sets the text in a relationship, whether obvious or concealed, with other texts".[1] Genette (who is inordinately fond of neologisms) uses the term "hypertextuality" for any relationship uniting a later text (which he calls the "hypertext") to an earlier text

[1] Gerard Genette, *Palimpseste: Literature in the Second Degree* (Lincoln: University of Nebraska, 1997) 1.

(which he calls "hypotext"), upon which it is somehow dependent. Genette's "hypotext" is what many other critics call the "intertext," though he means self-conscious and intended relations between texts.

New Testament scholars have not uncommonly adopted the term in a very narrow sense to mean (for example) citations, allusions and echoes of the Hebrew Bible or the Greek Septuagint in New Testament literature. The identification and analysis of such sources, however, has been a perennial concern of both classicists and New Testament scholars and is only part of what is meant by intertextuality. The term intertextuality has not been limited to literature, but has included criticism of film, painting, sculpture, music, architecture and photography, expanding the term "text" to encompass all of the arts.

2. Distinctive Features of Rev 17

Vision reports in apocalyptic literature characteristically contain lengthy detailed descriptions of highly symbolic dreams or visions which the apocalyptist has purportedly experienced together with their decoded meaning. The apocalyptist is typically accompanied by an angelic guide with whom he carries on a dialogue, with the apocalyptist typically asking simple-minded questions (e. g., "what is this?" "what does that mean?" etc.) with the interpreting angel providing the profound answers which constitute the basic message the author is trying to convey in the textual unit under consideration. Revelation 17 fits into this apocalyptic pattern nicely, but surprisingly, it is the only partial-text in the entire book which does. There are, in fact, several distinctive features of Revelation 17 which provoke the interest of interpreters.

For example, the presence of the interpreting angel in Revelation 17, while typical of other Jewish and Christian apocalypses, is a distinctive feature found only here within the Revelation of John. Only here does an angelic guide provide a running allegorical commentary on the features of John's vision. This strikes the reader as odd, because the book opens with an explicit mention that an angel was sent by God to John to make known "the revelation of Jesus Christ" (1:1), and concludes with the reappearance of this interpreting angel who tells John that "These words are trustworthy and true. And the Lord, the God of the spirits of the prophets, has sent his angel to show his servants what must soon take place" (22:6). This last speech is apparently attributed to the angel who gave John a guided tour of the New Jerusalem (21:9–22:9), but who never explains anything to him, though he does use a measuring rod to convey the size of the City.

A second distinctive feature is that the vision is *static*. That is, it does not consist of any movement or action, but rather has the character of a *tableau*. The vision consists of five main features: (1) The woman is sitting on a scarlet beast with seven heads and ten horns (v. 3b). (2) The woman has a lavish costume

(v. 4a). (3) The woman holds a golden cup filled with the abominations of her fornication (v. 4b). (4) On the forehead of the woman is a mysterious name: "Babylon the Great, the Mother of Prostitutes and of Earthly Abominations" (v. 5). (5) The woman was drunk from the blood of the righteous (v. 6a).

A third distinctive feature is that this vision is patently allegorical. While allegorical or symbolic visions are characteristic of Jewish apocalypses generally, such features are rare in the rest of the Revelation of John. One example is the appearance of Christ in Rev 1:12–20, walking in the midst of seven golden menorahs and holding seven stars in his right hand. At the end of this vision, Christ volunteers the following allegorical interpretation: "As for the mystery of the seven stars which you saw in my right hand, and the seven golden menorahs, the seven stars are the angels of the seven churches and the seven menorahs are the seven churches."

A fourth distinctive feature is that some of the symbols are polyvalent. For example, the seven heads of the beast are interpreted in v. 9b as seven mountains, but also as seven kings. Again, the woman is described as holding a golden cup containing the abominations of her fornication (v. 4), but is shortly thereafter described as drunk on the blood of the righteous (v. 6). The contents of the cup is construed in two quite different ways.

A fifth peculiar feature is that elements not found in the vision described in vv. 3b–6a are treated in the interpretation in vv. 7–18 as if they were. For example, in v. 15, the interpreting angel says that "The waters that you saw, where the prostitute resides, are peoples and crowds and nations and languages." Actually, John did not actually *see* the waters, for they are not referred to in the vision itself, but only in the angel's anticipatory description of what the seer will see in v. 1.

A sixth peculiar feature is the lack of symmetry between the vision and the interpretation. While the scarlet beast with seven heads and ten horns is referred to only briefly in the vision (v. 3), this complex figure dominates the allegorical interpretation (vv. 8–17, with the intrusive mention of the waters in v. 15). On the other hand, the description of the woman dominates the vision (vv. 3b–6a), but her symbolic significance is referred to only briefly and almost as an afterthought at the conclusion of the interpretive section (v. 18).

What are we to make of these peculiar features? They combine to suggest that the vision is a literary creation rather than a revelatory experience, and perhaps as a complex transformation of earlier texts as well.

3. The Dea Roma Coin

A number of years ago I was sitting in the library at the University of Trondheim working through some books on numismatics, searching for symbols and images which might illuminate the world of Revelation of John. I was stunned when

I saw the photograph of a sestertius minted in 71 CE in the Roman province of Asia during the reign of Vespasian (69–79 CE). Since the minting date was relatively close in both time and space to John's production of the Apocalyse, I was sure that there must be some relationship between the images on the reverse of this coin and Rev 17:9: "The seven heads are seven mountains upon which the woman is seated."

The obverse has a portrait of Vespasian encircled with his titles in a standard abbreviation: IMP CAESAR VESPASIANVS AVG PM TP PP COS III, meaning "Emperor Caesar Vespasian Augustus, Pontifex Maximus, Tribunicia Potestas ["Tribunal Power"], Pater Patriae [Father of the Fatherland], Consul for the third time." The reverse depicts the goddess Roma in military garb (some think modeled after Athena, others as an Amazon, others as a combination of the two), seated on the Seven Hills of Rome with a parazonium ("small sword") in her left hand with the point resting on her left knee. She is flanked on the left and right fields with the abbreviations "S" and "C," standing for *Senatus Consultum*, or "a resolution of the senate. Two other small groups are found on each side of her. An anthropomorphic personification of the river Tiber reclines on a mini-version of the Seven Hills to the right, which Dea Roma seems to be touching with her left foot. Another group consisting of the famous she-wolf with the twins Romulus and Remus is located on the lower left.

Despite my initial excitement, further investigation revealed that a number of other scholars had made the connection between the Dea Roma coin and Rev 17:9. How many other scholars? Only about 3,741 (slight exaggeration). That took some of the wind out of my sails until I realized that, for the most part, they had failed to exploit the identification in any meaningful interpretive sense. After some reflection, I concluded that the vision in Rev 17 is static because it was basically an ekphrasis, or a description of a work of art.

There is some agreement among historians of ancient art that this particular version of Dea Roma was modeled after an actual marble or bronze frieze, though no example of this particular group has survived. It is generally true that representations of temples and statues on Roman coins were reproduced with some fidelity to the originals and that rarely are non-existent architectural monuments or statues depicted.

4. Literary and Rhetorical Uses of Ekphrasis

Ekphraseis were used in epic and prose narratives primarily as digressions. Among the more celebrated ekphraseis that are found in the Homeric epics, the earliest Greek literature, include the relatively lengthy description of the shield of Achilles (*Iliad* 18.478–608), and the relatively brief description of the cup of Nestor (*Iliad* 11.632–5). Both became literary models for later authors. Most ekphraseis, like these two Homeric examples, are descriptions of works of art or handcraft, such as beautiful garments (the mantle of Jason in Apollonius Rhodius *Argonautica* 1.721–67, the very lengthy description of the shield of Dionysus in Nonnus *Dionysiaca* 25.380–567, and the shield of Euryplus in Quintus Smyrnaeus *Posthomerica* 6.471–92. In addition to works of art, landscapes, places and buildings were also the subject of ekphraseis, including the palace and garden of Alkinoos (*Odyssey* 7.84–132), the palace of Aeëtes (Apollonius Rhodius *Argonautica* 3.213–48), and the cave of the nymphs (Quintus Smyrnaeus *Posthomerica* 6.471–92).

By the second cent. CE, descriptions of paintings were frequently used to introduce entire compositions or large sections of compositions. A painting depicting the story of Europa and the bull (closely corresponding to similar scenes on coins from Sidon) is described at the beginning of Achilles Tatius *Leucippe and Clitophon* 1.1–2, and later the author includes descriptions of a painting depiating Perseus and Andromeda (3.6–7) and Prometheus (3.8).

The ekphrasis was eventually transformed from a constituent literary form used as a digression in narrative texts to an independent literary form, evident in such literary works as the *Imagines* ("Paintings") of Philostratus Major, the *Imagines* of Philostratus Minor (apparently a family business), Cebes *Tabula* and Callistratus *Descriptiones* (descriptions of fourteen statues). During the Roman period, ekphraseis became a very popular literary form. One first century CE work which became increasing popular during the medieval period because of its moralizing content was the *Tabula* of Cebes, which consists of a lengthy discussion of the contents and significance of a picture on a votive tablet in a temple. The work is essentially a discussion of the major themes of popular morality. The *Tabula* is a dialogical ekphrasis in which a group of visitors to a temple see a votive tablet with a picture on it that they cannot understand, i. e., they sense that the picture carries a symbolic meaning. An old man offers to explain the meaning of the picture and provides a moralizing allegorical explanation of the various figures depicted. The ensuing dialogue between the old man and the visitors is replete with questions and answers, often varied forms of "What is this? Or "Who is this?", coupled with answers introduced with "This is" or "That is."

The term ekphrasis (Latin: *descriptio*) is not regularly used in rhetoric until the Second Sophistic (2nd cent. CE). It frequently appears in the Progymnasmata (Hermogenes *Prog.*10; Aphthonius *Prog.* 12; Theon *Prog.* 11; Nicolaus *Prog.* 12). Theon defines ekphrasis as "a descriptive account bringing what is illustrated vividly before one's sight" (*Progymnasmata* 7; Spengel 1853–54:3.491). Thus the purpose of the ekphrasis is ἐναργεία ("vividness"). Nicolaus suggests that "ekphrasis undertakes to fashion spectators out of auditors" (*Prog.* 12; Spengel 1853–54:3.49). Though ekphrasis is commonly defined as "the rhetorical description of a work of art" (*OCD* 377), this is somewhat restrictive for the rhetorical handbooks listing the topics appropriate for ekphrasis include persons, circumstances, places, periods of time, customs, festivals, and assemblies, as well as statues and paintings.

There are two major approaches to the use of ekphraseis by the time of the Second Sophistic during the second cent. CE. One approach centers on the importance of understanding and interpreting the work of art itself. The other focuses on the hidden meanings conveyed by the work of art, which are usually revealed through allegorical interpretation. There are two subtypes of such allegorizing descriptions: (1) those whose meaning is obvious (as in Lucian *De mercede conductis* 42 [in which the *Tabula* of Cebes is specifically mentioned] and Lucian *Calumniae* 4–5), and (2) those whose meaning is not apparent and must be carefully explained by someone who is knowledgeable (Lucian *Hercules*; Cebes *Tabula*). In both Lucian's *Hercules* and Cebes' *Tabula*, the narrator is puzzled over the meaning of the representation.

5. Hebrew Bible Anti-Babylon Texts in Rev 17

Before arguing more closely that Rev 17 constitutes an ekphrasis of the Dea Roman sculpture, however, I need to reconstruct the lens through which the author read that work. He makes it relatively easy for us to do so, since he makes several transparent allusions to two anti-Babylon Jeremiah passages from the Hebrew Bible. First, however, it is important to know that Rome was widely associated with Babylon by Jews and Christians after 70 CE. The reason is that just as Babylon had captured and destroyed Jerusalem in 587 BCE, so Rome had captured and destroyed Jerusalem in 70 CE. A slightly later (early 2nd cent. CE) Jewish pseudepigraphical work, the *Paralipomena Ierimiou*, similarly plays with the image of Babylon as a codename for Rome.

The first Biblical allusion is found in Rev 17:1, which refers to "the judgment of the great whore seated by many waters." This is likely an allusion to Jer 51:13, part of a prophetic denunciation of Babylon: "O you who dwell by many waters, rich in treasures, your end has come." Since peoples and armies are often symbolized by "many waters" Rev 17:12–14 (Ps 144:7; Isa 8:6–7; 28:17; Jer 47:2), this suggests the allegorical interpretation offered in v. 15: "The waters which you saw, where the whore resides, are peoples and crowds and nations and languages."

Another clear allusion is found in v. 4 of the vision, where the woman is described as holding a golden cup in her hand. This is an allusion to Jer 51:7:

> Babylon was a golden cup in the Lord's hand,
> making all the earth drunken;
> the nations drank of her wine,
> therefore the nations went mad.

Yahweh is presented by Jeremiah as compelling his enemies to drink from a cup. It is obvious, however, that the author has transposed part of this allusion to v. 2, the introduction which prepares the author for what he will see: "with whom the kings of the earth have fornicated, and with whom the inhabitants of the earth have become drunk from the wine which is her immorality." The references to the cup, the wine and the nations becoming intoxicated all anticipate the explicit mention of the cup in v. 4. The association of Babylon's cup with sexual immorality (which apparently symbolizes political and economic domination) has been added to the Jeremiah allusion by the author. He is enamored with this expansion of Jer 51:7, however, for he uses it four times (including Rev 17:2). When Babylon is first mentioned in the Apocalypse in 14:8 in a brief angelic announcement, we read:

> Fallen, fallen is Babylon the great,
> She who made all nations drink the wine of her passion.

Similarly, the expanded allusion to Jer 51:7 occurs again in Rev 18:2–3:

> Fallen, fallen is Babylon the great!
> ...
> for all nations have drunk the wine of her immoral passion
> and the kings of the earth have committed fornication with her.

A final and less obvious allusion is found in Rev 19:2:

> He has judged the great harlot
> who corrupted the earth with her fornication,
> and he has avenged on her the blood of his servants.

We need to ask where the author got his reference to "kings of the earth" and why he personifies Babylon as a woman. First, it is clear that the author has a deep familiarity with the anti-Babylon material in both Jeremiah and Isaiah. In another passage in Jeremiah, the cup image occurs without reference to Babylon (Jer 25:15–16):

> Thus the Lord, the God of Israel, said to me:
> "Take from my hand this cup of the wine of wrath,
> and make all the nations to whom I send you drink it.
> They will stagger and be crazed because of the sword
> Which I am sending among them."

Jeremiah takes the cup and forces a long list of peoples and kings to drink, beginning with (Jer 25:18–19):

> Jerusalem and the cities of Judah, its kings and princes, ...
> Pharaoh king of Egypt, his servants, his princes, all his people and all the foreign folk among them ...
> And all the kings of the land of Uz
> And all the kings of the land of the Philistines ...

Finally, as far as personifying Babylon as a female figure is concerned, Jeremiah does not exploit the imagery of Babylon as a woman, though he does refer to Babylon with feminine pronouns (e. g., Jer 51:47, 52, 53) and he refers to Babylon once as "the daughter of Babylon". The female personification of Babylon is much more important in the lamentation over Jerusalem found in Deutero-Isaiah 47:1–15. There feminine imagery dominates the passage for the prophet addresses Babylon as the "virgin daughter of Babylon," the "daughter of the Chaldaeans," "the mistress of kingdoms" (v. 5), and finally as a "widow" (v. 8).

A brief survey of these allusions suggests that the author is not only aware of these Babylon texts in the Hebrew Bible, but that he has used them to mutually interpret one another. It is this textual construct which he uses as a hermeutic to parody the Dea Roma image.

6. Revelation 17 as an Ekphrasis

With this interpretive framework in place, I want to argue in more detail that the sculpture or frieze which formed the subject for the Dea Roma sesterius of Vespasian can be construed as the hypotext which the author has transformed into the hypertext which constitutes Revelation 17.

First, the centrally important figure of the female figure who functions as a personification can easily be identified with the figure of Dea Roma on the coin, though there appears to be nothing immediately evident in the image which would associate Dea Roma with a prostitute. However, on the lower left-hand field of the reverse, there is a representation of the well-known Roman legend of the infants Romulus and Remus being nurses by a she-wolf. The Latin term *lupa* means both "female wolf" and "prostitute." The luxurious clothing and jewelry of the great whore (v. 4a) are not part of the depiction of Dea Roma on the coin, but are drawn from the stereotypical description of prostitutes in ancient literature which was sometimes applied to cities. Pericles reportedly contemned the extensive building program in Athens by comparing the city to a gaudy prostitute (Plutarch *Pericles* 12.2): "We are gilding and beautifying our city which, like a shameless woman, adds to her wardrobe precious stones and costly statues and temples worth millions."

Second, the woman is described as "seated by many waters (vv. 1b, 15). The Dea Roma sesterius depicts the goddess as seated beside, and even touching with her left foot, the personification of the Tiber, reflecting the historical location of Rome on the banks of that river. This feature also characterizes historical Babylon, described in Jer 51:13 as "you who dwell near many waters."

Third, while the woman is described in the vision as seated on the beast with seven heads and ten horns, the interpretive section of the vision interprets the seven heads of the beast as "seven mountains on which the woman is seated" (v. 9). The image of Dea Roma seated on the seven hills on the reverse of the Vespasian sestertius is clearly the most obvious and striking link between the coin and Revelation 17.

Fourth, the golden cup "filled with the abominations and impurities of her fornication" (v. 4b), has no obvious correspondence with the Dea Roma coin. This metaphor is rather an allusion to Jer 51:7, though there the metaphor represents Babylon itself: "Babylon was a golden cup in the Lord's hand, making all the earth drunken; the nations drank of her wine; therefore the nations went mad." An analogous metaphor analogy is found in Cebes 5.1–3 where a woman named Apate ("Deceit") is described as seated on a throne holding a cup and leading astray people who drink of it (i. e., those who are about to enter the world through the gateway of life).

Fifth, the mysterious name inscribed on the forehead of the great whore in v. 5 may be connected to the name "ROMA" on the Vespasian sestertius. Rome was widely thought to have a secret name. Plutarch asks (*Quaestiones Romanae* 61): "Why is it forbidden to mention or to inquire after or too call by name that deity, whether it be male or female, whose special province it is to preserve and watch over Rome?" His answer is essentially the same as the one found in Servius (*Comm. in Verg. Aen* 2.351): "The Romans wish to keep secret the identity of the god who cared for Rome, and therefore their priestly regulations decreed that the gods of Rome should not be invoked by their proper names that they might not be enticed away." Johannes Lydus (6th cent. CE) maintained that Rome had three names, a political name known to all (Roma), a hieratic name also widely known (Flora), and a ritual name used only by the Roman priests (*De mensibus* 4.73). Lydus thought that Rome's ritual name was "AMOR," i. e., the Latin term for "love" which was "ROMA" spelled backwards. This may have been the view of the unknown graffiti-artist who scribbled the square anagram based on the name Roma on a wall in Pompeii:

R	O	M	A
O			M
M			O
A	M	O	R

Since Romans regarded themselves as descendants of Aeneas, the son of Venus, the god of love and sexuality, the name "Amor" would not have been thought inappropriate. For the author of the Apocalypse, "amor" could easily have been construed as illicit sexual passion.

Sixth, the vision describes the woman as "drunk with blood of the saints and the witnesses to Jesus" (v. 6), despite the fact that this is clearly an interpretation rather than something visually perceptible. The fact that Dea Roma holds a parazonium meant to symbolize the military might of Rome might suggest the many Jews and Christians who had been killed by Rome, both during the Neronian persecution following the great fire in Rome in 64 CE, and the first Jewish revolt in 66–72 CE.

Seventh, and finally, the puzzled narrator is a stock literary device found in late ekphraseis of pictures with obviously allegorical significance. After describing a strange picture of Hercules, the narrator of Lucian's *Hercules* (4) says: "I had stood for a long time, looking and wondering and fuming," when a Celt offered to explain the riddle of the picture. Similarly in Cebes *Tabula* 2.1, the narrator sees a painting he cannot understand. Fortunately, an old man is standing by who can explain the allegorical significance of the painting. Finally, in Callimachus *Imagines* 6, the narrator describes a statue of Lysippus and then state, "Such was the marvel, as it seemed to us," but a man who was skilled in the arts explained the meaning of the statue.

7. Conclusions

While most residents of Roman Asia thought that the world was a pretty good place and that Rome was a benevolent mother, John saw it differently. A resident alien who was probably a Palestinian refugee following the capture and destruction of Jerusalem in 70 CE, he used a palette of traditional apocalyptic colors to paint a different picture. Aiming at the Christian minority, at least some of whom he thought had swallowed Roman propaganda hook, line and sinker, John gave them an unforgettable lesson in remedial reading. The positive picture of the benevolent Mother was turned into the negative image of a conniving, carousing, murderous, debauched whore. They could never look at the Dea Roma friezes or coins again with the same innocent eyes.

The Prophetic Circle of John of Patmos and the Exegesis of Revelation 22:16

David Hill, to whom this article is respectfully dedicated, has cautiously argued that the nine references to "prophets" in Rev (10:7; 11:10, 18; 16:6; 18:20, 24; 22:6, 9) refer primarily to Christian prophets who constituted a special group within the churches of the Roman province of Asia, though they did not hold formal offices or exercise institutional authority over other Christians.[1] Hill also suggested that John addressed his apocalypse directly to these community prophets (1:1; 22:16), whose task it was to mediate John's revelatory message to the seven churches.[2] He maintains, however, that John himself was not a typical Christian prophet, but rather a prophet who consciously stood in the Israelite-Jewish prophetic tradition. Since Christian prophets were subject to community authority and restricted themselves to oral prophesying, John did not compose his book in his capacity as a Christian prophet, but rather (on analogy with the ancient Israelite prophets) in direct response to the command of the risen Lord "with authentic prophetic consciousness".[3] My purpose in the present article is to focus on a close reading and exegesis of Rev 22:16 in defense of what I take to be Hill's essentially correct understanding of that passage, an interpretation which has been disputed by a number of other scholars.[4]

---

[1] David Hill, "Prophecy and Prophets in the Revelation of St. John," *NTS* 18 (1971–72), 406–11.

[2] Hill, "Prophecy," 413.

[3] Hill, "Prophecy," 415 f.; *idem, New Testament Prophecy* (Atlanta: John Knox, 1979) 87. This is undoubtedly the weakest of Hill's three proposals. The view was first proposed in 1959 by Gerhard Friedrich (*TDNT,* 6.849 f.), generally approved by Elizabeth Schüssler Fiorenza ("The Quest for the Johannine School: The Apocalypse and the Fourth Gospel," *NTS* 23 [1977], 425), and defended more recently in a particularly imaginative and vulnerable form by Wayne A. Grudem (*The Gift of Prophecy in* 1 *Corinthians* [Washington, DC: University Press of America, 1982] 106–109). For a critique of this view see M. Eugene Boring, "The Apocalypse as Christian Prophecy," *Society of Biblical Literature* 1974 *Seminar Papers,* ed. George MacRae (Cambridge, MA: Society of Biblical Literature, 1974) 2. 56; David E. Aune, *Prophecy in Early Christianity and the Ancient Mediterranean World* (Grand Rapids: Eerdmans, 1983) 205–208; Adela Yarbro Collins, *Crisis and Catharsis:* The *Power of the Apocalypse* (Philadelphia: Westminster, 1984) 39 f.

[4] Most recently by Yarbro Collins, *Crisis,* 34–46.

I.

Rev 22:16 reads as follows: Ἐγὼ Ἰησοῦς ἔπεμψα τὸν ἄγγελόν μου μαρτυρῆσαι ὑμῖν ταῦτα ἐπὶ ταῖς ἐκκλησίαις, "I, Jesus, sent my angel to attest this message to you for the churches". This statement, attributed to the exalted Jesus, is metatextual since the pronoun ταῦτα probably refers to the entire message of Revelation which has just been presented (1:4–22:5).[5] Along with 22:6 this verse has several similarities to 1:1 which (in the context of 1:1–3) is also a metatextual statement which explicitly introduces the book which follows, presented as a statement of the author to his audience.[6]

The central problem in interpreting Rev 22:16 is that of determining the referents of the plural pronoun ὑμῖν (a dative of indirect object) and the plural noun ταῖς ἐκκλησίαις. The options are limited. Commentators usually understand ὑμεῖς to refer either to a group of Christian prophets (who mediate John's message to the seven churches),[7] or to the Christian members of the seven churches to whom John addressed his book (1:4).[8] With a few exceptions, most scholars

[5] While most commentators interpret ταῦτα in this way, some argue that it refers only to the immediate context, i.e., the promises and threats in 22:12–15; see Berhard Weiss, *Die Johannes-Apokalypse: Textkritische Untersuchungen und Textherstellung* (Texte und Untersuchungen, 7.1; Leipzig: J.C. Hinrichs, 1891) 112, and Martin Karrer, *Die Johannesoffenbarung als Brief* (Göttingen: Vandenhoeck & Ruprecht, 1986) 224 n. 14.

[6] A helpful analysis of the literary framework of Revelation is that proposed by Lars Hartman, "Form and Message: A Preliminary Discussion of 'Partial Texts' in Rev. 1–3 and 22,6 ff," *L'Apocalypse johannique et l'Apocalyptique dans le Nouveau Testament,* ed. J. Lambrecht (Leuven: University Press; Gembloux: J. Duculot, 1980) 129–49; cf. David Hellholm, "The Problem of Apocalyptic Genre and the Apocalypse of John," *Society of Biblical Literature* 1982 *Seminar Papers,* ed. K.H. Richards (Chico: Scholars Press, 1982) 157–98.

[7] Wilhelm Bousset, *Die Offenbarung Johannis* (6th edn; Göttingen: Vandenhoeck & Ruprecht, 1906) 459; Isbon T. Beckwith, The *Apocalypse of John* (New York: Macmillan, 1919) 777; R.H. Charles, *A Critical and Exegetical Commentary on the Revelation of St. John* (Edinburgh; T. & T . Clark, 1920) 2.219 (a secondary possibility); Martin Kiddle, The *Revelation of St. John* (London: Hodder & Stoughton) 454; Emst Lohmeyer, *Die Offenbarung des Johannes* (3rd edn; Tübingen: J.C.B. Mohr [Paul Siebeck], 1970) 180; Schüssler Fiorenza, "The Quest for the Johannine School," 425; Ugo Vanni, *La Struttura Letteraria dell'Apocalisse* (2nd edn; Brescia: Morcelliana, 1980) 80; Elisabeth Schüssler Fiorenza, "Apocalypsis and Propheteia: The Book of Revelation in the Context of Early Christian Prophecy," *L'Apocalypse johannique et l'apocalyptique dans le Nouveau Testament,* ed. J. Lambrecht (Leuven: Leuven University Press; Gembloux: J. Duculot, 1980) 120 f.; Ulrich B. Müller, *Offenbarung,* 370; David E. Aune, "The Social Matrix of the Apocalypse of John," *Biblical Research* 26 (1981) 19; Ulrich B. Müller, "Literarische und formgeschichtliche Bestimmung der Apokalypse des Johannes als einem Zeugnis frühchristlicher Apokalyptik," *Apocalypticism in the Mediterranean World and the Near East,* ed. David Hellholm (Tübingen: Mohr Siebeck, 1983) 616.

[8] Henry Barclay Swete, The *Apocalypse of St John* (Grand Rapids: Eerdmans, n.d.) 309; Charles, *Revelation* 2.219; Akira Satake, *Die Gemeindeordnung in der Johannesapokalypse* (Neukirchen-Vluyn: Neukirchener Verlag, 1966) 25; Eduard Lohse, *Die Offenbarung des Johannes* (Göttingen: Vandenhoeck & Ruprecht, 1976) 113; Robert H. Mounce, The *Book of Revelation* (Grand Rapids: Eerdmans, 1977) 394; J.P.M. Sweet, *Revelation* (Philadelphia: Westminster, 1979) 315, 317; G.R. Beasley-Murray, The *Book of Revelation* (Grand Rapids:

simply choose one of these two views without providing supportive arguments.[9] These are not the only possible views, however, and we will introduce other possibilities below.

The exegesis of the phrase μαρτυρῆσαι ὑμῖν ἐπὶ ταῖς ἐκκλησίαις must begin with the recognition that in Greek it is only a remote linguistic possibility that the plural dative pronoun ὑμῖν and noun ταῖς ἐκκλησίαις can refer to the same entity. While the author of Revelation was not a native speaker of Greek and consequently his composition exhibits numerous syntactical irregularities,[10] the phraseology of Rev 22:16 is unusual but clearly within the boundaries of conventional Greek usage. The presence of the preposition ἐπί indicates that the substantive ταῖς ἐκκλησίαις is more remote from the action described by the infinitive μαρτυρῆσαι than is the pronoun ὑμεῖς. This means that the view that ὑμεῖς and αἱ ἐκκλησίαι *both* refer to Christians in general is *a priori* untenable.[11] Since αἱ ἐκκλησίαι very probably refers to the seven Christian communities in the Roman province of Asia, ὑμεῖς must refer to a *different* group.

The problematic character of the phrase ἐπὶ ταῖς ἐκκλησίαις centers on the relatively uncommon use of the preposition ἐπί. There are several ways in which ἐπί with the dative can be construed. (1) ἐπί with the dative can function as a marker of persons *benefited* by an event, i. e., the *dativus commodi.* μαρτυρῆσαι ὑμῖν ἐπὶ ταῖς ἐκκλησίαις can therefore be translated "to testify *for* [the benefit of] the churches,"[12] or even "on account of," or "for the sake of the churches".[13] This is the preferable way of understanding ἐπί, one which assumes that the referent of ὑμεῖς mediates revelation to the referent of αἱ ἐκκλησίαι. (2) ἐπί can also function as "a marker of the experiences, often with the implication of an action by a superior force or agency."[14] Though this way of construing the significance

Eerdmans, 1981) 342; Jürgen Roloff, *Die Offenbarung des Johannes* (Zürich: Theologischer Verlag, 1984) 212. Pierre Prigent (*L'Apocalypse de Saint Jean* [Lausanne and Paris: Delachaux & Niestlé, 1981] 357) argues that the ὑμεῖς in 22:16 is modeled after 22:6 and represents a secondary addition which accompanied the inclusion of the proclamations to the seven churches, and therefore it refers to the churches.

9 Three exceptions are Beasley-Murray, *Revelation,* 342, Vanni, *La Struttura,* 180, and Yarbro Collins, *Crisis,* 39.

10 On this problem see T. Cowden Laughlin, The *Solecisms of the Apocalypse* (Princeton: C. S. Robinson, 1902), and G. Mussies, The *Morphology of Koine Greek as Used in the Apocalypse of John: A Study in Bilingualism* (Leiden: Brill, 1971).

11 Most of the commentators cited above in note 7 (with the exception of Swete) hold that both ὑμῖν and ταῖς ἐκκλησίαις refer to Christians in the seven churches.

12 Johannes Louw and Eugene Nida (eds.), *Greek-English Lexicon of the New Testament Based on Semantic Domains* (2 vols.; New York: United Bible Societies, 1988) I, § 90.40.

13 Moses Stuart, *Commentary on the Apocalypse* (2 vols.; Andover: Allen, Morrill & Wardwell, 1845) 2. 393; Paul S. Minear, *I Saw a New Earth: An Introduction to the Visions of the Apocalypse* (Washington and Cleveland: Corpus Books, 1968) 364, provides this translation of Rev 22:16a: "It is I, Jesus, who sent my angel to confirm these things to you, for the sake of the congregation."

14 Louw-Nida, *Greek-English Lexicon,* I, § 90.57.

of ἐπί, is less probable, the problematic phrase could then be translated "to testify *to* the churches." (3) Several scholars have argued that ἐπί with the genitive can mean "about, concerning," citing John 12:16 in addition to Rev 10:11 and 22:16.[15] According to Yarbro Collins, "The testimony is thus not given to others "for" the congregations, but to them, and is "about" them."[16] The chief difficulty with this view is that the message of Reveleation (with the exception of Rev 2–3) is not primarily *about* the churches, though it is clearly *for* them.[17] Though ἐπί in Rev. 10:11 is often referred to as a parallel usage,[18] that assumption is problematic. Rev 10:11 reads: "It is necessary that you prophesy again to many peoples [ἐπί λαοῖς … πολλοῖς] and nations and tongues and kings." Since the content of Revelation from that point on fits that injunction, in this context ἐπί, can reasonably be construed to mean "about, concerning, on the subject of".[19] This is an unusual meaning of ἐπί with the dative, however, which would normally be expressed with ἐπί and the genitive.[20] Since John's message to the nations is primarily one of *judgment,* however, the use of ἐπί with the dative in 10:11 is best construed in the sense of "to prophesy *against* the people" (i. e. ἐπί with the *dativus incommodi*).[21]

The difficulty of understanding how to construe ἐπί with the dative in Rev 22:16 is reflected in the variant readings for ἐπί. The original reading was certainly ἐπί,[22] which is the *lectio difficilior* because of the relatively unusual meaning of the preposition in this context.[23] The easiest scribal correction was

[15] Charles, *Revelation,* 1.cxxxiii; ἐπί in Rev 22:16 is translated as "au sujet de" by Allo (*L'Apocalypse,* 359 f.) and Prigent (*L'Apocalypse,* 357), both of whom refer to the parallel use of ἐπί in 10.11. Walter Bauer, *Wörterbuch zum Neuen Testament* ed. K. & B. Aland 6th edn; (Berlin and New York: Walter de Gruyter, 1988) col. 582 (II.1.b.δ); this meaning of ἐπί, however, is both rare and problematic. Of the six texts cited by Bauer-Aland as examples of this usage, both Rev 22:16 and Heb 11:4 do not fit the gloss. On the latter passage see Harold W. Attridge, *The Epistle to the Hebrews* (Philadelphia: Fortress, 1989) 316 f.; ἐπί τοῖς δώροις probably means "upon the gifts," or "over the gifts," perhaps referring to a legendary fire sent to consume the offering.

[16] Yarbro Collins, *Crisis,* 39; cf. Satake, *Gemeindeordnung,* 24 who then translated 22:16a: "Ich, Johannes, sandte euch meinen Engel, um dieses zu bezeugen, nämlich über die Gemeinden (über das Schicksal der Gemeinden)."

[17] Satake (*Gemeindeordnung,* 24) anticipates this objection and argues that the author is less interested in the entire Cosmos than he is in the fate of Christians, and therefore he directs his book to them.

[18] Bousset, *Offenbarung,* 166; Allo, *L'Apocalypse,* 360; Prigent, *L'Apocalypse,* 357 n. 19; Kraft, *Offenbarung,* 281; Bauer-Aland, *Wörterbuch,* col. 582 (II.1.b. d).

[19] Bauer-Aland, *Wörterbuch,* col. 582 (II.1.b.δ).

[20] Bauer-Aland, *Wörterbuch,* col. 580 (I.1.b.γ).

[21] Louw-Nida, *Greek-English Lexicon,* I, § 90.34: ἐπί + dative or accusative can function as "a marker of opposition in a judicial or quasi-judicial context" meaning "against," i. e., with the *dativus incommodi.*

[22] Josef Schmid, *Studien zur Geschichte des griechischen Apokalypse-Textes* (München: Karl Zink, 1955) 2. 34.

[23] א *1611 1854 2050 2053–2062* (a small but very important group of witnesses); *Andreas family f2023; Byzantine;* the reading is accepted by most modern editions.

the simple omission of the problematic ἐπί, a textual alteration found in the influential *Commentary on the Apocalypse* by Andreas of Caesarea (written ca. 600 CE).[24] This omission was probably motivated by a desire to read ταῖς ἐκκλησίαις in apposition to ὑμῖν, "to you, that is, to the churches". This scribal alteration suggests the difficulty which native speakers had in understanding ὑμῖν and ἐπὶ ταῖς ἐκκλησίαις as referring to the same group.

Another widespread correction, which has found some modem scholarly support, was the substitution of ἐν for ἐπί.[25] This substitution was a correction which could mean "I, Jesus, have sent my angel to you in the churches," i.e., it stresses the fact that individual Christians are members of the seven Christian communities.[26] The view that it could mean "*before* the churches," i.e., "in the community gatherings,"[27] involving the oral reading of Revelation before the assembled Christian communities by lectors, is problematic since the term ἐκκλησία does not have that meaning elsewhere in Revelation.[28]

While the occurrence of ὑμεῖς in 22:16 is unexpected, second-person plural pronouns (and verb forms) are used in direct address in two different contexts in Revelation, in the epistolary prescript (1:4) and in some of the proclamations to the seven churches (2:12–29). The closest apparent parallel to 22:16 is found in 1:4 in the epistolary prescript: "John to the seven churches [ταῖς ἑπτὰ ἐκκλησίαις] which are in Asia, grace to you [ὑμῖν] and peace."[29] Here, in contrast to 22:16, the plural dative noun ταῖς ἐκκλησίαις and pronoun ὑμῖν clearly refer to the same entity; ταῖς ἐκκλησίαις is a dative of indirect object, while ὑμῖν is a *dativus commodi.* Furthermore, this is the only place in Revelation where all seven Christian communities are collectively addressed with a plural pronoun. However, ὑμεῖς occurs here within a nominal clause which constitutes a stereotypical epistolary

---

24 *051 209 598 Andreas;* cf. Josef Schmid, *Der Apokalypse-Kommentar des Andreas van Kaisareia,* Part 1.1 of *Studien zur Geschichte des griechischen Apokalypse-Textes* (München: Karl Zink 1955) 260; *Arethas; Primasius* (*vobis septem ecclesiis);* Heinrich J. Vogels, *Untersuchungen zur Geschichte der Lateinischen Apokalypse-Übersetzung* (Düsseldorf L. Schwann, 1920) 164.

25 ἐν is supported by A (lacuna in C) *1006–1841* (these, with 911 which has a lacuna here, constitute an important family); *2329 Andreas fam f2073 i l* 94 (for a list of MSS comprising these families, see Schmid, *Studien,* I/2, pp. 1–78; *gig* (*testari haec in ecclesiis;* Vogels, *Untersuchungen,* 175); *Tyconius*[2] (*testari vobis haec in ecclesiis;* Vogels, *Untersuchungen,* 190); *Beatus* (*testari vobis haec in ecclesiis;* Vogels, *Untersuchungen,* 208); *vulg* (*testificari vobis haec in ecclesiis).* This reading is accepted as original by B. *Weiss, Johannes-Apokalypse,* 224; Charles, *Revelation,* 2.382; Hadorn, *Offenbarung,* 217 f. (it is also included as a marginal reading in Westcott and Hort).

26 Satake, *Gemeindeordnung,* 24.

27 Weiss, *Johannes-Apokalypse,* 112, 224; Hadorn, *Offenbarung*, 218.

28 While ἐκκλησία can mean "assembly" in the sense of a group of citizens gathered for social or political activities (cf. Acts 19:39; cf. Louw and Nida, *Greek-English Lexicon,* I, § 11.78), there are no instances in Revelation in which ἐκκλησία means "Christian assembly;" cf: Karrer, *Johannesoffenbarung*, 224 n. 13.

29 Vanni, *La Struttura Letteraria,* 180.

salutation of the kind typical of early Christian letters, particularly those attributed to Paul. The second context within which second-person plural pronouns are used in Revelation is in the proclamations to the seven churches in 2:12–29. Though the author uses the literary device of addressing each proclamation to an angel who functions as the *alter ego* of each community, he does not consistently maintain that fiction. He can refer to the *entire* community with second-person plural verbs (2:10) and pronouns (παρ' ὑμῖν; 2:13), or he can address a particular group within a community in a similar way (2:10, 14–15, 20–22, 24). None of these uses of ὑμεῖς can be regarded as a satisfactory parallel to the ὑμεῖς of Rev 22:16.

II.

Since it is virtually certain that ὑμεῖς and αἱ ἐκκλησίαι in Rev 22:16 must be understood as referring to two *different* (though possibly overlapping) entities, we must evaluate the various proposals which have been made in the attempt to identify the two groups. H. B. Swete, aware that two groups are necessarily in view, distinguishes the ὑμεῖς, which he thinks refers to Christians in the seven communities addressed by John, from the αἱ ἐκκλησίαι immediately following, which refers to Christians everywhere, the church universal.[30] The term αἱ ἐκκλησίαι occurs thirteen times in Revelation (only in 1–3 and 22:16), seven times in the formula "what the Spirit says to the churches" (2:7, 11, 17, 29; 3:6, 13, 22). In four of the remaining occurrences, the *seven* churches to whom the Revelation is addressed are specifically in view (1:4, 11, 20 [2x]); the two remaining occurrences are 2:23 and 22:16). In all these references with the possible exception of 22:16, it is either clear or probable that the seven churches are specifically in view. There is no evidence to suggest that αἱ ἐκκλησίαι as a collective term refers to any group other than the seven specific Christian communities to whom the book as a whole is addressed.

Since the phrase αἱ ἐκκλησίαι in Rev 22:16 undoubtedly refers to the seven Christian communities of Roman Asia addressed by John, ὑμεῖς must refer to a *different* group. There are four possible options which have been suggested: (1) *potential martyrs,* i. e., particularly faithful Christians who faced the possibility of dying for their faith, (2) *lectors* whose task it was to read Revelation to the congregations, (3) *envoys* whose task it was to deliver copies of Revelation to each of the seven churches, or (4) a group of John's *prophetic colleagues.*

1. G. B. Caird is alone, so far as I can determine, in proposing that the testimony is given only to those who are ready and willing to lay down their lives

---

[30] Swete, *Apocalypse,* 309.

for their faith.[31] Though he does not support this opinion with evidence, it is true that particular rewards are promised to "the one who conquers" (2:7, 11, 17, 26 f.; 3:5, 12, 21; cf. 16:15), and martyrs are certainly accorded special status in the author's eschatological scenario (20:4–6). However, there is nothing to suggest that the ὑμεῖς of 22:16 should be identified with this elite group.

2. Theodor Zahn is one of the few who have suggested that ὑμεῖς refers to the *lectors* whose task it would be to read the book of Revelation to Christians at their assemblies.[32] This proposal has the advantage that "the one who reads" and "those who hear," referred to in Rev 1:3, are two distinct entities. Since the author intended that Revelation be read in assemblies of all the seven churches by different lectors, they could conceivably be referred to as a group, i. e., οἱ ἀναγινώσκοντες. Further, since several verbal and thematic links exist between 22:16 and 1:1–3, this view would tie them even closer together.

3. While no commentator to my knowledge has suggested that the ὑμεῖς of Rev 22:16 could refer to the *envoys* responsible for carrying copies of Revelation to their destinations, that possibility deserves consideration. While there is no way of knowing whether or not John was still an exile when Revelation was completed, it is nevertheless likely that others were entrusted by him to deliver copies of the book to some if not all of the seven churches. Who these individuals were cannot be determined, and how they performed their task cannot be known, except by analogy. In the ancient world private letter carriers often played an active role in the delivery of a written message by accompanying it with an oral message.[33] Paul's letters reflect a network of Christian communities interconnected by frequent visits by Christians of various stations, traveling for secular as well as for religious reasons, among whom were messengers carrying letters from those unable to be physically present.[34] Tychicus is an example of a Christian who is presented as an envoy of Paul whose task it was to carry a letter to the Colossians and provide an oral report of Paul's personal situation (Col 4:7).[35]

---

[31] G. B. Caird, *A Commentary on the Revelation of St. John the Divine* (New York: Harper & Row, 1966) 286.

[32] Theodor Zahn, *Die Offenbarung des Johannes* (lst, 2nd, 3rd edn; (Leipzig and Erlangen: A. Deichert, 1924–26) 2.626 n. 89, 628. This view was briefly articulated earlier by B. Weiss (*Johannes-Apokalypse,* 112, 224) and also appears to be the view of Johannes Panagopoulos, "Die urchristliche Prophetie: Ihre Charakter und ihre Funktion," *Prophetic Vocation in the New Testament and Today,* ed. J. Panagopoulos (Suppl NovT, 45; Leiden: Brill, 1977) 22.

[33] John L White, *Light from Ancient Letters* (Philadelphia: Fortress, 1986) 216. White translates the closing lines of a letter written in 257 BCE: "The rest (i. e., anything else that remains) learn from the one who carries the letter to you. For he is no stranger to us."

[34] Wayne A. Meeks, The *First Urban Christian:* The *Social World of the Apostle Paul* (New Haven: Yale University, 1983) 109 f.

[35] E. A. Judge, "The Early Christians as a Scholastic Community," *Journal of Religious History* 1 (1960–61), 134 f. Though Colossians is probably pseudonymous (cf. Mark Kiley, *Colossians as Pseudepigraphy* [Sheffield: JSOT Press, 1986]), which would have had little or no effect on the presentation of typical social customs and roles.

Further, Tychicus is not presented as a subordinate, but as a "beloved brother, faithful minister and fellow servant [σύνδουλος]" of Paul. Perhaps the closest analogy to the envoys of John who must have delivered copies of Revelation to their destinations is found in Hermas *Vis.* 2.4.3, where the Ancient Lady tells Hermas what to do with the revelation she has given him:

> You shall therefore write two little books and send one to Clement and one to Grapte. Clement shall then send it to the cities abroad for that is his duty; and Grapte shall exhort the widows and orphans; but in this city you shall read it yourself with the elders who are in charge of the church.

Those whom Hermas is instructed to send out with copies of his book are envoys and lectors, though not prophets. Another close parallel from Greco-Roman paganism, from second-century CE Anatolia, involves envoys who are prophets. Lucian reports that the oracular prophet Alexander of Abonuteichos sent χρησμολόγοι (roughly "collectors and interpreters of oracles") to cities throughout the Roman empire with predictions of plagues, fires and earthquakes (*Alex.* 36). Understanding the ὑμεῖς of Rev 22:16a as envoys coheres well with the way in which that passage should be translated: "I, Jesus, sent my angel to attest this message to you for the churches."

4. The widespread view that the ὑμεῖς of Rev 22:16a refers to a group of prophets associated with John,[36] is usually based on two inferences: (a) Rev 22:9 indicates that John is one of several Christian prophets, and (b) the term "servants" in Rev 22:6, like the phrase "servants of God" elsewhere in Revelation, refers to Christian prophets.

a. In Rev 22:9, the angelic revealer claims that "I am [εἰμι] a fellow servant [σύνδουλός] of you and your brothers the prophets and those who obey the contents of this book." By including this statement, John clearly implies that he is a prophet, a self-conception corroborated by his characterization of the book he is writing as a "prophecy" (1:3) and a "prophetic book" (22.7,10,18,19). While it is clear that a plurality of prophets is in view in Rev. 22:9, the problem is whether this refers to (a) John and ancient Israelite prophets, (b) John, other contemporary Christian prophets and ancient Israelite prophets, or (c) John and other contemporary Christian prophets. While some scholars think that all nine references to prophets in Revelation refer to Christian prophets,[37] others argue that these references (with the exception of 11:10) can be understood as referring exclusively to ancient Israelite prophets.[38] It is important to note that the phrase "your brothers the prophets" is coordinated with "those who obey [τῶν τηρούντων] a present substantival participle] the words of this book". Since the latter group

[36] See note 7 above.

[37] A.T. Nikolainen, "Über die theologische Eigenart der Offenbarung des Johannes," *TLZ* 93 (1968), 161–70.

[38] Yarbro Collins, *Crisis and Catharsis,* 44.

is one contemporaneous with John, the likelihood that the former phrase also describes contemporaries is increased. This interpretation is confirmed by Rev 19.10, which not only contains verbal parallels to 22:9, but which also is one of two structurally similar conclusions of a pair of angelic disclosures (17:1–19:19; 21:9–22:9).[39] Rev 22:9 therefore has an important parallel in 19:10.

Then I fell down at his feet to worship him, but he said to me, You must not do that! I am a fellow servant [σύνδουλός] with you and your brothers who hold the testimony [τὴν μαρτυρίαν] of Jesus. Worship God. For the testimony [ἡ μαρτυρία] of Jesus is the spirit of prophecy.

Here a single group contemporaneous with John is mentioned, "your brothers who hold the testimony of Jesus." Their prophetic function is suggested by the gloss with which the verse concludes, which identifies ἡ μαρτυρία Ἰησοῦ (a subjective genitive) with τὸ πνεῦμα τῆς προφητείας. The conclusion is inescapable that the glossator is trying to make it abundantly clear that the "brothers who hold the testimony of Jesus" are *prophets*. This strengthens the case that the prophets mentioned in 22:9 are Christian prophets contemporaneous with John, and further that they are the most likely group referred to by the ambiguous ὑμεῖς of 22:16.

b. If "servants" (δοῦλοι) in 22:6 is intended to refer to "prophets," that would provide further evidence for a prophetic community associated with John in Asia:

And the Lord, the God of the spirits of the prophets [τῶν πνευμάτων τῶν προφητῶν], has sent his angel to show [δεῖξαι] his servants [τοῖς δούλοις] what must soon take place.

This statement has close verbal parallels with both 22:16 and 1:1, and in all likelihood belongs to the final redaction of Revelation. The term "servants" is used in several ways in Revelation: (1) literally of "slaves" (6:15 [sing.]; 13:16; 19:18), (2) figuratively of Christians generally (2:20; 7:3; 19:5; 22:3); (3) figuratively in the phrase "[God's] servants the prophets" of prophets (10:7; 11:18);[40] (4) figuratively of John himself (1:1), (5) figuratively of Moses (15:3). The ambiguous passages (1:1; 22:6) could thus refer to Christians generally (2), or to prophets (3) and (4). The use of the verb δεικνύναι narrows the choice somewhat, for it is used six times of visionary revelations to John (4:1; 17:1; 21:9, 10; 22:1, 8), and twice with the ambiguous term δούλοις used as an indirect object (1:1; 22:6). If the term "servants" in 22:6 and 1:1 refers to prophetic associates of John, then it is clear that Revelation has been entrusted by John to prophetic colleagues and envoys for distribution and presentation to the seven

---

[39] Charles H. Giblin, "Structural and Thematic Correlations in the Theology of Revelation 16–22," *Biblica* 55 (1974), 487–504; cf. Vanni, *La Struttura Letteraria*, 283–86.

[40] In Rev 11:18, the phrase τοῖς δούλοις σου τοῖς προφήταις refers to *one* group rather than two, since in lists of groups of people found in Revelation are polysyndetic, with καί consistently used to link each individual group.

churches. This understanding has the advantage of providing a reason why John prefaced an apocalypse framed as a letter with a prologue in 1:1–3. The prologue functions to legitimate the fact that the revelation which John has received and written is in possession of prophetic envoys charged with its dissemination.

III.

References to prophets and prophecy in Revelation are both maddeningly general and intriguingly ambiguous. Only one prophet, Jezebel, is specifically mentioned, though with a pejorative codename (2:20). She has followers (2:22 f.), but they are not styled prophets, though the original Jezebel did maintain a stable of 450 prophets of Baal and 400 prophets of Asherah (1 Kgs 18:19). The Two Witnesses of Revelation 11 are presented as Christian prophets (11:3, 10), and regardless of their symbolic significance, suggest that John's conception of the prophetic role was modeled after Old Testament prototypes. Prophetic guilds led by master prophets are religious phenomena found in ancient Israel and early Christianity.

There is considerable evidence in the OT for the existence of prophetic schools (called "sons of the prophets"), which sometimes practiced group prophecy and were led by master prophets given the title "father."[41] Elisha led one such school (1 Kgs 20:35; 2 Kgs 2:3,5, 7, 15; 4:1–38). Even classical prophets such as Isaiah had disciples (Isa 8:16–18), who were probably responsible for writing down, collecting and editing of their oracles into the complex and layered books that bear their names.

Groups of prophets also functioned in early Christianity, though the evidence is scanty and problematic. Migaku Sato has recently argued that the sayings source Q arose in just such a prophetic community.[42] 1 Cor 14:29–33 suggests that a group of prophets functioned in a special way in the Corinthian church. The odist responsible for the *Odes of Solomon* seems to represent a group of inspired singers, perhaps as their leader, who constituted a distinct group within the community (cf: *Odes Sol.* 7.16b–20).[43] A similar prophetic school may lie behind the pseudonymous Ascension of Isaiah (cf: ch. 6), a Jewish work with an extensive Christian addition completed in the second century CE. While little is known of any of these Christian prophetic groups, they do provide a model for understanding the prophetic circle of John of Patmos.

---

41 Aune, *Prophecy in Early Christianity*, 83.

42 Migaku Sato, *Q und Prophetie: Studien zur Gattungs-und Traditionsgeschichte der Quelle Q* (WUNT, 29; Tübingen: Mohr Siebeck, 1988).

43 David E. Aune, "The Odes of Solomon and Early Christian Prophecy," *NTS* 28 (1982), 448 f. Reprinted below, pp. 320–46.

IV.

In this article I have argued for the following positions: (1) From a syntactical standpoint it is highly unlikely that both ὑμῖν and ταῖς ἐκκλησίαις in Rev 22:16 refer to the same group or entity. (2) Since αἱ ἐκκλησίαι in all probability refers to the seven Christian congregations addressed by John, the ὑμεῖς necessarily refers to a *different,* though perhaps overlapping, group or entity. (3) Of the groups which have some claim to be identified with the ὑμεῖς of Rev 22:16 (envoys, lectors and prophets), the prophets referred to in 22:9 have the strongest claim, though it is likely that they also served both as envoys and lectors in the distribution and presentation of Revelation to the seven churches. (4) The existence of such a prophetic circle is made more probable by hints of analogous prophetic groups in Judaism and early Christianity.

God and Time in the Apocalypse of John

1. Introduction

While God is frequently referred to in the Apocalypse of John as the focal presence in numerous scenes set in the heavenly throne room and the primary recipient of the worship and hymns of praise offered by members of the heavenly court, he is only given a speaking role twice in the entire book. The first instance is toward the beginning of the book, at the conclusion of the prologue (1:8): "'I am the Alpha and the Omega,' says the Lord God, 'who is and who was and who is to come, the Almighty'" (the NRSV, I think incorrectly, does not enclose the last phrase in quotation marks as I have done here). The second instance occurs in a climactic position in the eschatological drama which constitutes the focus of Rev 4:1–22:9. Following the destruction of the first heaven and the first earth and the appearance of the new heaven and the new earth, God is given a longer speech (21:5–8), near the middle of which we find two further titles uttered as self-predications: "I am the Alpha and the Omega, the Beginning and the End" (v. 6b; I have capitalize the last two nouns, though the NRSV does not).

The two passages just quoted have a striking similarity that I want to explore further in this essay, written in honor of my esteemed colleague and friend, Paul J. Achtemeier. Both passages contain self-predications introduced by "I am" (*ego eimi*): "'I am the Alpha and the Omega,' says the Lord God, 'who is and who was and who is to come'" (1:8), and "I am the Alpha and the Omega, the beginning and the end" (21:6). These two "I am" sayings contain three divine titles, all of which are found in other contexts in the Apocalypse of John, and all of which appear to have temporal as well as cosmological aspects. A closely related title which does not appear in these two "I am" sayings is "the First and the Last," which is associated with two titles we have already met, "the Alpha and the Omega," and "the Beginning and the End" (Rev 22:13), suggesting that it is part of a set. In this essay, I will argue that this series of interrelated temporal metaphors that function as divine titles were specifically crafted by the author to encapsulate his apocalyptic vision of God as the sovereign and almighty One who at the end restores both the cosmos and humankind to the pristine perfection of the beginning.

There are, then, four divine titles in the Apocalypse of John that have an implicit relationship to the notion of time: (1) "[he] who is and who was and who is to come" occurs three times in a tripartite form, twice in the form just quoted (1:4, 8), and once in a slightly modified tripartite form as "who was and is and is to come" (4:8), while the related bipartite form "who are and who were" occurs twice (11:17; 16:5), (2) "the First and the Last" (1:17; 2:8; 22:13), (3) "the Beginning and the End" (21:6; 22:13), and (4) "the Alpha and the Omega" (1:8; 21:6; 22:13).

There are several arresting features about these titles which are of obvious interest. *First*, with the exception of the first (which is a temporal continuum in both its three- and two-part forms), the other three titles are expressed in terms of two extremes of a continuum embracing all that lies between. *Second*, while the first title is applied exclusively to God in the Apocalypse and the second is applied exclusively to Christ, the third and fourth are applied both to God (1:8) and to Christ (21:6; 22:13). What may appear as a blurring of the distinction between God and Christ is in fact an attempt to use conceptions of God to characterize Christ, a theological move which needs closer examination. *Third*, there is a tendency for some of these titles to cluster, for two are found together in 1:8 and 21:6, while three are found side by side in 22:13. This suggests that, in these three passages at least, these titles are in some sense synonymous as well as mutually interpretive. *Fourth*, each of these titles is used as a self-predication of God or Christ following "I am" [*ego (eimi)*] (1:8, 17; 21:6; 22:13):

1:8 "'I am [*ego eimi*] the Alpha and the Omega,' says the Lord God, 'who is and who was and who is to come, the Almighty.'"

1:17 "I am [*ego eimi*] the First and the Last and the Living One, and I was dead but behold I am living for ever."

21:6 "And he said to me, 'It is finished. I am [*ego (eimi)*] the Alpha and the Omega, the Beginning and the End.'"

22:13 "I [*ego*] (am) the Alpha and the Omega, the First and the Last, the Beginning and the End."

The titles "the Alpha and the Omega" and "the Beginning and the End" are, in fact, used *only* in "I am" self-predications. *Fifth* and finally, it is striking that none of these titles occur elsewhere in the NT or other early Christian literature prior to the third century CE.

After exploring the significance of each of the four divine titles individually, I will examine the possible relationships between these titles and the conceptions of time characteristic of Jewish apocalypses in general and the Apocalypse of John in particular.

2. Four Divine Titles

The One who is and who was and who is to come

This striking tripartite formula occurs twice in this form (1:4, 8) and once in a slightly revised form exhibiting a more chronological arrangement: "who was and is and is to come" (4:8). A variation also occurs in two occurrences of a bipartite form of the title using just the first two of the three predicates: "who is and who was" (11:17; 16:5). In each context the predicates are used of God alone, a fact which suggests that some God-language was thought appropriate only for God. Surprisingly, neither the tripartite or bipartite versions of this formula occur elsewhere in early Jewish or early Christian texts before the third cent. CE. The predicate "the One who is" (*ho ōn*), however, occurs with some frequency in Greco-Jewish texts, ultimately based on the LXX version of Ex 3:14 (Josephus *Ant.* 8.350; LXX Jer 1:6; 4:10; 14:13; 39:17; Philo *Mosis* 1.75; *Somn.* 1.231; *Quod Deus* 110). In these Hellenistic Jewish contexts, the predicate is used in an *ontological* rather than a temporal sense, and can therefore be translated as "the Existent One."

The predicate "the One who is" also occurs in some comparatively late pagan philosophical and magical texts, though the latter may well have been the result of the pagan fascination with Jewish divine names. The possible temporal significance of the phrase "the One who is" (*ho ōn*) only becomes evident when it is associated in the Apocalypse with the predicates "the One who was" (*ho ēn*) or with "the One who was and who is coming" (*ho ēn kai ho erchomenos*). Further, the final predicate "the One who is to come" gives the whole not only a temporal, but more specifically an eschatological significance.

Very similar to the tripartite title in the Apocalypse of John is Plato's discussion of the traditional Greek way of referring to God (the principle of unity in the cosmos, not Zeus, the foremost Olympian deity) using past, present and future forms of the verb "to be" found in *Timaeus* 37e: "We say that it [Eternal Being] was and is and will be [*legomen gar dē hōs ēn esti te kai estai*]." Plato, however, rejects this as a naive and inaccurate way of speaking of Eternal Being:

> All these [days, nights, months, years] are all divisions of time, just as "was" [*to ēn*] and "shall be" [*estai*] are generated forms of time, though we apply these terms reflexively though improperly and incorrectly to the eternal being. For we say that "he is" or "he was" or "he will be," though actually only "he is" [*to esti*] is appropriate.

Of the many other texts which indicate that the verbal reference to past, present and future was indeed a traditional way of using temporal categories to refer to the eternality of the divine being (e.g., Plato *Leges* 4.715e; Plutarch *De Iside et Osiride* 354c; *Asclepius* 134.25–26), I will cite just three of the relevant parallel texts. Pausanias 10.12.10 preserves a hexameter formula which he attributes to the female priestesses of Zeus at the famous oracle at Dodona: "Zeus was, Zeus is, Zeus shall be." The Zeus who can be so described, however, is not the Zeus of Greek mythology (the normal Greek view is that the cosmos is eternal but the gods came into existence in time), but rather is an attempt to transfer the name of the central Olympian deity of traditional Greek myth and cult to the god of the philosophers, who is identical with the basic principle of the universe (i. e., with the universe itself) and who was thought to provide it with a basic and inclusive Unity. According to the *Asclepius* 14.17–18: *deus aeternus nec nasci potest nec potuit; hoc est, hoc fuit, hoc erit semper*, "the eternal God neither can nor could have come to be, that which is, which was, which always will be." Here the past, present and future forms of *sum* are explicitly used to indicate the eternality of God. The third text is a fragment 14(21) of Empedocles: "From them [fire, air, water] comes all that was and is and will be hereafter." In this instance, the tripartite formula is not used of god but of the basic constituents of the cosmos, regarded as god in philosophical tradition. Here it is clear that the tripartite formula is understood in a temporal manner as a metaphor for the eternity of god. With regard to Revelation, it has been frequently noticed that the third predicate of the tripartite formula has been modified from a future form of the verb "to be" (*eimi*), either *estai* or *essetai*, to the present substantival participle *ho erchomenos*, "the One who comes."

Martin McNamara has argued that the Aramaic equivalent to the tripartite divine name found in Rev 1:4, 8; 4:8 is in some way dependent on similar formulations found in several Targumic texts. One example he cites is *Exod. Rab.* 3:14: "R. Isaac [ca. 300 CE] said: The Holy One Blessed be He said to Moses: Say to them: 'I am he who was and I am he (who is) now and I am he (who will be) forever.' Wherefore is it said thrice, 'I am'." He suggests that an even closer parallel can be found in *Tg. Ps.-J.* Deut 32:39: "When the Memra of the Lord will be revealed to redeem his people he will say to all the nations: 'See now that I am He who is and who was and I am he who will be and there is no other God beside me.'" McNamara's view that the author of the Apocalypse was dependent on these Targumic traditions rather than on LXX Exod 3:14 or on the pagan Hellenistic tradition discussed above, however, is problematic because of the late date of the Targums. It is worth noting that the Targums agree with the Hellenistic parallels in using the future tense of the verb "to be" in the formula, suggesting dependence on the Hellenistic parallels discussed above, while the author of the Apocalypse has substituted a present participle with future significance: "the One who is coming." What really matters, of course, is not where the tripartite formula came from, but how and why the author has modified it and what it means in the Apocalypse of John.

The tripartite and bipartite versions of the formula occur in a variety of contexts in the Apocalypse, each of which sheds some light on the meaning or function of the title. The first occurrence of the tripartite formula is in the epistolary salutation in Rev 1:4–5:

Grace to you and peace from him who is and who was and who is to come, and from the seven spirits who are before his throne, and from Jesus Christ, the faithful witness, the firstborn of the dead, and the ruler of the kings of the earth.

While the form of this salutation is very similar to the salutations found in the superscriptions to the Pauline letters, the content is distinctive. A typical Pauline or Deutero-Pauline salutation (though some are expanded and varied), would be "grace and peace from God our Father and the Lord Jesus Christ" (e. g., 1 Cor 1:3; 2 Cor 1:2; Phil 1:2; 2 Thess 1:2; Eph 1:2). The inclusion of the tripartite divine title in the superscription of Rev 1:4, in the slot where Christians familiar with the Pauline letters would expect a more conventional salutation, suggests that the author is making a special point of emphasizing this particular divine title.

Similarly in Rev 1:8, where the tripartite title is repeated, this time in one of just two brief speeches attributed to God in the entire book, the reader or hearer cannot fail to miss the importance and distinctiveness of the formula, for here it is framed by two other divine titles in the form of a complex "I am" saying: "'I am the Alpha and the Omega,' says the Lord God, 'who is and who was and who is to come, the Almighty.'" The author is fond of clusters of three elements, and has used this group of three titles to mutually reinforce one another. "The Alpha and the Omega" (see below) is an abbreviated metaphor for the comprehensiveness expressed in a different way than the tripartite formula. The designation "Almighty" (*pantokrator*), again juxtaposed with the tripartite formula in Rev 4:8, occurs some 170 times in the LXX as a translation for the Hebrew word *tsěbāʾôt* ("hosts"), a traditional Israelite epithet of God linking him to warfare, found frequently in the OT in the archaic phrase *yhwh tsěbāʾôt*, "Lord of hosts." The Greek term *pantokrator*, which means "all powerful" or "all mighty," was chosen by the LXX translators to convey the meaning they found in *tsěbāʾôt* in the third cent. BCE, and also represents the significance which the author of the Apocalypse attributes to "the Alpha and the Omega" as well as the tripartite formula.

In a hymnic context in Rev 4:8, the tripartite formula appears in a slightly revised form in a more chronological order: "Holy, holy, holy, the Lord God Almighty, who *was* and is and *is to come*." While the first part of this acclamation closely follows the Hebrew text of Isa 6:3 (where the LXX transliterates rather than translates *tsěbāʾôt*, the tripartite formula represents an addition by the author of the Apocalypse, perhaps based on traditional Jewish exegesis of Exod 3:14 and Deut 32:39, though nowhere in Jewish literature does the *Qeduššah*, or *Sanctus*, occur with the tripartite formula.

The bipartite formula "who are and who were" occurs in two other hymnic contexts in Rev 11:17 and 16:5. The omission of the epithet "who is to come" is probably due to the fact that from a dramatic perspective, God has *already* visited the earth in judgment earlier in the narrative of each passage (11:18a:

"The nations raged, but your wrath *came*"; 16:5: "You are just in these your judgments"), as well as salvation (11:18b: "[the time came] for rewarding your servants"). In 11:17, God is also addressed as "the Lord God Almighty," so that the title *pantokrator* actually occurs in company with the tripartite formula in two of its three occurrences (1:8; 4:8) and with the bipartite version of the formula in this context (11:17). In Rev 16:5 the bipartite title "who are and who were" is followed by a relatively rare predicate "Holy One" (*hosios*).

The results of this sequential discussion of the uses of the tripartite and bipartite formulas in their respective contexts are two: (1) The epithet "who is to come," present in three occurrences of the tripartite formula (1:4, 8; 4:8) is missing in the bipartite versions (11:17; 16:5), presumably because the judgment of God has already come in the narrative context. This suggests that "who is to come" is a divine epithet narrowly focused on the "coming" of God understood primarily as a divine visitation in eschatological judgment and salvation. (2) The title most frequently associated with the tripartite and bipartite formula is "Almighty," a traditional title of God in early Judaism which suggests the author's primary understanding of the significance of the tripartite and bipartite formulas.

The Alpha and the Omega

This divine title, which does not occur earlier than the Apocalypse of John, is used twice of God (1:8; 21:6) and once of Christ (22:13). In all three instances it is a predicate nomination in an "I am" statement. The author clearly intends the reader to associate this title with the other antithetical titles, for it is found with "the Beginning and the End" in 21:6 and with "the First and the Last" and "the Beginning and the End" in 22:13. The context of the divine self-predications "I am the Alpha and the Omega, the Beginning and the End" in Rev 21:6 is extremely significant, for it is part of 21:5–8, the second speech attributed to God in the Apocalypse (the first is in 1:8) a divine utterance which follows the destruction of the first heaven and the first earth.

Since Alpha and Omega are the first and last letters of the Greek alphabet, the author apparently intends an association with the speculation which surrounded the letters of the alphabet. In later Jewish alphabet symbolism, *'emet*, the Hebrew word for "truth," was interpreted as a designation of God as the beginning, middle and end (*Yer. Sanh.* 18a). Yet the basic conception must surely have been Hellenistic in origin (see Plato *Laws* 4.716A; Josephus *Against Apion* 2.190), since *mu* is the twelfth letter of the twenty-four letter Greek alphabet (as close to the middle as possible, given the even number of letters). While *aleph* and *tau* are the first and last letters of the Hebrew-Aramaic alphabet, *mem* is not the middle letter of these alphabets, but rather the thirteenth of twenty-two letters.

Hellenistic alphabet speculation also involved the vowels. The Greek alphabet had seven vowels, aeēiouō, thought by some to constitute the true name of God. According to Eusebius (*Preparation for the Gospel* 519d):

> [The Hebrews] say also that the combination of the seven vowels contains the enunciation of one forbidden name, which the Hebrews indicate by four letters and apply to the supreme power of God, having received the tradition from father to son that this is something unutterable and forbidden to the multitude.

While the Tetragrammaton (literally "four letters") refers to the four Hebrew consonants in *yhwh*, the unspoken name of God, reference to the seven Greek vowels similarly reflects the belief that aeēiouō somehow contains the pronunciation of that unutterable divine name. This tradition is also preserved in *PGM* XIII.39: "Write the great name with the seven vowels," and again in *PGM* XXI.11–12: "Your name which is seven-lettered in harmony with the seven vowel sounds." The seven vowels can also be used in self-predications following "I am," as in *PGM* III.661: "I am aeēiouō aeēiouō."

In *On Style* 2.71, a first century CE essay mistakenly attributed to Demetrius of Phaleron (late fourth cent. BCE), there is a reference to Egyptian priests who used the seven vowels in singing hymns in praise of the gods. Again (despite the supposed Egyptian provenance of the tradition) the mention of seven vowels indicates that *Greek* vowels are in view, and it is likely that this tradition preserves the notion that the seven vowels are construed as a divine name, as they frequently are in the magical papyri (nearly all of which originated in Egypt). Alpha and omega can be understood as an abbreviation of the seven vowels by contraction, one common ancient type of abbreviation in which the first and last letters or a word, or the first two and last two letters of a word are used as an abbreviation of the entire word.

The temporal significance of "the Alpha and the Omega" seems to have been left in the dust. However, the phrase must have been polyvalent, since when juxtaposed with "the Beginning and the End" (21:6) and "the First and the Last" and "the Beginning and the End" (22:13), it seems to take on the notions of preeminence and superiority. In *PGM* IV.487–8, the significance of the seven vowels is construed in terms of priority or preeminence: "First origin of my origin, aeēiouō, first beginning [*archē prōtē*] of my beginning."

The First and the Last

The divine title "the First and the Last" (*ho protos kai ho eschatos*) occurs three times in the Apocalypse, always as the predicate of an "I am" declaration, and always a self-predication of the exalted Christ (1:17; 2:8; 22:13). Since this title is associated with two others in 22:13, which are used elsewhere of God in the Apocalypse (the Alpha and the Omega and the Beginning and the End), it is appropriate to explore its significance in this paper. This title is almost certainly based on the Hebrew text of Isaiah 44:6b (cf. 48:12), which is an "I am" self-predication of "the Lord, the King and Redeemer of Israel, the Lord of Hosts," which can be literally translated "I am the first and the last" (for whatever reason, the LXX never uses the term *eschatos* to translate *'achărôn*). The context is a lengthy speech attributed to God (42:14–44:23), which contains a section toward the end (44:6–8) in which God emphasizes the fact that he is absolutely sovereign and that there are no other gods beside him. The fact that the author of the Apocalypse presents the exalted Jesus as claiming this predication of himself is significant christologically, for from the perspective of the OT such a predication is appropriate only to the God of Israel.

Rev 1:17–18, in the context of an appearance of the exalted Jesus, is in the familiar form of an oracle of assurance: "Stop being afraid. I am the First and [*kai*] the Last, even [*kai*] the Living One. I died and behold I am alive for evermore" (my translation). It is possible, with the NRSV to translate the clause "I am the First and the Last and the Living One" (here I have capitalized the titles) under the assumption that the self-predication has a tripartite form. However, the fact that the bipartite title "the First and the Last" occurs without elaboration in 22:13 suggests that the *kai* following the bipartite form in 1:17 is epexegetical or explanatory, suggesting that "the First and the Last" is also the Living One. The phrase "the Living One" appears to be a double entendre, for it is immediately interpreted by reference to the death and resurrection of Jesus, yet "the Living One" primarily calls to mind the numerous OT references to God as "the living God" (Deut 5:26; 1 Sam 17:26, 36; Jer 10:10; 23:36; Dan 6:27). Further, the phrases "the One who lives forever" and "the God who lives forever" are used by the author to refer to God four times in the Apocalypse (4:9, 10; 10:6; 15:7), indicating its relative importance.

The second occurrence of the title in Rev 2:8, though expressed in the third person, clearly refers back to the previous use of the title in 1:17–18 in the inaugural christophany: "These are the words of the First and the Last, who was dead and came to life." Here it is clear that "who was dead and came to life" is not a title but rather a particular way of identifying Jesus as "the First and the Last." The third and final occurrence of the title is the "I am" predication of the exalted Jesus in 22:13: "I am the Alpha and the Omega, the First and the Last, the Beginning and the End." Here, finally, all three of these antithetical titles occur in the same context mutually defining one another. Since the exalted Jesus has the last word here, the functional equivalency between himself and God is intentionally emphasized. Each of these antithetical titles attempts to capture a divine characteristic by implying that, since God is both extremes he encompasses the continuum defined by the antithesis. Since "the Alpha and the Omega" is twice attributed to God in "I am" sayings (1:8; 21:6), and "the Beginning and the End" is also a define self-predication in part of a short speech attributed to God in 21:6, it is clearly the author's purpose to identify the exalted Jesus with God.

The Beginning and the End

Finally, "the Beginning and the End," as we have seen above, is a self-predication of God in the "I am" statement of Rev 21:6, and is similarly a self-predication of the exalted Jesus in the "I am" statement of Rev. 22:13. From the standpoint of narrative strategy, it is not only clear that the author wants us to understand that God and the exalted Jesus are somehow functionally identical, but also that the categories for conceptualizing the cosmic significance of Jesus are based on language primarily associated with God. This title, which is sometimes found in extra-biblical sources with a reference to the middle, i.e., "the Beginning and the Middle and the End," is drawn from Hellenistic philosophical and religious traditions and has cosmological as well as temporal signification. The Derveni papyrus, found preserved through carbonization in a Macedonian grave and dating to ca. 350 BCE, contains a fragment from an earlier Orphic poem: "Zeus is the beginning, Zeus is the middle, all things are fulfilled by Zeus." A similar Orphic fragment is preserved in Plato *Laws* 4.715E: "God … holds the beginning and the middle and the end of all things which exist," a statement quoted by a number of early Christian authors (Ps.-Justin *Cohort.* 25; Irenaeus *Adv. haer.* 3.25.5; Hippolytus *Ref.* 19.6; Clement Alex. *Strom.* 2.22; Origen *Contra Celsum* 6.15). God is referred to as "the beginning and end of all things" by both Philo (*Plant.* 93) and Josephus (*Ant.* 8.280), but this title is rarely found in early Christian writers. "Beginning and End" is also a divine epithet found in many magical texts, including the Greek magical papyri. In *PGM* IV.2836–7, part of a hexameter hymn to Hekate (a Greek goddess who acquired cosmic significance in some circles): "Beginning and end [*archē kai telos*] are you [Hekate], and you alone rule all. For all things are from you and you alone rule all." Here, remarkably, Hekate is assigned a cosmic significance which is expressed through a different metaphor in *Orphic Hymns* 1.7 where she is designated as "key-bearing mistress of the entire cosmos." The last line quoted above from *PGM* IV.2837 is significant as a gloss interpreting one way of construing the title "the Beginning and the End": "For all things are from you and you alone rule all."

Summary

To this point we have discussed four titles for God and/or Christ which we have argued are similar in both form and meaning. Three of the four titles use different metaphors to conceptualize a continuum bounded by extremes: the Alpha and the Omega, the First and the Last, the Beginning and the End. Only the One who is and who was and who is to come (and its variations) does not fit this pattern. This last title does not consist of elements which frame a continuum, so much as points plotted along a temporal continuum based on the ancient perception of the three basic tenses of the Greek verb: past, present and future. As observed above, this was a widespread metaphor for expressing the eternality of the cosmos or of the one God (capitalized in translations of Greek sources only when understood as equivalent to the cosmos). As we have noted, the author of the Apocalypse has modified the third term of this traditional formulation by substituting "the One who comes" for the more conventional Hellenistic phrase "the One who will be." This title in the Apocalypse is based on the three basic tenses of the Greek language: past, present and (implied) future, or on two tenses: past and present.

3. Biblical and Apocalyptic Perspectives on Time

In this section, I want to review some of the work on the Biblical conceptions of time to determine their utility for our investigation of the focal four divine titles this essay.

Conceptions of Time in Biblical Theology

The theological significance of the Biblical conception of time has been a topic of major interest explored by a number of OT and NT scholars associated with the Biblical theology movement during the middle third of the Twentieth Century. Many of these scholars, however, tended to underrate apocalypticism and hence ignored the temporal perspectives of Biblical (and extra-biblical) apocalypses and apocalyptic passages. Reacting against the history-of-religions school's conception of the faith of Israel and early Christianity as syncretistic amalgams of the myths, ideas and practices of pagan societies and cultures in their environment, these scholars identified theological features and presuppositions of the faith of Israel and the early Church which they considered historically and culturally unique. In their view, uniqueness was itself a strong argument for truth. This perspective pervades the nine-volume *Theological Dictionary of the New Testament*, a major monument of the Biblical theology movement (1933–73; English translation 1964–74).

Not surprisingly, adherents of the Biblical theology movement found the Hebrew conception of time, inherited by early Christianity, to be in sharp contrast to (as well as superior to) the Greek view. In Oscar Cullmann's classic book *Christ and Time: The Primitive Christian Conception of Time and History* (1945; English translation 1950), he contrasted Hebrew and Greek conceptions of time, proposing that the former was linear, while the latter cyclical. For primitive Christianity and Biblical Judaism, he argued, the most appropriate metaphor for time was the "upward sloping line" moving irreversibly toward the goal of complete fulfillment. The mid-point of this upward sloping line is the

Christ event, from which all preceding and subsequent events receive meaning (the division of western time to "Before Christ" and "Anno Domini" are two expressions of the historical centrality of the Christ event). The two ideas which most clearly express the NT concept of time, he argued, were expressed by two Greek words for time, *kairos*, referring to a point of time, i.e., time defined by its content, and *aiōn*, designating a duration or extent of time which could be understood as limited or unlimited. According to Cullmann, time and eternity are not contrasted, as in Greek philosophy (e.g., Plato *Timaeus* 37D), but time is contrasted with endless time.

In *The Fulness of Time* (1952), John Marsh argued that a cyclical, abstract conception of time was characteristic of Greek thought (represented by the Greek word *chronos*), which he called "chronological" time a perspective which deprived history of any real significance. On the other hand "realistic" time located an event by its content and was, he claimed, the hallmark of the Hebrew conception of time inherited by early Christianity (represented by the Greek term *kairos*). In a short appendix, Marsh criticized Cullmann's linear model since it implied a concept of "chronological time" which he thought was lacking in the OT. He further found the linear view is misleading since the end of the linear process (the Christ event) has appeared in the middle of the line as the center of history, rather than at the end of the line (a point of view which Cullmann had developed at great length). Both Marsh and Thorlief Boman (a Norwegian OT scholar influenced by Johannes Pedersen) thought that neither the line nor the circle (nor any other spatially-oriented metaphor) adequately conveys the Hebrew conception of time. Marsh was also critical of the cataclysmic view of history (by which he apparently means the apocalyptic view), since once the end occurs, the process leading up to it ceases to have significance.

In the early 1960's, James Barr published two monographs which severely critiqued the linguistic methodology that characterized many articles in the *Theological Dictionary of the New Testament*, as well as several studies on the Greek and Hebrew conceptions of time written by Biblical scholars. Barr used three basic lines of argument. First, attempts to connect the Hebrew and Greek conceptions of time with the aspectual verbal system of Hebrew and the temporal verbal system of Indo-European (specifically Greek) were methodologically invalid. Second, Greek and Hebrew words have distinct semantic meanings which must not be blended by an "illegitimate totality transfer," i.e., words are not "concepts" which contain all latent semantic meanings in all contexts. Third, not all Greek conceptions of time were cyclical, while cyclical conceptions of time are also found in the Hebrew Bible. Momigliano, in essential agreement with Barr, argued that a cyclical view of time is absent from the histories of Herodotus and Thucydides, while on the other hand, the Israelite festival of Passover is a prime example of cultic and cyclical time.

Malina's Model of Ancient and Modern Time

The problem of time in the Apocalypse of John has been raised more directly by Bruce Malina, who objects to labeling the book an "apocalypse" and has questioned the propriety of using the term "eschatology" to describe the temporal perspective of the work. Both terms, he argues, are modern theological concepts imposed anachronistically on the Apocalypse. What scholars label "eschatology" was not concerned with life after death or the future, he maintains, but with life in the *present*. Since John's prophecy has just two temporal dimensions, past and present, there is nothing particularly "eschatological" about it.

Malina's view of the conception of time in the Apocalypse was based in part on earlier research on social conceptions of time in the ancient and modern world published in an article entitled "Christ and Time: Swiss or Mediterranean?" There he presented a model for understanding the conception of time held by an ancient Mediterranean person, using a variety of modern social scientific studies. Unlike modern Americans, he argues, who have a highly abstract notion of time and a predominantly *future* orientation, ancient Mediterranean peasants had a primarily *present* orientation, dividing time into *experienced* time and *imaginary* time. "Experienced time" is the perception of duration within the horizon of actual experience, i. e., a broad conception of "the present," which focuses on processes which include the recent past, the present and that which is forthcoming (i. e., the unfolding or developing horizon of the experienced present). "Imaginary time" on the other hand, refers to everything which does not exist in the present, i. e., the past and the future.

In a second set of antithetical conceptions, Malina argues that modern Americans have a "linear separable time" which is monochronic (they can do only one thing at a time), while traditional peoples have a social time conception which is polychronic (they can do several things at once). The ancient Mediterranean had no conception of "linear separable time," and could not experience urgency based on scheduled time. The social time of traditional peoples had both "cyclical" and "procedural" dimensions. Cyclical time is rooted in the regular motion of the sun, moon and stars, pegged to recurrent human activity, while "procedural time" perceives the experience of singular and infrequent occurrences like biological processes which must be brought to completion (e. g., marriage, birth of a firstborn son, old age).

Malina then presents a third set of antitheses consisting of modern "abstract historical and operational time" over against "traditional historical and operational time." The latter understands historical time primarily for its present significance (like "imaginary time"), while "modern historical time" (a post-Renaissance development in the west) is a sense of history which assumes that people in the past were different from people in the present, i. e., human societies do not have to be the way they are.

In the following chart, I have simplified Malina's relatively complex model of Mediterranean time to call attention to the basic three sets of antithetical features of the ancient or traditional and modern conceptions of time described above.

Malina's Antithetical Conceptions of Time

Modern Conceptions	*Ancient Mediterranean Conceptions*
Modern Abstract Time	Traditional Experienced and Imaginary Time
Modern Linear Separable Time	Traditional Cyclical and Procedural time
Abstract Historical and Operational Time	Traditional Historical and Operational time

One of the strengths of Malina's approach is that he does not rely on simple graphic metaphors, such as the line, circle or spiral, but rather provides detailed verbal descriptions of the ways in which he thinks time was conceptualized by both ancients and moderns. He observes that the distinction which Biblical theologians make between linear time and cyclical time is not very clear, for the so-called linear time of the Bible is actually cyclical, but in the sense that the cycle occurs only once, not indefinitely. Malina's antithetical constructions of time are remarkably similar to Marsh's "chronological" time versus "realistic" time dichotomy (the latter was designated "psychological" time by Boman). While "chronological" time was characteristic of Greek thought and "realistic" time of Hebrew thought for Marsh, corresponding to Cullmann's characterization of the Greek conception of time as "cyclical," and the Jewish and early Christian conception of time as "linear," Malina lumps all ancients together (Greeks, Romans, Hebrews), arguing that they had a *present* orientation consisting of *experienced* and *imaginary* time, while modern Americans have an *abstract* notion of time with a *future* orientation. In the end, such simplistic antithetical conceptions are problematic, for most of the social constructions of time discussed by Malina (and many which are not) are found in both the modern and ancient worlds, though in widely varying proportions and differing from culture to culture. The antithetical conceptualization of temporal constructs is a rhetorical strategy to privilege one side of the antithesis over the other. The Biblical theologians explicitly regarded the Hebrew conception of time superior to the Greek conception, while Malina implicitly regards ancient experiential conceptions of time as superior to modern abstract conceptions.

Malina's rejection of the terms "apocalyptic" and "eschatology" as modern temporal conceptions imposed on ancient thought is based in part on a misrepresentation of their meaning in modern scholarship. Scholars do not generally use these terms to refer to the distant future, but rather to the imminent future transformation of the world, i. e., the end of history. Further, Malina's insistence that ancients were *present* oriented (though he defines the "present" broadly to consist of "this generation," i. e., forty years) is based on the reductionist view that language about the future really functions exclusively to control and direct present social behavior. Eschatological language certainly does functioned in this way, but it functions in other ways as well.

Reflections on Models for Time

While time and space provide the basic grid for the human perception of reality, both can be conceptualized in an astonishing variety of ways. Time, unlike space, involves change, and the experience of the movement of time is often conceptualized through the spatial metaphors of the "line" or the "circle," often thought to be antithetical. As a counterpart to Cullmann's "upward sloping line," it is equally possible to conceive of time as a "downward sloping line," i. e., as headed in a negative degenerative direction which includes cultural and moral decline. This is essentially the conception of time reflected in Jewish apocalyptic literature, but is also the view of the seventh cent. BCE Greek poet Hesiod. In *Works and Days* 109–201, he describes five successive races of humans, each representing a further decline in culture and morality. A similar decline is implicit in Daniel's vision of four sequential empires represented by four beasts, each worse than the last (7:1–8). There are two features implicit in the linear time model (whether straight, upward or downward sloping): (1) Primacy is placed on the past or on what is perceived as the first in a series of events, i. e., past events are implicitly understood as the causes of present and future events. (2) The linear sequence consisting of three isolable dimensions of time (past, present, future) implies that each temporal category is consistent with the other.

There are, of course, other possible metaphors. The "spiral," for example, suggests that there are cyclical movements of events which are never identically repeated, combining the progressive character of the linear metaphor with the repetitive character of the cyclical metaphor, and of course the spiral can go up or down. The spiral is a metaphor appropriate for the repeated historical cycles of apostasy-punishment-repentance-deliverance narrated in the book of Judges (since no cycle is exactly repeated in the narrative), or the sin-exile-return cycle in prophetic passages in the *Testaments of the Twelve Patriarchs*, or the lengthy eschatological vision which understood human history as a series of six dark rain showers, or times of falsehood, and six bright rain showers, or times of truth (*2 Bar* 53:1–74:4). The dark showers which follow the twelfth bright showers represent the future, consisting of a period of warfare and chaos culminating in the assembly of hostile nations which will be judged by the Messiah and punished or rewarded depending on how they have treated Israel (71:1–72:6). The final bright showers represent the period following the Messiah's complete victory over all opposition in the world, when he sits down in peace for ever on the throne of his kingdom introducing an apparently permanent idyllic period (73:1–74:4).

The "zigzag" (proposed by Steensgaard) can be used to convey the perception of sudden changes in history, reflecting (for example) the notion that while the God of Israel intervenes to judge and to save, people are free to obey or disobey (since history is not predetermined), thus changing the course of history continually, giving it a "zigzag" character, though this can also be conveyed through the spiral. Or, one could perhaps even conceptualize time under the metaphor of a line of dashes, that is, by a series of events separated from each other by the fact that each is perceived as having a beginning and an end. However, these metaphors must be recognized for what they are: crude ways of understanding time, a dimension of reality which can be conceptualized in a great number of ways.

Summary

Each in their own way, the proposals of the Biblical theologians and of Bruce Malina represent general conceptions imposed on, rather than elicited from, the Biblical text, and to that extent they are unsatisfactory. Time is a phenomenon which can be conceptualized in a multiplicity of ways and various social and psychological constructions of time can exist side-by-side without any perception of conflict or contradiction. When I make an appointment with my physician for 3:15 p.m., I understand that to mean strict clock time, and I will probably arrive at least ten minutes early. After sitting in the waiting room for thirty to sixty minutes, I will eventually be ushered into an inner cubicle to wait another eternity (perhaps fifteen to twenty minutes) for the appearance of the physician. This time lag, which makes everyone who experiences it angry, occurs for the simple reason that the physician is not operating according to time on his watch, but rather must complete a series of tasks defined by the specific complaints of a series of patients. Between this "abstract" time of my world and the "experiential" time of the physician's world, the nurse-receptionist, pretending that the arrival of the physician is imminent, is the one who mediates between two very different conceptions of time.

3. Restoration in the Apocalypse of John

The four divine titles reviewed above cohere particularly well with the notion of "restoration" which is characteristic of Jewish apocalyptic literature in general and the Apocalypse of John in particular. "Restoration" is a conception which has an essentially temporal character and which can be imagined as a cycle which occurs just once, returning to the place where it began.

Throughout the ancient world, both east and west, the imagined past was commonly considered the primary basis for assessing the legitimacy of the present and envisioning the shape of the future. There is a continuing debate about the legitimacy of the second of two rival concepts of history in the Greek world: while the notion of history as deterioration from an original Golden Age is widely accepted as representing the ancient Greek view, the notion of history as progress from primitive beginnings is often considered an anachronistic view attributed to the Greeks. Ancient thinkers such as Democritus, Aristotle and Protagoras are sometimes thought to have conceived of history as holding out the possibility of the infinite progress of human culture (the second notion), but the problem with that assessment lies in the probability that they understood progress as the attainment of perfection within a closed or limited ideal. Viewing the ideal past as paradigmatic for the present as well as the future, at any rate, was particularly characteristic of apocalyptic eschatology, which was preoccupied with the problem of evil. Salvation, the ultimate solution to the negative impact of evil on individuals and society, was not thought to occur through divine intervention in history, but rather through the elimination of history by the destruction of the old world order and its replacement by a new order. The ultimate solution of the human predicament was projected into the eschatological future where both the punishment and salvation of responsible moral agents would be meted out by God. Salvation, the positive aspect of the solution, was the divinely arranged restoration of individuals within their social matrices to the ideal state which they had enjoyed at the beginning. The conception that the End should recapitulate the perfect and paradigmatic Beginning, forms the basic horizon of the apocalyptic view of history, for the imperfections of the present constitute a low point between the perfections of the distant past and the perfections of the imminent future.

Apocalyptic eschatology centers on the expectation of God's imminent intervention into human history to save his people and punish their enemies by destroying the existing cosmic order and by restoring or recreating the cosmos to its original pristine perfection. It is the world view which is characteristic of "apocalypses," a literary form which flourished between 250 BCE and 150 CE, when Palestine was successively dominated by the Greeks (both the Ptolemies and the Seleucids) and then the Romans.

The restoration theme in apocalyptic literature has both nationalistic and universalistic aspects in apocalyptic literature, both of which are represented in the Apocalypse of John. Nationalistic restoration includes such elements as the restoration of sovereignty over the land of Palestine, the restoration of kingship, i. e., the reestablishment of theocratic monarchy in the ideal form of the Davidic messiahship, the regathering of the twelve tribes of Israel, and the final restoration of the city of Jerusalem and the Temple. Universalistic restoration, on the other hand, lacks an ethnic focus, but rather envisions the restoration of creation, the restoration of Edenic conditions and the restoration of human society generally.

While various constituent themes of national restoration are found in the Apocalypse of John, the constituent themes of universal or cosmic restoration are of direct and particular relevance for understanding the four titles of God or Christ. Particularly significant is the speech of God in the Apocalypse (Rev 21:5–8), at the center of which we find the self-predications "I am the Alpha and the Omega, the Beginning and the End" (v. 6). The immediate context indicates that these titles must be understood within the framework of cosmic restoration. Rev 21:5–8 is arguably the most important single passage in the Apocalypse, for here the central message of the book is articulated by God himself, including emphases on his sovereignty and power, the trustworthiness of the revelation transmitted by John, and the salvation or judgment awaiting the conquerors and the enemies of God respectively. The summative character of the passage is indicated by the fact that it is a pastiche of words and phrases drawn from elsewhere in the book, and the passage itself is carefully composed of seven sayings:

(1) Then the One sitting on the throne said, "Behold I am making everything new" [v. 5a].
(2) He also said, "Write, for this message is trustworthy and true" [v. 5b].
(3) He also said to me, "It is finished" [v. 6a].
(4) "I am the Alpha and the Omega, the Beginning and the End" [v. 6b].
(5) "I will freely give some water to the one who is thirsty from the well of living water" [v. 6c].
(6) "Those who conquer will inherit these things, for I will be their God and they will be my children" [v. 7].
(7) "But as for the cowards and the unbelievers and the abominable and murders and the immoral and sorcerers and idolaters and all who lie, they will experience the lake that burns with fire and sulphur, which is the second death" [v. 8].

Here the phrase "I am making everything new" emphasizes God's role in the recreation or renewal of a fallen cosmos, while "It is finished" refers not to the end of the first heaven and the first earth, but rather to the completion of God's planned restoration of the world to its original perfection. Despite the relative infrequency of references to God as creator in the Apocalypse (4:11; 10:6; 14:7), this passage alludes to Isa 43:19 ("Behold I am doing a new thing"), but reinterprets it to emphasize God's role as renewer or recreator. Rev 21:5–8 follows the brief narrative mention of the appearance of the new heaven and the new earth following the apparent destruction of the first heaven and the first earth, and the descent of the holy city Jerusalem (21:1–3).

In the Apocalypse of John, the focus of the new or renewed creation is the New Jerusalem (21:1–22:9), which represents a combination of the eschatological themes of national restoration (the restoration of Jerusalem and of the twelve tribes) with the two focal themes of universal restoration (renewal of creation and the restoration of Paradise). In Rev 21:12, the New Jerusalem is described as having a wall with twelve gates, each inscribed with the names of "the twelve tribes of the sons of Israel." This implies that the New Jerusalem is not simply a city but rather the center for a reinhabited land. The expectation of the eschatological restoration of Jerusalem has antecedents in the eschatological Jerusalem of Ezekiel, which has twelve gates, three on each side, named after the twelve tribes of Israel (Ezek 48:30–35), as well as in the reconstructed apocalypse found in many fragmentary copies at Qumran entitled "Description of the New Jerusalem" (inspired by Ezekiel) which also depicts the eschatological Jerusalem as having twelve gates named after the twelve tribes of Israel (4Q554 frag. 1,I.9–II.11). Similarly in the Temple Scroll, the twelve gates of the eschatological Jerusalem are named after the twelve tribes of Israel (11QTemple 39.12–13; 40.11–14), anticipating the final realization of one of the central concerns of Jewish eschatology, the restoration of all Israel, which is repeatedly mentioned in post-exilic OT and early Jewish literature. However, in none of these texts is the eschatological restoration of Jerusalem, carefully linked to the restoration of the people, made part of the cosmic restoration as it is in the Apocalypse of John.

In the Apocalypse of John the restoration of Jerusalem is also linked to the restoration of Paradise. In Rev 2:7 (cf. 22:14) this is suggested in the promise that the exalted Christ will grant the conqueror the privilege of eating of the tree of life in the Paradise of God. Rev 22:2 uses Edenic imagery (refracted through Ezekiel (31:8–9) to describe the New Jerusalem, for the Apocalyptist describes how, on either side of the river of living water flowing through the city, there are trees of life each with twelve kinds of fruit each producing fruit monthly.

4. Concluding Observations

In the hermeneutically significant speech of God in Rev 21:5–8, placed in the narrative context of the restoration of creation through replacement and restoration of Paradise through the renewed access to the tree of life in the New Jerusalem, the divine titles "the Alpha and the Omega" and "the Beginning and the End" (21:6) appear to be linear conceptions for understanding God's relationship to his creation. Yet since the line proceeds from the original creation to a new creation and from a Paradise lost to a Paradise regained, the "line" is essentially a "circle" which ends up where it began.

If we regard Rev 21:5–8 as a passage of central significance in the theology of the Apocalypse, the title "the Alpha and the Omega" there is paired elsewhere with "the One who is and who was and who is to come," used of God in 1:8, and later used as a self-predication of Christ in 22:13, where it occurs in conjunction with "the First and the Last" and "the Beginning and the End" (the latter also found applied to God in 21:6).

The exclusive application of the title "the One who is and who was and who is to come" to God in the Apocalypse perhaps needs some qualification. In Biblical tradition Yahweh is "the coming One," a tradition based in part on the Sinai tradition. God "comes" to *judge* (Pss 95:13; 97:9; Isa 30:27; 66:15–16; Jer 21:13;

Mic 1:3; Mal 3:1–2) as well as to *save* (Isa 35:4; 40:10–11; 59:20; Ezek 43:1–5; Ps 49:2; Zech 2:10; 14:5). This opens the possibility, then, that the tripartite name serves as a theological motto for the Apocalypse of John signifying that the eternal God is about to visit the world bringing both judgment and salvation.

Yet in the Apocalypse of John, though God is identified as "the One who is coming," there is not a single explicit reference to God as "coming." It is rather his wrath that "comes" (11:18). But as we have seen, the omission of the third predicate "the One who is to come" in Rev 11:17–18 and 16:5 from the normally tripartite formula suggests that, at least from a narrative perspective, God has in fact "come" in judgment in the plagues of the seven trumpets and in the plague unleashed by the third bowl angel. However, these "comings" cannot be identified with the final and climactic coming of God to judge the world. Two different verbs meaning "to come" (*erchomai* and *hēkō*) are used to refer to the impending coming of Christ (1:7; 2:5, 16, 25; 3:3 [twice], 11; 16:15; 22:7, 12, 20). However, four of these texts cannot refer to the Parousia, but rather must refer to a "coming" in judgment which must be understood as preliminary to the final and climactic Parousia of Christ (2:5, 16; 3:3 [twice]). The difference is that God "comes" to judge the wicked with preliminary plagues, while Christ "comes" to judge the Christian community. In these texts, the author of the Apocalypse uses language traditionally applied God as a basis for exploring the function and significance of Christ.

Charismatic Exegesis in Early Judaism and Early Christianity

1. Introduction

"Charismatic exegesis" is one of several terms that have been used in recent years to describe various types of Biblical interpretation practiced in early Judaism and in early Christianity,[1] whose distinctive feature is the implicit or explicit claim that the interpretation itself has been divinely revealed. The phrase "charismatic exegesis" itself was coined by H. L. Ginsberg, in conversation with William Brownlee, to describe the type of biblical interpretation practiced in the Qumran Community by the author of the Habakkuk commentary (1QpHab).[2] Despite the fact that "charismatic exegesis," or one of its aliases, is frequently referred to in scholarly discussion, there are many misconceptions about it that require clarification.[3] One of the results of this discussion will be to suggest that "charismatic exegesis" is an infelicitous umbrella term used to designate a wide variety of claims that share the common conviction that the interpretation of sacred or revealed texts carries divine authority. The main problem with the term "charismatic exegesis" is its individualistic, psychological focus which limits its application to the phenomenon of an inspired interpreter through whom God reveals the true meaning of the sacred text.

Most scholars would agree that charismatic exegesis exhibits several characteristics: (1) it is *commentary*, (2) it is *inspired*, (3) it has an *eschatological* orientation, and (4) it was a prevalent type of *prophecy* during the Second Temple period. At this point I wish to unpack each of these points briefly and to point out some of the main problematic issues that must be examined in more detail in the rest of this paper.

---

[1] Other essentially synonymous terms include "inspired eschatological exposition" (E. E. Ellis, "'Spiritual' Gifts in the Pauline Community," *Prophecy and Hermeneutic in Early Christianity* [Grand Rapids: Eerdmans, 1978] 26), and "spiritual exegesis," i. e., "exégèse spirituelle" (L. Cerfaux, "L'exégèse de l'Ancien Testament par le Nouveau Testament," in P. Auvray (ed.). *L'Ancien Testament et les Chrétiens* [Paris: Editions du Cerf, 1951] 138).

[2] W. H. Brownlee, "Biblical Interpretation among the Sectaries of the Dead Sea Scrolls", *BA* 14 (1951), 61 n. 4.

[3] For an earlier attempt to grapple with this issue, see David E. Aune, *Prophecy in Early Christianity and the Ancient Mediterranean World* (Grand Rapids: Eerdmans, 1983) 339–46: "Appendix: Christian Prophecy and Charismatic Exegesis."

1. As *commentary* on Scripture, the practice of charismatic exegesis implies the primary religious authority of the biblical books.[4] Yet this commentary is not characterized by the consistent application of particular methods or procedures of biblical interpretation (such as the seven rules of Hillel, the thirteen rules of R. Ishmael, or the thirty-two rules of R. Eliezer ben Jose Ha-Gelili).[5] Nor is such commentary restricted to particular literary genres, though the biblical texts interpreted are usually considered neither halakah nor haggadah but eschatological prophecy. Further, as commentary, the interpreter's understanding of the text is not confused with the text itself (though the text can be altered to reflect the particular interpretation that is being imposed on it), but is separated from the text. Further, the interpretation of the text, despite its revealed character, is not regarded as equal in authority to the text being interpreted.

2. Certainly the *sine qua non* of charismatic exegesis is the belief or claim that the interpretation is ultimately based on divine inspiration. Yet here we enter into a problematic area, for while early Judaism presupposed the divine authority of the Torah and the Prophets (even though the latter was not strictly defined until the first or second century CE), there was no widely shared theory or explanation of how divine inspiration actually worked.[6] Though there is ample evidence that the Qumran Community believed *that* God revealed the truth to them, there is precious little evidence to suggest *how* they thought that the Spirit revealed truth.[7] There is therefore the danger that phrases like "divine inspiration" and "Holy Spirit",[8] which can mean and have meant many different things, will be defined in a synthetically uniform or even anachronistic manner, perhaps even in ways ultimately derived from, or at least influenced by, Christian dogmatics. If some kind of claim for the divine authority of an interpretation is not implicitly or explicitly present in the text, there is no way to be sure that we are dealing with charismatic exegesis. The claim for inspired interpretation, in turn, often implies a particular hermeneutical approach to the text in which its true meaning

---

[4] H.M. Orlinsky has emphasized the fact that *books* of the Hebrew Bible were canonized, not *texts* ("The Septuagint and its Hebrew Text," *The Cambridge History of Judaism* [4 vols.; Cambridge: The University Press, 1984–] 2.557–62). Therefore the phenomenon of the alteration of the sacred text, or the conscious selection of particular variant readings to bring the text more into line with the interpreter's understanding of the text, occurs both in early Judaism and early Christianity and does not contradict the sacred status of such biblical books.

[5] Many of these exegetical procedures, which are often associated with midrash, were practiced during the late Second Temple period even though they did not have formal labels; this is convincingly demonstrated for the Qumran literature by Brooke, *Exegesis at Qumran*, 166–67, 279–323.

[6] J. Barton, *The Oracles of God: Perceptions of Ancient Prophecy in Israel after the Exile* (New York and Oxford: Oxford University Press. 1986) 116–28.

[7] O. Betz, *Offenbarung und Schriftforschung in der Qumransekte* (Tübingen: Mohr Siebeck, 1960) 137–38.

[8] See A. E. Sekki, *The Meaning of RUAḤ at Qumran* (SBLDS, 110; Atlanta: Scholars Press, 1989).

is not evident, but requires a certain perspective or insight not shared by all who revere the same sacred text. There is, however, a generic sense in which Judaism regarded the interpretation of Scripture to be revelatory.[9]

3. Finally, charismatic exegesis may be *eschatological*, a characteristic exhibited in both the midrash pesher commentaries from Qumran, and in certain phases of early Christianity. What this means in practice is that the interpreter is convinced that he is living in the last days and that the particular scenario of events in the immediate past, present and future, were predicted by the biblical writers.

4. In light of the Jewish view that prophecy ceased in Israel with the activity of Haggai, Zechariah and Malachi (*b. Sot.* 48b), some scholars have argued that charismatic exegesis was a form of prophecy widely found in Judaism during the Second Temple period,[10] or more cautiously expressed that one strand of prophecy in early Judaism followed an interpretive-exegetical tradition.[11] It is possible to understand prophecy in early Judaism in at least two ways: (1) the direct inspiration of the prophet, or (2) the indirect inspiration of the prophet, that is, inspiration as mediated through the sacred text.

2. Biblical Interpretation in Early Judaism

The sanctity of the Torah and the Prophets was a central and unifying feature of early Judaism. Yet the Bible, like all sacred foundational texts (whether oral or written), was subject to manipulation through interpretation. Different understandings of the same sacred texts served to legitimate the often conflicting views held by diverse groups. While there were many formal and informal principles and procedures used to interpret Scripture in early Judaism, the written product of these methods was expressed in a variety of literary forms.[12] Some, though not all, of these were adopted by early Christians, who tended to see Scripture either in terms of eschatological prophecy or in terms of typological anticipations of the Christian dispensation.

These forms include:[13] 1. *Paraphrastic translation*, in which particular understandings of the text are folded into a translation (Aramaic Targumim,

[9] Daniel Patte, *Early Jewish Hermeneutic in Palestine* (SBLDS, 22; Missoula, MT: Scholars Press, 1975) 7.

[10] M. Hengel, *The Zealots* (Edinburgh: T.+T. Clark, 1989) 234–35.

[11] G. Dautzenberg, *Urchristliche Prophetie: Ihre Erforschung, ihre Voraussetzungen im Judentum und ihre Structur im ersten Korintherbrief* (Stuttgart: Kohlhammer, 1975) 43–121.

[12] Patte, *Early Jewish Hermeneutic*.

[13] All of the following literary forms are subsumed under the broad definition of midrash advocated by R. Bloch, "Midrash", *DBSup*, V, cols. 1263–81, who regards it as an approach to Scripture rather than as a literary form.

the earliest examples of which are 4QtgLev, 4QtgJob and 11QtgJob,[14] and the Septuagint).[15] 2. *Rewritten Scripture*, whereby portions of the Hebrew Bible were understood in new or different ways through additions, deletions and modifications (intracanonical example: 1–2 Chronicles; extracanonical examples: *Jubilees*, *Ps.-Philo*, or *Liber Antiquitatem Biblicarum*, the Genesis Apocryphon or 1QapGen; the Temple Scroll or 11QTemple; Philo, *De vita Mosis*; Josephus, *Jewish Antiquities*). 3. *Anthological style*, in which the biblical text is not explicitly cited and commented upon but is woven into the style of the composition (1QH, apocalypses).[16] 4. *Commentaries*, in which the biblical text is quoted and interpreted (pesharim, midrashim; many of Philo's works including *Legum allegoriae, De cherubim,* etc.),[17] which can again be subdivided into verse-by-verse commentary or thematic commentary. There are examples of all four of these genres which are attributed to divine revelation. One way of viewing these various literary forms of biblical interpretation is in terms of their degree of proximity or distance from the biblical text: *paraphrastic translations* present themselves as the sacred text, *rewritten Scripture* is at once more distant from the biblical text, yet may be intended to replace that text, the *anthological style* links a new composition in often very subtle ways to biblical texts, while *commentaries* carefully distinguish the text from the interpretation.

By the Second Temple period, the Jewish concern with the study of the Torah was increasingly expressed in terms of the necessity of receiving divine enlightenment to understand it. This theme is reiterated in Ps. 119 (vv. 12, 18–19, 27, 33–35, 73); v. 18 is typical: "Open my eyes, that I may behold wondrous things out of thy law." This motif is also evident in the famous description of vocation of the sage in Sir. 39.1–11, esp. 39.6–7 (NRSV):

> If the great Lord is willing, he will be filled with the spirit of understanding (πνεύματι συνέσεως ἐμπλησθήσεται); he will pour forth words of wisdom and give thanks to the Lord in prayer. He will direct his counsel and knowledge aright, and meditate on his secrets (ἐν τοῖς ἀποκρύφοις).

---

[14] E. Schürer, *The History of the Jewish People in the Age of Jesus Christ (175 BC–AD 135)* (3 vols.; rev. G. Vermes and F. Millar; Edinburgh: T. & T. Clark, 1973–87) 99–114; R. Le Déaut, *Introduction à la littérature targumique* (Rome: Pontifical Biblical Institute, 1966); *idem*, "The Targumim", in W.D. Davies and L. Finkelstein (eds.), *The Cambridge History of Judaism* (4 vols.; Cambridge: Cambridge University Press, 1984–) 2.563–90.

[15] R. Bloch ("Midrash", *DBSup*, V, col. 1278) argues that the Septuagint and other early versions should be analyzed not only from the standpoint of textual criticism but also from the perspective of the history of exegesis.

[16] A. Robert, "Les attaches littéraires bibliques de Prov I–IX", *RB* 43 (1934), 42–68, 172–204, 374–84; 44 (1935), 344–65, 502–25; cf. *idem,* "Littéraires (Genres)", *DBSup*, V, col. 411: the anthological procedure is "remployer, littéralement ou équivalemment, les mots ou formules des Ecritures antérieures."

[17] P. Borgen, "Philo of Alexandria", *Jewish Writings of the Second Temple Period* (CRINT, 2.2; Assen: Van Gorcum; Philadelphia: Fortress Press, 1984) 233–41.

In part this may be based on the association and even identity of Torah and Wisdom. Sir. 24.1–33, entitled 'Αινέσις Σοφίας, "Praise of Wisdom" in the three great Greek uncial manuscripts, identifies Wisdom with Torah in v. 23: "All this is the book of the covenant of the Most High God, the law which Moses commanded us as an inheritance for the congregations of Jacob" (see also Wis. 6.18; Bar. 3.29–4.4).[18] A similar view is frequently expressed by the author of the *Hodayot:* "[How] shall I look, unless Thou open my eyes? Or hear, [unless Thou unstop my ears]?" (1QH 18.19; trans. Vermes); "These things have I known because of your understanding; for you have uncovered my ear to marvelous mysteries" (1.21); "the man by whose mouth you have established the teaching and within whose heart you have set understanding" (2.17-18).[19] The result of this early Jewish conviction that God himself must reveal the true significance of his Torah is perhaps the implicit supposition behind the Jewish belief that Torah is not limited to the Pentateuch, nor even to the entire Hebrew Bible, but presupposes the unity and authenticity of the oral as well as the written Torah and therefore includes the interpretation of the sages right up to the present day.[20] There is therefore some truth to the notion that in early Judaism, *all* biblical interpretation involves "charismatic exegesis" in its broadest sense, that is, divinely gifted insight into the meaning of Torah.

Just as the gift of divine wisdom is necessary to understand and obey Torah, so the insight of the sage, also a gift from God, is necessary to interpret dreams and visions (e.g. Joseph in Gen. 40–41, and Daniel in Dan 2, 4–5). This "mantic wisdom" (as distinct from "proverbial wisdom", with which it is closely related),[21] links the techniques and terminology of dream interpretation (a major form of divination), the pesher interpretation of the Qumran *Hodayot,* and the explanations of the meanings of visions by the *angelus interpres* in Jewish apocalyptic literature.[22] Three important terms, רז ("mystery"), גלה ("disclose", "reveal") and פשׁר ("interpretation") occur together in Dan 2:30, where Daniel,

[18] The identification of Wisdom and Torah is made elsewhere in Sirach, though less forcefully (1:1–30; 6:32–37; 15:1; 19:20; 21:6; 23:27); see G.T. Sheppard, "Wisdom and Torah: The Interpretation of Deuteronomy Underlying Sirach 24.23", in G.A. Tuttle (ed), *Biblical and Near Eastern Studies* (Grand Rapids, MI: Eerdmans, 1978) 166–76.

[19] G. Vermes, *The Dead Sea Scrolls in English* (London: Penguin Books, 3rd edn, 1987). For further references, see 10.5–7; 11.4–5, 9–10, 16–17; 12.11–14, 32–34; 13.18–19; 18.10–11, 19–21. Knowledge, often equated with enlightenment, is extremely important in the Qumran literature; see H. Ringgren, *The Faith of Qumran* (Philadelphia: Fortress Press, 1963) 114–20.

[20] E.E. Urbach, *The Sages* (Cambridge, MA: Harvard University Press, 1987) 286–314; J. Neusner, *The Way of Torah* (Belmont: Wadsworth Publishing, 4th edn, 1988) 81–85.

[21] H.-P. Muller, "Mantische Weisheit und Apokalyptik", in J.A. Emerton *et al.* (eds.), *Congress Volume, Uppsala 1971* (VTSup, 22; Leiden: Brill, 1972) 283–85.

[22] A. Finkel, "The Pesher of Dreams and Scripture", *RevQ 4* (1960), 357–70; L.H. Silberman, "Unriddling the Riddle: A Study in the Structure and Language of the Habakkuk Pesher", *RevQ 5* (1961), 323–64; K. Elliger, *Studien zum Habakuk-Kommentar vom Toten Meer* (Tübingen: Mohr Siebeck, 1953) 154–57.

after telling the king that the future has been revealed to him in a dream by "the revealer of mysteries [MT: גלה רזיא; LXX: ὁ ἀνακαλύπτων μυστήρια]", that is, God, explains (nrsv):

But as for me, this mystery [MT: רזא; lxx: τὸ μυστήριον] has not been revealed [mt: גלי; lxx: ἐξεφάνθη] to me because of any wisdom that I have more than any other living being, but in order that the interpretation [MT: פש רא; LXX: τοῦ δηλωθῆναι] may be known to the king and that you may understand the thoughts of your mind.

In the Aramaic part of Daniel, רז ("mystery") is regularly the object of פשׁר (2:19, 28–30, 47), with a single exception (2:22); the means whereby God reveals mysteries is through night visions (2:19).

The terms רז ("mystery") and פשׁר ("interpretation") are used in similar ways in both Daniel and the Qumran pesharim,[23] and it appears that there is more similarity between the methods of exegesis in Daniel and the pesharim than between the pesharim and later rabbinical midrashim.[24] It is likely that the final redaction of Daniel during the mid-second century BCE was contemporaneous with the earlier literary activity of the Qumran community. While the Genesis narrator presents various people who relate their dreams to Joseph (Gen. 40–41), Daniel must know *both* the dream and its interpretation (Dan. 2:17–45), a feature that suggests the close connection between charismatic exegesis and prophecy.[25]

3. The Qumran Pesharim

Several types of biblical interpretation are evident in the surviving literature from Qumran.[26] One of the more significant types of interpretation is represented by the biblical commentaries or pesharim. Following Carmignac and Dimant, we distinguish three types of *pesharim*: (1) "Continuous pesharim" (i. e. verse-by-verse commentaries on entire books, e. g., 1QpHab), (2) "Thematic pesharim" (i. e. quotations from various biblical books grouped around a theme, e. g., 4QpIsa^{e}; 4QFlor 1–2 i 14; 11QMelch 12, 17), and (3) Isolated pesharim, the use of one or two verses from the Hebrew Bible interpreted using the pesher method and terminology, but within the framework of a larger composition (e. g.

23 F. F. Bruce, *Biblical Exegesis in the Qumran Texts* (Grand Rapids: Eerdmans, 1959) 7–17; Silberman, "Unriddling the Riddle", 323–64.

24 Elliger, *Studien zum Habakkuk-Kommentar,* p. 164; cf. A. Szorényi, "Das Buch Daniel, ein kanonisierter Pescher?", in J.A. Emerton *et al.* (eds.), *Congress Volume, Geneva 1965* (VTSup, 15; Leiden: Brill, 1966) 278–94.

25 J.L. Kugel and R.A. Greer, *Early Biblical Interpretation* (Philadelphia: Westminster Press, 1986) 58–59.

26 G. Vermes ("Biblical Proof-Texts in Qumran Literature", *JSS* 34 [1989], 493–508) enumerates four categories of proof-texts: (1) eschatological actualization, (2) direct proof (without explanation), (3) reinforced proof (with explanation), and (4) proof of historical fulfillment.

CD 19.5–13 on Zech. 13:7; 1QS 8.13–15 on Isa. 40:3).[27] Fragments of at least eighteen commentaries on portions of the Hebrew Bible have been found at Qumran,[28] including fourteen on the prophets,[29] and three on the Psalms,[30] and one which is unidentified.[31] In two passages in 1QpHab, the author articulates the basic presuppositions which informed his understanding of the biblical text. The first statement is found in 1QpHab 2.7–10 (trans. Vermes):[32]

> They, the men of violence and the breakers of the Covenant, will not believe when they hear all that [is to happen to] the final generation from the Priest [in whose heart] God set [understanding] that he might interpret (לפשור) all the words of His servants the prophets, through whom he foretold all that would happen to His people and [His land].

The second passage is found in 1QpHab 7.1–5 (trans. Vermes):

> And God told Habakkuk to write down that which would happen to the final generation, but He did not make known to him when the time would come to an end. And as for that which He said, *That he who reads may read it speedily*: interpreted (פשרו) this concerns the Teacher of Righteousness, to whom God made known (הודיעו) all the mysteries (רזי) of his servants the Prophets.

There are several presuppositions expressed in these texts:[33] 1. The events of the final generation have been predicted beforehand by God through the biblical prophets. 2. The true meaning of the Biblical text relates primarily to that period in which the text is being interpreted, that is, it refers to historical events that have occurred or will occur in the "final generation",[34] which center not on world

---

27 J. Carmignac, "La document de Qumran sur Melkisédeq", *RevQ* 7 (1969–70), 360–61; D. Dimant, "Qumran Sectarian Literature", in M.E. Stone (ed.), *Jewish Writings of the Second Temple Period* (CRINT, 2.2; Assen: Van Gorcum; Philadelphia: Fortress Press, 1984) 504–505.

28 A careful critical examination of each of these texts is available in M.P. Horgan, *Pesharim: Qumran Interpretations of Biblical Books* (CBQMS, 8; Washington, DC: Catholic Biblical Association of America, 1979); cf. *idem,* "The Bible Explained (Prophecies)", in R.A. Kraft and G.W.E. Nickelsburg (eds.), *Early Judaism and its Modern Interpreters* (Philadelphia: Fortress Press; Atlanta: Scholars Press, 1986) 247–53.

29 1QpHab, 1QpMic (1Q14), 1QpZeph (1Q15), 3QpIsa (3Q4), 4QpIsa^{a} (4Q161), 4QpIsa^{b} (4Q162), 4QpIsa^{c} (4Q163), 4QpIsa^{d} (4Q164), 4QpIsa^{e} (4Q154), 4QpHos^{a} (4Q166), 4QpHos^{b} (4Q167), 4QpMic (4Q168), 4QpNah (4Q169), 4QpZeph (4Q170).

30 1QpPs (1Q16), 4QpPs^{a} (4Q171), 4QpPs^{b} (4Q173).

31 4QpUnid (4Q172).

32 Vermes, *The Dead Sea Scrolls in English.*

33 Horgan, *Pesharim,* 229.

34 The relationship between the *pesharim* and the historical traditions they may contain remains a problematic issue which has yet to be adequately investigated; see P.R. Davies, "Eschatology at Qumran", *JBL* 104 (1985), 48. Outside the *pesharim,* there is no trace of a confrontation between the Teacher of Righteousness and the Man of the Lie. The probability is that there was no single Wicked Priest or Man of Lies but rather a series of such figures; cf. A.S. van der Woude, "Wicked Priest or Wicked Priests? Reflections on the Identification of the Wicked Priest in the Habakkuk Commentary", *JJS* 33 (1982), 349–59; W.H. Brownlee, "The Wicked Priest, the Man of Lies, and the Righteous Teacher – The Problem of Identity", *JQR* 73 (1982), 1–37.

or national history, but on the opposition experienced by the community.[35] 3. The words of the prophets are mysteries (רזים), the meaning of which God has revealed to the Teacher of Righteousness (probably identical with the Priest,[36] cf. 4QpPs[a] 3.15). Though several scholars subsume the Qumran commentaries under the rubric of "midrash",[37] and Vermes has even categorized them as targumic,[38] there is a prevailing tendency to regard the pesharim as constituting a distinct literary genre.[39] The structure of the pesharim is consistent and exhibits the following pattern: 1. a series of brief sections (varying from a phrase to five verses), that is, lemmata, are quoted from a particular biblical book in order, followed by 2. the interpretation of the biblical passage introduced by the term פשרו.[40] In virtually every instance of the use of the term פשר in the literature from Qumran, the term is used as a stereotyped formula to introduce the interpretation of a biblical text. Analyses of the lemmata of the pesharim suggest that the authors have altered the biblical text to bring it more into line with their understanding of the true meaning of the text.[41]

For the purpose of this essay, of course, the crucial issue is the claim that the pesharim preserved revealed interpretations of Scripture. Here it must be observed that the *author* of 1QpHab does not claim divine insight into the meaning of Scripture for himself, but rather attributes such insight to the founder or leader

---

[35] E. Jucci, "Interpretations e storia nei *pesharim qumranici", BO* 29 (1987), 163–70.

[36] B. E. Thiering, "Once More the Wicked Priest", *JBL* 97 (1978), 191–205; W. H. Brownlee, *The Midrash Pesher of Habakkuk* (Missoula, MT: Scholars Press, 1979) 57.

[37] Bloch, "Midrash", cols. 1276–78; Bloch, who provides a broad definition of midrash, finds a close relationship between midrash and apocalyptic (the latter is a type of the former), and therefore between midrash and 1QpHab (col. 1277): "Le *Commentaire d'Habacuc,* qui est une paraphrase actualisante des deux premiers chapitres d'Habacuc, met en oeuvre tous les procédés midrashiques connus." A. G. Wright considers 1QpHab to be haggadic midrash ("The Literary Genre: Midrash", *CBQ* 28 [1966], 418–22). G. Brooke argues that the *pesharim* constitute a type of midrash, but that to regard them as an independent genre unnecessarily multiplies generic categories ("Qumran Pesher: Towards the Redefinition of a Genre", *RevQ* 10 [1981], 483–503).

[38] G. Vermes, "A propos des commentaires bibliques découverts a Qumrân", *RHPR* 35 (1955), 96–102.

[39] Horgan, *Pesharim,* 229–59; I. Fröhlich, "Le genre littéraire des *pesharim* de Qumrân", *RevQ* 12 (1986), 383–98. I. Rabinowitz argues that the *pesharim* are not midrashim, but have a closer affinity with apocalyptic ("*Pesher/Pittaron.* Its Biblical Meaning and its Significance in the Qumran Literature", *RevQ* 8 [1973], 219–32). See also K. G. Friebel, "Biblical Interpretation in the *Pesharim* of the Qumran Community", *Hebrew Studies* 22 (1981) 13–24.

[40] The term פשר occurs within several stereotyped phrases: על הדבר פשר ("the interpretation of passage concerns"), על פשרו ("its interpretation concerns"), אשר פשרו ("its interpretation is that"), with variations (Brownlee, *Midrash Pesher,* 23; Horgan, *Pesharim,* 239–44).

[41] T. H. Kim, "Eschatological Orientation and the Alteration of Scripture in the Habakkuk Pesher", *JNES* 49 (1990), 185–94. The author cites 1QpHab 12.1–10 and 5.8–12 as specific examples. See also the alterations of Isa. 6.9–13 in 1QIsa[a] 6.2–10 discussed by C. A. Evans, "1Q Isaiah[a] and the Absence of Prophetic Critique at Qumran", *RevQ* 11 (1984), 537–42.

of the Community.[42] Further since the claim that the true meaning of the mysteries of Scripture have been revealed to the Teacher of Righteousness occurs just twice in the pesharim, such a claim cannot be considered a generic feature of these commentaries.[43] The revealed character of this interpretation is evident in 1QpHab 2.8, where the Teacher of Righteousness is described as:

הכוהן אשר נתן אל ב[לבו בינ]ה
לפשור את כול דברי עבדיו הנביאים

The priest into whose heart God placed understanding to interpret all the words of his servants the prophets.

The idiom נתן אל־לבב, "to put into the heart", occurs in Neh 2:12 and 7:5 where it refers to the divine guidance of Nehemiah's plans for Jerusalem (the same idiom occurs in Greek in Rev 17:17).[44] A similar gift of divine understanding is claimed for the Teacher of Righteousness in 4QpPs[a] 4.27, and recurs several times in the *Hodayot,* of which he may have been the author (1QH 2.13; 4.27–29; 7.27; 14.8).[45] A special revelation of the meaning of the Torah that has been granted to the community is mentioned in 1QS 5.8–10 (trans. Knibb):[46]

He [initiants] shall undertake by a binding oath to return to the law of Moses with all his heart and soul, following all that he has commanded, and in accordance with all that has been revealed from it (לכול הנגלה ממנה) to the sons of Zadok, the priests who keep the covenant and seek his will, and to the multitude of the men of their covenant who together willingly offer themselves for his truth and to walk according to his will.

This is one of several statements in 1 QS reflecting the belief that the community's interpretation of Scripture was given by revelation (1QS 1.9; 8.15; 9.13).[47] While it is true that the verb גלה in the Dead Sea Scrolls is used only of the community's

---

[42] This implies that the interpretations in the *pesharim* had their origin in some form of communal study of the Scriptures at which the Teacher of Righteousness presided. Some suggestions regarding the *Sitz im Leben* of the *pesharim* have been made by J. T. Milik, "Fragments d'un midrash de Michée dans les manuscrits de Qumran", *RB* 59 (1952), 418: during the daily watch when a group probably read and interpreted a biblical book verse by verse (cf. 1QS 6.6–8). Elsewhere Milik suggested that the commentaries might be linked to interpretations of Scripture presented during community meetings for worship (*Ten Years of Discovery in the Wilderness of Judaea* [trans. J. Strugnell; London: SCM Press, 1959] 41).

[43] Thus the claim by F. García Martínez ("El pesher: Interpretación profética de la Escritura", *Salmanticensis* 26 [1979], 125–39), that the chief distinction between pesharim and midrashim is that the former claims to be divinely revealed, must be treated with caution. Similarly, M. Horgan has called them "revealed interpretations of revealed mysteries concerning history" ("The Bible Explained [Prophecies]", 251).

[44] For parallels to this idiom, see G. von Rad, "Die Nehemia-Denkschrift", *ZAW* 76 (1964), 176–87.

[45] The identification of the Teacher of Righteousness as the author of the *Hodayot* is disputed by D. Dombkowski Hopkins, "The Qumran Community and 1Q Hodayot: A Reassessment", *RevQ* 10 (1981), 323–64.

[46] M.A. Knibb, *The Qumran Community* (Cambridge: Cambridge University Press, 1987).

[47] Josephus claims that some Essenes profess to predict the future, an ability apparently

understanding of the Hebrew Bible, not of the Bible itself, the former was certainly presupposed.[48] The revelation granted to the community is the focus of 1QS 8.15 (trans. Knibb):

This (way) is the study of the law [which] he commanded through Moses, that they should act in accordance with all that has been revealed from time to time (ככול הנגלה עת בעת) and in accordance with what the prophets revealed by his holy spirit (גלו הנביאים ברוח קודשו).

The phrase ככול הנגלה עת בעת, "according to all that has been revealed from time to time", which occurs again in 1QS 9.13, suggests that the insight into the true meaning of Scripture was not based on a single revelation, but rather on a continuing series of revelatory insights. Further, while the Holy Spirit is never mentioned in connection with the charismatic interpretation of Scripture, it is mentioned here as the instrument of prophetic revelation. There is no indication, however, that the revealed interpretation of Scripture, whether disclosed to the Teacher of Righteousness or to the "sons of Zadok" or perhaps other members of the community, is linked to particular exegetical techniques.[49]

4. Josephus and Charismatic Exegesis

Josephus preserves important information about prophecy in Judaism during the Hellenistic and Roman periods.[50] He may have been particularly interested in the subject because he considered himself as a prophet, though perhaps not equal in status or authority with the biblical prophets.[51] Understandably sensitive about his surrender to the Romans, he presents a brief apology for his actions in *War* 3.351–54 (trans. Thackeray in LCL):

---

based on their study of the Hebrew Bible, but he does not claim that their predictions are inspired *(War* 2.159).

48 *Contra* H.-J. Zobel, *TDOT,* 2.487.

49 This is the view of G. J. Brooke, but it is based only on inference: "Inspiration, if any, does not lie in the result of the exegesis as such, in its content, but rather in the ability of any member of the community and especially the Teacher of Righteousness to interpret scripture through the correct application of exegetical techniques" *(Exegesis at Qumran,* 43–44). E. Slamovic has also argued that rabbinic methods of exegesis are present in Qumran literature in "Toward an Understanding of the Exegesis in the Dead Sea Scrolls", *RevQ* 7 (1969–71), 3–15.

50 Despite the rabbinic view that prophecy had ceased with the activity of Haggai, Zechariah and Malachi, early Judaism was extremely diverse, and there is abundant evidence to suggest that prophecy continued in altered forms to the end of the second temple period; see Aune, *Prophecy in Early Christianity,* 103–106, R.A. Horsley, "Popular Prophetic Movements at the Time of Jesus. Their Principal Features and Social Origins", *JSNT* 26 (1986), 3–27, and J.-C. Ingelaere, "L'inspiration prophétique dans le Judaïsme: le témoignage de Flavius Josèphe", *ETR* 62 (1987), 237–45.

51 J.L. Blenkinsopp, "Prophecy and Priesthood in Josephus", *JJS* 25 (1974), 239–62, and L.H. Feldman, "Prophets and Prophecy in Josephus", in D.J. Lull (ed.), *SBLSP 1988* (Atlanta: Scholars Press, 1988) 424–41.

He [Josephus] was an interpreter of dreams (περὶ κρίσεις ὀνείρων) and skilled in divining the meaning of ambiguous utterances of the Deity (τὰ ἀμφιβόλως ὑπὸ τοῦ θείου λεγόμενα); a priest himself and of priestly descent, he was not ignorant of the prophecies in the sacred books. At that hour he was inspired (ἔνθους γενόμενος) to read their meaning, and, recalling the dreadful images of his recent dreams, he offered up a silent prayer to God. "Since it pleases thee", so it ran, "who didst create the Jewish nation, to break thy work, since fortune has wholly passed to the Romans, and since thou hast made choice of my spirit to announce the things that are to come (τὰ μέλλοντα εἰπεῖν), I willingly surrender to the Romans and consent to live; but I take thee to witness that I go, not as a traitor, but as thy minister."

This text suggests a number of important features of Josephus' view of prophecy:[52] 1. the revelatory value of some dreams (a universal belief in the ancient world), 2. revelation can be ambiguous, 3. the possible link between priesthood and prophecy, 4. the importance of a knowledge of biblical prophecy, 5. inspiration enables an interpreter to understand dreams and prophecies correctly. The passage is particularly important because of the parallel between the interpretation of dreams and the interpretation of Scripture, a parallel which a number of scholars have recognized between the OT tradition of dream interpretation and the terminology of the Qumran pesharim (see below). Though the language of inspiration is Hellenistic (e.g. the term ἔνθεος), it is quite clear that Josephus claims, perhaps because of his priestly descent, that his understanding of the true meaning of both dreams and Scriptures was based on divine insight,[53] like that of Joseph or Daniel of old.

Martin Hengel, who holds that the charismatic interpretation of Scripture was characteristic of prophecy in the Judaism of the Hellenistic and Roman periods, has argued that Zealot prophecy during the first century CE (like prophecy in early Judaism generally) had three characteristics: 1. the charismatic interpretation of Scripture, 2. the eschatological possession of the Spirit, and 3. a historical and political orientation.[54] Hengel refers to Josephus *War* 6.312–13 (trans. LCL):[55]

But what more than all else incited them to war was an ambiguous oracle (χρησμὸς ἀμφίβολος), likewise found in their sacred scriptures (ἐν τοῖς ἱεροῖς εὑρημένος γράμμασιν), to the effect that at that time one from their country would become ruler of the world. This they understood to mean someone of their own race, and many of their wise men (πολλοὶ τῶν σοφῶν) went astray in their interpretation of it.

---

52 Ingelaere, "L'inspiration prophétique", 240.

53 When he speaks of the inspiration of the biblical prophets, he uses the phrase ἡ ἐπίπνοιαν ἡ ἀπὸ τοῦ θεοῦ (*Apion* 1.37), but he does use the term ἔνθεος of Saul when he prophesies (*Ant.* 6.56), and of Elijah (*Ant.* 8.346); cf. Feldman, "Prophets and Prophecy", 436.

54 Hengel, *Zealots*, 233–45.

55 Hengel, *Zealots,* 237. The same ambiguous prophecy is referred to in Tacitus *Hist.* 5.13 and Suetonius *Ves.* 4.5.

While this enigmatic passage suggests that, in Josephus's view, scholars called σοφοί, "sages", occupied themselves with the interpretation of this oracle. Despite the educated guesses of Hengel and others,[56] very little more can be said with any certainty about this passage, which is probably not less ambiguous than the oracle to which it refers. There is no clear indication that this oracle was circulated in Zealot circles. There is no clear indication that tile "ambiguous oracle" referred to Num. 24.17 (or even Dan. 7.13–14). Nor is there any evidence that a "prophetic charism" was involved in the interpretation of this oracle.

While little can be said about charismatic exegesis in Zealot circles, it appears clear that Josephus himself was a charismatic exegete in the sense that he regarded his ability to understand and interpret both revelatory dreams and Scripture as the product of divine enlightenment.

5. "Charismatic Exegesis" in Other Phases of Early Judaism

Recent scholarship has made it increasingly clear that a long process of explanation and adaptation is already reflected in the Hebrew Bible in the form of intracanonical interpretations that have become part of the biblical text itself.[57] One of the central convictions that permeated early Judaism was that the sacred texts of the past have a direct bearing on the present.[58] This conviction is reflected in the various literary genres in which various types of biblical interpretation find expression.

In many respects the Septuagint, the Old Greek translations of the Hebrew Bible (with additions from various sources), is also a subtle interpretative rendition of the Hebrew text.[59] Sometimes the additions to the Hebrew text are not so subtle, as in the extensive additions to Esther and Daniel found only in Old Greek translations.[60] Since this interpretative translation is coextensive with the biblical text itself, the "claim" for the divine inspiration and authority of this complex collection of exegetical subtleties is implied rather than expressed. One result of this implicit claim is the canonical status of the Septuagint in Eastern Orthodoxy. By the late second century BCE, the Septuagint was provided with

[56] This passage is discussed in some detail by Hengel, *Zealots,* 236–40.

[57] Bloch, "Midrash", col. 1270; Michael Fishbane, "Revelation and Tradition: Aspects of Inner-Biblical Exegesis", *JBL* 99 (1980), 343–61, *idem, Biblical Interpretation in Ancient Israel* (Oxford: Clarendon Press, 1985).

[58] Kugel and Greer, *Early Biblical Interpretation,* 38.

[59] E. Tov, "Die griechischen Bibel übersetzungen", in Wolfgang Haase and Hildegard Temporini (eds.), *ANRW* 2.II.20.1 (Berlin: Walter de Gruyter, 1987) 143–45, 147–51; S. Jellicoe, *The Septuagint in Modern Study* (Oxford: Clarendon Press, 1968) 318–24.

[60] Septuagint manuscripts often differ among themselves; the version of Tobit found in codex Sinaiticus (א), for example, is more paraphrastic than the versions of Tobit in the codices Alexandrinus (A) and Vaticanus (B).

a legend supporting its divine origin in the letter of Aristeas.[61] Similarly, the Targums are presented as the biblical text, yet they have a paraphrastic character resulting from the amplification of the Hebrew text, frequently including traditions with a popular character.[62] The Targums vary in the degree to which they amplify the underlying text; even the Targum Onqelos, which sticks closer to the Hebrew text than the various fragmentary Palestinian Targums, includes material not found in the underlying text.[63] Targums, then, must also be categorized as interpretations that present themselves as having an implicitly inspired character.

One of the techniques of apocalyptic writing often involved the attribution of predictions about the recent past, as well as the present and future, to ancient Israelite sages or angelic revealers. That is, both the visions and interpretations provided by supernatural revealers are part of a complementary revelatory process. Apocalypses use biblical texts in a complex variety of ways. In the partial texts of some apocalypses, prophetic books of the Jewish Scriptures are used as structural models, thereby legitimating new elements by dressing them in familiar garments.[64] Apocalypses also make frequent use of the "anthological style" in which Scripture is echoed in allusions placed within an interpretative framework, not formally quoted and matched with a separate commentary.[65] Apocalypses virtually *never* present formal interpretations of biblical texts separated from the text itself. The book of *Jubilees,* written during the second century BCE, is essentially a revised version of Genesis 1–Exodus 14, including many additions and deletions, all presented as a revelation transmitted to Moses by an angel on Mount Sinai *(Jub.* 1.1–6, 26–29). This retelling includes many features that are not found in the Pentateuch itself, but which are free compositions by the author.[66] Two examples are the elaborate explanation of why God had called Abraham

61 The author of the *Epistle of Aristeas* clearly regarded the Septuagint translators as inspired; see the recent arguments of Orlinsky, "The Septuagint and its Hebrew Text", II, 542–48; sec also D. Georgi, *The Opponents of Paul in Second Corinthians* (Philadelphia: Fortress Press, 1986) 110–11. The inspiration of the Septuagint translators is emphasized in Philo *(Vit. Mos.* 2.37, 40; he is familiar with *Epistle of Aristeas),* who claims that the translators of the Septuagint wrote "as though divinely inspired" (καθάπερ ἐνθουσιῶντες), and were not simply translators but hierophants and prophets (οὐχ ἑρμηνέας ἐκείνους ἀλλ' ἱεροφάντας καὶ προφήτας).

62 R. Le Déaut. *The Message of the New Testament and the Aramaic Bible (Targum)* (Rome: Biblical Institute Press, 1982) 13–15.

63 J.W. Bowker, "Haggadah in the Targum Onqelos", *JSS* 12 (1967), 51.65.

64 See J.-P. Ruiz, *Ezekiel in the Apocalypse: The Transformation of Prophetic Language in Revelation 16, 17–19, 10* (Frankfurt am Main: Peter Lang, 1989).

65 D.W. Suter *(Tradition and Composition in the Parables of Enoch* [SBLDS, 47; Missoula, MT: Scholars Press, 1979]) analyzes the "midrashic" use of Isa. 24.17–23 in *1 En.* 54.1–56.4 and 64.1–68.1. Suter uses the term midrash incorrectly, however, for no distinction is made in *1 Enoch* 37–71 between text and interpretation, and such a distinction is a *sine qua non* of midrash.

66 J.C. Endres has identified 25 pericopes freely composed by the author in *Jub.* 19–45 *(Biblical Interpretation in the Book of Jubilees* [CBQMS, 18; Washington. DC: Catholic Biblical Association of America, 1987] 197–98).

(*Jub.* 11.14–12.21), and the explanation of why God decided to test Abraham by ordering him to sacrifice his son Isaac (*Jub.* 17.15–18). The fact that the author altered the text in so many ways makes it obvious that his conception of "sacred text" was not identical with the modern conception of a sacred text as a "fixed text." It is clear that the author is consciously presented his work as an inspired interpretation of much of the narrative portion of the Pentateuch.[67]

The Temple Scroll (11QTemple), dating to the second century BCE, presents itself as a book of authoritative religious law which, like the five books of the Pentateuch, was regarded as having been given by God to Moses on Mount Sinai.[68] One of the more striking features of 11QTemple is the frequent introduction of first-person speeches attributed to God, thereby making the entire composition the revealed word of God.[69] The creation of the Temple Scroll is virtually identical to that postulated for the creation of the Torah itself.[70]

This brief consideration of the Septuagint, the Targumim and several pseudepigraphic compositions emanating from early Judaism (apocalypses, *Jubilees,* the Temple Scroll) has complicated the conventional conceptions of "charismatic exegesis." All of these compositions are vehicles for presenting various forms of biblical interpretation. The Septuagint and the Targumim blend exegetical traditions with the biblical text in such a way that the new amalgam implicitly presents itself as Scripture. *Jubilees* and 11QTemple are two of many examples of "Rewritten Scripture" in early Judaism, yet differ from the Septuagint and the Targumim only in the more extensive degree to which nonbiblical traditions are assimilated to a new presentation of the biblical text. It is not possible to determine whether these representations of biblical texts were intended by their unknown authors to supplement or to replace their canonical counterparts. Of the genres discussed in this section, certainly the apocalypses present interpretative traditions that make no pretense of being identified with portions of the biblical canon. Here the technique is quite different. Exegetical traditions (along with a pastiche of various types of cosmological and eschatological lore) are presented as divine revelation communicated to a seer by a supernatural revealer. All of these forms of biblical interpretation legitimate biblical interpretation either by linking it to texts already recognized as sacred, or by claiming fresh revelations.

---

67 Kugel and Greer, *Early Biblical Interpretation,* 60–61.

68 Y. Yadin, "Is the Temple Scroll a Sectarian Document?", in G. M. Tucker and D. A. Knight (eds.), *Humanizing America's Iconic Book: SBL Centennial Addresses 1980* (Chico, CA: Scholars Press, 1982) 153–69.

69 H.-A. Mink has characterized the Temple Scroll as "pseudepigraphic halakah" in "The Use of Scripture in the Temple Scroll and the Status of the Scroll as Law", *SJOT* 1 (1987), 20–50.

70 A. M. Wilson and L. Wills, "Literary Sources of the *Temple Scroll*", *HTR* 75 (1982), 275–88; G. Brin, "Concerning Some of the Uses of the Bible in the Temple Scroll", *RevQ* 12 (1987), 519–28.

6. Charismatic Exegesis in Early Christianity

The interpretation of the Jewish Scriptures was one of the central preoccupations of early Christianity. The focus of this interpretative activity was largely christological, that is, it centered on the interpretation of eschatological prophecies that demonstrated that Jesus was the Messiah and that his life, death and return were all anticipated in Scripture.[71] This focus on the *eschatological* significance of the Old Testament has close similarities with the concerns of early Judaism, particularly the Qumran Community. Yet there is no real parallel in early Christianity to the verse-by-verse commentary found in the Qumran pesharim.[72] Indeed, until at least the mid-second century CE, there is no evidence to suggest that early Christians adopted the genre of the verse-by-verse commentary on sacred books.[73] At most, one finds examples of what was designated above as "isolated pesharim" in both narrative and expository discourse in the New Testament, in which an Old Testament passage and its interpretation are juxtaposed but not blended. An example from narrative discourse is the series of Old Testament quotations with the distinctive ἵνα/ὅπως πληρωθῇ or πληρώθη formulas found at the conclusion of narrative episodes in Matthew (1:22; 2:15, 17, 23; 4:14; 8:17; 12:17; 13:35; 21:4; 27:9).[74] Examples of the use of Old Testament quotations in expository discourse are found throughout the genuine Pauline letters, though *only* in the so-called *Hauptbriefe,* with the greatest concentration in Romans.[75]

Christians believed, as did the Judaism from which they emerged, that because they were the people of God they had received special wisdom and insight from God (1 Cor 1:18–31; Eph 1:9; *Barn.* 5:3; Ignatius *Eph.* 14:1; Polycarp *Phil.* 12:1).

---

71 Some of the more important treatments of this subject include C.H. Dodd, *According to the Scriptures: The Sub-Structure of New Testament Theology* (London: James Nisbet, 1952); K. Stendahl, *The School of St Matthew and its Use of the Old Testament* (Philadelphia: Fortress Press, 1968 [1954]); B. Lindars, *New Testament Apologetic: The Doctrinal Significance of Old Testament Quotations* (London: SCM Press, 1961); D. Juel, *Messianic Exegesis: Christological Interpretation of the Old Testament in Early Christianity* (Philadelphia: Fortress Press, 1988).

72 J.J. Collins, "Prophecy and Fulfillment in the Qumran Scrolls", *JETS* 30 (1987), 267–78.

73 The first Christian known to comment on an entire biblical book was Heracleon, a Valentinian Gnostic whose activity was centered at Rome, ca. 170 CE. Fifty-one fragments of his comments on the gospels are preserved, largely in Clement of Alexandria, *Ecl.* 25.1 and *Strom.* 4.71–72, and Origen, *Comm. in Joh.* 13 (trans. in Werner Foerster, *Gnosis: A Selection of Gnostic Texts* [Oxford: Clarendon Press, 1972] I, 162–83). Earlier (ca. 160 BCE), the Valentinian Ptolemaeus had commented on the prologue to the Gospel of John (fragments in Irenaeus, *Adv. haer.* 1.8.5).

74 Stendahl, *The School of St Matthew*, 194–202 (where the similarities between Qumran pesher methods and Matthaean formula quotations are emphasized). Nowhere does Stendahl find it useful to apply terms like "charismatic exegesis" to early Christian biblical interpretation.

75 E.E. Ellis, *Paul's Use of the Old Testament* (Grand Rapids, MI: Eerdmans, 1957). On 139–47, Ellis argues for the similarity between "midrash pesher" (an interpretative reshaping of the text from an apocalyptic perspective) and Paul's exegetical technique.

This special insight was often attributed to the revelatory influence of the Spirit of God, believed to be present as the eschatological gift of God in the midst of the believing community (1 Cor 2:6–16; 1 Jn 2:20, 27).[76]

Various phases of early Christianity understood this gift of divine insight in very particular ways. The Johannine community, for example, was convinced the Spirit enabled them to understand the true meaning of the words of Jesus (Jn 14:26; 16:12–15; cf. 2:22; 12:16).[77] Here "charismatic exegesis" focuses on the oral transmission of Jesus traditions, presumably to legitimate the particular understanding of that tradition cherished by the Johannine church. For Paul and the author of Luke-Acts, this supernatural insight could be applied to the Old Testament (2 Cor 3:14–18; Lk 24:45).[78] In 1 Cor 2:6–16,[79] Paul claimed that the Spirit of God enabled Christians to understand the secret and hidden wisdom of God (i. e., the gospel of Jesus Christ) which had been concealed for ages but was now revealed to those who had received the Spirit. The notion of a "mystery of God hidden for ages but now revealed" has been designated the "revelation schema",[80] and occurs with some frequency in Pauline and Deutero-Pauline literature (Col 1:26–27; Eph 3:5, 9–10; Rom 16:25–26; cf. 2 Tim 1:9–10; Tit 1:2–3; 1 Pet 1:20). This "revelation schema" is specifically linked to the Christian understanding of the OT in Rom 16:25 (NRSV):

> Now to God who is able to strengthen you according to my gospel and the proclamation of Jesus Christ, according to the revelation of the mystery (ἀποκάλυψιν μυστηρίου) that was kept secret for long ages but is now disclosed (φανερωθέντος), and through the prophetic writings is made known to all the Gentiles.

Here the Greek term translated "disclosed" is in the passive voice, which functions here as a *passivum divinum,* that is, as a circumlocution used to avoid mentioning God as subject of a finite verb,[81] and can therefore be translated "God has disclosed." The widespread use of the "revelation schema", with its hidden-revealed dialectic, suggests that early Christians perceived that their

---

[76] See D. E. Aune, "The Presence of God in the Community: The Eucharist in its Early Christian Cultic Context", *SJT* 29 (1976), 451–59.

[77] M. E. Boring, "The Influence of Christian Prophecy on the Johannine Portrayal of the Paraclete and Jesus," *NTS* 25 (1978), 113–23.

[78] Cerfaux, "L'exégèse de l'Ancien Testament", 138.

[79] P. Stuhlmacher, "The Hermeneutical Significance of 1 Cor. 2:6–16", in G. F. Hawthorne (ed.), *Tradition and Interpretation in the New Testament: Essays in honor of E. Earle Ellis* (Grand Rapids, MI: Eerdmans; Tübingen: Mohr Siebeck, 1987) 328–47; see also K. O. Sandnes, "'*Paul – One of the Prophets?' A Contribution to the Apostle's Self-Understanding*" (Stavanger: Sandnes, 1987) 79–119 (now published in Tübingen: Mohr Siebeck, 1990).

[80] D. Lührmann, *Die Offenbarungsverständnis des Paulus und in paulinischen Gemeinden* (Neukirchen-Vluyn: Neukirchener Verlag, 1965) 113–17.

[81] J. Jeremias, *Neutestamentliche Theologie.* I. *Die Verkündigung Jesu* (Gütersloh: Gerd Mohn, 1971) 20–24. In the Targumim the passive voice is frequently used to replace the active voice when God is the subject of verbs in the Hebrew text (cf. *Targ. Jer.* 3.8; 8.4; 11.20; 16.17).

understanding of the christological significance of the Old Testament was radically different from Judaism. It is further likely, though scarcely demonstrable, that early Christian biblical interpreters shared the view that their understanding of the Old Testament was, in a general sense, the product of divine enlightenment. To go beyond this and to claim that early Christian interpreters considered themselves divinely inspired is to exceed the evidence.

The term "Christian prophet", however, is ambiguous, for it can refer to a role played by particular individuals, perhaps even an office (Acts 13:1–3; 1 Cor 12:10), but can also refer to those who prophesy, whether just once, a few times, or regularly (1 Cor 14:1). Gerhard Dautzenberg has demonstrated the extent to which prophecy in early Judaism and early Christianity was, at least in part, an *interpretative* phenomenon.[82] Glossolalia, clearly a type of prophetic activity, was (at least occasionally) subject to another type of prophetic gift, the ἑρμενεία γλωσσῶν, "*interpretation* of tongues" (1 Cor 12:10; 14:27–28). Similarly, prophetic speech was also subject to interpretation (1 Cor 14:29; perhaps to be identified with the gift of διακρίσεις πνευμάτων, mentioned in 1 Cor 12:10).[83]

One important issue to consider is whether or not Christian prophets were charismatic interpreters of Scripture.[84] The connection between prophets and Old Testament interpretation is often argued in the following way. 1. Prophecy played an important role in paraenesis, that is, moral exhortation, in early Christianity (Acts 4:36; 9:27; 13:15; 15:32; 1 Cor 12:7; 14:3).[85] 2. Further, exhortation is clearly associated with the exegesis of Scripture in Rom 15:4: "For whatever was written in former days was written for our instruction, so that by steadfastness and by the encouragement (παρακλήσεως) of the Scriptures we might have hope." 3. One could therefore conclude with E. Earle Ellis that "The interpretation of Scripture was indeed regarded, under certain conditions, as prophetic

---

[82] Dautzenberg, *Urchristliche Prophetie,* 43–121, 122–48.

[83] Dautzenberg, *Urchristliche Prophetie,* 122–48; W.A. Grudem, *The Gift of Prophecy in 1 Corinthians* (Washington, DC: University Press of America, 1982) 263–88 (an attempt to refute Dautzenberg's view that διακρίσεις πνευμάτων in 1 Cor 12:10 is another way of describing the διακρίνειν of prophetic speech in 1 Cor 14:29); Aune, *Prophecy in Early Christianity,* 217–29 (in which Dautzenberg's views are qualified).

[84] Scholars who have emphasized the role of Christian prophets as interpreters of Scripture include E.G. Selwyn, *The First Epistle of St Peter* (London: Macmillan, 1946) 134; L. Gaston, *No Stone on Another* (NovTSup, 23; Leiden: E.J. Brill, 1970) 50–51; É. Cothenet, "Les prophètes chrétiens comme exégètes charismatiques de l'Ecriture", in J. Panagopoulos (ed.), *Prophetic Vocation in the New Testament and Today* (NovTSup, 45; Leiden: E.J. Brill, 1977) 77–107; reprinted with some changes in É. Cothenet. *Exégèse et Liturgie* (Lectio Divina, 133; Paris: Les Editions du Cerf, 1988) 63–96; E.E. Ellis, "The Role of the Christian Prophet in Acts", *Prophecy and Hermeneutic in Early Christianity* (Grand Rapids: Eerdmans, 1978) 137–38; W.S. Hall, *Paul as a Christian Prophet in his Interpretation of the Old Testament in Romans 9–11* (ThD dissertation, Lutheran School of Theology at Chicago; Ann Arbor: University Microfilms, 1982).

[85] Ellis, *Prophecy and Hermeneutic,* 130–38.

activity."[86] Yet the evidence he adduces is inadequate to establish his thesis. The flaws in this line of reasoning are that paraenesis was never the exclusive province of either prophecy or biblical interpretation in the early church, and that prophets are never explicitly linked to the task of biblical interpretation. There is little evidence to substantiate the view that one of the major preoccupations of Christian prophets was the inspired exegesis of the Old Testament.

Since Paul probably regarded himself as a Christian prophet,[87] and frequently interprets the Old Testament in his main letters, it is appropriate to ask whether or not he should be regarded as a charismatic exegete. Winfield Hall has focused on this problem. While many scholars have used the term "charismatic exegesis" in vague ways, Hall has proposed that it has three characteristics that reflect the form, content and function of this inspired exegetical activity:[88] 1. the use of formulas such as "the Lord says" or "that it might be fulfilled", which suggest that the interpreter is emphasizing the inspiration of the oracle quoted (form), 2. the tendentious alteration of the text of Scripture to fit the situation of the interpreter (content), and 3. the OT prophecy is regarded by the interpreter as directly applicable to his or her own situation (function). Since Hall does not mention the *sine qua non* of charismatic exegesis, that is, the explicit or implicit claim that the interpreter or the interpretation has been divinely revealed, his three criteria are inadequate. Hall attempted to demonstrate that Paul was a charismatic exegete through a careful analysis of the way in which he interprets the Old Testament in Romans 9–11. In many ways, Romans 9–11 is ideally suited for such a task: 1. It is the single passage in the Pauline letters with the highest concentration of OT quotations and allusions. 2. It is a unit of text that concludes in Rom 11:33–36 with a literary form consisting of a prayer of praise and thanksgiving following a divine revelation.[89] 3. It occurs within a composition that concludes with a "revelation schema" in Rom 16:25 (quoted above), which links the hidden-revealed dialectic with the Christian interpretation of the Old Testament. Unfortunately, however, since the author's three characteristics of inspired exegesis apply to much of early Jewish and early Christian biblical interpretation and are incapable of distinguishing "charismatic exegesis" from any other form of interpretative activity, his informative discussion of Romans 9–11 falls short of demonstrating that Paul regarded himself as a charismatic exegete. Yet, in light of Paul's overall hermeneutic perspective (1 Cor 2:6–16), and with specific reference to his articulation of the "revelation schema" in Rom 16:25, and the role of Rom 11:33–36 as a prayer of thanksgiving following a divine revelation,

[86] Ellis, *Prophecy and Hermeneutic*, 138.

[87] Aune, *Prophecy in Early Christianity*, 28–62. Most recently, see Sandnes, *Paul*.

[88] Hall, *Paul as a Christian Prophet*, 133–48.

[89] Examples of this literary form: 2 Chron. 20:18–19; Dan 2:20–23; *1 En.* 90:40; *4 Ezra* 13:57–58; *2 Bar.* 75:1–8; Josephus, *War* 3:354; *Corpus Hermeticum* 1:31–32; Mt. 11:25–27 (and par. Lk 10:21–22); Hermas, *Vis.* 2.1.1–2.

it is appropriate to use the term "charismatic exegesis" of Paul's interpretation of the Old Testament. However, "charismatic exegesis" here is not used in the sense of the immediate inspiration of the interpreter, but rather with the more general meaning that the Christian community's insights into the christological significance of the Old Testament is the product of divine enlightenment.

6. Conclusion

The foregoing discussion suggests that "charismatic exegesis" is an extremely complex phenomenon which (at least for early Judaism and early Christianity) appears to be rooted in the belief that the Torah can only be properly understood if God himself grants divine insight to his people. Charismatic exegesis does not consist of a particular type of interpretation identifiable on the basis of its distinctive form, content or function. Rather, charismatic exegesis is essentially a *hermeneutical ideology* that provides divine legitimation for a particular understanding of a sacred text which is shared with others who understand the text differently. Yet charismatic exegesis must be understood in an even broader and more comprehensive way, since the phenomenon of "prophecy by interpretation" is not found only in early Judaism and early Christianity but is more widespread and can apparently occur under certain conditions in other religions and cultures.[90]

In conclusion let me suggest that "charismatic exegesis", or "revealed interpretation", exhibits the following morphological features: 1. it is a procedure applied to dreams, visions, oral communications or relatively stable and authori-

---

[90] The interpretative procedures of the Qumran *pesharim*, for example, are closely paralleled in the late third-century BCE *Egyptian Demotic Chronicle,* or the "Patriotic Oracles with Interpretation" (J. Bergman. "Introductory Remarks on Apocalypticism in Egypt", in D. Hellholm [ed.], *Apocalypticism in the Mediterranean World and the Near East* [Tübingen: Mohr Siebeck, 1983] 54–55); cf. F. Daumas, "Littérature prophétique et exégétique égyptienne et commentaries esséniens", in M. Jourjon *et al.* (eds.), *À la recontre de Dieu: Mémorial A. Gélin* (Le Puy: Editions Xavier Mappus, 1961) 203–211; J.J. Collins, "Jewish Apocalyptic against its Hellenistic Near Eastern Environment", *BASOR* 220 (1975), 27–36. An example of the use of *lemmata* followed by an explanation of the text may be taken from the *Demotic Chronicle*, col. 3, 11. 1–2 (based on W. Spiegelberg, *Die sogennante Demotische Chronik* [Leipzig: J.C. Hinrichs, 1914] 16):

> "Rejoice, then, Prophet of Harsaphes!"
> This means: The Prophet of Harsaphes rejoices concerning the Greeks, for they became rulers in Hnês.
> "May he open the furnaces! I have given him the cattle"–
> This means: The ruler, who will come, opens [the doors] of the temple and allows sacrifices to again be brought to the gods.

For an examination of the parallels between the Qumran *pesharim* and the Gnostic *Pistis Sophia,* see J. Carmignac, "Le genre littéraire du 'pesher' dans la Pistis-Sophia", *RevQ* 4 (1963–64), 497–522.

tative written texts that are regarded as having a divine origin. 2. These dreams, messages or texts are regarded as puzzling or enigmatic, as indeed revelatory communications are frequently held to be,[91] and therefore they stand in need of interpretation, clarification, updating and actualization.[92] 3. This interpretation can be presented orally, or fused with the text through revision (i. e. the incorporation of interpolations into the text during the process of recopying), or can be kept separated from the text itself. 4. This explication often exhibits a marked sectarian orientation, and the thrust of the interpolated or interpreted text serves to reinforce or legitimate the group's particular view of the present or program for the future.[93] 5. The interpretation is regarded as having a divine origin, either through the immediate inspiration of the interpreter, the consciousness of the interpreter that he or she participates in a tradition of revealed interpretation, or through the attribution of the interpretation ultimately to supernatural beings or God himself. 6. Since the interpretation has a divine origin, it has the potential of rivaling the original message of the text in authority, though it usually continues to be regarded as qualitatively subordinate to the original revelatory communication.

---

[91] G. van der Leeuw, *Religion in Essence and Manifestation* (2 vols.; trans. J. E. Turner; New York: Harper & Row. 1963) 2:564–65.

[92] J. Z. Smith, "Wisdom and Apocalyptic", *Map is not Territory: Studies in the History of Religions* (SJLA, 23; Leiden: E. J. Brill, 1978) 74–85. An example is found in Dan 9:2, 24–26, in which Jeremiah's prophecy that the exile would last seventy years (Jer 25:11–12; 29:10) is expanded to mean 70 weeks of years, i. e., 490 years, since the author lived in the second, rather than the sixth, century BCE; sec P. Grelot, "Soixante-dix semaines d'années", *Bib* 50 (1969), 169–86.

[93] Kugel and Greer, *Early Biblical Interpretation,* 37–39.

Christian Prophecy and the Messianic Status of Jesus

1. The Problem

Jesus of Nazareth was regarded by his followers as the Messiah of Jewish eschatological expectation, if not during his lifetime, then certainly within a very short interval after his crucifixion and resurrection.[1] Jesus was executed for treason, after all, for pretending to be "the King of the Jews" (Mk 15:26). One of the first and most significant stages in the development of the Christology of earliest Palestinian Christianity was the conviction that through his resurrection, understood as his exaltation or enthronement at the right hand of God,[2] Jesus had become both Lord (Aram.: *mar;* Gk.: *kyrios*) and Messiah (*Christos*).[3] Ps 110:1, the single OT passage most quoted and alluded to in the NT, played a key role in facilitating such a belief,[4] though it is also probable that 2 Sam 7:12–14 may have played an even more significant role in the development of the so-called two-stage christology, from son of David to son of God (Rom 1:3–4).[5]

In the seven undoubtedly genuine letters of Paul, the earliest extant Christian literature, the term *Christos* occurs 266 times. It is used in two primary ways: as a proper name for Jesus and as a name for a specific Messiah, Jesus (cf. Rom

---

[1] This statement is intentionally formulated in such a way that the problem of the messianic consciousness of Jesus is avoided.

[2] B. Lindars, *New Testament Apologetic* (Philadelphia: Westminster Press, 1961) 42; W. O. Walker, "Christian Origins and Resurrection Faith," *JR* 52 (1972) 44.

[3] Acts 2:32–36, 13:33; Rom 1:3–4; Phil 2:9–11; cf. Heb 1:3–13; cf. J. H. Hayes, "The Resurrection as Enthronement and the Earliest Church Christology," *Int* 12 (1968) 333–45; R. H. Fuller, *Foundations* of *New Testament Christology* (New York: Scribner's 1965) 184–86.

[4] See the important study with an extensive bibliography by D. M. Hay, *Glory at the Right Hand: Psalm* 110 *in Early Christianity* (Nashville: Abingdon, 1973). For an updated bibliography, see T. Callan, "Ps 110:1 and the Origin of the Expectation That Jesus Will Come Again," *CBQ* 44 (1982) 625, n. 11. There are five quotations of portions of Ps 110 in the NT (Mk 12:36 = Mt 22:44 = Lk 20:42–43; Acts 2:34–35; Heb 1:13), two quotations in the Apostolic Fathers (*1Clem* 36:5; Barn. 12:10), and nineteen allusions to Ps 110:1 in the NT (Mk 14:62 = Mt 26:64 = Lk 22:69; Mk 16:19; Acts 2:33; 5:31; 7:55, 56; Rom 8:34; 1 Cor 15:25; Eph 1:20, 2:6; Col 3:1; Heb 1:3, 8:1, 10:12–13, 12:2; 1Pet 3:22; Rev 3:21).

[5] E. Schweizer, "Rom. 1:3 f. und der Gegensatz von Fleisch und Geist vor und bei Paulus," *Neotestamentica* (Zurich and Stuttgart: Zwingli Verlag, 1963) 180–89; D. C. Duling, "The Promises to David and Their Entrance into Christianity – Nailing Down a Likely Hypothesis," *NTS* 20 (1973–74) 70–77.

9:5). According to N.A. Dahl, *Christos* is *never* used in these letters as a general term but always as a designation for Jesus – it is *never* used as a predication of Jesus (e.g. "Jesus is the Christ"), is *never* accompanied by a genitive (e.g. "the Christ of God"), and the form "Jesus *the* Christ" is not found in the oldest text of the epistles.[6] The situation is virtually the same in the six disputed Pauline letters which were probably written during the generation following Paul's death (Ephesians, Colossians, 2 Thessalonians, 1 Timothy, 2 Timothy, Titus), in which the term *Christos* occurs 113 times, always as a proper name for Jesus. In the seven general epistles, *Christos* occurs 50 times and again is consistently used as a name for Jesus. In 1 John, however, *ho Christos* is used 2 times as a title predicated of Jesus. 1 John 2:22 speaks of those who deny "that Jesus is the Christ," and 1 John 5:1 mentions the benefits possessed by one "who believes that Jesus is the Christ."[7] *Christos* occurs 12 times in Hebrews, 3 times in the traditional form "Jesus Christ" (10:10; 13:8, 21), and 9 times alone, usually with the article, as designations for Jesus (3:6, 14; 5:5; 6:1; 9:11, 14, 24, 28; 11:26). In Revelation, an apocalypse in an epistolary framework, *Christos* occurs 7 times–3 times in the traditional formulation "Jesus Christ" (1:1, 2, 5), 2 times in the articular form "his [i.e. God's] Christ" as a title for Jesus (11:15, 12:10), and 2 times in the articular form as a name for Jesus (20:4, 6).[8] In the heterogeneous group of texts comprising the Apostolic Fathers, *Christos* occurs 213 times, usually as part of the compound name "Jesus Christ," once as a general designation for the Jewish Messiah (*Barn* 12:10 alluding to Mk 12:35–37 and par.), and just twice in the titular form "Jesus *the* Christ" (1 *Clem* 42:1, Ignatius *Eph* 18:2). In summary, the messiahship of Jesus is assumed in the NT epistolary literature, and with the exception of 1 John 2:22 and 5:1, little or no interest is shown in the problem of specifically demonstrating the messianic status of Jesus.

The situation is completely different in the Gospels and Acts, where the issue of the messianic status of Jesus is a matter of central concern. The term *Christos* is found 80 times in the gospels and Acts–16 times as a proper name for Jesus (e.g. Mk 1:1; John 1:17, 17:3) and 64 times as a title, either as a general designa-

---

[6] Dahl, "Die Messianität Jesu bei Paulus," *Studía Paulína in Honorem Johannís de Zwaan* (Haarlem: Erren F. Bohn, 1953) 83.

[7] R.E. Brown in *The Epistles of John* (AB 30 [Garden City: Doubletoy, 1983] 172) observes that in Christianity the titles Christ and Son of God were more than just messianic titles derived from Judaism but were used to express the divinity of Jesus. Therefore the problem reflected in 1John 2:22 and 5:1, in Brown's view, is that the "secessionists" apparently refused to identify the earthly, human Jesus with the divine Messiah, the Son of God (Brown, *Epistles of John,* 352). According to Brown, "the opponents so stress the divine principle in Jesus that the earthly career of the divine principle is neglected" *(The Community of the Beloved Disciple* [New York: Paulist Press, 1979] 112).

[8] M. de Jonge, "The Use of the Expression *ho Christos* in the Apocalypse of John," *L'Apocalypse johannique et l'Apocalyptique dans le Nouveau Testament,* ed. J. Lambrecht (Leuven: University Press, 1980) 267–81.

tion for the eschatological Davidic king,[9] or less frequently but more importantly as a title predicated of Jesus (Mk 8:29 = Mt 16:16 = Lk 9:20; Mk 14:61 = Mt 26:63 = Lk 22:67; John 9:22; 11:27; 20:31; Acts 5:42; 8:5; 9:22; 17:3b; 18:5, 28). Statements such as "Jesus is the Christ" (Acts 17:3b, John 11:27), or "Jesus is the Christ, the Son of God" (John 20:31) are often and correctly categorized as short creedal statements or confessions.

This brief survey of the use of the *Christos* designation in the NT highlights a problem. The earliest surviving Christian literature, the genuine letters of Paul (written over a fifteen-year period, 49–64 CE) do not suggest either directly or indirectly that the messianic status of Jesus was a matter of particular concern during Paul's career. In Acts, on the other hand, Paul is presented as arguing that Jesus is the Messiah (9:22; 17:2–3; 18:5, 28). The simplest (though not the most satisfying) explanation is that Paul expressed different concerns when addressing Christian congregations on the one hand and unconverted Jews on the other. On the whole, the Gospels and Acts, written during the generation following the death of Paul, show a vital concern with the problem of Jesus' messianic status. This is peculiar since one would expect that the period during which the issue of Jesus' messiahship would be most prominent and controversial would be the years immediately following the crucifixion and resurrection of Jesus, the period when Christianity was a group within early Judaism. Aside from the Gospels and Acts, the messianic status of Jesus does not come up for serious discussion again until second-century apologists, such as Justin Martyr, engage in Jewish-Christian dialogue. Why do the Gospels and Acts, written ca. 70–100 CE, exhibit a seemingly anachronistic concern with the problem of Jesus' messianic status?

2. The Proposal

Preoccupation with the ultimate religious significance of Jesus of Nazareth was not the only striking feature of early Palestinian Christianity. Christians consciously constituted an elect community living in the last days. They experienced the presence and power of the Spirit of God in their midst, externalized and verified through prophesying and miracles of healing. In addition to his messianic status, Jesus was also, perhaps alternatively, categorized as a prophet or even as the eschatological Mosaic prophet.[10] One significant aspect of the continuity

---

[9] Mt 2:4, 24:5; Mk 12:35 = Mt 22:42 = Lk 20:41; Mk 13:21 = Mt 24:23; Mk 14:61 = Mt 26:63 = Lk 22:67; Mk 15:32 = Lk 23:35; Lk 3:15; 4:41; 23:2, 39; 24:26, 46; John 1:20, 25; 3:28; 4:25, 29; 7:26, 27, 31, 41b, 42; 10:24; 12:34; Acts 2:31; 3:18, 17:3a.

[10] The evidence is summarized in D. E. Aune, *Prophecy* in *Early Christianity and the Ancient Mediterranean World* (Grand Rapids: Eerdmans, 1983) 153–57.

between the early community and Jesus was that both were reportedly filled with the Spirit of God.[11]

In this paper I wish to link the two topics of Jesus' messianic status and the prophetic character of early Christianity by posing a question of potentially great significance, though one which is very difficult to answer: Is there any evidence to suggest that the recognition of Jesus' messianic status (however defined) was legitimated by prophetic speech or prophetic visions by early Christians during the period ca. 30–50 CE?

The prophetic legitimation of the messianic status of Jesus is a possibility which coheres well with ancient Israelite kingship ideology, since there is abundant evidence in the OT to suggest that prophets played a significant role in the prophetic identification and anointing of prospective kings. Samuel anointed Saul (1Sam 10:1–8), and David (1Sam 16:1–3); Ahijah anointed Jeroboam I (1Kgs 11:29–39; 14:7); Jehu ben Hanani anointed Baasha (1Kgs 16:1–2); an unnamed prophet anointed Jehu (2Kgs 9:1–6). It is also likely that prophets participated in coronation ceremonies, perhaps declaring the new status of the king as son of God. Ps 2:7 and Ps 110:4 may have originated as prophetic oracles proclaiming the royal status and divine sonship of prospective kings.[12] During the late fifth century BCE, Sanballat and Tobiah accused Nehemiah of hiring prophets to declare "There is a king in Judah" (Neh 6:7). Josephus, who considered himself a clerical prophet,[13] reportedly announced to Vespasian that he was Caesar: "You are Caesar, Vespasian, and emperor, you and your son here" (Josephus *War* 3.400–2), a role also attributed to Yohanan ben Zakkai in rabbinic literature: "Behold, you are about to be appointed king" (ARN [Rec. A], 4.5; *b.Gitt* 56a–b).[14] Of the many popular messianic movements in Palestine from the death of Herod the Great in 4 BCE to the second Jewish revolt of 132–35 CE led by Simon Bar Kosiba,[15] it was only Bar Kosiba who apparently made an explicit messianic claim. This claim was publicly recognized and announced by Rabbi Akiba.[16] According to *y. Taʿan* 68d, "Again, when R. Akiba saw Bar Kosiba [Kokhba], he cried out, 'This is King Messiah,'" using the typical

[11] H. Windisch, "Jesus und der Geist nach synoptischer Überlieferung," *Studies in Early Christianity,* ed. S.J. Case (New York and London: The Century Companys, 1928) 209–36; C.K. Barrett, *The Holy Spirit and the Gospel Tradition,* rev. ed. (Philadelphia: Westminster, 1966).

[12] H.-J. Kraus, *Theology of the Psalms,* trans. K. Crim (Minneapolis: Augsburg, 1986) 111–19.

[13] J. Blenkinsopp, "Prophecy and Priesthood in Josephus," *JJS* 25 (1974) 239–62.

[14] A. Schalit, "Die Erhebung Vespasians nach Flavius Josephus, Talmud, und Midrasch: Zur Geschichte einer messianischen Prophetie," *ANRW* 2.2, 208–377.

[15] For a survey, see R.A. Horsley and J.S. Hanson, *Bandits, Prophets, and Messiahs: Popular Movements at the Time of Jesus* (Minneapolis: Winston Press, 1985) 88–134.

[16] E. Schürer, *The History of the Jewish People in the Age of Jesus Christ (175 BC–AD 135),* rev. and ed. by G. Vermes and F. Millar (Edinburgh: T. & T. Clark, 1973) 1.543–52.

form of the recognition oracle.[17] Akiba reportedly referred to bar Kosiba as bar Kokhba, "son of a star," referring to Simon's messianic status by an allusion to the messianic prophecy of Num 24:17. Yet the title which Bar Kosiba preferred, according to numismatic and papyrological evidence, was not Messiah, but *Nasi* ("prince"), a traditional title of the Israelite king.

3. Ambiguities in the Term "Messiah"

Yet in the final analysis, the ultimate religious significance of Jesus could not be confined to messianic categories. When fewer and fewer Jews and more and more pagans were attracted to Christianity, Christological motifs derived from Israelite kingship ideology inevitably became less functional. Thus while it is probable that in the very early period of Aramaic-speaking Palestinian Christianity the messianic status of Jesus was of paramount importance, messiahship became a decreasingly useful way of conceptualizing the ultimate significance of Jesus. While various and sometimes contradictory reconstructions of Israelite enthronement ritual have been proposed on the basis of the two OT coronation accounts (1Kgs 1:32–48; 2Kgs 11:12–20),[18] and the important enthronement Psalms 2 and 110,[19] it was the *unction* of the new king (representing his election by Yahweh)[20] which was the most important feature of coronation. Consequently the nominal form *māšîah*, ("anointed one") is often used in the OT with various modifiers, with the connotation "the king who has been consecrated through unction with oil."[21] The rite of unction was closely associated with possession by the Spirit of God (cf. 1Sam 10:1, 9; 16:13; Isa 61:1; Zech 4:1–14), an association also reflected in the NT (Acts 10:38; 1John 2:20, 27). In the NT, the Gk. term *Christos* ("anointed") is a translation of the Heb. term *māšîaḥ* (twice

[17] Schürer, *History of the Jewish People,* 1.543, n. 130. J. Fitzmyer, "The Bar Cochba Period" in *Essays on the Semitic Background of the New Testament* (Missoula: Scholars Press, 1974) 314–15.

[18] R. de Vaux, *Ancient Israel: Its Life and Institutions,* trans. J. McHugh (New York: McGrew-Hill,, 1961) 102–7, suggests five stages of Israelite enthronement rituals: (1) investiture with insignia, (2) the anointing, (3) the acclamation (e. g. "Long live the king!"), (4) the enthronement, and (5) the homage.

[19] Basing his findings primarily on Ps 110 and Ps 2:7, H.-J. Kraus, *Theology of the Psalms,* 111–19, suggests that the protocol for bestowing authority on the new king consisted of three distinct phases: (1) A prophetic speaker declared that the king was the "son of God" (Ps 2:7; 110:3). (2) The king was then told to ascend the throne and sit at the right hand of God (Ps 110:1). (3) After ascending the throne the king was declared the legitimate heir (Ps 110:4).

[20] Baruch Halpern, *The Constitution of the Monarchy in Israel* Harvard Semitic Monographs, 25 (Chico, CA: Scholars Press, 1981) 14.

[21] Cf. such phrases as "Yahweh's anointed" (1Sam 16:6: 24:6, 10; 26:9, 16; 2Sam 1:14, 19:21; Lam 4:20), "my [i. e. Yahweh's] anointed" (1Sam 2:35; 1Chr 16:22; Ps 105:15; 132:17), "thy [i. e. Yahweh's] anointed" 2Chr 6:42; Ps 84:9; 89:38, 51; 132:10; Hab 3:13), and "his [i. e. Yahweh's] anointed" (1Sam 2:10; 12:3, 5; 2Sam 22:51; Ps 2:2, 18:50, 20:6, 28:8; Isa 45:1).

transliterated as *messias* in John 1:41 and 4:25). When used in the Gospels and Acts as a general designation, it unambiguously refers to the ideal future Davidic king of Jewish eschatological expectation (Mk 15:32, John 7:42). There is little indication of the ambiguity which surrounded the notion in early Judaism. The reasons why the title *Christos* became the central way of defining the ultimate religious significance of Jesus in early Palestinian Christianity is problematic since his career did not fit early Jewish messianic expectations.[22]

It has become increasingly evident that the conception of "*the* Jewish Messiah" is in reality a synthetic construct which masks the variety of messianic figures in early Jewish eschatological expectation.[23] The absolute form "the Messiah," without an accompanying genitive or possessive pronoun, occurs rarely and primarily in late first-century texts (*1Enoch* 48:10; 52:4; *2 Bar* 30:1; 70:9; *4 Ezra* 7:28, 29; 12:32).[24] When it does occur, it usually refers to the eschatological Davidic king. Yet a priestly Messiah and a royal Messiah, with the latter subject to the former, are mentioned in both the Dead Sea Scrolls (1QS 9.10–11; 1QSa 12–13; cf. CD 19.10–11; 20.1) and the Testaments of the Twelve Patriarchs (*TReu* 6:5–12; *TLevi* 18:2–9). Prophets could also be called "Yahweh's anointed" (e. g. Samuel in 1Sam 24:6, 10; 26:16; 2Sam 1:14, 16), or "anointed ones" (Ps 105:15; CD 2:12, 6:1; 1QM 11:7–8; 11QMelch 18). In the Mishnah (codified ca. 200 CE), the Davidic Messiah is mentioned only twice and the designation "the anointed one" is used of the high priest.

The messianic role of Jesus was not limited to the traditional though ambiguous title Messiah, but was also conveyed through other titles such as Son of God, Son of David, King, and Son of man. Since the king of Israel was occasionally designated as the Son of God (2 Sam 7:12–14, Ps 2:7), that title was also appropriate for the Messiah once those passages were understood in a messianic sense (cf. 4QFlor 1.10–13; cf. *4 Ezra* 7:28: "my son the Messiah"; cf. 13:32, 37).[25] Even though there were many ways of referring to the royal descendant of the Davidic dynasty, the specific title "son of David" occurs in pre-Christian Jewish texts only in *Pss Sol* 17:23.[26] Similarly the term *kyrios* could be understood in a messianic

---

[22] It is this problem which concerned W. C. van Unnik in "Jesus the Christ," *Sparsa Collecta: The Collected Essays of* W. C. *van Unnik,* part 2 (Leiden: E. J. Brill, 1980) 248–68. Van Unnik proposes that for early Christians messiahship did not consist in the outward activity of a king but in a person who possesses the Spirit of God (266).

[23] See R. A. Horsley, "Popular Messianic Movements Around the lime of Jesus," *CBQ* 46 (1984) 471–95; Horsley and Hanson, *Bandits, Prophets and Messiahs;* R. A. Horsley, "'Like One of the Prophets of Old': Two Types of Popular Prophets at the Time of Jesus," *CBQ* 47 (1985) 435–63.

[24] M. de Jonge, "The Use of the Word 'Anointed' in the Time of Jesus," *NovT* 7 (1966) 132–48; *idem, TDNT* 9.511–17.

[25] E. Schweizer, "The Concept of the Davidic 'Son of God' in Acts and Its Old Testament Background, *Studies in Luke-Acts*, ed. L. E. Keck and J. L. Martyn (Nashville: Abingdon, 1966) 186–93.

[26] See the evidence assembled by Duling, "The Promises to David," 55–69.

sense in hellenistic Jewish Christianity on the basis of Ps 110:1 (Mk 12:35–37; Acts 2:33–36; *Barn* 12:10–12), a passage which was probably interpreted messianically in early Judaism by the first century CE[27] The Son of man designation is the most problematic of all. In recent years it has become increasingly clear that in pre-Christian Judaism there was no concept of "the Son of man" as an eschatological heavenly redeemer figure. The Jewish and Christian texts which use the Son of man designation in a titular sense all date from the last half of the first century CE Though Jesus very likely used the "Son of man" idiom as an indirect way of referring to himself, its transformation into a messianic title based on Dan 7:13 was probably accomplished by the early church.

The evangelists and their sources used these titles to define the person and function of Jesus. By the time the traditions of Jesus were incorporated into Q (ca. 50 CE) and particularly into Mark and the other Gospels (ca. 70–100 CE), the more significant eschatological titles and titles of honor found in them had become, at least to some extent, synonymous with one another by virtue of their common application to Jesus.[28] Because the meaning of such titles varied from context to context in Jewish eschatological scenarios, the specific application of each title to a particular historical figure such as Jesus necessarily resulted in the transformation of the titles in light of the historical particularity of Jesus and the concommitant transformation of the historical image of the Jesus to whom they were applied. The transformation of the titles themselves was unavoidable since the varied and even contradictory associations with which they were associated could not be applied to a historical figure without eliminating some connotations in favor of others. The transformation of the historical image of Jesus himself was also inevitable in view of the power and resiliency which many of these eschatological titles carried with them.

The meaning of the title Messiah or *Christos* when applied to Jesus, however, was determined primarily by *Christian* conceptions of Jesus rather than by conventional *Jewish* messianic notions.[29] That means that the Christian conception of the *heavenly* coronation of Jesus as Messiah represents a spiritualization of the traditional Jewish understanding of an *earthly* coronation of the ideal

---

[27] Hay, *Glory at the Right Hand,* 19–33.

[28] The complex relationship between the christological titles in Mark, for example, has recently been treated by J.D. Kingsbury, *The Christology of Mark's Gospel* (Philadelphia: Fortress, 1983). In a recent book by S. Kim, *The Son of Man as the Son of God* (Grand Rapids: Eerdmans, 1985), the author intends to show that Jesus consciously used the title Son of man as a discrete way of revealing himself as the Son of God. He has really only succeeded in achieving the obvious – i.e. that the designations "Son of man" and "Son of God" are synonymous by virtue of their application to Jesus.

[29] S.J. Case, "The Rise of Christian Messianism," *Studies in Early Christianity,* ed. S.J. Case (New York and London: The Century Company, 1928) 313; W. Manson, *Jesus the Messiah* (London, 1943) 12; N.A. Dahl, "Die Messianität Jesu" 86; W.C. van Unnik, "Jesus the Messiah," 259; M. De Jonge, "The Earliest Christian Use of *Christos:* Some Suggestions," *NTS* 32 (1986) 321.

king of the future. It was the death of Jesus, however, which the early church regarded as the primary obstacle preventing the general Jewish recognition of Jesus as the Messiah of Jewish expectation. The church therefore tried to revise the Jewish conception of the Messiah by arguing from OT proof texts that both suffering and death were integral aspects of the divinely ordained role of the Messiah (Lk 24:46; Acts 3: 18, 17:3, 26:22–23; 1Cor 15:3). For this reason early creeds or confessions placed the motif of the *death* of Jesus in close association with *Christos*, which already tended to be used as a proper name for Jesus in pre-Pauline hellenistic Jewish Christianity (cf. 1Cor 15:3).[30] The problem of identifying Jesus as the Messiah, however, did not simply center on the fact of the Messiah's death (which in itself was not so problematic, cf. *4 Ezra* 7:29), so much as the fact that he died before accomplishing the tasks traditionally associated with the ideal future Davidic king. However, early Palestinian Christianity did not *deny* the traditionally messianic role to Jesus, but simply *postponed* that role into the imminent (though indefinite) eschatological future (Acts 1:6; 3:20–21; Rev 11:15; 12:10; 20:4, 6).

4. Oracular Legitimations of Royal Status

Introductory Considerations

The focus of this section is on one particular feature of sacral legitimation, the prophetic or oracular recognition of the king as one divinely ordained to rule. In an earlier study, I called attention to the recognition oracle, a form of prophetic speech found in many parts of the ancient Mediterranean world.[31] The basic function of this oracular form was to provide both supernaturally guaranteed identification and divine legitimation for individuals of singular importance. Sacral legitimation was an important feature of ancient coronation rituals and ancient kingship ideologies. While all kings are "sacred" in one way or another, in the ancient Mediterranean world all kingships were sacred kingships.[32] The essential feature of sacral kingship is the special connection thought to exist between kings and the divine world, by virtue of which the king is accorded the status of a superior human being. In the cultures of the ancient Near East and the ancient Mediterranean world, sacral kingship was conceptualized through two very different royal ideologies. The king could either be accorded divine quality or divine descent, or he could be regarded as divinely chosen or elected. One of the primary concerns of usurpers who interrupted dynastic succession and

---

[30] W Kramer, *Christ, Lord, Son of God,* trans. E. Hardy (SBT 50; Naperville: Allenson, 1966) 38–44.

[31] Aune, *Prophecy in Early Christianity,* 68–70.

[32] C. Grottanelli, "Kingship: An Overview," *Encyclopedia of Religion,* ed. M. Eliade (New York: Macmillian, 1987) 8.313.

found new dynasties was the sacral legitimation of their rule. Israelite kingship ideology saw the sacrality of the king in terms of the tradition of divine election. Since the eschatological fantasies of messianism in the ancient Near East were based on the hope of the reestablishment of native kingship, it was inevitable that sacral legitimation in particular should play a significant role in authorizing the ideal future savior-king.

The Example of Alexander the Great

Alexander the Great was interested in promoting his divine descent in order to legitimate his status as ruler over the many formerly independent kingdoms which he conquered and attempted to unify through the imposition of hellenistic language and culture. Callisthenes, the official eyewitness historian and propagandist of Alexander's expedition (in a fragment of a lost work preserved in Strabo 17.1.43), mentions oracles revealing Alexander's divine origin. The most famous were reportedly pronounced by an Egyptian prophet at the oracle of Zeus-Ammon at the Oasis of Siwah, the oracle of Apollo at Didyma, and the prophetess Athenais. Though nothing further is known of the oracles of Didymaean Apollo and Athenais (cf. Strabo 14.1.34), several fragmentary versions of Alexander's visit to Siwah survive (Arrian, *Anabasis Alexandri* 3.3–4; Plutarch, *Alexander* 27.5–11; Diodorus 17.49.2–51; Q. Curtius Rufus 4.25–30).[33] The most likely historical reconstruction is that the priest of Ammon greeted Alexander as a "son of Zeus" (following the conventional *interpretatio Graeca,* Zeus was identified with Ammon, and Alexander's recent conquest of Egypt had made him the successor to the pharaohs, who were considered to be incarnations of the god Horus and sons of Amun Ra). The form of this greeting is variously preserved as *[su ei] Dios hyios* (Strabo 17.1.43), or *O pai Dios,* "O son of Zeus," a phrase which, according to one ancient rationalizing tradition, was based on a mispronunciation of *O paidos,* "My son" (Plutarch, *Alexander* 27.9). At all events, while Alexander did enter into the innermost shrine of Amun to pose questions to the oracle, he never revealed either his questions or the answers he received. It was Callisthenes, doubtless with Alexander's approval, who turned the priest's greeting into an oracular announcement of Alexander's divine sonship.[34] Following Callisthenes, the many popular accounts of Alexander's visit to Siwah tended to repeat and amplify the fiction of an oracular recognition of Alexander's divine status as son of Zeus.

---

[33] For a review of the literature on the question of Alexander's visit to Siwah and the oracle of Ammon, see J. Seibert, *Alexander der Grosse* (Darmstadt: Wissenschaftliche Buchgesellschaft, 1972) 116–25. See also the reconstruction by R. L. Fox, *Alexander the Great* (London: Dial Press, 1973): Wissenschaftliche Buchgesellschaft, 200–14, 523–24. More recently, see A. Brunt, trans., *Arrian* (Cambridge and London: Harvard University Press, 1976), 1.467–80 (Appendix V: "The Visit to Siwah").

[34] Fox, *Alexander the Great,* 211–12; Brunt, 1.471–72.

Gospel Accounts of Jesus

The historical Jesus, in a manner characteristic of charismatic leaders of thaumaturgical movements,[35] used various strategies to legitimate his mission and message as ultimate and transcendent. The historical core of the miracle tradition, though later embellished and amplified, certainly functioned in this way. Equally important was Jesus' confident proclamation of the imminent arrival of the kingdom of God. Further, his prophetic actions (e. g. the cleansing of the temple, the triumphal entry) and his prophecies of the fate of Jerusalem and the temple, though also modified in the tradition, constituted another form of legitimation.[36]

There is, however, no historically reliable evidence to suggest that either Jesus himself or those around him appealed to revelation to specifically identify or legitimate his person and work.[37] Whether or not his intention was to legitimate his role as *a* prophet, *the* Prophet, or the Messiah, or he did not consciously play any scripted role, it is clear that the early Palestinian church regarded the designation *Messiah* as so central for conceptualizing the significance of Jesus that it was quickly transformed into a proper name in pre-Pauline hellenistic Jewish Christianity.

There are many instances in the Synoptic Gospels in which the messianic status of Jesus is affirmed through supernatural means. (1) Using the form of the recognition oracle, on the occasion of the baptism of Jesus a heavenly voice declares, "You art my beloved Son; with you I am well pleased" (Mk 1:11 = Mt 3:17 = Lk 3:22; cf. John 1:34), and in the episode of the transfiguration a heavenly voice announces, "This is my beloved Son; listen to him" (Mk 9:7 = Mt 17:5 = Lk 9:35).[38] (2) Demons, speaking through those in whom they reside, are depicted as providing supernatural confirmation of Jesus' identity.[39] An important example is the Markan summary (3:11): "And whenever the unclean spirits beheld him, they fell down before him and cried out, 'You are the Son of God." This is a significant passage because Mark, in summarizing the demonic identification of Jesus, casts his summary in the form of a recognition oracle. (3) Peter's confession to Jesus that "You are the Christ" (Mk 8:29 = Mt 16:16 = Lk 9:20) also exhibits the form and content, if not the function, of a recognition oracle in Mark and Luke. Yet that defect is rectified by Matthew, who specifically emphasizes the revelatory character of Peter's pronouncement in Mt 16:17: "Blessed are you, Simon Bar-Jona! For flesh and blood have not revealed this to

---

[35] B. R. Wilson, *Magic and the Millennium: A Sociological Study of Religious Movements of Protest Among Tribal and Third-World Peoples* (New York: Harper & Row, 1973) 102–95.

[36] D. E. Aune, *Prophecy,* 171–88.

[37] The revelatory discourses in the fourth gospel, in which the "I am" predications of Jesus occur, did not originate with the historical Jesus.

[38] Aune, *Prophecy,* 271–72.

[39] Demonic identifications of Jesus are found in Mk 1:24 (= Lk 4:34); Mk 3:11 (= Lk 4:41); Mk 5:7 (= Mt 8:29 = Lk 8:28).

you, but my Father who is in heaven." (4) Particularly in Luke a series of angelic disclosures and prophetic utterances reveal various aspects of the messianic status of Jesus.[40] Two oracles are attributed to the aged Simeon, who functions as a prophet in recognizing the messianic status of the infant Jesus (2:25–35). Luke then introduces the prophetess Anna, who also recognizes Jesus as the one who will redeem Jerusalem (2:36–38). To this should be added the angelic message to Mary (1:26–38) and the aged Zechariah's prophecy (1:67–79).

An extensive instance of the remolding of Jesus traditions in line with messianic motifs is found in the gospel accounts of the baptism of Jesus mentioned above (Mk 1:9–11, Mt 3:13–17, Lk 3:21–22; cf. John 1:29–34). While the event itself is certainly historical, and perhaps even functioned as a prophetic call for Jesus, tradition has overlaid the narrative with imagery appropriate to the preliminary divine designation of a future Israelite king as a *nagid,* usually understood as a private anointing ritual.[41] While the ritual washing practiced by John has nothing in common with the practice of anointing with oil associated with Israelite royal designation and confirmation rituals (two separate but related stages),[42] the author of Luke-Acts understood the baptism of Jesus as his divine unction with the Holy Spirit (Lk 4:18; Acts 4:27, 10:38). Luke is very careful in his version of the baptism of Jesus to dissociate John from that event. According to Luke, John had already been arrested (Lk 3:20) before the baptism of Jesus took place (Lk 3:21–22). Similarly Acts 10:38 refers to "the baptism which John preached" and the fact that "God anointed Jesus of Nazareth with the Holy Spirit" without explicitly equating the two events, though they can hardly be understood otherwise.

Another legendary embellishment of the baptismal scene, the heavenly voice or *bat qol* either proclaiming *to* Jesus, "You are my beloved Son; with you I am well pleased" (Mk 1:11; Lk 3:22), or proclaiming *about* Jesus, "This is my beloved Son; with whom I am well pleased" (Mt 3:17), a conflated allusion to Ps 2:7 and Isa 42:1.[43] Psalm 2 is a coronation hymn, and the declaration in vs. 7, "you are my son," is an oracular adoption formula spoken to the king by a prophetic participant in the consecration ritual. A further step in the embellishment of the baptism episode is found in the fourth gospel, where the baptism of Jesus is by John the Baptist himself. The baptismal scene is described as a

[40] C. H. Talbert, "Promise and Fulfillment in Lukan Theology," *Luke-Acts: New Perspectives from the Society of Biblical Literature Seminar,* ed. C. H. Talbert (New York: Crossroad, 1984) 91–103; *idem,* "Prophecies of Future Greatness: The Contribution of Greco-Roman Biographies to an Understanding of Luke 1:5–4:15," *The Divine Helmsman,* ed. J. L. Crenshaw and S. Sandmel (New York: KTAV, 1980) 129–41.

[41] See Z. Weisman, "Anointing as a Motif in the Making of the Charismatic King," *Bib* 57 (1976) 379–82; Halpern, *Monarchy,* 125–48.

[42] Halpern, *Monarchy,* 125.

[43] But see B. Chilton, *A Galilean Rabbi and His Bible* (Wilmington: Glazier, 1984) 125–31.

revelation to John, probably modeled after scenes in which God enables Samuel to recognize Saul and later David as the Lord's anointed in 1Sam 9:15–17 and 16:1–13. John claims that God had revealed to him that "'He on whom you see the Spirit descend and remain, this is he who baptizes with the Holy Spirit"' (John 1:33). He therefore concludes: "'And I have seen and have borne witness that this is the Son of God'" (John 1:34).

The Primitive Confession "Jesus Is Lord"

1Cor 12:3 has provoked a great deal of discussion among NT interpreters:

> Therefore I want you to understand that no one speaking by the Spirit of God ever says "Jesus be cursed!" and no one can say "Jesus is Lord!" except by the Holy Spirit.

It is possible that the negative confession "Jesus be cursed!" represents a Pauline construct formulated as the antithesis to the positive confession "Jesus is Lord!" Though this confession was widely used throughout early Christianity (John 20:28, Rom 10:9, Phil 2:11), only here is it evident that it was (or could be) an inspired oracular utterance. The title "Lord" *(mar)* was already used of Jesus in Aramaic-speaking Palestinian Christianity (cf. the famous *marana tha* prayer in 1Cor 16:22).[44] The title "Lord" is closely linked to the messianic status of Jesus, since the Christian confession "Jesus is Lord" can be understood as an affirmation that Jesus is the royal Messiah at the right hand of God (Acts 2:34, Rom 8:34, 1Cor 15:25, Eph 1:20, Col 3:1), i.e. the Lordship of Jesus is the result of the completion of his saving work, not the presupposition for it. In hellenistic Jewish Christianity, "Lord" was the title which replaced "Messiah," which had been the centrally significant title for Jesus in Palestinian Christianity. While the form of this prophetic saying or confession is that of the recognition oracle,[45] any specific allusion to Jewish messianic ideology is missing.

Conclusions

In the Gospels the oracular legitimations of the ultimate religious significance of Jesus abound. Yet without exception they appear to be *literary dramatizations* of the messianic status of Jesus overlayed on the Jesus traditions. With the single possible exception of 1Cor 12:3 (a problematic passage with many possible interpretations), there is no evidence that Christians exercised prophetic speech to legitimate the messianic status of Jesus. However, that does not mean that such prophetic legitimation did not occur, since it appears that very few authentic examples of Christian prophetic speech have been preserved.

---

[44] J. Fitzmyer, "The Semitic Background of the New Testament *Kyrios*-Title," A *Wandering Aramaean: Collected Essays* (Missoula: Scholars Press, 1979) 115–42.

[45] Aune, *Prophecy in Early Christianity,* 86, 140–41, 256–57, 270–74.

4. Visionary Revelations of Jesus' Messianic Status

When Paul claimed that God "was pleased to reveal his Son to me" (Gal 1:16), he was very likely referring to his experience on the road to Damascus in which he saw and recognized that the exalted Jesus was the Messiah. In Gal 1:16 he uses the designation *Son,* while in 1 Cor 9:1 he refers to the object of his Damascus experience as *Lord:* "Have I not seen Jesus our Lord?" He never connects the term *Christos* with his Damascus experience. For Luke, Paul's Damascus experience was linked to his recognition of the Messianic status of Jesus (cf. Acts 9:20, 22; 26:22–23). Similarly in 1Cor 15:8, after a list of various appearances of the risen Jesus, Paul claims that "he appeared [*ōphthē*] also to me." The fact that Paul used the same verb *ōphthē* three times in connection with five earlier resurrection appearances (1 Cor 15:5–7) indicates that he regarded resurrection appearances (whether to Peter or to himself) as revelatory visions.[46] Yet neither Paul himself, nor the three later accounts in Acts 9, 22, and 26, reveal very much about the character of visionary revelations of the messianic status of Jesus. There are two important passages in the NT, however, which may provide more information about the form and content of such visionary revelations, Acts 7:55–56 and Rev 1:12–16.

Acts 7:55–56: The Vision of the Enthroned Son of Man

Acts 7:55–56 is an account of Stephen's own prophetic witness to the messianic status of Jesus, i.e. the enthroned Son of man at the right hand of God. It could well have been the kind of visionary experience mentioned by Paul but never described. Acts 7:55–56 is one of several passages in early Christian literature which reflect the exegetical permutations of Dan 7:13 combined with Ps 110:1 (cf. Mk 14:62 = Mt 26:64 = Lk 22:69).[47] Mk 14:62 and Acts 7:55–56, in addition to their common allusions to Dan 7:13 in combination with Ps 110:1, share two other features. They are both introduced with a verb of seeing (though two different Gk. verbs are employed), and they are both presented as revelatory sayings (Mk 14:62 is presented as a prophecy of Jesus regarding a future vision by

[46] R.H. Fuller, *The Formation of the Resurrection Narratives* (New York: Macmillan, 1971) 31–32, 49, 170. It is perhaps going too far beyond the evidence to suggest that Paul realized that the resurrection was true on the basis of his Damascus experience, as S. Kim proposes in *The Origin of Paul's Gospel* (Grand Rapids: Eerdmans, 1982) 72. Regarding the Damascus experience, W Marxsen observes that "Paul therefore fails to indicate whether it was that experience which convinced him of Jesus' resurrection" *(The Resurrection of Jesus of Nazareth* [Philadelphia: Fortress, 1970] 101).

[47] A similar tradition combining Dan 7:13 with Ps 110:1 is found in Hegesippus in a quotation from a lost work preserved by Eusebius *(HE* 2.23.13):

> And he answered with a loud voice, "Why do you ask me concerning the Son of Man? He is sitting in heaven on the right hand of the great power, and he will come on the clouds of heaven."

the high priest, while Acts 7:55–56 presents a visionary experience of Stephen when he is at the point of death). The hypothesis that I wish to explore is that the tradition behind both Mk 14:62 and Acts 7:55–56 reflects a vision by a Christian prophet (rather than simply a *pesher* tradition formulated by a Christian exegetical school), confirming the heavenly messianic status of Jesus.

A review of the relevant texts is an important first step in our discussion. Mk 14:62 (and Mt 26:64) has a clear reference to both the *Sessio ad Dextram Dei* and the Parousia:

> And Jesus said, "I am, and you will see the Son of man seated at the right hand of Power, and coming with the clouds of heaven."

In the parallel in Lk 22:69 the reference to the Parousia is not found:

> "But from now on the Son of man shall be seated at the right hand of the power of God."

The Parousia motif is also missing from Acts 7:55–56:

> But he [Stephen], full of the Holy Spirit, gazed into heaven and saw the glory of God, and Jesus standing at the right hand of God; and he said, "Behold, I see the heavens opened, and the Son of man standing at the right hand of God."

Since Luke knew Mk 14:62, he may have deleted the reference to "coming with clouds" for theological reasons. Yet he may have been familiar with a combination of Dan 7:13 and Ps 110:1 which lacked the Parousia motif. In Dan 7:13 itself, the "one like a son of man" comes on clouds to the Ancient of Days who is enthroned in heaven. This interpretation of Dan 7:13, when combined with Ps 110:1, is found in three other texts – the *Apocalypse of Peter* (ca. 135 CE), Book 2 of the Christian Sibylline Oracles (c. 150 CE), and the Odes of Solomon (c. 125 CE). The first text is in the *Apocalypse of Peter* 6 (trans. Hennecke-Schneemelcher, II, 671–72):

> And all will see how I come upon an eternal shining cloud, and the angels of God who will sit with me on the throne of my glory at the right hand of my heavenly Father.

Here allusions to Dan 7:13 and Ps 110:1 are placed on the lips of Jesus in the form of a prophecy very similar to Mk 14:62. The second text is found in the Christian *Sibylline Oracles* 2.241–44 (trans. Hennecke-Schneemelcher, II, 715–16):

> There shall come on a cloud to the eternal, eternal himself, Christ in glory with his blameless angels, and shall sit on the right hand of Majesty, judging on his throne the life of the pious and the ways of impious men.

Finally, the third text is found in the *Odes of Solomon* 36:3 (trans. Charlesworth), which retains a two-stage christology with allusions to Dan 7:13 and Ps 110:1, and is presented in terms of a report of a visionary ascent to heaven through the eyes of Jesus himself; as in Acts 7:55–56, there is no mention of the Parousia:

[The Spirit] brought me forth before the Lord's face, and because I was the Son of Man [Syr. *br nšʾ*], I was named the Light, the Son of God [Syr. *brh dʾlhʾ*].

In *Odes Sol* 36:1–2, the speaker claims that the Spirit lifted him to heaven "And caused me to stand [Syr. *wʾgymtny*] on my feet in the Lord's high place." This motif of "raising up"[48] can be seen in connection with the two-stage christology derived from 2 Sam 7:12–14 and expressed in the pre-Pauline confession preserved in Rom 1:3–4.

There are three major solutions to the tradition-critical problem presented by Mk 14:62 and Acts 7:55–56 in the light of these texts: (1) The Parousia motif found in Mk 14:62 could have been added by the evangelist to a tradition similar to that reproduced in Acts 7:55–56 (B. Lindars).[49] (2) The absence of the Parousia motif in Acts 7:55–56 could be due to the fact that Luke consciously deleted it from Mk 14:62 or a similar tradition known to him from another source (H. Tödt).[50] (3) Mk 14:62 and Acts 7:55–56 represent independent developments and combinations of earlier stages of exegetical developments (A. J. B. Higgins, N. Perrin).[51] While the second possibility is the simplest, the first is more convincing since the absence of the Parousia motif from allusions to Dan 7:13 suggests that Luke had access to a more primitive tradition. The real problem is to account for how the Parousia motif was first associated with Dan 7:13.[52] Since Jesus was the Son of man, and the enthronement of the Son of man is implied in Dan 7:13–14, he is therefore the Messiah, since the enthronement of the Messiah is testified to in Ps 110:1. In Lk 22:69 the visionary character of the saying is changed by the omission of "you will see," a phrase which has been added to Acts 7:56 in the modified form "1 see," though a verb different from that in Mark 14:62 is used.[53]

The tradition history of Acts 7:55–56 is much more complex than that of Mk 14:62. First, vs. 56 is a doublet of vs. 55 and was either composed by Luke himself or (in my view more likely) was an independent prophetic logion which

---

[48] Duling, "The Promises to David," 70–77.

[49] Lindars, *New Testament Apologetic,* 48–49.

[50] H. E. Tödt, *The Son of Man* in *the Synoptic Tradition,* trans. D. M. Barton (Philadelphia: Westminster, 1965) 304–5; Lindars changed his earlier opinion (see n. 30) to the view that Luke has modified the saying found in Mk 14:26, cf. B. Lindars, *Jesus Son of Man* (Grand Rapids: Eerdmans, 1984) 142.

[51] A. J. B. Higgins, *Jesus as the Son of Man* (Philadelphia, 1964) 143–46; N. Perrin, "Mk 14:62: The End Product of a Christian Pesher Tradition?" in *A Modern Pilgrimage in New Testament Christology* (Philadelphia: Fortress, 1974) 16–18; idem, *Rediscovering the Teaching of Jesus* (New York: Harper & Row, 1967) 179–80.

[52] Though this specific problem is addressed by T. Callan, "Psalm 110:1 and the Origin of the Expectation That Jesus Will Come Again," *CBQ* 44 (1982) 622–36, his solution is unsatisfactory.

[53] Luke tends to replace *horaō* with other verbs for seeing; see H. J. Cadbury, *The Style and Literary Method of Luke* (Cambridge: Harvard University Press, 1920) 175–76.

the author modified and inserted at that point.[54] The reference to "Jesus" standing at the right hand of God" in vs. 55 is changed to "the *Son of man* standing at the right hand of God" in vs. 56, to make the identification of Jesus with the Son of man absolutely clear. In vs. 55 the narrator reports that Stephen "saw [*eiden*] the glory of God, and Jesus standing at the right hand of God." This may simply be a literary dramatization of an exegetical tradition based on Ps 110:1 and Dan 7:13. In my view it is a literary dramatization of a brief vision report which circulated independently (perhaps originally introduced with a verb of seeing and used in a past tense, e. g. "I saw [*eidon*]"), conceptually influenced by Ps 110:1 and Dan 7:13. In either case, the point is that Jesus of Nazareth is now enthroned in heaven as Lord and Messiah (cf. Acts 2:34–36). In Acts 7:56 there are only two possible allusions to Dan 7:13; the Son of man designation and (less probably) the participle "standing" (*hestota*), since the Son of man, like angels, could be imagined as standing in the presence of God.[55] The unique feature of this vision report is that *the vision is narrated as it is experienced.* Though without parallel in the NT, very close parallels are found in Philo (*Vita Mos* 2.250–52, 280–81) and Pseudo-Philo's *Liber Antiquitatum Biblicarum* 28:6–10, which include a description of the visionary's inspired state followed by a vision report using a verb of seeing in the present tense.[56] Without exception these *visionary announcements of judgment* are literary productions in which future events are seen as though present by the visionary.

[54] See the discussion in R. Pesch, *Die Vision des Stephanus* (Stuttgart: Katholisches Bibelwerk, 1966) 50–54, and G. Schneider, *Die Apostelgeschichte* (Freiburg: Herder, 1980, 1982) 1.473–75.

[55] On this dubious point see E. Haechen, *The Acts of the Apostles* (Philadelphia: Westminster, 1971) 292, n. 4. The unique reference to "the Son of Man *standing* at the right hand of God" (Acts 7:56) has never been satisfactorily explained, and sometimes for that very reason has been considered a feature of pre-Lukan tradition. However, the reference makes sense as part of an indirect piece of anti-Simonian polemic. Luke knew a great deal about Simon and Simonianism, perhaps more than he chose to reveal. In the Clementine literature it is said that Simon "intimates that he is the Messiah by calling himself the Standing One (ho *hestōs*). He uses this title to indicate that he shall always stand, and that there is no cause of corruption which can make his body fall (*Clem Hom* 2.22; cf. *Clem Rec* 2.7). In Samaritan and gnostic texts, "standing" can be used as a divine attribute referring to the eternality of God, and it can also be used in Samaritan texts of the eschatological Mosaic prophet (J. E. Fossum, *The Name of God and the Angel of the Lord* (Tübingen: Mohr Siebeck, 1985) 120–24; R. M. Grant, *Gnosticism and Early Christianity,* rev. ed. [New York: Harper & Row, 1966] 90–93). Simon reportedly claimed "I am the Son of God standing to eternity" ("filius dei stans in aeternum") (*Clem Rec* 3.47). The prophet whom God will "raise up" (Acts 7:37, alluding to Deut 18:15, 18), can be thought of as "standing"; R. M. Grant suggests the parallel in Deut 5:31 in which God addresses Moses and says, "You stand with me, and I will tell you all the commandments" (Grant, *Gnosticism,* 92). This is supported by the fact that the variant tradition in which an allusion to Dan 7:13 and Ps 110:1 is attributed to the dying James the Just by Hegesippus (Eusebius, *HE* 2.23.13), the phrase "the Great Power," meaning God, is found only in Samaritan sources apart from this one fragment of Hegesippus; see Fossum, *The Name of God,* 169.

[56] For a formal analysis of these and similar texts, see Aune, *Prophecy in Early Christianity,* 148–52, 270.

Though the precise exegetical reasons for combining Dan 7:13 with Ps 110 are now obscure,[57] it is likely that they were used to interpret the resurrection of Jesus in the Aramaic-speaking Palestinian church,[58] though some contend on philological grounds that Ps 110:1 could only have been applied to the resurrection in Hellenistic Jewish Christianity.[59] Dan 7:13 was used to identify Jesus, who probably used the "Son of man" idiom as an indirect way of referring to himself, as the vicegerent of God; none of the Son of man sayings which allude to Dan 7: 13 have a strong claim to authenticity.[60] If that is so, then Mk 14:62 (which, introduced with "you will see," is awkward in its present context) cannot be regarded as authentic and must be considered a later addition to the narrative of the trial of Jesus.[61] Since Ps 110:1 may have been understood messianically in first-century Judaism, it was probably used in combination with Dan 7:13 to understand Jesus' resurrection in terms of heavenly enthronement of the Son of man as Messiah. The combination of Dan 7:13 with Ps 110:1 clearly identified Jesus, recognized as the Son of man, with the Messiah, a necessary step since there was no concept of an apocalyptic Son of man in pre-Christian Judaism. Since the designation "Son of man" was not used as a title of Jesus in christologi-

---

57 W.O. Walker, "The Origin of the Son of Man Concept as Applied to Jesus," *JBL* 91 (1972) 482–90, argues that the missing link is provided by Ps 8:6b (LXX 8:7b): "thou hast put all things under his feet," since vs. 4 uses the expression "son of man," the whole Ps was applied to Jesus. The no less probable suggestion of N.A. Dahl is mentioned by Hay, *Glory at the Right Hand,* 26, n. 32, namely Ps 80:17: "But let thy hand be upon the man of thy right hand, the son of man whom thou hast made strong for thyself!" The same solution is proposed by O.J.F. Seitz, "The Future Coming of the Son of Man: Three Midrashic Formulations in the Gospel of Mk," *Studia Evangelica* 6 (1973) 482–88. The simplest solution, however, is to note the mention of thrones, on one of which the Ancient of Days took his seat in Dan 7:9. In a Messianic interpretation of the Son of Man figure quite separate from that found in the gospels and Acts, the enthronement of the Son of Man is a conclusion also drawn in *1En* 62:5, though without the aid of Ps 110:1: "and pain shall seize them when they see the Son of man sitting on the throne of his glory" *(OTP,* 1. 43); see *1 Enoch* 61:8; 69:29. Slightly later than the Similitudes of Enoch (*1 Enoch* 37–71, dated ca. AD 90) is the rabbinic tradition attributed to Akiba that the two thrones of Dan 7:9 were for God and the Davidic Messiah (*b.Hag* 14a; *b.Sanh* 38b); cf. Andre LaCocque, *Le livre de Daniel* (Neuchatel and Paris: Delechause & Niestlè, 1976) 108, n. 6. A very similar tradition is found in Mt 19:28: "the Son of man shall sit on his glorious throne," a passage which exhibits no influence from Ps 110:1, a fact made clear by the parallel in Mt 25:31: "When the Son of man comes in his glory, and all the angels with him, then he will sit on his glorious throne."

58 G. Loader, "Christ at the Right Hand – Ps. CX. 1 in the New Testament," *NTS* 24 (1977–78) 200. Without mentioning Ps 110:1, J. Fitzmyer argues that the absolute use of the *kyrios* title for Jesus originated within a Palestinian-Semitic religious background ("The Semitic Background of the New Testament Kyrios-Title," 115–42).

59 Fuller, *Foundations* of *New Testament Christology,* 184–86.

60 W.O. Walker, "The Son of Man: Some Recent Developments," *CBQ* 45 (1983) 595–98; M. Casey, *Son of Man,* 237.

61 Tödt, *The Son of Man,* 36–40; Leivestad, *Jesus in His Own Perspective: An Examination of His Sayings, Actions, and Eschatological Titles,* trans. D.E. Aune (Minneapolis: Augsburg, 1987) 159; Lindars, *Jesus Son of Man,* 110–12; A.J.B. Higgins, *The Son of Man in the Teaching of Jesus* (Cambridge: Cambridge University Press, 1980) 77–79.

cal confessions (a fact made obvious by Mt 16:13: "Who do men say that the Son of man is?"),[62] the primary purpose of combining Dan 7:13 with Ps 110:1 must have been to identify Jesus the Son of man with the Messiah.

Rev 1:12–16: The Heavenly Son of Man

Rev 1:9–20 is a vision report of John's divine commission to write messages dictated by the exalted Christ for transmission to the seven churches. The seer John describes the supernatural being he saw as "one like a son of man" (vss. 13–14), clearly alluding to Dan 7:13 without suggesting any awareness of the extensive use of the title in the gospels. Yet he does maintain the primitive Christian identification of Jesus as Son of man with the Jesus of heavenly exaltation. The figure is presumably standing, a posture explicitly mentioned when John describes the Lamb in Rev 5:6. In the MT of Dan 7:13 the "one like a son of man" is presented to the Ancient of Days, thus clearly distinguishing the two figures. Yet in Rev 1:13–14, the "one like a son of man" is described *as if he is identical* with the Ancient of Days (whose hair is white as wool according to Dan 7:6; cf. Rev 1:14). This identification was not original with John. It is already presupposed by the LXX version of Dan 7:13: "He came like a son of man, and like the Ancient of Days was present, and those who were near were present with him." This reading is found in the only two LXX manuscripts of Daniel, the Codex Chisianus (Ms. 88), and the incomplete Chester Beatty papyrus codex 967 (late second- or early third-century CE). Ms. 88 and the Syro-Hexapla version of Daniel are both dependent on Origen's Hexapla; Ms. 967 is one of the earliest extant copies of parts of the LXX and constitutes an important independent witness to the reading of Ms. 88.[63] Wherever and however it originated, this text intentionally identifies the "one like a son of man" with the Ancient of Days.[64] Thus despite the problematic relationship between the Apocalypse of John and the rest of the Johannine corpus, they do share an emphasis on the divinity of Jesus, an emphasis that goes beyond Jewish messianic categories. It is not John's purpose to provide divine legitimation for the messianic status of Jesus, but rather to provide legitimation for his own status as a prophet for the revelatory book he was composing.

---

[62] D. G. Dunn, *Unity and Diversity in the New Testament* (Philadelphia: Westminster, 1977) 35–40; R. Leivestad, *Jesus in His Own Perspective,* 153–54.

[63] This reading is neither the result of accident nor error (F. F. Bruce, "The Oldest Greek Version of Daniel," OTS 20 (1977) 25; J. Lust, "Daniel 7:13 and the Septuagint," *ETL* 54 (1978) 62–69), as J. Ziegler, who corrected it to agree with the MT, presumed (*Susana-Daniel-Bel et Draco* [Göttinger Septuaginta 16.2; Göttingen: Vandenhoeck & Ruprecht, 1954] *ad loc.*), though it probably does not preserve a variant Hebrew reading (against Lust, "Daniel 7:13," 68).

[64] The precedent for this exegetical step taken by the LXX translators may have been Ezek 1:26, in which Ezekiel saw God as one "in the likeness of a man" sitting on the "likeness of a throne."

Summary

The earliest revelatory visions of the resurrected Jesus probably involved revelatory perception of his heavenly messianic status. The prophetic tradition standing behind the series of texts we have examined, all of which allude to a combination of Dan 7:13 with Ps 110:1, may have originated as a prophetic vision of the messianic status of Jesus, the Son of man, enthroned at the right hand of God. The following arguments support this view: (1) The earliest combination of Dan 7:13 with Ps 110:1 lacked any reference to the Parousia and instead focused on identifying the Son of man as the enthroned Messiah. (2) The combined allusions to Dan 7:13 and Ps 110:1 tend to occur in literary contexts as a prophecy or as a vision report, a usage in harmony with the hypothetical original revelatory function of the saying. (3) Sayings combining Dan 7:13 with Ps 110:1 are usually introduced with a verb of seeing, a feature appropriate to an original vision report with the introductory formula "I saw." (4) Acts 7:55–56 coheres with what is known of visions of the resurrected Jesus known from 1Cor 15:5–8, from Acts 9, 22, 26, and allusions in Paul's letters to his Damascus experience. (5) The conceptual character of revelatory visions exhibits a marked dependence on canonical visions (e. g. Paul understood his Damascus vision in terms of Jeremiah's inaugural vision; cf. Gal 1:15, Jer 1:5), and an OT interpretation (e. g. Rev 1:9–20). (6) There is evidence to suggest that other short oracular and visionary forms were circulated orally in early Christianity (e. g. Rev 1:7).[65]

5. Conclusions

In this paper we have explored the issue of whether or not the problematic issue of the messianic status of Jesus was legitimated by the inspired speech or revelatory visions of early Christian prophets. The fact that early Christian prophetic speech and visionary experiences have survived only fragmentarily has made the task very difficult. It appears that the messianic status of the earthly Jesus was a concern of central importance for the transmitters of the Jesus traditions to the extent that the portrait of Jesus took on greater and greater messianic contours. The evidence for this literary transformation of the Jesus tradition is evident in all of the Gospels, though we have focused only on the literary use of oracles and prophecies of the true status of Jesus. In discussing the brief vision report reflected in Acts 7:55–56 and Rev 1:14–16 (and several related texts), we discovered in them a major concern with affirming the messianic status of Jesus as the exalted and enthroned Son of man. We further proposed that these texts have made use of a primitive prophetic vision report which both confirmed and legitimated Christian perceptions of Jesus as Messiah. While this hypothesis is

[65] See Aune, *Prophecy in Early Christianity,* 247–338.

necessarily speculative, given the paucity of the evidence, there is nevertheless a strong possibility that both the reception and transmission of such revelatory visions made a major contribution to the spread of faith in the fact that Jesus had not only risen from the dead but had also been exalted to the right hand of God as Messiah and Lord.

The *Odes of Solomon* and Early Christian Prophecy*

1. Introduction

Early Christian prophecy, a subject long neglected by New Testament scholarship, has recently become the focus of numerous articles and monographs.[1] Though the literary sources for our knowledge of early Christian prophecy are, for the most part, fragmentary, scattered, difficult to correlate and enigmatic, progress in research can be made through the patient examination, comparison and interpretation of the relevant data. The major literary witnesses for the phenomenon of early Christian prophecy are Paul's first letter to the Corinthians, the Apocalypse of John,[2] the *Didache* and the *Shepherd of Hermas*. These documents all diverge from one another in temporal, geographical as well as ideological ways; the portrait of Christian prophecy which they exhibit also diverges to such an extent that *the* phenomenon of Christian prophecy, or *the* Christian prophet, or *the* history of Christian prophecy cannot yet be synthesized.

One major witness to the phenomenon of early Christian prophecy which has not been included in the list of four documents mentioned above is the *Odes of Solomon*. This collection of early Christian hymns presents a very distinctive aspect of early Christian prophecy which, while it has correlations with the

---

* Shortened version of a paper presented to the Pseudepigrapha Seminar of the Studiorum Novi Testamenti Societas at its Annual Meeting in Toronto, Canada on August 25–30, 1980.

[1] Among the recent monographs on the subject, see G. Dautzenberg, *Urchristliche Prophetie: Ihre Erforschung, ihre Voraussetzungen im Judentum und ihre Struktur im ersten Korintherbrief* (Stuttgart: Kohlhammer, 1975); U.B. Müller, *Prophetie und Predigt im Neuen Testament; Formgeschichtliche Untersuchungen zur urchristlichen Prophetie* (Gütersloh: Verlagshaus Gerd Mohn, 1975); J. Reiling, *Hermas and Christian Prophecy: A Study of the Eleventh Mandate* (Leiden: Brill, 1973); David Hill, *New Testament Prophecy* (Atlanta: John Knox Press, 1979). A number of important essays are found in the symposium edited by J. Panagopoulos, *Prophetic Vocation in the New Testament and Today* (Leiden: Brill, 1977) and in the collected essays of E. Earle Ellis, *Prophecy and Hermeneutic in Early Christianity: New Testament Essays* (Grand Rapids: Eerdmans, 1978). An up-to-date bibliography is appended to Hill's book.

[2] The author of the Apocalypse has been regarded by some scholars as a unique Christian prophet with greater similarities in role and function to his Old Testament predecessors than his New Testament counterparts: G. Friedrich, *TDNT,* 6.849–50; David Hill, "Prophecy and Prophets in the Revelation of St. John," *NTS,* 18 (1971–2), 411–14. This view has been refuted by E. Schüssler Fiorenza, "Apokalypsis and Propheteia; The Book of Revelation in the Context of Early Christian Prophecy," *L'Apocalypse johannique et l'Apocalyptique dans le Nouveau Testament,* ed. J. Lambrecht (Leuven: The University Press, 1980) 105–28.

prophetic phenomena exhibited elsewhere, nevertheless stands out as a very distinctive phase of early Christian prophecy. The purpose of the present study is to describe the phenomenon of prophecy exhibited in the *Odes* and to compare and contrast this description with Israelite-Jewish, early Christian and Graeco-Roman prophetic and oracular traditions.

2. Methodological Presuppositions

One of the suppositions which informs the present study is that certain documents of early Christianity share such close conceptual affinities that they can be used to supplement and correct one another in reconstructing particular phases of early Christian history.[3] While nearly every aspect of the study of the *Odes of Solomon* has been the subject of heated debate, one proposition commands almost universal scholarly agreement: the Odes share the conceptual world of the Fourth Gospel, the letters of Ignatius of Antioch and the Dead Sea Scrolls (particularly the Hodayoth). Given the unique problems attendant upon the study of the Fourth Gospel, one might suppose that specialists in Johannine studies would avail themselves of the important comparative material readily available in the Odes. Surprisingly, the implications of the conceptual relationship of the Fourth Gospel and the Odes remain to be fully explored.[4]

[3] This method is described and applied in D. E. Aune, *The Cultic Setting of Realized Eschatology in Early Christianity* (Leiden: Brill, 1972).

[4] In the first edition of C. K. Barrett's commentary on the Fourth Gospel, only six references to the *Odes* occurred; in the second edition some sixty-four references to the *Odes* are found (C. K. Barrett, *The Gospel according to St. John: An Introduction with Commentary and Notes on the Greek Text,* 1st ed. (London: SPCK, 1955), 2nd ed. (Philadelphia: Westminster Press, 1978). In most of the references to the *Odes*, Professor Barrett calls attention to various themes, such as the image of fruit and fruitbearing (eleven references, 473), persecution (four references, 480), the critical stance toward the sacrificial worship of the Temple (three references, 236), Christ's role in creation (four references, 156), etc. The failure to utilize the *Odes* in discussion of the history and character of the "Johannine community" is a serious issue; that failure characterizes the following contributions to the discussion: R. E. Brown, "Johannine Ecclesiology – The Community's Origins," *Interpretation,* 31 (1977), 379–93; *idem,* "'Other Sheep Not of This Fold'; The Johannine Perspective on Christian Diversity in the Late First Century," *JBL,* 97 (1978), 5–22; *idem, The Community of the Beloved Disciple* (New York: Paulist Press, 1979); D. M. Smith, Jr., "Johannine Christianity: Some Reflections on Its Character and Delineation," *NTS,* 21 (1974–5), 222–48; J. Louis Martyn, *History and Theology in the Fourth Gospel,* rev. ed. (Nashville: Abingdon, 1979); *idem, The Gospel of John in Christian History: Essays for Interpreters* (New York: Paulist Press, 1978). Professor J. L. Martyn in particular confuses literary history with social history in his attempt to reconstruct the three major periods in the history and emergence of Johannine Christianity; this reconstruction is found in chapter three, "Glimpses into the History of the Johannine Community," in *The Gospel of John in Christian History,* 90–121. His reconstruction is based almost exclusively on the source critical, form critical and redaction critical analysis of the Fourth Gospel, unchecked by external literary or historical controls. Martyn's only "firm" link to the world outside of the Fourth Gospel is the Johannine references to excommunication, ἀποσυνάγωγος, in John 9:22;

The nature of the present study necessitates the bald statement of a number of assumptions regarding the origin and nature of the Odes without arguing for each position in detail. First, the *Odes* were originally composed in Syriac, and constitute the earliest extant Syriac literature.[5] Second, the *Odes* were probably composed during the half century extending from the last quarter of the first to the first quarter of the second century CE;[6] later rather than earlier in this period. Third, the *Odes* constitute a unified collection of hymns written by a single author.[7] Fourth, the *Odes* were composed in Syria, more probably in the region of Edessa than Antioch.[8] Fifth, the *Odes* were written for the purpose of being chanted or sung in liturgical settings.[9] Sixth, the *Odes* should be characterized neither as "non-Gnostic" nor "Gnostic," but should be regarded as a special form of Christianity.[10] Though they contain some features of a docetic character, the

---

12:42; 16:2, which he (with many others) relates to the *Birkat ham-minim* issued from Yavneh (*b. Berakot* 28b). Professor Martyn does, in addition, adduce "The Ascent of James," purportedly a Jewish-Christian fragment buried in the Clementine Recognitions as shedding some light on the persecution motif in the Fourth Gospel, though the results are quite insubstantial; see his "Persecution and Martyrdom," in *The Gospel of John in Christian History,* 55–89.

[5] J.A. Emerton, "Some Problems of Text and Language in the Odes of Solomon," *JTS,* 18 (1967), 372–406. See the bibliographical discussion of this issue in J.H. Charlesworth, *The Pseudepigrapha and Modern Research* (Missoula: Scholars Press, 1976) 189–90, and Aune, *Cultic Setting,* 167–9 (there I sided with the view that Greek was the original language; I have since opted for Syriac).

[6] A date within the first century was favored by J.R. Harris and A. Mingana, *The Odes and Psalms of Solomon* (Manchester: The University Press; London: Longmans, Green & Co., 1916–20) 2.61–9, 93, and more recently by J.H. Charlesworth, *The Odes of Solomon: The Syriac Texts,* corrected ed. (Missoula; Scholars Press, 1977) 44, 49, 69, 113, 128.

[7] This view is argued by J.H. Bernard, *The Odes of Solomon* (Cambridge: The University Press, 1912) 41, and Harris and Mingana, *The Odes and Psalms of Solomon,* II, 133–7.

[8] Greek dominated Antioch, while Syriac dominated the country districts of Syria during the Seleucid era; cf. W.W. Tarn, *Hellenistic Civilization,* 3rd ed. (Cleveland and New York: World Publishing Co., 1961) 160. Greek was also spoken in Edessa, though Syriac appears to have been the language of the Christian church there; cf. A.F.J. Klijn, *Edessa: Die Stadt des Apostels Thomas: Das älteste Christentum in Syrien* (Giessen: Neukirchener Verlag, 1965) 45. F.C. Burkitt claimed that Syriac dominated in Edessa in *Early Eastern Christianity* (London: John Murray, 1904) 10. On the Edessene provenance of the Odes, see J. de Zwaan, "The Edessene Origin of the Odes of Solomon," *Quantulacumque: Studies Presented to Kirsopp Lake,* ed. R. Casey (London: Christophers, 1937) 285–302, and R.M. Grant, "The Odes of Solomon and the Church of Antioch," *JBL,* 63 (1944), 377.

[9] Aune, *Cultic Setting,* 174–84. While the first person singular dominates the *Odes*, many plural imperatives are also found: "Open, open [*pthw pthw*] your hearts to the exultation of the Lord" (all translations of the *Odes* are taken from Charlesworth, *The Odes of Solomon,* unless otherwise noted); "Confess [*'wde*] His power, and declare [*whww*] His grace" (7.26); "Walk [*hlkw*] in the knowledge of the Lord" (23.4); "Fill for yourselves [*mlw lkwn*] water from the living fountain of the Lord" (30.1).

[10] See J.H. Charlesworth, "The Odes of Solomon – Not Gnostic," *CBQ,* 31 (1969), 357–69, and H. Chadwick, "Some Reflections on the Character and Theology of the Odes of Solomon," *Kyriakon: Festschrift Johannes Quasten,* ed. P. Granfield and J.A. Jungmann (Münster: Verlag Aschendorff, 1970) 1.266–70. See also the brief remarks, with bibliography, in J.H. Charlesworth, *Pseudepigrapha and Modern Research,* 189. The assumption of the Gnostic character

anachronistic use of labels from a later period serves no useful purpose in understanding and interpreting the *Odes*. J. de Zwaan regarded the *Odes* as products of eastern "Vulgärchristentum,"[11] a category which appears useful in view of the fact that the *Odes* originated before the polarization of eastern Christianity into "orthodox" and "heterodox" tendencies.[12] Seventh, the *Odes* exhibit a strong conceptual affinity with phases of early Judaism; for that reason the Christian community in which they arose may be designated "Jewish-Christian." Many scholars have linked the *Odes* to the Qumran Hodayoth, some directly and others by positing a common cultural milieu.[13] O. Cullmann has called attention to the "striking parallels" between the Fourth Gospel and the *Odes*, and sees both as independent of one another, yet sharing the common cultural milieu of a heterodox or nonconformist Judaism which is reflected in the Hodayoth.[14] Yet there appears little reason to label this Judaism as "heterodox" or "non-conformist," as if all divergence from "official" Judaism (the Court of the Temple) somehow shared very close affinities. Samuel Sandmel has suggested the useful categories "Temple Judaism" and "synagogue Judaism,"[15] while J.W. Doeve contrasts "official" with "popular" religion in Judaism.[16] Eighth, and finally, the Odes share the conceptual and spiritual milieu of the Fourth Gospel and the letters of Ignatius of Antioch.[17] The Odist seems to represent a Christian community which regarded itself as an oppressed minority group; this conclusion is supported by the relatively frequent references to persecution and opposition (5. 4–9; 18. 11–15; 23. 13–20; 24. 7–12; 25. 5; 28. 5–6; 33. 11; 35. 3; 39. 1–4),

---

of the *Odes* has led David Hill to question their value for the study of early Christian prophecy: "Despite attempts to provide the Odes with a Jewish-Christian origin and a date in the first-century AD, the view is still widely accepted that we have to do with a Gnostic hymn-book from the second century. If so, should we seek or expect to find in it evidence on which to base a theory about the consciousness and activity of primitive Christian prophets?" in *New Testament Prophecy,* 164.

[11] "The Edessene Origin," 289.

[12] Walter Bauer's treatment of early Syrian Christianity may prove to be the most durable part of his book *Rechtgläubigkeit und Ketzerei im ältesten Christentum,* 2. Aufl. (Tübingen: Mohr Siebeck,1964).

[13] K. Rudolph, "War der Verfasser der Oden Salomos ein "Qumran-Christ"? Ein Beitrag zur Diskussion um die Anfänge der Gnosis," *RQ,* 16 (1964), 523–55; J. Carmignac, "Un Qumranien converti au Christianisme: l'auteur des Odes de Salomon," *Qumran-Probleme: Vorträge des Leipziger Symposions über Qumran-Probleme vom 9 his 14. Oktoher 1961*, ed. H. Bardtke (Berlin: Akademie-Verlag, 1963) 75–108; J.H. Charlesworth, "Les Odes de Salomon et les manuscrits de la Mer Morte," *RB, 77* (1970), 522–49; Charlesworth suggests (549), that the Odist was an Essene converted to Christianity.

[14] Oscar Cullmann, *The Johannine Circle* (Philadelphia: Westminster Press, 1976) 36.

[15] *Judaism and Christian Beginnings* (New York: Oxford University Press, 1978).

[16] "Official and Popular Religion in Judaism," *Official and Popular Religion: Analysis of a Theme for Religious Studies,* ed. H. Vrijhof and J. Waardenburg (The Hague: Mouton Publishers, 1979) 325–39.

[17] This conceptual affinity is discussed in Aune, *Cultic Setting,* 23–8.

and by the ethical or soteriological dualism which pervades the *Odes*.[18] The most likely reconstructed situation is that the Odist represented a Jewish-Christian community which had experienced the hostility and rejection of synagogue Judaism, one feature of which was the result of the promulgation of the *Birkat ham-minim* by rabbinic authorities at Yavneh toward the end of the first and beginning of the second century CE. For the purposes of the present study it is important to mention one of the more striking features shared by the *Odes*, the Fourth Gospel and Ignatius. That is the absence of most of the features usually associated with apocalypticism and apocalyptic literature in all three corpora, and the presence of what may be designated "realized eschatology" in the *Odes* and the Fourth Gospel.[19] "Realized eschatology" may be defined as that function of religious language which presents events or conditions normally regarded as existing *only* in the eschatological future *as if* they had already occurred or been experienced in the present or past perfect.

3. The Odist's Claims to Divine Inspiration

In antiquity, a prophecy or oracle is a written or oral message from a god, occasionally encoded, mediated by a human spokesperson. Prophecy, whatever else it may be, is a form of social communication which must be recognizably "prophetic" or "oracular". This recognition is usually secured through distinctive forms of behavior (possession or trance), and/or a verbal claim that the forthcoming (or preceding) message has a supernatural origin.[20] One of the more prominent features of the *Odes of Solomon* is the claim to divine inspiration frequently made by the author (6. 1–2; 10. 1–3; 11. 4–6; 12. 1–2; 15. 3–4; 16. 5; 42.

---

[18] For a discussion of dualism in the *Odes*, see J. H. Charlesworth, "Qumran, John and the Odes of Solomon," *John and Qumran*, ed. J. H. Charlesworth (London: Geoffrey Chapman, 1972) 117–35; cf. Charlesworth, "Les Odes de Salomon," 524–9. For a discussion of dualism as an ideological response to the experience of social alienation, see Wayne Meeks, "The Man from Heaven in Johannine Sectarianism," *JBL*, 91 (1972), 44–72; J. Louis Martyn, *The Gospel of John in Christian History*, 105–7. The social correlation of dualism with the experience of alienation is emphasized by Paul Hanson, *The Dawn of Apocalyptic* (Philadelphia: Fortress Press, 1975).

[19] Realized eschatology is not found reflected in the letters of Ignatius (see Aune, *Cultic Setting*, 152–65). The reason appears to be the peculiar nature of the circumstances under which the letters were written. If realized eschatology is particularly at home in the context of worship, then the *community* is the locus of that experience. Ignatius, on the other hand, is obsessed with his personal destiny, a fact which may account for the dominance of futuristic language in his letters.

[20] Modern studies on the phenomenon of trance or possession have been handily summarized by R. R. Wilson, *Prophecy and Society in Ancient Israel* (Philadelphia: Fortress Press, 1980) 21–88.

6). *Ode* 6. 1–2, which constitutes a striking example of this claim, was connected with the Montanist movement by scholars earlier in the century:[21]

As the wind moves through the harp
And the strings speak,
So the Spirit of the Lord speaks through my members,
and I speak through His love.

The thought does not stop here, but continues on into vv. 3–4:

For He destroys whatever is alien,
And everything is of the Lord.
For thus it has been from the beginning
And (will be) until the end.

The whole passage is striking because of the play on words ("wind" = *rwh*; "Spirit" = *rwhh),* reminiscent of John 3:8 ("wind" = πνεῦμα; "Spirit" = πνεῦμα).[22] The metaphor of the harp (or lyre, or flute) for the human instrument of divinely inspired utterance was widely used in the Graeco-Roman world.[23] Further, the expression "from the beginning until the end" (Syriac: *mn rysyt' w'dm' l'hrt';* Greek: ἀπ' ἀρχῆς ἕως τέλους) is found three times in the *Odes* (6.4; 7.14; 11.4), yet in early Christian literature prior to the middle of the second century, it is found only in the Apocalypse of John 21:6 (God speaking), and 22:13 (Christ speaking). W. C. van Unnik has demonstrated the Graeco-Roman origin of this idiom.[24] For the Odist, according to v. 3, prophetic inspiration involves the (temporary) cessation of mortal weakness and corruption, a notion very similar to a very popular Greek theory of divine inspiration which viewed the physical body as a hindrance to the inherently prophetic powers of the soul.[25] In spite of the Semitic ambience of the *Odes*, in this short passage we find several reflections of the influence of Graeco-Roman religious ideas.

The Odist's claims to divine inspiration are occasionally followed by a passage in which it appears that Christ is the speaker (9.1–5; 10.1–3; 17.5; 36.1). *Ode* 10.1–3, for example, contains the Odist's claim to inspiration:

The Lord has directed my mouth by His Word,
And has opened my heart by His Light.

---

21 For references to such studies, see Charlesworth, *The Odes of Solomon,* 31, n. 4.

22 Unfortunately the text of H is damaged at this point. Charlesworth's suggestion that *rwh* should be read appears convincing (*The Odes of Solomon,* 30–31, n. 1), and is followed by M. Lattke, *Die Oden Salomos in ihrer Bedeutung für Neues Testament und Gnosis,* I (Fribourg: Editions Universitaires; Göttingen: Vandenhoeck & Ruprecht, 1979) 90.

23 Philo *Quis rer. div.* 266; *De spec. leg.* 4.48–51; the notion was adapted by many Christian writers, cf. Theophilus *Ad Autolyc.* 2.9; Ps.-Justin *Coh. ad Graec.* 8; Athenagoras *Leg.* 9.

24 W. C. van Unnik, *Het Godspredikaat "Het Begin en het Einde" bij Flavius Josephus en in de Openbaring van Johannes* (Amsterdam: B. V. Noord-Hollandsche Uitgevers Maatschappij, 1976).

25 Plutarch *De def. orac.* 39 (431D–432F); Philo *De migr. Abr.* 190–91.

And He has caused to dwell in me His immortal life,
And permitted me to proclaim the fruit of His peace.
To convert the lives of those who desire to come to Him,
And to capture a good captivity for freedom.

It is immediately followed in vv. 4–6 by a section which appears to be *ex ore Christi.* Though the introduction in v.v. 1–3 functions in much the same way that the Old Testament messenger formula "thus says the Lord" does, in the *Odes* introductions to prophetic speech which carry a claim to inspiration are never expressed in stereotyped locutions. In early Christian literature generally, the Old Testament prophetic messenger formula is rarely used to introduce prophetic speech, though the functional substitute "thus says the Spirit" and similar locutions do occur (cf. Acts 21:11; Rev 2:1, 8, 12, 18; 3:1, 7, 14).[26]

Just as the Odist can introduce prophetic speech with a claim to inspiration, so he can, in two instances (3.10; 18.15), conclude a prophetic speech with a claim to inspiration as a kind of prophetic signature. Old Testament prophetic speeches often conclude with a more stereotyped expression such as the so-called divine oracle formula "an oracle/utterance of Yahweh".[27] In *Ode* 3, vv. 10–11 form the conclusion :

This is the Spirit of the Lord, which is not false,
Which teaches the sons of men to know His ways.
Be wise and understanding and vigilant.

A similar prophetic signature, with both declarative and imperative elements as in *Ode* 3. 10–11, concludes each of the proclamations to the seven churches in Rev 2 and 3; e. g., 3:6:

He who has an ear, let him hear
what the Spirit says to the churches.

Here the first line calls for careful attention and understanding, while the second attributes the speech presented in Rev 3:1–5 to the Holy Spirit. Another example of a prophetic signature is found in 1 Cor 14:37–38:[28]

---

[26] Early Christian prophetic formulas which mention the Spirit of God are discussed in detail by K. Berger, *Die Amen-Worte Jesu* (Berlin: Walter de Gruyter, 1970) 117–24.

[27] F. Baumgärtel, "Die Formel *ne'um jahwe,*" *ZAW,* 78 (1961), 277–90; H. W. Wolff, *Joel and Amos* (Philadelphia: Fortress Press, 1977) 143–4.

[28] That 1 Cor 14:37–8. is a claim that the foregoing is a prophetic speech is held by, among others, J. Lindblom, *Gesichte und Offenbarungen: Vorstellungen von göttlichen Weisungen und übernatürlichen Erscheinungen im ältesten Christentum* (Lund, Gleerup, 1968) 132–3, 143. 1 Cor. 14:38, identified as a "sentence of sacral law" by E. Käsemann, is now frequently considered a prophetic saying: cf. H. Kraft, "Die altkirchliche Prophetie und die Entstehung des Montanismus," *ThZ,* 11 (1955), 254–5; U. B. Müller, *Prophetie und Predigt,* 180; Hans Conzelmann, *1 Corinthians* (Philadelphia: Fortress Press, 1975) 246.

If anyone thinks that he is a prophet, or spiritual, he should acknowledge that what I am writing to you is a command of the Lord. If anyone does not recognize this, he is not recognized.

The phenomenon of the prophetic signature, however, is quite rare in early Christian literature. The two examples in the *Odes*, the seven instances in the Apocalypse and 1 Cor 14:37–8, constitute all the occurrences of this phenomenon of which I am aware.

There are several other places in the *Odes* which deal with the subject of divine or prophetic inspiration, yet not in the form of a personal claim by the Odist. The most famous example is *Ode* 42.6, cited by R. Bultmann as an example of inspired men speaking in the name of the Risen Christ:[29]

Then I arose and am with them,
And I will speak by their mouths.

In view of the many passages in the *Odes* in which Christ apparently speaks in the first person (see below), this statement provides a general legitimation for that phenomenon.[30]

4. Visions and Auditions

The only possible term for "prophet" used by the Odist is the ancient term "seer" (*ḥzy'*), which occurs only once (in the plural) in *Ode* 7.18–19:

The Seers [*ḥzy'*] shall go before Him,
And they shall be seen [*wnthzwn*] before Him,
And they shall praise the Lord in His love,
Because He is near and does see [*wḥzy'*].

Yet the term *ḥzy'*, could perhaps equally well refer to pilgrims who come to the Temple to "see" the Lord (cf. Pss 27. 4; 63. 3).[31] However, the Odist's fondness for paronomasia[32] may have prompted him to select this particular term in view of its varied prophetic and cultic meanings. The term *ḥzy'*, if used here as a term for prophet, emphasizes the reciprocity of prophetic sight; the seer is himself seen by God. The Odist's choice of the term *ḥzy'* from among the traditional Israelite-Christian terms for prophet suggests that visions may have been integral

[29] R. Bultmann, *Die Geschichte der synoptischen Tradition,* 8. Aufl. (Göttingen: Vandenhoeck & Ruprecht, 1970) 135, n. 1. The use of this passage by Bultmann and others is argued against by David Hill, *New Testament Prophecy,* 160–4. While Bultmann over-generalizes on the significance of this passage, Hill errs by throwing it out of court.

[30] See section 5, "The Speeches of Christ".

[31] This suggestion was made to me by Professor Ithamar Gruenwald.

[32] J. H. Charlesworth, "Paronomasia and Assonance in the Syriac Text of the Odes of Solomon," *Semitics,* 1 (1970), 12–26.

to the prophetic role in the Odist's community. The occurrence of both visions and auditions is mentioned in 5.3–4:

> Eyes I have obtained in Him,
> And I have seen [*whzyt*] His holy day.
> Ears I have acquired,
> And have heard His truth [*lšrrh*].

Here the phrase "His holy day" (*lywmh qdyš*) refers, I think, to the kind of eschatological scene depicted in *Ode* 7.16b–20. The word 'truth' (*šrr*) occurs some thirty-four times in the *Odes* (cf. the eight occurrences of *šryr'*), where it often appears to carry the connotation "revelatory truth," as in 8.8:[33]

> Hear [*šm'w*] the word of truth [*ptgm' dšrr*]
> And receive [*wqblw*] the knowledge of the Most High.

This couplet has several interesting features. The two plural imperatives indicate a real or imagined congregation. The couplet introduces what appears to be a speech of Christ, which extends from vv. 8–19, and therefore functions as a prophetic "proclamation formula".[34] Another passage which combines vision with audition is *Ode* 16.9:

> For the eye sees His works,
> And the ear hears His thought.

For the Odist, there is continuity between the role of a prophet in the reception and promulgation of revelatory truth and that of the community of believers in general.

One remarkable feature of the *Odes* is the author's relatively frequent description of his heavenly journeys, a phenomenon particularly characteristic of early Jewish apocalyptic literature, but also found in Old Testament references referring to the presence of prophets at the heavenly council of Yahweh, in some Graeco-Roman apocalypses, and in some of the vision reports of early Christian martyr acts.[35] In *Ode* 36.1–2, the Odist describes a trip to the heavenly world where he continues to offer praise to God:

---

[33] Cf. *Ode* 12.1–2: "He has filled me with words of truth,/ That I may proclaim Him./ And like the flowing of waters, truth flows from my mouth,/ And my lips declare His fruits." See also 12.13; 14.7 ("Teach me the Odes of Thy truth"); 17.5 ("Then they spoke the truth,/ From the breath which the Most High breathed into them"); 31.2; 33.8. Truth is also identified in the *Odes* with Christ, in the phrase "Son of Truth" (*br' dšrr'*), in 23.18, and Truth is personified in *Ode* 38 in such a way that He plays the role customarily played by the *angelus interpres* in more conventional apocalyptic texts.

[34] The so-called "proclamation formula" in the Old Testament introduced oracles with the phrase "Hear the word of Yahweh" (Amos 7:16; Jer 2:4; 7:2; 19:3; 22:11; etc.), cf. H. W. Wolff, *Joel and Amos,* 92–3. A similar proclamation formula is used in introducing speeches of the gods in Greek literature (*Iliad* 19.101–5), as well as to introduce oracles uttered by human instruments of the gods (*Odyssey* 15.173–78).

[35] Cf. 1 Kgs 22:19–23; Isa 6:1–13; 40:1–8; Jer 23:18; Amos 3:7; Zech 3:1–7; on this

I rested on the Spirit of the Lord,
And She lifted me up to heaven [*lrwm'*];
And caused me to stand on my feet in the Lord's high place [*brwmh dmry'*],
Before His perfection and glory,
Where I continued glorifying (Him) by the composition of His odes.

A speech of Christ then follows to the end of the *Ode* (vv. 3–8), indicating that this brief recitation of a *Himmelfahrt* functions as an introduction to a prophetic speech. A similar *Himmelfahrt* experience forms the introduction to Ode 38 (an ode which has some striking similarities to conventional apocalyptic vision reports):

I went up into the light of Truth as into a chariot,
And the Truth led me and caused me to come.

Similarly, in *Ode* 21.6–7, the close parallels to *Ode* 36:1–2 suggest the presence of a conventional sequence of motifs:

And I was lifted up in the light,
And I passed before Him.
And I was constantly near Him,
While praising and confessing Him.

Perhaps the most striking instance of all is found in *Ode* 11.16–17 :

And He took me to His Paradise,
Wherein is the wealth of the Lord's pleasure.
[The Greek lines are omitted here only for the sake of brevity]
Then I worshipped the Lord because of His magnificence. And I said...

The vision report form, alluded to above, is a characteristic feature of apocalyptic literature also found in later sections of the Old Testament.[36] The vision reports found in the *Odes* occur within the framework of a *Himmelsreise,* a common convention among apocalyptists, but unknown in the Old Testament. *Ode* 38 contains a fascinating instance of this convention. The Odist begins in vv. 1–2 (quoted above) with a reference to the heavenly transport of the seer. Truth, a term with revelatory significance for the Odist, brought him to the place

subject see F. M. Cross, "The Council of Yahweh in Second Isaiah," *JNES,* 12 (1953), 274–7; E. C. Kingsbury, "The Prophets and the Council of Yahweh," *JBL,* 83 (1964), 279–87. For the Graeco-Roman world, see H. W. Attridge, "Greek and Latin Apocalypses," *Semeia,* 14 (1979), 159–86, and J. S. Hanson, "Dreams and Visions in the Graeco-Roman World and Early Christianity," *Aufstieg und Niedergang der römischen Welt,* ed. H. Temporini and W. Haase (Berlin: Walter de Gruyter, 1980) Part II, 23. 2, 1395–1427. One of the more interesting examples of such a *Himmelsreise* is found in the so-called "Dream of Scipio" at the conclusion of book six of Cicero's *De republica.* Among the early Christian martyrologies, see *Acts of Perpetua and Felicitas* 4.

36 B. O. Long, "Reports of Visions Among the Prophets," *JBL*, 95 (1976), 353–65.

of immortal life (v. 3b), and caused him to "rest" (v. 4a). Truth continues to guide the seer (vv. 7–11):

But Truth was proceeding on the upright way,
And whatever I did not understand He exhibited to me:
All the drugs of error,
And pains of death which are considered sweetness.
And the corrupting of the Corruptor,
I saw [*ḥz'*] when the Bride who was corrupting was adorned,
And the Bridegroom who corrupts and is corrupted.
And I asked the Truth, Who are these?
And He said to me: This is the Deceiver and the Error.
And they imitate the Beloved and His Bride,
And they cause the world to err and corrupt it.

Here Truth functions as an apocalyptic *angelus interpres,* and provides the Odist with a guided tour of the heavenly world where, it appears, he sees heavenly realities which prefigure earthly realities.[37] The question-and-answer revelatory dialogue is characteristic of Jewish revelatory literature and Graeco-Roman revelatory dialogues (which have received the modern designation ἐρωταποκρίσεις).[38] The brief vision dialogue of *Ode* 38 reflects an intermediate stage in the process of "de-apocalypticization" in which the content of the vision no longer reflects the typical concerns of apocalyptic literature, but rather gives expression to the cosmological dimensions of the ethical dualism which permeates the *Odes*. A similar process of "de-apocalypticization" appears to have preceded the composition of major segments of the Shepherd of Hermas.

One of the more discussed *Odes* in the collection is *Ode* 11, of which a Greek translation has been recovered. This Ode also contains an account of a *Himmelsreise,* which is preceded by an account of the experience of divine inspiration of the Odist in vv. 4–8 :

From the beginning until the end
I received His knowledge.
And I was established upon the rock of truth,
Where He had set me.
And speaking waters touched my lips
From the fountain of the Lord generously.
And so I drank and became intoxicated,
From the living water *[my'ḥy']* that does not die.
And my intoxication was not with ignorance,
But I abandoned vanity.

---

37 That events above are the basis for earthly events is a commonplace notion in antiquity and not simply a Platonic idea: see H. Bietenhard, *Die himmlische Welt im Urchristentum und Spätjudentum* (Tübingen: Mohr Siebeck, 1951) 13.

38 H. Dörrie and H. Dörries, "Erotapokriseis," *RAC,* 6 (1966), 342–70.

Here the reference to living water is not an allusion to baptism, but an image used to symbolize divine revelation.[39] A similar use of water imagery is found in 12.2, where it is part of the Odist's claim to divine inspiration:

He has filled me with words of truth,
That I may proclaim Him.
And like the flowing of waters, truth flows from my mouth,
And my lips declare His fruits.

Returning to the *Himmelsreise* of *Ode* 11, the Odist then relates his transport to Paradise with a synopsis of what he beheld there (v. 16, including 16a-f in the Greek version, which is probably genuine):

And He took me to His Paradise,
Wherein is the wealth of the Lord's pleasure.
I beheld blooming and fruit-bearing trees,
And self-grown was their crown. Their branches were sprouting
And their fruits were shining.
From an immortal land (were) their roots.
And a river of gladness was irrigating them,
And round about them in the land of eternal life.

In this report, the Odist relates his experience of an allegorical vision; unlike *Ode* 38, he does not require the interpretive skill of the truth to convey the symbolic meaning of that which he sees. The Odist in this vision is a kind of celestial window-shopper; the importance of previewing Paradise lies simply in the fact that it is the destiny of all Christians, who are symbolized by the "blooming and fruit-bearing trees" (v. 18 explicitly makes this connection). The two central features of this Paradise, the fruitful trees and the river of gladness, may have been conceptualized by combining Ezek. 47. 12 with the description of Eden in Gen. 2. 9 f. The last part of *Ode* 11 contains, in vv. 17–24, a distinct structural unit in which the Odist offers a song of thanksgiving and praise for that which he has seen. Immediately after the portion quoted above in 16 and 16a–f, the Odist says (vv. 17 f.): "Then I worshipped the Lord because of his magnificence. And I said...." From a form critical perspective, this section conforms to the convention of a "thanksgiving for a divine revelation" a literary form found in both early Jewish, Graeco-Roman and early Christian revelatory literature.[40]

In surveying these references to visions and auditions by the Odist, and in consideration of many of the forms which he uses to articulate his revelatory

---

[39] "Living water" is referred to in Odes 6.18; 11.7, and the expression "speaking water" (*my' mll'*) is found in *Ode* 11.6, with a very close parallel in Ignatius *Rom.* 7. 2. "Water of life" is referred to several times in the Apocalypse of John (7:17; 21:6; 22:1, 17), where it never appears to allude to baptism. On the side of early Judaism, see *Jub.* 24:19, 25; *1 Enoch* 17.4; 1QH8. 7, 16; CD 19. 34. See the discussion in Charlesworth, "Les Odes," 534–8.

[40] Examples of this form are found in Q (Mt. 11:25–30; Lk 10:21–22); *Corpus Hermeticum* 1.32.

experiences, it is apparent that he stands within what might be designated the prophetic-apocalyptic tradition of early Judaism and early Christianity. The Odist, to be sure, is no apocalyptist, yet he has used many of the conventions of apocalyptic literature as vehicles for his own distinctive message.

5. The Speeches of Christ

One of the most distinctive and puzzling features of the *Odes* is the change in speakers, a phenomenon which occurs without formal indications that such a change is about to occur. This phenomenon may in part be accounted for by the antiphonal or responsorial character of the *Odes*.[41] While the earliest specific reference to antiphonal singing in Judaism is Philo's description of the liturgical practices of the Therapeutae (*Vit. cont.* 11), many Old Testament psalms give evidence of antiphonal structure and many references to this type of singing are found in rabbinic literature.[42] One of the more interesting examples of antiphonal or dialogical structure in the *Odes* is found in *Ode* 41. In vv. 1–7, the first person plural verb forms and pronominal suffixes predominate; here is an example from vv. 3–4:

> We live [*ḥyynn*] in the Lord by His grace,
> And life we receive [*mqblynn*] by His Messiah.
> For a great day has shined upon us [*ln*],
> And wonderful is He who has given to us [*mn*] of His glory.

In what is probably intended as a short speech of Christ (see below), the first person singular forms prevail in vv. 8–10:

> All those who see me [*ly*] will be amazed,
> Because I [*'n'*] am from another race.
> For the Father of Truth remembered me [*'tdkrny*];
> He who possessed me [*dqnny*] from the beginning.
> For His riches begat me [*yldny*],
> And the thought of His heart.

The first person plural resumes again in v. 11:

> And His Word is with us [*'mn*] in all our way [*'wrḥn*],
> The Savior who gives life and does not reject ourselves [*npštn*].

---

[41] Harris and Mingana, *The Odes and Psalms of Solomon,* 2.46.

[42] C. C. Keet, *A Liturgical Study of the Psalter* (London: George Allen & Unwin, Ltd., 1928) 63–6. For a collection of references to antiphonal singing in rabbinic literature, see R. Deichgräber, *Gotteshymnus und Christushymnus in der frühen Christenheit: Untersuchungen zu Form, Sprache und Stil der frühchristlichen Hymnen* (Göttingen: Vandenhoeck & Ruprecht, 1967) 46–7.

Similarly, *Ode* 4 begins with a reference to "my God" (*'lhy*), yet by vv. 9f. a transition is made to the first person plural:

Thou hast given to us [*ln*] Thy fellowship,
Not that Thou wast in need of us [*mnn*],
But that we are always in need [*ḥsyrynn*] of Thee.

The shift of speakers from singular to plural is a relatively common feature in the *Odes* and one which provides a setting for the present discussion.

Commentators have often noted the apparent shift in speakers from the Odist (in his role as *filius adoptivus)* to Christ (as *filius proprius)*.[43] These transitions, however, are based on content rather than form, for in no instance is the speaker explicitly identified as Christ. In some instances, as in *Ode* 41, the changes in grammatical number indicate a shift in speakers, yet the identity of the speakers is never made explicit. The basis for the speeches *ex ore Christi* in the *Odes* is stated programmatically in *Ode* 42.6, a reference quoted earlier:

Then I arose and am with them,
And I will speak by their mouths.

The term "arose" (*qmt*) can only refer to the resurrection of Jesus, while the second line just as certainly refers to prophetic utterances pronounced in the name and person of the Risen Christ.[44] In the translations of the Odes by Harris-Mingana and Charlesworth, the label "(Christ speaks)" has been inserted before the following sections of the Odes: 8.8–21 (Charlesworth: 8.8–19); 10.4–6; 17. 6–15 (Charlesworth: 17.6–16); 22.1–12; 28.8–19 (Charlesworth: 28.9–20); 31.6–13; 36.3–8; 41.8–10; 42.3–20.[45] Several of these speeches are introduced by statements which function as indications of the inspired or oracular character of what follows. Introductory claims to divine inspiration preface three such speeches (10.1–3; 28.1–7; 36.1–2); a proclamation formula introduces a fourth (8.8). Three speeches *ex ore Christi* begin with an expression reflecting the astonishment of onlookers (17.6; 28.8; 41.1). The content of these speeches is usually such that they can only be attributed to Christ; cf. *Ode* 36.3:[46]

[The Spirit] brought me forth before the face of the Lord.
And although a Son of Man [*br 'nš'*],
I was named the Luminary, the Son of God [*brh d'lh'*].

[43] The distinction between *filius proprius* and *filius adoptivus* is made by R. Abramowski, "Der Christus der Salomooden," *ZNW*, 25 (1936), 57.

[44] This passage was used by R. Bultmann to show that many of the "I" sayings of the Synoptic Gospels, as well as many of the prophetic and apocalyptic sayings attributed to Jesus in the Gospels were in actuality the product of Christian prophets speaking in the name of the Risen Jesus. This view contains many problematic features, many of which are discussed by David Hill, *New Testament Prophecy,* 160ff.

[45] The list of speeches attributed to Christ by Bernard, *The Odes of Solomon,* 39–40, includes 8.10–22; 10; 17.11–14(15); 22.1–5; 28.8–18; 31.7–11; 33.6–11; 42.4–26.

[46] Quoted from the translation of Harris and Mingana, *ad loc.*

Again, in 10.6, we find a claim that could only be made by Christ or God:

> And they walked in my life and were saved,
> And they became my people for ever and ever.

Many similar passages occur in the *Odes* (8.15–20; 22.5; 28.17; 31.13).

If the Odist is able to speak as a prophet in the name and person of Christ, *why* does he do so, *what* (if anything) is the distinctive content of these speeches *ex ore Christi,* and perhaps most importantly, what is the *function* of these speeches? These questions cannot be satisfactorily answered within the framework of the present study, for they are among the most difficult interpretive issues in the study of the *Odes*. On the second question, the speeches of Christ in the *Odes* focus on his soteriological role, including his mysterious appearance, the persecution he endured which was frustrated by his resurrection; his task of calling forth believers whom he had predestined; his proclamation to the dead and their response to him. Of all these elements (and there are others, though less prominent), the *descensus ad inferos* appears only within the framework of these speeches *ex ore Christi* (17.8–15; 22.1–12). Thus the main emphasis of these oracular sections is the role of Christ in gathering his people. Related to this is the strange passage in *Ode* 10.5–6, in which the inclusion of the Gentiles in the people of God is treated apologetically by the speaker. The emphasis on the total redemptive mission of Christ is comprehensible if it were in conflict with another soteriological principle and required independent legitimation. If we hypothecate that the other conflicting principle was Torah, then the emphasis in the speeches of Christ in the *Odes* becomes readily comprehensible. Of course, the fact that Torah is not mentioned explicitly or implicitly tells against this proposal. Yet the fact that the *Odes* are liturgical and not apologetic literature may explain this omission. The theme of persecution often arises in the speeches of Christ, a theme which we have already found common in sections outside these speeches. The speaker's experience of opposition, persecution and ultimate victory (29.8–19; 31.8–13; 42.5) apparently provides a paradigmatic precedent for the experiences of the Odist's community. The first and third question both relate to the function of the speeches of Christ in the *Odes*. The liturgical recitation and repetition of these speeches function to remind the community that Christ is not distant but very near to them. Through these hymns he directly addresses the community through the Odist.

6. Congregational Prophecy and Realized Eschatology

Early Christian prophecy has commonly been regarded as *congregational* prophecy, that is, its primary setting has been considered to be the Christian community assembled for worship[47] However, evidence for congregational prophecy is almost entirely limited to 1 Cor. 12–14, *Did.* 10–13 and Hermas *Mand.* 11. In scholarly discussion, the debate often centers on the problem of whether all Christians were potential or actual prophets or whether prophecy was the special province of a group of religious specialists designated "prophets." In our discussion thus far, we have attempted to underline the prophetic or oracular character of the *Odes*, and at the same time have recognized that many of them have an antiphonal or responsory structure designed for use in public worshi Christian worship functions in such a way that paradigmatic events and conditions of the past, as well as particular anticipated events and conditions of the future, are spoken of *as if* the temporal boundaries between past and future had become collapsed into an eternal present. In this section of our study we shall first consider the congregational character of prophecy in the *Odes* and then correlate this with evidence for the phenomenon of realized eschatology.

In *Ode* 8.1–7 (followed by a speech *ex ore Christi* in vv. 8–19), we find what appears to be an injunction to congregational prophecy; cf. *Ode* 8.3–4:

> Rise up [*qwmw*] and stand erect [*w'tqymw*]
> You [*hnwn*] who were brought low.
> You [*hnwn*] who were in silence, speak [*mllw*],
> For your mouth has been opened.

Though very little is known of the protocol of congregational prophecy, Hermas *Mand.* xi. 9 (trans. K. Lake), does indicate that an introductory prayer could serve as a prelude to the exercise of the prophetic gift:

> Therefore, when the man who has the Divine Spirit comes into a meeting [συναγωγὴν] of righteous men who have the faith of the Divine Spirit, and intercession [ἔντευξις] is made to God from the assembly of those men, then the angel of the prophetic spirit rests [κείμενος] on him and fills the man, and the man, being filled with the Holy Spirit, speaks to the congregation as the Lord wills.

In this light, let us consider the possibility of regarding *Ode* 14.7–8 as an individual invocation for the gift of prophetic speech:

> Teach me the odes of Thy truth,
> That I may produce fruits in Thee.
> And open to me the harp of Thy Holy Spirit
> So that with every note I may praise Thee, O Lord.

Though the Odes resist theological systematization, enough clues are present to reconstruct the ritual protocol preceding the public performance of a prophetic hymn. In *Ode* 37.1–4 (the entire *Ode*), we read:

---

47. This has recently been emphasized by Jannes Reiling, *Hermas and Christian Prophecy,* and *idem,* "Prophecy, the Spirit and the Church," *Prophetic Vocation in the New Testament and Today,* ed. J. Panagopoulos (Leiden: Brill, 1977) 58–76.

I stretched out my hands toward the Lord,
And towards the Most High I raised my voice.
And I spoke with the lips of my heart,
And He heard me when my voice reached Him.
His Word came towards me,
That which gave me the fruits of my labors;
And gave me rest by the grace of the Lord.

The ritual sequence evident in this passage, with supplementation from other passages in the *Odes*, consists of the following elements: (1) assumption of the standing position (cf. 26.12 [*qwm*]; 7.16b–21), (2) raising the arms in a cruciform pattern (27. 1–3; 35. 7),[48] (3) a petition for the ability to utter inspired song is addressed to the Lord (cf. 14.7–8), (4) the Odist experiences "rest," i. e. the overwhelming consciousness of the presence of God, and (5) the Odist utters an inspired song. The term "fruit" (*p'r'*), referred to in 37.3, is found fourteen times in the *Odes*, and always in a metaphorical sense. The symbol of fruit is often connected with speech, particularly inspired or prophetic speech (cf. 8.2; 10.2; 12.2; 14.7; 16.2). Similarly, the word "rest" (various form of the root *nh* occur twenty-one times) which appears to have eschatological overtones, is closely intertwined by the Odist with the experience of divine inspiration. In *Ode* 26.10 we read:

Or who can rest [*dmttnyḥ*] on the Most High,
That from His mouth he may speak?

"Rest" is the state in which the singers stand and sing their odes, according to *Ode* 26.12:

For it suffices to know and to rest [*wlmttnhw*]
For in the rest [*bnyḥwt'*] the singers stand [*qymyn*].

The Odist can even characterize his compositions as "odes of His rest" (26.3). "Rest" is also a feature of existence in Paradise, according to *Ode* 20.7–8:

And come into His Paradise and make thee a garland from His tree;
And put it on thy head and be glad; And recline on His rest [*nyhwth*].

The living fountain is another feature of celestial geography whose water flows from the lips of the Lord (30.5), and which provides rest, according to *Ode* 30.2:

And come all ye thirsty and take a draught;
And rest [*w'ttnyḥw*] by the fountain of the Lord.

"Rest" is also a condition which precedes the *Himmelsreise* described in *Ode* 38; in v. 4 we find the following:

---

[48] Charlesworth, *The Odes of Solomon,* 125, n. 10.

And it [Truth] went with me and made me rest [*w'nyḥ*]
and suffered me not to err;
Because it was and is the Truth.

Who is the Odist and how widespread is the phenomenon of prophecy in the community he represents? The more common terms for "prophet" (Syriac: *nby'*) and "prophecy" (Syriac: *nby*), borrowed from Hebrew, do not occur in the *Odes*. The absence of these terms, together with the general failure of the Odist to imitate other features characteristic of Old Testament prophetic formulas and styles, suggests that prophecy in the *Odes* is not merely a literary imitation. The Odist twice designates himself a "priest" (*khan*') in *Ode* 20.1, yet this designation is patently metaphorical, referring to his role as intermediary or intercessor (an important function for many Old Testament prophets). One designation for those who functioned as prophets in the Odist's community may have been the ancient term "seer" (*hzy*') which occurs only once in the plural in *Ode* 7.18–19. This passage occurs in the midst of an eschatological scene depicted in vv. 16b–20 which deserves quotation in full:

And the Most High will be known by His holy ones [*bqdyšwhy*]
To announce to those who have songs [*mzmwr'*] of the coming of the Lord [*dmtyth dmry'*],
That they may go forth to meet Him and may sing [*wmzmrwn*] to Him
With joy and with the harp of many tones. The Seers [*ḥzy* '] shall go before Him,
And they shall be seen [*wmtḥzwn*] before Him.
And they shall praise the Lord in His love,
Because He is near and does see [*wḥzy'*].
And hatred shall be removed from the earth,
And with jealousy it shall be drowned.
For ignorance was destroyed upon it,
Because the knowledge of the Lord arrived upon it.

The eschatological character of this scene is indicated, not only by the use of imperfect verbs (this is one of the few such scenes actually predicted in the *Odes*; elsewhere they are described as if actually present), but also by the fact that what is envisaged is the ultimate purification of the terrestrial world. In spite of the eschatological character of this scene, it is not unlikely that the constituent features of this theophany are patterned after the basic structures of public worship known to the Odist and his community. The "holy ones" (*qdyš'*), though clearly used of Christians generally in the only other two uses of the plural substantive (22.12; 23.1; cf. the synonym *hswhy* in 9.6), seems to be used here as the designation of a particular group whose task is heralding the arrival of the Lord.[49] Another term is used in *Ode* 6.13 for the prophetic role in

[49] The expression "the holy ones" is also used frequently in the Apocalypse for Christians generally (5:8; 8:3, 4; 13:7, 10; 14:12; 22:21), yet in certain contexts it is not clear whether Christians in general or a particular group of Christians are being referred to (11:18; 16:6;

the Odist's community, "ministers of that drink" (*lmšmšnwhy dhw mšty'*) the Coptic translates *mšmšn'* with *diakōn*). The term "drink" (*mšty'*) is used only three times in the Odes and always in association with speech (6.12, 13; 30.2). Since the Odist frequently refers to his compositions (which are written, not just composed orally, 26.8), as "odes," or "songs" (*zmyrt'*), cf. 14.7; 26.2, 3, 8; 36.2; 40.3, he can probably be designated as one of the singers in the group mentioned in 26. 12. The inspired nature of the songs is indicated in that all six occurrences of the term "ode" (*zmyrt'*) are qualified by some reference to the Lord: "odes of Thy truth" (14.7); "1 will recite His holy ode" (26:2); "the odes of His rest" (26.3); "the odes of the Lord" (26.8); "the composition of His odes" (36.2); "my members are anointed by His odes" (40.3). Though the evidence is not as clear as one could wish, it appears that the Odist represents a group of inspired singers (perhaps even their leader) who constitute a defined and recognizable group within the community.

One notable characteristic of prophetic speech in the Old Testament is the fact that future events are sometimes spoken of as if they had already occurred. Grammarians have labeled this use of the Hebrew verb the *perfectum propheticum*. Similarly, a characteristic of some Graeco-Hellenistic and early Christian prophecies is the use of the present tense in making predictions; this use of the present has been variously labeled "futuristic present," "prophetic present" and "oracular present". Since for early Christianity the ritual of re-presentation of the paradigmatic saving events of the past (the cross and resurrection of Jesus, primarily) was often complemented by the ritual anticipation of the completion of the divine program of saving events in the future (the Parousia of Jesus, the resurrection of the dead, the destruction of the wicked, the reward of the righteous and a blissful eternity spent in the presence of God), it is likely that congregational prophecy played an important and distinctive role in the present realization of protological and eschatological events and conditions.[50] While most of the features of apocalypticism have counterparts (*mutatis mutandis*) in the *Odes of Solomon* (the major exceptions are the notion of a general resurrection, the temporal dualistic framework of this age/age to come and the synopses of world history presented as prophetic predictions), the structural relationship of these elements is considerably different and they have lost their objectivity. The Parousia is the central moment of a theophanic scene in 7.17. Elsewhere Christ is spoken of as conquering and assuming his rulership, yet in terms which

18:20, 24). In the latter passages "holy ones" is used in conjunction with the designation "prophets."

[50] *Did.* 10:7 suggests that prophets be permitted to hold their own distinctive form of eucharist. In discussing the relationship of the liturgical scenes in Heaven to those on earth, H. Kraft observes in the case of John the seer, "Denn Johannes beansprucht für sich selber prophetisches Charisma und macht darum von der prophetischen Freiheit Gebrauch. Diese prophetische Freiheit besteht aber unter anderem in der Freiheit von agendarischen Bindungen" (*Die Offenbarung des Johannes* [Tübingen: Mohr Siebeck, 1974] 102).

make it difficult to distinguish his first coming from his second coming (10.4; 22. 5–7; 23.22; 31.1). Jesus (the name itself never occurs in the *Odes*, just as it does not in the Shepherd of Hermas), is designated "Messiah" seven times, three times using the apparently primitive expression "his Messiah" (*mšyhh*), in 9.3; 41.3, 15; cf. "Lord's Messiah" (*bmšyhh dmry'*), in 29.6 (cf. 17. 17; 24.1; 39.11). Given the Jewish matrix of the *Odes*, it is impossible to suppose that the apocalyptic role of the Messiah was unknown to the Odist's community. Remnants of the notion of a final cosmic battle between good and evil are also found in the *Odes*, though interpreters are prone to see in such references a depiction of the spiritual warfare of Christians. *Ode* 9.6–11 (trans. Harris-Mingana) is an example of such a disputed passage:

> For I announce peace, to you His saints;
> That none of those who hear may fall in war [*bqrb'*]
> And that those who have known Him may not perish,
> And that those who receive (Him) may not be ashamed.
> An everlasting crown is Truth;
> Blessed are they who set it on their heads:
> A stone of great price (it is);
> And the wars [*wqrb'*] were on account of the crown.
> And righteousness hath taken it,
> And hath given it to you.
> Put on the crown in the true covenant of the Lord;
> And all those who have conquered shall be inscribed in His book.

The similarities between this passage and Rev 3:5, 11; 2:10 (crown and name inscribed in the book of life for perseverance), suggest that an apocalyptic theme has been applied to the historical experience of persecution. In early Christian literature the crown is primarily a symbol of eternal life or immortality, a fact evident in such phrases as "crown of life" (Rev 2:10; Jas 1:12), and "crown of immortality" (*Mart. Polyc.* 17.1; 19.2). Crown imagery is eschatologically oriented; that is, the crown is to be worn only in the future when one's earthly life has been successfully completed (2 Tim 4:8; Jas 1:12; 1 Pet 5:4; *Mart. Polyc.* 17:1; 19:2; Hermas *Sim.* 8.2.1). In the *Odes*, on the other hand, the crown is described as having been put on either in the past or the present. In *Ode* 17.1–2, in which the second couplet is synonymous with the first, we read:

> Then I was crowned by my God,
> And my crown is living.
> And I was justified by my Lord,
> For my salvation is incorruptible.

Since the Odist uses the image of crowning as an experience of the past or present,[51] and crowning is primarily a symbol of the presence of salvation,[52] he

[51] Harris and Mingana, *The Odes and Psalms of Solomon,* 11, 209.
[52] Charlesworth, *The Odes of Solomon,* 28, n. 15.

is clearly using the language of realized eschatology (cf. 1.1; 5.12; 9.11; 17.1; 20.7).

Crowning is one of many images used by the Odist to present immortality as a present possession, a conception similar to that frequently expressed in the Fourth Gospel.[53] The Odist is fond of the phrase "immortal life" (*hy' dl' mwt'*), which he uses seven times (3.8; 10.2; 15.10; 28.6; 31.7; 38.3; 40.6). "Immortal life" is regarded a present possession in *Ode* 10.2:

> And He has caused to dwell in me His immortal life;
> And has permitted me to proclaim the fruit of His peace.

An oblique reference to Paradise, the appropriate environment for the enjoyment of immortal life, is found in *Ode* 15.10:

> And eternal life has arisen in the Lord's land,
> And it has become known to His faithful ones,
> And been given without limit to all that trust in Him.

See also 5.14; 28.6–7; 31.7; 38.3; 40.6.

A corollary of the present possession of immortality is the absence of the negative aspects of mortality: sickness, weakness, ignorance, persecution. Immortality for the Odist is inseparable from the presence of God, and whenever the Odist and his community find themselves in that presence, there is a pervasive consciousness that all that is inconsistent with that presence has been banished from it. This is particularly evident in the Odist's accounts of his ascent to the divine presence, an example of which is found in *Ode* 21.1–4:

> I lifted up my arms on high
> On account of the compassion of the Lord.
> Because He cast off my bonds from me,
> And my Helper lifted me up according to His compassion and His salvation.
> And I put off darkness,
> And put on light.
> And even I myself acquired members.
> In them there was no sickness
> Or affliction or suffering.

A similar experience is narrated in the prelude to the *Himmelsreise* described in *Ode* 11.7–11:[54]

> And I drank and became intoxicated,
> From the living water that does not die [*my' ḥy' dl' mytyn*];
> And my intoxication was not with ignorance;
> But I abandoned vanity,
> And turned towards the Most High, my God,
> And was enriched by His favors.

---

[53] Aune, *Cultic Setting*, 105–21.

[54] See also 7.19–21; 13.1–4; 15.6; 18.1–3; 31.1–3; 38.6.

And I rejected the folly cast upon the earth,
And stripped it off and cast it from me.
And the Lord renewed me with His garment,
And possessed me by His light.

The Odes are permeated with the "Paradise tradition," i. e. that Judaeo-Christian tradition which conceptualized salvation in terms of a restoration of the Edenic conditions thought to have existed prior to the fall.[55] We have already suggested that the notion of "immortal life" (*hy' dl' mwt'*) is part of this tradition, since mortality was thought to have begun with man's expulsion from Paradise. Of the three most common elements in the Jewish conception of the physical features of Paradise, the tree(s) as a principle of fecundity, the (fountain of) living water, and the mountain,[56] the first two frequently occur in the *Odes*. In the Odist's visit to Paradise in *Ode* 11, he sees the many trees watered by the river of gladness in the land of eternal life (vv. 16, 16a-f, Greek version). The trees symbolize Christians; as vv. 18–21 make clear:

And I said, Blessed, O Lord, are they
Who are planted in Thy land [*b'r'k*],
And who have a place in Thy Paradise;
And who grow in the growth of Thy trees,
And have passed from darkness into light.
Behold, all Thy laborers (are) fair,
They who work good works,
And turn from wickedness to Thy pleasantness.
For they turned away from themselves the bitterness of the trees,
When they were planted in Thy land.

The heavenly Paradise and the earthly church have somehow merged into one entity. This is possible, of course, in view of the apocalyptic convention of regarding persons, events and conditions in the heavenly world as having earthly counterparts in the past, present or future. Several times the Odist uses the word "land" (*'r'*) as a synonym for Paradise (11, 12, 13, 18, 21; 15.10). The term "Paradise" (*prdys'*) occurs but five times in the *Odes*, and four of those occurrences are found in *Ode* 11. The fifth occurrence, in *Ode* 20.7–9, clearly reveals the realized eschatological dimension of Paradise as virtually identical with the Church:

But put on the grace of the Lord generously,
And come into His Paradise,
And make for thyself a crown from His tree.
Then put (it) on thy head and be joyful,
And recline upon His rest.

55 Aune, *Cultic Setting,* 37–42, 185–8.

56 J. Daniélou, «Terre et Paradis chez les Peres de l'Eglise,» *Eranos-Jahrbuch,* 22 (1953), 434–7.

For His glory will go before thee;
And thou shalt receive of His kindness and of His grace;
And thou shalt be anointed in truth with the praise of His holiness.

Here the concept of "rest," which belongs to the Paradise tradition of the *Odes*, and to which we have already called attention, is of central significance.

A second and perhaps complementary aspect of realized eschatology in the *Odes* concerns the final elimination of all God's enemies. This event is described in the *perfectum propheticum* in *Ode* 23.18–22:

And there was seen at its head, the head which was revealed,
Even the Son of Truth from the Most High Father.
And He inherited and possessed everything,
And then the scheming of the many ceased.
Then all the seducers became headstrong and fled,
And the persecutors became extinct and were blotted out.
And the letter became a large volume,
Which was entirely written by the finger of God.
And the name of the Father was upon it;
And of the Son and of the Holy Spirit,
To rule for ever and ever.

Here the theme of the cosmic dominion of Christ is accompanied by the necessary preliminary step of the total conquest of all opposition as a prelude to the inauguration of his eternal rule (cf. Phil. 2:5–11, where the same theme is also found within a hymn). A similar juxtaposition of the two motifs of conquest of enemies and assumption of rule is found in the brief speech *ex ore Christi* in *Ode* 29.8–10:[57]

And He gave me the sceptre of His power,
That I might subdue the devices of the Gentiles,
And humble the power of the mighty.
To make war by His Word,
And to take victory by His power.
And the Lord overthrew my enemy by His Word,
And he became like the dust which a breeze carries off.

In view of the apparent persecution and opposition experienced by the Odist's community, this prophetic vision of the complete destruction of their enemies functioned to avert their gaze from the enveloping situation and to fix instead their eyes on the heavenly glory and victory which they, as conquerors and victors, will ultimately experience.

---

[57] According to Harris and Mingana, *The Odes and Psalms of Solomon,* 365: "The discrimination of the parts of the Ode [29] in which Christ speaks is difficult. In some ways it looks more like a dialogue. Verses 6, 7 might be the poet's experience, verses 8–10 the Lord's and the closing verse again the poet."

7. The Phenomenon of the Prophetic Hymn

There can be little doubt that prayer and praise were two characteristic aspects of early Christian prophecy.[58] Col. 3:16 (followed by Eph. 5:19) refers to ψαλμοῖς ὕμνοις ᾠδαῖς πνευματικαῖς, using one adjective to modify three nouns; here πνευματικός should be translated "inspired by the Spirit." Though it is impossible to distinguish between "psalms" and "hymns" and "songs," and though we cannot be sure of the kind of compositions to which Paul and the Deutero-Pauline tradition referred, it is nevertheless clear that these compositions were understood as prophetic genres and that they were an integral part of early Christian worshi Elsewhere Paul refers to singing in an inspired state (ψαλῶ τῷ πνεύματι, 1 Cor 14:15), and David Hill has made the acute observation that a comparison of the lists in 1 Cor 14:26 and 14:6 reveals that "hymn" in the former takes the place of "prophecy" in the latter.[59]

In Mediterranean antiquity generally there was an elusive yet persistent association between prophecy, oracles and various types of song. This is partly attributable to the fact that prophecy and oracles in both ancient Israel and in regions under Greek influence were more frequently than not articulated in poetic form.[60] Musical instruments were often associated with prophetic inspiration, even if most scholars regard them as aids in controlling the onset of a trance. At some ancient Greek oracles, notably that of Clarian Apollo, a cult official designated as the θεσπιωδός or "oracle singer," would reproduce prose oracles in poetic form and sing them to the inquirers.[61] Plato refers several times to the χρησμῳδοί, "oracle singers," apparently freelance singers or reciters of oracles (*Apol.* 22c; *Ion* 534d). Prose oracles had become more common by the first century CE, judging by Plutarch's essay *De Pythiae oraculis*, which deals with the topic of why the oracles of Delphi are no longer given in verse. The Chaldean Oracles, written toward the end of the second century CE by Julianus the Theurgist, are in hexameter and have a hymn-like quality.[62] An oracular hymn which is frequently quoted as a parallel to Rev 1:8 is attributed by Pausanias to the Peleiae (literally, "doves"), or prophetic priestesses of the oracle of Zeus at Dodona:[63]

---

58 J. Panagopoulos, "Die urchristliche Prophetie, ihr Charakter und ihre Funktion," *Prophetic Vocation in the New Testament and Today* (Leiden: Brill, 1977) 22.

59 Hill, *New Testament Prophecy,* 210.

60 On the poetic character of Greek oracles, see most recently, Joseph Fontenrose, *The Delphic Oracle* (Berkeley and Los Angeles: University of California Press, 1978) 166–95.

61 O. Schneider, *Nicandrea* (Leipzig: Teubner, 1856) 18; K. Buresch, *Klaros: Untersuchungen zum Orakelwesen des späteren Altertums* (Leipzig: Teubner, 1889) 35; H. W. Parke, *Greek Oracles* (London: Hutchinson University Library, 1967) 139.

62 E. des Places, *Oracles Chaldaïques avec un choix de commentaires anciens* (Paris: Société d'Edition "Les Belles Lettres," 1971).

63 Pausanias 10.12.10 (translation of author). For other oracular hymns see the much-discussed Sarapis oracle cited in Macrobius *Sat.* 1.20.16–17; cf. R. van den Broek, "The Sarapis

Zeus Was, Zeus is, Zeus shall be; O mighty Zeus.
Earth sends up the harvest; therefore sing the praise of Earth as Mother.

On the Israelite side, Sigmund Mowinckel proposed the prophetic origin of a number of psalms in the Old Testament (Pss 20, 21, 50, 60, 72, 75, 81, 85:9 ff.; 89:20 ff.; 108; 110; 131; 132:11 ff.),[64] a suggestion which has been fully exploited by A. R. Johnson.[65] The disappearance of prophecy in ancient Israel has been widely regarded as in part the result of the inclusion of cult prophets into the ranks of the Levitical singers;[66] the Chronicler equates "singing" with "prophesying" (1 Chron 25:1, 3, 6), and narrates the prophetic activity of both Levites and priests (2 Chron 20:14–18; 24:20).

The Apocalypse of John is one product of early Christian prophecy which contains a number of hymns set within the framework of an extensive vision report. Yet while the *Odes of Solomon* are hymns which originated in a liturgical context in early Syrian Christianity, the hymns of the Apocalypse, though they certainly contain traditional material,[67] are not derived from early Christian liturgy, but are literary compositions fashioned by the author for their present setting.[68] Heinrich Kraft has suggested that John's liberty in reformulating and transforming liturgical traditions is to be attributed to his "prophetic freedom."[69] Regardless of the merits of this suggestion, it is not unlikely that the hymns of the Apocalypse were modeled after early Christian and perhaps early Jewish exemplars.[70] Despite many differences in form and content, the hymns of the

Oracle in Macrobius *Sat.* 1.20, 16–17," in *Hommages à Maarten I. Vermaseren* (Leiden: Brill, 1978) 1.123–41.

[64] S. Mowinckel, *The Psalms in Israel's Worship* (Nashville: Abingdon Press, 1962) 2.58–68; cf. A. S. Kapelrud, "Sigmund Mowinckel and Old Testament Study," *God and His Friends in the Old Testament* (Oslo: Universitetsvorlaget, 1979) 53–78.

[65] A. R. Johnson, *The Cultic Prophet and Israel's Psalmody* (Cardiff: University of Wales Press, 1979).

[66] A. R. Johnson, *The Cultic Prophet in Ancient Israel* (Cardiff: University of Wales Press, 1944) 68–74.

[67] For an emphasis on the traditional elements in the hymns, see J. O'Rourke, "The Hymns of the Apocalypse," *CBQ*, 30 (1968), 399–409. These elements are more carefully and thoroughly discussed in K.-P. Jörns, *Das hymnische Evangelium: Untersuchungen zu Aufbau, Funktion und Herkunft der hymnischen Stücke in der Johannesoffenbarung* (Gütersloh: Verlagshaus Gerd Mohn, 1971) 161–64.

[68] G. Delling, "Zum gottesdienstlichen Stil der Johannesapokalypse," *NovT,* 3 (1959), 134–5; R. Deichgräber, *Gotteshymnus und Christushymnus in der frühen Christenheit: Untersuchungen zu Form, Sprache und Stil der frühchristlichen Hymnen* (Göttingen: Vandenhoeck & Ruprecht, 1967) 178–9. The view that the hymns of the Apocalypse actually reflect early Christian liturgy is held by J. Kroll, *Die christliche Hymnodik bis zu Klemens von Alexandreia,* 2. Aufl. (Darmstadt: Wissenschaftliche Buchgesellschaft, 1968) 16–17.

[69] H. Kraft, *Die Offenbarung des Johannes* (Tübingen: Mohr Siebeck, 1974) 102.

[70] The Apocalypse of John and the Odes of Solomon contain the earliest evidence for Christian borrowing of the antiphonal hymn-structure from Judaism; cf. I. Elbogen, *Der jüdische Gottesdienst in seiner geschichtlichen Entwicklung,* 3. Aufl. (Frankfurt a. M.: J. Kaufmann, 1924) 494 ff.

Apocalypse and the *Odes of Solomon* both have a strong emphasis on realized eschatology. In this they differ from the hymns of the New Testament generally, which never speak of future events or conditions as if they were already present and accomplished. The eschatological perspective of the hymns of the Apocalypse varies from total anticipation (Rev 7:10b), to partial realization (11:15b; 12:10), to total realization (19:1–2).[71] In Rev 16:4–7, for example, the events regarded as future in 15:3–4 are regarded as actualized.[72] In 12:10–12, a number of eschatological events are regarded as realized, though the conclusion indicates that the full completion of the plan of God remains unfulfilled. Again, in Rev 19:1b–2, we see a perspective which views the eschatological judgment as fully realized:

> Hallelujah! Salvation and glory and power belong to our God,
> for his judgments are true and just;
> he has judged the great harlot who corrupted the earth with her fornication,
> and he has avenged on her the blood of his servants.

Realized eschatology in the hymns of the Apocalypse, then, consists of the view that some of the major events constitutive of the end of the present age have already occurred. Like the *Odes of Solomon*, these hymns strongly emphasize the establishment of the rule of Christ and the elimination of the enemies of the people of God. Unlike the *Odes of Solomon*, there is no emphasis on the present experience of immortality. In summary, the judgment of L. L. Thompson appears fully appropriate: "The writer of the Apocalypse used hymnic liturgical materials as they were used by prophets in the worship of the Christian community: to realize in the present realities otherwise apprehended only as future eschatological events.[73]

8. Conclusions

The *Odes of Solomon* constitute a unique witness to the character of early Christian prophecy in the Syrian theatre of the Roman world near the beginning of the second century CE. Their prophetic character is suggested not only by the frequent claims to divine inspiration made by the Odist and the numerous references to visions and auditions experienced and occasionally narrated, but also by the problematic speeches *ex ore Christi* in which the Risen and triumphant Jesus speaks through prophetic intermediaries to a community buffeted by opposition and persecution. While any comparison with the 'psalms, hymns and songs inspired by the Spirit' mentioned in Col 3:16 and Eph 5:19 would be

---

71 Jörns, *Das hymnische Evangelium*, 159.
72 Jörns, *Das hymnische Evangelium*, 138.
73 L. L. Thompson, "Cult and Eschatology in the Apocalypse of John," 49 (1969), 348 f.

both speculative and fruitless, the liturgical setting of the *Odes of Solomon* taken together with their prophetic character suggests that various types of hymns or songs of prayer and praise were important vehicles for the prophetic utterance of early Christian prophets. One centrally important feature of the *Odes*, and one with parallels in the hymns of the Johannine Apocalypse, is the imaginative presentation of events and conditions of the future as if they were features of present experience. Thus realized eschatology, no less than apocalyptic eschatology, was an important feature of prophetic utterances within the framework of early Christian liturgical celebration.

The Apocalypse of John and Graeco-Roman Revelatory Magic[1]

In honorem Morton Smith

The Apocalypse of John mirrors in a very distinctive way the social and cultural amalgam which constituted late first century Christianity. Though a Christian document, it is heavily indebted to Jewish religious and apocalyptic traditions. It also exhibits both the influences of and the reactions to Hellenism. The purpose of this paper is to examine selected Hellenistic magical traditions which have been taken up consciously by John and fashioned into an anti-magic apologetic.[2]

The Hellenistic features of the Apocalypse entered the conceptual world of the author through indirect and direct channels. Indirectly and unconsciously, John emerged from a Judaism already unevenly "orientalized" since the sixth century BCE (centering in Palestine and the eastern diaspora), and Hellenized since the sixth and fifth century BCE (centering in Palestine and the western diaspora).[3] The orientalization and Hellenization of Judaism are particularly

[1] Paper delivered to the Seminar on the Apocalypse at the 40th General Meeting of SNTS, held in Trondheim, Norway, August 19–23, 1985. This study was made possible by a 1985 Summer Stipend from the National Endowment for the Humanities. Further, Professor H. D. Betz kindly allowed me to examine the galley proofs of the forthcoming volume he has edited, *The Greek Magical Papyri in Translation including the Demotic Spells* (Chicago and London: University of Chicago Press, 1986), together with the preliminary computer printout of the English index for that volume.

[2] For earlier discussion of Hellenistic influence on the Apocalypse see Franz Boll, *Aus der Offenbarung Johannis: Hellenistische Studien zum Weltbild der Apokalypse* (Berlin: Teubner, 1914). Hans Dieter Betz describes the problem in "On the Problem of the Religio-Historical Understanding of Apocalypticism," *JTC* 6 (1969) 134–56. For a response to Betz, see Adela Yarbro Collins, "The History-of-Religions Approach to Apocalypticism and the 'Angel of the Waters' (Rev 16:4–7)", *CBQ* 39 (1977) 367–81.

[3] For a balanced approach to eastern influences on Jewish apocalyptic, see John J. Collins, "Jewish Apocalyptic Against Its Hellenistic Near Eastern Environment", *BASOR* 220 (1975), 27–36. The basic study on the Hellenization of early Judaism is Martin Hengel, *Judaism and Hellenism: Studies in Their Encounter in Palestine During the Early Hellenistic Period*, 2 vols. (Philadelphia: Fortress, 1974). See also Morton Smith, "On the Wine God in Palestine: Gen. 18, Jn. 2, and Achilles Tatius," *Salo Wittmayer Barron Jubilee Volume* (Jerusalem: American Academy of Jewish Research, 1975) 815–29; *idem*, "Helios in Palestine", *Eretz-Israel* 16 (1982) 199–214. This perspective, however, has not gone unchallenged, particularly by conservative Jewish scholars; cf. D. Flusser, "Paganism in Palestine," *The Jewish People in the First Cen-*

evident in apocalypticism which (like wisdom and magic) was nearly an international phenomenon in the ancient world characterized by similar eschatological scenarios and similar patterns of utilizing native mythological motifs of kingship and combat.[4] More directly and consciously, John adapted religious, mythical and cultural traditions for both positive and negative reasons. On the one hand, he used pagan imagery in order to communicate revelatory visions in linguistic, symbolic and mythical idioms widely understood in the ancient world (e. g. the Python-Leto version of the ancient combat myth reflected in the imagery of Rev 12).[5] On the other hand, he used pagan imagery and practices as part of a broad apologetic assault on Graeco-Roman culture itself (e. g., the use of imagery drawn from Roman imperial court ceremonial to characterize the heavenly court in contrast to its diabolical earthly imitation).[6] One of the more fascinating and problematic features of the Apocalypse is the extent to which the author consciously juxtaposed and blended traditions of diverse origin.

1. Graeco-Roman Magic

Like apocalyptic and wisdom, magic was an ecumenical phenomenon in the ancient world reflecting the broadly syncretistic tendencies of the Hellenistic and Roman periods.[7] Again like apocalyptic, though less true of wisdom, magic was a phenomenon which existed within the framework of particular nativistic religious traditions. Magic is often defined in opposition to religion as ritual procedures for manipulating and coercing supernatural beings for utilitarian ends, whereas religion supplicates and venerates them.[8] This conceptual model

tury, vol. 2 of *Compendia Rerum Iudaicarum ad Novum Testamentum* (Philadelphia: Fortress, 1976) 1065–1100; Louis H. Feldman, "Hengel's Judaism and Hellenism in Retrospect", *JBL* 96 (1977) 371–82.

[4] See particularly Jonathan Z. Smith, "Native Cults in the Hellenistic Period", *HR* 11 (1971) 236–49. The international character of apocalypticism is emphasized in David Hellholm, (ed), *Apocalypticism in the Mediterranean World and the Near East: Proceedings of the International Colloquium on Apocalypticism, Uppsala, August 12–17, 1979* (Tübingen: Mohr Siebeck, 1983). See also Jonathan Z. Smith, "Wisdom and Apocalyptic", *Map Is Not Territory: Studies in the History of Religions* (Leiden: Brill, 1978) 67–87 and Samuel K. Eddy, *The King is Dead: Studies in the NearEastern Resistance to Hellenism, 334–31 BC* (Lincoln : University of Nebraska Press, 1961).

[5] Adela Yarbro Collins, *The Combat Myth in the Book of Revelation* (Missoula: Scholars Press, 1976).

[6] D.E. Aune, "The Influence of Roman Imperial Court Ceremonial on the Apocalypse of John", *BR* 18 (1983) 5–26. Reprinted above, pp. 99–119.

[7] For more extensive arguments and documentation for the views expressed in this paragraph see D.E. Aune, "Magic in Early Christianity", *Aufstieg und Niedergang der römischen Welt*, ed. H. Temporini and W. Haase, Part II, 23/2 (Berlin and New York: De Gruyter, 1980) 1507–23. Reprinted below, pp. 368–420.

[8] J.G. Frazer, *The Golden Bough: A Study in Magic and Religion*, 3rd ed. (New York: Macmillan, 1910) Part 1, Vol. 1, 224–5.

emerged after the Reformation as a means for validating Protestant piety over against Roman Catholic superstition. When modern field anthropology began in the late nineteenth century, the model became an important conceptual framework for understanding the religious practices of small-scale societies. This was only natural since Protestant missionaries often functioned as amateur anthropologists because of their extensive field experience. Yet the manipulation/supplication model, precisely because of its now obvious ethnocentric character with an inherent system of values (manipulation is bad; supplication is good), is useless for a scientific approach to the study of religion. Alternate approaches are necessary. Using a sociological model, magic can be understood neutrally in terms of religious deviance. That is, magic is a form of religiosity which is generally disapproved and which is the object of social stigma and social control (e. g. prevention is attempted through enactment of legal penalties or other less formal types of control and prevention). Using the approach of the phenomenology of religion, magic can be distinguished from religion in view of its private, instrumental and illegal or antisocial character.

Graeco-Roman magic is known from a variety of sources including magical papyri, gems and amulets, curse tablets and literary notices.[9] For this study, however, the magical papyri are the most important source. What, we may ask, is so "magical" about this collection of papyri? They are categorized as magical because they include detailed instructions for the performance of certain ritual acts, the preparation of particular religious paraphernalia (*materia magica*), and the recitation of prescribed formulas, hymns and prayers, all for use in *private* (often secret) ceremonies for the achievement of specific utilitarian goals. These papyri are "magical," not because they fit the manipulation model, but because they are private instrumental rituals using a variety of rites and a vocabulary, and addressed to a set of gods for a set of purposes all of which were elements of a complex identified in ancient society as "magic." The magical papyri consist of spells or procedures which exhibit a variety of objective goals. The spells fall into four general categories: (1) protective and apotropaic magic (the primary function of magical gems and amulets), (2) aggressive and malevolent magic (a main function of the *defixionum tabellae* or curse tablets), (3) love magic and (4) revelatory magic.

Since the magical papyri nearly all come from Egypt and were produced primarily from the third through the sixth centuries, their use in understanding a document such as the Apocalypse of John may appear problematic. Several points can be made in support of their utility for comparative purposes. (1) While the bulk of the papyri were written from the third through the sixth centuries, the conservative nature of the religious formulas, hymns and rituals that they contain suggests that Graeco-Egyptian magic had achieved its basic form by

[9] For a survey of these sources, see Aune, "Magic in Early Christianity", 1516 ff.

the first century CE.[10] (2) Several magical papyri actually date from the last centuries BCE on palaeographical grounds;[11] some of these exhibit the same Graeco-Egyptian syncretistic patterns as the later papyri. (3) Even though the magical papyri have an obviously Egyptian character (Egypt was widely regarded as a centre of ancient magic, cf. Origen *Contra Celsum* 1.22, 28, 38, 68), they also exhibit a significant amount of Greek influence, particularly in the magical hymns in hexameter and trimeter and in Apollo-Helios and Hekate-Selene magic.[12] (4) Despite the obvious spatial and cultural distance between Asia Minor and Egypt, the Apocalypse does contain traditions which could only have been derived from Egypt, though the channels of transmission remain a mystery. Particularly perplexing examples of this phenomenon are the motifs of "the second death" and "the lake of fire", rarely found singly, but associated *only* in the Apocalypse (20:14; 21:8) and in the underworld mythology of ancient Egyptian mortuary literature (the Coffin Texts; the Book of the Dead).[13]

---

[10] A.D. Nock, "Greek Magical Papyri", *Essays on Religion and the Ancient World*, ed. Z. Stewart (Cambridge: Harvard University Press, 1972) I, 187.

[11] E.g. *PGM* XVI (no. 3378); XX (*P. Berol.* inv. 7504 + *P. Amh.* ii, Col. II [A] + *P. Oxy.* in- edit.); CXVII (*P. Mon. Gr.* inv. 216); CXXII (*P. Berol.* inv. 21243). Belonging to the first or second century CE are LVII (University of Michigan, Ann Arbor, uncatalogued), LXXII (*P. Oslo* III,75), LXXXV (*P. Harris* 56).

[12] M. Nilsson, "Die Religion in den Griechischen Zauberpapyri", *Opuscula Selecta* (Lund: Gleerup, 1960), III, 130–2 (on the hymns) 140 f. (on Apollo), 143–5 (on Hekate-Selene).

[13] The motifs of "τὴν λίμνην τοῦ πυρός" and "ὁ δεύτερος θάνατος" occur together in ancient Egyptian texts, e. g., Book of the Dead 175.1, 15, 20; cf. E.A.W. Budge, *The Egyptian Book of the Dead* (New York: Dover, 1967) 184, 186 f. The closest parallel in Jewish literature is Tg. Isa. 65.6 in which the fire of Gehenna and the second death are juxtaposed; however the text is relatively late and the concept of a lake of fire is not present. The motifs are rarely found separately in ancient literature, much less together. "The second death" is mentioned four times in the Apocalypse (2:11; 20:6, 14; 21:8), but not in the rest of the NT, second century Christian literature, or in pre-Christian Greek literature (but n. b. that the term διοθανής, "twice dead", is used to refer to Odysseus' visit to Hades, *Odyssey* 12.22, the "twice" referring to Odysseus" future death). The phrase occurs in Plutarch *De facie* 942F (he is very familiar with Egyptian myth and ritual; cf. J. Hani, *La religion Égyptienne dans la pensée de Plutarque* [Paris: Société d''Édition "Les Belles Lettres", 1976]) in a positive sense for the death of the soul on the moon (preceded by the death of the body on earth) which frees the νοῦς to ascend to a blissful existence on the sun (cf. G. Soury, *La démonologe de Plutarque* (Paris: Société d'Édition "Les Belles Lettres", 1942) 196–203). In Lucian *DMort.* 7.2, Menippus, speaking to the soul of Tantalus in Hades, contests the notion of a second Hades or a second death (θάνατος ἐντεῦθεν). The source of this motif in the Hellenistic world, though the means of transmission are not known, is the Egyptian conception of the second death (S. Morenz, *Egyptian Religion*, trans. A.E. Keep [Ithaca: Cornell University Press, 1973] 254; J. Bergman, "Introductory Remarks on Apocalypticism in Egypt", *Apocalyptic in the Mediterranean World and the Near East*, ed. D. Hellholm [Tübingen: Mohr Siebeck, 1983], 57). "To die the second death" (*mt m whm*) is a phrase occurring frequently in the Coffin Texts and the Book of the Dead: R.O. Faulkner, *The Ancient Egyptian Coffin Texts*, 3 vols. (Warminster: Aris & Phillips, 1973–78) I, 88 (Spell 83) I, 134 (Spell 156) I, 267 (Spell 203) II, 69 (Spell 423) II, 76 (Spell 438) II, 88 (Spell 458) II, 308 (Spell 787); J. Zandee, *Death as an Enemy according to Ancient Egyptian Conceptions* (Leiden. E.J. Brill, 1960) 186–8). It refers to the total destruction of the *ba* ("soul") after bodily death (Zandee, p. 14), a fate to be avoided at all costs. The Egyptian significance of second death and

2. Revelatory Magic and Apocalyptic

Graeco-Roman magical divination, or revelatory magic, is a phenomenon known to us primarily through two sources, the Greek and Demotic "magical" papyri (private ritual procedures for achieving various concrete goals), and literary accounts (apocalypses), which of ten include vision reports of ascents to heaven, descents to Hades, or of appearances on earth of messengers from either region.[14] In the recent translation of Greek, Coptic and Demotic magical papyri edited by Hans Dieter Betz, of the approximately 534 spells identified on

---

the lake of fire, i.e., complete and total destruction, *cannot* be meant in the Apocalypse (cf. 14:9–11; 20:10). Rather, as in Philo *De prem. et poen.* 70 and Tg. Isa. 65. 6, eternal torment is signified. The Hebrew expression for second death is *mwt šny*, first occurring in the ninth century CE work Pirqe de-Rabbi Eliezer 34, while the Aramaic *mwt' tnyn'* ("second death"), occurs only in the targumim, from which six texts are discussed by M. McNamara, *The New Testament and the Palestinian Targum* (Rome: Pontifical Biblical Institute, 1966) 118–24: Tg. Jer. 51. 39; 51. 57; Tg. Deut. 33:6; Tg. Isa. 22:14; 65:6; 65:15. McNamara, who does not discuss the parallels in Lucian or Egyptian literature, suggests that "the expression must have come from Judaism, unless it was coined by Christianity" (p. 118). The motif of "the lake of fire", which occurs six times in the Apocalypse (19:20; 20:10, 14–15 [three times]; 21. 8), has no close parallels in the OT, Jewish or Graeco-Roman literature, particularly in respect to the description of the place of eternal punishment as a λίμνη ("lake"). Cf. "Flammensee", *Lexikon der Aegyptologie* (Wiesbaden: Otto Harrassowitz, 1977) II, 259–60; H. Kees, *Totenglauben und Jenseitsvorstellungen der alten Aegypter* (Leipzig: Hinrichs, 1926) 294f. The image of the lake of fire does occur in the Book of the Dead (17. 40–42; 24. 4; 175. 15, 20), where it is located in the underworld (cf. Zandee, 133–42). Fire in the underworld as a means of eternal punishment is first mentioned in Judaism in Isa. 66:24 and frequently thereafter (*1 Enoch* 10:6, 13; Matt 5:22; 13:42, 50), and it became natural to think of the underworld as the site for a river of fire (*2 Enoch* 10. 2), a tradition taken up in Christian underworld mythology (*Apoc. Paul* 31, 34, 36). The specific conception of a *lake of fire*, however, when mentioned in early Christian texts (cf. *Apoc. Peter* [Akhmimic] 23), depends on the Apocalypse of John.

[14] The Greek magical papyri, with some Coptic materials, are conveniently collected in K. Preisendanz, *Papyri Graecae Magicae. Die Griechischen Zauberpapyri*, 2 vols., 2nd ed., ed. A. Henrichs (Stuttgart: Teubner, 1973–4). Most of the Demotic magical papyri are available in transliterated Demotic with a facing English translation in F. L. Griffith and H. Thompson, *The Leyden Papyrus: An Egyptian Magical Book* (New York: Dover, 1974; originally published in London, 1904). A translation of these and other related magical papyri is now available in H. D. Betz, ed. *The Greek Magical Papyri in Translation Including the Demotic Spells* (Chicago and London: University of Chicago Press, 1986); Betz includes 126 papyri, 45 more than in A. Henrichs' second edition of Preisendanz, though the oracle questions (LXXIII–LXXVI) and the Christian papyri are excluded. In this paper, all translations of these papyri, henceforth abbreviated as *PGM* (*Papyri Graecae Magicae*) or *PDM* (*Papyri Demoticae Magicae*) are taken from this translation unless otherwise noted. For a survey of Greco-Roman apocalypses see H. W. Attridge, "Greek and Latin Apocalypses," *Semeia* 14 (1979) 159–86. And for an overview of ancient ascent literature with an extensive bibliography, see A. F. Segal, "Heavenly Ascent in Hellenistic Judaism, Early Christianity and Their Environment", *Aufstieg und Niedergang der römischen Welt*, ed. H. Temporini and W. Haase, Part II, 23/2 (Berlin and New York: De Gruyter, 1980) 1333–94. See also H. D. Betz, "Fragments from a Catabasis Ritual in a Greek Magical Papyrus", *HR* 19 (1980) 287–95 (with bibliographical references); M. Smith, "Ascent to the Heavens and the Beginning of Christianity," *Eranos* 50 (1981) 403–29; H. D. Betz, "The Problem of Apocalyptic Genre in Greek and Hellenistic Literature: The Case of the Oracle of

formal grounds, 112 (or 21%) deal with revelatory divination. Revelation was obviously a major concern of ancient magic.[15]

Revelatory procedures in the magical papyri can be placed in two categories, magical divination and oracular magic.[16] Magical divination includes lamp divination (*lychnomanteia*, e. g. *PGM* VII.540–77), bowl divination (*lekanomanteia*, e. g. *PGM* III.276), saucer divination (*phialomanteia*, e. g. IV.3209–54), and divination by dreams (*oneiromanteia*, e. g. VII.1009–16). Oracular magic includes procedures for personal visions (*autoptikos*, *autoptos*, or *autopsia*, e. g., VII.319–34, 335–47) for acquiring foreknowledge (*prognosis*, e. g. VII.348–58), for acquiring an assistant divinity (I.1–42, 173–77), oracular questions and answers through a boy medium and certain types of bowl divination (those in which the divinity appears in the liquid). The fact that no firm distinction is made between technical divination (the first type) and natural divination (the second type) is typical for the Greek conception of revelatory media, in contrast to the views of early Judaism.

Hellenistic procedures for securing revelations and apocalypses have functional equivalents in Judaism in texts associated with Merkavah mysticism (how to get to the throne of God and what one will see and hear on the journey), and Jewish apocalyptic literature (a report of what one saw and heard during an "actual" revelatory experience). Ritual procedures for procuring magical revelation and apocalypses are complementary expressions of ancient revelatory conceptions and experience. The Merkavah literature and the Greek magical papyri provide instructions for revelatory experiences without including narratives of those experiences. Ancient apocalypses narrate revelatory experiences but omit references to the preparatory ritual techniques (if any). The connections between these two literary forms are apparent in several respects. Historically, it is likely that Merkavah mysticism emerged from Jewish apocalyptic.[17] Further, there are significant phenomenological similarities between the Merkavah texts and the Greek magical papyri.[18] From a literary standpoint, some Jewish and

Trophonius," *Apocalypticism in the Mediterranean World and the Near East*, ed. D. Hellholm (Tübingen: Mohr Siebeck, 1983) 577–97.

[15] The most comprehensive study of Greco-Roman revelatory divination is that of T. Hopfner, *Griechisch-aegyptischer Offenbarungszauber*, 2 vols. (Leipzig: Haessel-Verlag, 1921–4); cf. Hopfner's article "Mageia", in Pauly-Wissowa, *Realencyclopaedie der klassischen Altertumswissenschaft*, XIV, 1 (1928) 301–93.

[16] For a more detailed discussion with references, see D. E. Aune, *Prophecy in Early Christianity and the Ancient Mediterranean World* (Grand Rapids: Eerdmans, 1983) 44–7.

[17] P. Alexander, "3 (Hebrew Apocalypse of) Enoch", in *The Old Testament Pseudepigrapha*, Vol. 1: *Apocalyptic Literature and Testaments*, ed. J. H. Charlesworth (Garden City: Doubleday, 1983) 235.

[18] G. Scholem, *Jewish Gnosticism, Merkabah Mysticism, and Talmudic Tradition* (New York: The Jewish Theological Seminary of America, 1965) 75–83; M. Smith, "Observations on Hekhalot Rabbati", *Biblical and Other Studies*, ed. A. Altmann (Cambridge: Harvard Univer-

Christian apocalypses preserve brief references to revelatory techniques;[19] yet even Graeco-Roman apocalypses only briefly mention preparatory rituals.[20] An interesting case at point is the discovery of the conclusion of *Kestos* 18 of the third century Christian writer Julius Africanus (*P. Oxy.* 412), included as *PGM* XXIII. This "unexpurgated" text sandwiches a twenty-seven line magical hymn in dactylic hexameter between lines 50 and 5 1 of the description of Odysseus' ritual preparations for his entry into Hades (Odyssey 11), which Africanus thinks was suppressed.[21] Africanus himself has probably inserted two parenthetical descriptions of two sections of the hymn, "He has said what must be done" (line 14), and "He tells us what charms must be sung" (line 21), thus dividing the procedure properly into two parts, the *praxis* and the *epode*.[22] Though his view that the hymn was genuinely Homeric is absurd, the text is valuable for showing what a writer of the second century CE thought would be an appropriate preparation for a descent.

3. In Pursuit of Trivia

The prophetic call narrative in Rev 1:9–20 is a complex pastiche of imagery drawn from various sources. A supernatural revealer "like a son of man" appears to John and claims to possess "the keys *to* Death and Hades" (1:18b).[23] The

sity Press, 1963) 142–60. This connection is made more apparent by the third or fourth century CE. Jewish magical handbook *Sepher ha-Razim*.

19 A long prayer in preparation for revelation is narrated in *4 Ezra* 3:1–36 (cf. Dan 9:3; 10:2–3), and a seven-day period of fasting, mourning and prayer is mentioned in *4 Ezra* 5:20–23; 6:31–59; 9:23–37; 13:50–1. A seven-day preparatory period is often mentioned in the magical papyri. Revelatory ritual with close ties to Hellenistic magical divination appears in Hermas *Vis*. 2.1.1; 2.2.1; 3.1.1–2.

20 Betz, "Apocalyptic Genre," 581.

21 For the Greek text and commentary, see J.-R. Vieillefond, *Les "Cestes" de Julius Africanus* (Paris: Librairie Marcel Didier, 1970) 277–91. The text is also discussed in Hopfner, *Offenbarungszauber*, II, 150–2.

22 R. Wünsch, "Deisidaimoniaka," *ARW* 12 (1909) 3. Wünsch, who discusses the text extensively on pp. 2–19, dates it to the first or second centuries CE (p. 17).

23 The genitives τοῦ θάνατου and τοῦ ᾅδου could either be objective or possessive genitives (i.e., "the keys to Death and Hades", or "the keys *belonging* to Death and Hades"). If they are regarded as objective genitives, Death and Hades must be understood spatially (as in Rev 20:13–14), but if they are construed as *possessive* genitives, Death and Hades must be understood as personifications (as in Rev 6:8). The first possibility is preferable since Death is never (to my knowledge) described in ancient texts as possessing keys, and there are few if any ancient texts in which Hades is so described (Pausanias 5.20.3 describes a decorated table showing Ploutos holding a key, but the same text distinguishes him from Hades whom he has locked up). Furthermore, τοῦ ᾅδου is an abbreviation for τοῦ [οἴκου τοῦ] ᾅπδου. T. Holtz, for other reasons, also supports understanding the phrase "of Death and Hades" as an objective genitive in *Die Christologie der Apokalypse des Johannes*, 2. Aufl. (Berlin: Akademie Verlag, 1971) 86–7. The possessive genitive has been taken to reflect the myth of the *descensus ad inferos*, since if the keys once belonged to the personified Death and Hades (only in Rev 6:8),

image of the risen Jesus as keybearer is derived from Hellenistic conceptions of Hekate, though few scholars have made the connection.[24] After providing a brief introduction to the character and significance of Hekate, three arguments will be elaborated in support of this proposal: (1) Hekate's popularity during the Hellenistic and Roman periods centered in southwest Asia Minor, where the ideology of her universal sovereignty, particularly as Mistress of the Cosmos, would have made her an obvious rival of the Christ of Christianity. (2) In the Hellenistic world, Hekate is the primary mythological figure associated with the possession of the keys to the gates of Hades. (3) Hekate is the patron goddess of magic and sorcery, with *revelatory* magic as one of her central concerns. Asia Minor was an important centre for magical practices in antiquity and the Apocalypse reflects the author's opposition to such activities. Hekate and Christ had mutually exclusive franchises on divine revelation. The significance of this proposal lies in the fact that John, in effect, depicts the risen Jesus as one who has usurped the role of Hekate.

(1) Hekate is a very ancient and complex goddess with many associations. Hesiod's hymn to Hekate (*Theog.* 404–52) depicts her as an Olympian deity with none of her later chthonic features, though he may have suppressed this aspect.[25] In the final stage of the traditional Greek conception of the evolution of cosmic polity, Zeus ruled the sky, Poseidon the sea, Hades the underworld with all three sharing the earth. For Hesiod, Hekate was a kind of general practitioner assigned authority in three cosmic regions, the sky, the earth and the sea, with underworld associations notably absent.[26] Later the conception of Hekate *trimorphos* (= Latin *triformis*, "having three forms or shapes") was connected with her threefold identity as Juno Lucina, Trivia and Luna (Catullus 34.9), or Selene/Luna in heaven, Artemis/Diana on earth, and Persephone/Hekate in Hades.[27] Hekate *triprosopos* ("having three faces") is depicted as fighting on the

---

they must have been wrested away from them (Josef Kroll, *Gott und Hölle: Der Mythos vom Descensuskampfe* [Leipzig and Berlin: Teubner, 1932] 10 f.). This view has wide support; cf. W. Bousset, *Die Offenbarung Johannis* (Göttingen: Vandenhoeck & Ruprecht, 1906) 198; J. Jeremias, *TDNT* III, 746, and E. Lohse, *Die Offenbarung des Johannes*, 11. Aufl. (Göttingen: Vandenhoeck & Ruprecht, 1976) 21.

[24] To my knowledge the connection is made only by J.H. Moulton and G. Milligan, *The Vocabulary of the Greek Testament Illustrated from the Papyri and Other Non-Literary Sources* (Grand Rapids: Eerdmans, 1980) 345 (s. v. *kleis*). J. Kroll comes close to making the connection (*Gott und Hölle*, 476–7).

[25] Hesiod, *Theog.* 404–52; cf. M.L. West, *Hesiod, Theogony: Edited with Prolegomena and Commentary* (Oxford: Oxford University Press, 1966) 276–8.

[26] *Theog.* 412–15, 427; a view preserved in Orph. *Hymni* 1.2; cf. the references cited in M.A. Koops, *Observationes in Hymnos Orphicos* (Leiden: Brill, 1932) 3–4.

[27] The epithet *Trivia* ("she of the three ways") was used by Vergil (*Aen.* 6.35), and interpreted in the following way by Servius, *Comm. in Verg. Aen.* 4.511: "et cum super terras est, creditur esse Luna: cum in terris, Diana; cum sub terris, Proserpina" (G.C. Thilo and H. Hagen, *Servii Grammatici qui feruntur in Vergilii carmine commentarii* [Leipzig: Teubner, 1881] I, 557). Jo. Tzetzes identified the three forms of Hekate as Selene, Hekate and Artemis, though without

side of the Olympians in the Gigantomachy on the east frieze of the altar of Zeus from Pergamon.[28] This cosmic significance of Hekate led to conceptions of her as Mother of All, Mistress of All, Beginning and End. In *PGM* IV.2836 f., in the context of a hexameter hymn to Hekate in which she is explicitly identified with Mene, Artemis, Persephone and Selene, we read: "Beginning / and end [ἀρχὴ καὶ τέλος] are you, and you alone rule all. / For all things are from you, and you alone rule all. / For all things are from you, and in you do / All things, Eternal one, come to their end."[29] The "Beginning and End", of course, is precisely the self-predication of Christ in Rev 21:6; 22:13 (see below). In the Orphic Hymns, probably written during the early second century CE or later in Asia Minor (near in place and time to the composition of the Apocalypse),[30] Hekate's universal significance is reflected in the phrase "key-bearing mistress of the entire cosmos" (πάντος κόσμου κληδοῦχον ἄνασσαν, l. 7). In harmony with the tendency to universalize the significance of original local deities, Hekate was also identified with Isis,[31] though the claims of Hekate's protagonists never quite matched those of the Isis aretalogies.

During the Hellenistic and Roman periods, Hekate was particularly popular in southwest Asia Minor.[32] Though the worship of Hekate was primarily of a

identifying their spheres of influence; cf. W. J. W. Koster (ed), *Scholia in Aristophanem*, Pars IV: *Jo. Tzetzae Commentarii in Aristophanem*, Fasc. 1 (Groningen and Amsterdam: Bouma, 1960) 142 (In Plutum 594). Orphism emphasized the unity of Artemis, Persephone and Hekate (C. A. Lobeck, *Aglaophamus sive de theologiae mysticae Graecorum causis* [Königsberg: Bornträger, 1829] 543 ff.) The depiction of Hekate as *trimorphos* and *triprosopos* is by no means unique to her. In the Mediterranean world Geryon, Typhon and Hermes are similarly depicted, and the phenomenon is also found in Hinduism, Buddhism, Jainism and among several African peoples; cf. W. Kirfel, *Die dreiköpfige Gottheit* (Bonn: Ferd. Dümmlers Verlag, 1948).

[28] E. Rohde, *Pergamon: Burgberg und Altar* (Berlin: Henschelverlag Kunst und Geseilschaft, 1982) 84–5; E. Laumonier, *Les cultes indigènes en Cane* (Paris: E. De Boccard, 1958) 350.

[29] W. C. van Unnik, *Het godspredikaat "Het begin en het einde" bij Flavius Josephus en in de openbaring van Johannes*, Mededelingen der Koninklijke Nederlandse Akademie van Wetenschappen, Afd. Letterkunde, Nieuwe Reeks, Deel 39, No. 1 (Amsterdam: B. V. Noord-Hollansche Uitgevers Maatschappij, 1976) 57–9.

[30] K. Ziegler, "Orphische Dichtung", *Der Kleine Pauly*, IV, 357.

[31] Apuleius, *Met.* 11.5; in *P. Oxy.* 1380, 84 f. Isis is called "Artemis of three-fold nature". Cf. J. G. Griffiths, *Apuleius of Madauros. The Isis-Book (Metamorphoses Book XI)* (Leiden: Brill, 1975) 117–19, 152–1.

[32] T. Kraus, *Hekate: Studien zu Wesen und Bild der Göttin in Kleinasien und Griechenland* (Heidelberg: Carl Winter, 1960) 24–56 focuses on "Die kleinasiatische Hekate," and 166–8 contains a list of "Hekate-Zeugnis aus Karien und Phrygien." For numismatic evidence on Hekate's popularity in Asia Minor see F. Imhoof-Blumer, *Kleinasiatische Münzen*, 2 vols. (Hildesheim and New York: Georg Olms Verlag, 1974; originally published in 1901–2) I, 156 f., nos. 11, 12, 13. The goddess is represented as Artemis-Hekate on coins from Ephesus (I, p. 54, no. 42; p. 60, no. 66). This identification is found on a coin from Philadelphia minted under Domitian (I, p. 181, no. 6). For further numismatic evidence see *Sylloge Nummorum Graecorum Deutschland, Sammlung v. Aulock*, 18 vols. (Berlin: Gebr. Mann Verlag, 1957–68), s. v. "Hekate" in P. R. Franke, W. Leschhorn and A. U. Stylow, *Sammlung v. Aulock Index, Sylloge Nummorum Graecorum Deutschland* (Berlin: Gebr. Mann Verlag, 1981). Also important are

private nature (appropriate for her importance in Graeco-Roman magic), she also had a number of famous public cults.[33] Caria was both the likely region of her origin and the location of her main cult centre at the Hekateion at Lagina.[34] By Hellenistic times she became popular as the goddess of magic, of the spirits of the dead, and of Hades. She was worshipped at places where roads forked and received the epithet *Trioditis*, literally translated in Latin by *Trivia* ("she of the three roads"). Sacrifices of food to Hekate left at shrines at such intersections were called "Hekate's dinners", (*deipna Hekates*, *Hekataia* or *Hekatesia*) to which the poor often helped themselves.[35] An epithet used most frequently of Hekate is Enodia/ Einodia, "by the wayside" (Lucian, *Nav.* 15; Pausanias 3.14.9; Audollent, *Defixionum tabellae*, 41B.8), an epithet used in masculine form of Hermes, god of travellers. As part of the process of *interpretatio Graeca*, Artemis was assimilated to Carian Hekate (as Apollo was to Carian Helios),[36] and Hekate was similarly connected with a number of other goddesses in addition to Artemis (and her Roman approximation, Diana), including Selene ("Moon") and Persephone, and less importantly with Bona Dea, Magna Mater, Isis, Bendis, Brimo (*PGM* IV.2611), and Mene, "Moon".

(2) By Hellenistic times Hekate is associated with many symbols (semeia), including torches, the sword, snakes, the crescent moon, the stag, a basket, the

---

the volumes in B. V. Head, *A Catalogue of the Greek Coins in the British Museum* (Bologna: A. Forni-Editore, 1964), particularly Vol. 14 (Ionia) 104; Vol. 18 (Caria, Cos, Rhodes) 22, 148–51, 154–9; Vol. 22 (Lydia) 28, 192, 254, 355. For other basic studies on Hekate see J. Heckenbach "Hekate" Pauly-Wissowa, *Realencyclopaedje der klassischen Altertumswissenschaft* 7 (1912) 2769–82; W. H. Roscher, "Hekate," Ausfuhrliches Lexikon der griechische und römischen Mythologie (Leipzig: Teubner, 1886–90) 1/2, 1885–1910; L. R. Farnell, *The Cults of the Greek States* (Oxford: Oxford University Press, 1896) II, 501–19, 549–57); "Hekate," *Der Kleine Pauly*, II, 982–3.

[33] Important public cults include the public festivals at the temple of Hekate at Lagina (Strabo 14.2.25), the annual mysteries of Hekate celebrated in Aegina (Pausanias 2.30.2; Origen, *Contra Cels.* 6.22), Hekate's role in the Samothracian mysteries (A. Adler, *Suidae Lexicon* (Leipzig: Teubner, 1928–38) IV, 318, s. v. Samothrake), and her role in the myth connected with the Eleusinian mysteries (*Homeric Hymn to Demeter* 23–24, 51–9, 438; Cf. N. J. Richardson, *The Homeric Hymn to Demeter* [Oxford: Oxford University Press, 1974] 155–7, 293–5; G. E. Mylonas, *Eleusis and the Eleusinian Mysteries* [Princeton: Princeton University Press, 19611 192, 212). The Chaldaean Oracles may have functioned as a private cult with private mysteries of Hekate; cf. A. D. Nock, *Conversion* (Oxford: Oxford University Press, 1933) 117.

[34] Kraus, *Hekate*, 20; cf. E. Sittig, *De Graecorum Nominalibus Theophoris* (Halle: University of Halle, 1911) 61 f.; Laumonier, *Les cultes*), 344–425.

[35] K. F. Smith, "Hecate's Suppers," *Encyclopedia of Religion and Ethics*, VI, 565–67; Aristophanes, *Plutus*, 594–7; cf. W. G. Rutherford (ed.), *Scholia Aristophanica* (London and New York: Macmillan, 1896–1905) 1, 63; Demosthenes, *Or.* 54.39; Plutarch, *Quaest. conv.* 7.6.3 (708 f.); Adler, *Suidae Lexicon*, II, 214 (s. v. Hekate). Lucian, *Dial. mort.* 1.3; *Cataplus* 7; cf Scholium in Luciani *Vit. auct.* 8, where it is said that the offerings were made on new moons, i. e., the first of each month (H. Rabe, ed., *Scholia in Lucianum* [Stuttgart: Teubner, 1971; originally published in 1906] 125).

[36] Laumonier, *Les cultes*, 425.

patera, dogs and the keys to the gates of Hades.[37] Representations of Hekate *trimorphos* have three bodies including three heads and six arms; each arm holding a different symbol.[38] Hekate is often given the epithet κληιδοῦχος or κλειδοῦχος ("key-bearer").[39] *PGM* IV.1403 describes her as "key-bearing Persephassa" (a poetic form of Persephone, with whom Hekate is often identified).[40] One of Hekate's related epithets is ὑηξίχθων, "who break open the earth" (*PGM* IV.2722), indicating her control of the passageways between Hades and earth. This epithet is used eight times in a series of related curse tablets from Cyprus in the phrase "you who possess the keys of Hades, who break open the surface of earth."[41] The office of κλειδοφόρος ("key bearer") at Lagina, often mentioned on inscriptions, is connected to Hekate though the precise ritual and symbolic significance of the office remains a matter of speculation.[42] Residents of southwest Asia Minor (including the Christian communities to whom the Apocalypse was addressed), would have associated the possession of the keys to the gates of Hades primarily

---

[37] For lists of these *semeia* or *parasema* see *PGM* IV.2334 (bronze sandal, fillet, key, wand, iron wheel, black dog, thrice-locked door, burning hearth, shadow, depth, fire), *PGM* VII.780–85: ox, vulture, bull, beetle, falcon, crab, dog, wolf, serpent, horse, asp, goat, baboon, cat, lion, leopard, fieldmouse, deer, multiform virgin, torch, lightning, garland, herald's wand, child, key), and *PGM* LXX (virgin, bitch, serpent, wreath, key, herald's wand, golden sandal); cf Betz, "Catabasis Ritual," 291, esp. n. 20. One reference in the *Sepher ha-Razim* mentions those who have learned to "pour (libations) to their [i. e. angelic] names and cite them by their signs at the period when (prayer) is heard (so as) to make a magical rite succeed"; M. A. Morgan (trans.), *Sepher ha-Razim: The Book of Mysteries* (Chico: Scholars Press, 1983) 21. This is similar to *PGM* 111.536: "I have spoken your signs and symbols." This suggests that the recitation of symbols was a significant (if optional) part of a magical invocation, and one which lent itself to iconographic representation.

[38] Head, *Catalogue*, XVIII, p. 22, no. 49: Hekate triformis with six hands holding torches, a key, a serpent and a dagger (other object unclear), with a dog at her feet.

[39] Orph. *frag*. 316 (O. Kern, *Orphicorum Fragmenta* [Berlin: Weidmann, 1922] 324); Orph. *Hymni* 1.7 (cf. Koops, *Observationes*, 7 f.). See also Kohl, "Kleidouchos", Pauly-Wissowa, *Realencyclopaedie der klassischen Altertumswissenschaft*, XI (1921) 593–600; Dexler, "Kleidouchos", *Ausführliches Lexikon der griechischen und römischen Mythologie*, II, 1218; W. Koehler, "Die Schlüssel des Petrus: Versuch einer religionsgeschichtlichen Erklärung von Matth. 16,18.19", *ARW* 8 (1905) 214–43, esp. 220–36. Coins of Hekate occasionally show her carrying a key (B. V. Head, *Catalogue*, XVIII, 22). On her association with the keys to Hades, see *PGM* IV.1403, 2293, 2335; VII.785.

[40] In two prose curse tablets from Achaia the name (Hekate) is spelled in the Attic form "Pherrephatte" in A. Audollent, *Defixionum tabellae quotquot innotuerunt tam in Graecis Orient is quam in totius occidentis partibus praeter Atticas* (Paris: A. Fontemoing, 1904), citations are by text and line: 68A.2; 69A.9; 69B.2).

[41] Audollent, *Defixionum tabellae*, 22.53 f.; 23. 12 ff.; 26. 39; 29. 36; 31. 36; 32. 39; 35. 36; 37. 36.

[42] Strabo 14. 2. 25; cf. Heckenbach, "Hekate", 2779; Kraus, *Hekate*, pp. 48–50 (with a partial list of the relevant inscriptions). This epithet is both ancient and not the exclusive province of priests or priestesses of Hekate. Among the Linear B tablets from Pylos the title *Karawipora* (= *klawiphora*), "key-bearing priestess" is attested; W. Burkert, *Greek Religion* (Cambridge: Harvard University Press) 45.

with Hekate,[43] though various other deities throughout the Mediterranean world were also associated with the keys to the underworld, particularly Aiakos and Anubis.[44] The mythical motif of Hekate as guardian of the gates of Hades had a functionally analogous domestic application. She had both a cathartic and apotropaic function as the purifier of the home and protector of the doorway from malevolent beings and influences (Theophrastus, *Char.* 16.7). A small Hekateion could be found near the entrance of many homes (Porphyry, *Abst.* 2.16).

(3) The special type of Greek magic associated with Hekate (and her many aliases), became an important element in Graeco-Egyptian magic.[45] While the most prominent Greek deity in the papyri is Apollo-Helios (the sun god), known by other names in accordance with the eclectic *interpretatio magica* as Zeus, Mithras, Sarapis, Abraxas, Iao, Adonai and others,[46] the prominence of Hekate-Selene and her close association with the moon is complementary to Apollo-Helios. Apollo was, of course, the revelatory deity par excellence in the Greek world. The name "Hekate" occurs in the magical papyri sixteen times (ex-

---

43 Kraus, *Hekate*, 49; Roscher, "Hekate," 1906.

44 For Aiakos, see Apollodorus, *Bib.* 3.12.6, where it is said that "he guards the keys to Hades." Aiakos is also given the epithet κλειδοῦχος ("key holder") on several inscriptions (*Corpus Inscriptionem Graecarum*, III, 933, no. 6298; G. Kaibel, *Epigrammata Graeca ex lapidibus conlecta* [Berlin: G. Reimer, 1878] 262 f., no. 646), an assignment which was a later addition to his role as a judge in Hades (Plato, *Apol.* 41a; *Gorg.* 524a). For Aiakos" role as gatekeeper of Hades, with no mention of keys, see *PGM* IV.1462: "Aiakos gatekeeper of the eternal bars"; Lucian, *Dial. mort.* 6.1 (here Aiakos gives Menippus a tour of Hades in 6.1–6); 13.3. Anubis is also described as "keybearer" in *PGM* IV.1465, and the one "who holds the keys of the gates of Hades" (*PGM* IV.340 f., and two other very similarly worded papyrus texts (P. Köln Inv. T. 1.10–11; Kairo SB.7542 = *Supplementum Epigraphicum Graecum*, 8 [1937–8] 574) quoted and compared by D. Wortmann, "Neue magische Texte," *Bonner Jahrbücher*, 168 [1968] 69). Another similar text (*SEG* 1717), is quoted with commentary by G. H. R. Horsley, *New Documents Illustrating Early Christianity: A Review of the Greek Inscriptions and Papyri Published in 1976* (North Ryde: Macquarie University, 1981) 33–6. Anubis is shown holding a key on several magical gems (references in Wortmann, p. 70). Key-bearing is not a native attribute of Anubis but is attributable to Greek influence, cf. Morenz, *Egyptian Religion*, 249–50; for more detail see S. Morenz, "Anubis mit dem Schlüssel," *Religion und Geschichte des Alten Aegypten*, ed. E. Blumenthal and S. Herrmann with A. Onasch (Köln and Wien: Bohlau, 1975) 510–20. Plutos is described as possessing the keys to Hades in Pausanias 5.20.3 (cf. Koehler, "Die Schlüssel des Petrus," 222–3). A series of *defixiones* from Cyprus name an otherwise unknown divinity Sisochor as one who has the power to "lead out of the gates of Hades"; Audollent, *Defixionum tabellae*, 22.25–26; 24.13–14; 29.15–16; 32.15; 33.18; 37.16–17.

45 Nock, "Greek Magical Papyri," 185. In general see T. Hopfner, "Hekate – Selene – Artemis und Verwandte in den griech. Zauberpapyri," *Pisciculi: Studien zur Religion und Kultur des Altertums. Festschrjft F. J. Dölger*, ed. T. Klauser and A. Ruecher (Münster: Aschendorff, 1939) 125–45. On Hekate's general role in magic see T. Hopfner, "Mageia," Pauly-Wissowa, *Realencyclopaedie der klassischen Altertumswissenschaft*, XIV, cols. 304–5.

46 The name "Apollo" occurs ten times in *PGM*, while "Helios" occurs fifty-three times; cf. H. G. Gundel, "Vom Weltbild in den griechischen Zauberpapyri: Probleme und Ergebnisse," *Proceedings of the Twelfth International Congress of Papyrology*, ed. D. H. Samuel, American Studies in Papyrology, 7 (Toronto: Hakkert, 1970) 185–6.

cluding aliases),[47] and the most extensive magical handbook (the Paris papyrus, *PGM* IV, containing 3,274 lines) includes a collection of six general purpose Hekate-Selene spells (2441–2890), including two different versions of the same series of spells (2441–2621; 2622–2784). Hekate also figures prominently in the *defixiones* (particularly those from Cyprus, Achaia), where her name occurs sixteen times (again excluding aliases).[48] Hekate also plays a prominent role in magical revelation, part of her role as a patron goddess of magicians (Apollonius Rhodius 3. 248–52 [Medea], 477 f., 528–30; Eusebius, *Praep. ev.* 5.11–13). The Staatliche Museum in Berlin has a miniature bronze altar in triangular form with three reliefs of Hekate used for magical ritual; the altar is from Pergamon and is dated ca. 200–250 CE.[49] She was regarded as the mother of Circe and Medea, the two witches of Greek mythology (Diodorus 4.45.2–3). In consequence of the *interpretatio magica* which pervades the magical papyri and *defixiones*, she is functionally associated with or identified with a plethora of other chthonic deities, particularly those who function as gatekeepers and/or key bearers in Hades. These include Erischigal, the Babylonian goddess of the underworld, often used as a magical name (*PGM* IV.2749–50; VII.896), Persephone, Kore, Artemis and Selene. Hekate is said to prophesy through mediums and Porphyri quotes several of her oracles (Eusebius, *Praep. ev.* 3.16; 5.7, 8, 12, 13).

A widespread feature of the cosmologies of the ancient world was the notion that the three separate regions of the cosmos (heaven, earth, and underworld) were connected by a system of "doors" or "gates" which functioned to impede or facilitate communication and travel between regions (cf. Rev 4:1). The gatekeeper(s) who guarded the doors or gates and possessed the key(s) to them occupied positions of great power and authority. Just as the door to heaven provided a means for *ascent* to receive divine revelations or *descent* to earth for a heavenly revealer, so the door to Hades was the avenue for revelatory *descents* to the netherworld or the *ascent* of chthonic revealers to earth. Control of the entrance to Hades was essential for those who wanted to summon souls of the dead (*PGM* IV. 1467–68). The motif of the "opening of heaven" was used throughout the ancient world as a metaphor indicating the beginning of a revelatory experience.[50] It is therefore not surprising that Hekate, both by virtue of her control

[47] *PGM* III.46; IV.2118, 2610, 2632, 2692, 2713, 2730, 2815, 2880, 2957; XXXVI.188 (*bis*); LXX.4, 23; XCIII.5; CXIV.1. The name Hermekate, a combination of Hekate and Hermes occurs in III.46–7; cf. IV.2609 f.: "Hermes and Hekate together." Selene (= Hekate) occurs sixteen times: *PGM* I.148; IV.845, 2525, 2545, 2622, 2640, 2664–5, 2711, 2785, 2821, 2985; VII.669, 866, XIII.20, LII.4; LXII.9–10. Mene, "Moon" Hekate) occurs four times (IV.2264, 2278, 2609, 2815).

[48] Audollent, *Defixionum tabellae*, 22.35; 24.20; 26.24; 29.23; 30.28; 31.22; 32.23; 33.27; 35.22; 38.14; 41A.7, 11, 13; 71.4; 72.13 f.; 75a.4; 242.39.

[49] For a photograph, see J. Godwin, *Mystery Religions in the Ancient World* (San Francisco: Harper & Row, 1981) 23.

[50] For a survey of this motif see F. Lentzen-Deis, "Das Motiv der "Himmelsöffnung" in verschiedenen Gattungen der Umweltliteratur des Neuen Testaments," *Bib* 50 (1969) 301–27.

of the gates of Hades and in view of her role as a patron divinity of magic and sorcery, should figure prominently in Graeco-Roman *revelatory* magic. Though very little evidence has survived from sources other than the magical papyri, it is clear that one aspect of revelatory magic involved the magical control of the gates of Hades for the purpose of descent into the realm of the underworld. In the *Menippus* 6 ff. of Lucian of Samosata just such a ritual descent is parodied. Menippus reports that one of the magi in Babylon claimed "with certain incantations and rituals to open the gates of Hades and descend" (*Men.* 6). This was done by the magi, who called upon various chthonian gods including Hekate-Persephone.[51] Thereupon the ground was rent asunder (cf. Hekate's epithet ὑηξίχθων, "who break open the earth") and Hades became plainly visible below (9–10). For the ascent, the magician points Menippus to the light shining through the keyhole (κλειθρία) of the underworld side of the entrance to the oracle of Trophonius (22). H. D. Betz has identified part of one such descent ritual which survives in fragments in *PGM* LXX. In this ritual prescription, the user is instructed in the identity of Hekate-Erischigal using an "I am" formulation for protection against the dangers of descent (LXX.5). Epiphanies of Hekate from Hades are occasionally mentioned in response to the appropriate invocations.[52] Lucian describes her reported appearance: she is three hundred feet tall, carries a torch in her left hand and a sword in her right; she has snakes in place of hair (like Medusa), and is an anguipede; she could stamp her foot on the ground and break open a chasm to Hades (*Philopseudes* 23 f.). In Vergil's epic presentation of the role of the Cumaean Sibyl, the prophetess is the priestess of both Apollo and Hekate (*Aeneid* 6.35), and before opening the entrance to Hades for Aeneas, invokes "Hekate, power in heaven and hell" (*Hecaten caeloque Ereboque potentem*, 6.247), followed by a prayer for revelation (6.264–67). The underworld mythology of the *Aeneid* is similar to that parodied by Lucian and widely attested in other Graeco-Roman apocalypses.[53] The phenomenon of ritual ascent (*anabasis*) has its connections, not with Hekate, but, in Graeco-Roman magic at least, with Apollo-Helios. The best example is the so-called "Mithras Liturgy" (*PGM* IV.475–829).

Still indispensable is O. Weinreich, *Türöffnung im Wunder- Prodigien- und Zauberglauben der Antike, des Judenturns und Christentums*, TBAW, 5 (Stuttgart: Kohlhammer 1929) 200–464. Also important is M. Wälkens, *Die kleinasiatischen Türsteine* (Mainz: P. von Zabern, 1986), with representations of doors on gravestones.

[51] In *Men.* 9, Lucian quotes this line of hexameter: "And nocturnal Hekate and dreadful Persephone," which O. Bouquiaux-Simon has shown to be a modification of *Odyssey* 11.47: [prayer] "To mighty Hades and dreadful Persephone" (part of the preparatory ritual for Odysseus" entry into Hades), in "Lucien, citateur d"Homère," *L'Antiquité Classique*, 29 (1960) 5–17.

[52] "Catabasis Ritual," 287–95.

[53] Cf. Betz, "Apocalyptic Genre," 531–48.

A final important though complex feature of revelatory magic associated with Hekate is her use of angelic mediators. Not infrequently a divinity invoked to come sends an *angelos* in his or her stead (*PGM* XIII.603–11), though this is usually simply a "messenger" (i. e., a god, daimon, dream, person or even an animal), though *not* a member of a special class of supernatural beings. In one spell which appeals to Selene-Hekate, the goddess is entreated to "send forth your angel from among those who assist you," and "hear my words, and send forth your angel" (*PGM* VII.891, 898). As a term for a class of beings functioning as divine messengers intermediate between men and God, *angelos* was a common conception in Hellenistic Judaism; in Graeco-Roman cults, however, the term only began to gain currency in the first centuries CE, probably through Judaeo-Christian influence.[54] One of the epithets of Hekate herself was *Angelos*.[55] In an Attic curse tablet, Hermes, Hekate, Pluto, Kore, Persephone, etc. are called "subterranean messengers" (ἄγγελοι καταχθόνιοι).[56]

4. The Alpha and the Omega

"I am the First and the Last" is the first of three formulas which function as divine predicates in Rev 1:17b–18. This formula is found again at the conclusion of the Apocalypse as one of three self-predications of *Christ* (Rev 22:13): "I am the Alpha and the Omega, the First and the Last, the Beginning and the End. "The first and third formulas are used as self- predications of God in Rev 21:6: "I am the Alpha and the Omega, the Beginning and the End." In Rev 1:8, the author has placed three formulas together: "I am the Alpha and the Omega, says the Lord God, the one who is and the one who was and the coming one, the Almighty." This juxtaposition of varied elements drawn from Judaism and Hellenism exemplifies the author's tendency both to avoid the mechanical repetition of lists and to blend eastern and western traditions. These predicates also indicate a high Christology, since divine predicates used for God are also applied to Christ. Further, the listing of many divine predicates is relatively rare in early Christian literature but common in magical texts. As a divine predicate, the formula "the beginning and the end (and middle) [of all things]" (the last phrase implicitly understood), is drawn from Hellenistic religious and philosophical tradition and has a cosmological rather than temporal significance, as the important study of

---

[54] A. Dieterich, *Eine Mithrasliturgie*, 3rd ed. (Darmstadt: Wissenschaftliche Buchgesellschaft, 1966 [originally printed 1903]) 49.

[55] Scholium in Theocriti, *Idyll* 2.12; F. Deubner, *Scholia in Theocritum* (Paris: Editore Ambrosio Firmin Didot, 1849) 19; Hesychius s. v. *Angelos*; cf. Pindar, *Paean* 2.77–78; Farnell, *Cults*, II, 517 f.; Roscher, "Hekate," col. 1891.

[56] Audollent, *Defixionum tabellae*, 75a.2–3.

W.C. van Unnik demonstrates.[57] The origin of the formula "the first and the last" is usually assigned to Judaism on the basis of the Septuagint translations of Isa 44:6 (cf. 41:4; 43:10; 48:12), as well as on the temporal nature of the formula. Yet even this formula is found in Greek literature, and has a Hellenistic resonance.[58]

The formula with the closest associations with magical revelation, however, is the self-predication "I am the Alpha and the Omega", which occurs for the first time in the Apocalypse of John.[59] This formula is interpreted by the author through the parallel formulas "the Beginning and the End" (Rev 21:6; 22:13), "the First and the Last" (Rev 22:13), "the one who is and who was and the coming one," and the "Almighty" [*pantocrator*] (Rev 1:8). "Beginning and End" is a divine epithet found in the magical papyri (*PGM* IV.1125, 2836–7). In later Jewish alphabet symbolism the Hebrew word "truth," *'emet*, was interpreted as a designation of God as the beginning, middle and end. Yet the formula itself was of Hellenistic derivation (*mu* is the middle letter of the Greek alphabet, while the Hebrew or Aramaic *mem* is not).[60] The proposal that the Hebrew wordplay is derived from the hypothetical Greek acrostic ΑΜΩ,[61] is gratuitous.

Alpha and omega do occur together, separated by spaces from other "words," within the context of series of various combinations of the seven Greek vowels in magical spells.[62] It is likely that ΑΩ is an abbreviated way of referring to the chanting of all seven vowels.[63] In the magical papyri the seven vowels frequently function as a divine name. *PGM* XIII.39 commands "write the great name with the seven vowels," and in XXI.11–14 we read "your name which is seven-lettered [in] harmony with the seven [vowel sounds, which are pronounced according to] the twenty-eight forms of the moon" (followed by the

[57] Van Unnik, *Het godspredikaat*, 66, observes that the formula "the beginning and end" abbreviates the longer formula "the beginning and end *of all things*." Some of the texts which contain the formula include Plato, *Leg.* 4.715E, Josephus, *Ant.* 8.280; *Contra Ap.* 2.190; Philo, *Plant.* 93.

[58] Hesiod, *Theog.* 34; Theognis 1.3–4; cf. Van Unnik, *Het godspredikaat*, 74–6.

[59] In general see F. Cabrol, "A O", *Dictionnaire d'Archéologie Chrétienne et de Liturgie*, ed. F. Cabrol and H. Leclercq (Paris: Letouzey et Ané, 1924) I, 1–25 (emphasizing the use of the formula in Christian art and inscriptions beginning with the third century; E. Lohmeyer, "A und O", *Reallexikon für Antike und Christentum*, I, 1–4; F. Boll, *Sphaera: Neue griechische Texte und Untersuchungen zur Geschichte der Sternbilden* (Leipzig: Teubner, 1903) 469 ff.; R. Reitzenstein, *Poimandres Studien zur griechisch-aegyptischen und frühchristlichen Literatur* (Leipzig: Teubner, 1904) 156 ff.

[60] *b. Sanhedrin* 18a; cf. Lohmeyer, "A und 0," col. 2.

[61] Holtz, *Christologie*, 150.

[62] *PGM* IV.411, 528, 992, 993, 1224, 2351; V.363, 367; VII.476, 720; XIII.849–59 [*bis*], 931; XLIV (figure holding a staff with aleph written on the left and omega on the right); aleph omega are engraved on the back of a magical gem published by D. Wortmann, "Neue magische Gemmen," *Bonner Jahrbücher*, 175 (1975) 74; Audollent, *Defixionum tabellae*, 16, line 14 (p. 27); 252, line 13 (p. 348).

[63] W.B. Stanford, "The Significance of the Alpha and Omega in Revelation 1.8," *Hermathena*, 98 (1964) 43–4.

vowels). This seven-vowel divine name can be used in self-predications (under the influence of Egyptian magic where the magician pretends to be the deity): "I am AEHIOY[Ω AEHIOYΩ]" (*PGM* 111.661), or in *PGM* XIII.207: "Lord, I imitate [you by saying] the seven vowels … A EE HHH" etc. Occasionally AΩ occurs in conjunction with another divine name, as in "Abrasax AΩ" (*PGM* V.363, 367; cf. IV.528), or as a divine name (under the supposition that the seven vowels, individually, in various combinations and collectively symbolize the divine name), e.g.: "I call upon you with your name AΩ EY HOI" etc. (*PGM* IV.1182f.; cf. IV.992–93, 3238f.). Further, the letter aleph was associated with the concept of beginning or ἀρχή: "First origin of my origin, AEHIOYΩ, first beginning [ἀρχὴ … πρώτη] of my beginning" (*PGM* IV.487–8).

The divine name most frequently used in the magical papyri (sixty-six times) is Iaō, a name also used in conjunction with AΩ in sequences of vowel permutations functioning as *voces magicae* often juxtaposed with series of other divine names. In *PGM* IV.992–93, for example, we read: "god of gods, benefactor, AΩ IAΩ EAY, you who direct night and day, AI AΩ." Iaō almost certainly entered magical repertoire as a Greek transliteration of the divine name *yhw* ("Yahu") a shortened form of *yhwh* ("Yahweh") the covenant name of the God of Israel. This form is attested in the fifth century BCE Elephantine papyri and was presumably current in Egyptian Judaism.[64] A papyrus manuscript of Leviticus from Qumran (4Q LXX Lev b), late first century BCE to early first century CE, contains the divine name in phonetic Greek spelling IAΩ, rather than the expected *Kyrios*.[65] The only other occurrence of IAΩ in a Greek OT manuscript is in the sixth century Codex Q (Marchalianus) of the Prophets. Undoubtedly one of the attractions of the name Iaō was the fact that it contains three of the seven vowels; in magical papyri and *defixiones*, Iaō occurs many times in vowel sequences.[66] Iaō could be turned into the palindrome IAΩAI (*PGM* VII.375, 520, 521; XIII.811), or schematically reduced from IAΩ to AΩ to Ω (VII.220). It is likely that the Tetragrammaton (perhaps transliterated IAOYE) was occasionally transliterated using all seven vowels in the form IAΩOYHE (though this is difficult to substantiate).[67] Further, IAΩ is used several times in the magical papyri

---

[64] R. Ganschinietz, "Iao", Pauly-Wissowa, *Realencyclopaedie der klassischen Altertumswissenschaft*, IX (1914) 699–700; D.E. Aune, "Iao," *Reallexikon für Antike und Christentum* (Stuttgart: Anton Hiersemann, 1995), Band XVII, cols. 1–12; cf. the short discussion by J. Michl, "Engel V (Engelnamen)", *Reallexikon fürAntike und Christentum*, V, col. 216.

[65] See P.W. Skehan, "The Qumran Manuscripts and Textual Criticism," *Volume du Congrès, Strasbourg 1956*, Supplements to Vetus Testamentum, IV (Leiden: Brill, 1957) 157; H. Stegemann, "Die Gottesbezeichnungen in den Qumrantexten", *Qumran, sa piété, sa théologie et son milieu*, ed. M. Delcor (Leuven: University Press, 1978) 205; C.H. Roberts, *Manuscript, Society and Belief in Early Christian Egypt* (Oxford: Oxford University Press, 1979) 30.

[66] *PGM* II.16; III.458, 573ff., 582; IV.204ff., 962–3, 1034–5, 1040–1, 1043–4, 1220ff., 1560ff.; VI.28f.; VII.307ff., XIII.779f., 977–8; 1020–1, 1047.

[67] F. Kenyon, *Greek Papyri in the British Museum*, I (London: British Museum, 1893) 63; L. Blau, *Das altjüdische Zauberwesen* (Strassburg i.E. : Karl J. Truebner, 1898) 130; Stanford,

with the divine predicate "the one who is" (ὁ ὤν) in the formulaic phrase "strong lord, mighty ΙΑΩ ΟΥΩ ΙΩ ΑΙΩ ΟΥΩ, who exist [ὁ ὤν]" (*PGM* XIII.1020, 1045. *PGM* LXXI.3–4 has even more similarity to Rev 1:8, since both passages have the epithets "the one who is" and "pantokrator" (author's trans.): "the god who is, ΙΑΩ! Lord, ruler of all" (ὁ ὤν θεὸς ὁ Ἰάω, κύριος παντοκράτωρ).

Several conclusions emerge from a comparative study of the formula ΑΩ in the Apocalypse and in the magical papyri. (1) ΑΩ functions as a divine name in both the Apocalypse and the magical papyri, though in the latter it is one among many vowel permutations all of which can function as divine names. (2) ΑΩ is a prominent constituent of ΙΑΩ, the divine name which occurs most frequently in Graeco-Roman magical texts; for Jewish ears ΙΑΩ is connected to the Israelite name for God, an abbreviation of the name YHWH. (3) John adapted the divine predicate ΑΩ which was at home primarily in the world of Graeco-Roman magic for its symbolic connection with other formulas such as "the beginning and end", and "the first and the last", and because of its connection with ΙΑΩ.

(4) The fact that Christ himself and not a human practitioner utters this and other formulas as divine self-predicates suggests that he cannot be controlled by incantations but he is in fact the supreme Lord of the cosmos who is independent of all human control and manipulation, who now reveals his true name.

5. I Am Coming Quickly

Rev 22:20 contains a concluding promise of Christ, "surely I am coming quickly," together with the response of John, "Amen, come Lord Jesus." The second statement has the form of a liturgical invocation, or epiklesis, while the first resembles the kind of response attributed to the deity who appears. Most commentators correctly understand John's "invocation" as a Greek translation and modification of the Aramaic formula *marana tha* or *maran atha*, either of which may be translated "our Lord, come!" or "our Lord has come".[68] John, I argue, has added new nuances to this early Christian formula (cf. 1 Cor 16:22; *Did.* 10:6), by placing it in a literary setting in which it is paired with the announcement of Jesus, "surely I am coming quickly!" By giving the *maranatha*

"Significance," 43–4. Egyptian priests are describing as singing the seven vowels in Demetrius *De elocutione* 71 and Eusebius, *Praep.* 11.6.36 (519d), proposes that the seven (Greek) vowels contain the pronunciation of the secret name of God, spelled with four letters by the Jews.

68 The philological evidence (with an extensive bibliography) is discussed by K. G. Kuhn, *TDNT*, IV, 467–70. For more recent discussion with further bibliography see C. F. D. Moule, "A Reconsideration of the Context of *Maranatha*," *NTS* 6 (1959–60) 307–30; S. Schulz, "Maranatha und Kyrios Jesus," *ZNW* 53 (1962) 1 25–44; P. É. Langevin, *Jésus seigneur et l'éschatologie: exégèse de textes prépauliniens* (Bruges-Paris: Desclée de Brouwer, 1967) 168–298.

formula this interpretive overlay, the author appears to be alluding to liturgical invocations in the ancient world.

In the OT and Judaism, the presence of God is a religious idea of central importance. While the OT and Judaism knew or anticipated various modalities of the divine presence (in "nature", in the holy war, in the cult, in personal experience and at the eschaton), liturgical invocations requesting the deity to "come" are rare.[69] In the OT, Yahweh is frequently conceptualized as "the God who comes", for he is the subject of the verb *bô'* some thirty-three times. Most of these references, however, refer to past comings of Yahweh and are often found in the context of hymns of praise.[70] Cultic invocations for God to "come" in the Second Temple period occur only in Hellenized accounts of Israelite-Jewish religion (Josephus, *Ant.* 4.46; 20. 90). While the expectation of the eschatological coming or visitation (*pĕqûdāh*) of Yahweh frequently expressed in later sections of the OT (often in terms of the coming Day of Yahweh, Joel 2:1 ff.; 3:4; Zech 14:5; Mal 3:1), and in the literature of Second Temple Judaism, prayers requesting that coming are rare.

Throughout the history of Greek religion, on the other hand, the gods were invoked to "come" since they were conceived in terms of extension in space and must "come" in order to be present and really hear the supplicant.[71] These invocations were customarily expressed using imperative forms of a variety of verbs meaning "to come"; e. g., βάθι, δεῦρο, ἐλθέ, ἐρινίσεο, ἕρπε, ἧκε, μόλε, etc. Liturgical invocations of this type were used in ceremonies of dedication for new images and temples of the gods, for securing their presence during sacrifices, oracular consultations and prayers, and in private adaptations of public rituals by Graeco-Roman magicians. Zeus, at least in public liturgies, is never invited to come; he sees and acts from where he is. The most famous ancient Greek invocation for a god to come is found in Sappho *fr.* 1.5, 25. Although very few ancient Greek liturgical texts have been preserved,[72] their basic character is revealed in such fragmentary texts as the old Delphic hymn to Apollo embedded in *PGM* I.296–325, which begins "O lord Apollo, come with Paian. / Give answer to my questions, Lord. O Master / Leave Mount Parnassos and the Delphic Pytho / Whene'er my priestly lips voice secret words." Among the pre-Christian Homeric Hymns, only Hymn 24 to Hestia invokes the goddess to "come" (ἔρχεο). In

[69] Individual and communal laments in the Psalms and in the archaic holy war traditions call on God to "arise" (קום, Pss 3:8; 44:27; 74:22; Num 10:35 ff.). In such contexts the divine response "I will arise" occasionally occurs (Psa 12:6; Isa 33:10).

[70] Deut 33:2; Psa 96:13; 98:9; Isa 59:19–20; Hab 3:3–4, 16; Zech 2:14.

[71] E. Pax, *Epiphaneia. Ein religionsgeschichtlicher Beitrag z. bibl. Theologie* (München: Münchener Theologische Studien, 1955) 32 ff.; H. S. Versnel, "Ancient Prayer," in *Faith, Hope and Worship: Aspects of Religious Mentality in the Ancient World*, ed. H. S. Versnel (Leiden: Brill, 1981) 29–30.

[72] Cf. Dieterich, *Mithrasliturgie*, 213 ff., a collection of liturgical phrases; see also Betz, "Catabasis Ritual," 287–95.

contrast, the post-Christian Orphic Hymns often conclude with an invocation to the particular divinity addressed.[73] Invocations or epikleseis to various gods and supernatural beings to "come" pervade the magical papyri.[74] Phrases which bear a closer resemblance to Rev 22:20 include "come to me Lord!" (δεῦρό μοι κύριε, 12.238; ἦκέ μοι κύριε, 13.88, 603), and "Quickly, by your power now appear on earth to me, yea verily, god!" (1.89 f.). All of these passages from the magical papyri, however, belong to one of the major types of Graeco-Roman magic: magical divination, which typically requires the presence of a supernatural being as a revelatory medium.[75] Further, the appearance of the god, daimon or angel invoked is a private event in response to a secret ritual procedure performed in the magician's home. In dramatic and mythological literature, the responsorial counterpart to these invocations is the "I have come" speeches placed in the mouths of various divinities and supernatural revealers.[76]

In the phrase Surely I am coming quickly, used five times by John (2:16; 3:11; 22:7, 12, 20), "I am coming" (ἔρχομαι) is an oracular or prophetic present accompanied by the adverb ταχύ ("quickly"), making the phrase unique in early Christian literature. The ritual impatience of magicians is well known. In the Greek magical papyri, many spells end with various permutations of the formula ἤδη ἤδη, ταχὺ ταχύ, "now, now! quick, quick!" (III.123 f.; IV.1245, 1593, 1924, 2037, 2098). This impatience can also accompany invocations to the god or *daimon* to "come" quickly (I.89–90; IV.236–7; VI.14; VII.248 f., 329 ff.). Again John turns the table on contemporary magical practice and places the promise to come on the lips of the risen Jesus, adding the adverb "quickly" to make the parody obvious. As a prophet, John's role is reduced to a responsorial affirmation of the promise of Jesus.

6. Conclusions

For the original recipients of the Apocalypse, the validity of John's message depended on their acceptance of it at face value as a revelation of God through Jesus Christ to John for them. The author used a variety of rhetorical devices

---

[73] Orph. *Hymni praef.* 43; 1.9; 9.11; 11.4, 21; 12.14; 14.12; 27.11; 33.8; 34.1; 35.7;36.13; 40.8; etc. Nearly half the hymns conclude with such an invocation.

[74] "Come to me" (δεῦρό μοι): *PGM* I.163; II.2; III.129; 481, 564; IV.1171, 1605; VII.961, 962, 963, 964, 965; (ἐλθέ μοι): III.51; V.249; LXII.25.

[75] Hopfner, *Offenbarungszauber*, II, 40 ff.

[76] Athena in *Iliad* 1.207; Apollo in Euripides, *Orestes* 1628; Dionysius in Euripides, *Bacchae* 1; a ghost in Euripides, *Hecuba* 1; Poseidon in Euripides, *Troades* 1; Hermes in Euripides, *Ion* 5; a Syrian prophet in Origen, *Contra Celsum* 7.9; cf. O. Weinreich, "De Dis Ignotis Quaestiones Selectae," *Ausgewählte Schriften* (Amsterdam: B.R. Gruener, 1969) I, 285 ff., with other examples.

to ensure the proper reception of his revelation.[77] The quest for divine revelation, whether preserved from the past in written form or sought through various revelatory media in the present, was not an exclusive prerogative of Judaism or Christianity, but was a widespread concern throughout the Graeco-Roman world. In addition to the many popular public oracles, there was a thriving black market in magical revelation.

In this study we have discussed three complexes of religious motifs, one which occurs just once ("I have the keys to Death and Hades," Rev 1:18), and two which occur repeatedly ("I am coming quickly," five times; "I am the Alpha and the Omega," four times). These passages all have several features in common. First, they are all presented as words of the risen Jesus. Second, they are all located in the literary framework of the Apocalypse (Rev 1–3, 22), a fact capable of several kinds of explanations. Third, they all have striking parallels with the techniques, formulas and motifs of magical revelation as shown in the Greek and Demotic magical papyri. Fourth, these passages in the Apocalypse are all unique in early Christian literature, a fact which suggests (but does not prove) that John has not derived them intact from Christian tradition, but has consciously adapted them from Graeco-Roman tradition. Finally, an analysis of these passages in the Apocalypse in the light of Graeco-Roman magical divination suggests that these techniques, formulas and motifs from the world of pagan magical practice have been used by the author in such a way that the validity of the religious and magical assumptions behind them are implicitly denied. In other words, the author has devised an extensive and creative antimagical polemic the purpose of which is to nullify the revelatory claims of the pagan competitors of Christian prophets. John includes magical practices (φάρμακα) in the vice list in 9:20–1, and emphasizes the fact that magicians (φαρμακοί) will experience the second death (21:8) and be excluded from the Holy City (22:15). John also mentions the magical feats accomplished by the beast from the earth (13:13–15; cf. 19:20). These explicit references, in addition to linking the anti-magic apologetic of Rev 1–3 and 22 to the body of the document (Rev 4–21), only partially reveal the depth of the struggle which John waged against the widespread beliefs and assumptions of Graeco-Roman magical revelation.

[77] Many of these are discussed in D.E. Aune, "The Social Matrix of the Apocalypse of John," *BR* 26 (1981) 16–32. Reprinted above, pp. 175–89.

Magic in Early Christianity*

1. Introduction

Considered in relationship to early Christianity, magic has generally received a bad press. In one of the more recent articles on that subject, "Magie und Aberglaube an den Anfängen des Christentums" by N. Brox[1], the author describes magic *"als ständig drohende Dekadenz und als überall anwesende Perversion von Religion und auch von christlichem Glauben"*. Such was not always the case. Two generations ago the study of Graeco-Roman magic made a significant impact on New Testament studies through the careful, though sometimes erratic, studies produced by a number of German scholars associated with the so-called *religionsgeschichtliche Schule* (A. Dieterich, R. Reitzenstein, A. Deissmann, W. Heitmüller, F. Preisigke, O. Bauernfeind and others). More recently, the rise of the Biblical theology movement was accompanied by a strong reaction against the notion that ancient Mediterranean magic could have influenced early Christianity in any substantive way. The authors of many of the articles in the *Theologisches Wörterbuch zum Neuen Testament*, most of whom consider themselves Biblical theologians, write as if they were involved in a conspiracy to ignore or minimize the role of magic in the New Testament and early Christian literature. However, for those who know the ways of birds there are signs in abundance that Graeco-Roman magic is again being considered a potentially fruitful subject which may illuminate important aspects of the religion of early Christians.

One important influence in the renewed interest in Graeco-Roman magic has been the revision and republication of the large corpus of Graeco-Egyptian magical papyri originally edited by K. Preisendanz and published in two volumes in 1928 and 1931. Careful corrections together with the addition of some supplementary material characterize the second edition of Preisendanz, *Papyri Graecae Magicae: Die griechischen Zauberpapyri* [*PGM*], ed. A. Henrichs, I (Stuttgart: Verlag B.G. Teubner, 1973), II (Stuttgart: Verlag B.G. Teubner, 1974). Preisendanz' third volume, consisting mainly of elaborate sets of indices to the first

* The author wishes to express his gratitude to a number of colleagues whose comments, suggestions and corrections have been incorporated into this article: professors C. Thomas Brockmann, Hans Dieter Betz, David Schroeder and Morton Smith.

[1] *Trierer theologische Zeitschrift*, 83 (1974), 157.

two volumes, was printed in 1941 but almost completely destroyed (along with Verlag B.G. Teubner) in 1943. Students of Graeco-Egyptian magic, therefore, await with great anticipation Henrichs' revisions of this invaluable set of indices. Yet another important impetus for the renewed study of ancient Mediterranean magic was the discovery and publication by M. Margalioth, *Sepher ha-Razim* ["Book of Mysteries"] (Jerusalem, 1966), which was apparently a handbook of a Jewish magician, dated by Margalioth to possibly the third century CE. An English translation of this Hebrew magical handbook has been made by Michael Morgan and will soon be published by Scholars Press. Margalioth's edition has been severely criticized by I. Gruenwald of Tel Aviv University, who believes that a more accurate edition of *Sepher ha-Razim* is necessary.

A number of significant secondary studies which relate directly to the study of Graeco- Roman magic have appeared recently, a fact which further confirms a burgeoning scholarly interest in the subject. In M. Smith's *Clement of Alexandria and a Secret Gospel of Mark* (Cambridge: Harvard University Press, 1973), the author devoted a short but excellent discussion to affirming the widespread influence of ancient magic on Jesus and earliest Christianity (220–37). The next year saw appearance of J.M. Hull's *Hellenistic Magic and the Synoptic Tradition* (London: SCM Press, 1974), nearly half of which was devoted to a general discussion of the nature and features of Graeco-Roman magic; in spite of some rather serious flaws, Hull's book constitutes an important contribution to a seriously neglected subject. *Jesus the Magician* (New York: Harper & Row, 1978) is the title of another important book by M. Smith; in this study the author analyzes the New Testament evidence in the light of Graeco-Roman magical traditions, and concludes that Jesus is best understood in the role of a magician or sorcerer.

A number of shorter studies which pertain to our subject have also appeared which focus on the relationship between Christianity and magic in the third and fourth centuries of the Christian era. Mention should be made of A.A. Barb's "The Survival of Magic Arts" in: *The Conflict Between Paganism and Christianity in the Fourth Century*, ed. A. Momigliano (Oxford: Clarendon Press, 1963); like N. Brox, the author regards magic as a perversion of religion. Particularly noteworthy for an exemplary application of the structural-functional method of contemporary anthropological and sociological theory is P. Brown's "Sorcery, Demons and the Rise of Christianity", in: *Witchcraft: Confessions & Accusations*, ed. M. Douglas (London, 1970). Despite the title of N. Brox, "Magie und Aberglaube an den Anfängen des Christentums," *Trierer theologische Zeitschrift*, 83 (1974), 157–80, the author devotes most of his discussion to Origen, Chrysostom and Augustine; the stubborn persistence of magical practices among Christians despite official ecclesiastical opposition is attributed to the nature of *Volksglaube*. Brox' article, which has much to commend it, should be read in light of J. Engemann's "Zur Verbreitung magischer Übelabwehr in der nichtchristlichen und christlichen Spätantike," *Jahrbuch für Antike und Chris-*

tentum, 18 (1975), 22–48, in which evidence for magical practices in clerical circles is discussed.

All of the publications discussed above appear to be symptomatic of a basic shift in the intellectual climate in which ancient Mediterranean religion and society have been studied. The rise of the structural-functional method in sociology and anthropology and the phenomenological method in comparative religions have provided scholars with theoretical frameworks in which the value judgments of the observers are regarded as an improper intrusion into the subject matter. Hence it is becoming increasingly less intellectually respectable to regard ancient Mediterranean magic (no less than the magic of modern primitive societies) pejoratively. A different, but no less significant shift has occurred in the historical and cultural perspective from which New Testament scholarship has interpreted early Christian life and literature. The tendency of the *religionsgeschichtliche Schule* to regard early Christianity as a syncretistic phenomenon within the broader context of Graeco-Roman paganism gradually gave way to a more exclusive focus on Judaism as the primary social and religious matrix of early Christianity by the Biblical theology movement (a tendency reinforced by the discovery of the Dead Sea Scrolls in 1947). More recently there has begun a perceptible shift on the part of New Testament scholars toward a more comprehensive emphasis on Graeco-Roman society and culture as the broader context within which both Judaism and early Christianity must be understood.

The specific objectives of the present study are three in number: (1) to summarize and criticize much of the work that has already been accomplished on the subject of the relationship of ancient magic to early Christianity, (2) to provide a more comprehensive and consistent theoretical framework within which the study of magic and early Christianity might be pursued in a more satisfying and productive manner, and (3) to highlight the lacunae which currently exist in scholarly research. The vastness of the subject matter makes it necessary that our discussion be limited to the more important and relevant aspects of our topic.

2. The Nature and Function of Magic

For more than a century the nature and function of magic and its relationship to religion has been discussed endlessly. Prior to World War II, the discussion of magic was generally hampered by two widely-held presuppositions: that magic is easily separable from religion, and that magic is a decadent cultural phenomenon. Between the two World Wars, anthropologists turned from an earlier preoccupation with religious origins in primitive societies to more general ethnographical interests. Since World War II the seminal work of E. E. Evans-Pritchard, *Witchcraft, Oracles and Magic among the Azande* (Oxford: Clarendon Press, 1937), appears to have again made the study of religion and magic respectable, this time within a structural-functional framework. Evans-Pritchard himself recommended a moratorium on the anthropological use of the terms "religion" and "magic" as mutually exclusive phenomena capable of clear definition. He, with many other anthropologists, has come to speak more inclusively of "religio-magical" phenomena[2]. Two discrete notions lurk behind this hyphenated adjective: (1) the distinction between magic and religion is at best ambiguous, and (2) magic, in view of its interrelationship with religion, cannot be dismissed as unimportant. Evans-Pritchard regards the attempt to understand magic as a universal idea with a unique essence as a thoroughly hopeless task[3].

Recent anthropological studies on magic and religion have exhibited two divergent trends. One trend, strongly influenced by Evans-Pritchard, has tended to treat religio-magical phenomena only within the context of empirical studies of particular cultures thereby avoiding the temptation to formulate definitions which pretend universal validity[4]. The second trend has been the renewed consideration of the problem of the nature and function of magic and religion and their relationship to science and technology on the theoretical level[5]. Common to both trends is the emerging *communis opinio* among modern anthropologists that the older dichotomy between magic and religion is not only misleading, but that, regarded as strict categories, totally unworkable.

With few exceptions, classicists and New Testament scholars prior to World War II found it convenient to draw a distinction between magic and religion and to regard magic either as a vestige of an early stage of man's religious development[6], or as a perverse and corrupt form of religion[7]. M. Nilsson expressed the

---

[2] D. F. Aberle, "Religio-Magical Phenomena and Power, Prediction and Control," *Southwestern Journal of Anthropology,* 22 (1966), 221–30.

[3] E. E. Evans-Pritchard, *Theories of Primitive Religion* (Oxford: Clarendon Press, 1965) 111.

[4] Evans-Pritchard's analyses of primitive religions exemplify the emic approach whereby definitions, distinctions and values are derived from the actors themselves rather than imposed on them by the observer; cf. E. E. Evans-Pritchard, *Nuer Religion* (Oxford: Clarendon Press, 1956) 95; *idem, Witchcraft, Oracles and Magic among the Azande* (Oxford: Clarendon Press, 1937) 21. For a discussion of the terms "emic" and "etic" that have emerged from the so-called New Ethnology, see M Harris, The Rise of Anthropological Theory: A History of Theories of Culture (New York: Crowell, 1968) 568–604.

[5] Two articles which review the state of the question and offer new theoretical frameworks are M. and R. Wax, "The Notion of Magic, Current Anthropology," 4 (1963), 495–518, and K. E. Rosengren, "Malinowski's Magic: The Riddle of the Empty Cell, Current Anthropology," 17 (1976), 667–85.

[6] Wilamowitz-Moellendorff warned against mixing superstition and true religion, describing magic as *Urdummheit,* in: *idem, Der Glaube der Hellenen*, I (Berlin: Weidmannsche Buchhandlung, 1931) 28 ff., 31. W. Bousset regarded magic as the lowest rung on the ladder of human religious development (*Das Wesen der Religion dargestellt an ihrer Geschichte* [Halle: Gebauer-Schwetschke, 1903] 40 ff.).

[7] The Norwegian classicist S. Eitrem referred to the magical papyri as "interesting relics of degenerate religions and of the human mind gone astray" in the preface of *Papyri Osloensis*, Fasc. I (Oslo: Norske videnskaps-akademi, 1925). More recently E. R. Dodds observed that

view that the relationship to the gods in religion and magic was fundamentally different[8]. A.-J. Festugière regarded magic as the inverse of religion[9]. Karl Prümm, S.J. described magic as *widerreligiös*[10]. In spite of the unquestioned erudition of these scholars, it is clear that the common supposition underlying these judgments is the inclination to discredit magic in contrast to religion.

A.D. Nock, one of the more erudite historians of ancient Mediterranean religions, held a contrary opinion. "There is not, then", he claimed of the Graeco-Roman world, "as with us, a sphere of magic in contrast to the sphere of religion"[11]. He registered strong agreement with F. Pfiser, that "there exists no fundamental distinction between incantation and prayer, just as there is none between magic and religion"[12]. More recently, historians of ancient Mediterranean religions have begun to protest the rigid distinction formerly made between magic and religion[13]. Among historians of Graeco-Roman religions, as among contemporary anthropologists, a rigid dichotomy between magic and religion has become increasingly difficult to sustain. Even among those who do propose such a theoretical distinction, inconsistencies not infrequently arise in their empirical discussions of the features of Graeco-Roman magic[14].

Recognizing the difficulty of drawing a hard and fast line between magic and religion, anthropologist W.J. Goode has formulated a number of "nondichoto-

---

"the magical papyri constantly operate with the debris of other people's religion" (*Pagan and Christian in an Age of Anxiety: Some Aspects of Religious Experience from Marcus Aurelius to Augustine* [Cambridge: Cambridge University Press, 1965] 73).

[8] M. Nilsson, "Die Religion in den griechischen Zauberpapyri," in: *idem*, *Opuscula Selecta: linguis Anglica, Francogallica, Germanica conscripta*, III (Lund: C.W.K. Gleerup, 1960) 130.

[9] A.J. Festugière, *L'Idéal religieux des Grecs et l'Évangile* (Paris: Librairie Lecoffre, 1932) 289.

[10] K. Prümm, *Religionsgeschichtliches Handbuch für den Raum der altchristlichen Umwelt* (Rome: Päpstliches Bibelinstitut, 1954) 360.

[11] A.D. Nock, "Paul and the Magus," in: *idem, Essays on Religion and the Ancient World*, I, ed. Z. Stewart (Cambridge: Harvard University Press, 1972) 314.

[12] Quoted by Nock, "Paul and the Magus," 315.

[13] J. Ferguson, *The Religions of the Roman Empire* (Ithaca: Cornell University Press, 1970) 157f.; S.G.F. Brandon, "Magic and the Black Art," *The Modern Churchman*, n.s., 11 (1968), 75; E.R. Goodenough, *Jewish Symbols in the Greco-Roman Period*, II (New York: Pantheon Books, 1953) 155f.; M. Smith, *Clement of Alexandria and a Secret Gospel of Mark* (Cambridge: Harvard University Press, 1973) 221f. Even K. Prümm. who regards ancient magic as *Aberglaube* from the perspective of the norms of Christian theology, realizes that it must be viewed as "religion" from the perspective of *Religionswissenschaft* (*Religionsgeschichtliches Handbuch*, 362).

[14] Festugière admitted that some "magical" texts (e.g., *PGM* XL) are purely "religious" in nature (*L'Idéal religieux des Grecs*, 282); Nilsson too, in his discussion of the significance of the magical papyri remarked that "several of these invocations are quite beautiful and marked by a genuinely religious spirit" ("Die Religion in den griechischen Zauberpapyri," 155); also Dieterich, who normally demarcated magic from religion, noted the great extent to which magical texts drew on material from religious texts in: *idem*, *Eine Mithrasliturgie*, 2. Aufl. (Leipzig und Berlin: B.G. Teubner, 1910) 27f.

mous empirical differences" between magic and religion[15]: (1) magic tends to adopt a manipulative attitude toward "extra-ordinary" reality, while religion tends to adopt a supplicative attitude, (2) magical activities tend to be used instrumentally for specific goals, while religious activities tend to be regarded as ends in themselves, (3) magic tends to emphasize individual goals, while religion tends to focus on group goals, (4) magical activities tend to be private and individual, while religious activities tend to be carried out by groups, (5) magic tends to develop professional-client relationships, while religion tends to emphasize the "shepherd-flock" or "prophet-follower" relationship, (6) magic tends, in cases of failure, to introduce substitute techniques, while substitution is less characteristic of religion, and (7) magic tends to act impersonally with minimal emphasis on emotion, while religion tends to make greater use of emotion and to evoke attitudes of awe and worship. Goode is exceedingly wary of formulating universally valid statements about either religion or magic unless they are carefully qualified; his discussion has not received the attention it deserves.

Perhaps the most common way in which magic has been distinguished from religion, both by behavioral scientists and historians of religion, is based on a supposed difference in attitude toward supernatural powers: magic is said to be manipulative and coercive, while religion supplicates and venerates (the hazards of such psychologizing, however, remain generally unrecognized). Historians of religion, frequently concerned with formulating universally valid generalizations, have shown themselves particularly vulnerable to this notion. The article by J. De Vries, "Magic and Religion," *History of Religions*, 1 (1962), 214–21, sets forth just such a position; he claims that "it is generally agreed, of course, that [magic and religion] are fundamentally opposed" (214), and that magic in contrast to religion adopts an audaciously coercive attitude to that which the community regards as venerable (221). "The difference [between magic and religion] lies certainly not in the more or less social aspect but rather in the psychological attitude of the individual: in magic he desires to command, in religion he feels reverence" (218). The basic fallacy in absolutizing this attitudinal distinction between magic and religion is the fact that it is demonstrably false: magic not infrequently supplicates while religion not infrequently manipulates supernatural powers. In the fine study of magic in sixteenth and seventeenth century England by K. Thomas, *Religion and the Decline of Magic: Studies in Popular Beliefs in Sixteenth and Seventeenth Century England* (London: Weidenfeld and Nicolson, 1971), the author shows how Protestant theologians attacked Catholicism by differentiating magic from religion in terms of the manipulation/supplication dichotomy (51–77 and passim). One suspects that this theological distinction between magic and religion which has become so influ-

[15] W.J. Goode, "Magic and Religion: A Continuum," *Ethnos*, 14 (1949), 172–82; *idem*, *Religion among the Primitives* (Glencoe; Free Press, 1951) 50–55.

ential in western religious thought has replaced an earlier implicitly sociological definition of magic which not only dominated the pre-Reformation distinction between magic and religion in Christianity, but also appears to be the central way in which the two were distinguished in the Graeco-Roman world. The attitudinal distinction between magic and religion has been emphasized by a number of historians of ancient Mediterranean religions, most notably by M. Nilsson and A. J. Festugière.[16]

Before formulating a sociological definition of the relationship of magic to religion, let us first note other ways in which magical beliefs and practices have been distinguished from those of religion, particularly by historians of Graeco-Roman religions. One of the central presuppositions of magic is said to be an understanding of the principles of cosmic sympathy and antipathy[17], essential for the successful performance of magical rituals. However, the universal religious phenomenon of divination also operates on the basis of this presupposition[18], making it evident that the notion of the coherence and interrelationship of the apparently discrete parts of the cosmos is hardly unique to magic. Many historians of Graeco-Roman religions have focused on magical incantations[19] or magical ritual[20] as constitutive of the essence of magic. However, here too, it is difficult if not impossible to establish a phenomenological distinction between magical incantation and religious prayer or magical and religious ritual. In terms of beliefs and practices, there appears to be no thoroughly convincing way of distinguishing magic from religion. M. Mauss emphasized this point in an attempt to formulate a general theory of magic: "...the functions of magic are not specialized. Magical life is not compartmentalized like religion. It has not led to the growth of any autonomous institutions like sacrifice and priesthood"[21].

Beginning with E. Durkheim, the French Sociological School viewed magic as consisting of beliefs, practices and persons operating outside the religious collectivity, thereby emphasizing the individualistic, anti-social dimensions of

---

[16] *Supra*, notes 8 and 9.

[17] J. G. Frazer devoted a lengthy section of his *The Golden Bough*, I (3rd ed.; New York: The Macmillan Company, 1935), to the discussion of sympathetic magic (52–219), and magical sympathy and antipathy is discussed at length also in M. Mauss, *A General Theory of Magic* (London and Boston: Routledge and Kegan Paul, 1972). For the notion in Graeco-Roman magic, see T. Hopfner, *Griechisch-ägyptischer Offenbarungszauber*, I (Leipzig, 1921), paragraphs 97, 106, 378 ff.; J. Röhr, *Der okkulte Kraftbegriff im Altertum*, *Philologus*, Suppl. 17 (Leipzig, 1923).

[18] R. Bloch, *Les prodiges dans l'antiquité classique* (Paris: Presses universitaires de France, 1963) 4 ff: cf. V. Turner's analysis of metaphor and symbol in ritual indicative of similar "bonds of sympathy" in: *idem, The Ritual Process: Structure and Antistructure* (Ithaca: Cornell University Press,1969).

[19] K. H. E. De Jong, *Das antike Mysterienwesen in religionsgeschichtlicher, ethnologischer und psychologischer Beleuchtung* (Leiden: Brill, 1909) 143.

[20] Festugière, *L'Idéal religieux des Grecs*, 284 ff.; Prümm, *Religionsgeschichtliches Handbuch*, 371.

[21] Mauss, *A General Theory of Magic*, 88.

magic[22]. M. Mauss developed a more adequate view of magic and the magician on the basis of beliefs shared by the entire social unit, though magic itself was viewed as unauthorized, abnormal or at least not highly estimable[23]. Mauss saw the essence of magic in its illegality: "A magical rite is any rite which does not play a part in organized cult – it is private, secret, mysterious and approaches the limit of a prohibited rite"[24]. More recently, a contemporary historian of ancient Mediterranean religions, J.Z. Smith, has emphasized illegality as the one universal characteristic of magic[25]. Between Mauss and Smith, of course, we have the development of the structural-functional method in anthropology and sociology in which such labels as "magic" and "magician" are viewed as playing an important role in social definition and control[26].

The sociological description of the nature and function of magic in relation to religion, particularly within the framework of the structural-functional method as it has been developed since World War II, appears to be the most satisfying theoretical perspective from which to analyze magic in Graeco-Roman religions. One particular branch of sociological inquiry which has risen to great prominence in America in the last decade is the study of social deviance[27]. In spite of the enormous amount of literature on social deviance, there are only two primary theoretical approaches to the subject, symbolic interactionism and

---

22 E. Durkheim, *The Elementary Forms of the Religious Life* (New York: Free Press, 1965) 57 ff. In *Purity and Danger: An Analysis of Concepts of Pollution and Taboo* (New York: Praeger, 1966), M. Douglas properly criticizes Durkheim by claiming that he "advocated an altogether too unitary view of the social community. We should start by recognizing communal life for a much more complex experience than he allowed. Then we find that Durkheim's idea of ritual as symbolic of social processes can be extended to include both types of belief in contagion, religious and magical. If he could have foreseen an analysis of ritual in which none of the rules he called hygienic are without their load of social symbolism, he would presumably have been happy to discard the category of magic" (22).

23 Mauss, *A General Theory of Magic*, 24, 32.

24 *Ibid.*, 24.

25 J.Z. Smith, "Good News is No News: Aretalogy and Gospel," in *Christianity, Judaism and Other Greco-Roman Cults*, ed. J. Neusner, I (Leiden: Brill, 1975) 23.

26 Douglas, *Purity and Danger*, 102; J. Middleton and E.H. Winter (eds.), *Witchcraft and Sorcery in East Africa* (London: Routledge and Paul, 1963). However, the problems inherent in the use of the structural-functional method in this collection of essays are underlined by V. Turner's "Witchcraft and Sorcery: Taxonomy versus Dynamics," in *idem*, *The Forest of Symbols: Aspects of Ndembu Ritual* (Ithaca: Cornell University Press, 1967) 112–27.

27 Some significant studies of social deviance include D.C. Gibbons and J.F. Jones, *The Study of Deviance: Perspectives and Problems* (Englewood Cliffs: Prentice-Hall, 1975); D. Matza, *Becoming Deviant* (Englewood Cliffs: Prentice-Hall, 1969); E.M. Lemert, *Human Deviance, Social Problems & Social Control* (Englewood Cliffs: Prentice-Hall, 1967); N.J. Davis, *Sociological Constructions of Deviance: Perspectives and Issues in the Field* (Dubuque: W.C. Brown, 1975); M.B. Clinard, *Sociology of Deviant Behavior*, 3rd ed. (New York: Holt, Rinehart and Winston, 1968); K.T. Erikson, "On the Sociology of Deviance," in *The Collective Definition of Deviance*, ed. F.J. Davis and R. Stivers (New York: The Free Press, 1975).

structural-functionalism[28]. Labeling theory, which is frequently associated with the symbolic interactionist approach to social deviance, may equally well be adapted for use within a structural-functionalist perspective[29]. In spite of the fact that symbolic interactionism seems to have eclipsed structural-functionalism in contemporary American sociology, the structural-functionalist approach appears better suited for dealing with the particular problems with which this article is dealing: magic in early Christianity within the context of Graeco-Roman religions[30].

The claim that illegality is the one universal characteristic of magic, made by J.Z. Smith and others, is not completely satisfactory. A more adequate formulation of substantially the same point would be that magic is universally regarded as a form of deviant behavior[31]. Throughout the remainder of this study, therefore, magic is defined as that form of religious deviance whereby individual or social goals are sought by means alternate to those normally sanctioned by the dominant religious institution. Unless religious activities fit that definition, they will not be regarded as magical for the purposes of this study. Religious activities which fit this first and primary criterion must also fit a second criterion: goals sought within the context of religious deviance are magical when attained through the management of supernatural powers in such a way that results are virtually guaranteed. These two criteria incorporate many of the observations

[28] The most significant scholar associated with the structural-functional approach to social deviance is R.K. Merton, "Social Problems and Theory," in: *Contemporary Social Problems*, ed. R.K. Merton and R.S. Nisbet, 3rd ed. (New York: Harcourt, Brace, Jovanovich, 1971); R.K. Merton, *Social Theory and Social Structure*, rev. ed. (Glencoe: Free Press, 1957). We shall rely rather heavily on Merton's theory of anomie (131–94 in: *Idem*, Social Theory and Social Structure).

[29] One of the more balanced discussions of labeling theory is E.M. Schur, *Labeling Deviant Behavior: Its Sociological Implications* (New York: Harper & Row, 1971); two outstanding applications of labeling theory to the study of social deviance are H.S. Becker, *Outsiders: Studies in the Sociology of Deviance* (London: Free Press of Glencoe, 1963), and T.J. Scheff, *Being Mentally Ill: A Sociological Theory* (Chicago: Aldine Publishing Company, 1966).

[30] S. Cole, "The Growth of Scientific Knowledge: Theories of Deviance as a Case Study," in: *The Idea of Social Structure*, ed. L.A. Coser (New York: Harcourt, Brace, Jovanovich, 1975), 175–220.

[31] R.K. Merton defines deviant behavior as "conduct that departs significantly from the norms set for people in their social statuses" in *idem*, *Social Problems and Theory*, 824. Similar definitions are suggested by Gibbons and Jones, *The Study of Deviance*, 3, and Clinard, *Sociology of Deviant Behavior*, 28. N.K. Denzin has persuasively argued that a complete theory of social deviance must account for misconduct that does not come to the attention of the agencies of social control ("Rules of Conduct and the Study of Deviant Behavior: Some Notes on the Social Relationship," in *Deviance and Respectability*, [ed.] Jack Douglas [New York: Basic Books, 1970] 121). E.M. Lemert has done this by differentiating between "primary deviation" (norm-violating acts before a pejorative label is affixed), and "secondary deviation" (norm-violating acts after the pejorative label has been affixed) in *idem*, *Social Pathology: A Systematic Approach to the theory of Sociopathic Behavior* (New York: McGraw-Hill, 1951) 22 f., 75 f. In the same vein, T.J. Scheff formulated the concept of "residual rule-breaking", i.e., norm-violating behavior prior to labeling (*Becoming Mentally Ill*, 31–54).

of W. J. Goode within the theoretical framework of a structural-functionalist approach to social deviance.

With this definition of the role of magic in mind, let us briefly summarize the thrust of this section of our study in terms of a series of interrelated propositions: (1) Magic and religion are so closely intertwined that it is virtually impossible to regard them as discrete socio-cultural categories. (2) The structural-functional analysis of magico-religious phenomena forbids a negative attitude toward magic. (3) Magic is a phenomenon which exists only within the matrix of particular religious traditions; magic is not religion only in the sense that the species is not the genus. A particular magical system coheres within a religious structure in the sense that it shares the fundamental religious reality construction of the contextual religion. (4) Magic appears to be as universal a feature of religion as deviant behavior is of human societies.

3. Magic in Graeco-Roman Religions

The most comprehensive study of magic in the Graeco-Roman world is the unexcelled treatise of T. Hopfner, *Griechisch-ägyptischer Offenbarungszauber*, 2 vols. (Leipzig: H. Haessel, 1921–24), presented in condensed form by the author in an extensive article entitled "Mageia", in Pauly-Wissowa, *Real-Encyclopädie der klassischen Altertumswissenschaft*, XIV, 1 (1928), 301–93. A new synthesis of Graeco-Roman magic is needed in view of the many archaeological and papyrological discoveries since Hopfner's publications, as well as in consideration of the numerous contributions to scholarly research on the subject during the last two generations. Our knowledge of ancient Mediterranean magic is based on two primary classes of sources: (1) historical evidence (consisting of magical papyri[32], charms and amulets[33], *tabulae*

[32] In addition to the corpus of magical papyri originally edited by K. Preisendanz and now revised by A. Henrichs, see F. L. Griffith and H. Thompson (eds.), *The Demotic Magical Papyrus of London and Leiden* (London: H. Grevel, 1904–1909); A. M. Kropp, *Ausgewählte koptische Zaubertexte*, 3 vols. (Brussels: Édition de la Fondation égyptologique reine Élisabeth, 1930–31); V. Stegemann, *Die koptischen Zaubertexte der Sammlung Papyrus Erzherzog Rainer in Wien* (Heidelberg: C. Winter, 1934). In addition to these collections, other magical papyri continue to be published from time to time; some of these include: D. Wortmann, "Neue magische Texte," *Bonner Jahrbücher*, 168 (1968), 56–111; R. Daniel, "Two Love-Charms," Zeitschrift *für Papyrologie und Epigraphik*, 19 (1975), 249–64; G. M. Parassoglou, "Artificial Scripts and Magical Papyri," *Studia Papyrologica*, 13 (1974), 57–60; I. Proulx and J. O'Callaghan, "Papiro magico cristiano (P. Yale inv. 989)," *Studia Papyrologica*, 13 (1974), 83–88; H. Quecke, "Ein Fragment eines koptischen Zaubertextes," *Studia Papyrologica*, 8 (1969), 97–100. An extremely valuable commentary on *PGM* XXXVI in: S. Eitrem (ed.), Papyri Osloensis, Fasc. I (Oslo: Norske videnskap-akademi, 1925). Other important studies or reviews of the magical papyri include A. D. Nock, "Greek Magical Papyri," in *idem, Essays on Religion and the Ancient World*, I (Cambridge: Harvard University Press, 1972), 176–94 (originally published in 1929); S. Eitrem, "Aus 'Papyrologie und Religionsgeschichte': Die

execrationum[34], as well as a variety of historical and philological notices preserved in extant Graeco-Roman literature[35]), and (2) literary-folkloristic evidence (primarily analyses of magical types and motifs in Graeco-Roman folklore indicative of the myth-image, in contrast to the historical reality, of magicians and magic in the popular imagination of citizens of the ancient Mediterranean world[36]). Any narrative sources which describe either magical activities or miraculous events will require close examination to determine the intentionality of the description so that, if possible, actual magical activities and procedures may be separated from the imaginative embellishments of folkloristic processes.

---

magischen Papyri," in: *Papyri und Altertumswissenschaft. Vortrage des 3. internationalen Papyrologentages in München vom 4. bis 7. September 1933,* hrsg. von W. Otto und L. Wenger, *Münchener Beiträge zur Papyrus-Forschung*, 19 (Munich, 1934), 246–63; M. Nilsson, "Die Religion in den griechischen Zauberpapyri," in *idem, Opuscula Selecta*, III (Lund: C. W. K. Gleerup, 1960) 129–66; A. J. Festugière, "Excursus E: La valeur religieuse des papyrus magiques," in: *idem, L'Idéal religieux des Grecs et l'Évangile*, 281–328.

[33] The two most important studies of Graeco-Roman magical amulets are C. Bonner, *Studies in Magical Amulets (*Ann Arbor: University of Michigan Press, 1950), and A. Delatte and P. Derchain, *Les intailles magiques Gréco-Egyptiennes, Bibliothèque Nationale* (Paris: Bibliothèque Nationale, 1964). See also C. Bonner, "A Miscellany of Engraved Stones," *Hesperia*, 23 (1954), 138–57; D. Wortmann, "Neue magische Gemmen," *Bonner Jahrbücher*, 175 (1975), 63–82; G. M. Parassoglou, "A Christian Amulet against Snakebite," *Studia Papyrologica*, 13 (1974), 107–10; five amulets are discussed in: Wortmann, "Neue magische Texte," 102–6. Among secondary studies, see F. Eckstein and J. H. Waszink, "Amulett," *Reallexikon für Antike und Christentum*, I (1950), 397–411, and Goodenough, *Jewish Symbols*, II, 153–295.

[34] R. Wünsch, *Defixionum Tabellae Atticae* (Berlin, 1873); A. Audollent, *Defixionum Tabellae*…(Paris: A. Fontemoing, 1894); R. Wünsch, Sethianische Verfluchungstafeln aus Rom (Leipzig: B.G. Teubner, 1898); cf. F. Pradel, *Griechische und süditalienische Gebete, Beschwörungen und Rezepte des Mittelalters* (Gießen: A. Töpelmann, 1907); D. R. Jordan, "A Curse Tablet from a Well in the Athenian Agora," *Zeitschrift für Papyrologie und Epigraphik*, 19 (1975), 245–48; Jordan's announced edition of more than 100 lead curse tablets from the Athenian agora has not yet appeared (*American Journal of Archaeology*, 78 [1974], 169). The most recent and best general treatment of the subject is K. Preisendanz, "Fluchtafel (Defixion)," *Reallexikon für Antike und Christentum*, VIII (1972), 1–29 (an extensive bibliography may be found in cols. 28 f.); see also S. Eitrem and H. Herter, "Bindezauber," *Reallexikon für Antike und Christentum*, II (1954), 380–85.

[35] A. Abt, *Die Apologie des Apuleius von Madaura und die antike Zauberei* (Gießen, 1908); J. E. Lowe, *Magic in Greek and Latin Literature* (Oxford: Blackwell, 1929); J. G. Griffiths (ed.), *Apuleius of Madauros, The Isis-Book, Metamorphoses, Book XI* (Leiden: Brill, 1976). O. Herzig, *Lukian als Quelle für die antike Zauberei*, Diss. Tübingen 1933 (Tübingen, 1940); H. Hubert, «Magia,» *Dictionnaire des antiquités grecques et romaines*, III/2 (1904), 1494–1521.

[36] A. Aarne, *The Types of the Folktale*, trans. and rev. S. Thompson (Helsinki: Academia Scientarum Fennica, 1961); S. Thompson, *Motif-Index of Folk Literature*, 2nd ed., 6 vols. (Bloomington: University of Indian Press, 1955–58); though dated, A. H. Krappe, *The Science of Folklore* (London: Methuen, 1962), devotes a chapter to magic (287–300). A recent guide to bibliographical materials on the subject of folklore is J. H. Brunwand, *Folklore: A Study and Research Guide* (New York: St. Martin's Press, 1976).

The goals of Graeco-Roman magical activities have been classified by T. Hopfner in four major categories[37]: (1) protective and apotropaic magic, (2) aggressive and malevolent magic, (3) love magic and magic aimed at the acquisition of power and control, and (4) magical divination. Unfortunately, Hopfner has linked these primary objectives of magic in a fairly rigid way with what he regards as the three major varieties of the magical art, *Theurgie, Magie* and *Goëtie*[38]. The goals of Graeco-Roman magic then, very generally, may be characterized as providing protection, healing, success and knowledge for magical practitioners and their clients, and harm for their opponents. Formulated in this way, it can be seen at once that the goals of magic are very similar to the goals of religion. The difference lies primarily in the way in which goals are achieved. Graeco-Roman magic provided an alternate means whereby goals and benefits sanctioned by religion but not easily attainable through prescribed religious observances, could be achieved by individuals in ways which pretended to guarantee results. In other words, those who failed[39] to achieve the particular benefits promised by religion not infrequently turned to magic for an alternate means (and one generally regarded as socially deviant) for achieving their goals. What must have been a common situation in the Graeco-Roman world is encapsulated by Plutarch: "People with chronic diseases, when they have despaired of ordinary remedies and customary regimens turn to expiations and amulets and dreams" (de facie 920B).

Magical practices and practitioners were generally illegal throughout the history of the Roman empire[40], though that which the Roman authorities regarded as constitutive of "magic" varied considerably from one period to another. Opposition to magic was based primarily on social rather than religious grounds. Most of the terms for magical practitioners were always used in a pejorative sense (i.e., *magicus, ariolus,* γόης, ἀγύρτης)[41], though the term μάγος carried

[37] Hopfner, "Mageia," Pauly-Wissowa, XIV, 1 (1928), 378; *idem, Griechisch-ägyptischer Offenbarungszauber*, II, pars. 41 ff.

[38] Hopfner, *Griechisch-ägyptischer Offenbarungszauber*, II, paragraphs 41 ff., 70 ff. Hopfner, perhaps following the Neoplatonists, regards *Theurgie* as the *"höchste Stufe aller Zauberei"* (*ibid.*, par. 42).

[39] Merton, *Social Theory*, 131–94. Merton uses the term anomie to describe the disjunction which occurs when segments of a society find it difficult or impossible to achieve culturally valued goals by socially approved means. He presents a typology of five modes of adaptation: (1) conformity, (2) innovation, (3) ritualism, (4) retreatism, and (5) rebellion. Innovation, the pursuance of approved goals through deviant or illegitimate means, is a mode of adaptation which translated into a framework of socially approved religious goals is analogous to magic.

[40] R. Macmullen, *Enemies of the Roman Order: Treason, Unrest and Alienation in the Empire* (Cambridge: Harvard University Press, 1966) 125 ff. The author devotes a chapter to the discussion of magicians in the Roman empire (95–127).

[41] Macmullen, *Enemies of the Roman Order*, 110; cf. Plutarch's attitude in *De superstitione* 165F–166A. On γόης, see G. Delling, *Theological Dictionary of the New Testament*, I (1964), 737 f., W. Burkert, "ΓΟΗΣ," *Rheinisches Museum*, 102 (1962), 36–55; H.D. Betz (ed.), *Plutarch's writings and Early Christian Literature* (Leiden: Brill, 1975) 1 ff., 154.

with it a certain oriental mystique and so could be understood in both a positive and negative way[42]. With the lone exception of μάγος in Mt 2:1 ff., these terms invariably carry a pejorative connotation in the New Testament and early Christian literature.

During the first century CE, magic was a phenomenon which pervaded the various Graeco-Roman cults, Judaism and Christianity. For various reasons, magic increased in popularity from the second through the fifth centuries of the Christian era within all cults in the Roman empire. Some scholars have supposed that magic in this era was a kind of international fifth column, independent of religion and possessing a style and ethos of its own[43]. While it is true that the papyrological evidence for Graeco-Egyptian magic exhibits a thoroughly syncretic character[44], it would be more accurate to locate the phenomenon of syncretism as the primary level of religious cults with their accompanying ideologies. Since Graeco-Egyptian cults, as Graeco-Roman religious cults generally, are marked by strong syncretistic tendencies, it should hardly occasion surprise that magical substructures within such cults should exhibit syncretic characteristics. In H.G. Gundel's study of the world view expressed in the magical papyri, he found that the *Weltanschauung* of the papyri closely corresponded to that of Graeco-Egyptian religions[45]. Graeco-Roman magical traditions flourished within the matrix of the multivalent, syncretistic phenomenon of Graeco-Roman religions; if such magic had an international character, the basis for it was the international character of religious cults.

The matrix of early Christianity was a Palestinian Judaism which had been permeated by Hellenistic influences to such an extent that any rigid distinction between Palestinian and Hellenistic Judaism must be regarded as untenable[46].

---

42 Nock, "Paul and the Magus," 308–330; G. Delling, *Theological Dictionary of the New Testament*, IV (1967), 356 ff.

43 Hull, *Hellenistic Magic*, 7, 27 ff.

44 Eitrem, "Die magischen Papyri," 250; Nilsson, "Die Religion in den griechischen Zauberpapyri," 166; Goodenough, *Jewish Symbols*, 153 ff.

45 H.G. Gundel, "Vom Weltbild in den griechischen Zauberpapyri: Probleme und Ergebnisse," in *Proceedings of the Twelfth International Congress of Papyrology at Michigan* (Toronto: A.M. Hakkert, 1970) 185; this article should be read as a supplement to his earlier book, *idem*, *Weltbild und Astrologie in den griechischen Zauberpapyri* (München: Beck, 1968).

46 M. Smith, "Palestinian Judaism in the First Century," in: *Israel: Its Role in Civilization*, ed. M. Davis (New York: Seminary Israel Institute of the Jewish Theological Seminary of America, 1966) 67–81; I.H. Marshall, "Palestinian and Hellenistic Christianity: Some Critical Comments," *New Testament Studies*, 19 (1972–73), 271–87; M. Hengel, *Judaism and Hellenism*, I, trans. J. Bowden (Philadelphia: Fortress Press, 1974) 252,311 f.; D. Flusser, "Paganism in Palestine," *The Jewish People in the First Century*, Section I of *Compendia Rerum Iudaicarum ad Novum Testamentum*, I (Philadelphia: Fortress, 1976), 1065–1100; this last article should be supplemented with M. Smith's "On the Wine God in Palestine", in: *Salo Wittmayer Baron Jubilee Volume* (Jerusalem: American Academy for Jewish Research, 1975) 815–29; E.P. Sanders, *The Tendencies of the Synoptic Tradition* (London: Cambridge University Press, 1969) 190–255; B. Lifschitz, "L'hellénisation des juifs de Palestine," *Revue*

As Christianity expanded into the Graeco- Roman world it continued for a time to retain such a close relationship to Judaism that it was all but indistinguishable from it. During the second half of the first century, when various Christian groups began to emerge as distinct entities, Christianity became an anomaly in the ancient world: it became a religious tradition unrelated to nationality[47]. Graeco-Roman "religion" (one must remember that the Greeks had no comprehensive term for religion as a distinct socio-cultural phenomenon)[48] consisted of three major types: (1) state cults, (2) mystery cults, and (3) philosophical sects or schools. Within this framework, Judaism constituted a state cult with a large diaspora constituency until shortly after 70 CE.

For reasons which need not be elaborated here, Christianity was less syncretistic than most other Graeco-Roman cults, while Judaism was even less syncretistic than Christianity[49]. Both Christianity and Judaism retained a sense of self-identity partially expressed in the separation of Judaism from Christianity and the distance which both cults felt from other Graeco-Roman religio-cultural traditions. If magic is a general substructure of all religions, one would assume that both Judaism and Christianity would develop magical traditions in a manner consistent with their religious systems. I think that J. Trachtenberg is clearly in error when he denies the existence of a distinctive form of Jewish magic until the post-Talmudic period[50]. Similarly, the present study will attempt to make it clear that early Christianity rapidly developed a distinctive form of magic which cohered with its reality construction[51]; early Christian writers unwittingly mapped the contours of Christian magic in their apologetic program developed in rebuttal to pagan and Jewish charges that Christians practiced sorcery.

Early Christianity soon stood in an ambiguous and anomalous position between Judaism on the one hand and Graeco-Roman society on the other. Since Christianity began as a religious movement within Judaism and became institutionalized within the Graeco-Roman world, one suspects that there was never a time when magical traditions did not exert strong influences upon it. During the first centuries of the Christian era, magic (despite its deviant religious character) constituted a strong undercurrent in Judaism[52], and Jewish magic certainly be-

---

Biblique, 4 (1965), 520–38; W.D. Davies, "Paul and Judaism," in: *The Bible and Modern Scholarship*, ed. J.P. Hyatt (Nashville: Abingdon Press, 1965) 178–83.

[47] M. Nilsson, "Universal Religion," in: *idem, Opuscula Selecta*, III (Lund, 1960), 383; J.Z. Smith, "Native Cults in the Hellenistic Period," *History of Religions*, 11 (1971–72), 236–49.

[48] A.D. Nock, *Conversion* (Oxford: Clarendon Press, 1933) 10.

[49] D.E. Aune, "Orthodoxy in First Century Judaism," *Journal for the Study of Judaism*, 7 (1976), 1–10.

[50] J. Trachtenberg, *Jewish Magic and Superstition: A Study in Folk Religion* (New York: Berman's Jewish Book House, 1939) 11.

[51] Barb, The Survival of Magic Arts, 107.

[52] The standard treatment of ancient Jewish magic remains that of L. Blau, *Das altjüdische Zauberwesen*, 2. Aufl. (Straßburg i.E., 1914); S. Lieberman supplements and corrects Blau in:

came part of the Christian heritage[53]. As Christianity emerged from Judaism in consequence of its paganization, it continued to absorb magical traditions from the surrounding Graeco-Roman world[54].

Several particular features of magic in the Graeco-Roman world require comment prior to a more detailed discussion of magic in early Christianity.

1. One important feature of magic during this period was the irregularity of its utilization in contrast to the carefully structured recurrent observances of religious rituals. The very routine periodicity of religious observance tended to make the cult unresponsive to the irregularity and unpredictability of crises, particularly during the Hellenistic and Roman era. Magic was frequently resorted to as an alternate, though socially deviant, way of dealing with unanticipated needs and crises.

2. Magic appears to have been far more popular among the lower, uneducated classes in the Graeco-Roman world than among the upper classes[55]. Those who were educated and affluent associated magical practices with the uneducated and poor in the lower strata of society (Origen *contra Celsum* 6.41; 7.4; Philostratus *vit. sophist.* 523, 590). Certainly the Greek of the magical papyri is the unpretentious common language of the people, not the cultivated, literary and atticistic language of the educated[56]. Since the Graeco-Roman literature which is extant was produced and transmitted by the educated, rarely are the views of the common people adequately represented[57].

---

idem, Greek in Jewish Palestine (New York: The Jewish Theological Seminary of America, 1942) 91–114. Other important discussions include E. Schürer, *Geschichte des jüdischen Volkes im Zeitalter Jesu Christi*, III, 2. Aufl. (Leipzig: J. Hinrichs, 1911) 407–20; J. Trachtenberg, *Jewish Magic and Superstition*; M. Simon, *Verus Israel: étude sur les relations entre Chrétiens et Juifs dans l'Empire romain (135–425)* (Paris: E.D. Boccard, 1948) 394–431; E.R. Goodenough, *Jewish Symbols*, II, 151–295; J. Neusner, *A History of the Jews in Babylonia* (Leiden: Brill, 1965–70) II, 147–50; III, 110–26; IV, 330–62; V, 174–96, 217–43 (all excellent discussions); J. Goldin, "The Magic of Magic and Superstition," in: *Aspects of Religious Propaganda in Judaism and Early Christianity*, ed. E. Schüssler Fiorenza (Notre Dame: University of Notre Dame Press, 1976) 115–47; M. Hengel, *Judaism and Hellenism*, I, 239–41; II, 88 (n. 175); on magic at Qumran, see M. Delcor, "Recherches sur un horoscope en langue hébraique provenant de Qumran," *Revue de Qumran*, 5 (1966), 521–42; J. Carmignac, "Les horoscopes de Qumran," *Revue de Qumran*, 5 (1965), 199–217. For general bibliography see G. Delling, *Bibliographie zur jüdisch-hellenistischen und intertestamentarischen Literatur 1900–1965*, TU, 1961, 2. Aufl. (Berlin: Akademie Verlag, 1975) 177 f. ("Zaubertexte").

[53] R. Kraft, "The Multiform Jewish Heritage of Early Christianity," in Christianity, *Judaism and Other Greco-Roman Cults*, III, ed. J. Neusner (Leiden: Brill, 1975) 196 f.

[54] Effectively demonstrated by Brox, "Magie und Aberglaube," 158–61.

[55] N. Brox, "Der einfache Glaube und die Theologie: zur altkirchlichen Geschichte eines Dauerproblems," *Kairos*, 14 (1972), 161–87.

[56] Prümm, *Religionsgeschichtliches Handbuch*, 369.

[57] The dichotomy between the religion of the upper classes and that of the lower classes is the focus of M. Nilsson's "Problems of the History of Greek Religion in the Hellenistic and Roman Age," *Harvard Theological Review*, 36 (1943), 251–75; on 254, speaking of scholars who follow one of two major approaches to the study of Greek religion, he observes that "they

3. The popular distinction between magic and miracle has it that the latter is more "religious" than the former[58]. In reality, the magic/miracle dichotomy is not only an artificial distinction which presupposes an unambiguous difference between magic and religion, it also appears to have little value in interpreting the evidence available to us from the Graeco-Roman period[59]. J. M. Hull in his book *Hellenistic Magic and the Synoptic Tradition*, devotes a chapter to the discussion of "Miracle and Magic" (45–72). Hull suggests that a miracle is partly or wholly magical if it: (1) has no cause but the will of the wonder-worker, or (2) is based on a cause-and-effect theory of sympathetic bonds, or (3) is brought about by human effort through a ritual performance (54). This distinction between magic and miracle is based on Hull's substantive definition of magic as a belief that supernatural entities are linked by invisible bonds of sympathy to visible symbols of their powers in such a way that a knowledge of these powers, their sympathies, antipathies and symbols makes it possible to exert influence and control over the forces of the universe (37 f.). Hull's distinction between magic and miracle is unsatisfactory because there is little in the definition which is distinctive of magic in contrast to religion, and the sympathy/antipathy theory cannot be regarded as unique to magic (supra, n. 18). Besides, how can an event be "partly" magical? If we define "miracle" in a commonly accepted way – R. Swinburne, for example, has defined miracle as "an event of an extraordinary kind, brought about by a god, and of religious significance"[60] – it becomes evident that "miracle" is a product of mankind's mythopoetic capabilities. Extraordinary events which are categorized as magic should properly consist of the perceived results of ritualistic procedures which are believed to effect desirable goals within the framework of religious deviance. The fact that popular imagination credited magicians in the Graeco-Roman world with abilities to perform many impossible feats (bringing down the moon, flying through the air, walking on water, eclipsing the sun, transformation into non-human forms)[61], and magicians themselves were not infrequently taken in by their own act (PGM, XXXIV contains a number of astonishing claims)[62], means only that mythopoeism can structure experience as well as belief.

---

call attention to rites and magic, to ideas and doctrines without due regard to the social changes and stratifications of the population."

58 Prümm, *Religionsgeschichtliches Handbuch*, 360 f.; W. Heitmüller, "*Im Namen Jesu" Eine sprach.- u. religionsgeschichtliche Untersuchung zum Neuen Testament, speziell zur altchristlichen Taufe* (Göttingen: Vandenhoeck & Ruprecht, 1903) 159.

59 M. Nilsson, *Geschichte der griechischen Religion*, 2. Aufl. (München: Beck, 1961) 2.520–34.

60 *The Concept of Miracle* (London: Macmillan, 1970), 1.

61 Hopfner, "Mageia," 374 ff. Hippocrates *Morb. Sacr.* 4; Lucian *Philops.* 13 f.

62 J. Z. Smith, referring to the work of R.-L. Wagner (*"Sorcier" et "Magicien": Contribution à l'histoire du vocabulaire de la magie* [Paris: E Droz, 1939] 26–35), suggests that the distinction between the sincere and the charlatan magician is a significant and pervasive division in the phenomenology of magical practitioners. Sociologically, this psychological ap-

4. Finally, our sources reveal three relatively distinct functions of magic in the Graeco-Roman world, all of which require a setting in social deviance: (1) the pragmatic, goal-oriented utilization of deviant religious procedures and materials to achieve particular goals for individuals, (2) the imaginative literary and folkloristic portraits of magicians and magical activities which are based upon, but not limited to, the actual, historical practice of magic in the ancient Mediterranean world, and (3) the use of accusations of the practice of magic as a means of social control and definition. Religious propaganda of the Graeco-Roman era was replete with accusations that various individuals or groups practiced magic, together with the defense of those charges[63]. In view of the general illegality of magic in the Roman empire, the accusation of magic is, among other things a form of social control used by those within the dominant social structure to label and exert control on those in the ambiguous and unstructured areas of society[64]. In view of the fact that the charge of sorcery or magic is part of a constellation of accusations of antisocial behavior leveled at marginal or interstitial individuals and groups[65], from a sociological perspective the validity or invalidity of the charge itself becomes relatively unimportant, though from a historical perspective, however, it becomes crucial.

proach appears beset by many pitfalls. In the performance of social roles, to use E. Goffman's dramaturgical metaphor, the performer may be taken in by his own act or not (*The Presentation of Self in Everyday Life* [New York: Doubleday, 1955] 17). For sociological issues it is generally unnecessary to decide which is the more real, the fostered impression or the one the performer attempts to conceal from the audience (*Ibid.*, 65 f.). One can profitably study false performances to learn about honest ones (*Ibid.*, 66). The problem is further complicated by the fact that sincerity and fraud can be found in the same individual claiming to possess magical powers. Shamans apparently add fraud to their performances, yet still retain a belief in their own supernatural powers; cf. A. L. Kroeber, *The Nature of Culture* (Chicago: University of Chicago Press, 1952) 311, and C. Levi-Strauss, *Structural Anthropology* (2 vols.; New York: Basic Books, 1963–76) 161–80.

[63] A. B. Kolenkow, "A Problem of Power: How Miracle Doers Counter Charges of Magic in the Hellenistic World," *Society of Biblical Literature, 1976, Seminar Papers* (Missoula: Scholars Press, 1976) 105–10; P. Brown, "Sorcery, Demons and the Rise of Christianity," in *Witchcraft: Confessions & Accusations*, ed. M. Douglas (London: Tavistock, 1970); S. Isser, "Dositheus, Jesus, and a Moses Aretalogy," in: *Christianity, Judaism and Other Greco-Roman Cults*, IV, ed. J. Neusner (Leiden: Brill, 1975) 167–89.

[64] Douglas, *Purity and Danger*, 102; on this aspect of Ms. Douglas' work, see S. R. Isenberg and D. E. Owen, "Bodies Natural and Contrived: The Work of Mary Douglas," *Religious Studies Review*, 3 (1977) 1–17.

[65] M. Eliade, "Some Observations on European Witchcraft," *History of Religions*, 14 (1975), 149–72. In *Jewish Magic and Superstition*, 1–10, J. Tractenberg summarizes medieval legends of Jewish sorcery.

4. Jesus and Magic

The complex nature of the primary sources for our knowledge of the historical Jesus, the canonical gospels, is such that the authentic historical features of the life and activities of Jesus of Nazareth can only be extricated with great difficulty from the folkloristic embellishments, idealizations and editorial tendencies found in the gospels and the traditions of which they are constituted. Many of these traditions are directly relevant for a consideration of the nature and function of magic in the life and activities of Jesus. In this study we shall focus on the miracle tradition contained in the gospels, in spite of the fact that a full treatment of the subject of "Jesus and Magic" would include many other topics[66], though perhaps of less central significance. The miracle tradition of the gospels contains accounts of six exorcisms[67], seventeen healings[68], and eight so-called nature miracles[69]. Next in importance are the generalizing descriptions of Jesus' program of wonderworking[70], allusions to miracles performed by his disciples[71], references to specific miracles which are alluded to but not narrated[72], and various feats of Jesus wherein he appears to exercise supernatural powers[73]. Finally

---

66 A fuller approach to this subject is sketched out by M. Smith, *Clement of Alexandria*, 220–37.

67 (1) the Demoniac in the Synagogue (Mk 1:23–27; Lk 4:33–36); (2) the Gerasene Demoniac (Mk 5:1–20; Mt 8:28–34; Lk 8:26–39); (3) the Daughter of the Syrophoenician Woman (Mk 7:24–30; Mt 15:21–28); (4) the "Epileptic" Boy (Mk 9:14–29; Mt 17:14–21; Lk 9:27–43); (5) the Dumb Demoniac (Mt 9:32–34); (6) the Blind and Dumb Demoniac (Mt 12:22–23; Lk 11:15).

68 (1) Peter's Mother-in-law (Mk 1:29–31; Mt 8:14–15; Lk 4:38–39); (2) the Leper (Mk 1:40–45; Mt 8:1–4; Lk 5:12–16); (3) the Paralytic (Mk 2:1–12; Mt 9:1–8; Lk 5:17–26); (4) the Man with the Withered Hand (Mk 3:1–6; Mt 12:9–14; Lk 6:6–11); (5) the Daughter of Jairus (Mk 5:21–43; Mt 9:18–26; Lk 8:40–56); (6) the Woman with the Hemorrhage (Mk 5:25–34; Mt 9:20–22; Lk 8:43–48); (7) the Deaf Mute (Mk 7:31–36); (8) the Blind Man near Bethsaida (Mk 8:22–26); (9) Blind Bartimaeus (Mk 10:46–52; Mt 9:27–34; Lk 18:35–43); (10) the Young Man at Nain (Lk 7:11–17); (11) the Bent Woman (Lk 13:10–17); (12) the Ten Lepers (Lk 17:11–19); (13) the Man with Dropsy (Lk 14:1–6); (14) the Paralytic (Jn 5:1–9); (15) the Raising of Lazarus (Jn 11); (16) the Man Born Blind (Jn 9:1–41); (17) the Centurion's Servant (Mt 8:5–13; Jn 4:46–54).

69 (1) the Stilling of the Storm (Mk 4:35–41; Mt 8:23–27; Lk 8:22–25); (2) the Feeding of the Five Thousand (Mk 6:30–44; Mt 14:13–21; Lk 9:10–17; Jn 6:1–15); (3) the Feeding of the Four Thousand (Mk 8:1–10; Mt 15:32–39); (4) Walking on Water (Mk 6:45–52; Mt 14:22–33; Jn 6:16–21); (5) the Cursing of the Fig Tree (Mk 11:12–14, 20–26; Mt 21:18–22); (6) the Coin in the Fish's Mouth (Mt 17:24–27); (7) the Miraculous Catch of Fish (Lk 5:1–11; cf. Jn 21:1–11); (8) the Transformation of Water to Wine (Jn 2:1–11).

70 (1) Mk 1:32–34; Mt 8:16; Lk 4:40–41; (2) Mk 1:39; Mt 4:24; (3) Mk 3:10–11; Lk 6:17–18; (4) Mk 6:56; Mt 14:36.

71 (1) Mk 3:14–15; (2) Mk 6:7; Mt 10:1; Lk 9:1; (3) Mk 9:18, 28; Mt 17:16, 19; Lk 9:40; (4) Mk 16:17–18; (5) Lk 10:17–20.

72 Mary Magdalene is said to have been relieved of seven demons (Lk 8:2; cf. Mk 16:9).

73 Jesus possesses supernatural knowledge (Jn 1:47–51; 2:25; 6:70–71), he escapes miraculously from enemies (Lk 4:29–30; cf. Jn 8:59 [var. lec.]), and he has prophetic foreknowledge; many other such characteristics could be listed.

we have what appear to be the remnants of accusations leveled at the historical Jesus to the effect that he practiced magic[74].

Did the historical Jesus actually perform miracles? Predictably, conservative New Testament scholars argue for the complete historicity of the miracle tradition, but their arguments are theologically and apologetically motivated[75]. However, there is also general consensus among critical New Testament scholars that there is overwhelming evidence that Jesus did in fact perform exorcisms and healings[76]. The nature miracles, however, are generally regarded as legendary embellishments of the Jesus tradition. The historicity of the exorcisms is particularly emphasized by a number of prominent critical scholars[77].

While there is no infallible way of confirming or disconfirming the historicity of particular exorcisms or healings once the legendary embellishments have been stripped away, there are several general arguments which are used to affirm the essential historicity of the wonderworking activities of Jesus: (1) The fact that Jewish[78] and pagan[79] sources label Jesus as a magician can be regarded as independent evidence reflecting the fact that the historical Jesus was a wonderworker[80]. However, since much of this corroborative evidence does not antedate the second century, it may simply reflect attitudes toward the image of Jesus

---

[74] These will be discussed below in some detail.

[75] The most comprehensive recent attempt to demonstrate the historicity of Jesus' miracles is: H. van der Loos, *The Miracles of Jesus*, *NovT Suppl* 9 (Leiden: Brill, 1965).

[76] F.C. Conybeare, *Myth, Magic and Morals: A Study of Christian Origins* (London: Watts, 1910) 142 f.; R.M. Grant, *Miracle and Natural Law in Graeco-Roman and Early Christian Thought* (Amsterdam: North Holland Publishing Company, 1952) 168; A. Fridrichsen, *The Problem of Miracle in Primitive Christianity* (Minneapolis: Augsburg, 1972) 26; R. Fuller, *Interpreting the Miracles* (Philadelphia: Westminster Press, 1963) 18–29; R. Bultmann, *Jesus and the Word* (New York: Charles Scribner's Sons, 1958) 173.

[77] R. Bultmann, *Theologie des Neuen Testaments*, I (Tübingen: Mohr Siebeck, 1948) 28; R. Bultmann, "The Primitive Christian Kerygma and the Historical Jesus," in: *The Historical Jesus and the Kerygmatic Christ*, ed. C. Braaten and R. Harrisville (New York: Abingdon Press, 1964) 22; N. Perrin, *Rediscovering the Teaching of Jesus* (New York: Harper & Row, 1967) 65; S.V. McCasland, *By the Finger of God: Demon Possession and Exorcism in Early Christianity in the Light of Modern Views of Mental Illness* (New York: Macmillan, 1951) 54–82.

[78] Jewish traditions of Jesus as a sorcerer and magician have been collected by H.L. Strack, *Jesus, die Häretiker und die Christen nach den ältesten jüdischen Angaben* (Leipzig: J.C. Hinrichs, 1910); H.L. Strack and P. Billerbeck, *Kommentar zum Neuen Testament aus Talmud und Midrasch*, I (München: Beck, 1926) 38 ff., 84 ff., 631. For discussion, see Blau, *Das altjüdische Zauberwesen*, 29, 57, n. 4; R. Travers Herford, *Christianity in Talmud and Midrash* (London: Williams and Norgate, 1903) 35–41, 54–56; S. Krauss, "Jesus," *The Jewish Encyclopedia*, VII (1904), 170–73 (an excellent discussion); T. Klausner, *Jesus of Nazareth: His Life, Times, and Teaching* (Boston: Beacon Press, 1964) 18–47; H. van der Loos, *The Miracles of Jesus*, 156–75. Christian sources reflecting Jewish charges that Jesus practiced magic include Justin *Dial.* 69.5; *1 Apol.* 30; Origen *contra Celsum* 1. 28; Arnobius *adv. nat.* 1. 43; Lactantius *div. inst.* 4. 15. 1.

[79] Origen *contra Celsum* 1.6, 28, 38, 68; 2.9, 14, 16, 48, 49; 6.77. Celsus refers to Jesus' miracles as "inventions and myths" (πλάσματα καὶ μῦθοι) in 3. 27; 5. 51, 57; 7.77.

[80] Fuller, *Interpreting the Miracles*, 23; Perrin, *Rediscovering the Teaching of Jesus*, 65.

which had crystallized in Christian literature and teaching[81]. (2) The fact that the miracles of Jesus are found in every stratum of gospel tradition is indicative that the tradition has a historical core[82]. (3) Since the Jesuanic miracle tradition possesses some distinctive features unparalleled in Judaism, the Graeco-Roman world or early Christianity, those features necessarily derive from Jesus himself[83]. (4) Since most of the healings and exorcisms found in the tradition can be construed as psychosomatic cures, their occurrence is not an a priori historical impossibility[84]. (5) The title "Son of David", which is embedded in two exorcism stories (Mt 12:23; 15:22) and one healing story (Mk 10:47–48; Mt 9:27; 20:30 f.; Lk 18:38 f.) can now be understood as a possible reference to "Solomon" and to the very considerable tradition of magic and healing which was associated with that name[85]; since this connotation of the title was understood as little by New Testament authors as by modern New Testament scholars[86], it has a strong claim to historicity. On these bases, we regard it as entirely plausible that Jesus

---

81 *The Jewish Encyclopedia*, VII, 170 ff.; P. Winter, *On the Trial of Jesus* (Berlin: De Gruyter, 1961) 144. Winter briefly discusses one of the more important Jewish texts in the Babylonian Talmud on this subject, Sanhedrin 43a, and claims that it is based on Christian (literary) sources. E. Stauffer, on the other hand, regards b. Sanhedrin 43 a as evidence that Jesus was charged with sorcery (among other things) at his trial (*Jesus, Gestalt und Geschichte* [Bern und München: Francke Verlag, 1957] 19).

82 Perrin, *Rediscovering the Teaching of Jesus*, 65 (congruent with Perrin's "criterion of multiple attestation" discussed on 45 ff.); R. Bultmann, *The History of the Synoptic Tradition* (New York and Evanston: Harper & Row, Publishers, 1963) 239.

83 For example, "faith" in many of the miracle stories is used in an absolute sense and is not faith "in" or "on" anyone or any thing; this is claimed to be unique, cf. Perrin, *Rediscovering the Teaching of Jesus*, 130–42; J. Roloff, *Das Kerygma und der irdische Jesus* (Göttingen: Vandenhoeck & Ruprecht, 1970) 152–73.

84 J. D. G. Dunn, *Jesus and the Spirit* (Philadelphia: Westminster Press, 1975) 74 ff.; McCasland, *By the Finger of God*.

85 L. R. Fisher, "Can This Be the Son of David?" in *Jesus and the Historian*, ed. F. T. Trotter (Philadelphia: Westminster, 1968) 82–97; K. Berger, "Die königlichen Messiastraditionen des Neuen Testaments," *New Testament Studies*, 20 (1973), 3–9; Berger argues that "son of David" designates the Messiah as an exorcist and miracle worker, arguing against those that contend that Jewish messianic expectation was not tied to miracle working. See also E. Lövestam, "Davids-son-kristologi hos synoptikerna," *Svensk Exegetisk Årsbok*, 15 (1972), 198–210. Fisher, Berger and Lövestam are criticized by D. C. Duling, "Solomon, Exorcism, and the son of David," *Harvard Theological Review*, 68 (1975), 235–52. On the connection between the figure of Solomon and magic, see C. C. McCown, *The Testament of Solomon* (Leipzig: Harrassowitz, 1922), 48 f., and Strack-Billerbeck, *Kommentar zum Neuen Testament*, IV, 510 ff., 533 f. (Solomon as the patron of exorcists).

86 Cf. H. C. Kee, *Community of the New Age: Studies in Mark's Gospel* (Philadelphia: Westminster Press, 1977) 171: "the appropriateness of Bartimaeus' calling Jesus "Son of David" is not at all clear". Further, the major handbooks on New Testament Christology do not even mention the Solomonic tradition under the rubric of "Son of David"; cf. R. H. Fuller, *The Foundations of New Testament Christology* (New York: Charles Scribner's Sons, 1965); O. Cullmann, *The Christology of the New Testament*, rev. ed. (Philadelphia: Westminster Press, 1963); F. Hahn, *The Titles of Jesus in Christology* (New York and Cleveland: World, 1969).

performed deeds which both he and those about him regarded as miraculous feats of exorcism and healing.

Before considering the relationship of the miracle tradition to magic in greater detail, it is first necessary to discuss the context of the thaumaturgical activities of Jesus. Several scholars have noted that, when compared with Jewish or Graeco-Roman miracle stories, those in the Gospels are similar in content, but differ in context[87]. The supposed unique context of Jesus' miracles is their eschatological setting within the framework of Jewish apocalypticism. Jesus' miracles are unique in that, while non-Christian miracle stories exalt the person of the performer and are done as ends in themselves, those effected by Jesus have an eschatological significance in that they are subordinate to the proclamation of the nearness of the Kingdom of God[88]. While these arguments are not basically incorrect, they have been erroneously used to claim that Jesus' thaumaturgical activities cannot be considered magical.

Both historically and sociologically, the most appropriate designation for the role which Jesus assumed is that of messianic prophet[89]; the particular type of collective behavior which he sparked must correspondingly be labeled as a millennial movement[90]. Just as the comparative study of millennial movements has

---

[87] Grant, *Miracle and Natural Law*, 172; C.K. Barrett, *The Holy Spirit and the Gospel Tradition* (London: SPCK, 1966) 57.

[88] H.C. Kee, "The Terminology of Mark's Exorcism Stories," *New Testament Studies*, 14 (1967–68), 239, 245f. P. Achtemeier, "Gospel Miracle Tradition and the Divine Man," *Interpretation*, 26 (1972), 185; E. Schweizer, *Jesus* (Richmond; John Knox, 1972), 43; Kee, *Community of the New Age*, 23; H. van der Loos, *The Miracles of Jesus*, 150; R. Pesch, *Jesu ureigene Taten?Ein Beitrag zur Wundertaten* (Freiburg: Herder, 1970) 24f.

[89] The question of whether or not Jesus self-consciously played the role of a messiah is still hotly debated; I continue to maintain the position that he did in fact conceptualize his own role in a manner similar to other charismatic or prophetic-messianic leaders of millennial movements during the first century; cf. D.E. Aune, "The Problem of the Messianic Secret," *Novum Testament*, 11 (1969), 1–31; *idem,* "A Note on Jesus' Messianic Consciousness and 11Q Melchisedek," *Evangelical Quarterly*, 45 (1973), 161–65. It is of course a matter of historical record that no Jew explicitly claimed to be the messiah prior to Bar Kochba. However, the title "messiah" does not appear to have functioned as an exclusive label for this role prior to the late first century CE; cf. M. de Jonge, "The Use of the Word "Anointed" in the Time of Jesus," *Novum Testamentum*, 7 (1966), 133f. Completely unacceptable is the thesis propagated by some New Testament scholars that Jesus cannot be categorized in terms of psychology, comparative religion or general history; this position has been maintained by M. Hengel, *Nachfolge und Charisma* (Berlin: A. Töpelmann, 1968) 97f., and E. Käsemann, "The Problem of the Historical Jesus," in *idem, Essays on New Testament Themes* (London: SCM Press, 1964) 46.

[90] J.G. Gager, *Kingdom and Community: The Social World of Early Christianity* (Englewood Cliffs: Doubleday, 1975) 20–37; S.R. Isenberg, "Millenarianism in Greco-Roman Palestine," *Religion*, 4 (1974), 24–46. In B.R. Wilson's recent comparative study of millennial movements, *Magic and the Millennium: A Sociological Study of Religious Movements of Protest among Tribal and Third World Peoples* (New York; Harper & Row, 1973), the author suggests a schema of eight types of millennial movements, each of which constitutes a distinctive "supernaturalistic response to the world". The two ideal types proposed by Wilson which appear to be the most useful for analyzing the movement centering in Jesus are the thaumaturgical movement and the conversionist movement. The former centers on a religious

shown that magic functions in such a way that the leaders of such movements are supernaturally legitimated, so the thaumaturgical activities of Jesus appear to have functioned as a form of supernatural legitimation supporting his role as messianic prophet. Sociologically, millennial movements are a collective form of deviant behavior. Consequently, in line with the definition of magic which we have formulated above, we are disposed to regard wonderworking within the context of a millennial movement as essentially magical. Further, in B. Wilson's comprehensive study of millennial movements among Third World peoples, those who join such movements are generally conscious of being afflicted with evils that the contextual social system has been impotent to solve. According to Wilson, "The living god, the man who claims to be a messiah, must of necessity be a thaumaturge. He may not practice much and he may rely largely on legendary feats, but usually he will be obliged to appear and to manifest power … Casting out demons and countering such evils, healing the sick, and purging or curing wizards are his specialty"[91]. The subordinate function of magic within such movements gives it a dynamic role in contrast with the more mechanistic overtones which magical activities appear to have in other social settings. Nevertheless, magic is magic regardless of whether the context is individual or collective social deviance.

The millennial movement initiated by Jesus, though more successful ultimately than other such movements in Graeco-Roman Palestine, was nevertheless just one among a number of such movements[92]. Demonstrations of magical power appear to have been a central feature of those movements of which we have any knowledge. The revolt of Theudas (ca. 44–46 CE) is reported in Josephus *Ant.* 20. 97–98 and Acts 5:36; he attempted to lead a band of 400 dryshod over the Jordan in an apparent attempt to replicate the feat of Joshua. He was slain and his followers scattered by the Romans. Josephus refers to Theudas as a γόης, though he seems to have designated himself as a προφήτης. The revolt of Judas the Galilean is also reported by Josephus *Ant.* 18.1–10; 20. 102; Wars 2. 117f. and Acts 5:37; he also appears to have presupposed the assistance of God. An unnamed Samaritan led a revolt reported in Josephus *Ant.* 18. 85–87, and led a group of followers to Mt Gerizim in Samaria expecting to recover miraculously the ancient Temple vessels; he too must be regarded as having conceived of

practitioner or charismatic leader who, through his wonderworking, lays claim to supernatural forms of legitimation (133 f.). The leader must incorporate such magical activities as healing and exorcism into his role because those who join such movements characteristically believe in and demand supernatural communications and manifestations of power that have immediate personal significance (70).

[91] Wilson, *Magic and the Millennium*, 134.

[92] E. Meyer, *Ursprung und Anfänge des Christentums*, II (Stuttgart und Berlin: J. G. Cotta, 1925) 402–12; Hengel, *Nachfolge und Charisma*, 23–27; D. M. Rhoads, *Israel in Revolution: 6–74 CE, A Political History Based on the Writings of Josephus* (Philadelphia: Fortress Press, 1976); Isenberg, "Millenarianism in Greco-Roman Palestine."

himself as an eschatological prophet[93]. Again, in Josephus *Ant.* 20. 196–72; *Wars* 2. 261–63 and Acts 21:31, we read of an unnamed Egyptian who designated himself as a προφήτης; Josephus, however, labels him a ψευδοπροφήτης and a γόης. This revolutionary figure intended to lead a band of 30,000 followers to the Mount of Olives, from which vantage point he intended to cause the walls of Jerusalem to fall down.

Twice Josephus summarizes the activities of first century Palestinian millennial movements. In *Ant.* 20. 167 f., he makes this descriptive generalization:

> "Moreover, imposters and deceivers [γόητες καὶ ἀπατεῶνες ἄνθρωποι] called upon the mob to follow them into the desert. For they said that they would show them unmistakable marvels and signs [τέρατα καὶ σημεῖα] that would be wrought in harmony with God's design."

A similar summary is found in *Wars* 2. 259:

> "Deceivers and impostors [πλάνοι γὰρ ἄνθρωποι καὶ ἀπατεῶνες] under the pretense of divine inspiration fostering revolutionary changes, they persuaded the multitude to act like madmen, and led them out into the desert under the belief that God would there give them tokens of deliverance [σημεῖα ἐλευθερίας]."

The frequency and spontaneity of these several instances of collective deviant behavior in first century Palestine reveal the presence of deep-seated tensions and strains in that society. The mundane goals of the Jewish religion (peace, prosperity, long life, fruitfulness of the womb and field, health, etc.) were frustrated by both economic conditions[94] and the religious establishment[95]. Both Jesus' teaching and his wonderworking activities constituted alternate, though socially deviant, means of achieving acceptable goals; widespread experience of dissatisfaction and frustration virtually ensured his success.

At this point let us summarize the major features of Jesus' techniques of exorcism and healing as they appear in the gospel tradition. Exorcisms are generally distinguished from healings in the tradition[96]: exorcism relieves sufferers from the adverse effects of being possessed by malevolent supernatural beings (demons), while healing with a few major exceptions does not appear to presuppose that disease or physical malfunctions have a demonic cause[97]. A closer

93 M. F. Collins, "Hidden Vessels in Samaritan Traditions," *Journal for the Study of Judaism*, 3 (1972), 97–116.

94 S. Applebaum, "Economic Life in Palestine," *The Jewish People in the First Century*, Section I of *Compendia Rerum Iudaicarum ad Novum Testamentum*, II (Philadelphia: Westminster Press, 1976) 631–700.

95 S. R. Isenberg, "Power through Temple and Torah in Greco-Roman Palestine," in *Christianity, Judaism, and Other Greco-Roman Cults*, II, ed. J. Neusner (Leiden: Brill, 1975) 24–52.

96 S. Eitrem, *Some Notes on the Demonology in the New Testament*, 2nd ed. (Oslo: Universitetsforlaget, 1966) 34 f. Healings and exorcisms are differentiated in the following passages: Mk 1:32–34 (Mt 8:16; Lk 4:40 f.); 1:39 (Mt 4:24); 3:10–11 (Lk 6:17–18); Lk 13:32.

97 In the story of the healing of the woman with a "spirit of infirmity" (Lk 13:10–17), the cause of the woman's distress is specifically described as a "binding" (δεῖν) effected by Satan.

analysis of the healing narratives, however, reveals that they stand in a more fluid relationship to exorcism stories than first appears[98]. While Jesus' exorcistic and healing technique does not follow a rigid or invariable pattern, at least two generalizations can be made about it: (1) Jesus never touched demon-possessed individuals; on the other hand, the technique of touching was the characteristic way in which he healed the sick and infirm. (2) Jesus' own use of the authoritative word of command was perhaps the most characteristic technique which he used to effect both exorcisms and healings.

While the synoptic tradition (the Fourth Gospel is completely silent at this point) preserves only six accounts of Jesus' exorcisms, three sayings which deal specifically with exorcisms (Lk 11:19–20 [Mt 12:27–28]; 13:32; Mk 3:19–27 [Mt 12:25–26, 29; Lk 11:17–18a, 21–22]), and a few editorial summaries which mention his ministry of exorcism[99], they have a strong basic claim to historicity[100]. In an important article on the technique of exorcism, C. Bonner demonstrated that an ancient exorcist's work was most effectively carried out if the afflicting demon, before leaving the oppressed individual, was compelled to do one or more of the following: (1) reply to the practitioner's conjurations (demons effect "dumbness" in those they possess, presumably to frustrate the exorcist); cf. Mt 9:32; Mt 12:22 (Lk 11:14); Mk 9:17, 25; (2) tell his name or his nature; Mk 5:9 (Lk 8:30), or (3) provide visible proof that the possessing force was a demon and that he has actually left the afflicted individual; in Mk 1:26 (Lk 4:35) and 9:26, the exorcisms are accompanied by convulsions, while in Mk 5:13 (Mt 8:32; Lk 8:33) the demons leave the demoniac for a herd of swine which destroys itself in the sea[101]. Bonner does not draw any conclusions regarding the significance of these parallels, nor does he venture an opinion whether these techniques are traditional embellishments or characteristics of the exorcistic techniques of the historical Jesus[102].

For the magical use of δεῖν καὶ λύειν, see F. Büchsel, *Theological Dictionary of the New Testament*, II (1964), 60, n. 3. Since Jesus heals her by touch, some have argued that this is not an exorcism; however, the texts should not be interpreted that rigidly.

[98] Several miracle stories contain traces of exorcistic language; J. M. Robinson, *The Problem of History in Mark* (London: SCM Press, 1957) 40; O. Böcher, *Christus Exorcista: Dämonismus und Taufe im Neuen Testament* (Stuttgart: Kohlhammer, 1972) 70–76.

[99] For the six exorcisms, cf. supra, n. 67; for the editorial statements which mention exorcism: Mk 1:32 ff. (Mt 8:16; Lk 4:40 f.); 1:39 (Mt 4:24); 3:10 f. (Lk 6:17 f.); Lk 7:21; 8:2.

[100] Supra, n. 77.

[101] C. Bonner, "The Technique of Exorcism," *Harvard Theological Review*, 36 (1943), 39–49; Hull, *Hellenistic Magic*, 68 ff. amplifies some of Bonner's points with additional data.

[102] In an earlier article, "Traces of Thaumaturgic Technique in the Miracles," *Harvard Theological Review*, 20 (1927), 171–81, Bonner suggests that the magical techniques which he discusses entered into the miracle tradition in the process of their transmission. This suggests to me that, in some Christian circles at least, the portrayal of Jesus as a magician was not something that had to be avoided at all costs.

Yet another characteristic of the exorcistic technique of Jesus is the use of the verb ἐπιτιμᾶν in two exorcism stories, Mk 1:25 (Lk 4:35, 41) and 9:25 (Mt 17:18; Lk 9:42)[103]. In the "Genesis Apocryphon" (1QapGen), a first century BCE Aramaic document from Palestine, Abraham is described as performing an exorcism on the king of Egypt by rebuking the evil spirit (20:28 f.), after praying and laying hands on the monarch. The Aramaic verb *g'r*, which in all probability lies behind ἐπιτιμᾶν in those passages cited above, is interpreted by J. Fitzmyer to mean "to be exorcised" (i. e., driven out by a rebuke)"[104]. Although ἐπιτιμᾶν or its synonyms does not occur in exorcistic contexts in Graeco-Roman accounts or in other Jewish accounts[105], we have here a term of Palestinian provenance which may reflect the usage of the historical Jesus. It would appear that H. C. Kee's attempt to demonstrate that ἐπιτιμᾶν is a *terminus technicus* for "the word of command that brings hostile powers under control" is unsuccessful[106].

Another term with magical connotations which occurs in a gospel exorcism story is φιμοῦν (Mk 1:25; Lk 4:35), where it is really a formula for exorcism[107].

Of the six exorcisms of Jesus preserved in gospel tradition, two describe no exorcistic technique whatsoever (Mt 9:32 ff. and 12:22 ff.). In three exorcism stories, Jesus expels demons with short succinct commands: "Jesus rebuked [ἐπετίμησεν] him, saying "Be silent [φιμώθητι] and come out [ἔξελθε] of him!"" (Mk 1:25; Lk 4:35); "Come out [ἔξελθε] of the man, you unclean spirit!" (Mk 5:8; Lk 8:29); "He rebuked [ἐπετίμησεν] the unclean spirit and said to it, "I command you, come out [ἔξελθε] of him and never enter him again!"[108]"

---

[103] Elsewhere the term ἐπιτιμᾶν has entered into a legendary nature miracle, Jesus' rebuke of the wind in Mk 4:39. Also, in the Lukan version of the healing of Simon's mother-in-law (Lk 4:38 f.), Jesus "rebukes" the woman's fever. If this were a Lukan embellishment, it would be noteworthy as an instance in which magical technique (in contrast to legendary magical motifs) has entered into synoptic tradition. Based on what we know of Luke's not infrequent use of non-Markan variants of his Markan exemplar (cf. T. Schramm, *Der Markus-Stoff bei Lukas* [Cambridge: Cambridge University Press, 1971]), I would argue that the Lukan version of the healing of Peter's mother-in-law is in fact more original than the version preserved in Mk 1:29 ff.

[104] J.A. Fitzmyer, *The Genesis Apocryphon of Qumran Cave I* (Rome: Pontifical Biblical Institute, 1966) 123; cf. *idem*, "Some Observations on the Genesis Apocryphon," *Catholic Biblical Quarterly*, 22 (1960), 284.

[105] Kee, "The Terminology of Mark's Exorcism Stories," 241.

[106] *Ibid.*, 232–46. Kee's apparent purpose in this article is to provide a firm base within the synoptic miracle tradition itself for arguing the eschatological significance of Jesus' exorcisms. As they stand the exorcism stories themselves contain no clear connection with Jesus' eschatological program; neither the Spirit of God nor Satan are ever mentioned within the framework of such stories.

[107] Fridrichsen, *The Problem of Miracle*, 112; Eitrem, *Some Notes on Demonology*, 38; idem, *Papyri Osloensis*, Fasc. I, 76 f. Eitrem refers to E. Rohde's correlation of φιμοῦν with καταδεῖν in exorcisms involving the dead in his *Psyche*, II (New York: Harper 4 Row, 1966) 603 ff.

[108] Provision that demons never return is a constituent element of many ancient exorcisms

(Mk 9:25; Mt 17:18; Lk 9:42). The brevity of these exorcistic formulae has led some scholars to contrast them with the long adjurations of the magical papyri (cf. the famous "Recipe of Pibeches" in *PGM* IV, 3007–3086). Aside from the not unimportant observation that such a contrast is quantitative, not qualitative, it should be noted that most of the magical papyri come from the third through the fifth centuries CE during the great *Blütezeit* of Graeco-Roman magic; it appears that the older the magical forms, the shorter and more precise are the formulas[109]. Hull has claimed that the expression "come out" [ἔξελθε] is the usual form of address in exorcisms in the magical papyri[110]. However, since this verb in the imperative mode in exorcisms is only found four times (*PGM* IV, 1243, 1245, 3013; V, 158), that claim is hardly valid. Rather, the usual form of addressing a demon is an expression of adjuration followed by the naming of those supernatural powers being invoked, frequently accompanied by *voces magicae* (e. g., "I adjure you by" [ὁρκίζω σε κατὰ], cf. *PGM* III, 36; IV, 289; VII, 242 and passim). The purpose of the adjuration, of course, is to harness supernatural powers in order to effect the exorcism. In instances in which [ἐξ]ορκίζω is followed by an objective accusative and an infinitive (e. g., *PGM* IV, 3037 f.: ὁρκίζω σε … λαλῆσαι), once the adjuration has been completed the practitioner may then switch to the imperative mood (e. g. *PGM* IV, 3041, 3044: λάλησαν). When the practitioner has achieved control of the demon, he may exercise that control by commanding the demon to do any number of things: ἀπάλλαξον (*PGM* IV, 86; V, 125, 130, 133; Wortmann, "Neue magische Texte," 107); ὕπαγε … ἔγειρε … ἄπελθε (Wortmann, op. cit., 83); ἀπόστηθι (*PGM* IV, 1244); ἀκολούθησον (*PGM* V, 158); ὑπόταξον (*PGM*, V, 164), and many others. In fact the term [ἐξ]ορκίζω in exorcistic contexts can mean anything from "implore" to "command," dependent on the relative power which the practitioner sees in the supernatural powers upon whom he calls. Therefore, Jesus' use of the imperative mood in exorcisms is in fact a widely known and used form of adjuration in the ancient world[111]. The fact that Jesus can confidently command demons and expect instant obedience indicates that he already thought himself in possession of the necessary supernatural powers requisite for accomplishing such feats. The great gulf which some New Testament scholars would place between "the

(Josephus *Ant.* 8. 25; Philostratus *vit. Apoll.* 4. 20), and can be one of the many functions of amulets (*PGM*, IV, 1254).

[109] Nilsson, "Die Religion in den griechischen Zauberpapyri," 132; Festugière, *L'Idéal religieux des Grecs*, 283; W. R. Halliday, *Greek Divination: A Study of Its Methods and Principles* (London: Macmillan, 1913) 27.

[110] Hull, *Hellenistic Magic*, 68.

[111] Eitrem, *Some Notes on Demonology*, 40 (however, Eitrem contrasts the magical force of imperatives which are repeated many times with the simple imperatives of Jesus, 32, n. 3). Apollonius of Tyana is represented as using a command to exorcise a demon in Philostratus *vit. Apoll.* 4. 20, as are Hanina ben Dosa and Shimon ben Jochae (Strack-Billerbeck, *Kommentar zum Neuen Testament*, IV, 514, 534–35). In Acts 16:18, the only narrated exorcism of Paul, the verb παραγγέλλω is a synonym of ὁρκίζω.

powerful word of the Son" and "magical incantations" is simply nonexistent[112]. The short authoritative commands of Jesus to demons in the gospel narratives are formulas of magical adjuration[113].

Of the three sayings of Jesus in which exorcisms are mentioned, Lk 13:32 (though probably genuine) contributes little to our knowledge. The Beelzebul controversy (Mk 3:19b–27; Mt 12:22–26, 29; Lk 11:14–18a, 21–22), which has a strong claim to historicity[114], contains the charge by Jesus' adversaries that he was casting out demons through the agency of a more powerful demon[115]. Jesus is represented as refuting the charge by pointing out its contradictory presuppositions. Finally a third pericope (Lk 11:19–20; Mt 12:27) is widely recognized as authentic even though it has been inserted into an alien context[116]: "if it is by the finger of God [Mt: Spirit of God] testament demons,then the kingdom of God has come upon you." Jesus apparently regarded his exorcisms as signs of the coming kingdom of God; as such they were subordinate to a framework of apocalyptic eschatology. Jewish eschatology expected the removal of the evil spirit from the world at the end of days[117]. It was precisely this diffuse, distant and general religious goal which Jesus, within the framework of a socially deviant millennial movement, made a concrete and present reality by controlling spiritual power through magical techniques.

Turning now to the gospel healing stories, we have already noticed the central function of the rite of laying on of hands in the ministry of Jesus[118]. The use of

---

112 This artificial distinction is made by, among others, E. Stauffer, *Theological Dictionary of the New Testament*, II (1964) 626.

113 In *Das Neue Testament und die dämonischen Mächte* (Stuttgart: Kohlhammer, 1972), O. Böcher appropriately describes Jesus' commands to demons as *Wortzauber* (33 ff.). In a recent article by W. Kirchschläger, "Exorcisms in Qumran?" *Kairos*, 18 (1976), 135–53, the author correctly affirms the use of exorcism at Qumran, but erroneously concludes that both the Qumran writings and the Gospels rejected magical ideas.

114 S. E. Johnson, "Jesus and First Century Galilee," in: *In Memoriam Ernst Lohmeyer*, ed. W. Schmauch (Stuttgart: Evangelisches Verlagswerk, 1951) 80; Fridrichsen, *The Problem of Miracle*, 102–10 (an excellent discussion); Fuller, *Interpreting the Miracles*, 25 ff.; J. Jeremias, *New Testament Theology*, I (New York: Charles Scribner's Sons, 1971) 91; Barrett, *Holy Spirit*, 59–63.

115 The presuppositions behind this charge are briefly discussed in: Bonner, *Amulets*, 106.

116 H. Windisch, "Jesus und der Geist nach synoptischer Überlieferung," in: *Studies in Early Christianity*, ed. S. J. Case (New York and London: Century, 1928) 216 ff.; Perrin, *Rediscovering the Teaching of Jesus*, 63–68; Fuller, *Foundations of New Testament Christology*, 105. However, the saying is regarded as inauthentic by Fridrichsen, *The Problem of Miracle*, 74 f.

117 *1 Enoch* 54:4–6; 69:27–28; *Test. Levi* 18:12; *Test. Juda* 25:3; *Jub.* 23:29; *Ass. Moses* 10:1; 1QS 4:19–21; 1QM 14:10; 1QH 3:18; Zech. 13:2; cf. Aune, "The Problem of the Messianic Secret," 29; O. Betz, *Was Wissen Wir von Jesus?* (Stuttgart and Berlin: Kreuz-Verlag, 1965), 42–47; O. Betz, "Jesus heiliger Krieg," *Novum testamentum*, 2 (1957), 116–37.

118 In healing stories, the laying on of hands is referred to in Mk 1:31 (Mt 8:15); 1:41 (Mt 8:3; Lk 5:13); 5:41 (Mt 9:25; Lk 8:54); 7:33–34; 8:23, 25; 9:27; Lk 13:13 (cf. Lk 7:14). General references to the laying on of hands as a healing rite are found in Mk 5:23 (Mt 9:18); 6:5; 7:32; 8:22; 16:18; Lk 4:40 (cf. Mk 6:2). On the general subject see J. Behm, *Die Handauflegung im Urchristentum: Nach Verwendung, Herkunft und Bedeutung in religionsgeschichtlichem*

touch was unquestionably an authentic feature of Jesus' healing technique. In Hellenistic traditions, touch as a healing rite is used by the gods in legends and stories, but only very rarely by human miracle workers[119]. There is no association of the rite of laying on of hands with healing in Old Testament or rabbinic tradition[120]. However, the "Genesis Apocryphon" contains a brief reference to Abraham's exorcism of the king of Egypt through prayer, laying on of hands and rebuking the evil spirit (1 QapGen 20:28–29); this is the only instance of the laying on of hands as a healing rite in an ancient Jewish source[121]. In contrast to Jesus' technique, however, prayer plays a central role, just as it does in rabbinic miracle stories[122]. While prayer was apparently used in early Christian healing rituals (Jas 5:14–16), it is only rarely referred to in connection with Jesus' healings; those few references, however, are not insignificant. Jesus' reference in Mk 9:29 to the necessity of prayer for difficult exorcisms appears to derive from the early church rather than Jesus himself. In Mk 7:34, it is said of Jesus that "after looking up to heaven, he sighed [ἐστέναξεν]", and then proceeded to heal a deaf and dumb man. "Looking up to heaven" is a gesture of prayer (cf. Lk 18:13; Strack-Billerbeck, *Kommentar zum Neuen Testament*, II, 246 f.), and the groaning appears to be a form of "silent prayer", which is a conventional feature of the behavior of a wonderworker[123]. In Jn 11:41b–42 Jesus is described as addressing a prayer to God prior to a miracle (cf. Jn 9:31)[124]. Jesus' prayer prior to the multiplication of the loaves (Mk 6:41; Mt 14:19; Lk 9:16; Jn 6:11) is a

Zusammenhang untersucht (Leipzig: A. Deichert, 1911); J. Coppens, *L'imposition des mains et les rites connexes dans le Nouveau Testament* (Paris: J. Gabalda, 1925); S. Morenz, "Handauflegung," *Religion in Geschichte und Gegenwart*, 3. Aufl., III (Tübingen: Mohr Siebeck, 1959) 52 f.; Eitrem, *Some Notes on Demonology*, 41–46. O. Perels, I think erroneously, sees Hellenistic influences in the tradition of Jesus' healing by touch: *Die Wunderüberlieferung der Synoptiker in ihrem Verhältnis zur Wortüberlieferung* (Stuttgart: Kohlhammer, 1934), 91. A bibliography is found in *Theological Dictionary of the New Testament*, IX (1974), 424.

[119] O. Weinreich, *Antike Heilungswunder: Untersuchungen zum Wunderglauben der Griechen und Römer* (Gießen: Töpelmann, 1909) 45–48. The few examples which Weinreich cites are not earlier than the third century CE. In Roman literature, Tacitus preserves the story of Vespasian's healings at Alexandria in which one man's crippled hand is cured by a touch of the emperor's foot (*Hist.* 4.81; cf. Suetonius *Vesp.* 7). In European folklore traditions, note the tradition of the "king's touch"; cf. Thomas, *Religion and the Decline of Magic*, 192–204.

[120] E. Lohse, *Theological Dictionary of the New Testament*, IX (1974), 428.

[121] D. Flusser, "Healing through Laying On of Hands in a Dead Sea Scroll," *Israel Exploration Journal*, 7 (1957), 107 f.

[122] W. Schmithals, *Wunder und Glaube* (Neukirchen-Vluyn: Neukirchener Verlag, 1970), 20.

[123] Eitrem, *Some Notes on Demonology*, 54 f.; cf. C. Bonner, "Traces of Thaumaturgic Technique in the Miracles," *Harvard Theological Review*, 20 (1927), 171–74; Bonner does not sufficiently stress the prayer-like nature of the inarticulate groans.

[124] R. Bultmann, *The Gospel of John* (Philadelphia: Westminster Press, 1971) 408, interprets this prayer as a demonstration that Jesus is no magician or divine man who works by his own power; the same view is expressed by C. K. Barrett, *The Gospel According to St. John* (London: SPCK, 1958) 336. However, the apologetic motif which is clearly present in this prayer is in all probability a redactional overlay obscuring the original intent of the prayer .

stereotypical feature of Jewish piety. Jesus does place the performance of nature miracles in close connection with faith and prayer in Mk 11:23–24 (Mt 17:20; Lk 17:6). All that can be said is that prayer played a role in Jesus' wonderworking, but hardly a major one.

As in the case of the exorcisms, many of Jesus' healings were effected by a succinct command directed toward the afflicted individuals: "Be clean!" (Mk 1:41); "I say to you, rise up, take your pallet and go home!" (Mk 2:11); "*Talitha cumi*!" which Mark interprets as "Little girl, I say to you, arise!" (Mk 5:41); "Your faith has made you well; be healed of your disease!" (Mk 5:34); "*Ephphatha*!" which Mark renders as "Be opened!" (addressed, interestingly enough, to the deaf man's ear in Mk 7:34); "Go and show yourselves to the priests!" (Lk 17:14); "Young man, I say to you, arise!" (Lk 7:14); "Rise, take up your pallet and walk!" (Jn 5:8); "Lazarus, come out!" (Jn 11:43); "Go; be it done to you as you have believed!" (Mt 8:13). As in the case of the exorcisms, so here too the healing commands of Jesus must be regarded as magical formulas of adjuration. Only four healing stories lack a pronouncement by Jesus; in two (Mk 1:29–31; Lk 14:1–6), the stories are narrated so briefly that the pronouncement may have dropped out of the tradition. In Mk 5:25–34 the healing is effected (vv. 27–29) and only later is a pronouncement of healing made by Jesus (v. 34). Mk 8:22–26, therefore, is the only miracle story clearly lacking a pronouncement by Jesus in the tradition; here, however, an elaborate ritual involving sputum and touch effects the healing.

Two healing pronouncements of Jesus in particular have drawn a great deal of attention: the Aramaic commands "*Talitha cumi*," (Mk 5:41), and "*Ephphatha*" (Mk 7:34), neither of which are reproduced by Matthew or Luke. The fact that Aramaic was in all probability the mother tongue of Jesus means that these phrases, if indeed they are *ipsissima verba* of Jesus, could not have been used by him as *voces magicae*. Why then are these Aramaic healing formulas preserved in the tradition used by Mark? In view of the importance attributed to preserving adjurations and incantations in their original languages[125], these formulas were probably preserved for the purpose of guiding Christian thaumaturges in exorcistic and healing activities[126]. In early Christianity, therefore, these Aramaic phrases may have functioned as magic formulas[127].

---

[125] Iamblichus *de myst.* 7.4 f.; Lucian *Philops.* 9; Lucian *Alex.* 13; Origen *contra Cels.* 1.24 f.; 5.45; cf. A. Deissmann, *Bible Studies* (Edinburgh : T. & T. Clark, 1901) 355; Dieterich, *Eine Mithrasliturgie*, 39 f.; above all, see T. Hopfner, *Griechisch-ägyptischer Offenbarungszauber*, I, 706–68.

[126] M. Dibelius, *Die Formgeschichte des Evangeliums*, 6. Aufl. (Tübingen: Mohr Siebeck, 1971) 80–84; Eitrem, *Some Notes on Demonology*; D. Tiede, *The Charismatic Figure as Miracle Worker* (Missoula: Scholars Press, 1970) 267 f.

[127] O. Böcher, *Dämonenfurcht und Dämonenabwehr* (Stuttgart: Kohlhammer, 1970) 76; Böcher, *Das Neue Testament und die dämonischen Mächte*, 35; D. Strauss, *The Life of Jesus Critically Examined* (Philadelphia: Fortress Press, 1972) 448 f., and W. Wrede, *The Messianic*

Another feature of the gospel healing stories which demands some attention is the element of "faith" in such narratives; we have already noted that the distinctive meaning of faith in the miracle stories has led some scholars to affirm the essential historicity of Jesus' healing ministry[128]. Faith is an element in only two exorcism stories, where it is exercised by parents of afflicted individuals (Mk 9:23 f.; Mt 15:28). In healing stories, faith plays a significant role in four such narratives: Mk 5:34 (Mt 9:22; Lk 8:48); 10:52 (Lk 18:42); Lk 17:19; Mt 8:10, 13 (Lk 7:9); cf. Jn 11:26–27. Unfortunately a great deal of theological flummery has been occasioned by the retroactive importation of later Christian notions of faith into the use of the notion by Jesus[129]. Equally erroneous is the notion that faith played no part in Jewish or Graeco-Roman miracles[130]. The Greek word commonly rendered as "faith" in the synoptic healing and exorcism narratives could better be translated "trust". It simply refers to the naive and elemental confidence that Jesus possessed the requisite power to heal and cast out demons[131]. Since Jesus, according to tradition, only healed or exorcized those who came to him, the very fact of their coming indicated a hope that Jesus would effect a cure of their condition. The single indication that Jesus was not always successful is found in Mk 6:5–6 (Mt 13:58); here the view of Fridrichsen appears to be the most satisfactory: Jesus' help was not sought after in Nazareth, therefore he was not able to perform any exorcisms and only a few cures[132]. The necessity of a magician's credibility in the eyes of his clients is such a widespread phenomenon

Secret (Cambridge and London: James Clark, 1971) 147, n. 40 (both referred to in German editions by Dieterich, *Eine Mithrasliturgie*, 40). H. J. Cadbury, *The Peril of Modernizing Jesus* (New York: Macmillan, 1937) 81; Bultmann, *History of the Synoptic Tradition*, 213 f., refers to both Aramaic expressions as "magic words" (as does Böcher, in both references above). It is somewhat surprising that the Aramaic term *abba* (occurring once in the gospels, Mk 14:36; twice in the Pauline corpus, Rom 8:15; Gal 4:6) does not recur in magical contexts particularly since in form it is a palindrome (the term is not listed in the indices to Bonner, *Amulets* or Preisendanz, *PGM*, vol. 3). The cry from the cross, *eloi eloi lama sabachthani* (Mk 15:34; a curious mixture of Hebrew and Aramaic, is "corrected" in Mt 27:46) appears in a corrupted form in a Coptic charm published by A. M. Kropp, *Ausgewählte koptische Zaubertexte*, III, 59, 128, translated by E. Goodenough and described by him as the work of a Christian magician; *idem*, *Jewish Symbols*, II, 180.

128 *Supra*, n. 83.

129 Cf. A. Oepke, *Theological Dictionary of the New Testament*, III (1965), 210 f.

130 This view is expressed by Dunn, *Jesus and the Spirit*, 75; examples to the contrary from the cult of Aesklepios are cited by A. Oepke, *Theological Dictionary of the New Testament*, III, 210.

131 Fridrichsen, *The Problem of Miracle*, 78; Nock, "Paul and the Magus," 185; F. Preisigke, *Die Gotteskraft der frühchristlichen Zeit* (Berlin: W. De Gruyter, 1922) 4–6.

132 Fridrichsen, *The Problem of Miracle*, 80; T. Klausner's view that the miracles of Jesus were not always successful and that he was afraid to attempt them often is speculation, though not inherently improbable; *Idem*, *Jesus of Nazareth*, 272.

that the emphasis on "faith" in the gospel healing narratives cannot be considered a distinctive feature of the wonderworking activity of Jesus[133].

Four particular healing stories deserve special consideration: (1) the Woman with the Hemorrhage (Mk 5:25–34 and parallels), (2) the Deaf Mute (Mk 7:31–36), (3) the Blind Man near Bethsaida (Mk 8:22–26), and (4) the Man Born Blind (Jn 9:1–41). In the first story the healing is reported as accomplished, without the knowledge of Jesus, when the woman touched the border of his garment. Jesus is said to have perceived that "power had gone forth from him". This story has been intensively analyzed by the papyrologist F. Preisigke from the perspective of the materialistic view of divine "power" (δύναμις) on which the story focuses[134]. W. Grundmann, who was so preoccupied with denying that there was any connection between New Testament miracles and magic, found it unnecessary to refer to or discuss the notion of *dynamis* found in this story[135].

One of the more recent commentators on Mark, W. L. Lane, shows just how difficult it is to avoid the magical interpretation of this passage:

> Jesus possesses the power of God as the representative of the Father. Nevertheless, the Father remains in control of his own power. The healing of the woman occurred through God's free and gracious decision to bestow upon her the power which was active in Jesus. By an act of sovereign will God determined to honor the woman's faith *in spite of the fact that it was tinged with ideas which bordered on magic*[136].

The ideas expressed in the story of the woman's healing do not border on magic, they are of the essence of Graeco-Roman magical notions. Preisigke's discussion of this story, though he unfortunately focuses on the Lukan rather than the Markan version, is excellent, in spite of an overemphasis on the Egyptian origin of the concept of materialistic power presupposed in this miracle story. Consequently, Preisigke focuses on the term "fluid" which is a less than satisfactory conception for elucidating the idea of power found in the text[137]; δύναμις or πνεῦμα would perhaps have been more appropriate terms. One year after the appearance of Preisigke's small monograph, the more general treatment of the subject was published by J. Röhr, *Der okkulte Kraftbegriff im Altertum* (Leipzig: Dieterich 1923). The focal terms for Röhr's study are δύναμις (the most frequently used Greek word for "power"), and ἐνέργεια; to a lesser extent συμπάθεια

[133] V. Turner, "An Ndembu Doctor in Practice," in *Magic, Faith, and Healing*, ed. A. Kiev (New York: Free Press of Glencoe, 1964) 263; Thomas, *Religion and the Decline of Magic*, 210.

[134] *Die Gotteskraft der frühchristlichen Zeit* (Leipzig: W. De Gruyter, 1922).

[135] W. Grundmann, *Theological Dictionary of the New Testament*, II (1964), 284–317; *idem, Der Begriff der Kraft in der neutestamentlichen Gedankenwelt* (Stuttgart: Kohlhammer, 1932).

[136] W. L. Lane, *The Gospel According to Mark* (Grand Rapids, 1974) 192 f.

[137] Preisigke briefly notes these equivalencies on 39. The term "fluid" was picked up by E. Lohmeyer, even though it adds little to the discussion; E. Lohmeyer, *Das Evangelium des Markus* (Göttingen: Vandenhoeck & Ruprecht, 1959) 102, n. 6.

and ἀντιπάθεια, which (among other uses, scientific, philosophical and religious) are important for the ancient conception of magical power (77–95)[138]. Among Hellenistic miracle stories of healing discussed by Weinreich, those which are brought about by "*Heilende Statuen und Bilder*,"[139] in many ways form a close parallel to the Markan story. The fact that divine power resides in objects and persons and can be magically transferred or appropriated by those in need is found elsewhere in the New Testament[140].

The story of the healings of the Deaf Mute (Mk 7:31–37) and the Blind Man near Bethsaida (Mk 8:22–26)[141], appear to be closely related and have proven enigmatical to many commentators. Since these two pericopes have no synoptic parallels, some have assumed that they were absent from that edition of Mark used by Matthew and Luke. More probably, it has been conjectured that the first and third evangelists wished to delete the apparent references to magic[142]. The two stories have several common elements: (1) the afflicted individuals are healed in private, (2) saliva is used to effect the healing, (3) the affected organ is touched by Jesus, and (4) there is an emphasis on confidentiality. Attention should also be called to the use of the magic formula "*Ephphatha*" (Mk 7:34), the fact that Jesus is described as "looking up into heaven" and groaning (Mk 7:34), with the result that "his tongue was released" [ἐλύθη ὁ δεσμὸς τῆς γλώσσης αὐτοῦ][143]. Mk 8:22–26 has another unusual feature: the healing is accomplished in two stages, first saliva is applied to the man's eyes and Jesus lays his hands upon him with the result that he is only able to see indistinctly. In the second stage, Jesus touches the man's eyes directly and the complete healing is accomplished. The story of the Man Born Blind (Jn 9:11–41) also emphasizes the use of saliva mixed with clay to effect the restoration of sight (vv. 6–7). All of these techniques are well-known to both Jewish and Graeco-Roman magical practitioners. The fact that they are magical techniques is indicated not only by the deviant context in which they were performed, but also by the fact that Jesus made the general Jewish religious goal of health and longevity (Deut 6:2; Josh 1:8) individually and concretely available to particular persons by means which were thought guaranteed of success.

One of the more difficult aspects of our subject is the problem of determining to what extent the more obviously magical elements preserved in the gospel

[138] In the two publications by Grundmann (*supra*, n. 135), no account is taken of the work of Röhr.

[139] Weinreich, *Antike Heilungswunder*, 137–74.

[140] Cf. Acts 19:12, where cloths touched by Paul were used to heal the sick and cast out demons, and Acts 5:15 where Peter's shadow heals the sick.

[141] An excellent discussion of these passages is found in Roloff, *Das Kerygma und der irdische* Jesus, 127–31.

[142] F. W. Beare, *The Earliest Records of Jesus* (Nashville: Abingdon Press, 1962) 133 ff.

[143] A. Deissmann, *Light from the Ancient East*, 306 ff. calls this the clearest example of technical expressions taken from magic in the New Testament.

tradition can be traced back to the historical Jesus. R. Bultmann's judgment that the "Hellenistic origin of the miracle stories is overwhelmingly the more probable"[144] has been widely influential in modern discussions of the historicity of the miracle tradition. On the other hand, it has become increasingly evident that the neat form critical bifurcation between Hellenistic and Palestinian Jewish influences on the synoptic tradition is beset with difficulties, a product of the Teutonic compulsion for orderliness. The gospel miracle tradition has certainly been subject to folkloristic development and embellishment. However, whether these additions were made in a Hellenistic or Palestinian linguistic and cultural arena is extremely difficult to determine. H. C. Kee, who claims that the oldest layers of the tradition are uninterested in thaumaturgical details[145], in our opinion appears to have unwittingly demonstrated precisely the opposite. Eitrem's judgment that the miracle stories do not seem to have been embellished with more thaumaturgical details than were originally present in the tradition appears to me to be generally convincing[146], though careful research in this area is an urgent necessity. While there is some tendency to increase the magical techniques found in the gospel miracle stories[147], in most instances the exact opposite tendency appears to be at work. Here, of course, I am distinguishing between magical techniques and magical folkloristic motifs. The latter are clearly found in the nature miracles, most of which are creations out of whole cloth by the early communities. In the healing and exorcism stories, such motifs as healing from a distance, stopping the bier in a funeral procession, the impotence of rational medicine, are some of the more common folkloristic motifs[148].

The focal issue in this phase of our study has been to determine whether or not Jesus made use of magical techniques in his ministry of exorcism and healing, and if so, whether he should be labeled a magician. The thrust of our discussion to this point should make it abundantly clear that, in our opinion, Jesus did in fact make use of magical techniques which must be regarded as magical because they were effected within the socially deviant context of a millennial movement and because he was able to harness supernatural power in such a way that he and his followers believed that success was virtually guaranteed.

In a recent book entitled *Jesus the Jew* (New York: Macmillan, 1974), G. Vermes deals at some length with the historical significance of Jesus' exorcisms and healings. One type of exorcist in Palestinian Judaism, according to

---

[144] Bultmann, *History of the Synoptic Tradition*, 240.

[145] Kee, "The Terminology of Mark's Exorcism Stories," 245.

[146] Eitrem, *Some Notes on Demonology*, 63.

[147] M. Smith, *Clement of Alexandria*, 223; cf. *supra*, n. 103.

[148] The finest discussion of the constituent motifs in the synoptic miracle stories remains that of R. Bultmann, *History of the Synoptic Tradition*, 209–244. For a more recent discussion and analysis of the motifs in the miracle stories see G. Theissen, *Urchristliche Wundergeschichten: Ein Beitrag zur formgeschichtlichen Erforschung der synoptischen Evangelien* (Gütersloh: Verlaghaus Gerd Mohn, 1974) 57–128.

Vermes, flirted with magical techniques and was thought successful precisely because the appropriate rituals and incantations were flawlessly repeated (64). Jesus' exorcisms as depicted in the gospels, Vermes goes on to point out, are noticeably free from such magical or quasi-magical techniques (65). Even in Jesus' healings he rarely approximates the Noachic, Solomonic or Essene types of cures. Vermes concludes that

> the representation of Jesus in the Gospels as a man whose supernatural abilities derive, not from secret powers, but from immediate contact with God, proves him to be a genuine charismatic, the true heir of an age-old prophetic religious line [69].

Jesus, then, represents the Jewish "holy man" tradition, other illustrious examples of which were Honi (1st cent. BCE)[149] and Hanina ben Dosa (1st cent. CE). Jesus was a Galilean Hasid. Unfortunately, Vermes' discussion is flawed by an inadequate conception of magic: magical wonders are thought to be based on secret powers, while miracles of healing are the result of exceptional piety (i.e., an "immediate relationship to God"). The apocalyptic framework within which Jesus' activities and teachings took place has unaccountably receded into the background. Further, it should be observed that magical techniques vary with the particular conception of the divinity or supernatural powers held by the magical practitioner. In a Graeco-Roman polytheistic context, where many deities are noticeably lacking in such qualities as omnipotence, a different protocol is required than in a Jewish context in which Yahweh and his subordinates must be manipulated in a more covert manner.

The wonderworking activities of Jesus cannot be considered magical simply because his healing and exorcistic techniques have parallels in Graeco-Roman magic (though they in fact do), neither can they be considered non-magical because such traits are relatively infrequent. The wonders performed by Jesus are magical because they occur within a context of social deviance in which widely accepted but generally unattainable goals highly valued in Judaism are thought to be accomplished for particular individuals through the application of generally successful management techniques. While magical activities may constitute important aspects of the role of such figures as the shaman, the sage (both Graeco-Roman and rabbinic), the prophet and the messiah, each of these socio-religious roles involves different collections of specializations. Sociologically (and we shall have to remain with the vantage point with which we began), it would be problematic to categorize Jesus as a magician, since those magical activities which he used can be more appropriately subsumed under the role of messianic prophet.

---

[149] Cf. W.S. Green, "Palestinian Holy Men: Charismatic Leadership and Rabbinic Tradition," *ANRW* II 19, 2, ed. by W. Haase (Berlin and New York: Walter de Gruyter, 1979) 619–647.

5. Gospel and Aretalogy

In our discussion of the healings and exorcisms of Jesus as magical activities within the framework of the socially deviant millennial movement initiated by Jesus, we found compelling reasons to suppose that a solid core of authentic tradition lay behind the gospel accounts. The form critical analysis of the gospels has made it clear that, in some respects at least, Jesus' reputation as a thaumaturge was augmented and embellished through the creation of new stories as well as the amplification of older ones. In this section we shall consider three related issues: (1) the apologetic nature of the gospel genre, (2) the role of magic in the redactional activities of the evangelists, and (3) the influence of Graeco-Roman aretalogical traditions on the way in which the life of Jesus is depicted in the gospels.

A significant contribution to the question of the relationship of magic to the Gospel tradition has been made indirectly by J. Z. Smith in an article to which we have had occasion to refer above: "Good News is No News: Aretalogy and Gospel." Smith proposes that the primary characteristic of every major religious biography of the Graeco-Roman period is that of a double defense against (1) outsiders' charges that the subjects of these biographies were magicians, and (2) the sincere misunderstanding of insiders that these religious figures were wonderworkers or, in their terms, "divine men". Smith analyzes the *Vita Apollonii* of Philostratus and the *Vita Pythagorica* of Iamblichos from this perspective, demonstrating the important function of these two complementary motifs in the biographies and by implication their relevance for understanding the canonical gospels, particularly Mark. While Smith has little to say directly about the canonical gospels themselves, he assumes the relevance of his analysis for understanding Mark and John which he characterizes as reverse aretalogies in the sense that they appear to be combating the image of Jesus as magician-divine man.

A number of scholars, particularly P. Samain in his article "L'Accusation de magie contre le Christ dans les Évangiles," *Ephemerides Theologicae Lovanienses*, 15 (1938), 449–90, have contributed to our knowledge of the anti-magic apologetic found in the gospels. According to Samain, Jesus is never expressly charged with being a magician or practicing magic (454). Within a Jewish context, prophets and other divine emissaries were thought to accredit their missions by performing miracles; however, enemies of God in league with Satan could also perform wonders. To charge someone with having a pact with Satan, then, is to charge him with practicing magic (455 f.). Samain contends that the charge that Jesus was an imposter is equivalent to the more direct charge of practicing magic (456). The charge of imposture is found in Mt 27:63 (cf. Jn 7:12, 47) and many other passages; referring as well to parallels in Josephus and early Christian literature, Samain presents an iron-clad case for understanding the charge of imposture as an accusation that Jesus performed miracles by trickery or magical techniques (456–64). Turning to the Beelzebul pericope in Mk 3:22–30 and parallels, Samain correctly understands the phrase "by Beelzebul" as an ellipsis for the expression "in the name of Beelzebul" (466). At this point he refers to the statement of Origen, *Magi sunt, qui invocant Beelzebul* (*in Hom. in Num.* 13. 5). After citing a number of passages from the magical papyri which demonstrate that a divinity can be described as entering and inhabiting the magician (e. g., *PGM* III, 415 f., 470 ff.; IV, 710 f.), Samain then interprets the accusation that Jesus cast out demons by Beelzebul in this way:

> The Christ would be a magician: united to the leader of demons, he would compel him, since he possessed his name, to perform the prodigies which he desired and particularly exorcisms; no spirit or demonic power could resist him [469 f.].

In commenting on Lk 11:20; Mt 12:28, Samain observes that

> the distinction between an authentic miraculous deed and a magical act is less to be found in the procedure or result of the operation itself than in the supernatural powers which intervene there [471].

By exorcizing demons, Jesus has taken the part of God in making war against Satan; this is the opposite of the role of a magician (472). Turning to three passages in John (7:20; 8:48–53; 10:20 f.), all of which contain the phrase "you have a demon," Samain discusses them in detail (473–84), providing an amplified paraphrase of that charge: "You are only a pseudo-prophet charlatan, and your exaltation and your power are only products of the devil" (482). Finally, Samain turns to the pericopes in Matthew and Luke which deal with the temptation of Jesus (Mt 4:1–11; Lk 4:1–13), since such feats as changing stones to bread and flying through the air are not uncommon magical folklore motifs (484–90). Noting that the temptation story is commonly interpreted as relating to the question of religious vs. political messianism, and less commonly as the refusal of Jesus to use magical powers to accomplish his goals, Samain believes, probably correctly, that both views are correct (489)[150]. He concludes by observing that

---

[150] Only the third temptation in Matthew (4:8 ff.) and the second in Luke (4:5–8) have any connection with Jewish messianic expectations; the others relate to typical feats possible for a Hellenistic divine man or son of God, according to G. P. Wetter, *Der Sohn Gottes: Eine Untersuchung über den Charakter und die Tendenz des Johannes-Evangeliums* (Göttingen: Vandenhoeck & Ruprecht, 1916) 139 f. Fridrichsen, *The Problem of Miracle*, 121–28, sees the temptation story as reflecting two groups in the church, one which emphasizes the role of miracles, the other which, while not denying the reality and role of miracles, wishes to protect Christianity from declining into mere thaumaturgy. Eitrem, *Die Versuchung Christi* (Oslo: Grøndahl, 1924), quite properly emphasized the magical motifs in two of the three temptations and saw in the story an apologetic against the charge that Jesus was a magician. It would appear that Fridrichsen's and Eitrem's views are mutually exclusive. All of this has been ignored by C.K. Barrett, *The Holy Spirit*, 46–53.

the accusation that Jesus practiced magic is a motif which permeates the gospel tradition (490).

To the data provided by J.Z. Smith and Samain, we may add the contribution of C.H. Kraeling, "Was Jesus accused of Necromancy?," *Journal of Biblical Literature*, 59 (1940), 147–57, who defines necromancy as not only a means of divination in which the spirits of the dead playa central role but also as the use of such spirits for the accomplishment of magical feats (147, following T. Hopfner). Focusing on Mk 6:14–16, Kraeling is convinced that the evangelist thinks that both the common people and Herod believed that Jesus was John the Baptist *redivivus* in the Markan presentation (150). However, it is unclear how a resurrected John could be thought to perform miracles when he had not done so previous to his execution. Like Jesus (Mk 3:22; Jn 7:20; 8:48, 49, 52; 10:20), John the Baptist was accused of having a demon (Mt 11:18; Lk 7:33), that is, both were thought of as magicians "who had demonic spirits under their control, through whom they did unusual things" (154). The original notion reflected in Mk 6:14–16, and one which was not understood by Mark, according to Kraeling, is that "Jesus was using the spirit of John brought back from the dead to perform his miracles for him" (155).

A. Fridrichsen too made an important contribution to our knowledge of the anti-magic apologetic of the gospel tradition, not only in his 1925 book *The Problem of Miracle in Primitive Christianity*, but also in a later article entitled "The Conflict of Jesus with the Unclean Spirits," *Theology*, 22 (1931), 122–35. In *The Problem of Miracle*, Fridrichsen devoted a significant part of his treatment of miracles in early Christianity to a discussion of the hostile criticism which Jesus' miracles evoked (85–118). He isolated four major themes in an apologetic found in the gospels themselves and which live on in various Christian writers from the second through the third centuries. The four themes, shorn of the evidence which Fridrichsen adduces in their support, are: (1) The miracles of Jesus were not due to chance or magic, but were predicted by the Old Testament prophets. (2) Jesus' healings, in contrast with those of pagan wonderworkers, had a lasting effect. (3) Jesus used no devices in effecting healings and exorcisms in contrast with pagan magical practice. (4) Jesus sought no personal profit or advantage from miracles, but rather acted solely for man's salvation. In the very interesting and important dissertation of O. Bauernfeind, *Die Worte der Dämonen im Markusevangelium* (Stuttgart: Kohlhammer, 1927), the author examined the three sayings of demons preserved in Mk 1:24, 3:11 and 5:7 against the background provided by the magical papyri. He found that the words spoken by the demons have many parallels in magical incantations and that, in effect, the demons are presented as attempting to protect themselves, in vain, against Jesus by using magical formulas. By some quirk, Bauernfeind tries to show that this is not a folkloristic development in the gospel tradition, but that such demonic utterances actually correspond to actual occurrences in Jesus' ministry of exorcism (94). In "The Conflict of Jesus with the Unclean Spirits", Fridrichsen sets forth the much more probable view that the demonic exclamations were intended to defend Jesus from the accusation of being a magician in alliance with the prince of demons (125).

While it is clear that an anti-magic apologetic permeates the gospels, it is less clear whether and to what degree such accusations and their defense can be traced back to the historical Jesus. Here is another important area of research that requires scholarly attention.

In considering the role of magic in the redactions of the gospels, we must turn to the recent study of J. M. Hull, to which we have already referred. Hull's rather brief treatment of Mark (73–86) is marred by three factors: (1) He does not attempt to separate tradition from redaction in Mark; thus, while he does focus on many magical features of the Markan gospel, we are not presented with a careful delineation of the evangelist's perspective. (2) The anti-magical apologetic which is present in Mark (side-by-side with magical traditions!) is neither discussed nor evaluated by Hull[151]. (3) Recent work on the gospel as aretalogy, particularly relevant for the study of Mark, is not considered by Hull. Not only has the author not advanced our knowledge of the relationship between the Second Evangelist and Christian magical traditions, he has not even summarized many of the important contributions of studies already made.

Hull's treatment of the Gospel of Luke is more satisfactory, but still problematic. The chapter is entitled "Luke: The Tradition Penetrated by Magic", indicative of Hull's contention that the Lukan *Weltanschauung* is that of the "magical universe" (87). In contrast to McCasland, who asserts that Luke made no attempt to heighten the phenomena of exorcism[152], Hull attempts to show that Luke has in fact emphasized the phenomena of exorcism in various ways. Hull's views on Luke have received a telling critique by P. Achtemeier, "The Lukan Perspective on the Miracles of Jesus: A Preliminary Sketch," *Journal of Biblical Literature*, 94 (1975), 556–58, with which I find myself in complete agreement. Hull summarizes Preisigke's findings in the monograph to which we have already referred, *Die Gotteskraft der frühchristlichen Zeit* (Leipzig: De Gruyter, 1922), particularly as it relates to the story of the healing of the Woman with the Hemorrhage (109–114). Since the story occurred in Luke's Markan exemplar (Mk 5:25–34), the more appropriate place for discussing Preisigke's work would have been in Hull's chapter on Mark (Luke makes no substantial alteration in this pericope). Again, Hull ignores most of the recent redaction critical work on the Gospel of Luke, not to mention Lukan aretalogical elements.

---

[151] The two glaring omissions are the lack of any adequate discussion of the Beelzebul pericope (Mk 3:19b–30) and the failure to consider Bauernfeind's study *Die Worte der Dämonen im Markusevangelium*.

[152] McCasland, *By the Finger of God*, 49–51.

Hull's discussion of Matthew, in which he sees the tradition as purified of magic, is more satisfactory. The author is able to demonstrate convincingly the Matthaean suspicion of magical exorcism and healing. Again, however, recent redaction critical work on Matthew has been largely ignored. In sum, then, the central purpose of Hull's book, the analysis of the synoptic tradition from the perspective of ancient magic, is a task that the author has carried out in a very incomplete and unsatisfactory way. Redaction critical studies of the stance of each evangelist in relation to early Christian and Graeco-Roman magical traditions remain to be done.

The last decade has witnessed a dramatic increase in interest in the relationship between the gospel as a literary genre and Graeco-Roman aretalogical traditions[153]. A recent survey by P. Achtemeier, "Gospel Miracle Tradition and the Divine Man," *Interpretation*, 26 (1972), 174–97, concludes that in New Testament scholarship there appears to be an emerging inclination to see the gospels as attempts to combat the divine man image which had been superimposed on the figure of Jesus at earlier stages in the tradition (197). The original function of aretalogies was to praise various miracle-working divinities; by extension an aretalogy could recount the miracle-working activities of a charismatic figure, thereby demonstrating his status as a divine man. In a recent dissertation by D. L. Tiede, *The Charismatic Figure as Miracle Worker* (Missoula: Scholars Press, 1972), the author has attempted to demonstrate the existence of two discrete kinds of traditions, the aretalogies of the divine wise man and the aretalogies of the miracle-worker (5). Tiede's thesis has been rigorously challenged by M. Smith, both in a critical review of the dissertation in *Interpretation*, 28 (1974), 238–40, and in a paper presented on October 31, 1976 at the Society of Biblical Literature entitled "On the History of the Divine Man: A Critique of Tiede's Thesis", at which time Professor Tiede presented an oral response. The debate continues, and both New Testament scholars, students of Graeco-Roman religions and classicists alike will profit from an increasing focus on the nature and function of such charismatic figures in late antiquity. It is clear that particular individuals, such as Apollonius of Tyana and Jesus could be labeled a "divine man" by those

[153] Perhaps the best discussion of the general subject is M. Smith, "Prolegomena to a Discussion of Aretalogies, Divine Men, the Gospels and Jesus," *Journal of Biblical Literature*, 90 (1971), 174–99. See also H. D. Betz, *Lukian von Samosata und das Neue Testament*, TU, 76 (Berlin: Akademie-Verlag, 1961) 100–46; D. Georgi, *Die Gegner des Paulus im 2. Korintherbrief*, WMANT, 11 (Neukirchen-Vluyn: Neukirchen Verlag, 1964); M. Hadas and M. Smith, *Heroes and Gods: Spiritual Biographies in Antiquity* (London: Routledge and Kegan Paul, 1965); H. Koester, "One Jesus and Four Primitive Gospels," in *Trajectories through Early Christianity*, ed. H. Koester and J. M. Robinson (Philadelphia: Fortress Press, 1971) 187–93. H. D. Betz, "Jesus as Divine Man," in *Jesus and the Historian*, ed. T. Trotter (Philadelphia: Westminster Press, 1968) 114–33 (a German translation will appear in: A. Suhl, ed., *Der Wunderbegriff im Neuen Testament* [Darmstadt: Wissenschaftliche Buchgesellschaft, 1980]), and an extensive article (ca. 300 columns) on "Gottmensch", by H. D. Betz will appear in a forthcoming fascicle of *RAC*.

who approved of them, or as a "magician" by those who did not[154]. Smith is certainly correct when he notes that "the difference between these figures is one of social status and success"[155]. The process of labeling in such cases is entirely relative. As Becker has observed, "deviance is not a quality that lies in behavior itself, but in the interaction between the person who commits an act and those who respond to it"[156]. Both the gospels and Graeco-Roman biographies of such figures as Apollonius of Tyana and Pythagoras tend to "normalize" the deviant tendencies of such debated figures by showing them involved in fairly mundane and ordinary conduct as well as underlining their divine authentification in terms of unreproachable, if miraculous activities.

6. The Magical Use of the Name of Jesus

While there is no evidence to suggest that Jesus himself invoked the name of God or any other powerful names in the rituals which he used to effect exorcisms and healings[157], the gospels do contain traditions which indicate that the name of Jesus was used to perform exorcisms during his lifetime by disciples (Mt 7:22; Lk 10:17; cf. Mk 16:17), as well as by freelance Jewish exorcists not formally associated with Jesus (Mk 9:38 f.; Lk 9:49). These notices are generally regarded as historically reliable[158]. Acts contains several examples of the magical use of the name of Jesus in the performance of healings and exorcisms (3:6, 16; 4:7, 10, 30; 16:18; cf. 9:34; 19:13)[159], and Jas 5:14 describes a healing ritual in which the invocation of the "name of the Lord" is a central feature. The name of Jesus was so efficacious that it was incorporated into pagan exorcistic formulas[160]; Origen observes that the name of Jesus is so powerful that it is even effective when used by bad men (*contra Cels.* 1.6). Paul appears to use amulet imagery when he speaks of bearing on his body "the marks of Jesus" (Gal 6:17)[161], and the name of Jesus functions as a charm or amulet in Rev 14:1[162]. In early Christianity, the name of Jesus was used not only in the performance of exorcisms and healings and for apotropaic purposes, but also in prayers, prophecy and baptismal rituals.

---

154 G. Petzke, *Die Traditionen über Apollonius von Tyana und das Neue Testament* (Leiden: Brill, 1970) 47; cf. Wetter, *Der Sohn Gottes*, 73–82.

155 M. Smith, *Clement of Alexandria*, 228.

156 Becker, *Outsiders: Studies in the Sociology of Deviance*, 14.

157 Eitrem, *Some Notes on Demonology*, 10 f.

158 Eitrem, *Some Notes on Demonolgy*, 4–8; Heitmüller, "*Im Namen Jesu*," 241.

159 In Acts 9:40 Peter's short statement, "Tabitha, rise!" is expanded by the phrase *in nomine domini nostri Jesu Christi* in several versions (it, sy^h, sa, Cypr).

160 Many of these have been collected by Eitrem, *Some Notes on Demonology*, 8, n. 1.

161 Deissmann, *Bible Studies*, 358.

162 Heitmüller, "*Im Namen Jesu*," 249, n. 3; W. Bousset, *Die Offenbarung Johannes*, 6. Aufl. (Göttingen: Vandenhoeck & Ruprecht, 1906) 368.

The present discussion will focus on the use of Jesus' name in exorcisms and healings.

In considering the early use of the name of Jesus in the performance of healings and exorcisms in Acts, it must surely have appeared to Jewish and pagan observers that early Christian wonderworkers were practicing necromancy. As we have already indicated in connection with our discussion of Kraeling's article, necromancy is not only a form of divination, but also a means of accomplishing magical goals through the instrumentality of spirits of the dead (*PGM* IV, 333, 1914, 1950; LVII, 6). Thus, in Acts 9:34 when Peter exclaims "Aeneas, Jesus Christ heals you!" we have a phenomenon which could be regarded as necromancy by non-Christian observers. Like John the Baptist, Jesus was a βιαιοθάνατος, i. e., a person who had died a premature, violent death; in popular belief such spirits were readily available to become subject to the control of magicians (Tertullian *Apol.* 23.1). In Lucian *Philops*. 29, those who are decapitated (cf. John the Baptist) and those who are crucified (cf. Jesus) are so classified.

The Great Church drew a hard and fast line between Christian exorcists and pagan magicians[163]. In *2 Apol.* 6, Justin contrasts successful Christian exorcists who use the name of Jesus Christ, with others who use incantations and drugs. In referring to Jewish exorcists, Justin claims that exorcisms attempted in the names of Israelite kings (Solomon?), righteous men, prophets or patriarchs will not be successful, while those done in the name of the God of Abraham, Isaac and Jacob have a better chance of success (*Dial.* 85); in the same section he speaks against the use of fumigations and incantations by Jewish and gentile exorcists. Origen too, himself a firm believer in magic[164], attributed success to the use by both Jews and pagans of the various names for the God of the Jews in exorcisms (*contra Cels*. 4.33 f.). Christians too use the name of the supreme God as well as that of Jesus to perform exorcisms and healings which others found impossible to effect (*contra Cels*. 3.24).

The fundamental significance of the magical use of the names of divinities, supernatural beings or great men of the past is the supposition that such names share the being and participate in the power of their bearers; to possess a name is to possess power over the one who bears the name[165]. The most comprehen-

---

163 A. von Harnack, *Medicinisches aus der ältesten Kirchengeschichte* (Leipzig: Hinrichs, 1892) 111 (the entire chapter on exorcisms 104–124, is excellent). Several revisions later, an expanded chapter on exorcisms appeared in Harnack's *Die Mission und Ausbreitung des Christentums*, I, 4. Aufl. (Leipzig: J. C. Hinrichs, 1924) 151–70.

164 G. Bardy, «Origène et la Magie,» *Recherches de Science Religieuse*, 18 (1928), 126–42.

165 Deissmann, *Bible Studies*, 288 (he refers to Jas 2:19). On the general subject of the magical use of names, see B. Jacob, *Im Namen Gottes* (Berlin: S. Catvary, 1903) 72, 75 ff.; J. G. Frazer, *The Golden Bough*, I, 403–47; F. C. Conybeare, *Myth, Magic and Morals*, 35–50; Dieterich, *Eine Mithrasliturgie*, 109–116; Trachtenberg, *Jewish Magic and Superstition*, 78–103; H. Bietenhard, *Theological Dictionary of the New Testament*, V (1967), 242–83 (excellent

sive study of the magical use of the name of Jesus, within the general context of the magical use of names in both Judaism and Graeco-Roman paganism, is the still valuable study of W. Heitmüller, *"Im Namen Jesu": Eine sprach- und religionsgeschichtliche Untersuchung zum Neuen Testament, speziell zur altchristlichen Taufe* (Göttingen: Vandenhoeck & Ruprecht, 1903). Heitmüller makes a number of important points, two of which are particularly important for our present study: (1) The early Christian use of the name of Jesus shares the same magical presuppositions as the analogous use of powerful names in Judaism and Graeco-Roman paganism (253 f., cf. 148, 221). (2) Throughout the entire period encompassed by the first references to the use of the name of Jesus in the synoptic gospels until the time of Origen, essentially the same belief in the magical power of the name of Jesus is found in Christianity (236).

Jewish exorcists used the name of God in exorcisms (Josephus *Ant.* 2.275–76; 8.42–49; Irenaeus *adv. haer.* 2.4.6), sometimes in the formula "the God of Abraham, (the God of) Isaac, and (the God of) Jacob (Justin *Dial.* 85; 135; Origen *contra Cels.* 4.33 f.; 5.45; 1.22; cf. Acts 3:13–16)[166]. Alternate names for God, preserved in Hebrew transliterations, are frequently used in formulas in the magical papyri and on amulets (*PGM* IV, 1230 ff.; XII, 287 f.; XIII, 815 f., 975 f.); Origen mentions Sabaoth and Adonai as two such magical names used by Jews (*contra Cels.* 1.24), as well as "the God of the Hebrews" and "the God who drowned the King of Egypt and the Egyptians in the Red Sea" as exorcistic formulas (*contra Cels.* 4.34). In this last formula we have essentially a mini-aretalogy. In Graeco-Egyptian magical formulas the deeds of various gods are sometimes recounted in varying degrees of detail as an essential feature of the invocation[167]. Jewish exorcists also used angelic names[168], and in the Talmudic period, the name of a famous first century BCE rabbi, Joshua ben Peraḥiah was used in incantations inscribed on magical bowls[169]. It would appear that J. Trachtenberg's judgment that the invocation of names, especially angelic names, came to the fore only in the post-Talmudic period is in need of revision[170]. The lists of angelic names in the *Sepher-ha-Razim* and in the so-called "Angelic

---

bibliography on 242); Bietenhard claims that "there is in the NT no belief in magically potent names" (278).

[166] M. Rist, "The God of Abraham, Isaac, and Jacob: A Liturgical and Magical Formula," *Journal of Biblical Literature,* 57 (1938), 289–303; cf. Heitmüller, "*Im Namen Jesu,*" 180–82.

[167] Hopfner, "Mageia," Pauly-Wissowa, XIV, 1 (1928), 343; cf. T. Schermann, *Griechische Zauberpapyri und das Gemeinde- und Dankgebet*, TU, 34 (Leipzig: J.C. Hinrichs, 1909) 4–17.

[168] Heitmüller, "*Im Namen Jesu,*" 176–80.

[169] J. Neusner and J.Z. Smith, "Archaeology and Babylonian Jewry," in: *Near Eastern Archaeology in the Twentieth Century*, ed. J.A. Sanders, (Garden City: Doubleday, 1970) 331–47, esp. 337.

[170] Trachtenberg, *Jewish Magic and Superstition*, 88.

Liturgy" (4Q Serek) from Qumran, together with some of the other references we have cited should be sufficient to qualify Trachtenberg's view.

In response to Celsus' charge that Christians get the power they possess by pronouncing the names of certain demons and incantations, Origen counters that they do this by the name of Jesus and the recital of narratives about him (*contra Cels*. 1.6). We have already mentioned the quasi-aretalogical Jewish incantation in the name of "the God who drowned the king of Egypt and the Egyptians in the Red Sea" (*contra Cels*. 4.34). One of the more elaborate examples of such magical *historiolae* is found in the so-called "Recipe of Pibeches" (*PGM* IV, 3008 ff.); Eitrem refers to several other examples of the same phenomenon[171]. A closer inspection of the use of the name of Jesus in the performance of wonders from the New Testament era through to the time of Origen reveals that the name of Jesus was increasingly supplemented with other elements, in accordance with the general principle that magical formulas tend to expand in transmission. In Acts, the expressions "Jesus Christ" or "Jesus Christ of Nazareth" appear to suffice; in the Old Latin and Cyprianic variant of Acts 9:40, we find the expanded expression *in nomine domini nostri Jesu Christi.* By the time of Justin, the phrase "crucified under Pontius Pilate" is used to supplement the name of Jesus in formulas of exorcism (*2 Apol*. 6.6; *Dial*. 30.3; 76.6; 85.2)[172]. The notion that the crucifixion of Jesus spelled the destruction of demonic powers seems to underlie this expanded usage. The same formula occurs in Irenaeus *adv. haer*. 2.49.3: *in nomine Christi Jesu crucifixi sub Pontio Pilato* (cf. Irenaeus *Epideixis* 97). The same formula entered into baptismal liturgies (Justin *1 Apol*. 61), which originally functioned as magical rituals which expelled demons from baptismal candidates[173].

At this point a few remarks should be directed toward the eccentric article by E. G. Weltin, "The Concept of *Ex-Opere-Operato* Efficacy in the Fathers as an Evidence of Magic in Early Christianity," *Greek, Roman and Byzantine Studies*, 3 (1960), 74–100. After correctly observing that several early Christian rites acted independently of the persons who performed them in an *ex opere operato* manner (88–94), Weltin claims that "diverse magical formulae preclude an ascription of self-virtuous powers to any magical set of words" (76). Because early Christian exorcistic formulas exhibit variety in formulation, therefore, they do not possess *ex opere operato* power (85). Rather than argue that the demons

---

171 Eitrem, *Papyri Osloensis*, Fasc. I, 109.

172 E. F. Osborn, *Justin Martyr* (Tübingen: Mohr Siebeck, 1973) 63; Heitmüller, "*Im Namen Jesu*," 250, 334 ff.; Origene, *Contre Celse*, ed. M. Bourret, I (Paris: Les Éditions du Cerf, 1967) note on 1.6.

173 On the magical-exorcistic understanding of *"Onoma-Taufe"* in Justin, see C. Andresen, *Die Kirchen der alten Christenheit* (Stuttgart: Kohlhammer, 1971) 77; on baptism "in the name of Jesus" generally in the second century see Heitmüller, "*Im Namen Jesu*," 266–336; Böcher, *Christus Exorcista*, 66–80; F. J. Dölger, *Der Exorzismus im altchristlichen Taufritual* (Paderborn: F Schöningh, 1909).

copied the Christian mysteries, Justin should have argued (suggests Weltin) that since Christianity is a truly historical revelation with a legal contract enacted by the deity, the power to perform miracles is a permanent provision of this contractual relationship. "Magic", suggests Weltin, "is occult and knows no divine contract; it is unilateral and arises from man's ingenuity" (98). On 99 f., he expresses this view clearly:

> It is clearly not magical hocus-pocus or even presumptuous effrontery to draw payment on a permanent blank check at the express command of your Father. No classical god, as far as we have seen, or mystery deity that we know of, has been so lavish in his concern and so legal-minded as to have his contracts put into writing.

While the Gospels and Acts contain a great many narratives of healings and exorcisms, the epistolary literature of the New Testament refers to signs, wonders and mighty deeds only in very general terms (Rom 15:19; Gal 3:5; 1 Cor 12:10; 2 Cor 12:12; Heb 2:4). Only in Jas 5:14–16 do we find a specific healing ritual which is to be followed in cases of illness (1 Cor 12:9 refers to "gifts of healing" without further specification or elaboration). References to exorcisms occur only in the synoptic gospels and Acts and then are not referred to again until the middle of the second century in the writings of Justin Martyr. In a recent study of the relationship between rational medicine and miraculous or magical healing in early Christianity, M. Smith has pointed out the paradoxical nature of the evidence regarding the early Christian attitude toward health and illness[174]. While the Gospels and Acts contain many stories of miraculous cures, and Paul and others claimed that sickness could be miraculously healed, yet Paul himself was a sick man (2 Cor 12:7–10)[175]. Sickness was not uncommon in Christian communities, yet neither rational medicine (which was not unknown) nor miraculous or magical healing was resorted to. It would therefore appear that magical healing (in contrast to exorcism) was more firmly fixed in the ideology of Christian mission propaganda than in the experience of everyday life. The second century Neo-Platonist Celsus apparently charged that Christians avoided physicians (Origen *contra Cels.* 3.75), and Origen himself recommended in the third century that Christians ought to seek medical attention for physical ailments (*contra Cels.* 8.60). Origen recognized the effectiveness of names, demons and charms in combating illness, but emphasized at the same time that the truly pious man will avoid their use (*contra Cels.* 8.61).

---

[174] M. Smith, "Plutarch's *de tuenda sanitate praecepta* (Moralia 122 B–137E)," in: *Plutarch's Ethical Writings and Early Christian Literature*, ed. H.D. Betz (Leiden: Brill, 1978) 34–41.

[175] Harnack, *Medicinisches aus der ältesten Kirchengeschichte*, 93 f.

7. Glossolalia and *Voces Magicae*

One of the more peculiar characteristics of magical papyri and amulets from the Graeco-Roman period is the frequent occurrence of incomprehensible sequences of vowels and consonants, generally designated as *voces magicae*. Many of these *voces magicae* recur in precisely the same form in many magical texts, a fact which reveals their formulaic rather than extemporaneous nature. On the other hand such *voces magicae* frequently introduce or frame extemporaneous series of nonsensical sequences of vowels and consonants which are related to, yet different from the *voces magicae* themselves. Some of the more common sequences include the widely used "Ephesia grammata" and various palindromes (e.g., αβλαναθαναλβα, ιαωαι, αβερραμενθω, ουλερθεξαναξ, εθρελυωθμε, μαρεβα, etc.)[176]. This phenomenon, in combination with the interest which magical texts betray in foreign words and phrases and in the names of foreign divinities, has quite naturally led some scholars to suspect a close relationship between glossolalia and *voces magicae*[177]. Some deny any relationship[178], others affirm that the two are very closely related[179], while still others claim that the precise relationship, if any, cannot be determined[180]. Harnack, while he thought he recognized actual glossolalia behind the *voces magicae* in the *Pistis Sophia*, nevertheless concluded that "we certainly no longer have genuine glossolalia in the *Pistis Sophia*"[181].

Bonner contends that while the two might have sounded similar, glossolalia was "spontaneous, unmeditated utterance", while the *voces magicae* consisted of carefully transmitted, stereotypical formulas[182]. However, those who have heard the phenomenon of speaking in tongues in our day will notice that certain sequences of sound recur in this "spontaneous" utterance, leading one to suspect that the difference between spontaneous and formulaic ecstatic speech can easily be overdrawn.

---

176 See Preisendanz, *PGM*, 3.243–78 (index to magical words), and 279–80 (index to palindromes); on the last palindrome listed in our examples, see Eitrem, *Papyri Osloensis*, Fasc. I, 7 f.

177 J. Behm, *Theological Dictionary of the New Testament*, I (1964),723; S. Eitrem, *Orakel und Mysterien am Ausgang der Antike* (Zurich: Rhein-Verlag, 1947) 41; E.R. Dodds, *Pagan and Christian in an Age of Anxiety*, 55, n. 1; F. Dornseiff, *Das Alphabet in Mystik und Magie* (Leipzig and Berlin: B.G. Teubner, 1922) 45, 54 f.; H. Weinel, *Die Wirkungen des Geistes und der Geister im nachapostolischen Zeitalter bis auf Irenäus* (Freiburg: J.C.B. Mohr, 1899) 77.

178 A. Dietzel, "Beten im Geist," *Theologische Zeitung*, 13 (1957), 12 ff.

179 M. Smith, *Clement of Alexandria*, 233: "The spirit which spoke through the Christians and the spirits which spoke through pagan magicians spoke the same characteristic language."

180 W. Keilbach, *Religion in Geschichte und Gegenwart*, 3. Aufl., VI (1962), 1941.

181 A. von Harnack, *Über die Pistis Sophia*, TU, 7, 2 (Leipzig: J.C. Hinrichs, 1891) 88 f.

182 Bonner, *Amulets*, 189 f.

Unfortunately, while we are told that glossolalia was practiced in various places through brief (and late) narratives (Acts 2:1–13, in Jerusalem; 10:44–46, in Caesarea; 19:6, in Ephesus), and we receive some brief descriptive and theoretical statements on the subject by Paul (1 Cor 12–14), we apparently have no transcription of such utterances. I say apparently, because there is a possible exception in the term *abba* referred to by Paul in Rom 8:15 and Gal 4:6 together with an interpretation: *Abba!* "Father!" While many scholars interpret the στεναγμοὶ ἀλάλητοι in Rom 8:26 as glossolalia[183], they usually object to extending this interpretation to Rom 8:15. In form, *abba* is a palindrome of a foreign (Aramaic) word which would have been incomprehensible to gentile Roman Christians (or Galatian Christians) were it not for the fact that the utterance is interpreted. Paul, of course, insists that glossolalia be accompanied by an interpretation (1 Cor 14:13–19). In principle this use of *abba* functions no differently than the ecstatic cry εὐάν by devotees of Dionysos (Theophilus *ad Autolyc.* 2.28). I myself have heard the term *abba* used in the context of modern glossolalia several times; the fact that it is a *Lallwort* makes it easily adaptable to such contexts.

Furthermore, inarticulate speech, the speech of animals or other secret or incomprehensible languages can be part of the repertoire of the shaman[184]. Such speech also appears to be one possible characteristic of the prophet or diviner; Isa 8:19 speaks of wizards that squeak and gibber, and Celsus mentions the incoherent utterances of Syrian prophets (Origen *contra Cels.* 7.9 ff.; cf. Lucian *Alex.* 13)[185]. One major similarity between glossolalia and *voces magicae* is the fact that both are directed to a divinity; magicians in their incantations are calling upon supernatural powers just as Paul claims that those who speak in tongues are speaking to God (1 Cor 14:2, 28) in the "language of angels" (1 Cor 13:1)[186]. Iamblichus observes that unintelligible language used in holy rites reproduces the language of the gods (*de myst.* 7.4 f.; cf. Hopfner, *Griechisch-ägyptischer Offenbarungszauber*, I, 757). Similarly, the context of most transcriptions of *voces magicae* is that of an ἐπίκλησις directed to gods or other supernatural powers[187].

---

183 E. Käsemann, "The Cry for Liberty in the Worship of the Church," *Perspectives on Paul* (Philadelphia: Westminster Press, 1971) 127–34; *idem*, *An die Römer*, 3. Aufl. (Tübingen: Mohr Siebeck, 1974), 231 f.; H. Lietzmann, *An die Römer*, 5. Aufl. (Tübingen: Mohr Siebeck, 1933) 86; P. Althaus, *Der Brief an die Römer*, 6. Aufl. (Göttingen: Vandenhoeck & Ruprecht, 1966) 94; G. B. Cutten, *Speaking with Tongues* (New Haven: Yale University Press, 1927) 170 ff.

184 M. Eliade, *Shamanism: Archaic Techniques of Ecstasy* (New York: Pantheon Books, 1964) 96–99.

185 S. D. Currie, "Speaking in Tongues," *Interpretation*, 19 (1965), 274–94.

186 Eitrem, *Orakel und Mysterien*, 41.

187 The structure of the magical ceremony may be divided into two major parts, the [*epi*]-*klēsis* or invocation and the *praxis* or magical operation (Festugière, *L'Idéal religeux des Grecs*, 284–89). This morphology is more satisfactory than the more elaborate one of T. Hopfner, *Griechisch-ägyptischer Offenbarungszauber*, I, 869–81, followed by Prümm, *Religionsge-*

In sum, the available evidence in our judgment does not support the contention that glossolalia was a form of magical prayer closely related, if not identical to, the *voces magicae* of the magical papyri. The use of *voces magicae* in magical rituals appears always to have been directed toward the accomplishment of particular religious objectives. In contrast to this pragmatic, and hence thoroughly magical, function of the *voces magicae,* there is no evidence to suggest that glossolalia functioned similarly. Even that which some scholars regard as the clearest parallel to the phenomenon of glossolalia at Corinth, the incomprehensible speech of the Pythia which supposedly required prophetic interpretation to render Apollo's utterances comprehensible, turns out, on closer examination, to be a product of modern scholarly imagination[188]. There is no evidence that the Pythia's speech was incomprehensible.

8. Magical Prayer[189]

"In prayer", observed M. Weber, "the boundary between magical formula and supplication remains fluid"[190]. One of the most characteristic forms of magical prayer is the blessing and the curse. Blessing and cursing may be regarded as magical if, within the context of religious deviance, the act of invoking formulas of benison and malediction is regarded as tantamount to achieving the desired effect. In Graeco-Roman magic, formulas of cursing are the central feature of the so-called *tabulae execrationum*[191]. A curse has been defined by F. Büchsel as "a directly expressed or indicated utterance which in virtue of a supernatural nexus of operation brings harm by its very expression to the one against whom it is directed"[192]. The phenomenon of blessing and cursing permeates early Christianity[193], where it is certainly a magical phenomenon.

---

schichtliches Handbuch, 371–75. Hull, *Hellenistic Magic*, 42 ff. appears to be summarizing Festugière, but nowhere indicates that.

188 The traditional view is represented by Eitrem, *Orakel und Mysterien*, 42; H. Gunkel, *Die Wirkungen des heiligen Geistes*, 2. Aufl. (Göttingen: Vandenhoeck & Ruprecht, 1899) 18 f. The view expressed here is argued by J. Fontenrose, *The Delphic Oracle* (Berkeley: University of California Press, 1978) 212–24.

189 J. Leipoldt, "Gebet und Zauber im Urchristentum," in: *idem*, *Von den Mysterien zur Kirche: Gesammelte Aufsätze* (Leipzig: Koehler & Amelang, 1961) 104–115.

190 M. Weber, *The Sociology of Religion*, trans. E. Fischoff (Boston: Beacon Press, 1963) 26.

191 *Supra*, n. 34.

192 *Theological Dictionary of the New Testament*, I (1964), 449.

193 The most detailed investigation of this subject is L. Brun, *Segen und Fluch im Urchristentum* (Oslo: Jacob Dybwad, 1933), who does not deal with the magical complexion of blessing and cursing. Brun emphasizes the Jewish origin of these concepts in the New Testament and does not take seriously the form of the imprecations used, for example, by Paul. However, he does show the constellation of ideas which are involved in the "blessing/curse" topic.

Just as magical prayers are characterized by the use of imperatives (particularly toward their conclusion)[194], and by the lavish use of threats[195], so formulas of cursing also bear these two characteristic features. Curses are also closely related to "punitive miracles" in which harm is inflicted on persons or things; such *Strafwunder* are the inverse of *Heilungswunder*[196].

The Gospels preserve no narratives of punitive miracles performed by Jesus, with the single exception of the episode of the Cursing of the Fig Tree (Mk 11:12–14, 20–25; Mt 21:18–22). Brun notes that this narrative is not just a fortuitous exception, particularly in light of Lk 9:51–56 and Mt 26:53[197]. Further, the connection of this *Strafwunder* with Jesus' saying on faith (Mk 11:22–25; Mt 21:21–22) is probably not original[198], and appears to function in such a way as to diminish the magical character of the entire episode, which has a strong claim to historicity precisely because of its strange character. Jesus' pronouncement of woes upon various groups and individuals must also be considered under the rubric of cursing[199]. In the one instance in which Jesus pronounces a woe upon an individual (his future betrayer) in Mk 14:21 (Mt 26:24; Lk 22:22), the curse is fulfilled by the pitiful death of Judas (Mt 27:3–10; Acts 1:16–19). However, in this instance the contradictory accounts of Judas' demise indicate either a curse pronounced *ex eventu* by the Christian community or a story invented to report the fulfillment of the predicted woe.

In contrast to the gospels, *Strafwunder* occupy a very prominent position in the Acts of the Apostles where they are performed by both Peter and Paul[200]. In the story of Ananias and Sapphira, Peter presides over the death of Ananias (Acts 5:5), who dies without the invocation of a curse, while the death of his wife Sapphira (5:10) is preceded by a curse (5:9) which becomes immediately effective. In Acts 13:6–12, Elymas the magician is struck blind in consequence of an imprecation pronounced by Paul. These two punitive miracles, of course, are overshadowed by the numerically more frequent healings performed both by Peter (Acts 2:43; 3:1 ff.; 4:30; 5:12 ff.; 9:32 ff., 39 ff.) and by Paul (Acts 14:8 ff.; 16:16 ff.; 19:11 f.; 20:9 f.; 28:8 f.). The early Christian apologetic argument that Jesus' miracles (unlike those of Graeco-Roman magicians or divine men) were performed unselfishly and for the salvation of man, while apparently true of Jesus, could not as easily be applied to the Lukan portrait of apostolic activity. In early Christian apocryphal literature, the incidence of *Strafwunder* attributed

---

[194] Eitrem, *Papyri Osloensis*, Fasc. I, 46.

[195] Hopfner, *Griechisch-ägyptischer Offenbarungszauber*, I, 792; Eitrem, *Papyri Osloensis*, Fasc. I, 36.

[196] Weinreich, *Antike Heilungswunder*, 57–62, 138, 147–55.

[197] Brun, *Segen und Fluch*, 75 f.

[198] *Ibid.*, 76.

[199] *Ibid.*, 84–87.

[200] *Ibid.*, 78 ff.

to both Jesus and the apostles exhibits a marked increase in frequency[201], a feature which seems to indicate that the apologetic perspective of the more educated Christian authors was not fully shared or even understood by popular Christianity.

The Paul depicted in Acts 13:6–12 is fully consonant with the author of the Pauline letters. In an excellent recent study of the prayers of Paul, G. Wiles devotes a substantial section to considering blessings and curses in Paul's prayers[202]. The passages of central importance are the introductory curse (1:8 f.) and concluding blessing (6:16) of the letter to the Galatians, and the two curse passages in 1 Cor 5:3–5 (cf. Tim 1:20), and 16:22; in all of these passages imperative verbs are used. Many years ago Deissmann suggested that 1 Cor 5:3–5 be understood against the background of Graeco-Roman magic[203]. Deissmann demonstrated the presence of two technical terms from the magical ritual of execration; the chief difference between this early Christian curse formula and that of pagan magic being the Pauline substitution of "Satan" for pagan divinities. We must also reckon with the probability that this ritual execration was pronounced "in the name of the Lord Jesus" (1 Cor 5:4)[204]. The difficulty of interpreting this passage in a non-magical way is perhaps indicated by Wiles' lengthy discussion of it in its broader context[205]. For though the author recognizes that Paul's imprecations resemble Old Testament, Jewish and pagan usage, he opines that "it does not in itself necessarily imply a magical concept or a departure from his usual understanding of the limits of his own power and authority under God" (121). Wiles' difficulty in arguing against the magical interpretation of 1 Cor 5:3–5 becomes clear in his concluding statement: "Confident that no other protective course could be taken, he [Paul] acted as apostolic intercessor with a certainty that went far beyond his usual intercessory practice" (150).

The three other passages, Gal 1:8 f.; 6:16 and 1 Cor 16:22, differ from the one just discussed in that while 1 Cor 5:3–5 describes a ceremony of ritual execration, these passages imply that the letters to which blessings and curses are

---

[201] *Ibid.*, 81 ff.; cf. W. Bauer, *Das Leben Jesu im Zeitalter der neutestamentlichen Apokryphen* (Tübingen: Mohr Siebeck, 1909) 360–68.

[202] G. Wiles, *Paul's Intercessory Prayers: The Significance of the Intercessory Prayer Passages in the Letters of St. Paul*, SNTS Monographs, 24 (Cambridge: Cambridge University Press, 1974) 108–55.

[203] Deissmann, *Light from the Ancient East*, 303 ff.; *idem*, *Paul: A Study in Social and Religious History*, trans. W. E. Wilson (New York: Harper, 1927) 70; Brun, *Segen und Fluch*, 109.

[204] The grammatical problems are summarized by H. Conzelmann, *1 Corinthians*, trans. J. W. Leitch (Philadelphia: Fortress Press, 1975) 97; in interpreting the passage as we have, we are following Heitmüller, "*Im Namen Jesu*," 73 f. and W. Bousset, *Kyrios Christos*, 5. Aufl. (Göttingen: Vandenhoeck & Ruprecht, 1965) 87. R. Reitzenstein correctly describes the rite found in 1 Cor 5:3–5 as a *"Zauberhandlung"* in *idem, Die hellenistischen Mysterienreligionen nach ihren Grundgedanken und Wirkungen*, 3. Aufl. (Leipzig and Berlin: B. G. Teubner, 1927) 364.

[205] Wiles, *Paul's Intercessory Prayers*, 135–50

attached are thereby constituted as "magical letters"[206], a category of letters in antiquity. Deissmann demonstrated that the cognates ἀναθεματίζω and ἀνάθεμα in Gal 1:8f. and 1 Cor 16:22 were technical terms of magical execration in Graeco-Roman curse tablets[207]. The use of the imperative mood in the verbs of all of these formulas of execration makes it clear that we are dealing with the curse as a variety of magical prayer[208].

In J. Leipoldt's study "Gebet und Zauber im Urchristentum," the author proposed that, while prayer and magic cannot be clearly differentiated in Judaism or Graeco-Roman paganism, Jesus uniquely separated prayer from magic (109 ff.). Paul's prayers too, are non-magical (113–14). While Leipoldt's views on the relationship between prayer and magic in Graeco-Roman religions and Judaism are correct, we do not know enough about the prayers of Jesus to make an accurate judgment. Leipoldt's characterization of Paul's prayers as non-magical requires careful qualification in the light of the foregoing discussion.

One significant characteristic which dominates many magical prayers is the abundance of divine attributes, a feature not uncommon in Jewish and pagan prayers of the Graeco-Roman era[209]. Presumably influenced by Deissmann, T. Schermann, produced a study entitled *Griechische Zauberpapyri und das Gemeinde- und Dankgebet im I. Klemensbriefe*, TU, 34 (Leipzig: J. Hinrichs, 1909). Schermann's objective was to illuminate the formulation of the communal prayers of thanksgiving found in *1 Clement* 9–12; 20:1–12; 34:5–7; 59–61. After a consideration of various names and epithets of the gods in the prayers of the magical papyri (4–16), he provided a detailed analysis of the names and epithets of God in the thanksgiving prayers of *1 Clement* (22–50). Schermann concludes that while the content and form of the prayers in Clement are neither new nor original, neither are they dependent on pagan or Egyptian sources; the emphasis on the omnipotence of God in the creation and preservation of the world, the determination of the fate of mankind and governance over all beings forms a type of prayer which has close parallels in the Old Testament, Jewish apocryphal literature, Philo and the Greek magical papyri, not to mention *1*

---

206 H. D. Betz, "In Defense of the Spirit: Paul's Letter to the Galatians as a Document of Early Christian Apologetics," in *Aspects of Religious Propaganda in Judaism and Early Christianity*, ed. E. Schüssler Fiorenza (Notre Dame: University of Notre Dame Press, 1976) 112. See also H. D. Betz, "The Literary Composition and Function of Paul's Letter to the Galatians," *New Testament Studies*, 21 (1974/75), 378f., and H. D. Betz, *Galatians* (Philadelphia: Fortress Press, 1979) 25; there Betz refers to J. Schneider, "Brief," *RAC*, 2 (1954) 572f.; R. Stübe, *Der Himmelsbrief* (Tübingen: Mohr Siebeck, 1918), and J. Sykutris, "Epistolographie," Pauly-Wissowa, Suppl. V (1931), col. 207. The concluding curse in Rev 22:18–19 would appear to place that document in the category of a magical letter, since it has some formal features of ancient epistolary literature.

207 Deissmann, *Light from the Ancient East*, 92f.; cf. Brun, *Segen und Fluch*, 105.

208 Eitrem, *Papyri Osloensis*, Fasc. I, 46.

209 But, see the excellent article by H. D. Betz, "On the Problem of the Religio-Historical Understanding of Apocalypticism," *Journal for Theology and the Church*, 6 (1969), 134–56.

Clement (51). Thus, while Schermann's study does little to illuminate the features of magical prayer, it does underscore the proximity of "religious" prayer and "magical" incantation.

9. Magical Motifs in Early Christian Literature

The analysis of the various magical patterns and motifs which underlie some of the writings emanating from early Christianity is a task which has yet to be undertaken. In the New Testament, the Revelation of John has yet to be fully investigated from the vantage point of the history of religions, and it is precisely that document which shows the greatest impact of magical patterns and motifs in the New Testament. In the group of writings called Apostolic Fathers, it is the *Shepherd of Hermas* which appears to show the greatest number of such magical patterns and motifs. We shall first indicate a number of features in the Revelation of John which have magical parallels, and then turn to the important work of E. Peterson on the *Shepherd of Hermas*.

J.M. Hull has observed that magic has been "baptized" in the Apocalypse of John, and that "the relationship between Christianity and magic becomes creative, and magical images and customs are taken over wholesale without compromise to the essentially eschatological nature of the church's faith"[210]. In spite of the fact that the present study might question Hull's supposition of the alien nature of magic in early Christianity, his basic view of the Apocalypse of John is certainly correct. I would like to make a number of random observations regarding parallels between the Apocalypse and Graeco-Roman magic: (1) The use of the adverb "quickly" found not infrequently in the Apocalypse (1:1; 2:16; 3:11; 11:14; 22:6, 7, 12, 20) occurs regularly at the conclusion of magical incantations in the papyri. (2) The imagery of the plagues of the Jewish exodus used in the Apocalypse are strongly emphasized in *PGM* IV, 3007–86. (3) It has been noted by some scholars that certain passages of the Apocalypse (1:4, 8, 17; 21:6; 22:13) read like magical formulas[211]. (4) The creature with many eyes (Rev 4:6; 4:8) has striking parallels with the iconography of magical papyri and depictions on amulets[212]. (5) The verb νικᾶν found seventeen times in the Apocalypse, is a popular expression in magical literature used of the success of the magician[213]. (6) The rhetorical features of doxological prayers (cf. Rev 5:12) resemble those used by magicians[214]. (7) The name of God is a protective or apotropaic device

[210] Hull, *Hellenistic Magic*, 144.

[211] Eitrem, *Some Notes on Demonology*, 22; the author refers to the judgments of J. Weiss with approval.

[212] Hopfner, *Griechisch-ägyptischer Offenbarungszauber*, I, 213 ff.

[213] Eitrem, *Papyri Osloensis*, Fasc. I, 83.

[214] *Ibid.*, 89.

against evil powers (Rev 7:2, 3; 9:4; 14:1; 22:4), (8) similarly, the names of blasphemy are said to have been written on the head of an animal from the sea (Rev 13:1; 17:3), both notions which presuppose name-magic. (9) In Rev 20:1 f. (cf. 1:18; 9:1) an angel descends from heaven with the key of the Abyss and a chain to restrain Satan; here there are exact parallels in magical texts[215]. (10) The magical use of alpha and omega (Rev 1:8; 21:6; 22:3) has been commented upon by Dornseiff.[216] (11) The frequent use of the numbers three and seven in the Apocalypse has many magical parallels. (12) The "stone with the new name" (Rev 2:17) is a magical amulet[217]. Perhaps these random examples will serve as an indication of the extent to which the Apocalypse of John uses magical patterns and motifs.

In two important articles devoted to the *Shepherd* of Hermas, E. Peterson has convincingly demonstrated that the revelatory visions ostensibly received by Hermas are tricked out by terms and concepts from ancient magic and magical techniques, particularly as they relate to divination[218]. However, Peterson emphasizes that Hermas has produced a "*Buchprophetie*", and therefore "*weil sie Buchprophetie sind, können sie in ihrer Einkleidung Elemente aus der hellenistischen Offenbarungsliteratur übernehmen, ohne doch der magischen Handlung, die der hellenistischen Offenbarungsliteratur zugrunde liegt, Erwähnung zu tun*"[219]. In effect, the world of Hellenistic magic is indispensable for understanding some of the otherwise puzzling details of the visions, yet such borrowing must be considered primarily formal, since the two central revelatory figures found in the visions of Hermas are not compelled to appear through the use of magical formulas and rites[220]. R. Joly, referring to Peterson's work on Hermas, agrees on the formal nature of the Hellenistic magical influences[221], as does L. Pernveden.[222] J. Reiling, however, in his recent study on *Hermas and Christian Prophecy: A Study of the Eleventh Mandate*, NovTSup, 37 (Leiden: Brill, 1973), thinks that such magical influences on Hermas are more than just formal, and he regarded his own study as "an attempt to do for the 11th Mandate what Peterson did for the Visions" (21). At the conclusion of his study, Reiling states the following:

---

215 *PGM* IV, 3024 ff.; Wortmann, "Neue magische Texte," 69; Eitrem, *Some Notes on Demonology*, 11 f.

216 Dornseiff, *Das Alphabet*, 122–25.

217 Eitrem, *Papyri Osloensis*, Fasc. I, 41; Bousset, *Offenbarung Johannes*, 249; cf. supra, n. 161.

218 E. Peterson, "Beiträge zur Interpretation der Visionem im Pastor Hermae," in *idem*, *Frühkirche, Judentum und Gnosis* (Rom, Freiburg u. Wien: Herder, 1959) 254–70. A second article, "Kritische Analyse der fünften Vision des Hermas", is found in the same volume.

219 Peterson, "Kritische Analyse," 284.

220 Peterson, "Beiträge zur Interpretation," 268.

221 R. Joly (ed.), *Hermas le Pasteur*, SC, 53 (Paris: Les Éditions du Cerf, 1958) 54.

222 L. Pernveden, *The Concept of the Church in the Shepherd of Hermas* (Lund: C. W. K. Gleerup, 1966) 26, 34, 291.

If the conclusions drawn above are correct, there is reason to revise Peterson's judgment on the Hellenistic elements in the Visions. They are not just "Einkleidung", wording, which can, as it were, be detached without altering the portrait of the author's work and message, but there is good reason to see them as part of Hermas' work [174].

Reiling's own use of magical papyri to illuminate the 11th Mandate centers on the expression τὸ κενὸν πνεῦμα (41–48), which, he concludes, was a phrase associated with pagan divination used by Hermas to brand one who possessed such a spirit as utterly pagan (43), an explanation which assumes Hermas to be quite familiar with both the milieu and language of magical divination. Reiling places Hermas within the context of a Christianity within which there was an undercurrent of divinatory practices which had more in common with the religious ideas outside the church than with the theological positions of teachers within the church (81). In work currently in progress by the Swedish scholar David Hellholm at Uppsala, one hopes that the research of Peterson and Reiling will be supplemented so that a more accurate picture of the relationship between that enigmatical document and the world of Graeco-Roman magic will emerge[223].

10. Conclusions

The foregoing study, as incomplete as it necessarily is, has nevertheless attempted to summarize a great deal of the work which has been done during the last two generations on the relationship between magic and early Christianity. If we have found that magic was a characteristic feature of early Christianity from its very inception, that is because we have regarded magic as a constant if subordinate feature of all religious traditions. Unfortunately, the term "magic" itself has been a red herring in a great deal of the scholarly discussion. We have used the term without any pejorative connotations, referring only to the pragmatic and religiously deviant features of magic as a necessary and universally present substructure of religious systems. The study has also attempted to point to some of the critical areas where intensive research is required if the phenomenon of early Christianity is to be understood adequately.

[223] In discussing this matter with Mr. David Hellholm at the Institute for Antiquity and Christianity in Claremont, California in April, 1976, he gave me the impression that he would deal with this matter at some length in his Uppsala dissertation.

Index of Sources

Bible

Old Testament

New Testament

Early Christian Literature

Nag Hammadi Library

Early Jewish Literature

Dead Sea Scrolls

Greek and Latin Sources

Papyri and Inscriptions

Egyptian Literature

Index of Authors

Index of Subjects